Sixth Edition

Fundamentals of Organizational Behavior

Andrew J. DuBrin
Professor of Management, Emeritus
College of Business
Rochester Institute of Technology

Academic Media Solutions

Affordable - Quality Textbooks, Study Aids, & Custom Publishing

Cover photo: Sergey Nivens/Shutterstock

Fundamentals of Organizational Behavior, 6e, Andrew J. DuBrin

Paperback (black/white):   ISBN–13: 978-1-942041-73-3
                                    ISBN–10: 1-942041-73-X

Paperback (color):   ISBN–13: 978-1-942041-75-7
                                    ISBN–10: 1-942041-75-6

Loose-leaf version: ISBN–13: 978-1-942041-74-0
                                    ISBN–10: 1-942041-74-8

Online version: ISBN–13: 978-1-942041-76-4
                                    ISBN–10: 1-942041-76-4

Printed in the United States of America by Academic Media Solutions.

Brief Contents

Contents

6 Foundation Concepts of Motivation

111

7 Motivational Methods and Programs

137

PART 3 GROUPS AND INTERPERSONAL RELATIONS

8 Interpersonal Communication 161

9 Group Dynamics 191

10 Teams and Teamwork 215

11 Leadership in Organizations   235

12 Power, Politics, and Influence   263

16 Organizational Change and Innovation 359

17 Cultural Diversity and Cross-Cultural Organizational Behavior 383

Preface

Welcome to the sixth and updated edition of *Fundamentals of Organizational Behavior*. This book is designed for courses in organizational behavior and management that focus on the application of organizational behavior knowledge to achieve enhanced productivity and satisfaction in the workplace. Organizational behavior is about human behavior on the job. Knowledge of organizational behavior is, therefore, an important source from which any manager or corporate professional may draw. The same information that can drive a manager to excel can also assist individual organizational contributors in becoming more adaptive and effective. Nonmanagerial professionals, technology workers, sales representatives, and service providers benefit from the insight and analysis that organizational behavior provides, as do managers and prospective managers. All are welcome under the umbrella of organizational behavior.

Organizational behavior, because of its key contributions in driving workforce productivity, is a standard part of the curriculum in schools and colleges of business, management, and public administration. The case for the relevance of organizational behavior was stated recently by Bob Funk, the chairman, CEO, and founder of Express Employment Professionals, one of the nation's largest job agencies. Funk observes that getting ahead in today's world starts with skills. Yet hard skills and experience are only part of the equation, and not the important half. "So many people do not realize how important soft skills (essentially interpersonal skills) are to unlocking job opportunity," he says.*

As a result of interest in the field, research and writing about the field proliferates. To provide just an overview of this vast amount of information, many introductory textbooks are quite lengthy, easily filling 800 pages or more. To soften the impact of such encyclopedic approaches to the study of organizational behavior, many of these books also lavishly layer figures and photographs onto their extended narratives. Many of the new, briefer textbooks are simply condensed versions of the longer books.

Fundamentals of Organizational Behavior takes a briefer, more focused, and more applied approach to learning about the field. Instead of trying to dazzle with a baffling array of concepts, research findings, theories, and news clippings, this book concentrates on only the most useful ideas. It blends clear and thoughtful exposition of traditional topics, such as motivation, with topics of more recent origin, such as creativity, virtual teams, knowledge management, diversity, and cultural intelligence.

Although each chapter packs a lot of information, chapters consistently emphasize the essential and the practical. A major strategy was to de-emphasize elaborate theories and findings that are no longer the subject of active research, practice, or training programs. However, we did not permit our concern for brevity to strip the text down to a sterile outline devoid of human interest, examples, and useful applications. Most of the brief textbooks on organizational behavior sacrifice cases, self-quizzes, discussion questions, and in-action inserts. *Fundamentals of Organizational Behavior*, however, injects all of these elements into its pages and still stays concise.

The size and scope of this book are well suited to college courses that supplement a core textbook with journal articles, major projects, specialty textbooks, online information, or other instructional media. In addition, the comprehensiveness of *Fundamentals of*

---

*Quoted in William McGurn, "Bring Back the Work Ethic," *The Wall Street Journal*, September 5, 2017, p. A13.

Organizational Behavior, combined with its brevity, makes it suitable for workplace organizational training programs about human behavior. The student who masters this textbook will not only acquire an overview of and appreciation for organizational behavior research, literature, theory, and opinion, but will also develop a feel for managing and influencing others through the application of systematic knowledge about human behavior.

THE FEATURES

In addition to summarizing and synthesizing relevant information about essential organizational behavior topics and providing concrete examples of theories in action, *Fundamentals of Organizational Behavior* incorporates many useful features to make the material more accessible, collaborative, and incisive. It also works hard to be technologically relevant, such as by describing how information technology is used to enhance group decision making, how social media influence networking in organizations, and how artificial intelligence factors into decision making.

- *Learning Objectives* introduce the major themes of each chapter and provide a framework for study.
- *Boldfaced key terms* are defined in the margins, listed at the end of each chapter, and reinforced in an end-of-book glossary.
- *Opening vignettes* explore real organizational issues, highlighting the stake all types of organizations have in using human capital well.
- *Organizational Behavior in Action* boxes describe the actions of managers and professionals in dealing effectively with the human aspects of management, making visible the connection between theory and practice.
- *Self-Assessments and Skill-Development Exercises* support self-directed learning while driving the connections among research, theory, and practice down to the personal level. They not only provide a point of departure for students in understanding and valuing their own individual attitudes and behaviors, but they also serve to create an ongoing dialogue, as each assessment and exercise can be returned to many times over the course of a semester. The Self-Assessments and Skill-Development Exercises have been well-accepted features of the previous five editions.
- *Implications for Managerial Practice* sections, located near the end of each chapter, set off several smart suggestions for applying organizational behavior information in a managerial context.
- *Summaries of Key Points*, located at the end of each chapter, integrate all key topics and concepts into several cogent paragraphs and link them with the chapter's stated learning objectives.
- *Key Terms and Phrases* provide a useful review of each chapter's terminology.
- *Discussion Questions and Activities*, located at the end of each chapter, are suitable for individual or group analysis. Included are collaboration questions aimed at fostering group activity.
- *Case Problems*, located at the end of each chapter, illustrate major themes of the chapter and are suitable for individual or group analysis. Case Problems are uniquely designed to complement this textbook, and include relevant follow-up discussion questions.

THE FRAMEWORK

Fundamentals of Organizational Behavior is a blend of description, skill development, insight, and prescription. Divided into four parts, it moves from the micro to the macro, beginning with a brief introduction to the discipline. It then progresses to an exploration of the individual, to a discussion of groups and intergroup dynamics, and to an examination of organizational systems.

As just noted, Part 1 provides an introduction to organizational behavior. Chapter 1 focuses on the nature and scope of organizational behavior and provides the foundation for what is to come.

Part 2 includes six chapters that deal with the individual in the organization. Chapter 2 describes fundamental aspects of understanding individuals in terms of individual differences, mental ability, and personality. Chapter 3 describes individuals from the standpoint of learning, perception, and values. Chapter 4 describes attitudes, job satisfaction, and ethics as they relate to behavior in organizations. Chapter 5 is about individual decision making and creativity. Chapter 6 presents basic concepts of motivation, and Chapter 7 discusses techniques for enhancing motivation.

Part 3, about groups and intergroup relations, contains six chapters. Chapter 8 is about interpersonal communication, and Chapter 9 covers group dynamics, including the characteristics of an effective work group. Chapter 10 is devoted to teams and teamwork. Chapter 11 deals with leadership, a cornerstone topic in organizational behavior and management. Chapter 12 extends the study of leadership by describing power, politics, and influence. Chapter 13 describes the nature and management of conflict and stress. (This chapter deals in part with interpersonal phenomena and in part with individual phenomena.)

Part 4, about the organizational system and the global environment, contains four chapters covering macro issues in organizational behavior. Chapter 14 deals with organization structure and design. Chapter 15 is about organizational culture and knowledge management. Chapter 16 is about organizational change and innovation, but it also deals with the individual profiting from change. Chapter 17 covers cultural diversity and cross-cultural organizational behavior.

CHANGES IN THE SIXTH EDITION

The sixth edition updates the fifth edition as the knowledge base of organizational behavior continues to evolve. Fifteen of the seventeen chapter-opening vignettes and Organizational Behavior in Action boxes are new. Fifteen of the seventeen case problems are new, and new research findings can be found in every chapter. We have also selectively eliminated concepts that are essentially new names and labels for existing concepts. In several instances, we have eliminated the descriptions of research and focused on the conclusion of the research. We have reduced the number of technical terms, particularly where recent terms are variations of useful terms that already exist. Four new self-assessment quizzes and one new skill-development exercise are added to the book. Major additions and new or enhanced topical coverage are listed here, chapter by chapter:

Chapter 1: The Nature and Scope of Organizational Behavior

The history of organizational behavior includes a mention of artificial intelligence. A section on "The New Age Workplace" is added to the history of organizational behavior.

Chapter 2: Individual Differences, Mental Ability, and Personality

A self-assessment quiz about narcissism is added to the chapter. A brief section is now included about how performance is aided by having the optimum amount of a given personality trait. Information is presented about competencies associated with emotional intelligence.

Chapter 3: Learning, Perception, and Values

The link between modeling and social cognitive theory is added. An implication for managerial practice is added about not stereotyping workers who are talented in one aspect of work.

Chapter 4: Attitudes, Job Satisfaction, and Ethics

A key approach to enhancing ethical and socially responsible behavior is added: focus on the triple bottom line of profit, people, and the planet. Information is added about a meta-analysis of the positive consequences of ethical leadership on organizational performance.

Chapter 5: Individual Decision Making and Creativity

The classical/behavioral decision-making model is replaced by simply a decision-making model. Decision biases are added to the influences on decision making. Information is provided about how artificial intelligence influences managerial decision making.

Chapter 6: Foundation Concepts of Motivation

A discussion of grit as part of intrinsic motivation is added to the chapter. A self-assessment quiz about grit is also provided.

Chapter 7: Motivational Methods and Programs

A brief section is added about how having a purpose or cause contributes to meaningful work. Information is also provided about how a sense of purpose can be found in performing mundane or routine tasks. Information is added about how using personal strengths and performing tasks of interest contribute to job crafting.

Chapter 8: Interpersonal Communication

Additional information is presented about how the human touch can enhance the benefits of computer-mediated communication. A new point is added to overcoming cross-cultural communication barriers by recognizing cultural differences in behavior during meetings.

Chapter 9: Group Dynamics

Psychological safety is added as a characteristic of work group effectiveness. Another new section describes the problems of excessive collaboration including workflow bottlenecks and burnout.

Chapter 10: Teams and Teamwork

A brief summary is presented about how encouraging trust in a virtual team enhances collaboration. The role of prosocial motivation in building teamwork is explained.

Chapter 11: Leadership in Organizations

A self-assessment quiz about strategic thinking is added to the section about cognitive skills. A section is added on mindfulness as a leadership behavior. Crisis leadership is presented as a form of contingency leadership. We eliminate the section about the path-goal theory and substitutes for leadership to help reduce the complexity of the chapter.

Chapter 12: Power, Politics, and Influence

The *hubris syndrome* is presented as an explanation of how too much power can corrupt a leader. Bringing forth solutions rather than problems is added as an ethical political tactic.

Chapter 13: Conflict and Stress

More extensive information is presented about sexual harassment because of heightened interest in the topic. Abusive supervision is highlighted as a contributor to conflict. A self-assessment quiz is included about a person's approach to negotiation. The negotiation tactic of "use facts more than threats" is added. Another stressor is presented, *nomophobia*, referring to not having a smartphone accessible. More information is presented about organizational wellness programs.

Chapter 14: Organization Structure and Design

Information is presented about how organizational silos can be dysfunctional. Figure 14-3 is revised, showing the new product organizational structure at Caterpillar. A skill-development exercise is added about choosing an organization structure for your own company.

Chapter 15: Organizational Culture and Knowledge Management

Orientation toward serving customers and joy and happiness are added as dimensions of organizational culture. Two new consequences of organizational culture are added: emotional and physical safety of workers, and organizational health.

Chapter 16: Organizational Change and Innovation

A key addition is an influence model of the change process in organizations. A new tactic for overcoming resistance to change is added: leaders must change also. Artificial intelligence is added to the discussion of how information technology has changed organizations. The sections on linkage analysis and the process consultation are deleted because of their waning use. An eighth behavioral principle of innovation is added—imposing some constraints on innovation.

Chapter 17: Cultural Diversity and Cross-Cultural Organizational Behavior

Avoiding cultural gaffes is added to the section about the advantages of cultural diversity. Information is presented about SAP as a multicultural organization. A seventh cross-cultural negotiating tactic is added, related to integrative versus distributed outcomes. Recruitment of minority group members is added as a corporate diversity initiative, as is anti-bias training.

ONLINE AND IN PRINT

STUDENT OPTIONS: PRINT AND ONLINE VERSIONS

This sixth edition of *Fundamentals of Organizational Behavior* is available in multiple versions: online, in PDF, and in print as either a paperback or loose-leaf text. The content of each version is identical.

The most affordable version is the online book, with upgrade options including the online version bundled with a print version. What is nice about the print version is that it offers you the freedom of being unplugged—away from your computer. The people at Academic Media Solutions recognize that it is difficult to read from a screen at length and that most of us read much faster from a piece of paper. The print options are particularly useful when you have extended print passages to read.

The online edition allows you to take full advantage of embedded digital features, including search and notes. Use the search feature to locate and jump to discussions anywhere in the book. Use the notes feature to add personal comments or annotations. You can move out of the book to follow Web links. You can navigate within and between chapters using a clickable table of contents. These features allow you to work at your own pace and in your own style, as you read and surf your way through the material. (See "Harnessing the Online Version" for more tips on working with the online version.)

HARNESSING THE ONLINE VERSION

The online version of *Fundamentals of Organizational Behavior* offers the following features to facilitate learning and to make using the book an easy, enjoyable experience:

- *Easy-to-navigate/clickable table of contents*—You can surf through the book quickly by clicking on chapter headings, or first- or second-level section headings. And the Table of Contents can be accessed from anywhere in the book.

- *Key terms search*—Type in a term, and a search engine will return every instance of that term in the book; then jump directly to the selection of your choice with one click.

- *Notes and highlighting*—The online version includes study apps such as notes and highlighting. Each of these apps can be found in the tools icon embedded in the Academic Media Solutions/Textbook Media's online eBook reading platform (www.academicmediasolutions.com).

- *Upgrades*—The online version includes the ability to purchase additional study apps and functionality that enhance the learning experience.

INSTRUCTOR SUPPLEMENTS

In addition to its student-friendly features and pedagogy, the variety of student formats available, and the uniquely affordable pricing options that are designed to provide students with a flexibility that fits any budget and/or learning style, *Fundamentals of Organizational Behavior*, 6e, comes with the following teaching and learning aids:

- *Test Item File*—This provides an extensive set of multiple-choice, short answer, and essay questions for every chapter for creating original quizzes and exams.

- *Instructor's Manual*—This is a condensed version of the book offering assistance in preparing lectures, identifying learning objectives, developing essay exams and assignments, and constructing course syllabi.

- *PowerPoint Presentations*—Key points in each chapter are illustrated in a set of PowerPoint files designed to assist with instruction.

- *Online Video Labs with Student Worksheets*—A collection of high-quality, dynamic, and sometimes humorous video segments (contemporary and classic) produced by a variety of media, academic, and entertainment sources, accessed via the web. Organized by chapter, the video segments illustrate key topics/issues discussed in the chapters. Each video segment is accompanied by a student worksheet that consists of a series of discussion questions that helps students connect the themes presented in the video segment with key topics discussed in the specific chapter.

STUDENT SUPPLEMENTS AND UPGRADES (ADDITIONAL PURCHASE REQUIRED)

- *Lecture Guide*—This printable lecture guide is designed for student use and is available as an in-class resource or study tool. Note: Instructors can request the PowerPoint version of these slides either to use as developed or to customize.

- *Quizlet Study Set*—Quizlet is an easy-to-use online learning tool built from all the key terms from the textbook. Students can turbo charge their studying via digital flashcards and other types of study apps, including tests and games. Students are able to listen to audio, as well as create their own flashcards. Quizlet is a cross-platform application and can be used on a desktop, tablet, or smartphone.

- *Study Guide*—A printable version of the online study guide is available via downloadable PDF chapters for easy self-printing and review.

Acknowledgments

The final topical content and organization of this text were heavily influenced by the results of a survey of professors who expressed interest in using a shorter, more concise textbook. Instructors from 60 colleges provided their opinions on what subjects form the foundation of their courses. They also provided feedback on the types of pedagogical activities and features that provide real value to the introductory organizational behavior course. My writing also benefited from the suggestions of numerous reviewers, some of whom, for reasons of confidentiality, must remain anonymous. Grateful acknowledgment is made to

Lori Abrams
University of Minnesota

David C. Baldridge
Oregon State University

Talya N. Bauer
Portland State University

Dorothy Brandt
Brazosport College

Neil S. Bucklew
West Virginia University

Glenna Dod
Wesleyan College

Debi Griggs
Bellevue Community College

Mary Humphrys
University of Toledo

Avis L. Johnson
University of Akron

Marianne W. Lewis
University of Cincinnati

Jalane M. Meloun
Kent State University

Linda Morable
Richland College

Claire Marie Nolin
Eastern Connecticut State University

Regina M. O'Neill
Suffolk University

Douglas Palmer
Trinity College

Sarah Robinson
Indiana University–Purdue University Indianapolis

John W. Rogers
American International College

James Smas
Kent State University

Darrin Sorrells
Oakland City University

Bonnie Tiell
Tiffin University

Mary Anne Watson
University of Tampa

Thanks also to the staff at Academic Media Solutions (AMS) who worked with me to publish this new edition of *Fundamentals of Organizational Behavior*: Daniel C. Luciano, president/founder of AMS, and Victoria Putman of Putman Productions. My special thanks go also to Professors Douglas Benton of Colorado State University, Terri Scandura of the University of Miami, and Ann Welsh of the University of Cincinnati, who read the entire first-edition manuscript and made many valuable suggestions that continue to inform my work.

Finally, writing without loved ones would be a lonely task. My thanks therefore go to my family: Drew, Heidi, Douglas, Gizella, Melanie, Drake, Rosie, Clare, Camila, Sofia, Eliana, Julian, Carson, and Owen. I thank also Stefanie, the woman in my life, and her daughter, Sofie, for their contribution to my well-being.

Andrew J. DuBrin

About the Author

Andrew J. DuBrin is professor emeritus of management in the College of Business at the Rochester Institute of Technology, where he has taught courses and conducts research in management, organizational behavior, leadership, and career management. He has served the college as chairman of the management department and as team leader. He received his Ph.D. in industrial psychology from Michigan State University. His business experience is in human resource management, and he consults with organizations and with individuals. His specialties include leadership and career management.

Professor DuBrin is an established author of textbooks, scholarly books, and trade titles. He also has written for professional journals and magazines. He has written textbooks on leadership, the principles of management, political behavior in organizations, industrial psychology, and human relations. His scholarly books include the subjects of crisis leadership, impression management, narcissism, and the proactive personality. His trade titles cover many current issues, including coaching and mentoring, team play, office politics, coping with adversity, and tolerating ambiguity.

The Nature and Scope of Organizational Behavior

CHAPTER 1

Monkey Business Images/Shutterstock.com

Chapter Outline

Learning Objectives

After reading and studying this chapter and doing the exercises, you should be able to:

1. Explain what organizational behavior means.

2. Summarize the research methods of organizational behavior.

3. Identify the potential advantages of organizational-behavior knowledge.

4. Explain key events in the history of organizational behavior.

5. Understand how a person develops organizational-behavior skills.

Based in Fort Worth, Texas, the Starr Conspiracy is a marketing and advertising agency whose primary clients are enterprise software and services companies. Starr believes that it is changing the way marketing is done. The agency sees itself as the driving force behind the disruptors, the innovators, and the attention grabbers. Another self-descriptor is, "We are the agency of the future, and we explore beyond what currently exists—at an unmatched velocity."

Staff members at Starr have been collaborating closely on projects for four years. If you peek into the glass-walled conference rooms, notes chief executive Brett Starr, you will see people who would never sit together in a coffeehouse. These people are artists, marketers, data analysts, and software engineers. Yet Starr management saw a need for improvement in how well staff members collaborate and how smoothly they work together.

Starr engaged the services of a workplace behavior consultant to build self-directed teams responsible for coordinating their own work on client projects. Teams participate in face-to-face meetings with managers almost daily to give status reports or request support. Before these self-directed groups were formed, individual staff members were frequently interrupted by different managers with questions about projects, including a few that they were not ready to discuss at the time.

The consultant also trained Starr's 68 staff members to understand each other's communication and learning styles. For example, the top sales executive spoke so fast that other people could not process what he was saying. The executive had to learn to slow down so that the information he presented could be useful to others. An agency co-owner had to learn to listen more and give fewer presentations.

Starr employees say their projects and designs have become more creative and broader in scope, attributed to better cooperation and collaboration. Starr Art Director Nancy Crabb says, "Working across so many disciplines at once, we're able to tackle problems that I never would have tried previously."[1]

The story just presented illustrates how a company might make systematic use of knowledge of human behavior, including two relevant techniques to enhance the functioning of an organization. (The two techniques are self-directed teams and learning each other's communication and learning styles.) The purpose of this book is to present systematic knowledge about people and organizations that can be used to enhance individual and organizational effectiveness. Managers and potential managers are the most likely to apply this information. Yet the same information is important for other workers, including corporate professionals, sales representatives, customer service specialists, and technical specialists.

In the modern organization, workers at every level do some of the work that was formerly the sole domain of managers. Team members, for example, are often expected to motivate and train each other. One reason organizations get by with fewer managers than previously is that workers themselves are now expected to manage themselves to some extent. Self-management of this type includes the team scheduling its own work and making recommendations for quality improvement.

In this chapter we introduce organizational behavior from several perspectives. We will explain the meaning of the term, see why organizational behavior is useful, and take a brief glance at its history including current developments. After describing how to develop skills in organizational behavior, we present a framework for understanding the field. An important goal in studying organizational behavior is to be able to make sense of any organization in which you are placed, so that, for example, you might be able to answer the question: What is going on here from a human standpoint?

The Meaning and Research Methods of Organizational Behavior

A starting point in understanding the potential contribution of organizational behavior is to know the meaning of the term. It is also important to be familiar with how information about organizational behavior is acquired.

The Meaning of Organizational Behavior

Organizational behavior (OB) is the study of human behavior in the workplace, of the interaction between people and the organization, and of the organization itself.[2] The major goals of organizational behavior are to explain, predict, and control behavior.

Explanation refers to describing the underlying reasons or process by which phenomena occur. For example, an understanding of leadership theory would explain why one person is a more effective leader than another. The same theory would help predict which people (e.g., those having charismatic qualities) are likely to be effective as leaders. Leadership theory could also be useful in controlling (or influencing) people. One leadership theory, for example, contends that group members are more likely to be satisfied and productive when the leader establishes good relationships with them.

Data Collection and Research Methods in Organizational Behavior

To explain, predict, and control behavior, organizational-behavior specialists must collect information systematically and conduct research. The purpose of collecting data is to conduct research.

Methods of Data Collection

Three frequently used methods of collecting data in organizational behavior are surveys, interviews, and direct observation of behavior. The *survey questionnaire* used by a specialist in organizational behavior is prepared rigorously. Before preparing a final questionnaire, a scientist collects relevant facts and generates hypotheses (educated guesses) about important issues to explore. The questionnaire is carefully designed to measure relevant issues about the topic being surveyed. For example, participants in a study might be asked to evaluate their supervisor in various dimensions such as giving clear instructions and showing compassion. Among the surveys included in this textbook is the self-quiz about conscientiousness in Chapter 2.

Research about human behavior in the workplace relies heavily on the *interview* as a method of data collection. Even when a questionnaire is the primary method of data collection, interviews are usually used to obtain ideas for survey questions. Interviews are also helpful in uncovering explanations about phenomena and furnishing leads for further inquiry. Another advantage of interviews is that a skilled interviewer can probe for additional information. One disadvantage of the interview method is that skilled interviewers are required.

Naturalistic observations refer to researchers placing themselves in the work environment to collect much information about organizational behavior. Systematic observations

People engaged in highly technical work can also benefit from knowledge of organizational behavior because they too have frequent interactions with people and have to be creative.

LEARNING OBJECTIVE 1
Explain what organizational behavior means.

organizational behavior (OB)
The study of human behavior in the workplace, the interaction between people and the organization, and the organization itself.

LEARNING OBJECTIVE 2
Summarize the research methods of organizational behavior.

Direct observation of people is one method of data collection.

are then made about the phenomena under study. One concern about this method is that the people under observation may perform atypically when they know they are being observed. A variation of systematic observation is *participant observation*. The observer becomes a member of the group about which he or she collects information. For example, to study stress experienced by customer service representatives, a researcher might work temporarily in a customer service center.

Research Methods

Four widely used research methods of organizational behavior are case studies, laboratory experiments, field experiments (or studies), and meta-analyses.

Case information is usually collected by an observer recording impressions in his or her mind or on a notepad or tablet computer. People have a tendency to attend to information specifically related to their own interests or needs. Despite this subjective element in the case method, cases provide a wealth of information that can be used to explain what is happening in a given situation.

An *experiment* is the most rigorous research method. The essence of conducting an experiment is making sure that the variable being modified (the independent variable) influences the results. The independent variable (e.g., a motivational technique) is thought to influence the dependent variable (e.g., productivity). The dependent variable is also known as the *criterion* (or *measure*).

A major characteristic of the *laboratory experiment* is that the conditions are supposedly under the experimenter's control. For example, to study the effects of stress on problem-solving ability, a group of people might be brought into a room. The stressor the experimenter introduces is an electronic beeping noise. In a field setting, however, assuming the experiment was permitted, the experimenter might be unaware of what other stressors the subjects faced at that time. A key concern about laboratory experiments, therefore, is that their results might not apply to the outside world.

Field experiments (or *studies*) attempt to apply the experimental method to real-life situations. Variables can be controlled more readily in the laboratory than in the field, but information obtained in the field is often more relevant. An example of a field experiment would be investigating whether giving employees more power would have an effect on their motivation to produce a great quantity of work. The independent variable would be empowerment, while the dependent variable would be quantity of work.

meta-analysis A quantitative or statistical review of the literature on a particular subject; an examination of a range of studies for the purpose of reaching a combined result or best estimate.

A widely used approach to reaching conclusions about behavior is to combine the results of a large number of studies. A **meta-analysis** is a quantitative or statistical review of the literature on a particular subject and is also an examination of a range of studies for the purpose of reaching a combined result or best estimate. A meta-analysis is therefore a review of studies, combining their quantitative information. You can also view meta-analysis as a quantitative review of the literature on a particular subject. For example, a researcher might want to combine the results of 100 different studies about the job-performance consequences of group decision making before reaching a conclusion. Many of the research findings presented throughout this book are based on meta-analysis rather than on the results of a single study. Meta-analysis continues to gain in frequency of use, as reflected in the many published research studies based on the technique.

An important use of meta-analysis in organizational behavior is to understand how certain factors, referred to as *moderator variables*, influence the results of studies.[3] For example, in the experiment mentioned previously about stress and problem-solving ability, a moderator variable might be the amount of stress a study participant faces in personal life. Individuals who enter the experiment already stressed might be influenced more negatively by the electronic beeping noise.

Meta-analysis gives the impression of being scientific and reliable because so much information is assimilated, using sophisticated statistical tools. One might argue, however, that it is better to perform one rigorous study than to analyze many poorly conducted studies. A meta-analysis often consists of combining some carefully executed studies with a few of poor quality.

Quantitative versus Qualitative Research Methods

Another way to classify research methods is determining whether they are quantitative or qualitative.[4] Quantitative research involves collecting data, such as customer-satisfaction survey responses and production records. The data are then subject to a variety of statistical techniques including correlational analysis, regression analysis, and analysis of variance. Recording the results of experiments and meta-analysis are also examples of quantitative research methods.

Qualitative research involves the researcher interacting with the source of the data, such as talking to workers and even taking videos and still photos. Interviews and participant observations are qualitative research methods. Naturalistic observation (observing people in natural settings) is frequently used as a method of qualitative research. Recognize, however, that qualitative research closely resembles quantitative research when the data from the qualitative observations are coded. For example, while interviewing workers about their job satisfaction, every response that contains a certain topic might be assigned a code. To illustrate, when workers mention the topic of "consideration for my feelings," the response category of "consideration" would receive one entry. The entries would be tallied to yield a quantitative result. Many of the most important insights and theories in organizational behavior stem from qualitative research, such as uncovering what motivates people, and how organizations profit or learn from their experiences.

When management professors were asked to express their understanding of the difference between quantitative and qualitative research, one of the valuable insights that emerged was: "Quantitative research is about careful preparation and faithful execution of the plan laid out in the beginning; qualitative research is about exploring ideas."[5] Assume that a researcher wanted to study the conditions under which workers in a nonprofit organization are creative. Using a quantitative research method, he or she would prepare a lengthy questionnaire about organizational conditions related to creativity, and then administer the questionnaire to a large group of staff members in a few nonprofit organizations. Using a qualitative method, she might visit a few nonprofit agencies, and talk to workers about their creative problem solving.

How You Can Benefit from Studying Organizational Behavior

LEARNING OBJECTIVE 3
Identify the potential advantages of organizational-behavior knowledge.

Studying organizational behavior can enhance your effectiveness as a manager or professional. Yet the benefits from studying organizational behavior are not as immediately apparent as those derived from the study of functional fields such as accounting, marketing, purchasing, and information technology. Such fields constitute the *content* of managerial and professional work. Organizational behavior, in contrast, relates to the *process* of conducting such work. An exception may be seen with organizational-behavior specialists whose content, or functional knowledge, deals with organizational-behavior concepts and methods.

Visualize a woman industrial health specialist who has extremely limited interpersonal skills in communicating, motivating, and resolving conflict. She will have a difficult time applying her technical expertise to organizational problems. She will therefore fail in serving her clients because she lacks the ability to use effective interpersonal processes. In contrast, if the same health specialist had strong interpersonal skills, she could do a better job of serving her clients. (She would probably also hold onto her job longer.)

Studying and learning about organizational behavior offers four key advantages: (1) interpersonal skill development, (2) personal growth, (3) enhancement of organizational and individual effectiveness, and (4) sharpening and refinement of common sense.

Interpersonal Skill Development

Interpersonal skills remain of major importance in the modern workplace. These skills generally refer to getting along with people in a variety of ways such as motivating them,

Interpersonal skills are useful for people who wear a hard hat to work.

complimenting them, and being able to resolve conflict. People with good interpersonal skills are considered more rewarding to deal with.

Anil Singhal, the founder of NetScout Systems, a company that assists business firms and government agencies in managing their information technology networks, has helped many young employees make the transition to midcareer success. He believes that "primary skills" can take you only so far in your career. Singhal says that those talents by which you earned your college degree and first made your professional reputation can drive success for the first 10 years of a career. After that period, "secondary skills"—interpersonal skills such as the ability to interact well with coworkers—become key to continued success.[6]

More support for the key role of interpersonal skills in attaining career success stems from the observations of three economists. The trio found that high-paying occupations, including software engineer, financial advisor, and medical professional, require high-level interpersonal skills such as collaboration, empathy, and managing others.[7]

A major reason that interpersonal skill development is a key to success is that difficulty with interpersonal skills is a major reason behind career derailment. As Teddy Roosevelt said, "The most important single ingredient in the formula of success is to know how to get along with people."[8]

The distinction between *soft* skills and *hard* skills is relevant for understanding the importance of interpersonal skill development, as well as the development of other skills, in organizational behavior. Soft skills are generally interpersonal skills such as motivating others, communicating, and adapting to people of different cultures. Hard skills are generally technical skills, such as information technology and job design. Some skills, such as those involved with decision making, have a mixture of soft and hard components. To make good decisions you have to be creative and imaginative (perhaps a soft skill), yet you also have to weigh evidence carefully (most likely a hard skill).

Personal Growth through Insight into Human Behavior

As explained by Robert P. Vecchio, an important reason for studying organizational behavior is the personal fulfillment gained from understanding others.[9] Understanding fellow human beings can also lead to enhanced self-knowledge and self-insight. For example, while studying what motivates others, you may gain an understanding of what motivates you. Participating in the experiential exercises and self-assessments included in this textbook provides another vehicle for personal growth. A case in point is the study of motivation in Chapter 6. You will be invited to take a self-quiz about the meaningfulness of work to you. Taking the test and reviewing the results will give insight into the types of attitudes and behaviors you need to make your work more meaningful.

Personal growth through understanding others and self-insight is meritorious in and of itself, and it also has practical applications. Managerial and professional positions require sharp insights into the minds of others for tasks such as selecting people for jobs and assignments, communicating, and motivating. Sales representatives who can size up the needs of prospects and customers have a competitive advantage. Another value of understanding others and self-insight is that they contribute to continuous learning because the needs of others change over time, and so might your needs. For example, the recent prosperity and labor shortages have prompted many workers to demand exciting and meaningful work and worry less about job security.

Enhancement of Organizational and Individual Effectiveness

organizational effectiveness The extent to which an organization is productive and satisfies the demands of its interested parties.

A major benefit from studying organizational behavior is that it provides information that can be applied to organizational problems. An important goal of organizational behavior is to improve **organizational effectiveness**— the extent to which an organization is productive and satisfies the demands of its interested parties. Each chapter of this book contains information that is applied directly or indirectly by many organizations. One visible example is the widespread use of teams in the workplace. Certainly, organizational-behavior specialists did not invent teams. We suspect even prehistoric people organized some of their hunting forays by teams. Nevertheless, the conclusions of organizational-behavior researchers facilitated the shift to teams in organizations.

Individual effectiveness can be enhanced through studying organizational behavior.

Why does paying more attention to the human element improve business performance? One explanation Jeffrey Pfeffer offers is that people work harder when they have greater control over their work environment and when they are encouraged by peer pressure from teammates. Even more advantage comes from people working in a smarter way. People-oriented management practices enable workers to use their wisdom and to receive appropriate training. Another contribution to improved performance stems from eliminating positions that focus primarily on watching and controlling workers.[10] Much of organizational behavior deals with people-oriented management practices. Many of these practices will be described in later chapters.

Understanding organizational behavior also improves organizational effectiveness because it uncovers factors that contribute to or hinder effective performance. Among these many factors are employee motivation, personality factors, and communication barriers. Furthermore, an advanced understanding of people is a major contributor to managerial success. This is especially true because so much of a manager's job involves accomplishing tasks through people.

Organizational behavior also contributes insights and skills that can enhance individual effectiveness. If a person develops knowledge about subjects such as improved interpersonal communication, conflict resolution, and teamwork, he or she will become more effective. A specific example is that knowledge about organizational behavior can contribute to high performance. Executive coach Lisa Parker observes that managers sometimes neglect to give encouragement and recognition to good performers because these workers are already performing well. Yet if these same solid performers were given more encouragement, coaching in the form of advice, and recognition, they will often develop into superstars (very high performers).[11]

A frequent problem noted about managers is that they supervise too closely, or micromanage, the work of subordinates. One result is that employees can feel insecure and offended when their manager takes over a project that was assigned to them. If a present or future manager studies organizational behavior, he or she might become more aware of the problems of micromanagement, and then monitor his or her behavior to prevent micromanaging.[12]

The "Organizational Behavior in Action" box illustrates how a manager might use organizational-behavior knowledge in the form of paying attention to the human element to improve organizational effectiveness.

Sharpening and Refining Common Sense

A manager commented after reading through several chapters of an organizational-behavior textbook, "Why should I study this field? It's just common sense. My job involves dealing with people, and you can't learn that through a book." Many other students of organizational behavior share the sentiments expressed by this manager. However logical such an opinion might sound, common sense is not an adequate substitute for knowledge about organizational behavior. This knowledge sharpens and enlarges the domain of common sense. It markedly reduces the amount of time necessary to acquire important behavioral knowledge and skills, much as law school reduces the amount of time that a person in a previous era would have had to spend as a law apprentice.

Michelle Gass, the Kohl's CEO Who Combines Functional Skills with a Human Touch

After 17 years of experience in a variety of marketing roles at Starbucks, Michelle Gass (pronounced "Goss") was hired as the chief customer officer at the department store chain Kohl's. One of her first initiatives was to give a pep talk to employees at the retailer's headquarters in Menomonee Falls, Wisconsin. Gass sensed that a motivational talk was needed because, after several years of a post-recession growth, sales had begun to slip. As with other brick-and-mortar stores, competition from online retailers and boutiques was eating into sales.

Gass told the employees that Kohl's needed to think differently and that they should not be afraid to attempt new ideas, something most employees had been hesitant to do in the past. The willingness to change and to inspire employees were two of the reasons that Gass was chosen in 2017 to succeed Kevin Mansell as chief executive.

After graduating in 1966 from the Worcester Polytechnic Institute with a BS in chemical engineering, Gass decided to specialize in marketing. She received an MBA from the school of business at the University of Washington, followed by over five years of marketing experience at Procter & Gamble. Gass then spent nearly 17 years at Starbucks. Her last position at Starbucks was to head the company's unit that covered Europe, the Middle East, and Africa.

When Kohl's hired Gass, retail analyst Michael Exstein said that the retailer had "Gone outside the retail industry to hire someone with a pristine reputation in operations and strength in branding." While at Starbucks, Gass contributed significantly to the brand's turnaround. Gass was credited with the remake of Starbuck's Seattle's Best coffee brand. She also spearheaded the introduction of Frappuccino drinks and VIA instant coffee, as well as the My Starbuck's Rewards loyalty program. As a marketer, Gass was credited with always giving clear directions.

Her responsibilities as chief customer officer at Kohl's included marketing and e-commerce as well as acting as the chief merchandising officer for all products sold in the stores. Gass also pushed Kohl's to participate in the employee health and wellness trend.

Perhaps her boldest move was to form an alliance with Amazon whereby Kohl's sells several Amazon electronic products in selected stores. In addition, customers are allowed to return goods bought online at Amazon at over eighty Kohl's locations. Gass also convinced Under Armour Inc. to sell its gear at Kohl's, giving the retailer a strong presence in the activewear category.

Chip Bergli, the CEO of Levi Strauss & Co., has described Michelle Gass as a proven leader who has been a positive force for the retail business. Gass is recognized by work associates as quickly changing course when an idea an initiative fails. For example, Kohl's experimented with in-store coffee shops but abandoned the plan when the shops proved to be unprofitable. Mansell said that Gass has a "bias for action," meaning that she moves swiftly when making a tough decision such as closing an underperforming location.

Despite the increasing pressures facing her company as a retailer with stand-alone stores, Gass maintains a warm demeanor and smiles frequently in her interactions with coworkers and other employees.

QUESTIONS

1. What evidence that Michelle Gass combines functional (discipline-related) skills with a human touch is provided in this description?

2. Assuming that you wanted to apply your major to working in the retail field, how would you like to have Gass as your boss?

3. Relying on whatever current information you can quickly gather, how successful has Gass been as the CEO of Kohl's?

Source: Original case created from information in the following sources: Suzanne Kapner, "Kohl's Chooses Marketer as Next Chief Executive," *The Wall Street Journal*, September 17, 2017, p. B12; Rick Romell, "Mansell to Retire as Kohl's CEO: Former Starbucks Executive Gass to Succeed Him," *Milwaukee Journal Sentinel*, September 26, 2017, pp. 1–2; Sarah Halzack, "Michelle Gass Could Lead Department Stores Out of the Wilderness," www.bloomberg.com, December 21, 2007, pp. 1–6; Natalie Zmuda, "Starbucks Exec Michelle Gass Jumps to Kohl's as Chief Customer Officer," http://adage.com, pp. 1–4.

You may know through common sense that giving recognition to people is generally an effective method of motivating them toward higher performance. By studying organizational behavior, however, you might learn that recognition should be given frequently but not every time somebody attains high performance. (You specifically learn about intermittent rewards in your study of motivation.) You might also learn that the type of recognition you give should be tailored to the individual's personality and preferences. For example, some people like flamboyant praise, while others prefer praise focused tightly on the merits of their work. Formal knowledge thus enhances your effectiveness.

Organizational-behavior knowledge also refines common sense by challenging you to reexamine generally accepted ideas that may be only partially true. One such idea is that inactivity is an effective way to reduce stress from a hectic schedule. In reality, some hard-driving people find inactivity more stressful than activity. For them, lying on a beach for a week might trigger intense chest pains. For these people, diversionary physical activity—such as doing yard work—is more relaxing than inactivity.

If you study organizational behavior, you might become sensitized to the contribution of **evidence-based management**, or using research evidence to help make management decisions.[13] The Center for Evidence-Based Management points to four sources of evidence that should be considered, along with the quality of the evidence, when making a decision:

■ Findings from empirical (data-based) studies published in academic journals

■ Data, facts, and figures gathered from within the organization in which the decision maker is working

■ The experience and judgment of managers, professionals, and other practitioners

■ The values and concerns of the stakeholders (people involved with the organization) who may be affected by the decision[14]

Research and case-history evidence might be available for some types of decisions, but not all. The careful student of organizational behavior would look to see what evidence was available before making a decision. A relevant example is the movement toward employee engagement, or commitment to the work and company, as a way of enhancing organizational effectiveness. Some people regard employee engagement as a fad, yet evidence from hundreds of companies and over 60,000 employees indicates that employee engagement enhances organizational performance.[15]

An important caution about using evidence-based management is that you should not be frozen from making a decision just because relevant research on the topic is not available.[16] For example, a business owner might have the intuition that offering paternity leave to the men is his organization would boost employee loyalty and morale. He should make his decision now even if he cannot locate empirical research or other relevant data on this potential benefit of paternity leave.

A Brief History of Organizational Behavior

The history of organizational behavior is rooted in the **behavioral approach to management**, or the belief that specific attention to workers' needs creates greater satisfaction and productivity. In contrast to the largely technical emphasis of scientific management, a common theme of the behavioral approach is the need to focus on people. The behavioral approach to management was heavily influenced the work of psychologists and their study of individuals in the workplace. Furthermore, the fields of organizational psychology and organizational behavior resemble each other quite closely.

Scientific management did not ignore people altogether, and in some ways it contributed to organizational behavior. For example, scientific management heavily emphasized financial incentives to increase productivity. Yet the general thrust centered on performing work in a highly efficient manner.

Organizational behavior is also heavily influenced by social psychology, as well as sociology, the study of group behavior, organizational structure, diversity, and culture. In addition, the insights of cultural anthropologists contribute to an understanding of organizational culture (the values and customs of a firm), and they have been hired occasionally to help companies cultivate the right organizational culture. Organizational behavior also gains insights from political science by understanding the distribution of power in organizations.

Six key developments in the history of organizational behavior are the classical approach to management, the Hawthorne studies, the human relations movement, the

evidence-based management Using research evidence to help make management decisions.

LEARNING OBJECTIVE 4
Explain key events in the history of organizational behavior.

behavioral approach to management The belief that specific attention to the workers' needs creates greater satisfaction and productivity.

contingency approach to management and leadership, positive organizational behavior, and the Internet and social media era. The emergence of the new-age workplace might be considered the seventh key development.

The Classical Approach to Management

The study of management became more systematized and formalized as a by-product of the Industrial Revolution that took place from the 1700s through the 1900s. Managing these factories created the need for systems that could deal with large numbers of people performing repetitive work. The classical approach to management encompassed scientific management and administrative management and contributed some insights into understanding workplace behavior.

scientific management The application of scientific methods to increase worker's productivity.

The focus of **scientific management** was the application of scientific methods to increase an individual worker's productivity. An example would be assembling a lawn mower with the least number of wasted motions and steps. Frederick W. Taylor, considered the father of scientific management, was an engineer by background. He used scientific analysis and experiments to increase worker output. A key part of his system was to convert individuals into the equivalent of machine parts by assigning them specific, repetitive tasks.

Taylor tackled the dilemma of management wanting to maximize profits, and workers wanting to maximize possible wages. Disputes between management and labor centered on what each side saw as incompatible goals. Taylor believed that his system of scientific management could help both sides attain their goals, providing each would undergo a "mental revolution." Each side had to conquer its antagonistic view of the other. Taylor believed that management and labor should regard profit as the result of cooperation between the two parties. Management and labor each needed the other to attain their goals.[17] Scientific management is based on four principles, all of which direct behavior in the workplace.[18]

- Careful study of the jobs to develop standard work practices, with standardization of the tools workers use in their jobs
- Selection of each worker using scientific principles of personnel (human resources) selection
- Obtaining cooperation between management and workers to ensure that work is accomplished according to standard procedures
- Plans and task assignments developed by managers that workers should carry out

According to these principles of scientific management, there is a division of work between managers and workers. Managers plan and design work, assign tasks, set performance goals, and make time schedules. Managers also select and train workers to do the tasks according to standard procedures, and give the workers feedback about their performance. Workers are rewarded with financial incentives when they increase their productivity.[19]

administrative management A school of management thought concerned primarily with how organizations should be structured and managed.

Administrative management was concerned primarily with the management and structure of organizations. The French businessman Henri Fayol and the German scholar Max Weber were the main contributors to administrative management. Based on his practical experience, Fayol developed 14 management principles through which management engaged in planning, organizing, commanding, coordinating, and controlling. Weber suggested that bureaucracy is the best form or organization because it makes highly efficient management practices possible.

The core of management knowledge lies within the classical school. Its key contributions come from studying management from the framework of planning, organizing, leading, and controlling. The major strength of the classical school was providing a systematic way of measuring people and work that still exists in some form today. For example, United Parcel Service (UPS) carefully measures the output and work approaches of the delivery workers. The major limitation of the classical school is that it sometimes ignores differences among people and situations. In addition, some of the classical principles for developing an organization are not well suited to fast-changing situations.

The Hawthorne Studies

Many scholars pinpoint the Hawthorne studies (1923–1933) as the true beginning of the behavioral approach to management.[20] Without the insights gleaned from these studies, organizational behavior might not have emerged as a discipline. The purpose of the first study conducted at the Hawthorne plant of Western Electric (an AT&T subsidiary) was to determine the effect of changes in lighting on productivity. In this study, workers were divided into an experimental group and a control group. Lighting conditions for the experimental group varied in intensity from 24 to 46 to 70 foot-candles. The lighting for the control group remained constant.

The Hawthorne studies emphasized the climate of the work group.

As expected, the experimental group's output increased with each increase in light intensity. But unexpectedly, the performance of the control group also changed. The production of the control group increased at about the same rate as that of the experimental group. Later, the lighting in the experimental group's work area was reduced. This group's output continued to increase, as did that of the control group. A decline in the productivity of the control group finally did occur, but only when the intensity of the light was roughly the same as moonlight. Clearly, the researchers reasoned, something other than illumination caused the changes in productivity.

The relay assembly test room produced similar results over a 6-year period. In this case, relationships among rest, fatigue, and productivity were examined. First, normal productivity was established with no formal rest periods and a 48-hour week. Rest periods of varying length and frequency were then introduced. Productivity increased as the frequency and length of rest periods increased. Finally, the original conditions were reinstated. The return to the original conditions, however, did not result in the expected productivity drop. Instead, productivity remained at its usual high level.

One interpretation of these results was that the workers involved in the experiment enjoyed being the center of attention. Workers reacted positively because management cared about them. The phenomenon is referred to as the **Hawthorne effect**—the tendency of people to behave differently when they receive attention because they respond to the demands of the situation. In a research setting, this could mean that the people in an experimental group perform better simply because they are participating in an experiment. In a work setting, this could mean that employees perform better when they are part of any program—whether or not that program is valuable.

Hawthorne effect The tendency of people to behave differently when they receive attention because they respond to the demands of the situation.

The Hawthorne studies also produced other findings that served as the foundation for the human relations movement. Although many of these findings may seem obvious today, documenting them reinforced what many managers believed to be true. Key findings included the following:

1. Economic incentives are less potent than generally believed in influencing workers to achieve high levels of output.
2. Dealing with human problems is complicated and challenging.
3. Leadership practices and work-group pressures profoundly influence employee satisfaction and performance.
4. Personal problems can strongly influence worker productivity.
5. Effective communication with workers is critical to managerial success.
6. Any factor influencing employee behavior is embedded in a social system. For instance, to understand the impact of pay on performance, you have to understand the climate in the work group and the leadership style of the manager. Furthermore, work groups provide mutual support and may resist management schemes to increase output.

Despite the contributions of the Hawthorne studies, they have been criticized as lacking scientific rigor. The most interesting criticism contends that the workers in the control group were receiving feedback on their performance. Simultaneously, they were being paid more as they produced more. The dual impact of feedback and differential rewards produced the surprising results—not the Hawthorne effect.[21]

The Human Relations Movement

human relations movement An approach to dealing with workers based on the belief that there is an important link among managerial practices, morale, and productivity.

The **human relations movement** is based on the belief that there is an important link between managerial practices, morale, and productivity. Workers bring various social needs to the job. In performing their jobs, workers typically become members of several work groups. Often these groups provide satisfaction of some of the workers' needs. Satisfied workers, it was argued, would be more productive workers. The challenge for managers was to recognize workers' needs and the powerful influence that work groups can have on individual and organizational productivity.

A second major theme of the human relations movement is a strong belief in workers' capabilities. Given the proper working environment, virtually all workers would be highly productive. Significant amounts of cooperation between workers and managers prove critical to achieving high levels of productivity. A cornerstone of the human relations movement is Douglas McGregor's analysis of the assumptions managers make about human nature, delineated in two theories.[22] Theory X is a set of traditional assumptions about people. Managers who hold these assumptions are pessimistic about workers' capabilities. They believe that people dislike work, seek to avoid responsibility, are not ambitious, and must be supervised closely. McGregor urged managers to challenge these assumptions about human nature because they may be untrue in most circumstances.

Theory Y is an alternative, and optimistic, set of assumptions. These assumptions include the idea that people do accept responsibility, can exercise self-control, have the capacity to innovate, and consider work to be as natural as rest or play. McGregor argued that these assumptions accurately describe human nature in far more situations than most managers believe. He therefore proposed that these assumptions should guide managerial practice.

A large chunk of organizational behavior stems from the human relations movement. However, organizational behavior is more research-oriented than human relations and also develops more theories.

The Contingency Approach

Beginning in the early 1960s, organizational-behavior specialists emphasized the difficulties in finding universal principles of managing people that can be applied in all situations. To make effective use of knowledge about human behavior, one must understand which factors in a particular situation are most influential.

contingency approach to management The viewpoint that there is no one best way to manage people or work but that the best way depends on certain situational factors.

The **contingency approach to management** emphasizes that there is no one best way to manage people or work. A method that leads to high productivity or morale in one situation may not achieve the same results in another. The contingency approach is derived from the study of leadership styles. Experienced managers and leaders know that not all workers respond in the exact same way to identical leadership initiatives. A recurring example is that well-motivated, competent team members require less supervision than those who are poorly motivated and less competent. In Chapter 11, we present more information about the contingency approach to leadership.

The strength of the contingency approach is that it encourages managers and professionals to examine individual and situational differences before deciding on a course of action. Its major problem is that it is often used as an excuse for not acquiring formal knowledge about organizational behavior and management. If management depends on the situation, why study organizational behavior or management? The answer is that a formal study of organizational behavior or management helps a manager decide which factors are relevant in particular situations. In the leadership example just cited, the relevant factors are the skills and motivation of the group members.

Positive Organizational Behavior

A still-developing movement in organizational behavior is a focus on what is right with people. The human relations movement was a start in this direction. However, the movement toward focusing on strengths rather than weaknesses stems directly from *positive psychology*, with its emphasis on what is right with people, such as love, work, and play. Fred Luthans defines positive organizational behavior as the study and application of human resource strengths and psychological capacities that can be measured, developed, and managed for performance improvement.[23]

The criteria of being measurable and developmental are significant because they separate positive organizational behavior from simply giving pep talks and inspirational speeches to employees. An example would be the concept of *self-efficacy*, or having confidence in performing a specific task. A worker might be asked how confident he or she is to perform a difficult task, such as evaluating the risk of a particular investment. If his or her self-efficacy is not strong enough, additional experience and training might enhance the person's self-efficacy.

An everyday application of positive organizational behavior would be for a manager to focus on employee strengths rather than weaknesses. It is well accepted that encouraging a worker to emphasize strengths will lead to much more performance improvement than attempting to patch weaknesses. Assume that a person is talented in interpersonal relationships but weak in quantitative analysis. This person is likely to be more productive by further developing strengths in a position calling for relationship building. The less productive approach would be overcoming the weakness in quantitative analysis and attempting to become a financial specialist. (The point here is not that working on weakness is fruitless, but that capitalizing on strengths has a bigger potential payoff.)

In general, positive organizational behavior focuses on developing human strengths, making people more resilient, and cultivating extraordinary individuals, work units, and organizations. All of this is accomplished by careful attention to well-developed principles and research, rather than simply cheering people on.

positive organizational behavior The study and application of human resource strengths and psychological capacities that can be measured, developed, and managed for performance improvement.

The Internet and Social Media Era

As with every other field, how people behave in organizations has been affected by the Internet, including social networks. Rather than being a new approach to organizational behavior, these modern developments in information technology are incorporated into the work activities of the vast majority of workers at all levels in the organization. Rare exceptions do exist with respect to workers who do not have to use the Internet to accomplish their tasks. Among them are shoe shiners, street food vendors, hotel housekeepers, and circus clowns. Following are three of hundreds of possible examples of how the Internet and social media influence organizational behavior:

- Workers communicate and collaborate with each other through company social media networks, as well as public networks such as Facebook, Twitter, and Instagram.

- Team leaders motivate subordinates by sending them electronic messages in place of face-to-face meetings.

- Executives enhance their development of business strategy by gathering input from hundreds of company insiders and outsiders via a website dedicated for the purpose.

- Artificial intelligence (AI) is widely used to make more effective use of social media, such as targeting advertising to a person's unique profile of interests as revealed by previous clicks on shopping sites or news feeds. (The application of AI to decision making will be discussed in Chapter 5.)

The focus of our approach in this book as to how the Internet and social media affect organizational behavior will be in Chapter 8 about interpersonal communications.

The New-Age Workplace

new-age workplace Human-friendly spaces that accommodate both the digitalization of work and an emphasis on collaboration.

The new-age workplace refers to human-friendly spaces that accommodate both the digitalization of work and an emphasis on collaboration. Many of the demands for the new-age workplace come from millennials and other workers who have a strong desire for cooperation and teamwork. (The theme of collaboration is mentioned at various places in this book, and teamwork is explored in depth in Chapter 10.)

Advanced smart-building technologies enable workers to customize workspaces to their own needs and preferences, such as managing temperature, lighting, and even background music. Companies are also creating workspaces that encourage collaboration and team spirit, such as club rooms, meeting rooms that are warm and engaging, lounges, and whiteboard areas. Individual desks are still found widely, but they are often supplemented by tables for group seating in open-office plans. The freedom to work from remote locations is also part of the new-age workplace, even if not a new development.[24]

The physical aspects of the new-age workplace are tangible, but the intangible aspects are perhaps of greater significance. An emphasis on shared decision making, collaboration, and respecting the values of young and old, along with a more culturally diverse group of employees, are also an integral part of the new-age workplace.

Skill Development in Organizational Behavior

LEARNING OBJECTIVE 5
Understand how a person develops organizational-behavior skills.

Developing skill in organizational behavior means learning to work effectively with individuals, groups, and organizational forces. The greater one's responsibility, the more one is expected to work well at these three levels. Developing most organizational-behavior skills is more complex than developing a structured skill such as conducting a physical inventory or downloading an app for a mobile device. Nevertheless, you can develop organizational-behavior skills by reading this textbook and doing the exercises. The book follows a general learning model:

1. *Conceptual knowledge and behavioral guidelines.* Each chapter in this book presents research-based information about organizational behavior, including a section titled Implications for Managerial Practice.

2. *Conceptual information and examples.* These include brief descriptions of organizational behavior in action, generally featuring managers and leaders.

3. *Experiential exercises.* The book provides an opportunity for practice and personalization through cases and self-assessment exercises. Self-quizzes are included because they are an effective method of helping you personalize the information, assisting you in linking conceptual information to your own situation. For example, you will read about creative problem solving and also complete a quiz about creativity.

4. *Feedback on skill utilization, or performance, from others.* Feedback exercises appear at several places in the book. Implementing organizational-behavior skills outside the classroom will provide additional opportunities for feedback.

5. *Frequent practice.* Readers who look for opportunities to practice organizational-behavior skills outside the classroom will acquire skills more quickly. An important example is the development of creative thinking skills. The person who looks for imaginative solutions to problems regularly is much more likely to become a more creative thinker and be ready to think creatively at a given moment. Contrast this with the individual who participates in a creative-thinking exercise once, and then attempts the skill a year later when the need is urgent. As in any field, frequently practicing a skill the right way leads to skill improvement.

As you work through the book, keep the five-part learning model in mind. To help visualize this basic learning model, refer to Figure 1-1.

Developing organizational-behavior skills is also important because it contributes to your lifelong learning. A major theme of the modern organization is that to stay compet-

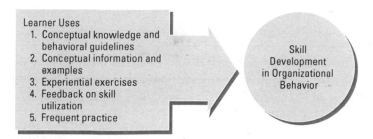

FIGURE 1-1 A Model for Developing Organizational-Behavior Skills

Organizational-behavior skills can be developed by using a systematic approach.

itive, a worker has to keep learning and developing. A relevant example is that as work organizations have become more culturally diverse, it is important to keep developing one's skills in working effectively with people from different cultures.

A Framework for Studying Organizational Behavior

A challenge in studying organizational behavior is that it lacks the clear-cut boundaries of subjects such as cell biology or Italian. Some writers in the field consider organizational behavior to be the entire practice of management. Others focus organizational behavior much more on the human element and its interplay with the total organization. Such is the orientation of this textbook. Figure 1-2 presents a basic framework for studying organizational behavior. The framework is simultaneously a listing of the contents of Chapters 2 through 17.

Proceeding from left to right, the foundation of organizational behavior is the study of individual behavior, presented in Chapters 2 through 7. No group or organization is so powerful that the qualities of individual members do not count. Visualize a famous athletic team with a winning history. Many fans contend that the spirit and tradition of

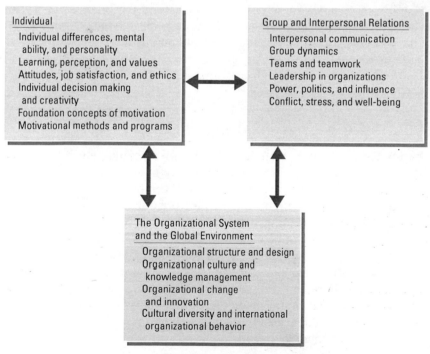

FIGURE 1-2 A Framework for Studying Organizational Behavior

To better understand organizational behavior, recognize that behavior at the individual, group, and organizational system, and global environmental levels are linked to one another.

the team, rather than individual capabilities, carry it through to victories against tough opponents. Yet if the team has a couple of poor recruiting years or loses a key coach, it may lose more frequently.

Key factors in understanding how individuals function include individual differences, mental ability and personality, learning, perception, attitudes, values, attribution, and ethics. It is also important to understand individual decision making, creativity, foundation concepts of motivation, and motivational programs.

As suggested by the arrows in Figure 1-2, the various levels of study are interconnected. Understanding how individuals behave contributes to an understanding of groups and interpersonal relations, the second level of the framework. This will be studied in Chapters 8 through 13. The topics include communication, group dynamics (how groups operate), teams and teamwork, and leadership. Although leadership relates directly to interpersonal relationships, top-level leaders are also concerned with influencing the entire organization. The study of power, politics, and influence is closely related to leadership. Conflict, stress, and well-being might be classified at the individual level, yet these processes are heavily dependent on interaction with others.

Finally, the third level of analysis in the study of organizational behavior is the organizational system and the global environment, as presented in Chapters 14 through 17. Components of the organizational and environmental level studied here include organizational structure and design, organizational culture, organizational change and knowledge management, cultural diversity, and international (or cross-cultural) organizational behavior. Cultural diversity and international organizational behavior could just as well have been studied before the other topics. Our position, however, is that everything else a person learns about organizational behavior contributes to an understanding of cross-cultural relations in organizations.

The connecting arrows in Figure 1-2 emphasize the interrelatedness of processes and topics at the three levels. Motivation provides a clear example. A person's motivational level is dependent on his or her individual makeup as well as work-group influences and the organizational culture. Some work groups and organizational cultures energize new members because of their highly charged atmospheres. The arrows also run in the other direction. Highly motivated workers, for example, improve work-group performance, contribute to effective interpersonal relationships, and enhance the organizational culture.

The influence of organizational-behavior factors may extend beyond the organization and lead to the firm's competitive advantage.[25] For example, the strongly talented individuals, high-performing teams, and high-performance culture that characterize Apple Inc. enhance its worldwide competitiveness.

Implications for Managerial Practice

Each of the following chapters includes a brief section explaining how managers and professionals can use selected information to enhance managerial practice. Our first lesson is the most comprehensive and perhaps the most important: Managers should raise their level of awareness about the availability of organizational behavior information. Before making decisions in dealing with people in a given situation, pause to search for systematic information about people and organizations. For example, if you need to resolve conflict, first review information about conflict resolution, such as that presented in Chapter 13. The payoff could be improved management of conflict.

Another key implication from this chapter is to search for strengths and talents in others and yourself, and then capitalize on these strengths as a way of improving organizational and individual effectiveness. Weaknesses should not be ignored, but capitalizing on strengths has a bigger potential payoff.

1. *Explain what organizational behavior means.* Organizational behavior is the study of human behavior in the workplace, the interaction between people and the organization, and the organization itself. Organizational behavior relates to the process, rather than the content, of managerial work.

2. *Summarize the research methods of organizational behavior.* Three frequently used methods of collecting data on organizational behavior are surveys (typically questionnaires), interviews, and direct observation of behavior. Four widely used research methods are case studies, laboratory experiments, field experiments, and meta-analysis. The essence of conducting an experiment is to make sure that the independent variable influences the results. Another way to classify research methods is whether they are quantitative or qualitative. Quantitative research is said to be about careful preparation and faithful execution of the plan laid out in the beginning; qualitative research is about exploring ideas.

3. *Identify the potential advantages of organizational-behavior knowledge.* Knowledge about organizational behavior offers four key advantages: interpersonal skill development, personal growth, the enhancement of organizational and personal effectiveness, and sharpening and refinement of common sense. Emphasizing the human factor increases productivity and gives a firm a competitive advantage. If you study organizational behavior, you might become more sensitized to the contribution of evidence-based management, or using research evidence to help make management decisions.

4. *Explain key events in the history of organizational behavior.* The history of organizational behavior parallels the behavioral approach to management, including contributions from classical management. The classical approach to management encompasses both scientific and administrative management, and contributes some insights into understanding workplace behavior. The behavioral approach formally began with the Hawthorne studies. Among the major implications of these studies were that leadership practices and work-group pressures profoundly influence employee satisfaction and performance.

The human relations movement and the contingency approach to management are also key developments in the history of organizational behavior. The human relations movement was based on the belief that there is an important link among managerial practices, morale, and productivity. Analysis of Theory X versus Theory Y (pessimistic versus optimistic assumptions about people) is a key aspect of the movement. The contingency approach emphasizes taking into account individual and situational differences in managing people. An emerging movement in the field is positive organizational behavior, which focuses on measurable human resource strengths and capacities. The Internet and social media era have influenced behavior in organizations because they are incorporated into the work activities of the vast majority of workers at all levels in the organization. The new-age workplace emphasizes collaboration and responding to the needs of millennials.

5. *Understand how a person develops organizational-behavior skills.* Organizational-behavior skills can be developed by following a general learning model that includes the use of conceptual knowledge and behavioral guidelines, experiential exercises, feedback on skill utilization, and frequent practice. The framework for studying organizational behavior in this textbook emphasizes the interconnectedness of three levels of information: individuals, groups and interpersonal relations, and the organizational system and the global environment.

Key Terms and Phrases

organizational behavior, p. 3

meta-analysis, p. 4

organizational effectiveness, p. 6

evidence-based management, p. 9

behavioral approach to management, p. 9

scientific management, p. 10

administrative management, p. 10

Hawthorne effect, p. 11

human relations movement, p. 12

contingency approach to management, p. 12

positive organizational behavior, p. 13

new-age workplace, p. 14

Discussion Questions and Activities

1. How might it be possible for a worker to not interact frequently with coworkers, yet still be a superior performer?

2. The term *belly-to-belly interview* used to be popular in market research. Why might this approach to data collection still be useful?

3. What contributions might organizational-behavior knowledge make in the Internet age?
4. What does it mean to say that organizational behavior relates to the *process*—as opposed to the *content*—of a manager's job?
5. Give a possible explanation why meta-analysis is considered so important in evaluating the effectiveness of prescription drugs.
6. Work by yourself, or form a small brainstorming group, to furnish an example from physical science in which common sense proves to be untrue.
7. How could a few principles of scientific management be applied to enhance the productivity of baristas at Starbucks?
8. Have you ever worked for a manager who held Theory X assumptions about people? What was the impact of his or her assumptions on your motivation and satisfaction?
9. It has often been said, that the higher you go in terms of management responsibilities, the more important interpersonal skills become. Why might this be true?
10. Get together with a few classmates. Develop a list of strengths of group members that you think if further developed would be career assets, and explain why these strengths might be assets.

CASE PROBLEM: Custodial Group Leader Danielle Attempts to Rev Up Her Staff

Danielle is the group leader, or supervisor, of a staff of 12 custodial workers at a large rural hospital. The hospital cares for patients from five different nearby counties. The custodians perform a variety of duties in relation to keeping the patient and administrative areas clean. Among these responsibilities are sweeping, mopping, dusting, and window cleaning. At times, a custodian has to clean up after a patient who did not make it to the restroom in time.

A high school diploma or its equivalency is not required for the position of custodial worker, and the starting pay is at the minimum hourly wage, with very small pay increases thereafter. Danielle believes that most of the group members are performing satisfactorily, with a few doing an outstanding job and a few performing poorly. The chief hospital administer, Nathan, receives the occasional complaint from patients and patient visitors about the cleanliness of the rooms. Nathan usually passes the negative information along to Danielle and encourages her to boost the performance of her custodial staff.

Danielle recognizes that she does not have much flexibility in terms of using financial incentives to boost the cleaning performance of her staff. She does give deserved praise to the group members. Although the praise appears to be appreciated, it does not have much impact on performance. After reading a few articles about motivating entry-level workers and getting them engaged in their work, Danielle concludes that if workers see the relevance of their work, they will perform well. She reflects, "If all the group members really understood how they were contributing to patient welfare, they would perform at a higher level."

Danielle's plan of action is to meet with her staff in groups of four for a 30-minute discussion of the meaning and purpose of their work. To give worker morale a small boost, Danielle explains to the workers that they are being paid for the time spent in the meeting. She also provides food and nonalcoholic beverages. Shortly into the meeting, Danielle says, "Now, I want you one by one to tell me how your custodial work is important to patients and helps the hospital."

The four group members have quizzical facial expressions, but Wendy speaks first: "Patients like the room clean. The people who run the hospital don't want to see a mess either. So I clean the best I can."

Roger volunteers to speak next and says with a pleased expression, "A shine on the floor brings a smile to the face of patients. So that's what I do."

Custodial worker Linda speaks next: "I've got something else to add. There are loads of germs floating through a hospital. We get rid of those nasty germs before any of our patients get sicker. So there you have it. We're pretty important."

Carmichael, the youngest custodian on the staff, then took his turn to speak: "I like what Wendy, Roger, and Linda said, but I see something else. It takes a giant team to run a hospital, and we all have an important position. If we don't keep the hospital clean, a lot of the medical care goes down the drain. It would be like throwing somebody into a sewer after knee surgery. We custodians are the front-line troops doing important work. And we cheer up our patients because we love them."

Danielle responded in an excited tone, "Carmichael you hit the nail on the head. Our group of custodians makes a big contribution to the health and welfare of our patients. Without you, our hospital would flop. We may not be neurosurgeons or surgical nurses, but we are all helping our patients get better. Keep that in mind as you go about your work this week and in the future."

Case Questions

1. What does this case suggest about the application of organizational-behavior knowledge by a first-level supervisor?

2. To what extent does it appear that Danielle is just playing "mind games" with her custodial staff to keep them working harder and not quitting?
3. If time permits, speak with a custodial worker and get the worker's opinion of the purpose and importance of his or her work. How does the information you uncover fit with what you read about in this case?

Sources: Original case base on some of the facts in in the following sources: Patty Onderko, "For the Greater Good: Leverage the Power of Self-Transcendence," *Success*, November, 2017, p. 12; Jessica Stillman, "What You Can Learn About Job Satisfaction From a Janitor," www.inc.com, June 7, 2013, pp. 1–2; Barry Schwartz, "Rethinking Work," *The New York Times*, August 28, 2015, pp. 1–6; David Zax, "Want to Be Happier at Work: Learn from These 'Job Crafters,'" www.fastcompany.com, June 3, 2013, pp. 1–3.

Endnotes

1. Original case created from information in the following sources: Sue Shellenbarger, "The Invisible Walls at Work," *The Wall Street Journal*, November 29, 2017, p. A11; "About the Starr Conspiracy," https://thestarrconspiracy.com, pp. 1–2. © 2018 THE STARR CONSPIRACY; "The Starr Conspiracy: Practice Manager, Content Strategy" (job posting) www.smartrecruiters.com, 2018, pp. 1–2.

2. Gregory Morehead and Ricky W. Griffin, *Organizational Behavior: Managing People and Organizations*, 4th ed. (Boston: Houghton Mifflin, 1995), p. 3.

3. Piers D. Steel and John D. Kammeyer-Mueller, "Comparing Meta-Analytic Techniques under Realistic Conditions," *Journal of Applied Psychology*, February 2002, p. 107.

4. Pratima (Tima) Bansal and Kevin Corley, "From the Editors—the Coming Age for Qualitative Research: Embracing the Diversity of Qualitative Methods," *Academy of Management Journal*, April 2011, pp. 233–237.

5. Pratima (Tima) Bansal and Kevin Corley, "From the Editors—Publishing in *AMJ*—Part 7: What's Different about Qualitative Research?" *Academy of Management Journal*, June 2012, p. 512.

6. Cited in Michael S. Malone, "The Secret to Midcareer Success," *The Wall Street Journal*, February 12, 2018, p. A17.

7. Cited in Lauren Weber, "Women Gain as Skills Shift for High-Paying Jobs," *The Wall Street Journal*, March 22, 2017, p. B5.

8. Quoted in Wendy L. Bedwell, Stephen M. Fiore, and Eduardo Salas, "Developing the Future Workforce: An Approach for Integrating Interpersonal Skills into the MBA Classroom," *Journal of Management Learning & Education*, June 2014, p. 171.

9. Robert P. Vecchio, *Organizational Behavior: Core Concepts*, 6th ed. (Mason, OH: South-Western/Thomson Learning, 2003), pp. 5–6.

10. Jeffrey Pfeffer, *The Human Equation* (Boston: Harvard Business School Press, 1998), p. 59.

11. Cited in Anne Fisher, "Turn Star Employees into Superstars," *Fortune*, December 13, 2004, p. 70.

12. Dori Meinert, "5 Types of Bad Bosses: Can They Be Fixed?" *HR Magazine*, August 2014, p. 29.

13. Rob B. Briner, David Denyer, and Denise M. Rousseau, "Evidence-Based Management: Concept Cleanup Time?" *Academy of Management Perspectives*, November 2009, p. 19.

14. Shonna Waters, "Evidence-Based HR: Gather Good Data to Make Better Decisions," *HR Magazine*, December 2017/January 2018, p. 68.

15. Susan Sorenson, "How Employee Engagement Drives Growth," *Gallup Business Journal*, June 20, 2013, p. 2.

16. Kevin Morrell and Mark Learmonth, "Against Evidence-Based Management for Management Learning," *Academy of Management Learning & Education*, December 2015, pp. 520–533.

17. Joseph E. Champoux, *Organizational Behavior: Essential Tenets* (Mason, OH: South-Western/Thomson Learning, 2003), pp. 11–12.

18. Frederick W. Taylor, *Principles of Scientific Management* (New York: W. W. Norton, 1911), p. 9.

19. Champoux, *Organizational Behavior*, p. 12.

20. E. J. Roethlisberger and W. J. Dickson, *Management and the Worker* (Cambridge, MA: Harvard University Press, 1939); Wertheim, pp. 2–3.

21. H. McIlvaine Parsons, "What Caused the Hawthorne Effect? A Scientific Detective Story," *Administration & Society*, November 1978, pp. 259–283.

22. Douglas McGregor, *The Human Side of Enterprise* (New York: McGraw-Hill, 1960), pp. 33–57.

23. Fred Luthans, "Positive Organizational Behavior: Developing and Managing Psychological Strengths," *Academy of Management Executive*, February 2002, p. 59; Carolyn M. Youssef and Fred Luthans, "Positive Organizational Behavior in the Workplace," *Journal of Management*, October 2007, p. 774.

24. Tom Carroll and Marie Puybaraud, "The New Age of the Tech-Enabled Workplace," *Promoda*, August 4, 2017, pp. 1–4; Johnny Karam, "New Age Workplaces Require a Changed Mindset," *Gulf News*, http://gulfnews.com/business/property/new-age-workplaces-require-a-changed-mindset-1.1705065, April 5, 2016; "A Guide to Design New-Age Workplace for Improved Productivity," *Entrepreneur India*, www.entrepreneur.com/article/280806, August 15, 2016, pp. 1–3.

25. Robert E. Ployhart, "Strategic Organizational Behavior (STROBE): The Missing Voice in the Strategic Human Capital Conversation," *Academy of Management Perspectives*, August 2015, p. 353.

Individual Differences, Mental Ability, and Personality

CHAPTER 2

kurhan/Shutterstock.com

Chapter Outline

Individual Differences

Mental Ability (Cognitive Intelligence)

Personality Differences

Emotional Intelligence

Implications for Managerial Practice

Learning Objectives

After reading and studying this chapter and doing the exercises, you should be able to:

1. Explain how individual differences influence the behavior of people in organizations.

2. Explain how mental ability relates to job performance.

3. Identify major personality variables that influence job performance.

4. Explain how emotional intelligence is an important part of organizational behavior.

Stacy Brown-Philpot is the CEO of TaskRabbit, an online and mobile marketplace that matches freelancers looking to perform everyday tasks for pay with consumers who need the tasks performed. Among the odd jobs "Taskers" perform are assembling furniture, yard work, cleaning, and repairing electronic devices. The average pay for these members of the gig economy is $35 per hour. Since its founding in 2008, the company has grown to 60,000 Taskers.

For three years prior to becoming CEO, Brown-Philpot was the chief operating officer (COO) of TaskRabbit. Before joining the company, she spent close to 10 years at Google heading online sales and operations. In 2015 she was appointed to the Hewlett-Packard (HP) Board of Directors, and she joined the board of retailer Nordstrom, Inc. soon thereafter. Brown-Philpot received a BS in economics from the Wharton School of Business and an MBA from Stanford University.

One of the first career shifts Brown-Philpot made was to leave a secure position in investment banking to attend graduate school. At Google, many people thought Stacy had the dream job. She says, "I had this corner office and everybody was like, 'This is amazing.' I felt comfortable, extremely comfortable, until I realized, I'm supposed to be taking chances. I said that I loved this, but it wasn't what I'm supposed to be doing." So she took the jump to TaskRabbit in order to help facilitate the gig economy. Brown-Philpot sensed the opportunity to provide thousands of people a chance to earn good money while performing tasks that people were unable or too overwhelmed to perform on their own.

Brown-Philpot made another adventuresome career decision in 2009 when she moved from the San Francisco Bay Area to Hyderabad, India, to become senior director of the online and sales operations for Google in that country. It was a difficult decision for her and her husband because they were planning to start a family at the time. One year later she returned to the Bay Area to rejoin her husband full time.

Brown-Philpot believes that getting "brain food" is vital for a person's career. "I read. I listen to talk radio, and fill myself with learning." Part of her learning early in her career was to ask her manager if there was anything he was doing that he did not like to do. She said that she would take it off his plate. Taking on these responsibilities helped her learn.

As CEO, Brown-Philpot focuses her efforts on strategy, people, and process. She regularly asks, "Do we have the right strategy? Do we have the right people to execute the strategy? Are the processes we run internally the ones that will allow us to execute well and win?"

As she looks toward the future, Brown-Philpot thinks that artificial intelligence (AI) will help expand the impact of TaskRabbit. Customers might be able to talk to their devices to set up tasks—for example, "Alexa, get me somebody over here quickly to assemble this bicycle." Another example of the application of AI would be if the filter in your refrigerator needed replacement, you would automatically get a Tasker to come over and replace the filter.

In an industry that has been accused of being underrepresented by women and African Americans in managerial and professional positions, Brown-Philpot is a rarity as a black woman heading a sizeable technology company.[1]

The story about the TaskRabbit CEO just presented illustrates how the combination of high intelligence and the personality trait of risk taking contributes to individual success and organizational effectiveness. The purpose of this chapter is to explain how individual differences affect performance. In addition, we describe key sources of individual differences: demographic diversity, mental ability, and personality. In Chapters 3 and 4, we will consider other sources of individual differences that influence behavior in organizations: learning, perception, values, attitudes, and ethics. Although our focus in this chapter is on individual differences, we also describe principles of human behavior that apply to everyone. For example, everyone has different components to his or her intelligence. We all have some capacity to deal with numbers, words, and abstract reasoning.

Individual Differences

People show substantial **individual differences**, or variations, in how they respond to the same situation based on personal characteristics. An extraverted production planner might attempt to influence a plant superintendent by taking him to lunch and making an oral presentation of her ideas. In the same situation, an introverted planner might attempt to influence the superintendent by sending him an elaborate report. Understanding individual differences helps to explain human behavior, but environmental influences are also important.

Variables on which individuals differ can be laid out on a continuum from stable to transitory. A person's propensity for creative problem solving tends to be stable. An example of a more transitory individual difference would be mood. Daphne might be a generally cheerful middle manager, but today is "Bring Your Pet to Work" day. A coworker's poodle bites her, placing Daphne in a bad mood for a couple of hours. As used in organizational behavior, the term *individual difference* generally refers to stable attributes.[2]

The importance of understanding individual differences for managing people is highlighted by the research of Marcus Buckingman, who studied over 80,000 managers, using both survey questionnaires and interviews. He concluded that exceptional managers come to value the particular quirks and abilities of their employees. Exceptional managers analyze how to capitalize on the strengths of workers and tweak the environment to adapt to employee strengths. For example, the manager might modify a job description so the worker can do more work that fits his or her talents, such as giving a very bright employee more opportunity to troubleshoot.[3]

A basic proposition of psychology states that behavior is a function of a person interacting with his or her environment.[4] The equation reads $B = f(P \times E)$, where B stands for behavior, P for the person, and E the environment. A key implication of this equation is that the effects of the individual and the environment on each other determine a person's behavior. For example, working for a firm that requires many levels of approval for a decision might trigger a person's tendencies toward impatience. The same person working in a flatter organization (one that requires fewer layers of approval) might be more patient. Have you ever noticed that some environments, and some people, bring out your best traits? Or your worst traits?

Another way of understanding the impact of individual differences in the workplace is to say that these differences *moderate* how people respond to situations. Assume that a new organizational structure results in most professional-level workers having two bosses. (Each worker has a manager in his or her own discipline, plus a project leader.) Workers who have a difficult time tolerating ambiguity (a personality trait) will find the new structure to be frustrating. In contrast, workers who tolerate ambiguity well will enjoy the challenge and excitement of having two bosses.

LEARNING OBJECTIVE 1
Explain how individual differences influence the behavior of people in organizations.

individual differences
Variations in how people respond to the same situation based on personal characteristics.

Rawpixel.com/Shutterstock.com

Individual differences are a key aspect of organizational behavior.

Here we identify seven consequences of individual differences that have a major impact on managing people:

1. *People differ in productivity.* A comprehensive analysis of individual differences illustrates the magnitude of human variation in job performance.[5] Researchers synthesized studies involving over 10,000 workers. They found that as jobs become more complex, individual differences have a bigger impact on work output. An outstanding industrial sales representative might produce 100 times as much sales revenue as a mediocre one. In contrast, an outstanding store cashier might produce only twice as much as a mediocre one. (An industrial sales position is more complex than the job of a cashier. Industrial selling involves a variety of activities, including persuading others, analyzing problems, and accessing relevant data.)

2. *Quality of work varies because people vary in their propensity for achieving high-quality results.* Some people take naturally to striving for high quality because they are conscientious, have a good capacity for precision, and take pride in their work. Workers who are less conscientious, less precise, and have little pride in their work will have more difficulty achieving quality targets.

3. *Empowerment is effective with some workers, but not with all.* People differ in how much they want to be empowered and involved. A major thrust of the modern workplace is to grant workers more authority to make decisions by themselves and to involve them in suggesting improvements. Many workers welcome such empowerment and enrichment because they seek self-fulfillment on the job. However, many other workers are not looking for more responsibility and job involvement. They prefer jobs that require a minimum of mental involvement and responsibility.

4. *A given leadership style does not work with all people.* People differ in the style of leadership they prefer and need. Many individuals prefer as much freedom as possible on the job and can function well under such leadership. Other individuals want to be supervised closely by their manager. People also vary with respect to the amount of supervision they require. In general, less competent, less motivated, and less experienced workers need more supervision. One of the biggest headaches facing a manager is to supervise people who need close supervision yet resent it when it is administered.

5. *People differ in their need for contact with other people.* As a by-product of their personality traits and occupational interests, people vary widely in how much human contact they need to keep them satisfied. Some people can work alone all day and remain highly productive. Others become restless unless they are engaged in business or social conversation with another employee. Some workers will often drop by the work area of other workers just to chat. Sometimes a business luncheon is scheduled more out of a manager's need for social contact than a need for discussing job problems.

6. *Company management will find that commitment to the firm varies considerably.* Some employees are so committed (or engaged) to their employers that they act as if they are part-owners of the firm. As a consequence, committed and loyal employees are highly concerned about producing high-quality goods and services. They also maintain excellent records of attendance and punctuality, which helps reduce the cost of doing business. At the other extreme, some employees feel little commitment or loyalty toward their employer, and therefore are not work engaged. They feel no pangs of guilt when they produce scrap or when they miss work for trivial reasons.

7. *Workers vary in their level of self-esteem, which, in turn, influences their productivity and capacity to take on additional responsibilities.* People with high self-esteem believe that they can cope with the basic challenges of life (self-efficacy) and also that they are worthy of happiness (self-respect). A group of economists found that self-esteem, as measured by a personality test, had a big impact on the wages of young workers. The researchers found that human capital—schooling, basic skills, and work experience—predictably had a significant impact on wages. Yet 10 per-

cent of this effect was really attributable to self-esteem, which highly correlated with human capital. It was also found that differences in productivity, as measured by comparative wages, related more to differences in self-esteem than to differences in human capital.[6]

The sampling of individual differences creating the consequences cited is usually attributed to a combination of genetic makeup and environmental influences. Some workers are more productive because they have inherited better problem-solving abilities and have lived since childhood in environments that encourage the acquisition of knowledge and skills. Many other personality traits, such as introversion, also are partially inherited.

Despite the importance of heredity, a person's environment—including the workplace—still plays a significant role in influencing job behavior. The manager must therefore strive to create a positive environment in which workers are able to perform at their best.

Mental Ability (Cognitive Intelligence)

Mental ability, or **cognitive intelligence** (the capacity to acquire and apply knowledge, including solving problems) is a major source of individual differences that affect job performance and behavior. Intelligent workers can best solve abstract problems. Research as early as 1917 and up to the present consistently indicates that intelligence, as measured by mental ability tests, is positively related to job performance.[7]

General mental ability is also a good predictor of job performance and success in training for a wide variety of occupations in the European community.[8] An example of the widespread use of mental ability tests to predict job performance is that most National Football League (NFL) teams use the Wonderlic Personnel Test, a standardized measure of cognitive ability, as part of the selection process. In general, quarterbacks—the position calling for the most analytical skills—tend to have the highest mental ability test scores.[9]

Few people seriously doubt that mental ability is related to job performance. Controversy does abound, however, about two aspects of intelligence. One is how accurately and fairly intelligence can be measured. It is argued, for example, that intelligence tests discriminate against environmentally disadvantaged people. The second controversial aspect is the relative influence of heredity and environment on intelligence. Some people believe that intelligence is mostly the product of genes, while others believe that upbringing is the key factor.

The argument that environment is the major contributor to intelligence centers on evidence that many people, if placed in an enriched environment, are able to elevate their intelligence test scores. People with genes favoring high intelligence will gravitate toward mentally enriching experiences, thereby relying on the environment to boost their natural cognitive advantage.[10] (If it is true that mental ability can be improved by a stimulating environment, giving employees ample opportunity to stretch themselves mentally will help them improve their intellectual skills.)

Based on hundreds of studies, it appears that heredity and environment contribute about equally to intelligence. This finding does not mean that a person with extremely limited mental capacity can be made super-intelligent through specialized training. Nor does it mean that a naturally brilliant person does not need a mentally stimulating environment.

Here we describe two aspects of mental ability that have implications for organizational behavior: the components of intelligence and practical intelligence. Emotional intelligence is described under the category of personality.

LEARNING OBJECTIVE 2
Explain how mental ability relates to job performance.

cognitive intelligence The capacity to acquire and apply knowledge, including solving problems.

Intelligence is a real asset in business.

Components of Intelligence

g (general) factor A major component of intelligence that contributes to problem-solving ability.

s (special) factors Components of intelligence that contribute to problem-solving ability.

Intelligence consists of multiple components. A component of intelligence is much like a separate mental aptitude. A standard theory of intelligence explains that intelligence consists of a g (general) factor along with s (special) factors that contribute to problem-solving ability. Another way of describing g is that it represents a general cognitive factor that pervades almost all kinds of mental ability. Scores on tests of almost any type (e.g., math or creative ability) are influenced by g. High scores on g are associated with good scholastic performance. In the workplace, g is the best predictor of success in job training, job performance, occupational prestige, and accomplishment within occupations. Also, g is related to many social outcomes, including early death due to vehicular accidents.[11] The g factor helps explain why some people perform so well in many different mental tasks—they have the *right stuff*.

Various researchers have identified different s factors contributing to overall mental aptitude. Figure 2-1 lists and defines seven factors that have been consistently noted. Being strong in any mental aptitude often leads to enjoyment of work associated with that aptitude. Conversely, enjoyment of an activity might lead to the development of an aptitude for that activity.

Practical Intelligence

practical intelligence The type of intelligence required for adapting to an environment to suit an individual's needs.

Many people, including specialists in organizational behavior, are concerned that the traditional way of understanding intelligence inadequately describes mental ability. An unfortunate implication of intelligence testing is that intelligence as traditionally calculated consists largely of the ability to perform tasks related to scholastic work. Thus, a person who scored high on an intelligence test could follow a complicated instruction manual but not have good common sense and judgment, which would be needed for an endeavor such as operating a successful small business. To overcome the limited idea that intelligence involves mostly the ability to solve abstract problems, the concept of **practical intelligence** has been proposed. This type of intelligence is required for adapting to an environment to suit an individual's needs.[12]

Practical intelligence helps explain why a person who has a difficult time getting through school can still be a successful businessperson, politician, or visual artist. It incorporates the ideas of common sense, wisdom, and street smarts. One reservation about practical intelligence derives from the implication that people who are highly intelligent in the

FIGURE 2-1 Special Factors Contributing to Overall Mental Aptitude

- *Verbal comprehension:* The ability to understand the meanings of words and their relationship to one another, and to comprehend written and spoken information.
- *Word fluency:* The ability to use words quickly and easily, without an emphasis on verbal comprehension.
- *Numerical:* The ability to handle numbers, engage in mathematical analysis, and do arithmetic calculations.
- *Spatial:* The ability to visualize forms in space and manipulate objects mentally, particularly in three dimensions.
- *Memory:* Having a good rote recall for symbols, words, and lists of numbers, along with other associations.
- *Perceptual speed:* The ability to perceive visual details, to pick out similarities and differences, and to perform tasks requiring visual perception.
- *Inductive reasoning:* The ability to discover a rule or principle and apply it in solving a problem, and to make judgments and decisions that are logically sound.

Source: These seven factors stem from the pioneering work of L. L. Thurstone, "Primary Mental Abilities," *Psychometric Monographs,* 1 (1938).

analytical sense are not practical thinkers. In truth, most executives and other high-level workers score quite well on tests of mental ability. Also, leaders at many levels in business who receive higher performance and actual productivity evaluations tend to score slightly higher on mental ability tests. These tests usually measure analytical intelligence.[13]

The relevance of practical intelligence was demonstrated in a study about entrepreneurs. The study was conducted by interviewing 22 printing industry CEOs and reviewing survey responses from 283 founders of early-stage printing and graphics businesses. Practical intelligence was measured by looking at responses to three scenarios directly relating to the printing industry, such as dealing with declining sales. The task requiring practical intelligence was to rank 10 different possible actions to deal with a specific problem. "Preferred action sequences" were ranked in terms of their effectiveness by industry experts. Two findings particularly relevant to the understanding of practical intelligence were as follows:

■ Industrial experience and practical intelligence are the most positively related when the entrepreneurs are strongly oriented to learn through concrete experience. Venture experience was also more closely related to practical intelligence when the entrepreneurs had a strong orientation to learn through concrete experience.

■ The positive relation between entrepreneurs' practical intelligence and new venture growth is stronger when the growth goals are high.[14]

A useful takeaway for the individual from this study is that experience helps develop practical intelligence. "Experience" in the study included both longevity and creating new ventures.

For organizations, an important implication about practical intelligence centers on problem-solving ability and age. Analytical intelligence may decline from early to late adulthood. As people become older, they compensate well for declining raw mental energy by focusing on things they do well. In job situations calling for wisdom, such as resolving conflicts, age and experience may be an advantage.

Personality Differences

LEARNING OBJECTIVE 3
Identify major personality variables that influence job performance.

Personality characteristics contribute to success in many jobs. Most job failures are not attributed to a person's intelligence or technical competence but to personality characteristics. The subject of personality is therefore important in organizational behavior. However, some controversy still centers on the concept of personality, despite hundreds of studies linking personality to job performance (several are referred to later). There is disagreement as to whether personality can be accurately measured and whether it is influenced more by heredity or environment.

personality The persistent and enduring behavior patterns of an individual that are expressed in a wide variety of situations.

Personality refers to the persistent and enduring behavior patterns of an individual that are expressed in a wide variety of situations. Your personality is the combination of attributes, traits, and characteristics that make you unique. Your walk, talk, appearance, speech, and creativity all contribute to your personality. Personality can therefore be regarded as the core of who you are.[15]

We approach the topic of personality by first describing nine key personality traits related to job performance and behavior, including a sampling of relevant research. Two experiential activities related to personality will also be presented.

Nine Major Personality Factors and Traits

According to the Five-Factor Model (also known as the *Big Five*) of personality, the basic structure of human

Our personality influences our interactions with coworkers.

personality is represented by five broad factors: neuroticism, extraversion, openness to experience, agreeableness, and conscientiousness. Each factor has more narrow traits that make up the factors. Although the Five-Factor Model of personality is well documented, other aspects of personality still have merit. We therefore present four other traits of particular significance to job behavior: self-monitoring, risk taking and thrill seeking, optimism versus pessimism, and narcissism. The subject of personality traits will be presented again when we discuss motivation in Chapter 6 and leadership in Chapter 11.

People develop all traits to different degrees, partially from growing up in a particular environment. For example, a person might have a natural tendency to be agreeable. An environment in which agreeableness was encouraged would help him or her become even more agreeable.

All nine traits have a substantial impact on job behavior and performance. The interpretation and meaning of these traits provide useful information because they help to pinpoint areas for personal development. Although these traits are partially inherited, most people can improve their development of them.

1. *Neuroticism (low emotional stability).* This trait reflects neuroticism versus emotional stability. People with high neuroticism are prone to psychological distress and coping with problems in unproductive ways. Traits associated with this personality factor include being anxious, insecure, angry, embarrassed, and worried. A person of low neuroticism—or high emotional stability—is calm and confident, and usually in control.

2. *Extraversion.* Traits associated with extraversion include being social, gregarious, assertive, talkative, and active. An outgoing person is often described as extraverted, whereas a shy person is described as introverted. Many successful leaders are extraverted, yet some effective leaders are introverted because they rely on other factors such as giving feedback and encouraging others. (Note that *extraversion* in everyday language is spelled *extroversion*.) Introversion is associated with work activities requiring critical and analytical thinking such as computer programming and engineering.

   A spinoff of studying extraversion and introversion is the recognition of people who blend both traits and are classified as *ambiverts*. These people tend to be adaptable and can change their approach to fit the situation. Ambiverts are also socially flexible in the sense of being comfortable in social situations as well as being alone.[16]

3. *Openness to experience.* People who score high with openness have well-developed intellects. Traits associated with this factor include being imaginative, cultured, curious, original, broad-minded, intelligent, and artistically sensitive. Many successful managers and professionals search printed information and the Internet for useful ideas. Also, many top-level executives support the arts.

4. *Agreeableness.* This factor reflects the quality of a person's interpersonal orientation. An agreeable person is friendly and cooperative. Traits associated with the agreeableness factor include being courteous, flexible, trusting, good-natured, cooperative, forgiving, softhearted, and tolerant. Agreeableness is a plus for customer service positions, such as a hotel receptionist.

5. *Conscientiousness.* A variety of meanings have been attached to the conscientious factor, but it generally implies dependability. Studies of conscientiousness suggest it consists of six sub-factors: industriousness, order, self-control, responsibility, traditionalism, and virtue.[17] Other related traits include being hardworking, achievement oriented, and persevering. Being conscientious to the extreme, however, can lead to workaholism and per-

Introversion can be an asset for performing analytical work.

marver/Shutterstock.com

SELF-ASSESSMENT 2-1

The Conscientiousness Quiz

Indicate the extent to which each of the following statements describes your behavior or attitude by circling one number. The numbers refer to Very Inaccurate (VI), Moderately Inaccurate (MI), Neither accurate nor inaccurate (N), Moderately Accurate (MA), and Very Accurate (VA). Consider enlisting the help of someone who knows your behavior and attitudes well to help you respond accurately to the statements.

Statement Related to Conscientiousness	VI	MI	N	MA	VA
1. I follow almost all rules on the job.	1	2	3	(4)	(5)
2. People who know me consider me to be quite dependable.	1	2	3	4	(5)
3. I frequently cut corners.	(5)	(4)	3	2	1
4. I am very involved in my work.	1	2	3	4	(5)
5. I go about my work methodically.	1	2	3	4	(5)
6. If somebody doesn't like the work I perform, it's that person's problem, not mine.	5	4	3	(2)	1
7. I typically plan my workday.	1	(2)	(3)	(4)	5
8. I attempt to avoid working too hard, so I have energy left over for life outside of work.	(5)	4	3	2	1
9. I go about my work with a sense of urgency.	1	2	(3)	4	5
10. I would strive for excellent performance only if I thought it would lead to a salary increase or bonus.	(5)	4	3	2	1
11. While at work, I regularly check personal e-mails, text messages, or my favorite websites.	(5)	4	3	2	1
12. I think I am much better organized than most of my coworkers.	1	2	3	4	(5)
13. I strive hard to reach the goals my supervisor has established for me.	1	2	3	4	(5)
14. I strive hard to reach the goals I have established for myself.	1	2	3	4	(5)
15. I lose patience easily when I am attempting to solve a difficult problem.	5	4	(3)	2	1

Scoring and Interpretation: Calculate your score by adding up the numbers circled:

60–75: You are a highly conscientious person who is probably also self-disciplined.

45–59: You have an average degree of conscientiousness, including dependability.

15–44: You are below average in conscientiousness, dependability, and self-discipline. Solicit feedback from others to see if this low score is warranted. If the score is accurate, strive to become more conscientious in order to do well in your career.

fectionism. Take the Self-Assessment 2-1 quiz to think about your tendencies toward being conscientious.

6. *Self-monitoring behavior.* The self-monitoring trait refers to the process of observing and controlling how we appear to others. High self-monitors are pragmatic and are even chameleon-like actors in social groups. They often say what others want

The Risk-Taking Scale

Answer true or false to the following questions to obtain an approximate idea of your tendency to take risks, or your desire to do so:

	True	False
1. I send and receive text messages while driving.	☐	☐
2. I think that amusement park roller coasters should be abolished.	☐	☐
3. I don't like trying foods from other cultures.	☐	☐
4. I would choose bonds over growth stocks for the majority of my investments.	☐	☐
5. I like to challenge people in positions of power.	☐	☐
6. I will eat fruit from a store or street vendor without first washing it.	☐	☐
7. I sometimes talk on my cell phone while driving at highway speeds.	☐	☐
8. I would love to be an entrepreneur (or I love being one).	☐	☐
9. I would like helping out in a crisis such as a product recall.	☐	☐
10. I would like to go cave exploring (or already have done so).	☐	☐
11. I would be willing to have at least 1/3 of my compensation based on a bonus for good performance.	☐	☐
12. I would be willing to visit a maximum-security prison on a job assignment.	☐	☐

Key: 1. T; 2. F; 3. F; 4. F; 5. T; 6. T; 7. T; 8. T; 9. T; 10. T; 11. T; 12. T.

Give yourself one point each time your answer agrees with the key. If you score 10–12, you are probably a high risk taker; 6–9: you're a moderate risk taker; 3–5: you are cautious; 0–2: you're a very low risk taker.

Source: The idea of a test about risk-taking comfort as well as several of the statements on the quiz, come from psychologist Frank Farley.

Conscientiousness is a key personality characteristic for helping others.

Photographee.eu/Shutterstock.com

to hear. Low self-monitors avoid situations that require them to adopt different outer images. In this way, their outer behavior adheres to their inner values. Low self-monitoring can often lead to inflexibility. People who are skilled at office politics usually score high on the self-monitoring factor.

7. *Risk taking and thrill seeking.* Some people crave constant excitement on the job and are willing to risk their lives to achieve thrills. The willingness to take risks and pursue thrills is a personality trait that has grown in importance in the high-technology era. Many people work for employers, start businesses, and purchase stocks with uncertain futures. Both the search for giant payoffs and daily thrills motivate these individuals.

A strong craving for thrills may have some positive consequences for the organization, including the willingness to perform dangerous feats such as setting explosives, capping an oil well, controlling a radiation leak, or introducing a product in a highly competitive environment. However, extreme risk takers and thrill seekers can create problems such as involvement in a disproportionate number of vehicular accidents and imprudent investments. Take the Self-Assessment 2-2 quiz to measure your tendency toward risk taking.

8. *Optimism* refers to a tendency to experience positive emotional states and to typically believe that positive outcomes will be forthcoming from most activities. The other end of the scale is *pessimism*—a tendency to experience negative emotional

states and to typically believe that negative outcomes will be forthcoming from most activities. Optimism versus pessimism is also referred to in more technical terms as *positive affectivity* versus *negative affectivity* and is considered a major personality trait. A person's tendency toward having positive affectivity (optimism) versus negative affectivity (pessimism) also influences job satisfaction. Being optimistic, as you would suspect, tends to enhance job satisfaction.[18] An appropriate degree of pessimism is helpful in many job situations, including being willing to point out a flaw in a group decision.[19]

9. *Narcissism* refers to an extremely positive and inflated view of the self, combined with limited empathy for others. The narcissist is self-absorbed, self-adoring, and self-centered, and has a grandiose preoccupation with his or her importance. Narcissism in the workplace has been researched and written about frequently because of its potentially negative relationship with job performance when work involves considerable contact with people. Many observers believe that narcissism has been on the rise in recent years, particularly with young people who received considerable praise early in life and want to be lavished with praise as workers. With a reasonable dose of narcissism, a person can be productive in a high-level position, such as a charismatic leader being self-confident, self-promoting, and flamboyant.[20]

In its extreme, the personality trait of narcissism can take the form of a personality disorder. Employees with this type of personality disorder are quick to take offense at criticism and are often looking for a fight, such as filing a lawsuit for being treated unfairly. A worker with a narcissistic personality disorder is often self-defeating and will engage in arguments with others even if it damages his or her reputation.[21]

Self-Assessment 2-3 provides you an opportunity to think about your own tendencies toward narcissism. (Of course, it may not be easy to recognize narcissistic behaviors and attitudes within yourself!)

Although personality is relatively stable, current research suggests that, as measured by the Five-Factor Model, some aspects of personality improve with age. Based on a sample of 132,000 subjects who took the personality tests on the Internet, it appears that people generally become more responsible, organized, and focused with age. The study examined traits over time. Conscientiousness tended to increase in adulthood, particularly in a person's 20s. Both men and women scored higher on agreeableness and openness as they reached age 30. Later research on the subject found that between the ages of 20 and 65, people perceive themselves to be stronger on positive traits, such as conscientiousness, and also to improve on negative traits, particularly in becoming less neurotic.[22] Personality theorists call this improvement in personality the *Maturity Principle*.[23] Readers interested in testing themselves on the Five-Factor Model of personality can visit www.outofservice.com.

Personality traits can also change slightly in response to unsettling career events, such as long-term unemployment. A study was conducted over time among 6,679 German workers who completed the Five-Factor Model personality test on two occasions, four years apart. Unemployed men and women showed a decline in agreeableness, conscientiousness, and openness in comparison to workers who had remained employed. Those individuals who lost their jobs but then were soon reemployed did not show personality changes.[24]

Research Evidence about Personality and Job Behavior and Performance

Depending on the job, any one of the nine personality factors mentioned previously can be important for good job performance. Here we review a few illustrative points from the vast number of studies relating personality factors to job performance.

1. *Conscientiousness.* The most consistent finding is that conscientiousness is positively related to job performance for a variety of occupations. Furthermore, the combination of intelligence ("can do") with conscientiousness ("will do") is especially important for job performance. In a study of 91 sales representatives for

Tendencies toward Narcissism

Many narcissists exhibit some of the behaviors and hold some of the attitudes listed here. To help you understand your tendencies toward narcissism, rate how strongly you agree with each of the following statements on a scale of 0 to 4, with 0 meaning not at all and 4 meaning very much.

1. When I am in a gathering of people I am usually the best-looking person in the room.		0 1 2 3 4
2. When I am in a gathering of people, I am usually the smartest person in the room.		0 1 2 3 4
3. I love me more than I love anybody else.		0 1 2 3 4
4. If I had an upset stomach, I would post that information on a social media website such as Twitter or Facebook.		0 1 2 3 4
5. I think that it is important that my contacts receive updated photos of me.		0 1 2 3 4
6. I don't think that anybody has the right to criticize me.		0 1 2 3 4
7. I don't think I should have to wait an entire year for a salary increase or bonus.		0 1 2 3 4
8. If I were dating, I would expect the person I am dating to fall in love with me by at least our fourth meeting.		0 1 2 3 4
9. I am destined for greatness.		0 1 2 3 4
10. If I wanted a consumer product or a vacation, and I didn't have the money, I would use my credit card without a second thought.		0 1 2 3 4
11. I get really upset when somebody criticizes me.		0 1 2 3 4
12. When I fail on a task, it is almost always because somebody else messed up.		0 1 2 3 4
13. I talk loudly on my phone when in public places like a restaurant or airport.		0 1 2 3 4
14. During a meeting (or in a classroom), I answer my phone even if the call is not urgent.		0 1 2 3 4
15. I would feel uncomfortable if a day went by without me being admired by somebody.		0 1 2 3 4
16. You don't find too many people as good-looking and smart as me.		0 1 2 3 4
17. I rarely worry about other people's problems.		0 1 2 3 4
18. People who know me are readily influenced by me.		0 1 2 3 4
19. I am a natural leader.		0 1 2 3 4
20. I enjoy being the center of attention.		0 1 2 3 4
21. I take many more selfies than other people I know.		0 1 2 3 4
22. When I read about famous people, I usually realize that I am equally as good as or better than they are.		0 1 2 3 4
23. I check search engines such as Google almost every day to see if there is a new mention of my name.		0 1 2 3 4
24. I am a very special person.		0 1 2 3 4
25. I am destined for outstanding success in my career and personal life.		0 1 2 3 4
26. Rather than discussing current events or sports with other people, I like to talk about myself and my accomplishments.		0 1 2 3 4
27. If I were not rated outstanding in a performance evaluation, I would regard it as an insult.		0 1 2 3 4
28. I don't take most rules seriously because I make my own rules.		0 1 2 3 4
29. I am "cool."		0 1 2 3 4
30. I am unusually charming.		0 1 2 3 4

SELF-ASSESSMENT 2-3

Tendencies toward Narcissism

Scoring and Interpretation:

91 or higher: You have strong narcissistic tendencies, to the extent that your work associates and personal contacts probably perceive you to be self-centered and preoccupied with your own importance. Some people most likely label you as a narcissist.

61–90: You have average narcissistic tendencies, to the extent that you have high self-esteem and self-confidence. Some people may regard you as self-centered but not to an annoying, bothersome level.

31–61: Your narcissistic tendencies are below average, to the extent that there are situations in which you appear too humble and modest. You could stand to focus attention on yourself a little more.

0–30: Your narcissistic tendencies are well below average, to the extent that your self-esteem and self-confidence could be suffering. You might consider developing a stronger appreciation of your good points and strengths.

Source: The idea for a few of the questions stem from Robert Raskin and Howard Terry, "A Principal Component Analysis of the Narcissistic Personality Inventory and Further Evidence of Its Construct Validity," *Journal of Personality and Social Psychology*, No. 5, 1988, p. 894.

an appliance manufacturer, the combination of intelligence and conscientiousness made accurate predictions of job success. Representatives who scored high on intelligence and conscientiousness tended to sell more appliances and receive better performance ratings from their supervisors. In a related study with the same sales representatives, extraversion was a good predictor of job performance.[25]

You may recall that moderator variables are important in understanding many aspects of organizational behavior, and this proves to be true with conscientiousness. A series of four studies of several different occupations found that workers needed good social skills for conscientiousness to be related to aspects of job performance and to interpersonal effectiveness.[26] For example, a conscientious sales rep still needs good social skill to close deals.

Conscientiousness itself often works as a moderator variable in contributing to job performance. An analysis of many studies suggests that people who are conscientious might engage in goal setting and be committed to their jobs, which are two factors that enhance job performance.[27]

2. *Self-Monitoring.* Self-monitoring is another personality factor whose relationship to job behavior has been supported by extensive research. Meta-analyses were conducted for 136 samples and over 23,000 employees to understand the relationship between work-related behaviors and self-monitoring. It was found that high self-monitors tend to receive better performance ratings and more promotions than low self-monitors. High self-monitors were also more likely to emerge as leaders.[28] In short, it pays to tell people what they want to hear if you want to succeed in business.

3. *Agreeableness Combined with Conscientiousness and Workplace Safety.* A meta-analysis of a number of studies involving 40,000 participants investigated how the personality traits included in the Five-Factor Model relate to workplace safety behaviors. Safe behaviors include such actions as following action-prevention procedures, obeying speed rules while driving a forklift truck, and wearing safety goggles as required. One major finding was that agreeableness and conscientiousness were negatively related to engaging in unsafe behaviors. In contrast, extraversion and neuroticism were positively associated with unsafe behaviors. The meta-analysis also found that agreeableness made the biggest difference in terms of avoiding unsafe workplace behaviors.[29]

4. *Extraversion.* A meta-analysis of 73 studies demonstrated a relationship between the Five-Factor Model and the two criteria of leadership effectiveness and stepping

forth as a leader. Extraversion was the factor most frequently associated with the two leadership criteria.[30] This finding is hardly surprising because in most leadership situations, being outgoing helps the leader relate to people. For the more analytical aspects of a leader's role, such as making strategic plans, some degree of introversion is helpful.

5. *Narcissism.* The relationship between narcissism and job performance has been studied most with respect to leadership. The stereotype that a narcissistic, self-absorbed leader is usually ineffective holds up in many situations. Yet a meta-analysis of 42 studies revealed that a moderate amount of narcissism contributes to leadership effectiveness. A conclusion was reached that there exists an optimal, midrange level of leader narcissism (as mentioned earlier in the description of narcissism).[31]

6. *Optimum Amount of Traits.* A major consideration about the relationship between personality and job performance is that most traits have a *curvilinear relationship* with job performance (as in relation to narcissism.) A curvilinear relationship means that an optimum amount of trait helps job performance, whereas being too low or too high in that trait might impair job performance. The optimum level is seen as having the ideal amount of a personality trait that enhances job performance, such as a manager having the right amount of extraversion to be warm toward people, yet still be a good listener and a careful thinker.[32]

Imagine a truck driver who is very low on conscientiousness. He or she will often be late with deliveries based on a lack of concern for timeliness. A driver with the right degree of conscientiousness will strive to be on time and overcome minor hurdles, such as a traffic jam. A super-conscientious driver might get into trouble in an effort to deliver the truckload of goods on time, such as attempting to drive through a blinding snowstorm and having an accident as a result.

A group of researchers conducted two studies in several work settings that generally supported the idea that both conscientiousness and emotional stability (low neuroticism) had a curvilinear relationship with job performance. One interpretation of their results is that workers who are too high on conscientiousness are rigid and inflexible. It is also conceivable that persons with very high emotional stability might become a little anxious when needed, such as worrying about achieving a sales quota. Another finding of the study was that the curvilinear relationship was less likely to appear for jobs of high complexity.[33] So don't worry if your computer security specialist or brain surgeon is highly conscientious and emotionally stable.

In general, favorable results when using personality measures to predict job performance are more likely to occur when the job requirements are carefully analyzed. For example, agreeableness is more important for an airline reservations assistant than a website developer. Another essential requirement for the use of personality testing for job selection and the development of employees is that the tests used must be scientifically constructed by experts in human behavior. Robert Hogan, a leader in the field of personality assessment in industry, contends that only a handful of personality tests are legitimate in terms of being substantiated by research.[34]

The Organizational Behavior in Action box illustrates how some companies rely on personality measures for key work assignments.

The role-plays in the Skill-Development Exercise give you an opportunity to practice managing for individual differences in personality. Remember that a role player is an extemporaneous actor. Put yourself in the shoes of the character you play and visualize how he or she would act. Because you are given only the general idea of a script, use your imagination to fill in the details.

Emotional Intelligence

The effective use of emotions has a major impact on career and personal success. **Emotional intelligence** refers to qualities such as understanding one's own feelings, empathy for others, and the regulation of emotion to enhance living. As the concept of emotional

Wealth Management Group Places More Emphasis on Introversion for Financial Consultants

The wealth-management group of a major national bank is responsible for managing the investment portfolios of bank clients with financial assets of a minimum of $1 million, not including the value of the client's residence. The financial consultants almost all have degrees in business or finance and usually have a minimum of 10 years' experience in banking and finance before working in the wealth-management group.

Applicants for wealth-management specialist positions (financial consultants) are also chosen on the basis of their personalities. Using both interview impressions and personality test results, extraversion is considered to be an important criterion for success as a financial consultant. The reasoning offered by bank executives and the human resources (HR) department is that a wealth manager has to be friendly toward clients and also be assertive enough to sell them investments.

Bank management began to observe that the wealth-management group did not appear to be attaining higher sales than comparable groups in other banks or at brokerage firms. Some data even suggested that the wealth-management financial consultants were performing at a below-average level. Top-level executives working with the HR group decided to hire an outside talent-selection specialist to examine their selection criteria for financial consultants.

The outside specialist concluded that the bank was basing its selection decisions on somewhat inaccurate stereotypes of a financial consultant's role. She noted that a financial consultant in a wealth-management group should be extraverted enough to be warm and supportive toward clients. Yet at the same time, the wealth managers should have a few qualities of the introvert, such as carefully listening to clients and being quite reflective and deliberate when making recommendations about investments.

Working with HR, the director of the wealth-management group made two key changes. One would be that any new financial consultants to be hired for the group should exhibit a mix of extraversion and introversion. The other initiative was to conduct interpersonal skill training for all wealth-management specialists in the art of carefully listening to clients and appearing to be more reflective and somber when making recommendations.

The consultant also explained that there is a growing recognition of the importance of professional workers being *ambiverts*, displaying a mix of extraversion and introversion. These personality types can adapt to the situation, such as being quiet and reflective when poring over data and warmly greeting clients who visit the office for the annual review of their investments.

A review of results 18 months after modifying the selection criteria for financial consultants and offering training about being more introverted suggested that the approach was providing good financial results. Revenue to the bank improved by 12 percent, and loss of clients was reduced by 9 percent.

QUESTIONS

1. In what type of selling do you think a high degree of extraversion would be a strong asset?

2. Visualize yourself as a wealth-management client. Explain whether you think that it would benefit you if your financial consultant displayed a balanced blend of extraversion and introversion (an ambivert).

Source: Original story with a couple of facts derived from the following sources: Deb Koen, "Introverts Can Leverage Skills to Succeed," *Democrat and Chronicle*, March 20, 2013, p. 5B; Elizabeth Bernstein, "Not Introvert, Nor Extravert: The Adaptable Ambivert," *The Wall Street Journal*, July 28, 2015, p. D2; Sumhathi Reddy, "How an Introvert Can Be Happier: Act Like an Extrovert," *The Wall Street Journal*, July 28, 2013, pp. D1, D2.

---

intelligence has surged in popularity, many definitions have been proposed, and more and more behavior has been incorporated into the concept. Emotional intelligence has to do with the ability to connect with people and understand their emotions. A worker with high emotional intelligence can engage in behaviors such as sizing up, pleasing, and influencing people.

Tests of emotional intelligence typically ask you to respond to questions on a 1 to 5 scale (never, rarely, sometimes, often, consistently). For example, indicate how frequently you demonstrate the following behaviors:

I can laugh at myself.	1	2	3	4	5
I help others grow and develop.	1	2	3	4	5
I watch carefully the nonverbal communication of others.	1	2	3	4	5

Personality Role-Plays

Run each role-play for about 7 minutes. The people not involved in the role-play will observe and then provide feedback when the role-play is completed.

1. *Narcissism.* One student plays the role of a worker whose creative ideas for saving the company about $1 million annually on shipping costs have resulted in a cash bonus and a letter of appreciation from the CEO. He decides to share this good news with a coworker who is a total narcissist, interested in talking about only his or her personal accomplishments. Another student plays the role of the narcissist.

2. *Openness.* One student plays the role of an experienced worker in the department who is told to spend some time showing around a new co-op student. It appears that this worker is open to experience. Another student plays the role of the co-op student, who is also open to experience and eager to be successful in this new position.

3. *Conscientiousness.* One student plays the role of a team member who is dependent on another team member for his or her contribution to a team project for which the entire team will receive the same grade. The second student was to have collected extensive data about how energy companies establish wholesale and retail prices for gasoline but is not ready with the input. The first team member has observed from the start of the group project that the second team member is the opposite of a conscientious person. The report is due in 5 days, and the professor is known for not accepting excuses for late papers.

Emotional intelligence is regarded by some researchers as an ability that focuses on the recognition and control of personal emotion. The person who insults the boss during a group meeting would be deficient in this regard. Researchers also view emotional intelligence as a combination of intellect and various personal traits and emotion.[35] Among the traits included in this approach would be insensitivity, such as making a derogatory comment about a coworker's hairstyle. Reflecting the broader view of emotional intelligence, Daniel Goleman and his associates regard this type of intelligence to include four key domains (or components):[36] Later research has identified 12 emotional intelligence competencies nested within each domain.[37] All 12 competencies are learnable capabilities that facilitate effectiveness in working with people as a leader or individual contributor. Figure 2-2 lists the four domains and associated competencies. You will observe that these competencies, such as influence, are quite broad in nature.

1. *Self-awareness.* The ability to understand one's own emotions is the most essential of the four emotional intelligence competencies. Having high self-awareness allows people to know their strengths and limitations and have high self-esteem. Effective individual contributors use self-awareness to accurately measure their own moods, and to intuitively understand how their moods affect others. Effective managers seek feedback to see how well their actions are received by others. A

FIGURE 2-2 Emotional Intelligence Domains and Competencies

	Domain	Associated Competency or Competencies
1.	Self-Awareness	Emotional self-awareness
2.	Self-Management	Emotional self-control; adaptability; achievement orientation; positive outlook
3.	Social Awareness	Empathy; organizational awareness
4.	Relationship Management	Influence; coach and mentor; conflict management; teamwork; inspirational leadership

manager with good self-awareness would recognize factors such as whether he or she was liked, or was exerting the right amount of pressure on people. (Emotional self-awareness is the competency associated with self-awareness.)

Emotional intelligence helps us interact smoothly with others.

2. *Self-management.* The ability to control one's emotions and act with honesty and integrity in a consistent and adaptable manner is important. The right degree of self-management helps prevent a person from throwing temper tantrums when activities do not go as planned. Effective workers do not let their occasional bad moods ruin their day. If they cannot overcome the bad mood, they let work associates know of the problem and how long it might last. A manager with high self-management would not suddenly decide to fire a group member because of one difference of opinion. (The competencies associated with self-management are emotional self-control, adaptability, achievement orientation, and positive outlook.)

3. *Social awareness.* Having empathy for others and having intuition about organizational problems are key aspects of this dimension of emotional intelligence. Socially aware leaders go beyond sensing the emotions of others by showing that they care. In addition, they accurately size up political forces in the office. A team leader with social awareness, or empathy, would be able to assess whether a team member has enough enthusiasm for a project to assign him or her to that project. A CEO who has empathy for a labor union's demands might be able to negotiate successfully with the head of the labor union to avoid a costly strike. (The competencies associated with social awareness are empathy and organizational awareness.)

4. *Relationship management.* This includes the interpersonal skills of being able to communicate clearly and convincingly, disarm conflicts, and build strong personal bonds. Effective leaders use relationship management skills to spread their enthusiasm and solve disagreements, often with kindness and humor. A corporate professional with good relationship management skills would not burn bridges and would continue to enlarge his or her network of people to win support when support is needed. (The competencies associated with relationship management are influence, coach and mentor, conflict management, teamwork, and inspirational leadership.)

Among the many practical outcomes of having high emotional intelligence is the ability to cope better with setbacks. A review of many studies concluded that low emotional intelligence employees are more likely than their high emotional intelligence counterparts to experience negative emotional reactions to job insecurity, such as high tension. Furthermore, workers with low emotional intelligence are more likely to engage in negative coping behaviors, such as expressing anger and verbally abusing an immediate supervisor for the organization failing to provide job security.[38]

A concern about the validity of the concept of emotional intelligence is that a person with good cognitive intelligence would also engage in many of the behaviors of an emotionally intelligent person. Another concern is that the popularized concept of emotional intelligence has become so broad it encompasses almost the entire study of personality. Some approaches to presenting emotional intelligence appear to present a long list of desirable qualities, such as resiliency and vision.[39]

Despite all its advantages, a high degree of emotional intelligence can have a downside. One potential problem is that a person with high emotional intelligence might have difficulty giving negative feedback to another person even if deserved. With too much sensitivity to the needs of others and too much empathy, the highly emotional intelligent person might not want to hurt another person's feelings by giving harsh feedback.[40]

Emotional intelligence underscores the importance of being practical-minded and having effective interpersonal skills to succeed in organizational life. Many topics included in the study of organizational behavior, such as communication, conflict resolution, and power and politics, are components of emotional intelligence. The message is an old one: Both cognitive and noncognitive skills are required for success!

Implications for Managerial Practice

A major implication of individual differences in cognitive ability and personality is that these factors have a major impact on the selection, placement, job assignment, training, and development of employees. When faced with such decisions, the manager should seek answers to such questions as the following:

- Is this employee intelligent enough to handle the job and deal with out-of-the-ordinary problems?
- Is this employee too intelligent for the assignment? Will he or she become bored quickly? Does this employee think that he or she is overqualified for the job?
- Is this employee's personality suited to the assignment? For instance, is the employee conscientious enough? Is the employee open to new learning?

Many employees perform below standard, not because they are not motivated, but their abilities and personality traits are not suited to the job. For instance, an employee who writes garbled update reports may be doing so because of below-average verbal comprehension, not low motivation. Another employee might perform poorly as a sales engineer because she dislikes the part of the job requiring direct contact with customers because she is introverted. Training programs and coaching can be useful in making up for deficits that appear on the surface to be motivational problems.

Summary of Key Points

1. *Explain how individual differences influence the behavior of people in organizations.* Understanding individual differences helps to explain human behavior. Nevertheless, behavior is a function of the person interacting with the environment, as expressed by the equation $B = f(P \times E)$. Seven consequences of individual differences that have an impact on managing people are (1) productivity, (2) quality of work, (3) effectiveness of empowerment, (4) leadership style, (5) need for social contact, (6) commitment and loyalty to the firm, and (7) self-esteem.

2. *Explain how mental ability relates to job performance.* Mental ability, or cognitive intelligence, is one of the major sources of individual differences that affect job performance and behavior. Intelligence consists of many components. One perspective is that intelligence includes a general factor (g) along with special factors (s) that contribute to problem-solving ability. A related perspective is that intelligence consists of seven components including verbal and numerical comprehension. To overcome the limited idea that intelligence involves mostly the ability to solve abstract

problems, the theory of practical intelligence has been proposed, referring to adapting to an environment to suit one's needs.

3. *Identify major personality variables that influence job performance.* Personality is one of the major sources of individual differences. Nine major personality traits are neuroticism, extroversion, openness to experience, agreeableness, conscientiousness, self-monitoring, risk taking and thrill seeking, optimism, and narcissism. Depending on the job, any one of these personality factors can be important for success.

4. *Explain how emotional intelligence is an important part of organizational behavior.* The concept of emotional intelligence helps explain how emotions and personality factors contribute to success. A worker with high emotional intelligence would be able to engage in such behaviors as sizing up, pleasing, and influencing people. The domains of emotional intelligence are self-awareness, self-management, social awareness, and relationship management. Twelve different competencies are associated with the four domains.

Key Terms and Phrases

individual differences, p. 23

cognitive intelligence, p. 25

g (general) factor, p. 26

s (special) factors, p. 26

practical intelligence, p. 26

personality, p. 27

emotional intelligence, p. 34

Discussion Questions and Activities

1. Why does having high self-esteem contribute to being more productive and earning a higher income?

2. Give an example from your own life of how $B = f(P \times E)$.

3. Ten years into the future, your classmates will show wide variations in terms of their career achievements. How might individual differences explain some of these differences in accomplishment?

4. Suppose you or a family member were taking an international flight. Would you want a pilot who claims he has good practical intelligence, even though he has below-average analytical intelligence? Explain your reasoning.

5. Research suggests that people with high cognitive ability earn more money and live longer. How would you explain this finding?

6. Provide an example that you have observed of a person who has very high analytical intelligence but is quite lacking in practical intelligence, including common sense.

7. If it is true that most millennials tend to be narcissistic, to what extent should managers lavish them with praise for ordinary accomplishments, such as being punctual?

8. Imagine that you are evaluating the performance of a subordinate, and that as you provide that person with some negative feedback, he or she begins to cry. How might you use your emotional intelligence to deal with the situation?

9. Provide an example of a person who destroyed his or her career because of poor self-management.

10. Explain why it might be true that today's production workers need to have above-average mental ability (cognitive intelligence) to succeed.

CASE PROBLEM: The Brand Called Amanda

As Amanda navigated the challenging highways toward her job interview in Los Angeles, she rehearsed in her mind the importance of communicating that she is a unique brand. "I have to get across the idea that I am special, even if my brand is not as well established as Coca-Cola or Mercedes. The customer-care position at the telecommunications firm will be a good way to launch my career and my brand." An excerpt of her job interview with the hiring manager, Sonya, follows:

Sonya: Welcome, Amanda. I am pleased that you made it through the online job application and the video screening interview. Tell me again why you would like to join our telecommunications company as a customer-care specialist.

Amanda: Oh, I don't really want to join you as a customer-care specialist. I would prefer the role of director of customer care, but I have to start somewhere. (Smiling) Seriously, I like the telecommunications business. It fits my brand called Amanda. I am a great support person and a great people person. I'm so unique because I'm great with details and great with people.

Sonya: Tell me specifically what key strengths you would bring to this job.

Amanda: As found in my brand called Amanda, I am into high-tech and high-touch. I'm a whiz at getting to the bottom of a technical problem, and I'm warm and wonderful with people. Come to think of it, have you seen my business card? It contains loads of detail about my skills and strengths on the back. The card is laminated so that it will last, and it contains my photo. It's even like a hologram, with a 3D look.

Another thing you should know is that I have received loads of compliments about my people skills. Just the other day, another customer in the supermarket said I was so nice and kind with the cashier. Many people have told me that I have made them feel relaxed.

Sonya: Yes, Amanda, I do have your card. You gave one to the receptionist, and she gave it to me. And why do you keep referring to yourself as a brand? Is this just a gimmick to get you noticed?

Amanda: Being a brand is the modern way to tell you that Amanda Logan is one of a kind. I've got a skill set that is hard to beat. Besides, I want to build a reputation fast that will propel me to the top as an executive in the telecom field.

Sonya: On the trip to the top, what do you plan to do for us as a customer-care specialist?

Amanda: I will live up to the brand called Amanda by getting customer care done big time. Just ask me to do something, and it will be done. Don't forget, I will be building my reputation and brand image during this beginning assignment. With my outstanding people skills and technical problem-solving skills, I am sure that customers will be feeding me ideas for improving the company. I will then pass on some of these suggestions to company management.

Sonya: Now let's talk about details like the job assignment, salary, and benefits.

Amanda: Fine with me. We have to deal with the mundane at some point.

Case Questions

1. What about Amanda's comments in the interview suggest that she is narcissistic?
2. What evidence do you find for any other personality trait that Amanda exhibits?
3. What recommendation can you offer Amanda to make her a more effective interviewee?

Endnotes

1. Original story created from facts and observations in the following sources: "Stacy Brown-Philpot: CEO, TaskRabbit," *Lean In*, February 28, 2018, pp. 1–2; Alexandra Wolfe, "Stacy Brown-Philpot: The TaskRabbit CEO Is Looking to the Future of Chores," *The Wall Street Journal*, August 5–6, 2017, p. C11; Zack Friedman, "How TaskRabbit CEO Stacy Brown-Philpot Conquers Everyday Tasks," *Forbes*, September 14, 2014, pp. 1–4; Wendy Naugle, "6 Ways to Make Your Next Career Risk Pay Off, from TaskRabbit CEO Stacy Brown-Philpot," *Glamour*, September 13, 2017, pp. 1–2.

2. Paul R. Sackett, Filip Lievens, Chad H. Van Iddekinge, and Nathan R. Kuncel, "Individual Differences and Their Measurement: A Review of 100 Years of Research," *Journal of Applied Psychology*, March 2017, p. 254.

3. Marcus Buckingham, "What Great Managers Do," *Harvard Business Review*, March 2005, pp. 70–79.

4. Kurt Lewin, *A Dynamic Theory of Personality* (New York: McGraw-Hill, 1935).

5. John E. Hunter, Frank L. Schmidt, and Michael E. Judiesch, "Individual Differences in Output Variability as a Function of Job Complexity," *Journal of Applied Psychology*, February 1990, pp. 28–42.

6. "The Vital Role of Self-Esteem: It Boosts Productivity and Earnings," *Business Week*, February 2, 1998, p. 26.

7. Sackett et al., "Individual Differences and Their Measurement," p. 255; Orlando Behling, "Employee Selection: Will Intelligence and Conscientiousness Do the Job?" *Academy of Management Executive*, February 1998, p. 78.

8. Jesús F. Salgado, et al., "A Meta-Analytic Study of General Mental Ability Validity for Different Occupations in the European Community," *Journal of Applied Psychology*, December 2003, pp. 1068–1081.

9. Sam Walker, "The NFL's Smartest Team," *The Wall Street Journal*, September 30, 2005, pp. W1, W10.

10. Research cited in Sharon Begley, "Good Genes Count, but Many Factors Make Up High IQ," *The Wall Street Journal*, June 20, 2003, p. B1.

11. Richard E. Nisbett et al., "Intelligence: New Findings and Theoretical Developments," *American Psychologist*, February/March 2012, p. 140.

12. Timothy A. Judge, Amy E. Colbert, and Remus Ilies, "Intelligence and Leadership: A Quantitative Review and Test of Theoretical Propositions," *Journal of Applied Psychology*, June 2004, pp. 542–552.

13. Robert J. Sternberg, *Beyond IQ: A Triarchic Theory of Human Intelligence* (New York: Cambridge University Press, 1995).

14. J. Robert Baum, Barbara Jean Bird, and Sheetal Singh, "The Practical Intelligence of Entrepreneurs: Antecedents and a Link with New Venture Growth," *Personnel Psychology*, No. 2, 2011, pp. 397–425.

15. "From 'Character' to 'Personality,'" *APA Monitor*, December 1999, p. 22.

16. Research reported in Elizabeth Bernstein, 'Not Introvert, Nor Extrovert: The Adaptable Ambivert," *The Wall Street Journal*, July 28, 2015, p. D2.

17. Brent W. Roberts, Oleksandr S. Chernyshenko, Stephen Stark, and Lewis R. Goldberg, "The Structure of Conscientiousness: An Empirical Investigation Based on Seven Major Personality Questionnaires," *Personnel Psychology*, Spring 2005, pp. 103–139.

18. Remus Ilies and Timothy A. Judge, "On the Heritability of Job Satisfaction: The Mediating Role of Personality," *Journal of Applied Psychology*, August 2003, pp. 750–759.

19. Research reported in Sumathi Reddy, "'A Perfect Dose of Pessimism': Is the Glass Half Full? Or Empty?" *The Wall Street Journal*, August 5, 2014, p. D1.

20. Emily Grijalva and P. D. Harms, "Narcissism: An Integrative Synthesis and Dominance Complementarity Model," *Academy of Management Perspectives*, May 2014, pp. 108–127; Andrew J. DuBrin, *Narcissism in the Workplace: Research, Opinion, and Practice* (Cheltenham, UK: Edward Elgar, 2012), pp. 1, 77.

21. Michael Farnsworth and V. John Ella, "Narcissists Inc." *HR Magazine*, May 2015, pp. 78–79.

22. Research reported in Rosemarie Ward, "Ripening with Age: Key Traits Seem to Improve as We Grow Older," *Psychology Today*, July/August 2003, p. 12.

23. Elizabeth Bernstein, "We Actually Get Nicer With Age," *The Wall Street Journal*, April 22, 2014, p. D1.

24. Christopher J. Boyce, Alex M. Wood, Michael Daly, and Constantin Sedikides, "Personality Change Following Unemployment," *Journal of Applied Psychology*, July 2015, pp. 991–1011.

25. These studies and similar ones are reviewed in Leonard D. Goodstein and Richard I. Lanyon, "Applications of Personality Assessment to the Workplace: A Review," *Journal of Business and Psychology*, Spring 1999, pp. 293–298.

26. L. A. Witt and Gerald R. Ferris, "Social Skill as Moderator of the Conscientiousness-Performance Relationship: Convergent Results across Four Studies," *Journal of Applied Psychology*, October 2003, pp. 809–820.

27. Sackett et al., "Individual Differences and Their Measurement," p. 260.

28. David B. Day, Deidra J. Schleicher, Amy L. Unckless, and Nathan J. Hiller, "Self-Monitoring Personality at Work: A Meta-Analytic Investigation of Construct Validity," *Journal of Applied Psychology*, April 2002, pp. 390–401.

29. Jeremy M. Beus, Lindsay Y. Dhanani, and Mallory A. McCord, "A Meta-Analysis of Personality and Workplace Safety: Addressing Unanswered Questions," *Journal of Applied Psychology*, March 2015, pp. 481–498.

30. Timothy A. Judge, Joyce E. Bono, Remus Ilies, and Megan W. Gerhardt, "Personality and Leadership: A Quantitative and Qualitative Review," *Journal of Applied Psychology*, August 2002, pp. 765–780.

31. Emily Grijalva, Peter D. Harms, Daniel A. Newman, Blaine H. Gaddis, and R. Chris Fraley, "Narcissism and Leadership: A Meta-Analytic Review of Linear and Nonlinear Relationships," *Personnel Psychology*, No. 1, 2015, pp. 1–47.

32. Nathan T. Carter et al., "Uncovering Curvilinear Relationships between Conscientiousness and Job Performance: How Theoretically Appropriate Measurement Makes a Difference," *Journal of Applied Psychology*, July 2014, pp. 564–586.

33. Huy Le et al., "Too Much of a Good Thing: Curvilinear Relationships between Personality Traits and Job Performance," *Journal of Applied Psychology*, January 2011, pp. 113–133.

34. Cited in Arielle Emmett, "Snake Oil or Science? That's the Raging Debate on Personality Testing," *Workforce Management*, October 2004, p. 90.

35. Dana L. Joseph and Daniel A. Newman, "Emotional Intelligence: An Integrative Meta-Analysis and Cascading Model," *Journal of Applied Psychology*, January 2010, pp. 54–78.

36. Daniel Goleman, Richard Boyatzis, and Annie McKee, "Primal Leadership: The Hidden Driver of Great Performance," *Harvard Business Review*, December 2001, pp. 42–51.

37. Daniel Goleman and Richard E. Boyatzis, "Emotional Intelligence Has 12 Elements. Which Do You Need to Work On?" *Harvard Business Review*, February 8, 2017, pp. 1–6.

38. Peter J. Jordan, Neal M. Ashkanasy, and Charmine E. J. Hartel, "Emotional Intelligence as a Moderator of Emotional and Behavioral Reactions to Job Insecurity," *Academy of Management Review*, July 2002, pp. 361–372.

39. Gerald Matthews, Moshe Zeidner, and Richard Roberts, *Emotional Intelligence: Science and Myth* (Cambridge, MA: The MIT Press, 2003), p. 531.

40. Tomas Chamorro-Premuzic and Adam Yearsley, "The Downsides of Being Very Emotionally Intelligent," *Harvard Business Review*, January 12, 2017, p. 3.

Learning, Perception, and Values

Rawpixel.com/Shutterstock.com

Learning Objectives

**After reading and studying this chapter and doing the exercises, you
should be able to:**

1. Explain the basics of modeling and shaping, cognitive learning, social
   cognitive learning, and e-learning.

2. Describe how learning styles influence workplace learning.

3. Describe key aspects of the perceptual process, along with common perceptual problems.

4. Describe how attribution theory and blaming others contribute to an understanding of human behavior in the workplace.

5. Summarize why values are an important part of organizational behavior.

Candice is the marketing director at the consumer appliance division of a large electronics company. She recently added to her staff a product planner named Blake who appears to be off to a good start after one month on the job. Yet as Candice walked by Blake's cubicle several times, she noticed that he was barefoot. The third time Candice observed that Blake was barefoot, she remarked, "Blake, why are you barefoot? This is an office, not a beach or a loft apartment."

Blake responded, "I am part of the new generation of professionals. We are not bound by old-fashioned dress codes. Besides, my role model is Adam Neuman, that incredible guy who started the shared office space company. I read in *Forbes* that his company is valued at $20 billion, and he often doesn't wear shoes and socks to the office. And he's not the only barefoot executive I have seen pictures of."

(Adam Neumann is the cofounder of WeWork, a company that provides office space for freelancers and sole proprietors who cannot afford an office staff of their own but still like the idea of working with other people. WeWork functions as a middleman, renting space from others at wholesale and then upgrading for cool design. In addition, WeWork provides flexible leases and built-in services like Internet access, Wi-Fi reception, mailroom services, and cleaning, along with free coffee and beer. Neuman thinks that the value added is an office atmosphere and culture for the independent workers. WeWork now has 163 locations in 52 cities worldwide and more than 2,900 employees.[1])

Candice said, "Neuman can do what he wants as the cofounder of a worldwide company, but you work here, and we want you to follow our dress code. Maybe you and I have different values when it comes to office decorum.

The story about the marketing director and the young product planner reflects how differences in values can influence how smoothly people work together. In this chapter, we describe four aspects of individual functioning: learning, perception, attributions, and values. Understanding these aspects of behavior helps managers deal more effectively with people. The same aspects of behavior should also make job seekers realize that technical skill alone is not enough to survive in today's digital economy.

Two Key Learning Processes and E-Learning

LEARNING OBJECTIVE 1
Explain the basics of modeling and shaping, cognitive learning, social cognitive learning, and e-learning.

learning A relatively permanent change in behavior based on practice or experience.

Given that most organizations emphasize continuous learning, it is useful to understand how people learn. Workers at all levels are expected to acquire both new hard skills and soft skills throughout their career. For example, a worker might have to learn the new technology to work at a call center and also develop an ability to understand the accents of people from different cultures, which is necessary to deal with call-center customers. **Learning** is a relatively permanent change in behavior based on practice or experience. A curiosity about learning is that it is possible to learn something and store it in your mind without changing your behavior.[2] For example, you might read that if you press "F12" in Word you open the "Save As" function. You keep it in mind, but do not use the command yet. The new knowledge is stored in your upper brain but is not yet put into action.

A person does not learn how to grow physically, digest food, hear sounds, or see light. These are innate patterns of behavior. But a person does learn how to conduct a performance evaluation, use an Internet search engine to access information, or prepare a report. Unless learning takes place, few employees would be able to perform their jobs satisfactorily.

Being able to learn well has gained in importance in organizations because many firms change too rapidly to predict what competencies will be needed even a few years into the future. As Claudio Fernández-Aráoz argues, the question is not what skills an employee currently possesses, but whether they have the potential to learn new ones. For example, a marketing manager might be hired by a company whose products are sold domestically.

Suddenly the company expands overseas, necessitating that the manager learn how to cope with international trade regulations.[3]

Employee learning has become necessary at all organizational levels for companies to stay competitive. (The purpose of training is for employees to learn skills, behaviors, and attitudes.) The Container Store emphasizes store associates interacting with customers, but it also has an online component. The CEO notes that the live chat and call centers are staffed with well-paid and well-trained workers in the home office with 10 to 15 years of experience. They have learned "1,000 different ways to use a dairy crate."[4]

Our concern here is with two methods of learning complex material: (1) modeling and shaping, and (2) cognitive learning, including informal learning. We also describe a popular method of delivering material for learning: e-learning. In recognition of the fact that people learn in different ways, we will also discuss learning styles.

Modeling and Shaping

When you acquire a complicated skill such as coaching a team member, you experience much more than the acquisition of a few habits. You learn a great number of habits, and you learn how to put them together in a cohesive, smoothly flowing pattern. Two important processes that help in learning complicated skills are modeling and shaping.

Modeling (or imitation) occurs when you learn a skill by observing another person perform that skill. Many sales representatives acquire sales skills by observing a competent sales representative in action. Apprenticeship programs are receiving new recognition for their importance in employee learning. Robert Lerman, an economics professor at American University, says that apprenticeships can offer a precise match between the skills that employers need and the training that workers receive.[5] Apprenticeships involve considerable modeling of more experienced workers by the apprentices.

> **modeling** Imitation; learning a skill by observing another person performing that skill.

Streamed videos and DVDs are widely used to facilitate modeling of skills such as interviewing, resolving conflict, and conducting a meeting. Modeling often brings forth behaviors that people did not previously seem to have in their repertoire. To model effectively, one must carefully observe the demonstration and then attempt the new skill shortly thereafter. Although modeling is an effective learning method, the learner must have the proper capabilities and motivation.

Modeling is a key aspect of **social cognitive theory**, which holds that observation, rather than trial and error and reward and punishment, is the key to learning. According to this theory, people learn not just from firsthand experience but also from observing what happens to other people or by hearing about what others have experienced. Another key observation of social learning theory is that we can learn new behaviors without actually performing them or being rewarded for demonstrating them.[6] For example, Claudia, a business administrator newly hired into a chain of hospitals, hears that staff members who purchase stock in the firm are viewed favorably by upper management. "A word to the wise is sufficient," so Claudia purchases 10 shares of the company stock.

> **social cognitive theory** Holds that observation, rather than trial and error and reward and punishment, is the key to learning.

Shaping occurs when a person learns through the reinforcement, or rewarding, of small steps that build up to the final or desired behavior. It is another way in which complicated skills are learned. At each successful step of the way, the learner receives positive reinforcement. As the learner improves his or her ability to perform the task, more skill is required to receive the reward.

> **shaping** Learning through the reinforcement or rewarding of small steps to build to the final or desired behavior.

A clerical worker might be shaped into an inside sales representative (taking telephone and online orders). He acquires a series of small skills, beginning with learning the inventory system. He receives a series of rewards as he moves along the path from a support specialist to an inside sales representative who can understand and satisfy customer requirements. Among the forms of positive reinforcement he receives are approval for his new skills, incremental pay increases, and the feeling of pride as new small skills are learned. Among the punishments he receives to assist learning are negative statements from customers when he fills an order incorrectly.

Cognitive Learning

cognitive learning theory A theory emphasizing that learning takes place in a complicated manner involving much more than acquiring habits and small skills.

Cognitive learning theory emphasizes that learning takes place in a complicated manner involving much more than acquiring habits and small skills. Learners also strive to learn, develop hunches, and have flashes of insight. Furthermore, they use many aspects of their personality (e.g., openness to experience) in acquiring knowledge. Suppose that a safety and health specialist discovers the cause underlying a mysterious rash on the skin of many employees. Cognitive learning theory would emphasize that the specialist may have reached the conclusion by acquiring bits of information that formed a cohesive pattern. The theory would also emphasize the goal orientation of the safety and health specialist, along with the person's reasoning and analytical skills. Dedication to the cause and problem-solving ability would also contribute to the learning.

informal learning A planned learning that occurs in a setting without a formal classroom, lesson plan, instructor, or examination.

Another type of learning in organizations that fits a cognitive theory explanation is **informal learning**. This is defined as any learning that occurs in which the organization does not determine or design the learning process. You might learn by observing others, asking tech support a question, or working with knowledgeable people.[7] The central premise of such learning is that employees acquire some important information outside of a formal learning situation. The employees capitalize on a learning situation outside of a formal structure, in which the rewards stemming from the learning situation are not explicit.

Informal learning can be spontaneous—such as receiving a suggestion on how to calculate the value of an American dollar in terms of a euro, and vice versa, while having lunch in a company cafeteria. Or the company might organize the work to encourage such informal learning. The company might provide common areas such as an atrium or food and beverage lounges that encourage employee interaction. Sometimes these common work areas are furnished with whiteboards and markers to facilitate exchanging ideas. Informal learning frequently does not have an expressed goal. You might be chatting in an atrium with a coworker and learn something valuable even though you had not established a learning goal for the conversation.

An important implication of informal learning for managers is that knowledgeable and well-motivated employees can help one another with learning. However, the manager must still be on guard against misinformed and poorly motivated employees who would create negative learning. Classroom training is helpful in increasing the chances that the right type of learning takes place.

A factor influencing how much cognitive learning takes place is the orientation of the learner. A *mastery orientation* relates to a dedication to increase one's competence with a task. These learners are eager to improve their ability with tasks. For example, a person might want to learn how to make more effective oral presentations so he or she could better enjoy presenting at meetings. With a *performance orientation*, learners focus on how well they perform a task and make comparisons with others. These learners are keenly interested in displaying their ability to others.

Evidence has been collected from college students that a mastery orientation is associated with greater effort and more complex learning strategies. (An example of a complex learning strategy would be paraphrasing and generating questions with answers.) In contrast, a performance orientation is associated with less effort devoted to the task and less frequent use of complex learning strategies.[8]

E-Learning

Important innovations in learning have taken place in both schools and industry through e-learning, also referred to as *distance learning*, *online learning*, or

Classroom interaction is effective for many types of learning.

remote learning. Here, the learner studies independently outside of a classroom setting and interacts with a computer in addition to studying course material. (Many readers of this book are doing so for an online course.) **E-learning** is a web-based form of computer-based training. An e-learning course usually is carefully structured with specific lessons plans for the student. E-learning is more of a method of delivering content than a method of learning, yet the process helps us understand more about learning.

e-learning A web-based form of computer-based training.

Mobile Devices

As much of computerized activity has shifted from desktop and laptop computers to mobile devices, so has e-learning. A substantial amount of online learning activities are now shifted to formats compatible with handheld devices. Simon Casuto explains that mobile learning is not simply e-learning on a mobile device. Instead, it involves self-paced, on-demand learning in bite-sized lessons.[9] For example, the 75,000 associates in North America for Keller Williams Realty Inc. use smartphones and tablet computers to view approximately 2- or 3-minute video lessons that build on the content learned in training rooms. Each lesson is accessed as streaming video or a podcast. The company director of video production says, "We need to better serve the agents who want to learn on their own time, even in the middle of the night."[10]

MOOCs

Another development in e-learning is in massive open-online courses, known as MOOCs. As originated by Sebastien Thrun, a Stanford University professor of computer science, these courses are designed to give hundreds of thousands of students across the world an opportunity to take courses free and outside of a university program. Many people who take these courses already have a college degree and want to explore an additional subject.[11] MOOCs are popular but have not lived up to their hype of becoming a dominant force in education, replacing colleges and traditional training programs.[12]

The link between MOOCs and organizational behavior is that some companies are developing, either on their own or by hiring contractors, MOOCs dealing with training content needed by the company. For example, the content could be productivity software or management courses. A business MOOC often follows this format: Hundreds or even thousands of workers enroll in a self-paced digital course that usually includes virtual lectures, online exercises, and extensive participation in collaborative online forums, including chats. Another way in which MOOCs could be used for online learning is for workers to take a MOOC course directly related to a job, such as creative thinking.[13]

A specific example of the business application of MOOCs is that Coursera, a large provider of massive online courses, has teamed up with several large financial and technology companies to provide job-relevant classes. The offerings are sponsored and partially designed by the corporations, and they focus on skill training and professional development.[14]

Geographic Dispersion of Employees

A major impetus behind e-learning is that many employees are geographically dispersed, making it difficult to gather them in one place for learning. With e-learning, employees in many different physical locations, including different parts of an office building or office complex, can readily participate in training. Although e-learning is technologically different from more traditional forms of learning, it still is based on basic methods of learning. For example, the learner will often need reinforcement to keep going, such as receiving an encouraging text message when he or she successfully completes a unit.

Motivation and Self-Discipline of the Learner

Another relevant aspect of e-learning here is that its success depends on cognitive processes of the learner, particularly self-motivation and self-discipline. Self-motivation is important because an assignment to take an e-learning course by the company is often not enough to motivate a person to work independently. Self-discipline is necessary to

Continuous learning is part of a successful career.

create a regular time for performing class work and to prevent distractions by work or home activities. In educational settings, successful distance learning also requires high motivation. Some students may not take e-learning seriously.

Blended Learning

E-learning has gained momentum, yet most companies prefer to use blended learning (web and classroom) because it combines the personal nature of classroom training with the cost efficiencies of learning via the Internet. The cost efficiencies include decreases in travel and lodging costs and payments to classroom instructors.[15] However, classroom training provides the difficult-to-measure benefit of employees spontaneously exchanging ideas that could lead to a creativity breakthrough. In general, e-learning is most effective in delivering conceptual subject matter such as product information, whereas classroom training is more effective for learning interpersonal skills.[16]

According to Lindsay Redpath, there is considerable evidence that online learning can be as effective as classroom learning, particularly when the instructor plays an active role, such as in leading discussions and summarizing key points.[17] Nevertheless, many workers at all levels enjoy the interaction with classmates and the instructor that is much more limited in e-learning.

Learning Styles

EARNING OBJECTIVE 2
Describe how learning styles influence workplace learning.

learning style A person's particular way of learning, reflecting the fact that people learn best in different ways.

Another important concept in understanding learning is **learning style**, the fact that people learn best in different ways. For example, some people acquire new material best through passive learning. Such people quickly acquire information through studying textbooks, manuals, online articles, and magazine articles. They can juggle images in their mind as they read about abstract concepts such as supply and demand, cultural diversity, and customer service. Others learn best by doing rather than by studying—for example, learning hands-on about customer service by dealing with customers in many situations.

Another key dimension of learning styles is whether a person learns best by working alone or cooperatively, such as in a study group. Learning by oneself allows for more intense concentration, and one can proceed at one's own pace. Learning in groups and through classroom discussion allows people to exchange viewpoints and perspectives. Considerable evidence has been accumulated that peer tutoring and cooperative learning are effective for acquiring knowledge.[18] Another advantage of cooperative learning is that it is more likely to lead to changes in behavior. Assume that a manager holds group discussions about the importance of achieving high customer satisfaction. Employees participating in these group discussions are more likely to assertively pursue high customer satisfaction on the job than those who only read about the topic.

A basic approach to learning styles is to divide them into three categories—visual, auditory, and kinesthetic, as illustrated in Figure 3-1. *Visual learners* learn best through seeing things as in reading, taking notes, and watching videos. *Auditory learners* learn best through hearing words and phrases, such as reading out loud, following spoken directions, and working in study groups. *Kinesthetic learners* learn best through experiencing and doing things, such as trying out a machine or piece of equipment, role-playing, and studying with others.[19] We emphasize the word *best* for all three learning styles because most people combine the three.

A manager can apply the concept of learning styles by asking group members to reflect on how they learn best. When new work-related material has to be learned, group members can select the learning method that is most effective for them. Some group members

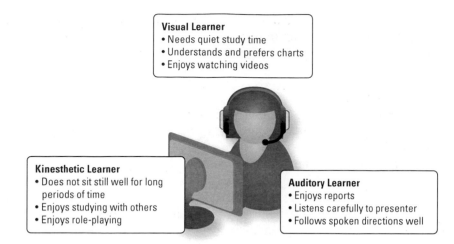

Visual Learner
- Needs quiet study time
- Understands and prefers charts
- Enjoys watching videos

Kinesthetic Learner
- Does not sit still well for long periods of time
- Enjoys studying with others
- Enjoys role-playing

Auditory Learner
- Enjoys reports
- Listens carefully to presenter
- Follows spoken directions well

FIGURE 3-1 The Visual, Auditory, and Kinesthetic Learning Styles

might study manuals, while others might find work in study groups valuable. A more cautious approach to capitalizing on learning styles is to encourage learners to use more than one mode of learning. They should invest some time in individual study and also interact with others to enhance learning.

Evidence suggests that when people are asked to learn with a method that does not match their preferred learning style, they can adapt to the situation and learn well anyway. A comprehensive review commissioned by the Association for Psychological Science concluded that there is almost no evidence that customizing instruction to match the preferred learning style of students leads to better achievement.[20] A general finding of this nature does not mean, however, that no learners profit from matching instruction to their preferred style.

Individual Differences Related to Skill Acquisition

The various approaches to learning, including learning styles, help us understand how people learn. How *much* people learn is another important consideration in understanding learning in the workplace. In general, people with higher cognitive intelligence and personality traits that allow them to concentrate better (such as emotional stability and conscientiousness) acquire knowledge and skills more readily.

A large-scale research study supports the idea that cognitive skills and personality traits contribute to a person profiting from training, and then using the acquired information to enhance job performance. The sample consisted of 9,793 trainees accepted into the Federal Aviation Administration (FAA) training program for air-traffic controllers. The average age of the trainee was 26 years; 84 percent were male, and 16 percent were female. Trainees took a cognitive skill test when applying for the program, whereas the personality test was administered as part of the medical examination of the air-traffic-control selection process.

The study found that air-traffic controllers who rate high on general cognitive ability demonstrated greater skills acquisition than controllers who rate lower on general cognitive ability. A combination of personality traits, known as *Factor A (warmth)*, proved useful in predicting skill acquisition. High Factor A people are warm, outgoing, attentive to others, cooperative, generous, and trusting. *Warmth* predicted skill acquisition,

Career-oriented people have to make time for learning.

particularly when training was based on group work. The study also demonstrated that trainees who performed well in the training program were more likely to achieve full performance status when employed as an air-traffic controller.[21]

Perception

LEARNING OBJECTIVE 3
Describe key aspects of the perceptual process, along with common perceptual problems.

perception The various ways in which people interpret things in the outside world and how they act on the basis of these interpretations.

Most of us interpret what is going on in the world around us as we perceive it—not as it really is. This tendency is much more pronounced when interpreting meanings rather than tangible physical phenomena. Five members of a team might give varying interpretations to receiving a 4-percent salary increase for the upcoming year. Yet the same five people would share the same accurate perception that an office tower is under construction across the street. **Perception** deals with the various ways in which people interpret things in the outside world and how they act on the basis of these interpretations. At times, however, perception could relate to internal phenomena. One person might wake up with an ache in the upper arm and perceive it to be an early indicator of a heart attack. Another person might dismiss a similar ache as having slept on the arm at an awkward angle.

Perceptions on the job are important. Many studies have investigated the consequence of employees' job perceptions. The results show that employees who perceive their job to be challenging and interesting have high job satisfaction and motivation. In addition, these favorable perceptions lead to better job performance.[22] Our concern here is with two aspects of perception of most concern to managerial workers: (1) perceptual distortions and problems, and (2) how people attribute causes to events.

Perceptual Distortions and Problems

Under ideal circumstances, people perceive information as it is intended to be communicated or as it exists in reality. For example, it is hoped that an executive from the home office who is assigned to a task force at a company division will perceive the assignment as a compliment. Yet the executive given such an assignment may perceive it as a way of being eased out the door. As shown in Figure 3-2, both characteristics of the stimulus and people's perceptual processes can lead to perceptual distortions. The late Chris

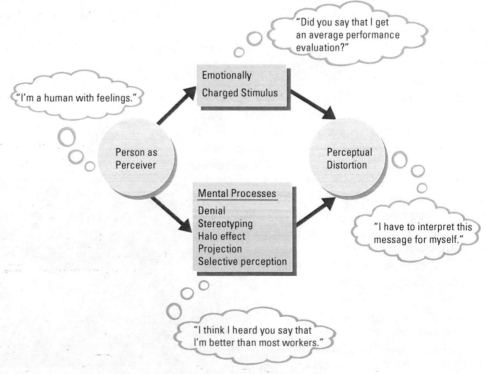

FIGURE 3-2 Contributors to Perceptual Distortions

Argyris observed that people are unaware of how they form perceptions; moreover, they are unaware that they are unaware.[23] Studying perception may therefore help reduce some of the mystery.

Characteristics of the Stimulus

Perceptual problems are most likely encountered when a stimulus or cue affects the emotional status of the perceiver. If you have strong attitudes about the issue at stake, you are most likely to misperceive the event. The perception of a stimulus or an event depends on the emotions, needs, attitudes, and motives of a person. Imagine that an irate customer sends an e-mail to a CEO complaining about shabby service received when asking for a refund on a defective product. The CEO widely distributes this letter by e-mail to company employees. Among the possible perceptions of this event are the following:

Interpretation by customer service manager: "I'm really in trouble now. It's my job to ensure top-quality service throughout the organization. The CEO thinks I've messed up big time."

Interpretation by customer service specialist immediately involved with the case: "It's nice to have a laugh once in a while. One customer out of 2,000 I've dealt with in the past year is upset. The other 99.9 percent have no gripe; so why worry?"

Interpretation by merchandising manager: "It's obvious the big boss is upset with the customer service group. I don't blame him. We get no complaints about the quality of merchandise. I hope those customer service reps can get their act together."

Mental Processes of People

The devices people use to deal with sensory information play a major role in creating perceptual problems. The general purpose of these perceptual shortcuts is usually to make the reality of a situation less painful or disturbing. As such, these mental processes are types of defensive behavior.

Denial If the sensory information at hand is particularly painful to us, we often deny to ourselves and others that the information even exists. A purchasing agent was confronted by her manager with the accusation that a supplier entertained her so lavishly that it was tantamount to a kickback. The purchasing agent replied that she thought the company was only concerned about sales incentives involving tangible goods or money. Yet the agent had been on a committee six months previously that formulated the new regulations on kickbacks.

Another frequently seen example of denial in organizations is when a manager ignores hints that he is falling out of favor and thus may soon lose his job. He then loses any advantage by not conducting a job search until he has been terminated.

The implication for the managerial worker is to stand ready for a message to be distorted by the receiver if the issue is emotional. Be prepared to clarify and repeat messages and to solicit feedback to ensure that the message was received as intended. Chapter 8 deals at length with the topic of overcoming communication barriers.

Stereotyping A common shortcut to the perceptual process is to evaluate an individual based on the group or class to which he or she belongs. Stereotypes reduce tension in an unusual way. Encountering a person who does not fit our stereotype of that person's group can be painful to our ego. We lessen the discomfort by looking for behavior that conforms to the stereotype. Assume that you believe that Chinese workers are meticulous. When you meet a Chinese worker on the job, you might have a tendency to search for evidence of meticulousness.

An important workplace consequence of stereotypes is that they typically lead to performance standards or expectations based on an individual's group membership. Manufacturing engineers from Germany have a positive reputation (stereotype) for their skill level. A manufacturing manager might therefore have very high standards of what he perceives to be superior work from a German engineer. At the same time, the manager might have lower standards of what constitutes superior engineering work from an engineer from another country.

The fact that stereotypes influence standards is not always harmful. When you say "My six-year-old nephew is great at math," you are using a different standard than when you say, "My statistics professor is great at math."

Halo Effect A tendency exists to color everything that we know about a person because of one recognizable favorable or unfavorable trait. When a company does not insist on the use of objective measures of performance, it is not uncommon for a supervisor to give favorable performance ratings to persons who dress well or smile frequently. The fine appearance or warm smile of these people has created a halo around them. Group members often create a positive halo about one member who is articulate and witty. In reality, the person's professional competence may be average.

Projection Another shortcut in the perceptual process is to project our own faults onto others instead of making an objective appraisal of the situation. A manager might be asked to recommend a group member for a difficult troubleshooting assignment out of town. The manager might hesitate, saying, "Most of the people in my group do not handle pressure well." In reality, handling pressure poorly is the manager's key weakness.

Selective Perception People use this mechanism when they draw an unjustified conclusion from an unclear situation. A feedback e-mail message from the manager might be interpreted as documentation to help the company build a case for firing the individual. Selective perception can have negative consequences when it leads to self-deception about potentially bad news. A worker planning for retirement, for example, might not pay attention to the trend toward companies doing away with traditional pensions. She observes only the encouraging news that many companies still do have traditional pensions. As a result, the worker may not embark on a serious investment program for retirement.

What can managerial workers do with knowledge about perceptual distortions? If it appears that a work associate is making obvious use of a perceptual distortion, one should gently confront the person about the discrepancy in his or her thinking. In the pension example, a coworker might have said, "Look, I claim no great foresight about our company pension plan, but our company could eliminate pensions at any time—particularly if we are bought out. If you want to fulfill your retirement dreams, you'd better start investing now."

LEARNING OBJECTIVE 4
Describe how attribution theory and blaming others contribute to an understanding of human behavior in the workplace.

Attribution Theory and Blame

Another important aspect of perception is how people perceive the causes of behavior in themselves and others. **Attribution theory** is the process by which people ascribe causes to the behavior they perceive. Two attribution errors are quite common. The **fundamental attribution error** is the tendency to attribute behavior to internal causes when focusing on someone else's behavior. We might therefore think that a vice president achieved that position because of his or her ambition and talent. The other error, **self-serving bias**, takes place when focusing on one's own behavior. People tend to attribute their achievements to good inner qualities, whereas they attribute failure to adverse factors within the environment. A manager thus would attribute increased productivity to his or her superior leadership skills but blame low productivity on poor support from the organization. (The self-serving bias takes place more frequently than the fundamental attribution error.)

attribution theory The process by which people ascribe causes to the behavior they perceive.

fundamental attribution error The tendency to attribute behavior to internal causes when focusing on someone else's behavior.

self-serving bias An attribution error whereby people tend to attribute their achievements to good inner qualities, whereas they attribute their failure to adverse factors within the environment.

Why Attributions Matter in the Workplace

Why attributions matter in organizations is more difficult to imagine than why topics such as leadership or motivation are relevant. A group of researchers conducted a meta-analysis of the outcomes or effects associated with attributions. The general finding was that attributions really do have a wide range of impacts. Here we present a sampling of their findings as related to whether people perceive an external versus an internal cause for events.[24]

1. The locus of attributions for favorable and unfavorable outcomes, or results, has a significant impact on performance. When workers made external attributions for external events (e.g., not attaining a goal), they were more likely to receive negative performance ratings. However, internal attributions for desirable results were positively associated with performance ratings. An example of the latter is that attributing goal attainment to one's own abilities promotes self-confidence in the ability to perform the task.

2. People tend to feel better when they attribute blame for negative outcomes to external factors and take credit for favorable outcomes. In other words, people feel better when they think they are responsible for good results, but can blame others for poor results.

3. Employees' internal attributions for favorable events were more strongly associated with improvements in the quality of their relationship with the leader. External attributions had a much smaller impact on the perception of improvements in quality of relationships with the leader. The point here is subtle, but it could mean that when we feel we are responsible for good results, it establishes a positive attitude that improves the relationship with the supervisor.

We often attribute successes to our own good qualities.

4. External attributions for employee negative results, or poor performance, are associated with a lesser intention to punish the employee. This finding fits common sense because a rational manager is less likely to punish an employee for poor performance that took place because of factors beyond the employee's control. For example, a massive hacking attack on customer credit-card information could result in a sudden drop in sales for a retailer.

A Basic Theory of Attribution

According to attribution theory as developed by Harold H. Kelley, people attribute causes after gathering information about three dimensions of behavior: consensus, consistency, and distinctiveness.[25]

- *Consensus* relates to comparing a person's behavior with that of peers. High consensus exists when a person acts similarly to others in the group, and low consensus exists when the person acts differently. If others cannot perform the same feat you can, your feat will be attributed to your internal qualities.

- *Consistency* is determined by assessing whether a person's performance on a given task is consistent over time. If you are consistent over time, people will attribute your accomplishment to your internal qualities.

- *Distinctiveness* is a function of comparing a person's behavior on one task with that person's behavior on other tasks. High distinctiveness means that the person has performed the task in question quite differently from his or her performance on other tasks. Low distinctiveness refers to stable performance or quality from one task to another. If you turn in high-quality performance on many tasks, your internal characteristics will receive credit.

Observe that consensus relates to other people, consistency involves time, and distinctiveness relates to other tasks. The combination of these factors leads to attribution of causes. People attribute behavior to external (or environmental) causes when they perceive high consensus, low consistency, and high distinctiveness. People attribute behavior to internal (or personal) factors when they perceive low consensus, high consistency, and low distinctiveness.

What might this approach to attribution theory mean in practice? A manager would attribute poor-quality work to external factors, such as poor equipment and resources,

To determine whether another person's behavior stems mainly from internal or external causes, we focus on three types of information: consensus, consistency, and distinctiveness.

The sales manager informs the group members that sales consultant Jen has just closed a deal on the sale of a $2 million digital printing press to a Fortune 100 company. To determine the cause of this feat, you make the following observations.

You conclude that...

Consensus		Consistency		Distinctiveness		Attribution
No one else made a sale like that (consensus is low)	+	Jen makes many big sales (consistency is high)	+	Jen performs well on other tasks also (distinctiveness is low)	→	Jen made the sale because of her talent (internal attribution)
Other reps have made giant sales (consensus is high)	+	Jen has not made other big sales (consistency is low)	+	Jen does not perform well on other tasks (distinctiveness is high)	→	Jen made the sale because of luck (external attribution)

FIGURE 3-3 Kelley's Theory of Attributing Causes—An Example

under these conditions: All workers are producing low-quality work (high consensus), the low quality occurs only one or two times (low consistency), and the low quality occurs on only one of several tasks (high distinctiveness). In contrast, the manager will attribute low quality to personal characteristics of the workers under these conditions: Only one person is performing poorly (low consensus), the low-quality work has persisted over time (high consistency), and the low-quality work occurs for several tasks (low distinctiveness). Figure 3-3 presents another example of this complicated attribution process.

A recent expansion of attribution theory focuses on the relationship between two workers, rather than focusing on internal or external attributions. The general idea is that events occur because of the interaction between two people, such as "We attained high performance because we worked well together," or "The failure of the project was our fault."[26] A doubles team in tennis might proclaim, "We won because we played so well together" or "We matched up well as a team."

Locus of Control

locus of control The way in which people look at causation in their lives.

A logical extension of attribution theory is the concept of **locus of control**—the way in which people look at causation in their lives. Some people have an internal locus of control because they perceive their outcomes as being controlled internally. As a result, they generally feel in control of their lives. Some people have an external locus of control because they perceive much of what happens to them as being controlled by circumstances.[27] People with an internal locus of control feel that they create their own opportunities in life, while those with an external locus attribute much of their success and failure to luck. Workers with an internal locus of control are generally more mature, self-reliant, and responsible.

New experimental research about locus of control suggests that people place more emphasis on environmental than internal factors when looking at causation. The internal self may still be important, but the environment receives more of the credit or blame.[28] For example, in evaluating the success of their investments, investors attribute some of their success or failure to internal qualities, but more weight is placed on economic conditions.

Attribution theory, including the locus of control theory, has another important implication for organizational behavior aside from those already mentioned. People search for causes of events and alter their behavior because of these perceptions. Managers should therefore invest time in explaining the causes of events to workers, to avoid misperceptions and counterproductive behavior.

Blame as an Attribution

Another aspect of attribution that merits highlighting is **blame,** the tendency to place the responsibility for a negative outcome on a person, a thing, or the environment. Thus, the workers may blame the CEO for sending work overseas, and the CEO blames the workers' high wages and benefits for making outsourcing essential. Blame is an innate tendency at least a million years old. Blame researcher Mark Alicke concludes that "the human impulse to blame grew out of the evolutionary need to avert harm."[29] Frequently, blame takes the form of blame shifting, as we attribute a negative outcome to someone other than ourselves.

Blaming others is a part of attribution.

Blame is most likely to take place when harmful events occur, from minor transgressions to international disasters. Blaming and punishing harm-doers will sometimes discourage people who imperil the physical and psychological well-being of others, such as blaming a bus driver for an accident that took place during an ice storm.[30]

A negative consequence of blame is that it can block problem solving. As the adage says, "Instead of fixing the problem, we fix the blame." Blame focuses on the past, whereas problem solving focuses on what needs to be done so the problem will not recur. A positive consequence of blame is that it can lead to change for the good. An airline company might blame high fuel costs for recent financial losses. As a result, the airline managers figure out a way to have passengers pay for more of the fuel costs, find a way to economize on fuel, or both.

blame The tendency to place the responsibility for a negative outcome on a person, a thing, or the environment.

Values

Another key factor influencing behavior in organizations is the values and beliefs of people. A **value** refers to the importance a person attaches to something that serves as a guide to action. Our values influence our perceptions because we tend to perceive positively those behaviors that support our values. For example, a person with strong humanitarian values would perceive positively the company donating surplus furniture to a mission for the homeless.

Values are also tied in with enduring beliefs that one's mode of conduct is better than the opposite mode of conduct. One person may highly value quantitative analysis and will look down on people who present a position without providing quantitative evidence. The topic of values is a perennial favorite, as baby boomers are compared with younger people in Generations X and Y. With baby boomers being more conservative and respectful of authority and hierarchy, the differences in values between the generations can cause job conflict. As with other group stereotypes, generation differences are often exaggerated. Figure 3-4 outlines several generational differences in values. Understanding generational differences is critical to managing people effectively.[31] For example, the oldest employees in an organization may prefer adhering closely to policies and procedures, whereas the youngest employees might prefer to improvise when faced with a problem. The manager may have to intervene to resolve these differences.

LEARNING OBJECTIVE 5
Summarize why values are an important part of organizational behavior.

value The importance a person attaches to something that serves as a guide to action.

Values help guide our workplace activities.

FIGURE 3-4 Value Stereotypes for Several Generations of Workers

Baby Boomers (1946–1964)	Generation X (1961–1980)	Generation Y (1981–2002) (Also referred to as Millennials, Connected Generation, or Digital Native Generation [born 1996–])
Uses technology as a necessary tool, but not obsessed with technology for its own sake	Tech-savvy	Tech-savvy to the point of regarding standard communication technology techniques such as e-mail to be old-fashioned
Tolerates teams, but values independent work	Prefers teamwork, dislikes hierarchy	Teamwork so important that individual decision making is often disliked
Strong career orientation	Strives for work–life balance but will work long hours for now	Strives for work–life balance, but will work very long hours to meet an urgent situation
Favors diplomacy	Candid in conversation	Ultra-candid in conversation
Believes that fully developed spoken communication is important	Perceives spoken communication to be a supplement to written electronic communication	Much prefers sending text messages and curt e-mails to coworkers rather than talking
Will multitask in front of work associates only when it seems necessary	Feels comfortable in multitasking while interacting with work associates	Assumes that multitasking, including texting while dealing with work associates, is acceptable behavior
Seeks feedback on performance at appropriate times, such as during performance evaluations or the end of a major project	Appreciates frequent feedback, but not impatient	Values self-absorption and narcissism, therefore demands almost daily feedback
Considers almost all work that is legal to be meaningful	Would enjoy doing meaningful work, such as helping the environment, but not obsessed with the idea	Prefers work with considerable meaning in terms of human impact
Sees the importance of loyalty to the organization	Loyal to the organization when thinking that organization is loyal in return	Places little importance on loyalty, prefers to switch employers whenever it suits own needs
Prefers doing work at the office	Enjoys working at the office but also appreciates opportunity for occasional telecommuting	Often questions why it is necessary to work at an office because information technology allows for working remotely

Source: Many of the ideas are from Henry G. Jackson, "Millennials @ Work," *HR Magazine*, May 2014, p. 8; Abby Ellin, "The Beat (Up) Generation," *Psychology Today*, April 2014, pp. 56–63; Max Mihelich, "Another Generation Rises," *Workforce Management*, May 2013, pp. 34–38; Gregg Hammill, "Mixing and Managing Four Generations of Employees," *FDUMagazine Online*, Winter/Spring 2005, p. 5; Kathryn Tyler, "Generation Gaps: Millennials May Be Out of Touch with the Basics of Workplace Behavior," *HR Magazine*, January 2008, pp. 69–72; Chris Penttils, "Talking about My Generation," *Entrepreneur*, March 2009, pp. 53–55.

Note: Disagreement exists about which age brackets fit baby boomers, Generation X, and Generation Y, with both professional publications and dictionaries showing slight differences.

We discuss values from three standpoints: how they are learned, how they are clarified, and the mesh between individual and organizational values. Values will be mentioned again in the discussion of ethics because values are the foundation of ethics.

How Values Are Learned

People are not born with a particular set of values. Rather, values are learned in the process of growing up; many values are learned by age 4. One important way we acquire values is through modeling. Often a person who takes considerable pride in work was reared around people who had a strong work ethic. Models can be parents, teachers, friends, siblings, and even public figures. If we identify with a particular person, the probability is high that we will develop some of his or her major values.

Communication of attitudes is another major way in which values are learned. The attitudes we hear expressed directly or indirectly help shape our values. If using credit to purchase goods and services was talked about as an undesirable practice among your family and friends, you might hold negative values about installment purchases.

Unstated but implied attitudes may also shape values. If key people in your life showed no enthusiasm when you talked about work accomplishment, you might not place a high value on achieving outstanding results. In contrast, if your family and friends centered their lives on their careers, you might develop similar values. (Or you might rebel against such a value because it interfered with a more relaxed lifestyle.)

Many key values are also learned through religion and thus become the basis for society's morals. A basic example is that all religions emphasize treating other people fairly and kindly. Members of the clergy teach many ethics courses and seminars because it is often assumed that a religious person has special expertise with constructive values.

Clarifying Values

The values you develop early in life are directly related to the kind of person you are now and will be, and the quality of relationships that you form.[32] Recognizing this fact has led to exercises designed to help people clarify and understand some of their own values. Value-clarification exercises ask you to compare the relative importance you attach to different objects and activities. Self-Assessment 3-1 gives you an opportunity to clarify your values. The Organizational Behavior in Action box illustrates how a group of recent college graduates put their values into action.

The Mesh between Individual and Organizational Values

Under the best of circumstances, the values of employees mesh with those required of the job and organization. When this state of congruence exists, job performance is likely to be higher. For example, a person who values workplace democracy is likely to perform better in a firm that gives workers more say in decision making than if he or she worked in one that was more authoritarian.

The values of Whole Foods Market, the upscale grocery chain now owned by Amazon, contain several values related to the food the company sells. Yet these values would apply to many other business firms.

- We sell the highest-quality natural and organic foods.
- We satisfy and delight our customers.
- We promote team member growth and happiness.
- We practice win-win partnerships with our suppliers.
- We create profits and prosperity.
- We care about our community and the environment.

Whole Food management communicates these values to every employee and job applicant, emphasizing that the values are stable and represent the underpinning of the

Clarifying Your Values

Directions: Rank from 1 to 21 the importance of the following values to you. The most important value on the list receives a rank of 1, the least important a rank of 21. Use the space next to the two "Other" blanks to include important values of yours not on the list.

_____ Having my own place to live

_____ Performing meaningful work

_____ Having one or more children

_____ Having an interesting job and career

_____ Owning a detached house, condominium, or apartment

_____ Having good relationships with coworkers

_____ Having good health

_____ Receiving lots of praise and recognition

_____ Participating in sports or other pastimes

_____ Being neat, clean, and orderly

_____ Being active in a professional society in my field

_____ Being a religious person

_____ Helping people less fortunate than myself

_____ Loving and being loved by another person

_____ Having physical intimacy with another person

_____ Earning an above-average income

_____ Being in good physical condition

_____ Being a knowledgeable, informed person

_____ Leading a digital lifestyle, including having up-to-date high-technology devices to be in touch frequently with work associates, friends, and family

_____ Other

_____ Other

QUESTIONS

1. Discuss and compare your ranking of these values with the person next to you.

2. Perhaps your class, assisted by your instructor, can arrive at a class average on each of these values. How does your ranking compare to the class ranking? What evidence will you need before you conclude that a given rank is representative of the class?

3. Are there any surprises in the class ranking? Which values did you think would be the highest and lowest?

4. How do you think average ranks for these values would be influenced by a person's culture?

---

company culture.[33] The customer base of the company suggests that the majority of its customers are in tune with Whole Food values.

Not every business firm claiming to have such values carries them out in practice. As a result, problems are created for some employees. When the demands made by the organization or a manager clash with the basic values of the individual, he or she suffers from **person–role conflict.** The employee wants to obey orders but does not want to perform an act that seems inconsistent with his or her values. A situation of this type might occur when an employee is asked to help produce a product or service that he or she feels is unsafe or of no value to society.

Unfortunately, both safety and value to society are not easy to specify objectively. Assume that a person is a supervisor in the pet insurance department of an insurance company. She might suffer from role conflict because she believes that pet insurance policies are a waste of resources. Yet many human resource professionals believe that pet insurance is an employee benefit that builds company loyalty, reduces worries for pet caretakers, and helps animals. One could argue that any product or service is of value to society because it creates employment for somebody.

What constitutes a good fit between personal values and organizational values may change at different stages of a person's career because of a change in values. At one point in a person's career, he or she may think that founding a business is important because the new firm might create employment. At another stage of the same person's career, he or she might believe that working for the nonprofit sector is more meritorious.

A starting point in finding a good fit between individual and organizational values is to identify what type of work would be the most meaningful. After identifying a passion

person-role conflict A condition that occurs when the demands made by the organization or a manager clash with the values of the individual.

Venture for America Provides an Opportunity for Recent Graduates to Do Good

Venture for America (VFA) is a program for young, talented, and enthusiastic college graduates to spend 2 years in the trenches of a startup business. The expectation is that the experience and knowledge they gain in these small companies will facilitate the fellows (as they are called) in these programs to start enterprises of their own. In turn, the new companies will create jobs in communities where new jobs are needed. The far-reaching goal of the Venture for America program is to create 100,000 new jobs in the United States by 2025.

Venture for America trains top college graduates and sends them to startups in cities where new business creation is a priority, such as Detroit, Philadelphia, New Orleans, Cleveland, and Baltimore. The intensive 5-week training program is conducted at Brown University, where experts from industry and business schools prepare the fellows with the skills and mindsets they will need to overcome the challenges they will face when they build a company. The subjects taught included entrepreneurship, product design, web design, finance, and public speaking.

After boot camp, the fellows spend 2 years helping grow the companies to which they are assigned and learning about entrepreneurship at the same time. The startup companies are in industries including e-commerce, biotechnology, finance, media, and clean technology. The starting salaries are less than $40,000 per year, with raises and stock options at the discretion of their employer. The fellows are given more responsibility and opportunity for decision making than they would have in most entry-level positions. During their tenure at the startup companies, the fellows typically live in group housing with other Venture for America fellows. For example, in Providence, Rhode Island, five fellows live together in a house and learn to live a simple lifestyle.

Venture for America was founded by Andrew Yang, the former chief executive of Manhattan GMAT, a test-preparation company. He was selected by the White House as a Presidential Ambassador for Global Entrepreneurship and a Champion of Change based on his inspiring and high-impact work in many communities. During his time with the test-prep company, Yang said he saw firsthand how a growing company creates opportunities for many people including teachers, the office staff, and customer support teams. He said, "We had someone go from an entry-level hire to running a department and lifting her entire family's standard of living out of the Bronx. Seeing that play out dozens of times makes you want to do as much of it as possible."

The VFA mission has three components, as follows:

- To revitalize American cities and communities through entrepreneurship.
- To enable our best and brightest to create new opportunities for themselves and others.
- To restore the culture of achievement to include value creation, risk and reward, and the common good.

Brentt Baltimore, a graduate of Claremont McKenna College, had this to say about the training camp: "I was challenged to think in a way I hadn't before. It was a once-in-a-lifetime chance to connect with and be pushed by really talented and passionate entrepreneurs."

Scott Lowe, a graduate of the University of Oklahoma, worked with three other fellows and raised $16,000 for their project Rebirth Realty, which buys and rehabilitates houses in Detroit. He said this about his post-VFA plans: "I'm going to start a company in Detroit because I want to create and I want to empower others to do the same. With my startup experience and VFA's growing network and resources, I'm set up to succeed."

QUESTIONS

1. Which values do you think would lead a young college graduate to join Ventures for America?

2. What impact do you think living together in a group would have on the values of the fellows at Ventures for America?

3. Almost all members of Venture for America are millennials. How does their behavior fit the value stereotypes of these people (a) wanting to do meaningful work, and (b) being narcissistic and self-absorbed?

Source: Original story created from facts and observations in the following sources: Renwei Chung, "Venture for America Founder Andrew Yang on Fostering Community, Culture, and Entrepreneurship," *Above the Law*, April 21, 2017, pp. 1–4; Hannah Seligson, "No Six-Figure Pay, but Making a Difference," *New York Times*, July 13, 2013, pp. 1–6; Emily Glazer, "For Grads Seeking to Work, Do Good," *The Wall Street Journal*, January 12, 2012, p. B5; Laura Baverman, "Venture for America Launches Young Entrepreneurs," *USA Today*, February 2, 2014, pp. 1–4; Andrew Yang, *Smart People Should Build Things* (New York: Harper Business, 2014).

in terms of work, one would then seek an employment opportunity that provides such work. For example, a manager might discover that helping young people learn useful job skills brings her the most professional excitement. She might then seek an opportunity to manage a manufacturing apprenticeship program in her company.

Implications for Managerial Practice

In addition to the suggestions made for applying information throughout this chapter (as is done in all chapters of this book), here we make a few additional practical suggestions.

1. Be aware of the pervasive effect of selective perception in organizational behavior. Many of the perceptions that people have, for example, are based on their needs at the time. A manager who has to fill a position by a tight deadline may judge the qualifications of applicants too positively. The judgment of a second party, who is not facing the same need, can be helpful in arriving at an objective judgment.

2. Employees who are talented in one aspect of work might become stereotyped as being capable of and interested in only that type of work. An example would be thinking that a competent financial analyst wants to remain in the finance department and would have no interest in serving on a product development team. Managers who form rigid opinions about what workers can and cannot do might waste the talents of these employees, and deny them the broad experience they need to advance.[34]

3. Company values can be readily forgotten in the press of everyday business activities. It is therefore worthwhile to discuss and reinforce organizational values occasionally. Company website postings and particularly chat sessions about values might prove helpful in reminding workers about and reinforcing values.

4. An important interpersonal skill in the workplace is to recognize both generational and individual values, and then make some concessions to satisfy the reasonable job demands stemming from these values. For example, to appeal to the value system of the stereotypical member of Generation Y, you would grant that person flexibility in choosing methods of work and working hours, frequent feedback, and meaningful projects. If you were working with a member of the veteran generation (born between 1922 and 1943), you would make concessions to his or her interests in abiding by rules and regulations.

Summary of Key Points

1. *Explain the basics of modeling and shaping, cognitive learning, and e-learning.* Modeling and shaping, and cognitive learning are two ways of learning complex material. Modeling involves imitating another person performing the task correctly, and then repeating the task. Modeling can be considered part of social cognitive learning. Shaping occurs when a person learns through the reinforcement of small steps that build up to the final or desired behavior.

   In cognitive learning, learners strive to learn, develop hunches, have flashes of insight, and use many aspects of personality. Cognitive learning includes informal learning, which occurs outside a formal learning situation.

   An important innovation in learning is e-learning, whereby the learner studies independently outside a classroom setting and interacts with a computer in addition to studying course material. E-learning is a web-based form of computer-based training. Although e-learning is different from traditional forms of learning, it still is based on basic methods of learning. Self-motivation and self-discipline are required for successful e-learning. The most successful e-learning experiences combine features of technology-based learning with the emotional support and interaction possible in the classroom.

2. *Describe how learning styles influence workplace learning.* People learn best in different ways; for example, some people acquire information best through passive learning. A preference for working alone versus cooperatively is another difference in learning style. A basic approach to learning styles is to divide them into three categories—visual, auditory, and kinesthetic. Most people combine the three learning styles.

   In general, people with higher cognitive intelligence and personality traits that allow them to concentrate better acquire knowledge and skills more readily.

3. *Describe key aspects of the perceptual process, along with common perceptual problems.* Perception deals with the various ways in which people interpret things in the outside world and how they act on the basis of these perceptions. Perceptual problems are most likely encountered when interpreting meanings rather than tangible physical phenomena. The devices people use to deal with sensory information play a major role in creating perceptual problems. Among these devices are denial, stereotyping, the halo effect, projection, and selective perception.

4. *Describe how attribution theory and blaming others contribute to an understanding of human behavior in the workplace.* Attribution theory is the process by which people ascribe causes to the behavior they perceive. The fundamental attribution error is to attribute behavior to internal causes when focusing on the behavior of others. This self-serving bias leads us to attribute good results to ourselves, and poor results to the environment.

People attribute causes after gathering information about consensus (comparison among people), distinctiveness (comparison across tasks), and consistency (task stability over time). Blame is an important part of attribution that sometimes blocks problem solving, yet at other times leads to positive change. Attributions have an impact in the organization on such matters as performance ratings, feeling good about attaining results, and the quality of relationships with the leader.

A logical extension of attribution theory is locus of control, or the way in which people look at causation in their lives. Blame is also a part of attribution and is most likely to take place in the presence of harmful events.

5. *Summarize why values are an important part of organizational behavior.* A *value* refers to the importance a person attaches to something that serves as a guide to action. Many values are acquired early in life, often through modeling. The values a person develops early in life are directly related to the kind of person he or she is now and will be, as well as the quality of his or her personal relationships. Job performance tends to be higher when there is congruence between individual and organizational values. A person suffers from person–role conflict when the demands made by the organization or a manager clash with the basic values of the individual.

Key Terms and Phrases

learning, p. 44	e-learning, p. 47	locus of control, p. 54
modeling, p. 45	learning style, p. 48	blame, p. 55
social cognitive theory, p. 45	perception, p. 50	value, p. 55
shaping, p. 45	attribution theory, p. 52	person-role conflict, p. 58
cognitive learning theory, p. 46	fundamental attribution error, p. 52	
informal learning, p. 46	self-serving bias, p. 52	

Discussion Questions and Activities

1. Give an example from your own life in which you have learned through modeling.
2. What relatively inexpensive steps might a company take to promote informal learning among employees?
3. If e-learning is so effective, why haven't most colleges and universities shifted almost entirely to distance learning?
4. How can a person capitalize on the halo effect in managing his or her career?
5. Work together in a group to supply several examples of how you might have different performance standards for people from different demographic groups.
6. Create a scenario in which, according to attribution theory, most people would agree that the success of a person who picked a winning stock was caused by his or her inner qualities.
7. What evidence have you seen that many workers over age 60 place a high value on communication technology?
8. Give an example of a situation in which you would most likely experience person-role conflict within the organization.
9. How well do you think that Google as an organization is true to its expressed value of avoiding doing evil?
10. The film and entertainment industries have been accused of widespread sexual harassment. To what extent might this problem be considered to be related to organizational values?

CASE PROBLEM: Branch Manager Abigail Blames Automated House Appraisals

Abigail is a branch manager of Property Appraisals LLC, a regional company whose primary business is appraising the value of residential properties. The appraisals serve a couple of important purposes. Sellers sometimes use the appraisals to provide guidelines for setting the price of a property that is placed on the market. A more extensive use of the appraisals, however, is by mortgage lenders, such as banks, that want an accurate value of a house before issuing a mortgage. Abigail has a staff of four property appraisers plus an administrative assistant.

Branch revenue has shown a decline for nine consecutive quarters even though residential sales in Abigail's city have shown a slight increase over the same period. Gwenn, the CEO of Property Appraisals, has been upset with declining number of appraisals conducted at Abigail's branch. During a face-to-face meeting with Abigail at her branch, Gwenn asked, "Will you please explain why you cannot stop the decline in business?"

Abigail responded, "As you well know, the property appraisal field is suffering from automation, and particularly algorithms. A lot of potential customers are simply visiting Zillow.com to figure out how much their home is worth. The Zesimate provided is absolutely free. Stan Humphries, the chief analytics offer at Zillow, boasts that the company values about 100 million homes every night, with an error rate of 4.3 percent. That's pretty tough competition."

Gwenn then countered, "Okay, I can see that if somebody wants a quick estimate of the value of a house, they might use Zillow. But what about when a person wants an appraisal that is not simply plucked off the Internet?"

Abagail said with a pained expression, "You must be aware that people are getting estimates supplied by firms in India for about $25. The India firm never gets near the property. They access information from the Internet, including Google photos, and make their estimates using software. Again, that type of competition is hard to beat when we charge about $375 for an appraisal."

Gwenn said, "I am aware of the problems the home appraisal industry is facing, but I still think that your office can do better. There is still a demand for customized, professionally prepared appraisals of residential properties. Stop blaming automation, and look at what you could be doing to enhance revenue in your branch."

Case Questions

1. What does this case have to do with attribution theory?
2. To what extent do you think Gwenn is justified in her criticism that Abigail is blaming outside forces for her problem?
3. What advice can you offer Abigail to deal with the problem she is facing with Gwenn?

Source: A few of the facts in this case are from the following sources: "Why Automation Is Killing the Property Appraisal Business," *Knowledge@*Wharton, August 21, 2017, pp. 1–4; Joe Light, "Mamas, Don't Let Your Babies Grow Up to Be Appraisers," *Bloomberg Businessweek*, July 17, 2017, pp. 29–30.

Endnotes

1. The facts are from Steven Berton, "The Way We Work," *Forbes*, October 24, 2017, pp. 68–72.

2. John W. Donahoe and David C. Palmer, *Learning and Complex Behavior* (Boston: Allyn & Bacon, 1994), p. 2.

3. Claudio Fernández-Aráoz, "21st-Century Talent Spotting," *Harvard Business Review*, June 2014, p. 49.

4. Shelly Banjo, "Clutter Buster's Next Foray," *The Wall Street Journal*, March 21, 2013, p. B7; "What We Stand For," *The Container Store*, http://standfor.containerstore.com, June 7, 2016, pp. 1–5.

5. Lauren Weber, "Here's One Way to Solve the Skills Gap," *The Wall Street Journal*, April 28, 2014, p. R3.

6. Rebecca A. Clay, "Albert Bandura Receives National Medal of Science," *Monitor on Psychology*, March 2016, p. 8; Charles G. Morris and Albert A. Maisto, *Psychology: An Introduction*, 11th ed. (Upper Saddle River, NJ: Prentice Hall, 2002), p. 221.

7. Nancy Day, "Informal Learning Gets Results," *Workforce*, June 1998, p. 31; Jay Cross, *Internet Time Group* (http://internettime.com), May 8, 2003, p. 2.

8. Sandra L. Fisher and J. Kevin Ford, "Differential Effects of Learner Effort and Goal Orientation on Two Learning Outcomes," *Personnel Psychology*, Summer 1998, pp. 397–420; Don VandeWalle, William J. Cron, and John W. Slocum, Jr., "The Role of Goal Orientation Following Performance Feedback," *Journal of Applied Psychology*, August 2001, pp. 629–640.

9. Simon Casuto, "Five Trends Driving the Growth of Mobile Learning in Corporate Education," *Forbes*, April 23, 2016, pp. 1–3.

10. Bill Roberts, "From E-Learning to Mobile Learning," *HR Magazine*, August 12, 2012, p. 61.

11. Douglas Belkin and Caroline Porter, "Job Market Embraces Massive Online Courses," *The Wall Street Journal*, September 27, 2013, p. A3.

12. Rebecca A. Clay, "MOOCs 2.0," *Monitor on Psychology*, July/August 2015, pp. 52–55.

13. Garry Kranz, "MOOCs: The Next Evolution in E-Learning?" *Workforce*, April 2014, p. 10.

14. Douglas Belkin, "At Coursera, Lessons in Skill Training," *The Wall Street Journal*, August 12, 2015, p. B4.

15. Michael A. Tucker, "E-Learning Evolves," *HR Magazine*, October 2005, p. 78.

16. Joe Mullich, "A Second Act for E-Learning," *Workforce Management*, February 2004, p. 52.

17. Lindsay Redpath, "Confronting the Bias against Online Learning in Management Education," *Academy of Management Learning & Education*, March 2012, pp. 125–140.

18. Wanda L. Stitt-Gohdes, "Teaching and Learning Styles: Implications for Business Teacher Education," in *The 21st Century: Meeting the Challenges to Business Education* (Reston, VA: National Business Education Association, 1999), p. 10.

19. Grace Fleming, "Learning Styles," http://homeworktips .about.com, © 2014.

20. Christopher Chabris and Daniel Simons, "Using Just 10% of Your Brain? Think Again." *The Wall Street Journal*, November 17–18, 2012, p. C3.

21. David W. Oakes et al., "Cognitive Ability and Personality Predictors of Training Program Skill Acquisition and Job Performance," *Journal of Business and Psychology*, Summer 2001, pp. 523–548.

22. Ricky W. Griffin, "Effects of Work Redesign on Employee Perceptions, Attitudes, and Behaviors: A Long-Term Investigation," *Academy of Management Journal*, June 1991, p. 426.

23. Chris Argyris, *On Organizational Learning* (Oxford, England: Blackwell, 1994), p. 7.

24. Paul Harvey, Kristen Madison, Mark Martinko, T. Russell Crook, and Tamara A. Crook, "Attribution Theory in the Organizational Sciences: The Road Traveled and the Path Ahead," *Academy of Manager Perspectives*, May 2014, pp. 132–133.

25. Harold H. Kelley, "The Process of Causal Attribution," *American Psychologist*, February 1973, pp. 122–123.

26. Marion B. Eberly, Erica C. Hulley, Michael D. Johnson, and Terence R. Mitchell, "It's Not Me. It's Not You, It's *US*! An Empirical Examination of Relational Attributions," *Journal of Applied Psychology*, May 2017, pp. 711–731.

27. Julian P. Rotter, "Generalized Expectancies for Internal vs. External Control of Reinforcement," *Psychological Monographs*, *80* (1966), pp. 1–28.

28. Russell E. Johnson, Christopher C. Rosen, Chu-Hsiang (Daisy) Chang, and Szu-Han (Joanna) Lin, "Getting to the Core of Locus of Control: Is It an Evaluation of the Self or the Environment?" *Journal of Applied Psychology*, September 2015, pp. 1568–1578.

29. Cited in Jeffrey Zaslow, "'It's All Your Fault': Why Americans Can't Stop Playing the Blame Game," *The Wall Street Journal*, September 15, 2005, p. D1.

30. Mark D. Alicke, "Culpable Control and the Psychology of Blame," *Psychological Bulletin*, *4*, July 2000, pp. 1–30.

31. Ron Zemke, "Generation Veneration," in *Business: The Ultimate Resource™* (Cambridge, MA: Perseus Books, 2002), pp. 39–40.

32. David C. McClelland, "How Motives, Skills, and Values Determine What People Do," *American Psychologist*, July 1988, p. 816.

33. "Our Core Values," Whole Food Markets, www .wholefoodsmarket.com/mission-values/core-values, 2018.

34. Carol Hymowitz, "Bosses Who Pigeonhole Workers Waste Talent, Contribute to Turnover," *The Wall Street Journal*, May 24, 2005, p. B1.

Attitudes, Job Satisfaction, and Ethics

CHAPTER 4

Andrey_Popov/Shutterstock.com

Chapter Outline

Attitudes and Emotions

Job Satisfaction and Attitudes

Job Satisfaction and Organizational Citizenship Behavior

Ethics

An Eight-Step Guide to Ethical Decision Making

Organizational Approaches to Enhancing Ethical and Socially Responsible Behavior

Implications for Managerial Practice

Learning Objectives

After reading and studying this chapter and doing the exercises, you should be able to:

1. Describe the importance of attitudes and emotions to behavior in organizations.

2. Describe the nature of and contributors to job satisfaction.

3. Describe how organizational citizenship behavior contributes to individual and organizational effectiveness.

4. Describe three ethical decision-making criteria, along with several explanations for the existence of ethical problems.

5. Describe the eight-step guide to ethical decision making.

6. Describe what organizations can do to enhance ethical and socially responsible behavior.

Founded in 1853, Levi Strauss is the manufacturer of Levi jeans, a brand known throughout the world. Less well known is the Levi Strauss & Co. Worker Well-Being initiative. It is a forward-looking approach to supply chain management that goes beyond factory walls to improve the lives of workers who make the company's products. The Worker Well-Being initiative surpasses meeting basic labor standards. It attempts to help workers in a variety of ways, such as managing finances, avoiding diseases, eating well, and working under comfortable conditions in old factories. Forty-two vendors that employ about 140,000 workers are involved in the program.

The thrust of Worker Well-Being is to partner with suppliers throughout the world and local organizations to design and deliver programs that meet worker needs, such as reporting to considerate supervisors. Before any program is implemented, suppliers administer a survey to factory workers to obtain direct information about their needs and demands. Focus groups that include group conversations are also used to gather data. A senior program manager at Levi Strauss acts as a focus-group facilitator. She asks questions such as the following: You're a young woman, how many children are you supporting? Are you cash-strapped? Are you living in a home that isn't safe or stable? Do you have access to potable water? Do you feel threatened at home? What are your goals?

After challenges are identified, suppliers partner with local nonprofits and nongovernmental organizations (NGOs) in order to implement programs that will meet the needs identified. For example, some workers might be getting sick frequently because of contaminated drinking water.

One of the major lessons Levi Strauss & Co. learned through Worker Well Being is the importance of partnerships with suppliers. By demonstrating positive business results to suppliers, the company was able to gain their support and financial investment. When suppliers see the return on investment, the Well-Being initiatives continue without direct funding from Levi Strauss, creating a sustainable model. Two examples of these successful initiatives are as follows:

- In Haiti, workers participating in or aware of Well-Being reported a 91 percent level of job satisfaction according to an independent evaluation. The high job satisfaction considerably reduced involuntary turnover.
- The HERhealth woman's health program in Egypt generated a four-dollar return from every dollar invested, for reasons such as less absenteeism due to illness.

The most popular improvements so far have met basic needs: water fountains with cool water; cooler air provided by fans; and kinder, more communicative supervisors.

Management at Levi Strauss has worked with the Center for Health and the Global Environment at Harvard University to gather more data to make the business case for why suppliers should invest in the well-being of workers. So far, the results are promising. The initiative also appears to be improving worker welfare and company profitability.

An expansion of Worker Well-Being is planned to enable Levi Strauss to produce more than 80 percent of its products in Worker Well-Being factories by 2020 and reach 30,000 workers by 2025. As company leadership sees it, Worker Well-Being can and should become the new norm for how apparel companies throughout the world do business.[1]

The story about the Levi Strauss initiatives for helping relatively low-paid apparel workers improve their lives illustrates how business executives can be highly ethical and socially responsible. Ethical conduct and socially responsible behavior are two topics presented in this chapter about attitudes, emotions, job satisfaction, and ethics. Understanding these aspects of behavior helps managers to deal more effectively with people and also to guide their own behavior toward high performance.

Attitudes and Emotions

"You've got an attitude," said the supervisor to the store associate, thus emphasizing the importance of attitude to job performance. For mysterious reasons, the term *attitude* in colloquial language often connotes a *negative* attitude. More accurately, an **attitude** is a predisposition to respond that exerts an influence on a person's response to a person, a thing, an idea, or a situation. Attitudes are an important part of organizational behavior because they are linked with perception, learning, emotions, and motivation. For example, your attitude toward a coworker influences your perception of how favorably you evaluate his or her work. Also, emotions such as joy and anger contribute to attitude formation. First, we examine the components of attitudes and their relationship to organizational behavior, and then explain how emotions influence behavior in the workplace.

An example of the importance of attitudes in the workplace is the research of Adam Grant of the Wharton School of the University of Pennsylvania. He has demonstrated that an attitude of wanting to help others, and then actually helping them, enhances both satisfaction and productivity. For example, when call-center workers were introduced to a customer who talked about the impact of their work, the productivity of the call-center workers spiked 400 percent in weekly productivity.[2]

LEARNING OBJECTIVE 1
Describe the importance of attitudes and emotions to behavior in organizations.

attitude A predisposition to respond that exerts an influence on a person's response to a person, a thing, an idea, or a situation.

Components of Attitudes

Attitudes are complex, having three components. The *cognitive* component refers to the knowledge or intellectual beliefs an individual might have about an object (an idea, a person, a thing, or a situation). A market researcher might have accumulated considerable factual information about statistics (e.g., sampling procedures) and software for analyzing data. The researcher might therefore have a positive attitude toward statistics. The feeling, or *affective* component, refers to the emotion connected with an object or a task. The market researcher mentioned might basically like statistical analysis because of some pleasant experiences in college associated with statistics. The *behavioral* component refers to how a person acts. The market researcher might make positive statements about statistical methods or emphasize them in his or her reports.

The cognitive, affective, and behavioral aspects of attitudes are interrelated. A change in one of the components will set in motion a change in one or both of the others. If you have more facts about an object or process (cognitive), you form the basis for a more positive emotional response to the object (affective). In turn, your behavior toward that object would probably become more favorable. For example, if you have considerable information about the contribution of feedback to personal development, you might have a positive feeling toward feedback. When receiving feedback, therefore, you would act favorably.

At times, people do not experience the type of consistency just described, and they feel compelled to search for consistency. **Cognitive dissonance** is the situation in which the pieces of knowledge, information, attitudes, and beliefs held by an individual are contradictory. When a person experiences cognitive dissonance, the relationship between attitudes and behaviors is altered. People search for ways to reduce internal conflicts when they experience a clash between the information they receive and their actions or attitudes. The same process is used when a person has to resolve two inconsistent sets of information.

A typical example of cognitive dissonance on the job might occur when a worker believes that the report she submits to team members is of high quality; her teammates, however, tell her the report is flawed and

cognitive dissonance The situation in which the pieces of knowledge, information, attitudes, and beliefs held by an individual are contradictory.

The behavioral component of an attitude refers to how a person acts.

michaeljung/Shutterstock.com

requires substantial revisions. To reduce the dissonance, the worker might conveniently ignore the criticism. Or the worker might reason that she is the resident expert on the topic of the report, and her teammates are therefore not qualified to judge the merits of her report.

Another important aspect of attitudes in the workplace is their strength. If you have a strong attitude toward something or somebody, it will have more impact on your job satisfaction and performance. Attitude strength is therefore a moderator variable.[3] You might have a strong attitude about having a supervisor who listens to your suggestions. If your supervisor does listen, it is likely to enhance your job satisfaction and performance. In contrast, you might have a weak attitude about the décor in the office. The appearance of your office would therefore have a minimal impact on your job satisfaction and performance.

Emotions in the Workplace

A traditional viewpoint contends that emotions in the workplace should be minimized, and decisions should be based on rational analysis. Nevertheless, the importance of emotion in influencing job behavior has long been recognized. For example, customer-contact workers need training to deal with angry customers, and supervisors have been trained how to give emotional support to a distressed group member. Interest in workplace emotion has surged, as evidenced by the growth of research and writing in this area.[4]

emotion A feeling, such as anger, fear, joy, or surprise, that underlies behavior.

In Chapter 2, we described the importance now attached to having emotional intelligence. An **emotion** is a feeling—such as anger, fear, joy, or surprise—that underlies behavior. Emotions might lead an employee who has just solved a difficult problem to shout "Yes!" and punch his or her fist into the air. Unfortunately, intense negative emotion might trigger an employee to stab another employee with a knife. A study commissioned by the Department of Homeland Security found that corporate insiders who attack computer systems are typically angry over disciplinary actions, missed promotions, or layoffs.[5]

The example just presented indicates that emotion can have an impact on the work behavior (attacking a computer system). Work behavior also has an impact on emotion, such as satisfactorily completing a difficult task giving a person an emotional lift. In contrast, failing a task can result in negative feelings. A study with nurses found that when they performed well in terms of patient care, they had more positive feelings after their shift. Correspondingly, when they failed at a patient care assignment, they experienced negative feelings after the shift.[6]

Similar to an attitude, an emotion consists of three interacting components: (1) internal physiological arousal, (2) expressive behavior in the face or body, and (3) a cognitive appraisal.[7] Visualize a production worker who has just been informed that he has won a $50,000 award for a suggestion that will save the company millions of dollars. The worker will experience a surge of physiological arousal, such as an accelerated pulse or an elevated breathing rate. His facial expressions will most likely communicate joy and surprise. The cognitive appraisal deals with quick thoughts, such as saying to himself, "Now, I will get the respect I deserve," and "Here's my chance to buy something great for my family and invest a little money also."

Managing Emotion

Neal M. Ashkanasy and Catherine S. Daus regard emotion in the workplace as an important challenge facing managers.[8] Given that every worker, top executives included, is an organism governed partly by emotion, constructive use should be made of emotion. Two suggestions by Ashkanasy and Daus provide practical starting points in managing emotions well. First, the manager should create a friendly emotional climate by setting a positive example. Managers might serve as a model of healthy emotional expression that includes being emotionally perceptive. ("Kelly, I notice that you are quite anxious about the credit-card–processing unit possibly being outsourced. How can I help you with your concerns?") Warm and sincere expression of positive emotion is usually effective, as is appropriate expression of negative emotion. The leader might indicate, for example, that he or she is also worried about a downturn in sales that could lead to cutbacks.

Another recommendation is to include a positive attitude as one factor in selecting individuals and teams. A candidate might be evaluated in part based on his or her emotional skills demonstrated during a job interview, and by checking his or her references. Within the organization, teams might be selected for key assignments in part based on their cheerful outlook. Positive attitudes contribute to organizational health, whereas consistently negative attitudes create an unfavorable work climate.

A caution to workers about emotional regulation is that anger derived from one set of interactions might be displaced toward others, with the result being poor coworker relationships.[9] For example, a call-center technician angry with customers or the boss might take out this anger on other call-center technicians.

Another perspective on anger in the workplace is that it can be a powerful force motivating us to achieve. Evidence from several fields suggests that anger may fuel the ambitions and creativity of some workers. Surprisingly, anger can help people calm down and get ready to address a problem. Anger appears to stimulate the frontal cortex, the part of the brain associated with pushing us to pursue desired goals and rewards in a logical, systematic manner.[10] The late Steve Jobs of Apple Corp. was admired for his creative approach to product design. At the same time, he was an angry, explosive person who would regularly belittle and demean people who disagreed with him. In short, anger within limits may be a positive force in the workplace, so managers and coworkers should not discourage all anger, such as getting angry about a product defect.

A highly practical aspect of dealing with emotions in the workplace is whether to vent, or openly and loudly express, negative emotion. Research suggests that after venting, people typically become angrier and more aggressive. A hostile vent directed toward coworkers or a supervisor can wind up alienating a person or might make him or her appear to be a candidate for anger management. The ready availability of social media, e-mail, and texting makes it easy to vent (or e-vent), such as cursing one's employer or boss.[11] Discipline, including being fired, often follows swiftly.

Emotional Labor

Another aspect of emotional behavior of importance in the workplace is the problem of faking emotions. **Emotional labor** is the process of regulating both feelings and expressions to meet organizational goals. Emotional labor involves both surface acting and deep acting. *Surface acting* means faking expressions, such as smiling, whereas *deep acting* involves controlling feelings, such as suppressing anger toward a customer whom you perceive to be uncivil.

Sales workers and customer service representatives carry the biggest emotional labor among all workers because so often they have to take on facial expressions and feelings to please customers.[12] Observations suggest that Uber drivers experience considerable emotional labor. The company suggests that drivers "stay calm, patient, and polite with riders" in order to obtain the best ratings. Uber drivers who fall below a certain rating might be deactivated.[13]

A meta-analysis of 116 studies provides new insights into the different impacts of surface acting versus deep acting on behavior and performance for workers in a variety of service jobs in a variety of industries. Three outcomes of emotional labor were studied: (a) job satisfaction, (b) stress and exhaustion from work, and (c) job performance. Surface acting proved to have more serious consequences than deep acting with respect to job satisfaction and stress/exhaustion. However, surface acting had little impact on performance. In contrast, the deep acting aspect of emotional labor tended to enhance satisfaction, decrease stress and exhaustion, and enhance job performance.[14] Deep acting may be less stressful because, if you change how you feel, you are no longer faking emotion. The lack of authenticity might be the true source of stress.

A study conducted in a call center in China provided more evidence that surface acting is more damaging to the customer-service worker than deep acting. Emotional labor and customer treatment were measured by paper-and-pencil questionnaires. A statement about bad customer treatment was, "venting their bad mood out on you." The results

emotional labor The process of regulating both feelings and expressions to meet organizational goals.

showed that employees engaging in more surface acting were more likely to receive negative treatment from customers. As a result, the workers experienced more negative affect and emotional exhaustion. In contrast, customer-service workers engaging in deep acting were more likely to receive positive treatment from customers, leading to more positive affect for the workers.[15] (It could be that customers can see through surface acting, and they find such behavior to be annoying.)

Emotional dissonance is a key aspect of emotional labor, referring to the mismatch between felt and expressed emotions. The greater the gap between actual and expressed feelings, the more frequently workers report feeling emotional exhaustion, dissatisfaction with their jobs, and cynicism toward customers.[16] Imagine making a PowerPoint presentation to top management and being interrupted with what you perceive to be foolish questions and ridicule. You want to retaliate, but instead, keep smiling and making comments such as "good question."

A variation of emotional labor can occur when workers create a façade in relation to conforming to corporate values. Façade creation might include conforming to the dress code despite disliking such attire, expressing agreement with one's manager although one thinks the manager is wrong, and going along with a group decision that one thinks is ridiculous. Maintaining a façade for a long time can lead to emotional distress.[17]

The potential negative effects of emotional labor can also be lessened with financial rewards for providing good customer service, as revealed in a series of three studies by Alicia A. Grandey and two colleagues. The studies involved U.S. workers, a call-center simulation with college students, and workers in sales companies in Taiwan. When customer service workers in the studies believed that they gained financially from positive emotional displays with customers, they achieved satisfaction from performing emotional labor.[18] In short, it can be fun if you are paid for acting nice with customers.

One implication of emotional labor is that managers need to take into account job characteristics in creating rules for displays of emotion. Rules that conflict with job characteristics may trigger unhealthy levels of tension. For instance, asking cashiers to be overly polite to customers may conflict with a fast work pace. Cashiers facing a long line of impatient customers may need to decrease displays of courtesy to avoid having customers wait even longer. (It takes more time to be polite and conversational.)[19]

Job Satisfaction and Attitudes

LEARNING OBJECTIVE 2
Describe the nature of and contributors to job satisfaction.

job satisfaction The amount of pleasure or contentment associated with a job.

Another reason attitudes are important in the study of organizational behavior is that they form the basis for how satisfied people are with their jobs. **Job satisfaction** is the amount of pleasure or contentment associated with a job. Workers will have high job satisfaction when they have positive attitudes toward job factors such as the work itself, recognition, and opportunity for advancement. Meaningful work is a key contributor to job satisfaction, as well as motivation, and will be discussed in Chapter 6 in relation to motivation.

According to a 2016 Pew Research Center survey, about one-half (49 percent) of U.S. workers were very satisfied with their jobs. Approximately 30 percent were somewhat satisfied, and about 6 percent were very dissatisfied. The survey results highlight the impact that wages have on job satisfaction, with workers earning more than $75,000 being the most satisfied. Only 39 percent of workers making under $ 30,000 were satisfied. A confounding factor about the relationship between income and satisfaction is that people earning higher income may also be performing more interesting work, adding to their satisfaction.

Job type has a big impact on satisfaction. Management workers were the most likely to say they were very satisfied (62 percent). Fifty-two percent of workers occupying professional and other salaried positions reported being very satisfied, and 48 percent of workers doing physical labor said they were very satisfied.[20]

Figure 4-1 provides a sampling of issues that influence employee satisfaction.

A practical view of job satisfaction is that it centers on employees having fun on the job. *Fun* can be anything from doing exciting work to engaging in sports during the lunch break.

FIGURE 4-1 A Sampling of Factors Influencing Employee Job Satisfaction in a Variety of Work Settings

1. Opportunities to use professional skills and abilities, and variety of work
2. Opportunity to do meaningful work (work that has an impact on others)
3. Autonomy and independence to make decisions
4. Job giving a sense of identity
5. Career development opportunities for learning and professional growth
6. Recognition for a job well done
7. Job security
8. Compensation, including pay, bonuses, and benefits
10. Communication between employees and senior management
11. Positive relationship with immediate supervisor
12. Good working conditions (e.g., spacious work areas and adequate lighting)
13. Realistic workload
14. Convenient work schedule
15. Trust between employees and senior management
16. Respectful treatment of all employees at all levels
17. Flexible working hours, including some opportunity to work remotely
18. Job-specific training
19. On-premises workout facilities

Question

Which several of the previous factors would be the most important for your job satisfaction? Why do you think so?

Source: "Employee Job Satisfaction and Engagement Survey: The Doors of Opportunity Are Open," Society for Human Resource Management, www.shrm.org/hr-today/trends-and-forecasting/research-and-surveys/pages/2017-job-satisfaction-and-engagement-doors-of-opportunity-are-open.aspx, 2017, pp. 1–9; "How Americans View Their Jobs," Pew Research Center, www.pewsocialtrends.org/2016/10/06/3-how-americans-view-their-jobs/, October 6, 2016, pp. 1–2; Colleen Leahy, "10 Top Perks from Best Companies, 2014," Fortune, http://fortune.com/tech/10-top-perks-from-fortunes-best-companies-to-work-for-2014/, January 16, 2014, pp. 1–11.

Companies today are likely to provide a working environment that provides key satisfying elements, such as casual dress, flexible working hours, and telecommuting. Happiness guru Shawn Anchor preaches that positive thinking, including happiness, produces better business results. His thinking is supported by the field research of positive-psychology pioneer Martin Seligman. Seligman discovered that the top 10 percent of optimists at MetLife Inc. outsold the bottom 90 percent by 90 percent. Based on these results, MetLife used a positive mental mindset as a screening factor for sales representatives. The new agents outsold already-hired pessimistic agents by 21 percent the next year and by 57 percent the following year.[21]

Managers are concerned about maintaining high levels of job satisfaction, including enthusiasm, because of the consequences, which include those in the following list. The relationship between job satisfaction and these outcomes has been demonstrated consistently over time.

- High productivity when the work involves contact with people
- A stronger tendency to achieve customer loyalty
- Loyalty to the company
- Low absenteeism and turnover
- Less job stress and burnout
- Better safety performance
- Better life satisfaction, including a better mood at home[22]

A satisfying job contributes to a positive outlook on life.

Low job satisfaction can lead to low work engagement.

The job satisfaction consequence of loyalty is especially important because it enhances employee retention (keeping valuable employees). Employee turnover is particularly expensive, involving costs such as recruitment, selection, training, and lost productivity while the replacement is trained. Management consultant Diane Arthur observes that if employees feel loyal to a company, they are likely to be more productive and make an extra effort for the employer. They are also likely to stay with the company, keeping the firm stable and allowing management to concentrate on sales, operations, and earnings, not hiring replacement workers.[23]

Many of the methods and techniques described in this book, such as empowerment and modified work schedules, are aimed at sustaining job satisfaction. Almost any positive management practice, however, might be linked to improving job satisfaction.

Organizational and managerial practices can only go so far in bringing about job satisfaction because personality factors such as optimism versus pessimism also influence satisfaction with the job and the company. An extreme optimist will find some joy in almost any job, whereas an extreme pessimist will usually be dissatisfied no matter what the job. Workers with high levels of self-esteem are also more likely to experience high job satisfaction because they typically feel good about what they are doing.[24] But again, we see a reciprocal influence in organizational behavior. Feelings of self-esteem can stem from doing meaningful work as well as from having a high-status position.

Job Satisfaction and Organizational Citizenship Behavior

LEARNING OBJECTIVE 3
Describe how organizational citizenship behavior contributes to individual and organizational effectiveness.

organizational citizenship behavior (OCB) Behaviors that express a willingness to work for the good of an organization even without the promise of a specific reward.

A broader consequence of job satisfaction is that it contributes to organizational citizenship behavior (OCB), or the willingness to work for the good of the organization even without the promise of a specific reward. Such behavior is discretionary; it is helpful to the company but not absolutely required by employers.[25] Organizational citizenship behavior has many components or sub-behaviors. A particularly useful distinction is between *affiliation-oriented* and *challenge-oriented* citizenship behaviors.[26]

Affiliation-oriented behaviors are interpersonal and cooperative, and tend to solidify or preserve relationships with others. An example would be sending a note of appreciation to a coworker who has won a patent. Challenge-oriented behaviors are change oriented and come with the risk that they could hurt relationships with others because they criticize the status quo. An example would be a technician going out of the way to suggest that the majority of company business trips could be replaced with videoconferencing.

New dimensions of organizational citizenship behavior emerge as the nature of work continues to change, such as more employees working from remote locations and more reliance on collaborative problem solving. A focus-group study with Google employees revealed two new affiliation-oriented OCBs that are particularly relevant for knowledge workers:

- *Employee sustainability* refers to participating in activities to maintain and improve one's health and well-being, or to support others' efforts to maintain their health and well-being.
- *Social participation* refers to taking part in social activities during the workday that are not directly related to core job tasks.[27]

A good organizational citizen contributes to a positive work atmosphere.

People who are good organizational citizens are likely to achieve some of the consequences of job satisfaction, including higher customer loyalty, higher productivity, better safety performance, and lower turnover. Although OCB is often a consequence of job satisfaction, personality factors are sometimes linked to OCB. Workers may be predisposed to being good (or poor) organizational citizens. A study of customer-contact workers supports the personality–OCB link. The employee-disposition (or personality) factors of service orientation and empathy were found to be related to engaging in good citizenship behavior in relation to customers. Four examples of service-oriented OCBs are when a person does the following:

- Encourages friends and family to use the firm's products and services
- Follows up in a timely manner to customer requests and problems
- Contributes many ideas for customer promotions and communication
- Frequently presents creative solutions to customer problems[28]

A concern about the construct (similar to a concept) of organizational citizenship behavior is that some employees may perceive going beyond their job description as part of their job. An employee might think, for example, "I'm paid a good salary to do whatever it takes to make my company successful, whether or not it is strictly my job."

Although OCB benefits the organization and will often facilitate career growth, being an exceptional organizational citizen may have negative consequences for the individual. A study of 98 couples investigated the impact that one type of organizational citizenship behavior—individual initiative—has with adverse personal consequences. Examples of individual initiative include working on weekends, taking work home, and working longer than most others. These types of initiative were rated by spouses or significant others. The results indicated that greater initiative was positively associated with feelings of being overworked, job stress, and conflict between work and family.[29] A study conducted with faculty members working at private universities in Taiwan revealed that fatigue stemming from citizenship behavior was less likely when organizational support was perceived to be high. An example of a questionnaire item measuring organizational support is, "How willing are other members of your department to help finish work that was assigned to you?"[30]

A related concern is that investing too much time in organizational citizenship behavior can result in lowered task performance. A study showed that a person who spends too much time helping others might neglect key job responsibilities.[31] An implication coming from these two studies is that managers should discourage good organizational citizens from going overboard.

Ethics

Our last key factor for understanding individuals in organizations is **ethics**, the set of moral choices a person makes. Ethics is based on an individual's beliefs about what is

LEARNING OBJECTIVE 4
Describe three ethical decision-making criteria, along with several explanations for the existence of ethical problems.

ethics An individual's moral beliefs about what is right and wrong or good and bad.

right and wrong or good and bad. Ethics can also be regarded as the vehicle that converts values into action. You might value a clean environment; the corresponding ethical behavior is not to place a television set or computer in a landfill. Ethics is a major consideration in studying the actions of managerial workers and the functioning of organizations. The prominent scandals in business during recent years have intensified recognition of the importance of ethics. We will therefore refer to ethics at various places in this book.

Here we approach ethics as it relates to individuals from four perspectives. First, we look at three somewhat philosophical criteria for making ethical decisions. Second, we describe major causes of ethical problems. Third, we present an eight-part guide to ethical decision making. Fourth, we describe the role of organizations in promoting ethical and socially responsible behavior.

Ethical Decision-Making Criteria

A standard way of understanding ethical decision making is to understand the philosophical basis for making decisions. When attempting to decide what is right and wrong, people can focus on (1) consequences; (2) duties, obligations, and principles; or (3) integrity.[32]

Focus on Consequences

When attempting to decide what is right and wrong, people sometimes focus on the consequences of their decision or action. According to this criterion, if nobody gets hurt, the decision is ethical. Focusing on consequences is often referred to as *utilitarianism*. The decision maker is concerned with the utility of the decision. What really counts is the net balance of good consequences over bad.

To focus on consequences, the decision maker would have to be aware of all the good and bad consequences of a given decision. A financial vice president might decide that if all travel-expense reimbursements were delayed by 10 days, the company could earn $1 million per year nationwide. The earnings would stem from holding on to money longer, thus collecting interest. How would this vice president know how many family arguments and how much job stress would be created by these delayed reimbursements? How many good performers would quit in disgust?

Focus on the Rights of Individuals

Another approach to making an ethical decision is to examine one's duties in making the decision. The theories underlying this approach are referred to as *deontological*, from the Greek word *deon* (or duty). Deontology also refers to moral philosophies that center on the rights of individuals and the intentions associated with a particular behavior. A fundamental idea of deontology is that equal respect must be given to all persons. The deontological approach is based on universal principles such as honesty, fairness, justice, and respect for persons and property. Rights, such as the right to privacy and safety, are the key aspects. From a deontological perspective, the principles are more important than the consequences. If a given decision violates one of these universal principles, it is automatically unethical, even if nobody gets hurt.

The financial vice president pondering whether to defer payments on travel expenses would not have to spend much time with deontology. She would say to herself, "Delaying these payments may earn the company another $1 million per year, but it is not honest, fair, or just. Furthermore, employees have a right to prompt payment."

Focus on Integrity (Virtue Ethics)

The third criterion for determining the ethics of behavior focuses on the character of the person involved in the decision or action. If the person in question has good character and genuine motivation and intentions, he or she will be judged to have behaved ethically. The criteria for good character will often include the two other ethical criteria. For example, one might judge a person to have good character if he or she follows the right principles and respects the rights of others.

Trustworthiness has emerged as a virtue of major importance for managers and professionals, in part because of many well-publicized incidents of executives being untrustworthy. The decision maker's environment, or community, helps define what integrity means. You might have more lenient ethical standards for a person selling you investment derivatives (high-risk investments used to hedge other investments, with their value derived from the existence of other securities) than you would for a bank vice president who accepted your cash deposit.

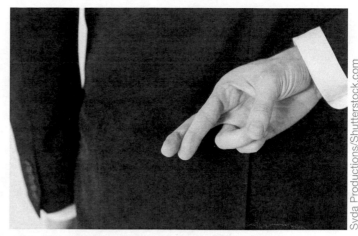

Poor ethics is a continuing problem in business.

Major Causes of Ethical Problems

Ethical problems in organizations are a global phenomenon. The Ethics and Compliance Initiative explores worker experiences in 13 countries, in both the private and public sectors. In 10 of the countries surveyed, more than one-half of respondents said they observed ethical violations. In 11 of the 13 countries, at least one in three respondents experienced retaliation for having reported ethical violations. The most frequently reported problems in nearly every country were lying (26 percent) and abusive behavior (25 percent). Approximately 16 percent of respondents observed bribery and corruption, with over one-half indicating that bribery involved management.[33] Figure 4-2 presents a sampling of unethical behavior in business.

Major contributors to unethical behavior are an *individual's greed* and *gluttony*, or the desire to maximize self-gain at the expense of others. Another key contributor to a person's ethics and morality is his or her *level of moral development*.[34] Some workers are morally advanced, while others are morally challenged—a condition that often develops early in life. People progress through three developmental levels in their moral reasoning. At the *preconventional level*, a person is concerned primarily with receiving external rewards and avoiding punishments. A manager at this level of development might falsify earnings statements for the primary purpose of gaining a large bonus.

At the *conventional level*, people learn to conform to the expectations of good behavior as defined by key people in their environment, as well as societal norms. A manager at this level might be just moral enough to look good, such as being fair with salary increases and encouraging contributions to the United Way campaign. At the *postconventional level*, people are guided by an internalized set of principles based on universal, abstract principles that may even transcend the laws of a particular society.

A manager at the postconventional level of moral behavior would be concerned with doing the most good for the most people, whether or not such behavior brought him or her recognition and fortune. If the manager just described wanted to direct an apprenticeship program, he or she might also be at the postconventional level of moral behavior.

Another major contributor to unethical behavior is an *organizational atmosphere that condones such behavior*. If leaders at the top of the organization take imprudent, quasi-legal risks, other leaders throughout the firm might be prompted to behave similarly. For example, top management at an investment banking firm might sell securities based on exceptionally high-risk loans, including car loans and mortgages on distressed properties.

Unethical behavior is often triggered by *pressure from higher management to achieve goals*, such as attaining overseas sales even if bribes are necessary. Research conducted by the Harvard Business School suggests that unrealistic goal setting can encourage workers to make compromising choices in order to reach targets. The unrealistic goals invite managers and other workers to cheat in two ways. The will cut corners to achieve a goal, such as using low-quality components to attain cost-cutting goals. Or, workers might lie when reporting how much of a goal they have actually attained.[35]

A final cause of unethical behavior to be mentioned here is *unconscious biases* that lead to unfair judgments and discriminatory practices. Suppose a real-estate manager

FIGURE 4-2 Four Examples of Unethical Behavior in Business

- Wells Fargo & Co., the giant bank, was involved in perhaps the biggest bogus-account scandal of all time. Going back over a decade, employees were pressured to meet aggressive sales goals set by company executives. About two million accounts were opened in customers' names without permission. CEO John Stumpf, who resigned in 2016, established the goal of eight accounts per household to be generated by cross-selling—getting customers to sign up for multiple products, including checking accounts, mortgages, and credit cards. Another revelation was that the bank had overcharged some auto-loan and mortgage customers.

  Wells Fargo agreed to a multimillion-dollar settlement in 2016 and fired over 5,300 employees involved in the scandal. Furthermore, over 500 brokers quit the firm because they no longer wanted to be associated with Wells Fargo.

- Prime Healthcare Service Inc. of California received a complaint from the Department of Justice (DOJ) alleging that the organization's management was closely involved in driving up hospital admission rates regardless of medical necessity. President and CEO Prem Reddy, MD, was accused of instructing hospitals to set arbitrary inpatient quotas at 20 to 30 percent. The DOJ said Reddy personally reprimanded emergency room doctors who did not meet these quotas or missed opportunities to admit Medicate beneficiaries, even for minor medical problems such as colds, back pain, or ear infections. The DOJ stated that hospitals within the system "received millions of dollars in inflated reimbursements for medically unnecessary inpatient admissions."

  A lawsuit was filed by a Prime Healthcare employee and joined by the DOJ in May 2016, under the False Claims Act. The suit alleges that Dr. Reddy pressured emergency room physicians in 14 Prime hospitals to admit patients instead of holding them for observation because Medicare generally pays more for admissions. Reddy was also alleged to have pressured physicians to "embellish" medical records to justify stays in the hospital.

- Vibram USA, the manufacturer of FiveFingers shoes, settled a multimillion-dollar class-action lawsuit. The charge was that the company deliberately misled customers about the health benefits of "barefoot" running shoes. A specific charge was that Vibram's claims that the shoes reduced the risk of foot injury and strengthened foot and leg muscles constituted false advertising.

- Hewlett-Packard Co. (H-P) paid $108 million to resolve bribery investigations about business transactions in Russia, Mexico, and Poland. The bribes involved cash, jewelry, and tours of the Grand Canyon and expense-paid trips to Las Vegas. H-P pleaded guilty to violating the Foreign Corrupt Practices Act that prohibits bribing government officials to obtain business.

Questions

1. What would prompt a company like Hewlett-Packard with over $100 billion in annual sales to bribe foreign government officials to obtain a contract?
2. What impact, if any, would the charges made above have on your willingness to maintain an account with Wells Fargo, stay at a Prime Healthcare hospital, purchase shoes from Vibram, or purchase equipment from H-P?

Source: Laura J. Keller and Shahien Nasiriour, "Wells Fargo's Uphill Battle," *Bloomberg Businessweek*, March 5, 2016, pp. 31–33; Matt Egan, Jackie Wattles, and Cristina Alesci, "Wells Fargo CEO John Stumpf Is Out," CNN Money, http://money.cnn.com/2016/10/12/investing/wells-fargo-ceo-john-stumpf-retires/index .html, October 12, 2016, p. 1; Melanie Evans, "Hospital Chain's CEO Faces Suit," *The Wall Street Journal*, August 1, 2016, p. B7; Evan Sweeney, "DOJ Complaint Levels New Allegations Against Prime Healthcare," www.fiercehealthcare.com/antifraud/doj-complaint-offers-revealing-new-allegations-against-prime -healthcare, June 28, 2016, pp. 1–3; Jessica Hulett, "FiveFinger Shoe Owner? Come Get Your Refund." *The Christian Science Monitor*, www.csmonitor.com/Business/Saving-Money/2014/0512/FiveFinger-shoes -owner-Come-get-your-refund , May 15, 2014, p. 1; Spencer E. Ante and Don Clarke, "H-P Settles Bribery Case," *The Wall Street Journal*, April 10, 2014, p. B1.

believes that women are much better at selling homes than men are, and the manager is not aware of his bias. His unconscious belief may lead him to hire a woman rather than a man when the two have comparable qualifications. It is difficult to overcome an unconscious bias, yet progress can be made by remembering to broaden one's options when making a workplace decision.[36]

An Eight-Step Guide to Ethical Decision Making

Linda K. Treviño and Katherine A. Nelson have developed a guide to ethical decision making that incorporates the basic ideas found in other ethical tests.[37] After studying this guide, you will be asked to ethically screen a decision. The eight steps to sound ethical decision making are described here.

LEARNING OBJECTIVE 5
Describe the eight-step guide to ethical decision making.

1. *Gather the facts.* When making an important business decision, it is necessary to gather relevant facts. Ask yourself such questions as: Are there any legal issues involved here? Is there a precedent in our firm with respect to this type of decision? Do I have the authority to make this decision? Are there company rules and regulations governing such a decision?

2. *Define the ethical issues.* The ethical issues in a given decision are often more complicated than suggested at first glance. When faced with a complex decision, it may be helpful to talk over the ethical issues with another person. The ethical issues might involve common ethical problems such as lying to customers, sexual harassment, and overstatement of the capability of a product or service.

3. *Identify the affected parties.* When faced with a complex ethical decision, it is important to identify those who will feel the impact of the decision. Brainstorming may be helpful to identify all the parties affected by a given decision. Major corporate decisions can affect thousands of people. If a company decides to shut down a plant and outsource manufacturing to a low-wage country, thousands of individuals and many different parties are affected. Workers lose their jobs, suppliers lose their customers, the local government loses out on tax revenues, and local merchants lose many of their customers.

4. *Identify the consequences.* After you have identified the parties affected by the decision, the next step is to predict the consequences for each party. It may not be necessary to identify every consequence. Yet it is important to identify the consequences with the highest probability of occurring and those with the most negative outcomes. Both short-term and long-term consequences should be specified. The company closing a plant might create considerable short-term turmoil, but might be healthier in the long term. A healthy company would then be able to provide for more workers. The short-term consequences of delaying expense reimbursements might be a few grumbles; ill will probably will be created for the long term.

5. *Identify the obligations.* When making a complex decision, identify the obligations and the reason for each one. A manufacturer of automotive brakes has an obligation to produce and sell only brakes that meet high safety standards. The obligation is to the auto manufacturer who purchases the brakes, and more importantly to the ultimate consumer, whose safety depends on effective brakes. The ultimate reason for the obligation to make safe brakes is that lives are at stake.

6. *Consider your character and integrity.* A core consideration when faced with an ethical dilemma is to consider how relevant people would judge your character and integrity. What would your family, friends, significant others, teachers, and coworkers think of your actions? How would you feel if your actions were publicly known through e-mail, social media, or the local newspaper? If you would be proud for others to know what decision you made when you faced an ethical dilemma, you are probably making the right decision.

7. *Think creatively about potential actions.* When faced with an ethical dilemma, put yourself in a creative-thinking mode. Stretch your imagination to invent several options rather than thinking you have only two choices—to do or not to do something.

Ethical Decision Making

Working in small groups, take one or both of the ethical dilemmas presented in this exercise through the eight steps for an ethical screening of contemplated decisions. Compare your answers for the various steps with other groups in the class.

Scenario 1: The Enormous Omelet Sandwich by Burger King. You and three other students are placed on an ethics task force at Burger King being asked to investigate the ethics of selling the Enormous Omelet Sandwich. The sandwich is composed of one sausage patty, two eggs, two American cheese slices, and three strips of bacon on a bun, and contains 730 calories and 47 grams of fat. The Enormous Omelet sells particularly well with males between 18 and 35. "Food police" outside the company claim that the Enormous Omelet is so loaded with fat and bad cholesterol that it could lead to heart disease.

Yet the position of company management is that there are plenty of options on the Burger King menu for customers who want to make healthy choices. The Enormous Omelet Sandwich has been a major financial success for the restaurant chain. You and your teammates are asked to present top management with an evaluation of the ethics of continuing to sell the Enormous Omelet Sandwich.

Scenario 2: The High-Profit Toys. You are a toy company executive starting to plan your holiday-season line. You anticipate that the season's hottest item will be RoboWoman, a battery-operated crime fighter and superheroine. RoboWoman should have a wholesale price of $25.50 and a retail price of $45.00. Your company anticipates a gross profit of $15 per unit. You receive a sales call from a manufacturing broker who says he can produce any toy you want for one-third of your present manufacturing cost. He admits that the manufacturer he represents uses prison labor in China but states that his business arrangement violates no law. You estimate that your firm can earn a gross profit of $19 per unit if you do business with the manufacturing broker. The decision you face is whether to do business with him.

Creative thinking may point toward a third choice, or even more alternatives. Visualize the ethical dilemma of a purchasing agent who is told by a sales rep that he will receive a Galaxy phone as a token of appreciation if his company signs a contract. The agent says to himself, "I think we should award the contract to the firm, but I cannot accept the gift. Yet if I turn down the gift, I will be forfeiting a valuable possession that the company simply regards as a cost of doing business."

By thinking creatively, the agent finds another alternative. He tells the sales rep, "We will grant the contract to your firm because your product fits our requirements. I thank you for the offer of the Galaxy, but instead, please give it to the Southside Young Entrepreneur's Club in my name."

8. *Check your intuition.* So far we have emphasized the rational side of ethical decision making. Another effective way of conducting an ethics screen is to rely on intuition. How does the contemplated decision feel, taste, and smell? Would you be proud of yourself or would you be disgusted with yourself if you made the decision? Of course, if a person lacks a conscience, checking intuition is not effective.

The Skill-Development Exercise gives you an opportunity to practice the eight-part guide to ethical decision making.

LEARNING OBJECTIVE 6
Describe what organizations can do to enhance ethical and socially responsible behavior.

corporate social responsibility
The idea that firms have an obligation to society beyond their economic obligations to owners or stockholder and also beyond those prescribed by law or contract.

Organizational Approaches to Enhancing Ethical and Socially Responsible Behavior

Establishing an ethical and socially responsible workplace is not simply a matter of luck and common sense. Top-level managers, assisted by other managers and professionals, can develop strategies and programs to enhance ethical and socially responsible attitudes and behavior. **Corporate social responsibility** is the idea that firms have obligations to society beyond their economic obligations to owners or stockholders, and also beyond those prescribed by law or contract. Both ethics and social responsibility relate to the goodness or morality of a firm. However, corporate social responsibility is broader than ethics because it relates to an organization's impact on society beyond doing what is ethical.

Focus on the Triple Bottom Line: Profit, People, and Planet

A comprehensive approach to being ethical and socially responsible is for an organization to focus on the **triple bottom line**. The idea is that organizations should prepare three different and separate bottom lines: the corporate bottom line; people in terms of their well-being; and the planet, referring to environmental responsibility.[38] Many businesses of all sizes make a conscious effort to focus on the triple bottom line. Keeping costs below revenue pays attention to the corporate bottom line. Many programs described in this book, such as employee engagement and stress management, attempt to enhance worker well-being. A focus on the planet takes many forms, such as recycling waste or a package-delivery service such as UPS using algorithms to find efficient truck routes, thereby reducing the amount of pollutants sent into the air.

triple bottom line The idea that companies should prepare three different and separate bottom lines: the corporate bottom line; people in terms of their well-being; and the planet, referring to environmental responsibility.

Amazon pays attention to profits and the planet simultaneously by attempting to ship each order in one correctly sized package instead of multiple boxes. Shipping costs are reduced, and at the same time, Amazon responds to consumers' concerns about the negative environmental impact and general nuisance of all the cardboard. Suppliers are involved in the process because Amazon requests that they make smaller packaging specifically for online sales, not store shelves.[39]

Leadership by Example and Establishing an Ethical Culture

A high-powered approach to enhancing ethics and social responsibility is for corporate leaders to behave in such a manner themselves. Leading by example contributes to establishing a culture in which ethical behavior is expected, and unethical behavior is not tolerated. The Worker Well-Being program established by leadership at Levi Strauss described in the chapter opener qualifies as being highly ethical and socially responsible.

An ethical culture sets the tone for ethical behavior. If people throughout the firm believe that behaving ethically is "in" and behaving unethically is "out," ethical behavior will prevail. A Society for Human Resource Management Foundation report describes an ethical workplace culture as one that gives priority to employee rights, fair procedures, and equity in pay and promotion. Furthermore, the culture should promote tolerance, compassion, loyalty, and honesty in the treatment of customers and employees.[40]

Written Codes of Ethical Conduct

Many organizations use written codes of conduct as guidelines for ethical and socially responsible behavior. Such guidelines are important because many organizations have fewer managers, and therefore workers have less day-to-day contact with a manager. Some general aspects of these codes require people to conduct themselves with integrity and candor. Here is a statement of this type from the Kraft Heinz Company, one of the world's largest food and beverage companies. The company's code of ethics consists of 10 short rules of behavior that all employees must follow:

1. Make food that is safe to eat.
2. Market responsibly.
3. Treat people fairly.
4. Respect the free market.
5. Compete fairly.
6. Respect the environment.
7. Deal honestly with the government.
8. Keep honest books and records.
9. Never trade on inside information.
10. Give Kraft Heinz foods your complete business loyalty.

A whistle-blower will report on wrongdoing in the organization.

Accepting Whistle-Blowers

A **whistle-blower** is an employee who discloses organizational wrongdoing to parties who can take action. Whistle-blowers will sometimes report wrongdoing to a company insider such as a vice president, or blow the whistle externally, such as to a government agency. Some of the revelations of the account fraud at Wells-Fargo stemmed from whistle-blowers. Emotion is a mediating factor in whistle-blowing. A team of researchers concluded that to the extent potential whistle-blowers experience anger and resentment toward the perceived wrongdoers, they will decide to blow the whistle.[41] For example, a manager angry about top management using the corporate jet for personal travel might report top management's misdeeds to the board.

whistle-blower An employee who discloses organizational wrongdoing to parties who can take action.

More than half the time the pleas of whistle-blowers are ignored. It is important for leaders at all levels to create a comfortable climate for legitimate whistle-blowing. Dori Meinert, a specialist on the topic, recommends that, to minimize the risk of whistle-blower lawsuits, managers and HR professionals should make employees comfortable reporting misconduct internally. Furthermore, whistle-blowers should be protected from retaliation.[42] The manager needs the insight to sort out the difference between a troublemaker and a true whistle-blower. Careful investigation is required because only 15 percent of complaints made to the U. S. government are found to have merit, according to the Department of Labor.

Training in Ethics and Social Responsibility

Many companies train managerial workers about ethics. Forms of training include messages about ethics and social responsibility from company leadership, classes on ethics at colleges, and exercises in ethics. These training programs reinforce the idea that ethically and socially responsible behavior is both morally right and good for business. Much of the content of this chapter reflects the type of information communicated in such programs.

Social Entrepreneurship

A direct approach to corporate social responsibility is to reach out into the environment to find new ways of doing social good as an entrepreneur or as a unit within a larger organization. **Social entrepreneurship** is an entrepreneurial approach to social problems such as homelessness, contaminated drinking water, and extreme poverty. Business people who take an entrepreneurial approach to solving social problems are classified as *social entrepreneurs*.

social entrepreneurship An entrepreneurial approach to social problems such as homelessness, contaminated drinking water, and extreme poverty.

A key aspect of social entrepreneurship in contrast to entrepreneurship in general is that social entrepreneurship addresses important social needs in a way that is not dominated by direct financial payoffs to the entrepreneur.[43] Social entrepreneurs are reformers and revolutionaries with a social mission, such as Muhar Kent, the former chairman and CEO of the Coca-Cola Company, who founded the Coca-Cola African Foundation to improve drinking water and sanitation in underdeveloped countries within Africa. One of the goals of the foundation is to reduce the number of children who die from preventable diseases.[44]

The example presented in the accompanying Organizational Behavior in Action could readily be described as social entrepreneurship.

Awareness of Cross-Cultural Influences on Ethics

A key part of encouraging ethical behavior is to know what constitutes good ethics. The answer is not so easy to ascertain in dealing with companies from other countries, which

Edwins Leadership & Restaurant Institute Gives Former Prisoners a Second Chance

Brandon Edwin Chrostowski believes strongly that every human being, regardless of his or her past, has the right to be given a second chance to re-enter society in an honorable way. This belief led to the founding of Edwins Leadership & Restaurant Institute in Cleveland, Ohio. The Institute is a nonprofit organization that runs a program to prepare former prisoners for careers in the hospitality field, particularly in high-end restaurants. An upscale restaurant serving French food is part of the Edwins Institute.

At Edwins, the students spend six demanding months studying details about the upscale restaurant business, from the history of sauce-making to serving and seating. To remain in the program, the students must show improvement. From 30 to 40 students are trained at a given time, with a new class starting every eight weeks. In excess of 30 percent of the students fall out of the program during the first week alone. The students who do graduate quickly find employment in fine restaurants.

Most applicants to the program are accepted, with the exception of those with a terribly negative attitude or those who come to the interview drunk or high. Chrostowski says, "Our real interview process is those first three weeks of training." After graduation, the participants continue to receive appropriate help. "We keep working with them to make sure they're moving forward by helping with child care issues, transportation issues, and the like," says Chrostowski.

Edwins Institute received considerable community support when it was founded in 2014. Donors and a crop of local and national chefs helped raise $1 million for the project. Partners added demolition and construction manpower, free legal services, and promotional services. Habitat for Humanity contributed some furniture, washing machines, and dryers for the apartments used to house students in need of a place to live.

The idea for Edwins stemmed from a short stretch in jail as a teenager for running when police broke up an adolescent gathering that involved drugs. Instead of a decade-long prison sentence, Chrostowski received a second chance in the form of probation. The basic strategy behind the Edwins program is to arm those reentering society with a skill set and a smile.

Chrostowski began his career in Detroit and has trained in some of the world's finest restaurants in Europe and the United States. He received an associate's degree in culinary arts and a bachelor's degree in business and restaurant management from the Culinary Institute of America. Chrostowski chose to establish his institute in Cleveland because of its high rate of poverty and incarceration, yet it is also a region where people understand reentry and its potential for helping society. The program began in a prison before establishing an outside institute. Some of the training still takes place in prisons. In addition to teaching culinary skills, the program addresses problems of health care and substance abuse.

Today the Edwins Institute graduates over 100 students a year between the prison program and the campus program. Ninety-seven percent of graduates find employment in fine restaurants in Cleveland and elsewhere, with a 1 percent recidivism (return-to-prison) rate. The success of the Edwins Institute's work has earned Chrostowski dozens of awards, including the CNN Hero Award.

QUESTIONS

1. In what way would you consider Edwins to be socially responsible?

2. How fair is it for the Edwins Institute to exclude people who want to learn a trade but are not former prisoners?

3. Assuming that you were a high-end restaurant owner or manager, explain whether you would hire former prisoners as staff members.

Source: Original story created from facts and observations in the following sources: Mark Feffer, "Working with Conviction: Know the Risks and Benefits of Hiring Someone with a Criminal History," *HR Magazine*, October 2016, pp. 28–34; Michelle Jarboe, "Edwins Second Chance Campus Comes Together on Cleveland's Buckeye Road," *The Plain Dealer*, September 14, 2015, pp. 1–5; Ron Lieber, "Restaurant Report: Edwins Leadership & Restaurant Institute in Cleveland," *The New York Times*, July 2, 2015, pp. 1–2; 'Our Mission,' *edwinsrestaurant.org*, 2018. Copyright EDWIN's Restaurant & Institute.

vary in what they consider to be ethical and socially responsible behavior. For example, both the United States and China make extensive use of prison labor—an activity some countries would consider highly unethical. Bribes to foreign officials to conduct business within their country are usually considered unethical and illegal. Yet, these bribes, reclassified as *offsets*, are widespread in international business. An offset is presenting a lavish package to a foreign government for the right to do business in their country. Offsets can be any form of financial or nonfinancial aids, such as direct investments, agreements to help countries export their goods, agreements to use more foreign components in the products sold, and even outsourcing production jobs overseas.

Mary C. Gentile, a specialist in values and leadership at the University of Virginia, Darden School of Business, reports an amusing incident illustrating the financial aspects of cross-cultural ethics. While directing an ethics seminar in Delphi, India, a participant told her, "Madam, we are happy to have you here and we listen to what you have to say about ethics and values in the workplace. But this is India, and we are entrepreneurs. We can't even get a driver's license without paying a bribe."[45] (We are not certifying the accuracy of this entrepreneur's perceptions.)

Organizational Performance Consequences of Being Ethical and Socially Responsible

The initiatives for ethics and social responsibility just described can benefit the organization, including attracting talented people to the organization. Also of note, a study conducted in 17 countries found that when employees perceived their employer to have good corporate social responsibility, they developed a stronger emotional commitment to the organization. The financial consequence is that workers with emotional ties to the organization are less likely to quit, therefore saving the company money.[46]

High ethics and social responsibility are sometimes related to different aspects of organizational performance, as suggested by a comprehensive analysis of the subject. Thomas W. H. Ng and Daniel C. Feldman conducted a meta-analysis of 101 samples published over a 15-year period, involving 29,620 study participants. Ethical leadership in the studies was usually measured by subordinates' evaluations of their supervisor or manager. A major result of the analysis was that ethical leadership was positively related to job attitudes, job performance, and overall evaluation of the leaders. Another key finding of the meta-analysis was that ethical leadership was slightly related to task performance and good organizational citizenship behavior and was also helpful in reducing counterproductive work behavior. A contributing factor to the findings of the study was that ethical leaders are more trusted by employees, and trust often results in positive job attitudes and behaviors.[47]

The relationship between social responsibility and profits can also work in two directions. More profitable firms can better afford to invest in social responsibility initiatives, and these initiatives can in turn lead to more profits. For example, the Coca-Cola Company clean-water initiative mentioned above along with similar initiatives, have enhanced the company's goodwill and sales throughout the world.

Implications for Managerial Practice

In addition to the suggestions made for applying information throughout this chapter (as is done in all chapters of this book), here we make two additional practical suggestions:

1. Recognize emotion in the workplace as a potentially constructive force rather than a human condition to be ignored or suppressed. For example, enthusiasm and joy should be encouraged because they are symptoms of feelings of accomplishment and high job satisfaction. Also, anger can be a constructive force if directed toward overcoming problems.
2. Being a good organizational citizen is usually an asset to your career because the behavior suggests that you are proactive and care about the good of the organization. Nevertheless, it is best to engage in an optimal amount of organizational citizenship behavior. If you spend too much time engaging in tasks outside your role, your own performance may suffer, such as in not attaining your work goals.
3. When facing a major decision, you will want to use many of the guidelines for problem solving and decision making presented in the next chapter. In addition, major decisions should be subject to the eight-step guide for ethical decision making presented here. For a quick check on the ethical soundness of your decisions, use steps 6 (consider your character and integrity) and 8 (check your intuition).

4. Helping to preserve the planet is an important managerial and organizational responsibility. Yet as ethics specialist Jim Nortz reminds us, a CEO of a manufacturing company is not compelled to throw dollars at every conceivable pollution-reduction measure.[48] Instead, the CEO should look at the big picture and ask such questions as, (a) "What, if any, environmental impact does the current pollutant discharge create?" (b) "Can these same environmental dollars be better spent to abate a greater environmental impact or safety risk association with the manufacturing operation?"

Summary of Key Points

1. *Describe the importance of attitudes and emotions to behavior in organizations.* Attitudes influence organizational behavior in many ways. The three components of attitudes are cognitive, affective, and behavioral. A state of cognitive dissonance leads people to reduce their internal conflict when they experience a clash between the information they receive and their actions or attitudes.

   An emotion consists of three interacting components: internal physiological arousal, expressive behavior, and a cognitive appraisal. Emotional labor takes place when workers adjust their feelings and expressions to meet organizational goals, such as pleasing customers. Managers should make good use of emotions. Two key steps are to establish a friendly emotional climate and to include a positive attitude as one factor in selecting individuals and teams.

2. *Describe the nature of and contributors to job satisfaction.* Attitudes are especially important because they are the basis for job satisfaction. Workers will have high job satisfaction when they have positive attitudes toward job factors such as the work itself, recognition, and opportunity for advancement. A practical view of job satisfaction is that it centers on employees having fun in their jobs. Satisfaction is linked to important consequences such as loyalty, absenteeism and turnover, and job stress. Loyalty is important for avoiding costly involuntary turnover.

3. *Describe how organizational citizenship behavior contributes to individual and organizational effectiveness.* Job satisfaction also contributes to organizational citizenship behavior. The good organizational citizen goes above and beyond the call of duty, or engages in extra role behavior. A particularly useful distinction in organizational citizenship behaviors is between affiliation-oriented and challenge-oriented behaviors. Personality factors, such as service orientation and empathy, contribute to organizational citizenship behavior. Low organizational citizenship behavior has been linked to turnover. When workers perceive their organizational support to be high, they are less likely to be fatigued by engaging in citizenship behavior. Being too strong an organizational citizen by taking on extra work can lead to conflict in personal life, and also to the neglect of regular job responsibilities.

4. *Describe three ethical decision-making criteria, along with several explanations for the existence of ethical problems.* A philosophical approach to understanding ethics gives three possible focuses: on consequences; on duties, obligations, and principles; or on integrity. When focusing on consequences, the decision maker is concerned with the utility, or net balance of good and bad consequences, of a decision. The deontological approach focuses on the rights of individuals and is based on universal principles such as honesty, fairness, justice, and respect for persons and property. The integrity, or virtue, criterion focuses on the character of the ethical action.

   Major causes of ethical problems include an individual's greed and gluttony; an individual's level of moral development; a culture that condones unethical behavior; pressure from higher management including unrealistic goals; and unconscious biases.

5. *Describe the eight-step guide to ethical decision making.* An eight-step guide to ethical decision making follows these steps: (1) gather the facts, (2) define the ethical issues, (3) identify the affected parties, (4) identify the consequences, (5) identify the obligations, (6) consider your character and integrity, (7) think creatively about potential actions, and (8) check your intuition. Choosing between two rights, or defining moments, may require an ethical test.

6. *Describe what organizations can do to enhance ethical and socially responsible behavior.* Managers can develop strategies and programs to enhance ethical and socially responsible attitudes and behaviors. Among these approaches are: focus on the triple bottom line, leading by example and establishing an ethical culture, establishing written codes of ethical conduct, accepting whistle-blowers, giving training in ethics and social responsibility, engaging in social entrepreneurship, and gaining awareness of cross-cultural influences on ethics. The preceding initiatives often lead to improved organizational performance, including profits.

Key Terms and Phrases

attitude, p. 67

cognitive dissonance, p. 67

emotion, p. 68

emotional labor, p. 69

job satisfaction, p. 70

organizational citizenship behavior (OCB), p. 72

ethics, p. 73

corporate social responsibility, p.78

triple bottom line, p. 79

whistle-blower, p. 80

social entrepreneurship, p. 80

Discussion Questions and Activities

1. What does it mean when executives and human resource professionals contend that they "hire more for attitudes than skills"?

2. For what reasons do you think most workers are reluctant to cry in front of other workers when something goes wrong, such as receiving a poor performance review or losing data on their computer? How does your answer fit with the idea that emotional expression is supposed to be welcome on the job?

3. There is some evidence that more intelligent workers are more likely to experience job satisfaction. How might you explain this relationship between intelligence and job satisfaction?

4. Why do you think it is true that flexible working hours boost job satisfaction for so many people?

5. What impact do you think permitting employees to use their own mobile devices to perform company work has on the job satisfaction of these employees?

6. Give an example of any job you have held where you did or might have demonstrated *challenge-oriented* citizenship behavior.

7. Why do so many believe that to succeed in business, you have to be a little unethical?

8. The Vice Fund (www.usamutuals.com) bills itself as a vice fund because it puts investors' assets into four industry sectors often associated with vice: tobacco, gambling, liquor, and defense. What is your opinion of (a) the ethics of the founders of the fund and (b) the advisability of investing money in such a fund?

9. What can a company as big as Kraft Heinz do to ensure that its employees are following its code of ethics?

10. Before accepting a job, how much weight would you place on whether the potential employer exhibited strong social responsibility? Explain your reasoning.

CASE PROBLEM: Financial Consultant Chloe Bites Her Tongue

Chloe is a financial consultant at Lake River Capital, a company whose primary service is managing the investments of high-income individuals. Although the field of wealth managers and financial advisors is crowded, Lake River has survived for 45 years. The company emphasizes frequent face-to-face meetings with clients.

As with other financial consultants or advisors within the office, part of Chloe's bonus is based on the amount of money in her clients' portfolios at the end of the year. To attain a large bonus, as well as retain clients, Chloe has to make smart investments and maintain a good relationship with clients. For the last year, Chloe has experienced increasing difficulty in being agreeable and warm toward some of her clients. She explains why as follows.

"One of my clients, Darwin, has asked me several times to find him a couple of investments that would help him reduce his income tax. I told him once politely that Lake River is committed to complying fully with tax regulations and that we make no exceptions. But Darwin makes the same demand frequently either by phone or in person. He knows enough not to put that kind of shady request in an e-mail. I want to tell Darwin how angry I am with him, but I don't dare.

"Another client of mine is a young guy, Jud. He thinks that because he is the client, he can hit on me. He has told me several times that he thinks I am cute and that he would like to have dinner with me. I told him that I do not socialize with clients except in our yearly client appreciation dinner. I also told Jud that I am married. Once when he left my office, he insisted on hugging me, even though I backed away. I wanted to scream at Jud and maybe even punch him in the face. But no, I smiled and told him to have a nice day.

"Lauren, an older client, really bugs me. During the last year, she has canceled our two appointments and asked to be rescheduled. One time, she canceled our rescheduled appointment and wanted another appointment later in the day. I wanted to scream at Lauren and tell her to find another financial consultant. Instead, I said politely that it would be helpful if she could make our scheduled appointments, but I would do the best I could to accommodate her,

"Another client, Constance, drives me crazy because of her unrealistic requests. She keeps telling me to find her the next great stock investment, such as Amazon or Apple, in its early days. Constance tells me that she wants Lake River to make her a multimillionaire. I have explained to Constance that we would have to make hundreds of risky investments with her money to find one Amazon or Apple. I really want to tell Constance to stop making the same stupid request every time she sees me. Instead, I smile and say we will keep our eyes open for a promising growth stock for her.

"All this biting my tongue and holding back on my true feelings is stressing me out. I like my job otherwise, but I don't know what to do with a few unreasonable clients."

Case Questions

1. In what way is this case about emotional labor?
2. What do you recommend that Chloe do differently so that she doesn't have to "bite her tongue"?
3. What about Chloe accepting the reality that "the customer is always right"?
4. If you were Chloe's manager, what would you do to help make her job less stressful?

Endnotes

1. Original story created from facts and observations in the following sources: Erika Fry, "The Ties That Bind at Levy's," *Fortune*, September 15, 2017, pp. 104–110; Adele Peters, "How Levi's Is Building Well-Being Programs Where They Matter Most: In Its Factories," *Fast Company*, www.fastcompany.com/3064477/how-levis-is-building-well-being-programs-where-they-matter-most-in-its-factories, October 13, 2016, pp. 1–3; "The LS & Co. Worker Well-Being Initiative," UN Global Compact, http://supply-chain.unglobalcompact.org/site/article/205, 2018, p. 1; "How Levi Strauss & Co.'s Worker Well-Being Program Is 'Changing the World'," *Unzipped* (blog), www.levistrauss.com/unzipped-blog/2017/09/levi-strauss-co-makes-fortunes-change-world-list/, September 9, 2017p. 1; "Sustainability: People," Levi Strauss & Co., www.levistrauss.com/sustainability/#people, 2018, pp. 1–5.

2. Rik Kirkland, "Wharton's Adam Grant on the Key to Professional Success," *McKinsey & Company* (www.mckinsey.com), June 2014, p. 3.

3. Debra J. Schleicher et al., "It's All in the Attitude: The Role of Job Attitude Strength in Job Attitude-Outcome Relationships," *Journal of Applied Psychology*, July 2015, pp. 1259–1274.

4. Neal M. Ashkanasy, Ronald H. Humphrey, and Quy Nguyen Huy, "Integrating Emotions and Affect in Theories of Management," *The Academy of Management Review*, April 2017, pp. 175–189.

5. Department of Homeland Security study cited in "U.S. Studies Root of Sabotage," Associated Press, May 17, 2005.

6. Allison S. Gabriel, James M. Diefendorff, and Rebecca J. Erickson, "The Relation of Daily Task Accomplishment Satisfaction with Changes in Affect: A Multilevel Study in Nurses," *Journal of Applied Psychology*, September 2011, pp. 1095–1104.

7. Saul Kassin, *Psychology*, 3rd ed. (Upper Saddle River, NJ: Prentice-Hall, 2001), p. 330.

8. Neal M. Ashkanasy and Catherine S. Daus, "Emotion in the Workplace: The New Challenge for Managers," *The Academy of Management Executive*, February 2002, pp. 82–83.

9. Stéphane Côté, "A Social Interaction Model of the Effects of Emotion Regulation on Work Strain," *Academy of Management Review*, July 2005, p. 525.

10. Joann Ellison Rodgers, "Go Forth in Anger," *Psychology Today*, April 2014, pp. 72–79.

11. Research reported in Elizabeth Bernstein, "Venting Isn't Good for Us," *The Wall Street Journal*, August 11, 2015, pp. D1, D4.

12. Alicia A. Grandey, "Emotion Regulation in the Workplace: A New Way to Conceptualize Emotional Labor," *Journal of Occupational Health Psychology*, 5(1), 2000, pp. 95–110; Grandey, "When the 'Show Must Go On': Surface Acting and Deep Acting as Determinants of Emotional Exhaustion and Peer-Related Service Delivery," *Academy of Management Journal*, February 2003, pp. 86–96.

13. Luke Stark, "Recognizing the Role of Emotional Labor in the On-Demand Economy," *Harvard Business Review*, August 26, 2016, pp. 2–3.

14. John D. Kammeyer-Mueller et al., "A Meta-Analytic Structural Model of Dispositional Affectivity and Emotional Labor," *Personnel Psychology*, Number 1, 2013, pp. 47–90.

15. Yujie Zhan, Mo Wang, and Junqi Shi, "Interpersonal Processes of Emotional Labor: The Role of Negative and Positive Customer Treatment," *Personnel Psychology*, No. 3, 2016, pp. 525–557.

16. Neal M. Ashkanasy, Charmine E. J. Härtel, and Wilfred J. Zerbe (eds.), *Emotions in the Workplace: Research, Theory, and Practice* (Westport, CT: Quorum Books/Greenwood, 2000).

17. Patricia Faison Hewlin, "And the Award for Best Actor Goes to…: Facades of Conformity in Organizational Settings," *Academy of Management Review*, October 2003, pp. 633–642.

18. Alicia A, Grandey, Nai-Wen Chi, and Jennifer A. Diamond, "Show Me the Money! Do Financial Rewards for Performance Enhance or Undermine the Satisfaction from Emotional Labor?" *Personnel Psychology*, No. 3, 2013, pp. 569–612.

19. Review of Ashkanasy, Härtel, and Zerbe, *Emotions in the Workplace*.

20. "How Americans View their Jobs," Pew Research Center, www.pewsocialtrends.org/2016/10/06/3-how-americans-view-their-jobs/, October 6, 2016, pp. 1–2.

21. Ed Frauenheim, "The Power of Positive Tinkering," *Workforce*, September 2013, pp. 44, 47.

22. Timothy A. Judge, Howard M. Weiss, John D. Kammeyer-Mueller, and Charles L. Hulin, "Job Attitudes, Job Satisfaction, and Job Affect: A Century of Continuity and of Change," *Journal of Applied Psychology*, March 2017, pp. 364–366; Judge and Remus Ilies, "Affect and Job Satisfaction: A Study of Their Relationship at Work and at Home," *Journal of Applied Psychology*, August 2004, pp. 661–673.

23. "Success Linked to Worker Loyalty," *Associated Press*, May 13, 2002.

24. Hamid Raza Alavi and Mohammed Reza Askaripur, "The Relationship between Self-Esteem and Job Satisfaction of Personnel in Government Organizations," *Public Personnel Management*, Winter 2003, pp. 591–600.

25. Kathryn H. Dekas, Talya N. Bauer, Brian Welle, Jennifer Kurkoski, and Stacy Sullivan, "Organizational Citizenship Behavior, Version 2.0: A Review and Qualitative Investigation of OCBs for Knowledge Workers at Google and Beyond," *Academy of Management Perspective*, August 2013, p. 219.

26. Scott B. Mackenzie, Phillip M. Podaskoff, and Nathan P. Podaskoff, "Challenge-Oriented Organizational Citizenship Behaviors and Organizational Effectiveness: Do Challenge-Oriented Behaviors Really Have an Impact on the Organization's Bottom Line?" *Personnel Psychology*, Number 3, 2011, p. 560.

27. Dekas et al., "Organizational Citizenship Behavior, Version 2.0," pp. 228, 233.

28. Lance A. Bettencourt, Kevin P. Gwinner, and Matthew L. Meuter, "A Comparison of Attitude, Personality, and Knowledge Predictors of Service-Oriented Organizational Citizenship Behaviors," *Journal of Applied Psychology*, February 2001, pp. 29–41.

29. Mark C. Bolino and William H. Turnley, "The Personal Costs of Citizenship Behavior: The Relationship between Individual Initiative and Role Overload, Job Stress, and Work-Family Conflict," *Journal of Applied Psychology*, July 2005, pp. 740–748.

30. Mark C. Bolino, Hsin-Hua Hsiung, Jason Harvey, and Jeffrey A. LePine, "'Well I'm Tired of Tryin'!' Organizational Citizenship Behavior and Citizenship Fatigue," *Journal of Applied Psychology*, January 2015, pp. 56–74.

31. J. Kemp Ellington, Erich C. Dierdoff, and Robert S. Rubin, "Decelerating the Diminishing Returns of Citizenship on Task Performance: The Role of Social Context and Interpersonal Skill," *Journal of Applied Psychology*, July 2014, pp. 748–758.

32. Linda K. Treviño and Katherine A. Nelson, *Managing Business Ethics: Straight Talk about How to Do It Right* (New York: Wiley, 1995), pp. 66–70; O. C. Ferrell, John Fraedrich, and Linda Ferrell, *Business Ethics: Ethical Decision Making and Cases*, 4th ed. (Boston: Houghton Mifflin, 2000), pp. 52–61.

33. "Surveys on Business Ethics 2016," Institute of Business Ethics, www.ibe.org.uk/userassets/briefings/b56_surveys2016.pdf, February 2017, pp. 1–2.

34. Research synthesized in Richard L. Daft, *Leadership: Theory and Practice* (Mason, OH: Thomson South-Western, 2003), pp. 369–370.

35. Ron Carucci, "Why Ethical People Make Unethical Choices," *Harvard Business Review*, December 16, 2016, p. 3.

36. Mahzarin R. Banaji, Maz H. Bazerman, and Dolly Chugh, "How (Un)ethical Are You?" December 2003, pp. 56–64.

37. Treviño and Nelson, *Managing Business Ethics*, pp. 71–75.

38. Rhonda Abrams, "Entrepreneurs, Mind the 'Triple Bottom Line,'" *USA Today*, January 24, 2018, pp. 1–2; "Triple Bottom Line," *The Economist*, November 17, 2009, pp. 1–2.

39. Laura Stevens and Erica E. Phillips, "More Amazon Orders, Fewer Boxes," *The Wall Street Journal*, December 21, 2017, p. B3.

40. Dori Meinert, "Creating an Ethical Culture," *HR Magazine*, April 2014, p. 24.

41. Michael J. Gundlach, Scott C. Douglas, and Mark J. Martinko, "The Decision to Blow the Whistle: A Social Information Processing Model," *Academy of Management Review*, January 2003, p. 112.

42. Dori Meinert, "Are You Listening?" *HR Magazine*, June 2014, p. 59.

43. Johann Mair and Ignasi Marti, "Social Entrepreneurship Research: A Source of Explanation, Prediction, and Delight," *Journal of World Business*, Issue 1, February 2006, pp. 36–44.

44. "WaterAid Joins Forces with the Coca-Cola Africa Foundation to Bring Safe Drinking Water," *Financial News Making Money* (www.finchannel.com), May 11, 2013, pp. 1–3.

45. Mary C. Gentile, "Talking about Ethics across Cultures," *Harvard Business Review*, December 23, 2016, p. 2.

46. Karsten Mueller, Kate Hattrup, Sven-Oliver Spiess, and Nick Lin-Hi, "The Effects of Corporate Social Responsibility on Employees' Affective Commitment: A Cross-Cultural investigation," *Journal of Applied Psychology*, November 2012, pp. 1186–1200.

47. Thomas W. H. Ng and Daniel C. Feldman, "Ethical Leadership: Meta-Analytic Evidence of Criterion-Related and Incremental Validity," *Journal of Applied Psychology*, May 2015, pp. 948–965.

48. Jim Nortz, "Steer an Ethical Course by Keeping an Eye on All Your Eggs," *Rochester Business Journal*, March 2, 2018, p. 16.

Individual Decision Making and Creativity

Chapter Outline

Jacob Lund/Shutterstock.com

Learning Objectives

After reading and studying this chapter and doing the exercises, you should be able to:

1. Work through the decision-making model when faced with a major decision.

2. Identify and describe factors that influence the effectiveness of decision making.

3. Understand the nature of creative decision making in organizations.

4. Enhance your creative problem-solving ability.

Rob McEwen is the chief executive officer of a gold, silver, and copper company called McEwen Mining Inc., yet he remains a legend for a breakthrough idea he had when he was the chairman and CEO of a Canadian company, Goldcorp. He knew at the time, about 20 years ago, that the company's Red Lake site in northwestern Ontario could be highly profitable. The problem was that nobody at Goldcorp could figure out where to find high-grade ore. The terrain was almost impossible to access, operating costs were high, and the unionized staff was on strike. The company had a gold mine that was functioning as a nonperforming asset.

An inspirational idea struck McEwen, whose background was in finance, not mining. While attending a conference about recent developments in information technology, McEwen was enamored with the open-source movement. Combating the advice of traditional thinkers in his own company, McEwen created the Goldcorp Challenge. The company posted Red Lake's closely guarded topographic data online and offered $575,000 in prize money to any individual or group who could identify gold-rich drill sites. To the amazement of many people in the mining industry, more than 1,400 scientists, engineers, and geologists in 50 countries tackled the problem. As the entries rolled in, the panel of five judges was astonished by the creativity of the submissions.

The winners of the challenge were two Australian teams working together that pinpointed locations that have made Red Lake one of the world's richest gold mines. The team members did not even visit the mine but instead developed a powerful 3-D graphical depiction of the mine. McEwen said that the contest was a gold mine. He said, "We have drilled four of the winners' top five targets and have hit on all four. But what's really important is that from a remote site, the winners were able to analyze a database and generate targets without ever visiting the property. It's clear that this is part of the future."[1]

The story about the Red Lake gold mine illustrates that going beyond traditional thinking can lead to a breakthrough idea. To be an effective decision maker, a person must think creatively. In this chapter, we study creativity in the context of individual decision making in organizations. First, we describe a model of the decision-making process; then we examine key influences on decision making, followed by a careful look at the nature and development of creativity. We return to the study of decision making in Chapter 9 with a description of group decision making. In Chapter 16 we include a discussion of innovation, which can be considered an extension of creativity. The creative aspects of decision making are emphasized in this chapter because employee creativity contributes enormously to organizational success. IBM conducted a survey of more than 1,500 CEOs across 33 industries and 60 countries about the number-one attribute they look for in hiring. The attribute was creativity because every company wants to be at the forefront of its industry and also be an innovation leader. For those outcomes, you need highly creative employees.[2]

A Decision-Making Model

LEARNING OBJECTIVE 1
Work through the decision-making model when faced with a major decision.

decision The act of choosing among two or more alternatives in order to solve a problem.

problem A discrepancy between the ideal and the real.

A **decision** takes place when a person chooses among two or more alternatives in order to solve a problem. People attempt to solve problems because a **problem** is a discrepancy between the ideal and the real. The ability to make good decisions is enormously valuable for a person's career and job performance. Choosing the right career will most likely mean more job satisfaction, less stress, and a longer life. (Stress-related disorders often shorten life.) Making good business decisions is more complex and difficult than most people recognize.

Managers and corporate professionals may make decisions in a generally rational framework. Nevertheless, at various points in the model (e.g., choosing creative alternatives), intuition and judgment come into play. Research stemming back to the 1980s has demonstrated that individual decision making is not always rational. In 2017, behavioral

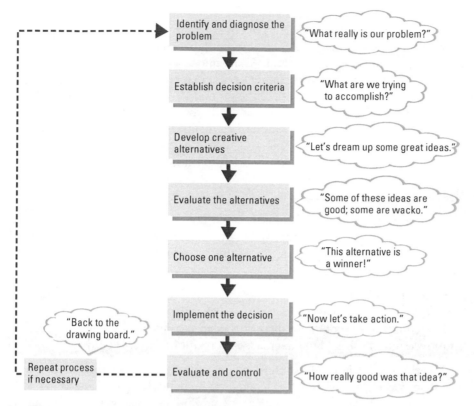

FIGURE 5-1 The Decision-Making Process

economist Richard Thaler was awarded a Nobel Prize for his studies demonstrating that individuals do not always make rational decisions about their future and finances.[3]

The seven steps in the decision-making process are outlined in Figure 5-1 and described in the following paragraphs. The model is useful for making complex decisions of both a personal and an organizational nature. You might therefore want to use the model in purchasing a car, choosing a career, or deciding whether to drop a product line.

Identify and Diagnose the Problem

Problem solving and decision making begin with the awareness that a problem exists. In other words, the first step in problem solving and decision making is identifying a gap between desired and actual conditions. A problem occurs when something has gone wrong or has deviated from the norm. At times, a problem is imposed on a manager, such as a demand from upper management to increase retailing sales by 20 percent. At other times, the manager has to search actively for a worthwhile problem or opportunity. For example, a human resources manager sought a unique way for her firm to celebrate cultural diversity.

Finding a problem lies at the heart of being a successful entrepreneur. A classic example is why Howard Schultz expanded Starbucks into a chain of cafés in the United States. (Starbucks already existed as a seller of coffee beans to stores.) According to legend, Schultz was traveling in Italy when he noticed that Italians were passionate about strong coffee and their local cafés. The insight hit him that "If it works in Italy, why not at home too?" He would offer Americans something they were not used to, thereby creating a new market.[4]

Dwayne Spradlin is the president and CEO of InnoCentive, an online marketplace that connects organizations with freelance problem solvers with different specialties. He contends that, when faced with innovation challenges, companies often neglect to spend enough time to define the problem they are trying to solve or to specify the importance of the problem to the organization. An example he cites is of a manufacturer that was looking for the right lubricant for its manufacturing machinery. Digging into the problem, the company soon recognized that it needed a new way to make the product, not a lubricant.[5] Such a decision is of great importance to the organization.

A thorough diagnosis of the problem is important because the real problem may be different from the one suggested at first look. To diagnose a problem properly, you must clarify its true nature. For example, what might at first glance seem like a problem of product defect is really one of consumer misuse of the product. To resolve the problem, one would need to better inform the consumer, not modify the product. An extreme example is that of an owner of a new digital camera complaining that the camera shot only partial images, with a horizontal dark spot across the pictures, when the true problem was that the camera user held his index finger across the lens while shooting photos.

Establish Decision Criteria

decision criteria The standards of judgment used to evaluate alternatives.

When solving a problem, it pays to know what constitutes a good decision. **Decision criteria** are the standards of judgment used to evaluate alternatives. The more explicit the criteria, the better the decision will be. In seeking to reduce costs, several of the decision criteria might include the following:

1. Product (or service) quality should not suffer as a result of the cost cutting.
2. Profits should increase as a result of the cost cutting.
3. Employee turnover should not increase because of the cost cutting.
4. Employee morale should not decrease as a result of the cost cutting.

A good starting point in establishing decision criteria, according to the late management guru Peter Drucker, is to ask, "What needs to be done?" rather than "What do I want to do?"[6] In the present example, the manager would ponder whether cost cutting is even worthwhile. Perhaps increasing spending would lead to improvements that would more than pay for themselves, such as hiring a highly talented worker who would make money for the company.

Develop Creative Alternatives

The third step in decision making is to generate alternative creative solutions. All kinds of possibilities are explored in this step even if they seem unrealistic. Often the difference between effective and mediocre decision makers is that the former do not accept the first alternative they think of. Instead, they keep digging until they find the best solution. For example, a corporate executive who was downsized out of a job wanted to purchase a business to operate. Impatient to renew his career, he purchased a well-known—but poorly performing—franchise. Trying to make the franchise operation profitable drained the rest of his cash reserve and he sold back the franchise at a big loss. Had he researched better alternatives, he might have succeeded. Creativity is such a key part of decision making that it receives separate treatment later in this chapter.

Evaluate the Alternatives

The next step involves comparing the relative value of the alternatives. The problem solver examines the pros and cons of each alternative and considers its feasibility. Part of evaluating the pros and cons of alternative solutions is to compare each against the decision criteria established in the second step. Some alternatives appear attractive, but implementing them would be impossible or counterproductive. For example, one alternative solution a couple chose for increasing their income was to open an entirely new restaurant and bar in a mall. When they discovered that the start-up costs would be approximately $600,000, they decided that the alternative was impossible for the time being.

Choose One Alternative

After investing a reasonable amount of time in evaluating the alternative solutions, it is time to choose one of them—to actually make a decision. An important factor influencing this process is the degree of uncertainty associated with it. People who prefer not to take risks choose alternatives that have the most certain outcomes. In contrast, risk takers are willing to choose alternatives with uncertain outcomes if the potential gains appear to be substantial. Despite a careful evaluation of the alternatives, in most decisions ambiguity remains. The decisions faced by managers are often complex, and the factors involved in them are often unclear.

Implement the Decision

Converting the decision into action is the next major step. Until a decision is implemented, it is not really a decision. Many decisions represent wasted effort because nobody is held responsible for implementing them. Much of a manager's job involves helping group members implement decisions. A fruitful way of evaluating a decision is to observe its implementation. A decision is seldom a good one if workers resist its implementation or if it is too cumbersome to implement.

Evaluate and Control

The final step in the decision-making framework is to evaluate how effectively the chosen alternative solved the problem and met the decision criteria. The results of the decision obtained are controlled when they are the ones set forth during the problem-identification stage. Getting back to the example in the section Establish Decision Criteria, the decision to cut costs would be considered good if service did not suffer, profits were higher, turnover did not increase, and morale did not decrease.

Influences on Decision Making

Decision making is usually not entirely rational because so many factors influence the decision maker. Research and opinion emphasize that humans use problem-solving strategies that are reasonably rapid, reasonably accurate, and that fit the quantity and type of information available.[7] In short, people do the best with what they have while making decisions.

LEARNING OBJECTIVE 2
Identify and describe factors that influence the effectiveness of decision making.

Most decision makers do not have the time or resources to wait for the best possible solution. Instead, they search for decisions, or those that suffice in providing a minimum standard of satisfaction. Such decisions are adequate, acceptable, or passable. Many decision makers stop their search for alternatives when they find a sufficient one.

Accepting the first reasonable alternative may only postpone the need to implement a decision that truly solves the problem and meets the decision criteria. For example, slashing the price of a pickup truck to match the competition's price can be regarded as the result of a sufficient decision. A superior decision might call for the firm to demonstrate to end users that the difference in quality is worth the higher price, which in the long term will increase sales.

According to decision theorist Julia Galef, the correct way of understanding rationality in decision making is that rationality depends on emotions. She explains that rationality is not about getting rid of emotions but analyzing them and taking them into account when making decisions.[8] Imagine that an entrepreneur wants to start a new business. At the same time he recognizes that a major reason for starting the new business is to get revenge on the employer who recently fired him. The entrepreneur must keep in mind not to make foolish decisions about investing in a new enterprise just to satisfy his motive of revenge.

Partly because of the need to make decisions quickly , decision makers often use simplified strategies, also known as **heuristics**. A heuristic becomes a rule of thumb in decision making, such as the policy to reject a job applicant who does not smile during the first 3 minutes of a job interview. A widely used investing heuristic is as follows: The percent of equity in your portfolio should equal 100 minus your age, with the remainder being invested in fixed-income investments including cash. (Some financial advisors recommend 110 instead of 100.) A 25-year-old would therefore have a portfolio consisting of 25 percent interest-bearing securities such as bonds, and 75 percent in stocks. Heuristics

heuristics Simplified strategies that become rules of thumb in decision making.

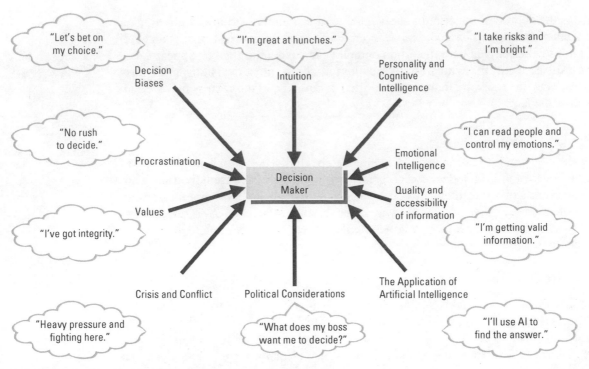

FIGURE 5-2 Influences on Decision Making

help the decision maker cope with masses of information, but their oversimplification can lead to inaccurate or irrational decision making.

A host of influences on the decision-making process contribute to decision effectiveness and quality. We describe nine such influences, as outlined in Figure 5-2.

Intuition

Intuition is a key personal characteristic that influences decision making. Effective decision makers do not rely on analytical and methodological techniques alone. Instead, they also use hunches and intuition. **Intuition** is an experience-based way of knowing or reasoning in which weighing and balancing evidence are done automatically. Intuition can be based mostly on experience, or mostly on feeling.[9]

intuition An experience-based way of knowing or reasoning in which weighing and balancing evidence are done automatically.

When relying on intuition, the decision maker arrives at a conclusion without using a step-by-step logical process. The fact that experience contributes to intuition means that decision makers can become more intuitive by solving many difficult problems. An unusual example is that of Guy Laliberté, the cofounder of Cirque Du Soleil, who believes that intuition has helped him in business life, particularly in sizing up people. He honed his intuition as a street performer—a fire-breather—on the streets of Montreal. "Sometimes you have a fraction of a second to evaluate, when you first meet someone, whether they might stab you or become your friend," said Laliberté.[10]

Tim Cook, the CEO at Apple Corp, provides an example of the importance of intuition in decision making. He explains that intuition is extremely critical in his job. According to Cook, the most important things in life, whether they are professional or personal, are decided on intuition. Although quantitative analysis is helpful, the decisions that are the most important are "gut calls."[11] Cook's analysis follows the Apple tradition of using imagination rather than market research or focus groups to decide what might captivate consumers.

Although the use of intuition in organizational decision making is now widely recognized, researchers have also found limitations to intuition. When the stakes are high, such as a CEO contemplating

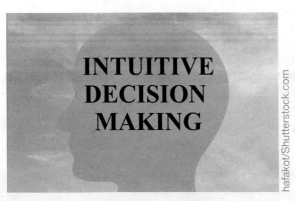

Intuition facilitates decision making.

acquiring a company in a different field, rational analysis is recommended. The analysis might include receiving input from many people and asking knowledgeable people loads of questions.[12] At the same time, however, intuition could help point the executive in the right direction, such as sizing up the overall merits of the company to be acquired. In short, you need to use your intuition to decide when intuition or extensive rational analysis is best!

Personality and Cognitive Intelligence

The personality and cognitive intelligence of the decision maker influence his or her ability to find effective solutions. A starting point is that the personality trait of risk taking and thrill seeking strongly influences the propensity to take risks. A real estate developer with a strong risk-taking and thrill-seeking tendency might be willing to take a chance and erect a new apartment building in a distressed area of town. Part of her reasoning would be that the new building will start to improve the neighborhood, thereby attracting tenants and gradually improving property values.

Similar relevant personality dimensions are cautiousness and conservatism. Being cautious and conservative can lead to indecisiveness where the decision maker has a tendency to avoid or delay making a decision. Because a key part of a manager's role is to make decisions, indecisiveness can be a major flaw and highly frustrating to subordinates who await a decision from the manager.[13] At the other extreme from indecisiveness is impulsiveness, where the decision maker jumps quickly to a decision without much analysis.

Perfectionism is another personality factor that has a notable impact on decision making. People who seek the perfect solution to a problem are usually indecisive because they are hesitant to accept the fact that a particular alternative is good enough. **Self-efficacy**, the feeling of being an effective and competent person with respect to a task, also has an influence. Researchers note, for example, that having the right amount of "gall" contributes to innovative thinking.[14] If you have high self-efficacy for many tasks, your self-confidence will increase, leading to more innovative thinking and risk taking.

self-efficacy The feeling of being an effective and competent person with respect to a task.

Optimism versus pessimism is another relevant personality dimension. Optimists are more likely to find solutions than pessimists are. Pessimists are also likely to give up searching because they perceive situations as being hopeless.

Cognitive intelligence has a profound influence on the effectiveness of decision making. In general, intelligent and well-educated people are more likely to identify and diagnose problems and make sound decisions than are those who have less intelligence and education. A notable exception applies, however: Some intelligent, well-educated people have such a fondness for collecting facts and analyzing them that they suffer from analysis paralysis.

Emotional Intelligence

Emotional intelligence is important for decision making because how effectively you manage your feelings and read other people affects the quality of your decisions. For example, if you cannot control your anger, you are likely to make decisions that are motivated by retaliation, hostility, and revenge. You might shout and swear at your team leader because of a work assignment you received.

Emotional intelligence also contributes to the problem of making decisions impulsively. The emotionally intelligent individual is able to control his or her impulses to avoid making a decision too quickly. Creating a space of even several seconds between an event and a reaction can prevent an impulsive decision, such switching suppliers because of a minor problem.[15]

Your emotional intelligence could also influence career decision making. If you understand your own feelings, you are more likely to enter an occupation or accept a position that matches your true attitudes. A common problem is that many people pursue "hot" and/or well-paying fields even

Self-efficacy helps in making good decisions.

Michael Kowalski/Shutterstock.com

when they are not passionate about the field. As a result, they are likely to become discouraged and leave the field—even as early as switching majors. Admitting this lack of passion to oneself might prevent misdirected time and effort.

Quality of Information and Big Data

Reaching an effective decision usually requires high-quality, valid information. One of the most important purposes of information systems is to supply managers and professionals with high-quality information. A vice president of manufacturing might contemplate the establishment of a manufacturing plant in a distant city. He or she would more likely make an effective decision if the information systems group had accurate information about factors such as the caliber of the workforce and environmental regulations.

Big Data Enormous amounts of data that have the potential to be mined for information.

Big Data refers to enormous amounts of data that have the potential to be mined for information. The use of the term *Big Data* recognizes the importance of collecting vast amounts of data from many sources and then analyzing the data to squeeze out valuable information and insights about customers and employees. Big Data might also be used to predict events, such as future health insurance costs based on the lifestyle choices of current employees. A business example of Big Data is to predict which retail stores are likely to survive or close by analyzing mobile phone calls, demographic information, credit-card bills, and other unconventional data. Such information could be helpful to investors.[16]

The specialist who analyzes Big Data attempts to coax treasure out of messy, unstructured data.[17] Making sense out of data is a real contribution because decision makers typically have more information available than they can absorb and integrate. For example, a company might use embedded employee badges that collect data on when employees enter the premises, how often they leave the building and return, and which employees enter and exit the building at the same time. But what useful insights might stem from all this information? One potential insight might be that some employees need help with overcoming tardiness.

A major purpose of analyzing masses of data is to help managers make decisions on the basis of evidence, rather than relying too heavily on intuition. A marketing example is that online booksellers have been able to track Big Data about which books customers bought, what else they looked at, and how much they were influenced by promotions, along with other information. Soon the booksellers developed algorithms to predict which books individuals might be interested in purchasing next.[18] (Defined simply, an algorithm is a step-by-step procedure for problem solving, particularly for a computer.) These algorithms may enhance sales somewhat, but they can also result in loads of useless e-mails sent to customers. For example, you might have purchased a book about cocker spaniels as a gift for a friend, but you are not interested in purchasing five other books about dogs. (More about algorithms as used in artificial intelligence is presented next.)

artificial intelligence The ability of a computer program or machine to think and learn in a manner that emulates human intelligence.

Decision makers often have to sort through Big Data.

Rawpixel.com/Shutterstock.com

The Application of Artificial Intelligence

Today's managerial decision maker is often influenced by both Big Data and its use of artificial intelligence. **Artificial intelligence** (AI) is the ability of a computer program or machine to think and learn in a manner that emulates human intelligence. The machine-learning aspect of AI means that the program learns from the patterns and associations it detects. Predictions have been made that soon AI will be as important for companies as is the Internet.[19] Very few business enterprises could survive without the use of the Internet.

A variety of companies have reported that the algorithms produced by artificial intelligence make them more efficient and give employees increased opportunities to perform new types of work. The same software is starting to take on management tasks such as scheduling and guiding strategic projects. For example, Royal Dutch Shell PLC uses machine-learning software to match workers and projects.[20]

In almost all cases the artificial intelligence is produced by data scientists, software engineers, or statisticians, yet the manager or corporate professional uses the data and decides whether or not is the data are useful. For example, an executive recruiting agency might use AI to identify the ideal candidate for a client's chief financial officer opening. Yet the members of management team should decide for themselves on such vital factors as how well they would enjoy working with this candidate and whether he or she would fit in with the company culture.

The accompanying Organizational Behavior in Action illustrates how a well-known company has effectively applied AI to enhance sales.

Political Considerations

Under ideal circumstances, organizational decisions are made on the basis of the objective merits of competing alternatives. In reality, many decisions are based on political considerations, such as favoritism, alliances, or the desire of the decision maker to stay in favor with people who wield power. Political factors sometimes influence which data are given serious consideration in evaluating alternatives. The decision maker may select data that support the position of an influential person whom he or she is trying to please. For instance, a financial analyst was asked to investigate the cost-effectiveness of outsourcing the payroll department, so he gave considerable weight to the "facts" supplied by a provider of payroll services. This allowed him to justify having an outside firm assume responsibility for the payroll function—a decision he knew that the influential person favored. Political factors in decision making, therefore, present an ethical challenge to the decision maker.

Pressure from top management has been cited as a political force that leads managers to make overly optimistic forecasts in analyzing proposals for substantial investments. By inflating the probable benefits of a project and minimizing the downside, these managers lead the organization into initiatives that are likely to fall short of expectations.[21] An example would be top management placing heavy pressure on an automotive marketing executive to come up with a dramatic new model that will enhance the company's prestige and profits. Facing this pressure, the marketing executive makes an optimistic proposal for a new vehicle that will compete against the Rolls Royce. The company proceeds to build a $375,000 luxury sedan that becomes a complete flop, partially because the automobile company is perceived by the public as a producer of ordinary—not prestigious—vehicles.

Crisis and Conflict

In a crisis, many decision makers panic. They become less rational and more emotional than they would be in a calm environment. Decision makers who are adversely affected by crisis perceive it to be a stressful event. As a consequence, they concentrate poorly, use poor judgment, and think impulsively. Under crisis, some managers do not bother dealing with differences of opinion because they are under so much pressure. A smaller number of managers perceive a crisis as an exciting challenge that energizes them toward their best level of problem solving and decision making. Conflict is related to crisis because both can be an emotional experience. For example, a CEO might be

Facing a conflict can sometimes hamper decision making.

Harley-Davidson Uses Artificial Intelligence to Generate Sales Leads in New York City

The president of Harley-Davidson, New York City, Asaf Jacobi, said that a big challenge of doing business in New York City is that it is a highly competitive environment. To get the response rates a brand wants and needs to make a profit, the brand has to reach a large number of people. Jacobi said that after doing a number of radio ads and print advertising campaigns, it was apparent that digital advertising and marketing were best suited to reaching the right audience.

Artificial intelligence plays a key role in this situation. Jacobi began reading about how artificial intelligence can boost online marketing, so he contacted An AI marketing firm called Adgorithms. Jacobi began using Albert, an AI-driven marketing technology developed by Adgorithms, for the company's e-commerce advertising.

Adgorithms used machine learning to automatically detect the characteristics of existing customers and build an online profile for lookalike prospects—those whose demographic characteristics and personal preferences are similar to those of existing customers. "Lookalikes" are also those people who resemble previous high-value customers and are therefore more likely to purchase a motorcycle. Albert gets its client's campaigns out across different devices, such as desktops and mobiles, and paid channels such as social media and Internet search, along with e-mail messages. Albert found that consumers likely to purchase diamonds were also likely to purchase luxury motorcycles.

Harley-Davidson launched its first AI campaign, "48 Bikes in 48 Hours," in 2016 to reduce overstock and see how quickly AI could find out enough relevant information about customer prospects to meet sales goals. Jacobi reported some outstanding results since the application of artificial intelligence and its algorithms to marketing its line of motorcycles. Prior to Albert, the New York City division's best sales record was eight motorcycles in a single weekend. In the first two-day campaign using Albert, 15 motorcycles were sold.

Within three months, average daily website visits surged by 566 percent. In May 2016, the number of leads skyrocketed by 2,930 percent, one-half of which were lookalikes. At last report, Jacobi was attributing 40 percent of Harley-Davidson New York sales to Albert. So many calls were generated by Albert that Jacobi built a six-person call center to deal with the deluge of telephone calls. An example of a specific Albert discovery was that ads with the term "call" were performing 447% better than ads with the term "buy." As a result, ads were modified accordingly.

Harley-Davidson NYC used to project that only 2 percent of the population in New York City was poten-tial buyers for its motorcycles. Albert identified new audiences by correlating online behaviors with their likelihood of conversion. Ads could then be targeted to these potential customers. Albert drove in-store traffic by generating qualified leads, defined as customer prospects who express an interest in speaking to a sales representative by filling out a form on the dealership's website.

The advantage of AI for Harley-Davidson of New York was that it evaluated what was working across digital channels and what failed to work. Albert allocated resources only to what had been proven to work, thereby increasing the return on investment of digital marketing.

Jacobi said, "For there to be a technology that knows nothing about us, yet can come in and outdo us in its first shot, was incredible." Five other Harley franchises are now using Albert, with about 10 more evaluating the possibility.

QUESTIONS

1. Harley-Davidson is still struggling to find customers nationwide and in other countries as the pool of potential motorcycle buyers shrinks. If artificial intelligence was so helpful in boosting online sales in the New York City area, why hasn't Harley-Davidson used AI to boost sales in every Harley franchise in the country?

2. Based on the success of Albert, explain whether you would recommend that Harley-Davidson now stop all traditional advertising, such as print ads in magazines and television commercials.

3. Instead of spending money on Albert, what about Harley-Davidson management using common sense? Why not search online for people who have bought leather jackets, high leather boots, and bandanas?

Source: Original story created from information in the following sources: Brad Power, "How Harley-Davidson Used Artificial Intelligence to Increase New York Sales Leads by 2,930%," *Harvard Business Review*, https://hbr.org/2017/05/how-harley-davidson -used-predictive-analytics-to-increase-new-york-sales-leads-by -2930, May 20, 2017, pp. 1–7; "Harley-Davidson Says Artificial Intelligence Drives 40% of New York Sales," www.emarketer.com/ Article/Harley-Davidson-Says-Artificial-Intelligence-Drives-40-of -New-York-Sales/1014642, October 26, 2016, pp. 1–2; David Kaplan, "Speed Marketing: How Harley-Davidson Used AI to Drive 40% of Motorcycle Sales," www.geomarketing.com/speed -marketing-how-harley-davidson-used-ai-to-drive-40-percent-of -motorcycle-sales, July 10, 2017, pp. 1–4; Jamie Grill-Goodman, "Harley-Davidson Bets on Artificial Intelligence," https://risnews .com/harley-davidson-bets-artificial-intelligence, May 25, 2017, pp. 1–3.

in conflict with a member of the executive team over whether retirement benefits should be frozen. The conflict upsets the CEO to the point that he makes the poor decision of firing the executive in question.

Values of the Decision Maker

Values influence decision making at every step. Ultimately, all decisions are based on values. A manager who places a high value on the personal welfare of employees tries to avoid alternatives that create hardship for workers, and therefore implements decisions in ways that lessen turmoil. Another value that significantly influences decision making is the pursuit of excellence. A manager or professional who embraces the pursuit of excellence (and is therefore conscientious) will search for the high-quality alternative solution.

Attempting to preserve the status quo is a value held by many managers, as well as others. Clinging to the status quo is perceived as a hidden trap in decision making that can prevent people from making optimal decisions. People tend to cling to the status quo because they think they can prevent making a bad decision simply by not taking action at all.[22] If you value the status quo too highly, you may fail to make a decision that could bring about major improvements. For example, the sales manager might want to maintain a large outside sales force even though the vast majority of customers prefer to purchase online. Keeping more outside sales reps on the payroll than necessary prevents lowering the cost of selling company goods.

Procrastination

Many people are poor decision makers because they **procrastinate**, or delay taking action, without a valid reason. Procrastination results in indecisiveness and inaction and is a major cause of self-defeating behavior. People can overcome procrastination by learning how to become more self-disciplined. Part of the process involves setting goals for overcoming procrastination and conquering the problem in small steps. For example, a person might first practice making a deadline for a decision for a minor activity, such as responding to a group of e-mail inquiries.

procrastinate To delay taking action without a valid reason.

Biases that Influence Decision Making

The description of personality traits, values, and political factors as influences on decision making hints at the problem of biases when making decisions. These biases lead to predictable mistakes because the decision maker repeats the same error systematically. Among the many such biases investigated by decision theorists is overconfidence.[23] According to this bias, most of us are overconfident in our ability to estimate and we therefore do not acknowledge the true uncertainty. Overconfidence in our decisions can lead to ignoring some of the potential negatives in the situation. One of the managerial problems associated with overconfidence is that the person is likely to overlook the importance of contingency plans. For example, the executive cited above in relation to political pressures did not develop a plan to exit the super-luxury sedan business.

Another bias that affects decision makers after they have made a decision is confirmation bias, which refers to the idea that we pay the most attention to information that supports the decision we have made. At the same time, we dismiss or minimize information that does not support our decision. A problem with the confirmation bias is that it may interfere with profiting from decision mistakes. An example of confirmation bias in practice would be an executive who decides to outsource manufacturing to one supplier and stop outsourcing to another supplier. The executive now looks for examples of satisfactory products from the new supplier and ignores problems.

A decision-making bias that resembles narrow-minded thinking is the not-invented-here (NIH) syndrome. NIH is a negative attitude toward knowledge derived from an external source.[24] A marketing office experiencing the NIH syndrome might ignore useful new ideas from people in other departments, in disciplines outside of marketing, and from other companies. It takes a lot of deliberate effort to avoid rejecting ideas from external sources. A couple of the ideas about enhancing and improving creativity presented later in this chapter are helpful in overcoming the NIH syndrome.

The Nature of Creativity

Creativity in organizations has surged in importance in recent years for several reasons. First, the high-velocity economy requires that business firms come up with new ideas frequently. Second, a creative business culture attracts, retains, and often motivates knowledge workers. Third, using creative techniques helps generate ideas that the normal mode of brain functioning might miss.[25] **Creativity** can be defined simply as the process of developing good ideas that can be put into action. The term **innovation** emphasizes the commercialization part of creativity, such as developing an innovative product, as will be discussed in Chapter 16 about organizational change and innovation. We approach the nature of creativity from three perspectives: steps in the creative process, characteristics of creative people, and conditions necessary for creativity.

Steps in the Creative Process

Understanding the steps involved in creativity helps a person become more creative and better manage creativity among others. An old but well-accepted model of creativity can be applied to organizations. The model divides creative thinking into five steps, as shown in Figure 5-3. Not all creative thinking follows these steps exactly, but the model works much of the time.

Step 1 is *opportunity or problem recognition*: A person discovers that a new opportunity exists or a problem needs resolution. Step 2 is *immersion*: The individual concentrates on the problem and becomes immersed in it. He or she will recall and collect information that seems relevant, dreaming up alternatives without refining or evaluating them. Step 3 is *incubation*: The person keeps the assembled information in mind for a while. He or she does not appear to be working on the problem actively, yet the subconscious mind takes over. While the information simmers, it is arranged into meaningful patterns. One way to capitalize on the incubation phase of creativity is to deliberately take a break from creative thinking. Instead, engage in a routine activity such as updating your electronic address book or sorting through e-mail. By immersing yourself in an entirely different and less taxing mental activity, a solution to the creative problem may emerge.

Step 4 is *insight*: The problem-conquering solution flashes into the person's mind at an unexpected time, such as on the verge of sleep, during a shower, or while running. Insight is also called the *aha! experience*; all of a sudden, some-

The insight step in the creative process is essential.

Sangoiri/Shutterstock.com

FIGURE 5-3 Steps in the Creative Process

thing clicks. Step 5 is *verification and application*: The individual sets out to prove that the creative solution has merit. Verification procedures include gathering supporting evidence, logical persuasion, and experimenting with new ideas. Application requires tenacity because most novel ideas are at first rejected as being impractical.

Characteristics of Creative People

Creative workers are different in many ways from their less creative counterparts. The characteristics of creative people, including creative leaders, can be grouped into three key areas: knowledge, intellectual abilities, and personality. Yet, as explained by Robert J. Sternberg, so many things are true about some creative people, but there are exceptions. For example, most creative people are high in self-esteem, but not all. Yet one consistent attribute of creative people stands out—the decision to be creative. Creative people decide that they will forge their own path and follow it, for better or worse.[26]

Knowledge

Creative problem solving requires a broad background of information, including facts and observations. This is particularly true because creativity often takes the form of combining two or more existing things in a new and different way. Internet search engines become more profitable by combining the exquisite technology of the search engines with the concept behind the Yellow Pages. For example, if you search for a singer, you will receive pop-up ads selling his or her music.

Intellectual Abilities

Creative problem solvers tend to be bright rather than brilliant, even though some of the best-known creative people are brilliant. An example of a brilliant creative person is Elon Musk, the CEO of Tesla Motors. He is also one of the founders of the company that became PayPal, as well as the space exploration company, SpaceX. He is currently spearheading the construction of an underground Hyperloop between New York and Washington, a ride that will take 30 minutes. Musk holds undergraduate degrees in physics and business (reflecting more of his high intelligence!). A good sense of humor and intellectual playfulness are outstanding characteristics of a creative problem solver. Humor helps release creativity, and some creativity is required to be funny.

Creativity can stem from both *fluid intelligence* and *crystallized intelligence*. Fluid intelligence depends on raw processing ability, or how quickly and accurately we acquire information and solve problems. Like raw athletic ability, fluid intelligence begins to decline by age 30, partly because our nerve conduction slows. Crystallized intelligence is accumulated knowledge that increases with age and experience. The implication for a manager who wants to assemble a creative group is to staff it with workers of varying ages. Generation X members of the group might have the wildest, most unique ideas. However, the baby boomers might have better intuition as to what will work.

Creative people maintain a youthful curiosity throughout their lives. The curiosity is not centered just on their field of expertise; they are enthusiastic about solving puzzling problems. Creativity consultant Juanita Weaver notes that when viewing the world with open and curious eyes, anything can trigger a new idea.[27] A person might be playing with a cat and observe how the cat's claws extend and contract based on the needs of the moment. Voila! The cat-watcher thinks of a new concept for a studded snow tire.

Creative people think divergently. They can expand the number of alternatives to a problem, thus moving away from a single solution. Yet the creative thinker also knows when it is time to think convergently, narrowing the number of useful solutions so innovation can occur.

Personality

Creative people tend to have a special type of self-confidence labeled **creative self-efficacy**, the belief that one can be creative in a work role. The major contributors to creative self-efficacy are self-efficacy about the job in general, experience on the job, and a

creative self-efficacy The belief that one can be creative in a work role.

supervisor who serves as a good model and persuades the worker that he or she is capable of finding imaginative solutions.[28]

Creative people can tolerate the isolation necessary for developing ideas. Talking to others is a good source of ideas, yet at some point the creative problem solver has to work alone and concentrate. Creative people are frequently nonconformists and do not need strong approval from a group. Many creative problem solvers are risk takers and thrill seekers who find developing imaginative solutions to problems to be a source of excitement. As Todd Yellin, vice president of product at Netflix, explains it, "If you're not falling on your face, you're not leaning far enough forward to take risks."[29] (Netflix staffers are required to be creative.)

Creative people are also persistent, which is especially important because so many alternatives might have to be explored before finding a workable solution. Creative people enjoy dealing with ambiguity and chaos. Less creative people become quickly frustrated when task descriptions are unclear and disorder exists.

Conditions Necessary for Creativity

Certain individual and organizational conditions are necessary for—or at least enhance—the production of creative ideas. The most consistent of these conditions are described here.

Expertise, Creative-Thinking Skills, and Internal Motivation

Teresa M. Amabile has summarized 22 years of research about the conditions necessary for creativity in organizations, and later on, other observers have reported similar findings. Creativity takes place when three components join together: expertise, creative-thinking skills, and the right type of motivation.[30]

Expertise refers to the knowledge necessary to put facts together. The more facts floating around in your head, the more likely you are to combine them in some useful way. *Creative thinking* refers to how flexibly and imaginatively individuals approach problems. If you know how to keep digging for alternatives and avoid getting stuck in the status quo, your chances of being creative multiply. Persevering, or sticking with a problem to a conclusion, is essential for finding creative solutions. A few rest breaks to gain a fresh perspective may be helpful, but the creative person keeps coming back until a solution emerges. Quite often an executive will keep sketching different organizational charts on paper or with a graphics program before the one that will help the firm run smoothly surfaces.

The right type of motivation is the third essential ingredient for creative thought. A fascination with or passion for a task is more important than searching for external rewards. People will be the most creative when they are motivated primarily by the satisfaction and challenge of the work itself. Although Jeff Bezos ultimately became wealthy from building Amazon.com, he was primarily motivated by the challenge of finding a way to capitalize on the potential of the Internet as a marketing vehicle. Research conducted by Adam M. Grant and James W. Berry adds a new dimension to the link between intrinsic motivation and creativity. A series of three studies using both field and laboratory data found that when workers are motivated to help others, intrinsic motivation makes a stronger contribution to being rated as creative by the supervisor.[31]

experience of flow Being "in the zone"; total absorption in one's work.

Passion for the task and high intrinsic motivation contribute to a total absorption in the work and intense concentration, which is known as the **experience of flow**. When an experience is engrossing and enjoyable, the task becomes worth doing for its own sake regardless of the external consequences.[32] Perhaps you have had this experience when completely absorbed in a hobby or being at your best in a sport or dance. (*Flow* also means being "in the zone.") A highly creative businessperson, such as an entrepreneur developing a plan for worldwide distribution of a product, will often achieve the experience of flow. Self-Assessment 5-1 gives you an opportunity to think about your powers of concentration.

Environmental Need

Three factors outside the person play a key role in fostering creativity. An environmental need must stimulate the setting of a goal. This is another way of saying, "Necessity is the

SELF-ASSESSMENT 5-1

A Checklist of Behaviors and Attitudes Reflecting Good Concentration and Focus

Attitude or Behavior	Yes	No
1. I rarely miss a deadline on a work project.	X	
2. When I begin a work activity, I am able to get started almost immediately.	X	X
3. When I am introduced to a person for the first time, I usually catch his or her name clearly.	X	X
4. I rarely read an entire news article from a print or electronic newspaper.	X	X
5. I find messages longer than a tweet difficult to follow.	X	X
6. I haven't read an entire book, except when reading a book was required for a course.	X	X
7. I have been able to perform well in a mental activity such as playing poker, chess, checkers, or doing a crossword puzzle.	X	
8. I am good at spotting typographical and spelling errors while I am reading.	X	
9. It is difficult for me to watch a movie, television program, or sporting event without sending a tweet or a social media post about every 5 minutes.	X	
10. I enjoy activities that force me to concentrate, such as meditation or yoga.		X
11. A few minutes after meeting a person for the first time, I can recall the color of his or her eyes.	X	X
12. I rarely ever lose or misplace items such as keys, handbag or wallet, gloves, or smartphone.		X
13. I have considerable difficulty in sticking with one activity for more than 10 minutes.	X	X
14. While at the grocery store or supermarket, I usually neglect to purchase one or two items, even if they are on my shopping list.	X	X
15. It is easy for me to listen carefully to the words when my national anthem is being played, such as at a sporting event.		X
16. I can fall asleep readily by thinking intently about something.	X	X
17. It is uncomfortable for me to have a meal without background noise such as a television show, the radio, or other people talking around me.	X	X
18. At work or at play, I am so focused on what I am doing it seems that I am wearing blinders as do horses.	X	
19. I enjoy studying the details of whatever I am doing.	X	
20. I spend far too much time trying to find electronic or paper documents.	X	X

Scoring and Interpretation: The answers suggesting good concentration and focus are as follows:

1. Yes	5. No	9. No	13 No	17. No
2. Yes	6. No	10. Yes	14. No	18. Yes
3. Yes	7. Yes	11. Yes	15 Yes	19. Yes
4. No	8. Yes	12. Yes	16. Yes	20. No

The higher you scored out of the 20 questions, the more likely it is that you have good concentration and focus. Also, if it was a struggle for you to complete the checklist, you may have a problem with concentration and focus.

mother of invention." So often the light bulb is mentioned as an example of creativity, and there is a modern version to this tale. Light bulb manufacturers have observed that many aging people want to appear younger. In response to this need, the manufacturers have introduced dozens of new bulbs, including a flattering array of fluorescent, halogen, and new incandescent bulbs that are an improvement over soft light. These "natural light" bulbs make wrinkles and blemishes appear less evident. By responding to this new environmental need, light bulb sales have increased about 6 percent.[33] Facing a conflict or struggle can also present an environmental need, such as a company needing a way of getting a new product to market fast in order to survive.

Encouragement from Others and Having Creative Coworkers

Another external factor in creativity is encouragement, including a permissive atmosphere that welcomes new ideas. A manager who encourages imaginative and original thinking, and does not punish people for making honest mistakes, is likely to receive creative ideas from employees. A study suggests that encouragement from family and friends, as well as from a supervisor, enhances creative thinking on the job. The participants in the study were both administrative and production employees in the Bulgarian knitwear industry. Support for creativity was measured by questions such as, "My family and friends outside this organization give me useful feedback about my ideas concerning the workplace." Supervisors rated employee creativity. The researchers concluded that (a) supervisors and coworkers and (b) family and friends each made their own contribution to worker creativity.[34]

Mood

You may have noticed that you think more creatively when you are in a good mood. A positive mood apparently also contributes to creative job performance, even if mood might not be truly classified as a condition necessary for creativity. One finding from a larger study suggests that managers with high emotional intelligence can sometimes trigger enough positive affect in their subordinates to enhance their creativity.[35] In other words, if the manager can help workers feel good, those workers might be better creative problem solvers.

A study of 222 employees in seven companies in three high-tech industries indicated that a positive mood made a positive, significant contribution to creativity. However, only weak evidence was found that producing a creative idea enhanced one's mood. Measurements of creativity were taken through both self-ratings and coworker ratings.[36]

Moderate Time Pressures

Some people are at their creative best when facing heavy time pressures. Several studies, however, suggest that feeling crunched leads to a creativity drop for most people. The greater the time pressure, the less likely workers are to solve a tricky problem, envision a new product, or have the type of "aha!" experiences that lead to innovation. Time pressure is a creativity dampener because it limits people's freedom to reflect on different options and directions. When workers believe they are faced with an urgent mission, the negative effects of time pressures are reduced.[37]

Enhancing and Improving Creativity

LEARNING OBJECTIVE 4
Enhance your creative problem-solving ability.

A unifying theme runs through all forms of creativity training and suggestions for creativity improvement: Creative problem solving requires an ability to overcome traditional thinking. The concept of traditional thinking is relative and hard to pin down but generally refers to a standard and frequent way of finding a solution to a problem. A traditional solution to a problem is thus a model or recurring solution. For example, traditional thinking suggests that to increase revenue, a retail store should conduct a sale. Creative thinking would point toward other solutions, such as increasing revenue by holding dramatic in-store demonstrations of a few products.

The central task in becoming creative is to break down rigid thinking that blocks new ideas. A conventional-thinking manager might accept the long-standing policy that spending more than $5,000 requires three levels of approval. A creative leader might ask, "Why do we need three levels of approval for spending $5,000? If we trust people enough to make them managers, why can't they have budget authorization to spend up to $10,000?"

Overcoming traditional thinking is often characterized as *thinking outside the box*, an expression that has become a cliché to the point that many people find it annoying. A "box" in this sense is a category that confines and restricts thinking. During the aftermath of Hurricane Katrina that hit the Gulf Coast in 2005, rescue specialists thought outside the box regarding where to lodge rescue workers and construction workers. Cruise ships were hired, giving the workers temporary living quarters offshore. Here we describe several illustrative approaches and techniques for enhancing employee creativity. Recognize also that the conditions for creativity just described can be converted into techniques for creativity enhancement. For example, a manager might be able to enhance creativity by encouraging imaginative thinking.

1. *Brainstorming.* Brainstorming, which most of us have already done, is the best-known technique for developing mental flexibility. The technique is also widely used to find solutions for real problems. Brainstorming is also accomplished online—participants from different locations enter their suggestions into a computer. Each participant's input appears simultaneously on the screens of the other participants. In this way, nobody feels intimidated by a dominant member, and participants think more independently. To increase the efficiency of brainstorming, participants are sometimes told in advance of the problem or problems to be solved. Prethinking can result in some more refined ideas being brought to the brainstorming session.

Refinements to brainstorming continue to evolve, such as having group members draw their solutions the best they can if they are not skilled at drawing. One reason drawing as a brainstorming technique can be effective is that some people have difficulty describing a process or thing strictly in words, making diagrams helpful.[38] Clyde, a member of a brainstorming team at a brewery, might say, "I've got an idea that will make our beer bottles stand out from the competition. Let me sketch if for you on the whiteboard."

The Skill-Development Exercise gives you a chance to apply brainstorming to a practical business problem.

Brainstorming can be done in small groups.

goodluz/Shutterstock.com

2. *Idea quotas.* A straightforward and effective technique for enhancing worker creativity is to simply demand that workers come up with good ideas. Being creative therefore becomes a concrete work goal. Thomas Edison used idea quotas, with his personal quota being one minor invention every 10 days and a major invention every 6 months. Google company practice (not quite a formal policy) permits some technical employees to devote 20 percent of their time to thinking up great new ideas, even with an uncertain financial payoff. Note that this Google practice refers to a *time* quota for ideas, yet the time allotted to ideas is likely to result in generating ideas. Another aspect of forcing the generation of ideas at Google is an intranet (internal website) that regularly collects fresh ideas from employees. Every employee spends a fraction of the workday on research and development. Two of the tangible outcomes of the intranet technique and the thinking time allotment are Gmail and AdSense.[39]

3. *Heterogeneous groups.* Forming heterogeneous groups can enhance creativity because a diverse group brings various viewpoints to the problem at hand. Key diversity factors include professional discipline, job experiences, and a variety of demographic factors. Diverse groups encourage diverse thinking, which is the essence of creativity.[40] The most influential aspects of diversity are inner qualities such as personality, values, and abilities, also known as deep-level diversity.[41] In building a diverse group for creativity, it would be helpful to choose people from different demographic and cultural groups who have a variety of personalities, values, and abilities.

   Individual differences in creative self-efficacy can influence the contribution of group heterogeneity to creativity. A study of 318 employees and 68 teams from Chinese companies found that cognitive team diversity facilitated individual creativity mostly when the team members were high in creative self-efficacy. (Cognitive team diversity refers to perceived differences in thinking styles, knowledge, skills, values, and beliefs among individual team members.)[42]

4. *Financial incentives.* A variety of laboratory studies have concluded that working for external rewards, particularly financial rewards, dampens creativity.[43] If you focus on the reward, you may lose out on the joy (internal reward) of being creative. In work settings, however, financial incentives are likely to spur imaginative thinking. Such incentives might include paying employees for useful suggestions and paying scientists royalties for patents that become commercially useful. For example, IBM is consistently one of the leading companies with respect to being awarded patents. IBM employees who are awarded patents are paid cash bonuses.

5. *Architecture and physical layout.* Many companies restructure space to fire up creativity, harness energy, and enhance the flow of knowledge and ideas. Any configuration of the physical environment that decreases barriers to divergence, incubation, and convergence is likely to stimulate the flow of creative thinking.[44] The reasoning is that creative thinking is more likely to be enhanced by cubicles rather than corner offices, by elevators rather than escalators, and by atriums rather than hallways. In short, creating the opportunity for physical interaction facilitates the flow of ideas, which in turn facilitates creative thinking. However, as described in Chapter 2, some workers dislike open work areas because it interferes with their concentration and creative thinking.

   Closely related to using physical layout to enhance creativity, several companies assign designated employees to share office space with employees of other companies in order to share and cross-fertilize ideas. The concept is part of coworking in which freelancers share office space with other freelancers to save office costs, but also to exchange ideas with other freelancers and remote workers. Nearly one in ten coworkers is employed by large or medium-sized businesses. Twitter has deployed coworking in teams in the United States, and Google has done the same in London. A spokesperson said that Google is less interested in saving rent than in meeting smart people.[45] The purpose of meeting these smart people is to spark creative thinking.

6. *Inspiration.* A leadership strategy for enhancing creativity and innovation is to inspire workers to think creatively. Inspiring creativity encompasses a wide range of

behaviors, including establishing a permissive atmosphere. Similarly, when workers believe they are working for a cause, such as helping people plan their financial futures, or curing a disease, they are more likely to be creative. The unusual creativity of Elon Musk has inspired workers throughout the companies he heads, and those he has headed the past, to think creatively.

7. *Feedback seeking.* An effective way for managers to facilitate creativity is to encourage workers to seek feedback on their own creative performance. A conclusion derived from a multitude of analyses is that individuals can enhance their creative problem solving by actively seeking feedback on their work from various sources. The proactive behavior of actively seeking feedback is important because external sources may not always provide their feedback spontaneously or at the right time. It is also likely that the external sources, such as supervisors and coworkers, may not be aware of the employee's need for support.[46] An example of asking or feedback from an external source would be to present an idea to a coworker and ask, "Have you ever seen anything like this before?"

8. *Creativity training.* A standard approach to enhancing individual and organizational creativity is to offer creativity training to many workers throughout the organization. Much of creativity training encompasses the ideas already covered in this chapter, such as learning to overcome traditional thinking and engaging in some type of brainstorming. Various techniques are used to encourage more flexible thinking, such as engaging in child's play, squirting each other with water guns, and scavenger hunts. An extreme technique is to deprive participants of food and rest for 24 hours so their defenses are weakened, and they are then mentally equipped to "think differently." Other creativity training techniques are more cerebral, such as having participants solve puzzles and ask "what if" questions.

   Creativity training would be of little value if creativity could not be taught. The comments of Wharton School professor Ron Schrift are representative about the teaching of creativity. He notes first that there are individual differences in creativity, with this ability following a normal distribution. Within these limits, he adds that, if you train yourself, you can become more creative. "Because creativity can be developed; it can be taught."[47]

Implications for Managerial Practice

1. A widely recommended decision tool for finding the root cause of a problem is to ask a series of questions, called the *Seven Whys* (or sometimes *Five Whys*). By asking "why" seven times, you are likely to get to the core issue of a problem. For example, as a CEO you observe that turnover is way above average in one division. The questioning might proceed in this manner:

   Question 1: "Why is turnover high?"

   Answer 1: "Because we have loads of people who decide to leave the firm."

   Question 2: "Why are they leaving?"

   Answer 2: "I guess they are not too happy."

   Question 3: "Why aren't they happy?"

   Answer 3: "They may not like the working conditions here too much."

   Question 4: "Why don't they like the working conditions?"

   Answer 4: "It's kind of a high-pressure atmosphere."

   Question 5: "Why is it a high-pressure atmosphere?"

   Answer 5: "The supervisors stay on people's backs."

   Question 6: "Why do the supervisors stay on people's backs?"

   Answer 6: "Most of them think that the best way to get results is to keep the pressure on employees."

Question 7: "Why don't supervisors know more about supervising workers?"

Answer 7: "A lot of them need more training in managing people, or they shouldn't have been chosen for supervisory positions in the first place."

2. Learning to be more creative is like learning other skills: Patience and time are required. As a manager, by practicing techniques and attitudes, you will gain the confidence and skill to build a group (or company) where creative thinking is widespread. A desirable goal is to find a way to tap the creativity of everyone for whom you are responsible.[48]

3. A basic approach to enhancing your own creativity is to give yourself some quiet time to think, and free up space in your brain to allow new ideas to emerge. Taking walks and meditating often enhance creativity because you have the opportunity to relax your brain. Peter Sims, the CEO of think tank Parliament, Inc., explains, "If you want people to be inventive, they need space. Steve Jobs took lots of walks. I see Mark Zuckerberg taking walks on the roof of Facebook's new headquarters."[49]

Summary of Key Points

1. *Work through the decision-making model when faced with a major decision.* A decision takes place when a person chooses from among two or more alternatives in order to solve a problem. The decision-making model presented here incorporates the ideas that managers make decisions in a generally rational framework, yet intuition and judgment also enter into the model. The seven steps in the model are as follows: (1) identify and diagnose the problem, (2) establish decision criteria, (3) develop creative alternatives, (4) evaluate the alternatives, (5) choose one alternative, (6) implement the decision, and (7) evaluate and control.

2. *Identify and describe factors that influence the effectiveness of decision making.* Heuristics are often used to simplify decision making. A host of influences contribute to decision-making quality, including intuition, personality and cognitive intelligence, emotional intelligence, quality of information and Big Data, the application of artificial intelligence (AI), political considerations, crisis and conflict, the values of the decision maker, procrastination, and decision-making biases.

3. *Understand the nature of creative decision making in organizations.* Understanding the steps involved in creativity can help a person become more creative and better manage creativity among others. The steps are as follows: (1) opportunity or problem recognition, (2) immersion, (3) incubation, (4) insight, and (5) verification and application.

Creative workers are different from others in several key areas. They typically have a broad background of knowledge and tend to be bright rather than brilliant. Both fluid intelligence and crystallized intelligence contribute to creativity. Creative people have a youthful curiosity and think divergently. Creative workers tend to have a positive self-image, including creative self-efficacy, and are often nonconformists who enjoy intellectual thrills, along with ambiguity and chaos.

For creativity to occur, three components must join together: expertise, creative-thinking skills, and internal motivation characterized by a passion for the task. Total absorption in the work, also known as the *experience of flow*, is also important. An environmental need should be present, including facing a conflict, as well as encouragement from others and having creative coworkers. A positive mood also contributes to creativity, as do moderate time pressures.

4. *Enhance your creative problem-solving ability.* A unifying theme runs through all forms of creativity training and suggestions for creativity improvement: Creative problem solving requires an ability to overcome traditional thinking. Techniques for enhancing creativity include brainstorming, imposing idea quotas, forming heterogeneous groups, offering financial incentives for creative problem solving in work settings, and using a physical layout conducive to creative thinking. Also helpful are inspiration for creative thinking, seeking feedback on creativity, and creativity training.

Key Terms and Phrases

decision, p. 88

problem, p. 88

decision criteria, p. 90

heuristics, p. 91

intuition, p. 92

self-efficacy, p. 93

Big Data, p. 94

artificial intelligence, p. 94

procrastinate, p. 97

creativity, p. 98

innovation, p. 98

creative self-efficacy, p. 99

experience of flow, p. 100

1. Can you give an example of an outstandingly successful decision in business? Explain why you consider the decision to be an outstanding success.
2. A handful of businesspersons who have earned billions of dollars stand ready to, or already have, purchased a professional sports team. To what extent do you think emotions influenced their decision to purchase the team?
3. Which decision criteria are relevant for you in choosing a career?
4. Provide an example from your own Internet use that you think illustrates the use of Big Data to influence you to make a purchase. To what extent did you feel manipulated or exploited?
5. A technique for creative problem solving is to remind oneself of a problem just before going to sleep. Upon waking up, a good solution often presents itself. How does this technique relate to the steps in the creative process?
6. Plastic straws have been under considerable attack in recent years from environmentalists and politicians. At the same time, many consumers complain that paper straws are inadequate because they disintegrate quickly. How can companies that produce drinking straws go about finding a creative solution to the threats to their industry?
7. Work together in a small group to reach a conclusion about several new products or services the world really needs. Explain why you need creative thinking to answer this question.
8. Recent experiments suggest that walking improves the free flow of ideas and creativity. If you can squeeze in the time, take a 30-minute walk sometime during the next week and observe if you can then think more creatively about any problem you are facing.
9. Shopping malls continue to show a gradual decline in terms of occupancy throughout North America. What creative suggestion can you offer mall owners to fill more of their space? (Maybe you can sell your idea after answering this question.)
10. Ask an experienced worker what he or she believes is the most important action a manager can take to enhance creative thinking among group members. Compare the response you get with the information in this chapter.

CASE PROBLEM: Real Estate Agent Bree Wants to Become More Creative

Thirty-year-old Bree is a commercial real estate agent, working for Coalition Properties in Vermont. Although she works for Coalition, the only money she earns is from sales commissions, usually about 6 percent of the sale price of a property. Bree also pays part of the advertising expenses for properties for which she is the listing agent.

Bree is earning enough money to keep her satisfied, but the owner of the agency, Courtney, is not totally satisfied with her performance. Courtney recently said to Bree during a review of monthly sales, "Bree, I want to you to break through with some bigger sales. You are closing sales here and there, but Coalition needs some bigger sales to make a respectable profit."

Bree responded, 'I am not disputing what you say, but could you give me an example of the type of bigger sale you are referring to?"

"I've got a good example for you," said Courtney. "We are the listing agent for a 35-acre plot on Castle Road that sits across from private homes and a senior residence. The property has been for sale for 20 years with no buyer yet. You haven't even generated one lead for the property."

Bree responded, "True enough, but that great big property had been sitting there for many years before I joined Coalition. The problem seems to be that the property is zoned for residential, and there are already enough housing developments close by. No developer wants to risk such a big development."

"I think I see the problem," said Courtney. "You would be earning more income for yourself and the Coalition if you were less conventional in your thinking. You are a valuable member of our team, but you would be even more valuable if you were a more creative real estate agent."

With a quizzical expression, Bree said, "I am creative with respect to decorating my house, cooking, and choosing gifts for friends and family members. But being creative in commercial real estate sales is pretty tough. Either someone wants to buy a property or not. Let me think about how I can become more creative, and I'll get back to you with my plan."

Case Questions

1. What is your opinion of Bree's belief that it is difficult to be creative in a field such as commercial real estate selling?
2. What practical steps might Bree take to become more creative in her selling?
3. What role should Courtney play in helping Bree become more creative as a real estate agent?

Endnotes

1. Original story created from facts and observations in the following sources: Olivier Leclerc and Mihnea Moldoveanu, "Five Routes to More Innovative Problem Solving," *McKinsey Quarterly*, April 2012, pp. 1–9; Gordon Pitts, "Rob McEwen: Mining Magnate with a Vision," *The Globe and Mail*, February 3, 2012, pp. 1–3; Linda Teschler, "He Struck Gold on the Net (Really)," *Fast Company*, May 31, 2002; Eric Jackson, "Rob McEwen Interview: On Gold Prices, Gold Miners and Bitcoin," Forbes, www.forbes.com/sites/ericjackson/2013/08/20/rob-mcewen-interview-on-gold-prices-gold-miners-and-bitcoin/#48d44dc07506, August 20, 2013, pp. 1–7.

2. Survey cited in Emma Seppala, "How Senior Executives Find Time to Be Creative," *Harvard Business Review*, https://hbr.org/2016/09/how-senior-executives-find-time-to-be-creative, September 12, 2016, pp. 1–2.

3. Ben Leubsdorf and David Gauthier-Villars, 'Nobel Goes to Economist Richard Thaler," *The Wall Street Journal*, October 10, 2017, p. A2.

4. "Starbucks' Schultz Played a Hunch," *Executive Leadership*, July 2004, p. 8.

5. Dwayne Spradlin, "Are You Solving the Right Problem?" *Harvard Business Review*, September 2012, pp. 86–87.

6. Quoted in "How to Succeed in 2005," *Business 2.0*, December 2004, p. 118.

7. Gerd Gigerenzer and Reinhard Selten (eds.), *Bounded Rationality: The Adaptive Toolbox* (Cambridge, MA: MIT Press, 2001).

8. Cited in Angela Chen, "To Achieve Success, Be More Logical and Take a Scientific View of Your Emotions," *The Wall Street Journal*, December 31, 2013. p. D1.

9. Eugene Sadler-Smith and Erella Shefy, "The Intuitive Executive: Understanding and Applying 'Gut Feel' in Decision-Making," *The Academy of Management Executive*, November 2004, pp. 76–91.

10. "Intuition by Guy Laliberté." *Forbes*, September 25, 2017, p. 139

11. Josh Tyrangiel, "Tim Cook's Freshman Year," *Bloomberg Businessweek*, December 16, 2012, p. 78.

12. C. Chet Miller and R. Duane Ireland, "Intuition in Strategic Decision Making: Friend or Foe in the Fast-Paced 21st Century?" *The Academy of Management Executive*, February 2005, pp. 19–30.

13. Jared Sandberg, "Deciders Suffer Alone; Nondeciders Make Everyone Else Suffer," *The Wall Street Journal*, November 8, 2005, p. B1.

14. Michael A. West and James L. Farr (eds.), *Innovation and Creativity at Work: Psychological and Organizational Strategies* (New York: Wiley, 1990).

15. Rasmus Hougaard, Jacqueline Carter, and Gitte Dybkjaer, "Spending 10 Minutes a Day on Mindfulness Subtly Changes the Way You React to Everything," *Harvard Business Review*, https://hbr.org/2017/01/spending-10-minutes-a-day-on-mindfulness-subtly-changes-the-way-you-react-to-everything, January 18, 2017, pp. 1–3.

16. Rachel Evans and Claire Boston, "Crunching Data to Predict Stores' Death," *Chicago Tribune*, October 22, 2017, p. 3.

17. Thomas H. Davenport and D. J. Patil, "Data Scientist: The Sexiest Job of the 21st Century," *Harvard Business Review*, October 2012, p. 70.

18. Andrew McAfee and Erik Byrnjolfsson, "Big Data: The Management Revolution," *Harvard Business Review*, October 12, p. 62.

19. Interview with Brian Krzanich, "Companies Must Use AI—or Else," *The Wall Street Journal*, October 24, 2017, p. R9.

20. Sam Schechner, "Algorithms Move into Management," *The Wall Street Journal*, December 11, 2017, p. B1.

21. Dan Lovallo and Daniel Kahneman, "Delusions of Success: How Optimism Undermines Executives' Decisions," *Harvard Business Review*, July 2003, p. 56.

22. John S. Hammond, Ralph L. Keeney, and Howard Rafia, "The Hidden Traps in Decision Making," *Harvard Business Review*, September–October 1998, p. 50.

23. Max H. Bazerman, *Judgment in Managerial Decision Making*, 5th ed. (New York: Wiley, 2002), pp. 31–33.

24. David Antons and Frank T. Piller, "Opening the Black Box of 'Not Invented Here': Attitudes, Decision Biases, and Behavior Consequences," *Academy of Management Perspectives*, May 2015, p. 193.

25. Juanita Weaver, "The Missing Think," *Entrepreneur*, January 2003, p. 68.

26. Robert J. Sternberg, "Creativity as a Decision," *American Psychologist*, May 2002, p. 376.

27. Juanita Weaver, "The Mental Picture: Bringing Your Definition of Creativity into Focus," *Entrepreneur*, February 2003, p. 69.

28. Pamela Tierney and Steven M. Farmer, "Creative Self-Efficacy: Its Potential Antecedents and Relationship to Creative Performance," *Academy of Management Journal*, December 2002, pp. 1137–1148.

29. Quoted in "The 100 Most Creative People in Business," *Fast Company*, June 2017, p. 39.

30. Teresa M. Amabile, "How to Kill Creativity," *Harvard Business Review*, September–October 1998, pp. 78–79.

31. Adam M. Grant and James W. Berry, "The Necessity of Others Is the Mother of Invention: Intrinsic and Prosocial Motivations, Perspective Taking, and Creativity," *Academy of Management Journal*, February 2011, pp. 73–96.

32. Mihaly Csikszentmihalyi, "If We Are So Rich, Why Aren't We Happy?" *American Psychologist*, October 1999, p. 824.

33. Sally Beatty, "The 2,500 Watt Makeover," *The Wall Street Journal*, August 5, 2005, p. W1.

34. Nora Madjar, Greg R. Oldham, and Michael G. Pratt, "There's No Place Like Home? The Contributions of Work and Nonwork to Creativity Support to Employee's Creative Performance," *Academy of Management Journal*, August 2002, pp. 757–767.

35. Michael R. Parke, Myeong-Gu Seo, and Ellad N. Sherf, "Regulating and Facilitating: The Role of Emotional Intelligence in Maintaining and Using Positive Affect for Creativity," *Journal of Applied Psychology*, May 2015, pp. 917–934.

36. Teresa M. Amabile, Sigal G. Barsade, Jennifer S. Mueller, and Barry M. Staw, "Affect and Creativity at Work: A Daily Longitudinal Test," *Harvard Business School Working Papers*, 2002–2003.

37. Research cited in Bridget Murray, "A Ticking Clock Means a Creativity Drop," *Monitor on Psychology*, November 2002, p. 24; Teresa M. Amabile, Constance N. Hadley, and Steven J. Kramer, "Creativity under the Gun," *Harvard Business Review*, August 2002, pp. 52–61.

38. Art Markman, "Your Team Is Brainstorming All Wrong," *Harvard Business Review*, https://hbr.org/2017/05/your-team-is-brainstorming-all-wrong, May 18, 2017, pp. 1–4.

39. Christopher Mims, "Google's '20% Time,' Which Brought You Gmail and AdSense, Is Now as Good as Dead," https://qz.com/115831/googles-20-time-which-brought-you-gmail-and-adsense-is-now-as-good-as-dead/, August 16, 2013, pp. 1–5.

40. Leigh Thompson, "Improving the Creativity of Organizational Work Groups," *Academy of Management Executive*, February 2003, p. 102; G. Pasacal Zachary, "Mighty Is the Mongrel," *Fast Company*, July 2000, p. 272.

41. Tomas Chamorrow-Premuzic, "Does Diversity Actually Increase Creativity?" *Harvard Business Review*, https://hbr.org/2017/06/does-diversity-actually-increase-creativity, June 22, 2017, pp. 1–6.

42. Shung J. Shin, Tae-Yeol Kim, Jeong-Yeon Lee, and Lin Bian, "Cognitive Team Diversity and Individual Team Member Creativity: A Cross-Level Interaction," *Academy of Management Journal*, February 2012, pp. 197–201.

43. Beth A. Hennessey and Teresa M. Amabile, "Reward, Intrinsic Motivation, and Creativity," *American Psychologist*, June 1998, pp. 674–675.

44. Dorothy Leonard and Walter Swap, "Igniting Creativity," *Workforce*, October 1999, pp. 87–89.

45. Greg Lindsay, "Working Beyond the Cube," *Fast Company*, March 2013, pp. 34–38.

46. Katleen E. M. De Stobbeleir, Susan J. Ashford, and Dirk Buyens, "Self-Regulation of Creativity at Work: The Role of Feedback Seeking Behavior in Creative Performance," *Academy of Management Journal*, August 2011, pp. 811–831.

47. "Can Creativity Be Taught?" Knowledge@Wharton, http://knowledge.wharton.upenn.edu/article/can-creativity-be-taught/, August 27, 2014, pp. 1–3.

48. Juanita Weaver, "Food for Thought," *Entrepreneur*, March 2003, pp. 62, 63.

49. Quoted in Seppala, "How Senior Executives Find Time to Be Creative," p. 4.

Foundation Concepts of Motivation

kurhan/Shutterstock.com

Learning Objectives

After reading and studying this chapter and doing the exercises, you should be able to:

1. Explain how worker engagement is part of employee motivation.

2. Describe several need theories of motivation, including the needs hierarchy, the two-factor theory, and the achievement–power–affiliation triad.

3. Summarize the key propositions of goal theory and reinforcement theory.

4. Explain the expectancy theory of motivation and its tie-in with self-efficacy.

5. Explain how equity theory and social comparison contribute to motivation.

6. Use social learning theory to motivate yourself.

7. Recognize the importance of both intrinsic and extrinsic motivators.

8. Explain how personality and cultural factors are related to motivation.

CarMax, with headquarters in Richmond, Virginia, is the largest retailer of used cars in the United States. The company operates more than 185 stores in 39 states nationwide, with all the stores having the sparkling look of a new-car dealership. CarMax leadership regards itself as having revolutionized the used-car business by delivering the high-integrity car-buying experience customers want and deserve. CarMax is known for reducing the stress that is often associated with purchasing a vehicle by offering a no-haggle, no-hassle experience, along with an extensive selection of vehicles.

CarMax employs 24,000 nationwide. During a recent 12-month period, the company retailed 671,000 used cars and sold 391,686 vehicles wholesale at its in-store auctions. A major factor contributing to the success and growth of CarMax is the company's effort to keep its workforce motivated by satisfying the needs and interests of its associates. CarMax president and chief executive officer Bill Hash said, "Our associates are our most important asset and strongest differentiator." CarMax's chief human resources officer and senior vice president, Diane Long Cafritz, plays a key role in developing programs to satisfy the needs of associates. She also advises managers throughout the company on how to motivate and retain associates.

CarMax operates a committee to ensure that employee morale is high. Managers are expected to be good listeners and to be able to incorporate feedback from associates into their approach to leadership and management. CarMax offers extensive training programs and opportunities to help employees grow professionally and personally.

One of the ways in which CarMax fosters employee success is by assigning mentors to all new hires. According to one associate, the company's nurturing environment "helped me become a better person." Employees in most positions receive more than 40 hours per year of job training. Managers emphasize helping employees to develop their self-confidence.

CarMax recognizes top-performing store associates through membership in the President's Club. The honor includes being recognized at company meetings and the use of demo cars at certain levels of accomplishment. Each fall, members of the President's Club are invited, along with a guest, to a formal recognition gala in Las Vegas with the senior management team. CarMax pays the travel expenses plus the cost of a one-night hotel stay. The event includes dinner, dancing, and special entertainment.[1]

The story about CarMax illustrates the initiatives many employers take to keep their workforces motivated, satisfied, and engaged in their work. Employee engagement is one of the foundational aspects of motivation presented in this chapter, and it has become the major thrust of work-motivation efforts in recent years. In the following chapter, we describe managerial techniques designed to enhance motivation, all based on motivation theory. This chapter also touches on practical approaches to motivation, but it starts with the basics of motivation.

Knowledge of and skill in motivating people are topics of perennial interest to managers and professionals and important contributors to their eventual success. Motivation (in a work setting) is the process by which behavior is mobilized and sustained in the interest of achieving organizational goals. We know a person is motivated when he or she actually expends effort toward goal attainment. Motivation is complex and encompasses a broad range of behaviors, many of which are described in this and the following chapter.

Employee Engagement for Motivation

Employee engagement has become a positive buzzword in business and other organizations. In popular use, the term has come to mean almost any favorable attitude a worker has about a job. The more scientific meaning of employee engagement refers to high levels of personal investment in the work tasks performed on the job.[2] Engagement centers on an individual's involvement, satisfaction, commitment, and enthusiasm for work. The

---

motivation In a work setting, the process by which behavior is mobilized and sustained in the interest of achieving organizational goals.

LEARNING OBJECTIVE 1
Explain how worker engagement is part of employee motivation.

employee engagement High levels of personal investment in the work tasks performed on the job.

engaged worker has a positive motivational state that propels him or her to find meaning in work.[3]

If you are work engaged, you invest emotional energy into the job, and the job becomes part of your self-image. As a result, you are motivated to accomplish work and attain goals. The engaged worker will also be a good organizational citizen. A recent State of Employee Engagement Survey indicated that in today's workplace, employee demand for continuous professional development, accelerated career growth, and "always-on" engagement is getting stronger.[4]

Self-Assessment 6-1 provides you an opportunity to relate the concept of work engagement to yourself.

Although the quiz you just took might imply that worker engagement is a constant, engagement does show some variation within the same person from time to time. Research conducted in a variety of industries suggests that work engagement is subject to moderate fluctuations day by day around an average level of engagement.[5] A highly engaged person is therefore unlikely to be totally detached from work on a given day, but that person will occasionally show a decline in engagement.

Jim Harter, the chief scientist of employee engagement and well-being at the Gallup Organization, observes that engaged workers have bought into the purpose of the organization, and are trying to make a difference. This is a primary reason they are usually the most productive employees. The engaged worker stands out because, according to research with thousands of organizations, only 30 percent of employees are committed to doing a good job. Approximately 50 percent of employees do enough work just to get by. About 20 percent of employees act out their discontent in counterproductive ways such as spreading negative attitudes to coworkers, staying home from work, and driving away customers through poor service.[6] Worker engagement in the studies mentioned in this section is measured by questionnaires similar to the one presented, My Work Engagement Tendencies.

A broad perspective on why work engagement is important for the individual is that he or she contributes to the prosperity of the organization, and therefore contributes to a winning team. As the organization prospers, so does the individual in terms of compensation and opportunities for advancement.

The positive outcomes described can also be attributed to the fact that engaged employees want to come to work, understand their jobs, and understand how their individual work contributes to the success of the total organization. In the words of Jim Harter, "Engaged workers are more attentive and vigilant. They look out for the needs of their coworkers and the overall enterprise because they personally 'own' the result of their work and that of the organization."[7] Based on close to 50,000 work units and 1.4 million employees, organizations that had high levels of employee engagement experienced the following outcomes:

- Higher customer satisfaction ratings
- Higher profitability
- Higher productivity (the amount of resources used to attain a desired output)
- Lower voluntary employee turnover (workers the employer did not intentionally let go)
- Fewer accidents involving injuries to people and damage to equipment
- Less shrinkage (theft by customers and employees)
- Lower absenteeism
- Fewer safety incidents with patients (observed in medical settings)
- Fewer quality defects[8]

In general, work units scoring in the top half of employee engagement nearly doubled their chances of attaining these positive results compared with those in the bottom half. Furthermore, work units in the top 1 percent of employee engagement were four times more likely to be successful than those in the bottom 1 percent.[9]

SELF-ASSESSMENT 6-1

My Work Engagement Tendencies

Indicate the extent to which each of the following statements describes your behavior or attitude by circling one number. If you are not currently working, relate the statements to any previous position you have held. The numbers refer to disagree strongly (DS), disagree (D), neither agree nor disagree (N), agree (A), and agree strongly (AS). Consider enlisting the help of someone who knows your behavior and attitudes well to help you respond accurately to the statements.

Statement about Job and Work	DS	D	N	A	AS
1. I feel filled with energy while at work.	1	2	(3)	4	(5)
2. My work usually starts to get a little dull after the first couple of hours on the job.	5	4	3	(2)	1
3. I am very proud of my work.	1	2	3	(4)	5
4. I plan to quit my job as soon as a better one comes along.	5	4	(3)	2	1
5. While at work, I often daydream about how nice it would be to be retired.	5	4	(3)	2	1
6. My job is a key part of who I am.	(1)	2	3	4	5
7. I think that helping my coworkers is an important part of my job.	1	2	3	4	(5)
8. I feel an emotional attachment toward my company.	(1)	2	3	4	5
9. I look forward to each workday with loads of excitement.	1	2	(3)	4	5
10. I should really find a different line of work.	5	4	3	2	(1)
11. The most exciting thing about my job is the fact that I get paid.	5	4	3	2	(1)
12. I really care about the welfare of my company.	1	2	3	4	(5)
13. It is really boring answering these questions about my job and work.	(5)	4	3	2	1
14. Almost every detail of my job interests me.	1	2	3	(4)	5
15. My job inspires me.	1	2	(3)	4	5

Scoring and Interpretation: Calculate your score by adding up the numbers circled:

60–75: You are intensely engaged and involved in your work and job, which should contribute substantially to your job satisfaction as well as your job performance.

30–59: You have an average degree of engagement and commitment in your work and job.

15–29: You are below average in work engagement and commitment. Solicit feedback from others to see if this low score is warranted. If the score is accurate, exercise self-discipline to look for aspects of your work that you find interesting, and build on these as a foundation to become more engaged in your work.

Source: A few of the statements in the quiz are based on questionnaire items presented in Wilmar B. Schaufeli, Arnold B. Baker, and Marisa Salanova, "The Measurement of Work Engagement with a Short Questionnaire: A Cross-National Study," *Educational and Psychological Measurement*, August 2006, p. 714.

Employers engage in a wide variety of activities to bring about worker engagement that include providing for professional growth opportunities and performance bonuses, as well as designing jobs to be meaningful and exciting. Among the many approaches to enhancing engagement are (a) providing the right tools employees need to succeed in their roles, (b) providing training and coaching, (c) listening to employees, (d) providing loads of employee recognition, and (d) fostering close connections among coworkers. An example of the last point is that at shutter manufacturer Timberlane, woodworkers built a beanbag toss game for employees to use at company parties.[10]

A caution about employee engagement is similar to the concerns about organizational citizenship behavior mentioned in Chapter 4: Too much engagement can have harmful side effects. Highly engaged workers can become so involved in their jobs that they neglect other important aspects of their lives. Studies have suggested that highly engaged workers tend to suffer from work interfering with family life. Employees who fail to take enough time off from work, or even thinking about work, might damage their physical health.[11]

Employee engagement is not a specific theory of work motivation or a group of well-defined methods. Yet engagement receives much more attention from HR managers, managers in general, and researchers than any of the theories of motivation described in this chapter. Engagement has emerged as the most widely used approach to employee motivation, particularly because it is so comprehensive, even including adequate worker compensation.

Need Theories of Motivation

The simplest explanation of motivation is one of the most powerful: People are willing to expend effort toward achieving a goal because it satisfies one of their important needs. Self-interest is thus a driving force. This principle is referred to as "What's in it for me?" or WIIFM (pronounced "wiff 'em"). Reflect on your own experience. Before working hard to accomplish a task, you probably want to know how you will benefit. If your manager asks you to work extra hours to take care of an emergency, you will most likely oblige. Yet underneath you might be thinking, "If I work these extra hours, my boss will think highly of me. As a result, I will probably receive a good performance evaluation and maybe a better-than-average salary increase."

To apply the WIIFM principle, you need to analyze the situation from the other person's point of view. A store manager might think that employees should be willing to restock merchandise after hours without compensation because they should be grateful to have a job. Yet from the employees' standpoint, they do not perceive that much is in it for them. From their point of view, the desire to be paid for overtime is stronger than the feeling of gratitude for having a job. (Paying for overtime is a legal requirement, yet widely ignored.)

Here we describe three classic need theories of motivation: the need hierarchy, the two-factor theory, and the achievement–power–affiliation triad.

Maslow's Hierarchy of Needs

Based on his work as a clinical psychologist, Abraham M. Maslow developed a comprehensive view of individual motivation.[12] **Maslow's hierarchy of needs** arranges human needs into a pyramid-shaped model with basic physiological needs at the bottom and self-actualization needs at the top (see Figure 6-1). Lower-order needs must be satisfied to ensure a person's existence, security, and requirements for human contact. Higher-order needs are concerned with personal development and reaching one's potential. Before higher-level needs are activated, the lower-order needs must be satisfied. The five levels of needs are described next.

1. *Physiological needs.* At the first level are basic bodily needs such as the need for water, air, food, rest, and sleep. Should these needs be unfulfilled, the individual will be preoccupied with satisfying them. Once met, the second level of needs emerges.

LEARNING OBJECTIVE 2
Describe several need theories of motivation, including the needs hierarchy, the two-factor theory, and the achievement power–affiliation triad.

Maslow's hierarchy of needs A classical theory of motivation that arranges human needs into a pyramid-shaped model, with basic physiological needs at the bottom and self-actualization needs at the top.

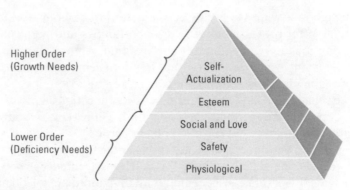

Higher Order
(Growth Needs)

Self-Actualization

Esteem

Social and Love

Lower Order
(Deficiency Needs)

Safety

Physiological

FIGURE 6-1 Maslow's Hierarchy of Needs

2. *Safety needs.* At the second level are needs relating to obtaining a secure environment without threats to well-being. These include needs for security and freedom from environmental threat. Many employees who work at dangerous jobs, such as loggers and miners, would be motivated by the chance to have safer working conditions. Sexual harassment is an example of the safety need for security from becoming frustrated, because the harassed person is subjected to an environmental threat. After a person feels safe and secure, a third level of needs emerges.

3. *Social and love needs.* Needs at this level include belonging to a group, affiliating with people, giving and receiving love, and engaging in sexual activity. Frustration of needs at this level can lead to serious personal problems. Managers can contribute to the satisfaction of social needs by promoting teamwork and encouraging social interaction in matters concerning work problems. When social and love needs are reasonably met, the person seeks to satisfy esteem needs.

4. *Esteem needs.* Needs at this level include self-respect based on genuine achievement, respect from others, prestige, recognition, and appreciation. Occupations with high status satisfy esteem needs. Managers can satisfy the esteem needs of employees by praising their work and giving them the opportunity for recognition. After reasonable satisfaction of esteem needs, most people will strive to achieve more of their potential through self-actualization.

5. *Self-actualization needs.* At the top of the hierarchy are needs for self-fulfillment and personal development and the need to grow to one's fullest potential. Self-actualized people are those who have become what they are capable of becoming.

Genuine achievement enhances self-esteem.

Managers can help employees move toward self-actualization by giving them challenging assignments, including the chance to do creative work.

A key principle of the needs hierarchy is that, as needs at a given level are gratified, they lose their potency (strength). The next level of need is then activated. A satisfied need ceases to be a motivator. For instance, once employees can pay for the necessities of life, they ordinarily seek opportunities for satisfying social relationships.

Many people think that, for the vast majority of workers, the only sensible way to motivate them is to satisfy higher-level needs. Furthermore, it has been argued that more companies today than when the need hierarchy was formulated are operating in knowledge and service economies. These modern organizations aim to fulfill a wide range of needs, including conveniences like meals and gyms.[13] Many exceptions still exist. A program of providing backup child care helps workers deal with social and love needs. Another consideration is that, even during prosperous times, there are many corporate downsizings that pose a threat to satisfying basic needs, such as security. Many manufacturers and retailers pay entry-level employees wages that make paying for food and housing a major struggle. The practical implication here is that many workers today can be motivated by offering them an opportunity to satisfy basic needs through such means as job security and a living wage.

Herzberg's Two-Factor Theory

The study of the needs hierarchy led to the two-factor theory of work motivation. According to the research of Frederick Herzberg, there are two different sets of job factors.[14] One set, the motivators or satisfiers, can motivate and satisfy workers. The other set, dissatisfiers, or hygiene factors, can only prevent dissatisfaction. Motivators relate to higher-order needs, while hygiene factors relate to lower-order needs.

The **two-factor theory of work motivation** explains how to design jobs to make them motivational. The motivational elements are the intrinsic (or job content) factors that make a job exciting. Motivator factors include achievement, recognition, advancement, responsibility, the work itself, and personal growth possibilities. The extrinsic (or job context) factors are hygienic. Although they are health maintaining and desirable, they are not motivational (according to this old theory). Examples of hygiene factors are pay, status, job security, working conditions, and quality of leadership. Herzberg believed that motivation increases when one combines pay with a motivator such as challenging work. (Money is so widely used to enhance motivation that the topic will be treated separately in Chapter 7.)

two-factor theory of work motivation Herzberg's theory contending that there are two different sets of job factors. One set can satisfy and motivate people (motivators or satisfiers); the other set can only prevent dissatisfaction (dissatisfiers or hygiene factors).

According to the two-factor theory, only the presence of motivator factors leads to more positive, energized behavior. For example, challenging work will motivate many people to exert increased effort. If intrinsic factors such as challenging work are not present, the result is neutral rather than negative, and the worker will feel bland rather than angry or unhappy. Although the presence of hygiene (or extrinsic) factors is not motivational, their absence can cause dissatisfaction as in the following illustration. A police captain reported that when officers were assigned old patrol cars, they complained frequently. However, when assigned brand new patrol cars, they did not express much appreciation. Nor did they increase their productivity as measured by the number of citations issued.

The two-factor theory has made two lasting contributions to work motivation. First, it has helped managers realize that money is not always the primary motivator. Second, it has spurred much of the interest in designing jobs to make them more intrinsically satisfying. The enrichment of individual jobs led to the enrichment of work group activities, which in turn spurred the development of self-managing work teams. All these topics are discussed in subsequent chapters.

A major problem with the two-factor theory is that it glosses over the importance of hygiene factors in attracting and retaining workers. Hygiene factors such as good benefits and company management satisfy and motivate many people. Many working parents will work extra hard to keep their jobs at a company that offers on-site child care or flexible working hours. Another problem with the two-factor theory is that some workers show no particular interest in such motivators as opportunities for growth and advancement. They work primarily so they can pay their bills and enjoy their time with family and friends.

McClelland's Achievement–Power–Affiliation Triad

Many other needs influence job behavior in addition to those mentioned specifically in the need hierarchy. (One example is the need for thrill seeking, as implied from the discussion of the trait for risk taking and thrill seeking described in Chapter 2.) David C. McClelland and his associates have provided a useful explanation of several of these needs.[15] They have proposed a theory of motivation based on the premise that people acquire or learn certain needs from their culture. Among the cultural influences are family, peer groups, television shows, and social media and other websites. When a need is strong enough, it prompts a person to engage in work activities to satisfy it. Three key acquired needs or motives driving workers are achievement, power, and affiliation.

The Need for Achievement

The **need for achievement** is the desire to accomplish something difficult for its own sake. People with a strong need for achievement frequently think of how to do a job better. Responsibility seeking is another characteristic of people with a high need for achievement. They are also concerned with how to progress in their careers. Workers with a high need for achievement are interested in monetary rewards primarily as feedback about how well they are achieving. They also set realistic yet moderately difficult goals, take calculated risks, and desire feedback on performance. (A moderately difficult goal challenges a person but is not so difficult as to most likely lead to failure and frustration.) In general, those who enjoy building a business, activities, and programs from scratch have a strong need for achievement. Figure 6-2 outlines the preferences of workers with a strong achievement need.

Achievement-oriented people get excited about attaining difficult goals.

need for achievement The desire to accomplish something difficult for its own sake.

need for power The desire to control other people, to influence their behavior, and to be responsible for them.

The Need for Power

The **need for power** is the desire to control other people, to influence their behavior, and to be responsible for them. Managers with a high need for power wish to control resources (e.g., money and real estate) in addition to people. A person with a strong need for power spends time thinking about influencing and controlling others and about gaining a position of authority and status. Wanting to make a positive impact is also part of the power motive. Executives who have buildings named after them or buy professional athletic teams have strong power needs. One problem with someone with a strong power drive in a large company is that he or she will attempt to accomplish too much personally rather than spread the task among many workers.[16]

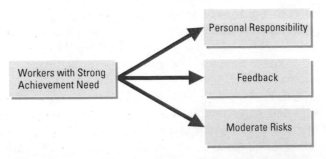

FIGURE 6-2 Preferences of Workers with a Strong Achievement Need

The Need for Affiliation

The **need for affiliation** is the desire to establish and maintain friendly and warm relationships with others. People motivated this way care about restoring disrupted relationships and soothing hurt feelings. They want to engage in work that permits close companionship. Successful managers have low affiliation needs, but managers with an extremely low need for affiliation may not show adequate concern for the needs of others.

need for affiliation The desire to establish and maintain friendly and warm relationships with others.

The acquired needs theory has made an important contribution in identifying needs related to managerial performance. For example, many studies have shown that successful executives have a strong need for power. Another consistent finding is that entrepreneurs have a strong need for achievement. However, the achievement–power–affiliation triad is not a complete explanation of work motivation, because it focuses on just several key needs. Similarly, needs theories in general explain only part of motivation. The remaining sections of the chapter describe other approaches to understanding work motivation.

The direct implication of needs theories for managing and leading people is that to get the most from workers' talents, it is necessary to "push their hot buttons." Two examples are as follows:

- Employees with strong security needs are likely to seek assurance, be cautious, and carefully stay within their job description. The manager might encourage risk taking from these workers by telling them about other employees who have tried something new and been successful. It is best to avoid surprises about change and offer frequent feedback.

- Employees with strong achievement needs are likely to display initiative and set personal goals, work well independently, take pride in work well done, and seek recognition for their good work. The manager might include them in the process of establishing work goals, give them ample resources, give them feedback on their work outcomes, and encourage professional growth opportunities.[17]

Goal Theory

Goal setting is a basic process that is directly or indirectly part of all major theories of work motivation. Managers widely accept goal setting as a means to improve and sustain performance. Based on several hundred studies, the core finding of goal-setting theory is as follows: Individuals who are provided with specific hard goals perform better than those given easy, nonspecific, or "do your best" goals—or no goals at all. At the same time, however, the individuals must have sufficient ability, accept the goals, and receive feedback related to the task.[18] Our overview of goal-setting theory elaborates on this basic finding.

LEARNING OBJECTIVE 3 Summarize the key propositions of goal theory and reinforcement theory.

The premise underlying goal-setting theory is that behavior is regulated by values and goals. A **goal** is what a person is trying to accomplish. Our values create within us a desire to behave consistently with them. For example, if an executive values honesty, he or she will establish a goal of trying to hire only honest employees. The executive would therefore make extensive use of reference checks and honesty testing. Edwin A. Locke and Gary P. Latham have incorporated hundreds of studies about goals into a theory of goal setting and task performance.[19] Figure 6-3 summarizes some of the more consistent findings, along with more recent developments. The list that follows describes these findings.

goal What a person is trying to accomplish.

1. *Specific goals lead to higher performance than do generalized goals.* Telling someone to "do your best" is a generalized goal. A specific goal would be: Decrease the cycle time on customer inquiries via the company website to an average of 3 hours. (Here is an example in which common sense can be wrong. Many people believe that telling others to "do your best" is an excellent motivator.)
2. *Performance generally increases in direct proportion to goal difficulty.* The more difficult one's goal, the more one accomplishes. An important exception is that when goals are too difficult, they may lower performance. Difficulty in reaching the goal leads to frustration, which in turn leads to lowered performance. At times when a major goal seems overwhelming, establishing smaller, interim goals is more motivational.

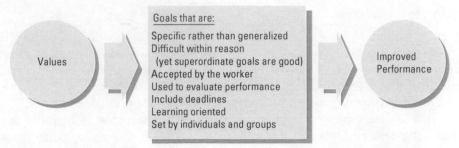

FIGURE 6-3 Goal-Setting Theory

superordinate goals
Overreaching goals that capture the imagination of people.

Goal theory now recognizes the importance of **superordinate goals**, overreaching goals that capture the imagination of people.[20] The superordinate goal is similar to a vision because it relates to an ideal and is often inspirational. The construction manager of a sewer-pipe company might explain to all workers that "We are working together to improve sanitation and help rid the world of deadly diseases stemming from poor sewage systems." Smaller goals then support the superordinate goals, such as installing a new sewer pipe under a given street within 10 days.

3. *For goals to improve performance, the worker must accept them.* If one rejects a goal, one will not incorporate it into planning. This is why it is often helpful to discuss goals with employees, rather than imposing goals on them. Accepting a goal implies that the goal is something the worker actually wants to accomplish, such as acquiring a skill that will help his or her professional development. Later research, however, suggests that the importance of goal commitment may be overrated. Two meta-analyses of laboratory studies about the effect of goal commitment on performance concluded that commitment has a small impact on performance. Goals appeared to improve performance whether or not people participating in the studies felt committed to their goal.[21]

Despite these recent findings, many managers think employee commitment to goals is important. For example, accepting goals often implies that the worker accepts the values and purposes of the organization.

4. *Goals are more effective when they are used to evaluate performance.* When workers know that their performance will be evaluated in terms of how well they attained their goals, the impact of goals increases. If goals are used to evaluate performance, workers should receive feedback on their progress toward goals and be rewarded for reaching them. **Feedback** is information about how well someone is doing in achieving goals. Rewarding people for reaching goals as a motivational technique is perhaps the most widely accepted principle of management.

feedback Information about how well someone is doing in achieving goals. Also, messages sent back from the receiver to the sender of information.

5. *Deadlines improve the effectiveness of goals.* For most people, goals are more effective when they include a deadline for completion. Deadlines serve as a tool of time control and increase the motivational impact of goals. Knowing that a deadline is approaching, the typical worker will invest more effort into completing the work. Yet when deadlines are too tight, particularly in complex jobs, work quality may suffer.[22]

6. *A learning goal orientation improves performance more than a performing goal orientation.* A person with a learning goal orientation wants to develop competence by acquiring new skills and mastering new situations. In contrast, the person with a performing goal orientation wants to demonstrate and validate his or her competence by seeking favorable judgments and avoiding negative judgments.

7. *Group goal setting is as important as individual goal setting.* Having employees work as teams with a specific team goal, rather than as individuals with only individual goals, increases productivity. Furthermore, the combination of compatible group and individual goals is more effective than either individual or group goals alone.

An effective way to apply goal theory is for the manager to set short-term goals or to encourage others to do the same. The short-term goals should support the organization's long-term goals but are established in "bites" that are more readily achievable. Assume, for example, that a manufacturing site wants to reduce absenteeism from 20 percent to 5 percent to remain competitive. Going from 20 percent to 5 percent in 3 months might not be achievable. However, moving down 2 percent per month would be feasible. As each 2-percent reduction in absenteeism is achieved, employees are fed back the results. The feedback serves as a reward for further progress.

Despite the many advantages of goal setting, goals can have negative consequences. A major concern is that some workers may behave unethically in the pursuit of goals, such as manipulating figures to attain a financial goal. Or a CEO might weaken an organization through cost cutting in order to reach a profit or stock price goal. Workers in the pursuit of individual goals may become so preoccupied with their own goals that they are reluctant to help others.[23] Also, the continual pursuit of stretch goals can be stressful, as workers keep extending their work week to "make their numbers."

The Skill-Development Exercise gives you an opportunity to practice setting goals for people in the workplace.

The Organizational Behavior in Action box illustrates how a major international corporation uses high-level goal setting (or superordinate goals) to motivate an entire workforce toward sustaining the environment.

Reinforcement Theory

A well-established explanation of motivation is **reinforcement theory**, the contention that behavior is determined by its consequences. The consequences are the rewards and punishments people receive for behaving in particular ways. In Chapter 7 we describe incentive programs that apply reinforcement theory to enhance motivation. Reinforcement theory, unlike needs-based theories of motivation, de-emphasizes understanding the needs a person attempts to satisfy. Instead, the manager looks for rewards that will encourage certain behaviors and punishments that discourage other behaviors.

At the foundation of reinforcement theory is **operant conditioning**, or learning that takes place as a consequence of behavior. More specifically, people learn to repeat behaviors that bring them pleasurable outcomes and to avoid behaviors that lead to uncomfortable outcomes. After people learn a behavior through operant conditioning, they must be motivated by rewards to repeat that behavior.

reinforcement theory The contention that behavior is determined by its consequences.

operant conditioning Learning that takes place as a consequence of behavior.

Positive reinforcement is a natural motivator.

Audacious Goal Setting at Consumer Products Giant Unilever

Even if you have not heard much about Unilever, you are probably familiar with a few of the household brands produced by the huge international company, such as Lifebuoy soap, Dove Body Wash, Surf, and Ben & Jerry's ice cream. The Anglo-Dutch company has 300 factories across the world that produce about 400 brands for an estimated 2.5 billion customers. When Paul Polman entered as CEO in 2009, he triggered fast growth and record profits despite the economic recession. He and his staff focused on emerging markets, selling the company's household products in very small quantities at prices of 10 cents to 15 cents.

Polman has become acclaimed throughout the world for embedding environmental and social goals into Unilever's business strategy—and also for earning substantial profits. The audacious goal Polman set 10 years ago was to double the size of the company and reduce its environmental impact simultaneously. One of the objectives was to source all the company's agricultural materials in a sustainable (in terms of environmental protection) way. Polman says, "If you set these audacious goals, you get people out of a comfort zone, and that makes them do amazing things."

A specific example of how Unilever contributes to sustaining life is through the hand-washing soap Lifebuoy. Product sales have been growing at a double-digit rate because the soap helps children in emerging markets reach the age of five through the basic act of hand washing. Knowledge of this accomplishment unleashes enormous energy in Unilever's employees.

The Unilever Sustainable Living Plan is built around three major goals. The first is improving health and well-being: "By 2020 we will help more than a billion people take action to improve their health and well-being." The second is reducing environmental impact: "By 2030 our goal is to halve the environmental footprint of the making and use of our products as we grow our business." The third is environmental livelihoods: "By 2020 we will enhance the livelihoods of millions of people as we grow our business."

Polman believes that Unilever has attained some great results from the Sustainable Living Plan. He believes that the plan contributes to business growth because the company sees consumers responding to campaigns by the Sustainable Living Brands, such as Hellmann's, on issues ranging from sustainable sourcing to water scarcity. At the same time, many managers believe that these audacious goals motivate the workforce to work hard to help attain a grand purpose.

QUESTIONS

1. How could such major goals related to sustainability affect the daily work of a factory worker?

2. How should a factory supervisor react to a production worker who says, "Why doesn't the company pay us more instead of spending so much money on trying to save the planet?"

Source: Original story created from facts and observations in the following sources: Geoff Colvin, "From High-Minded to High Value," *Fortune*, December 22, 2014, p. 38; "About Our Strategy," Unilever, www.unilever.com/sustainable-living, pp. 1–3, © Unilever 2018; Vivienne Walt, "Unilever CEO Paul Polman's Plan to Save the World," *Fortune*, March 1, 2017, pp. 1–25; Jeff Gowdy, "The Leaders and Laggards of Sustainability Goals," *New Metrics*, www.sustainablebrands.com/news_and_views/new_metrics/jeff_gowdy/leaders_laggards_sustainability_goals , p. 1, © 2007–2018 Sustainable Life Media Inc.

According to the famous experimental psychologist, the late B. F. Skinner, to train or condition people, and then later motivate them, the manager does not have to study the inner workings of the mind. Instead, the manager should understand the relationships between behaviors and their consequences. After these relationships are understood, the manager arranges contingencies to reward desirable behaviors and discourage undesirable behaviors.[24] Four basic strategies exist for arranging contingencies that can modify individual (or group) behavior: positive reinforcement, avoidance motivation, extinction, and punishment.

positive reinforcement The application of a pleasurable or valued consequence when a person exhibits the desired response.

Positive reinforcement is the application of a pleasurable or valued consequence when a person exhibits the desired response. After positive reinforcement, the probability increases that the behavior will be repeated. The term *reinforcement* means that the behavior (or response) is strengthened or entrenched. A manager who expresses appreciation when a team member works late strengthens the worker's propensity to work late.

avoidance motivation Rewarding by taking away an uncomfortable consequence.

Avoidance motivation is rewarding people by taking away an uncomfortable consequence. The process is also referred to as *negative reinforcement* because a negative situation is removed. Negative reinforcement is thus a reward, not a punishment, as commonly thought. Avoidance motivation is a way of strengthening a desired response by making the removal contingent on the right response. Assume that an employee is placed on probation because of poor attendance. After 30 consecutive days of coming to work, the employer rewards the employee by removing the probation.

Extinction is weakening or decreasing the frequency of undesirable behavior by removing the reward for such behavior. It is the absence of reinforcement. Suppose an employee engages in undesirable behavior such as creating a disturbance just to get a reaction from coworkers. If the teammates ignore the disturbance, the perpetrator no longer receives the reward of getting attention and therefore stops the disturbing behavior. The behavior is said to be extinguished.

Punishment is the presentation of an undesirable consequence for a specific behavior. An example of a punishment would be to suspend a worker for 2 weeks without pay for having violated a company rule. An indirect form of punishment is to take away a privilege, such as working on an interesting project, because of some undesirable behavior.

The most direct managerial application of reinforcement theory is to reward those behaviors that support the goals of the organization. Punishment is widely used to maintain discipline within the organization, such as not giving an employee a pay raise because of his or her poor performance. Avoidance motivation has less application than positive reinforcement and punishment, and extinction is mostly used to decrease disruptive or gross behaviors that are not rule violations.

The application of reinforcement theory is more obvious for basic jobs such as data entry or order shipment, yet the positive reinforcement can also be applied to sustain the motivation of managers and professionals. For example, a plant manager who reduced pollutants emanating from the factory might be given recognition on the company social media website.

Reinforcement theory is so widely used and well accepted that most managers and professionals are not even aware that many of their actions are based on the theory. For example, it is just natural to many managers to praise a worker for a job well done.

Expectancy Theory of Motivation and Self-Efficacy

According to **expectancy theory**, motivation results from deliberate choices to engage in activities in order to achieve worthwhile outcomes. People will be well motivated if they believe that a strong effort will lead to good performance and good performance will lead to preferred outcomes. The basic version of expectancy theory shown in Figure 6-4 is useful to managers and professionals. Components of the model including an update about the effects of emotion are described next, followed by the guidelines for motivation stemming from expectancy theory.[25]

Expectancy, Instrumentality, and Valence

The key components of expectancy theory are expectancy, instrumentality, and valence. Each one of these components exists in each situation involving motivation. An **expectancy** is a person's subjective estimate of the probability that a given level of performance will occur. The effort-to-performance (E → P) expectancy refers to the individual's subjective hunch about the chances that increased effort will lead to the desired performance. If a person does not believe that he or she has the skill to accomplish a task, that person might not even try to perform.

extinction Weakening or decreasing the frequency of undesirable behavior by removing the reward for such behavior.

punishment The presentation of an undesirable consequence for a specific behavior.

LEARNING OBJECTIVE 4
Explain the expectancy theory of motivation, and its tie-in with self-efficacy.

expectancy theory The theory that motivation results from deliberate choices to engage in activities in order to achieve worthwhile outcomes.

expectancy A person's subjective estimate of the probability that a given level of performance will occur.

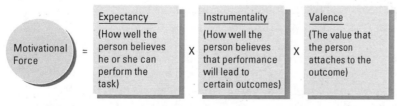

FIGURE 6-4 **A Basic Version of Expectancy Theory**

Self-efficacy leads to a high expectancy of accomplishing a task.

The importance of having high expectancies for motivation meshes well with a conception of work motivation that emphasizes the contribution of self-efficacy. If you have high self-efficacy about the task, your motivation will be high. Low self-efficacy leads to low motivation. Some people are poorly motivated to skydive because they doubt they will be able to pull the ripcord while free-falling at 120 mph. The following definition, which is more complete than the one presented in Chapter 5, will help you appreciate the contribution of self-efficacy to motivation:

Self-efficacy refers to an individual's convictions (or confidence) about his or her abilities to mobilize the motivation, cognitive resources, and course of action needed to successfully execute a specific task within a given context.[26]

An **instrumentality** is the individual's estimate of the probability that performance will lead to certain outcomes. The (P → O) instrumentality refers to the person's subjective evaluation of the chances that good performance will lead to certain outcomes. Among the outcomes might be an increase in status and salary, a promotion, more job security, and appreciation from management. Performance almost always leads to multiple outcomes. In formulating the instrumentality, the employee seeks a subjective answer to the question: "If I do perform well, will the organization really make good on promises to me?" Expectancies and instrumentalities range from 0.00 to 1.00 because both are probabilities.

Valence refers to the value a person places on a particular outcome. People attach positive valences to rewards and negative valences to punishments. An advertising copywriter might place a high positive valence on making a presentation to a client and assign a high negative valence to having his work insulted by the manager or client. The maximum value of a positive valence is +100, while the maximum value of a negative valence is –100. Neutral outcomes (indifference) carry a valence of zero. (Most versions of expectancy theory limit the range of valences from –1.00 to +1.00. However, such a limited range fails to capture the intensity of highly preferred or feared outcomes.) The numerical values of valences are unknown in most situations, yet it is reasonable to assume that people attach values of "good," "bad," and "neutral" to potential outcomes derived from their efforts.

instrumentality The individual's subjective estimate of the probability that performance will lead to certain outcomes.

valence The value a person places on a particular outcome.

The Calculation of Motivation

In expectancy theory, motivation force $M = (E \rightarrow P) \times (P \rightarrow O) \times V$. The potential of an expected outcome increasing motivation can be high only if the expectancies, instrumentalities, and valences are high. Because anything multiplied by zero is zero, a zero value for (E → P), (P → O), or V will reduce motivation to zero. Suppose an employee places a maximum value on receiving a raise (V = 100). The employee is confident that he or she can perform the task required (E → P = 0.85). And the employee is even more confident that the firm will come through with the raise if he or she performs well (P → O = 0.90). Note that the values of 0.85 and 0.90 are subjective estimates, not true calculations. The employee's motivation is consequently (100) × (0.85) × (0.90) = 76.5 (above average on a scale of –100 to +100).

A note of caution: The simple formula just presented does not tell the entire story because each task involves multiple expectancies, instrumentalities, and valences. Desirable and undesirable outcomes may cancel one another out, resulting in zero valence and therefore producing zero motivational force. For example, a person might not strive for a promotion because its positive valences (e.g., more money and status) are neutralized by its negative valences (e.g., having to relocate and leave friends behind).

To create a situation of high motivation, the manager should take steps to elevate expectancies, instrumentalities, and valences. One approach would be for the manager to make sure the worker had the right training and to boost the worker's self-confidence—thus elevating expectancies. Assuring the worker that good performance would lead to a reward could boost instrumentalities. Choosing meaningful rewards would elevate the valences.

The Influence of Affect on Expectancy Theory

We have already mentioned the influence of affect on attitudes and creativity (Chapters 4 and 5). Positive affect may also exert influence on the components of expectancy theory, as suggested by two laboratory studies with 97 college students. The task was solving anagrams (rearranging letters to make new words such as *item* from *mite*). Affect, or mood, was manipulated by giving students in the experimental group a bag of candy. A key finding was that when the link between performance and outcomes was specified, being in the positive affect group increased expectancies, instrumentalities, and valences.[27]

The implication is that managers might be able to increase the effectiveness of expectancy theory by finding ways to elevate the mood of group members. Dispensing bags of candy would be a short-term expedient because, as Chapter 7 will describe, the same reward repeated too often can become stale. Creating a positive work climate would probably be more effective at sustaining positive affect.

Equity Theory and Social Comparison

Expectancy theory emphasizes the rational and thinking side of people. Similarly, another theory focuses on how fairly people think they are being treated in comparison to certain reference groups. According to **equity theory**, employee satisfaction and motivation depend on how fairly the employees believe they are treated in comparison to peers. The theory contends that employees hold certain beliefs about the outcomes they receive from their jobs, as well as the inputs they invest to obtain these outcomes.

The outcomes of employment include pay, benefits, status, recognition, intrinsic job factors, and anything else stemming from the job that workers perceive as useful. The inputs include all the factors that employees perceive as being their investment in the job or anything of value that they bring to the job. These inputs include job qualifications, skills, educational level, effort, trust in the company, support of coworkers, and cooperative behavior.

The core of equity theory is that employees compare their inputs and outcomes (making social comparisons) with others in the workplace.[28] When employees believe that they receive equitable outcomes in relation to their inputs, they are generally satisfied and motivated. When workers believe that they are being treated equitably, they are more willing to work hard. Conversely, when employees believe that they give too much as compared to what they receive from the organization, a state of tension, dissatisfaction, and demotivation ensues. The people used for reference are those whom the employee perceives as relevant for comparison. For example, an industrial sales representative would make comparisons with other industrial sales reps in the same industry about whom he has information. Another way of looking at equity theory is that workers search for justice in terms of being treated fairly.

There are two kinds of comparisons. People consider their own inputs in relation to outcomes received, and they also evaluate what others receive for the same inputs. Equity is said to exist when an individual concludes that his or her own outcome/input ratio is equal to that of other people. Inequity exists if the person's ratio is not the same as that of other people. All these comparisons are similar to those judgments made by people according to expectancy theory—they are subjective hunches that may or may not be valid. Inequity can be in either direction and of varying magnitude. The equity ratio is often expressed as follows:

$$\frac{\text{Outcomes of Individual}}{\text{Inputs of Individual}} \quad \text{compared to} \quad \frac{\text{Outcomes of Others}}{\text{Inputs of Others}}$$

equity theory The theory that employee satisfaction and motivation depend on how fairly the employees believe they are treated in comparison to peers.

According to equity theory, the highest level of motivation occurs when a person has ratios equal to those of the comparison person. When people perceive an inequity, they are likely to engage in one of the following actions:

1. *Alter the outcome.* The person who feels mistreated might ask for more salary or a bonus, promotional opportunities, or more vacation time. Some people might even steal from the company to obtain the money they feel they deserve. Others might attempt to convince management to give less to others.

2. *Alter the input.* A person who feels treated inequitably might decrease effort or time devoted to work. The person who feels underpaid might engage in such self-defeating behavior by faking sick days to take care of personal business. Another extreme would be to encourage others to decrease their inputs so they will earn less money.

3. *Distort the perception.* To combat feelings of inequity, people can distort their perceptions of their own (or others') inputs or outcomes. Recognizing that he or she is overpaid in comparison to coworkers, a financial analyst might say, "Of course, I attended a much tougher program at college, so I deserve more money." Another distortion would be to look for evidence that coworkers are contributing less effort.

4. *Change the reference source.* A convenient way of restoring equity is to change to another reference source whose outcome/input ratio is similar to one's own. A recently graduated MBA accepted a job offer for $20,000 less per year than average compared to other graduates of her program. At first she grumbled about being underpaid but then reanalyzed the situation. Her conclusion was, "The MBAs I was comparing myself with took jobs in New York City or San Francisco where the cost of living is much higher. If I compare myself to MBAs getting hired outside of New York or San Francisco, I'm being paid well."

5. *Leave the situation.* As an extreme move, the person who feels treated inequitably might quit a job. He or she would then be free to pursue greater equity in another position.

Equity theory has much face validity and has direct relevance for pay systems. No matter how well designed a program of productivity or cost cutting might be, it must still provide equitable pay. Otherwise, the negative perceptions of workers might lead to less effort to accomplish the goals of management. With equitable pay, many employees will feel that justice has been done.

Social Learning Theory

LEARNING OBJECTIVE 6
Use social learning theory to motivate yourself.

social learning The process of observing the behavior of others, recognizing its consequences, and altering behavior as a result.

As described in Chapter 3, people learn various behaviors by observing and imitating others. At a later point, they are motivated to repeat the learned behaviors. **Social learning** is the process of observing the behavior of others, recognizing its consequences, and altering behavior as a result. According to social learning theory, individual behavior is influenced by a combination of a person's cognitions and social environment. A person has to make some interpretations of the efficacy and suitability of the behavior being observed; otherwise the model will not be imitated.

Social learning does not take place automatically just because environmental models are available. If social learning were that easy, almost every employee would be a model worker. Effective social learning, and therefore motivated behavior, is most likely to take place when several of the following conditions are met:[29]

1. The person should have high expectancies that he or she can learn the observed behavior, and high instrumentalities that the learned behavior will result in valued rewards. The high expectancies center on the person having high self-efficacy. Social learning will be facilitated when the person is confident of performing well in the modeled task.

2. Self-administration of rewards should take place. The person doing the modeling should find the behavior intrinsically satisfying and not have to rely exclusively on extrinsic rewards such as increased compensation and recognition. Modeling the

new behavior should result in personal satisfaction and an enhanced self-image. Assume that you learned how to negotiate effectively by observing a mentor negotiate a deal. You would most likely experience increased personal satisfaction from having acquired a valuable new business skill. At a later point, external rewards would be forthcoming if your new skill led to a higher performance evaluation or saving money when purchasing a home.

3. The behavior to be learned should involve mostly tangible, mechanical, and verbal activities such as physical and interpersonal tasks. It is thus easier to be motivated by watching another person negotiate than engage in strategic planning. We cannot readily imitate the cognitive processes of another person.

4. Social learning can take place only when we possess the physical and mental ability needed to imitate the behavior. A frail person cannot learn to move furniture by simply watching others do it correctly. Also, one cannot imitate effective negotiating practices if he or she is not intelligent enough to figure out what the other side really wants.

Social learning may appear to be more about learning than motivation, but the motivational aspects are still important. Workers typically model the behavior of people from whom they seek approval, such as superiors and high-performing teammates. Part of the motivation for learning and repeating the target behavior is to receive approval from significant people in the work environment. Have you ever noticed how people from the same organization often talk alike?

Intrinsic versus Extrinsic Motivation

Many management experts contend that if you make jobs more interesting, there may be less need for motivating people with external rewards. The two-factor theory of motivation is based on this idea. Also, attempting to motivate people by extrinsic rewards may not be sufficient. Motivating people through interesting work is based on the principle of **intrinsic motivation**. It refers to a person's beliefs about the extent to which an activity can satisfy his or her needs for competence and self-determination. The intrinsically motivated person has energy and passion for the task,[30] as implied in the discussion in Chapter 5 about the experience of flow. Values contribute to intrinsic motivation. People who highly value work tend to be intrinsically motivated, while people who place a low value on work have low intrinsic motivation. Meaningful work leads to intrinsic motivation and will be linked to the discussion of job enrichment in Chapter 7.

A useful observation about intrinsic motivation is that it can be experienced among a wide variety of workers, even those who are thought to work primarily for money. A study was conducted with on-demand workers (freelancers) who provide expertise to clients on a short-term-project basis. The expertise offered to clients included health-care, financial, and legal information. On-demand workers are often thought to be performing tasks for others primarily for money. A major conclusion reached was that intrinsic motivation increases when the on-demand work fulfills important personal needs, such as autonomy (working independently) and relating to other people.[31]

Self-Determination Theory and the Rationale behind Intrinsic Motivation Theory

Intrinsic motivation and self-determination theory are closely related. According to **self-determination theory**, workers are active agents of, rather than passive reactors to, environmental forces. Two factors influence the perception of intrinsic motivation. Certain characteristics of a

LEARNING OBJECTIVE 7
Recognize the importance of both intrinsic and extrinsic motivators.

intrinsic motivation A person's beliefs about the extent to which an activity can satisfy his or her needs for competence and self-determination.

self-determination theory The idea that workers are active agents of, rather than passive reactors to, environmental forces.

ASDF_MEDIA/Shutterstock.com

Internal rewards can be effective motivators.

task, such as challenge and autonomy, promote intrinsic motivation because they allow a person to satisfy the needs for competence and self-determination. Workers' perceptions of why they perform a task can also affect intrinsic motivation. Such motivation is likely to increase when people perceive that they perform tasks for themselves rather than for an external reward. To understand intrinsic motivation, visualize a coder joyously working until midnight to write software that will give her company a competitive edge in satisfying customers. She is so wrapped up in her work that she is unaware of the time. Furthermore, she gives no particular thought to whether she will receive a bonus for her outstanding work.

When an individual performs a task to achieve an external reward such as money or recognition, a shift occurs. The individual believes that the external reward caused the behavior, and money or recognition now controls his or her actions. The worker no longer perceives that he or she is self-determining. As a result, intrinsic motivation may decrease.[32]

Kenneth W. Thomas presents a view, shared by many others, of the importance of intrinsic motivation in today's workplace. He reasons that the world of work has evolved from the command-and-control era to one in which encouraging workers to manage themselves plays a major role in leading workers. Intrinsic motivation is necessary for self-management because self-management implies that you find your work rewarding in itself.[33]

Grit as Part of Intrinsic Motivation

grit Perseverance and passion for long-term goals.

Another perspective on intrinsic motivation is that it includes grit. As defined by Angela L. Duckworth and her colleagues, who have researched this human quality, **grit** is perseverance and passion for long-term goals.[34] The person with grit often wins out over even the more talented person because grit gives you the stamina for the long haul. As is frequently observed by industrial sales managers, the sales representatives who earn the most commissions are not necessarily those with the best persuasive skills and personal appearance. Instead, the winningest reps are those who have decent natural sales skills and who keep plugging along with logical proposals for the long haul. Indeed, the person with grit pursues external goals, but at the same time, he or she enjoys the excitement and inner satisfaction derived from working toward the goal.

A useful way of understanding the nuances of grit is to take the Self-Assessment 6-2. The scoring and interpretation are important, but equally valuable is to reflect on how the statements in the quiz might apply to you and whether you see need for improvement. Statement 17, "Determination to keep going is one of my greatest strengths," is particularly revealing. If you agree strongly with this statement, it would be one indicator that you have strong willpower and grit. If you disagree strongly, you have identified an area for self-improvement in terms of attaining career and personal goals.

The idea that grit is necessary for high achievement evolved during interviews conducted by Duckworth and her colleagues with professionals in a variety of fields, including investment banking, painting, journalism, college teaching and research, medicine, and law. When asked which personal attribute distinguishes star performers in their field, the professionals pointed to grit or a close synonym as frequently as they mentioned natural talent. Many of the interviewees were highly impressed by the achievements of colleagues who did not seem particularly gifted at first but whose sustained commitment to attaining their goals was intense and exceptional. Even more penetrating was the observation that many of the more gifted colleagues did not reach the top of their field. These interviews led to the development of a grit questionnaire, similar in nature to the one just presented.

Encouraged by the interview findings, Duckworth and her colleagues conducted a series of studies about the impact of grit. One study simply found that adults of approximately the same age with higher grit scores on the test completed more years of education—the implication being that it requires high persistence to attain a degree. The second study showed that college students who scored higher on the grit test achieved higher grades than their peers even though they had slightly lower SAT scores. An implication of this study is that given a reasonable amount of aptitude, grit is even more important than aptitude for performing well in college courses. Scholastic aptitude remains important, but grit might provide the extra edge for performing well in college.

Collectively, the findings of these studies suggest that the achievement of difficult goals requires not only talent but also sustained and focused application of talent over the long haul. Another conclusion drawn from the studies is that effort is not just intensity, as in a burst of effort to attain a goal. Rather, it is consistency and duration, or grit and self-discipline, that lead to long-term successful outcomes. These studies fit the observation that long-term effort is required in most fields to attain a high level of success, often ten years. However, we recognize that there are many extraordinarily successful teenagers in fields such as athletics and software development.

Problems Associated with Extrinsic Rewards

Intrinsic motivation theory is based on the fact that external rewards have disadvantages. Extrinsic rewards can sometimes lower a person's job performance and be demotivating, particularly when a creative task is involved. The appeal of extrinsic rewards can also cause people to

- focus narrowly on a task;
- rush through a job to get a reward;
- regard the task as a drudgery that must be suffered to receive a reward;
- see themselves as less free and less self-determining;[35]
- overlook the possible joy and excitement of the work because of the focus on rewards.

Despite these problems, a firm should not abandon financial bonuses and other forms of extrinsic motivation. Even the people who enjoy work intensely still expect to be paid well and crave recognition from management. Also, people who love their work, such as top executives, successful novelists, entertainers, and athletes, demand huge fees. The sensible solution is for managers to balance intrinsic and extrinsic rewards. For example, a purchasing agent who saved the company $300,000 by finding a low-price alternative for a component might be rewarded with the opportunity to work on a cross-functional team. He or she might also be given a hefty year-end bonus.

The Influence of Personality and Culture on Motivation

Personality and culture can both influence a person's level of drive and the rewards he or she thinks are relevant. For many people, being well motivated comes easily because they have personality traits that predispose them to this. Two key examples are *conscientiousness* and the *achievement need*. (A need usually functions like a personality trait.) The conscientious person will strive to get the job done, and the achievement-driven person welcomes accomplishing tasks. Conversely, it will be more difficult for the manager to motivate people who score low on conscientiousness and have a weak achievement need.

A study involving 164 telemarketing sales representatives at a large financial services firm provides empirical evidence for the link between personality factors and motivation. As most readers would suspect, high motivation is crucial to perform well as a telemarketer—particularly in light of all the rejection a telemarketer encounters. One of the study's findings was that conscientiousness and extraversion were both associated with better sales performance.[36] Extraversion often helps a person to be motivated to sell because the person feels comfortable in interacting with others and being assertive about his or her own ideas.

Cross-cultural factors influence which rewards or outcomes are most likely to have the highest valence for a particular group. Latinos, for example, generally favor outcomes that enable them to maintain cordial relations with other members of the work group. Also, Asians would ordinarily prefer not to receive rewards that singled them out for attention.

LEARNING OBJECTIVE 8
Explain how personality and cultural factors are related to motivation.

The Grit Quiz

Indicate the extent to which each of the following statements describes your behavior or attitude by circling one number. The numbers refer to disagree strongly (DS), disagree (D), neither agree nor disagree (N), agree (A), and agree strongly (AS). Consider enlisting the help of someone who knows your behavior and attitudes well to help you respond accurately to the statements.

Statement Related to Willpower and Grit	DS	D	N	A	AS
1. I get discouraged quickly when I receive a setback.	5	4	3	2	1
2. If I am scheduled to engage in a physical activity, I will go ahead even if I have a minor ache or pain.	1	2	3	4	5
3. If I am reading an important article, and I come across a paragraph that I do not understand, I usually stop reading.	5	4	3	2	1
4. I rarely stick with the same hobby or interest for more than a few months.	5	4	3	2	1
5. I sometimes shout and scream at another person when we have a disagreement.	5	4	3	2	1
6. I engage in physical exercise regularly.	1	2	3	4	5
7. If I am working on an important project, I am able to resist checking my e-mail or text messages for at least one hour.	1	2	3	4	5
8. I know what I want to accomplish in my career.	1	2	3	4	5
9. Instead of planning my future, I just let things happen.	5	4	3	2	1
10. I work much harder than most people I know.	1	2	3	4	5
11. My body weight is rarely where I would like it to be.	1	2	3	4	5
12. My living quarters are a mess.	5	4	3	2	1
13. If I have an important errand to run, I will postpone it if I consider the weather conditions outside to be unfavorable.	5	4	3	2	1
14. At least two people I have worked for mentioned that I am dependable and hardworking.	1	2	3	4	5
15. I frequently make statements on the job that I wish I could take back.	5	4	3	2	1
16. I frequently make statements in personal life that I wish I could take back.	5	4	3	2	1
17. Determination to keep going is one of my greatest strengths.	1	2	3	4	5
18. I often set small, short-term goals to reach a bigger goal, such as advancing my career.	1	2	3	4	5
19. After I set a goal, I will often check my progress on attaining that goal.	1	2	3	4	5

The Grit Quiz (continued)

Statement Related to Willpower and Grit	DS	D	N	A	AS
20. It would be very difficult for me to turn down an invitation to lunch even if I were working against a tight deadline.	5	4	3	2	1
21. I truly believe that I am pushing myself to my limits.	1	2	3	4	5
22. It is ridiculous to me that a person age 65 or older would bother completing a college degree.	5	4	3	2	1
23. I have been pursuing the same career goal for a long time.	1	2	3	4	⑤
24. My idea of what would be a satisfying career for me has changed several times so far in my life.	5	4	3	2	1
25. I keep trying to attain an important goal of mine, whether or not I receive positive feedback along the way.	1	2	3	4	5

Scoring and Interpretation:

85–125: You have exceptional grit, which, if combined with the right amount of intelligence and talent, should be a major asset to you in your work and personal life.

41–84: You have a reasonable degree of grit, which, if combined with the right amount of intelligence and talent, should get you through most challenges in life.

25–40: Your level of grit appears to be below average. If after serious self-reflection, this appears to be true, you would do well to work on strengthening your grit. It will take some willpower and self-discipline to accomplish this goal.

American managers are urged to be careful in assuming that rewards that are effective in their culture necessarily work well in other cultures. For example, increasing the salaries of one group of Mexican workers motivated them to work fewer, not more hours. As the Mexicans explained their behavior, "We can now make enough money to live and enjoy life in less time than previously. Now, we do not have to work so many hours." (The Mexicans placed a high valence on spending more time with family and friends.)

Another example of how culture influences the effectiveness of a reward—an expatriate manager in Japan rewarded a Japanese sales representative by promoting him to a management position (a status reward). However, the new manager experienced a decline in effort and performance. The promotion, an individualistic reward, separated the new manager from his colleagues and embarrassed him. As a result, he invested less effort in work.[37]

An extreme cross-cultural difference is that the promise of steady work and a regular wage is not a strong motivator in a select few cultures. To illustrate, several Canadian firms began mining for precious metals in Nunavut, Canada, several years ago. Many of the miners were recruited from the Inuit native population. On sunny days, many of the workers chose to seal hunt or fish (a strong cultural tradition) instead of reporting to work even if it meant losing wages at the mine. Because some of the seal hunting and fishing generates revenue, we cannot assume that the Inuit are not motivated by money.

Implications for Managerial Practice

1. The explanations of motivation presented in this chapter all have implications for managerial practice. Nevertheless, we emphasize suggestions derived from

expectancy theory because its components include ideas from other theories, and also mention how procrastination influences goal attainment:

a. *Determine what levels and kinds of performance are needed to achieve organizational goals.* Motivating others proceeds best when workers have a clear understanding of what needs to be accomplished. At the same time, managers should make sure that the desired levels of performance are possible.

b. *Train and encourage people.* Managers should give group members the necessary training and encouragement to be confident that they can perform the required task. Some group members who appear to be poorly motivated simply lack the right skills and self-confidence.

c. *Understand individual differences in valences.* To motivate workers effectively, managers must recognize individual differences in preferences for rewards. An attempt should be made to offer workers rewards to which they attach a high valence. Cross-cultural differences in valences may also occur.

d. *Use positive reinforcement more than punishment.* At times, punishment is necessary. Yet it can produce such negative side effects as anxiety and retaliation against the firm, including employees making costly mistakes intentionally.

e. *Be aware that procrastination can block goal attainment.* No matter how carefully goals are established in accordance with goal theory, an employee who procrastinates will not achieve a given goal on time. A worker who appears to be procrastinating will need to be confronted about the problem and encouraged to get moving to attain the goal. To help the worker overcome the procrastination, managers should emphasize attaining the easiest goal among the many goals involved in the task, such as establishing a computer file for the task.

2. Another implication for managerial practice with respect to motivation is that a manager's motivation to carry out a particular responsibility can influence the motivation level of subordinates to act accordingly. This managerial spillover effect was demonstrated in a study of customer service representatives in a large travel agency franchise that had adopted a new service technology tool. When managers were motivated to adopt the new technology themselves, the representatives were more likely to be motivated to do the same.[38]

Summary of Key Points

1. *Explain how worker engagement is part of employee motivation.* Motivation is the process by which behavior is mobilized and sustained in the interest of achieving organizational goals. Employee engagement centers on an individual's involvement, satisfaction, commitment, and enthusiasm for work. An engaged worker is motivated to accomplish work and attain goals, yet the engagement level can vary from time to time. Engaged workers are the most productive employees, and they contribute to the prosperity of the organization. Organizations with high levels of employee engagement have such outcomes as higher customer satisfaction ratings, greater profits and productivity, lower absenteeism, and fewer quality defects.

2. *Describe several need theories of motivation, including the needs hierarchy, the two-factor theory, and the achievement–power–affiliation triad.* As reflected in need theories of motivation, self-interest is a driving force. According to Maslow's needs hierarchy, human needs fall into five groups: physiological, safety, so-

cial and love, esteem, and self-actualization. As needs at one level are gratified, they lose their strength and the next level of needs is activated.

Herzberg's two-factor theory of work motivation divides job factors into motivators or satisfiers versus maintenance factors or dissatisfiers. Motivational factors are the intrinsic or job content factors (e.g., achievement and recognition) that make a job rewarding. Maintenance factors are the extrinsic aspects of the job (e.g., working conditions and benefits). Dissatisfaction stems from substandard extrinsic factors.

McClelland's acquired needs theory explains that certain needs people strive to satisfy are acquired or learned from the culture. His research centers on three needs of particular significance in understanding entrepreneurs and managers: achievement, power, and affiliation. The need for power is the primary motivator of successful managers.

3. *Summarize the key propositions of goal theory and reinforcement theory.* Goal setting is an important part of all major theories of motivation. Specific and

difficult goals result in higher performance than generalized goals. Goals must be accepted by workers and goals are more effective when they are used to evaluate performance and linked to feedback and rewards. Deadlines improve the effectiveness of goals. A learning goal orientation is more effective than a performance goal orientation and group goal setting is as important as individual goal setting.

According to reinforcement theory, behavior is determined by its consequences, or rewards and punishments, for behaving in particular ways. At the foundation of reinforcement theory is operant conditioning, or learning that takes place as a consequence of behavior. People learn to repeat behaviors that bring them pleasurable outcomes and to avoid behaviors that lead to uncomfortable outcomes. The four basic strategies for arranging contingencies to modify behavior are positive reinforcement, avoidance motivation, extinction, and punishment.

4. *Explain the expectancy theory of motivation and its tie-in with self-efficacy.* Expectancy theory is based on the idea that work motivation results from deliberate choices to engage in certain activities in order to achieve worthwhile outcomes. The three components of expectancy theory are effort-to-performance expectancies, instrumentalities, and valence. Individual differences can influence valence. Most situations have multiple outcomes and valences. Motivational force is the result of the multiplication of expectancies, instrumentalities, and valence. Positive affect may enhance any of these factors.

5. *Explain how equity theory and social comparison contribute to motivation.* Equity theory explains that workers compare their inputs and outcomes with relevant people in the workplace. When employees believe that they are receiving equitable outputs in relation to their inputs, they are generally satisfied and motivated. When workers believe they are giving too much in relation to what they are receiving from the organization, dissatisfaction ensues. Another way of looking at equity theory is that people search for justice in terms of being treated fairly. People will usually take action to bring their equity ratio into balance. Two such actions would be seeking greater outputs or decreasing input.

6. *Use social learning theory to motivate yourself.* According to social learning theory, individual behavior is influenced by a combination of a person's cognitions and social environment. People learn by imitating a model and becoming motivated to repeat the behavior. Conditions favoring social learning include high expectations, self-administration of rewards, observation of tangible behavior to imitate, and the necessary physical and mental ability.

7. *Recognize the importance of both intrinsic and extrinsic motivators.* The theory of intrinsic motivation, or self-determination, emphasizes that people are active agents rather than recipients of environmental forces. Passion and energy are part of being intrinsically motivated. Intrinsic motivation is tied in with needs for competence and self-determination. A person with a high level of grit pursues external goals, yet at the same time experiences strong intrinsic motivation in accomplishing tasks and goals.

Extrinsic rewards can sometimes lower a person's job performance and be demotivating, particularly when a creative task is involved. A combination of intrinsic and extrinsic rewards is best for motivation, although intrinsic motivation is essential for self-management.

8. *Explain how personality and cultural factors are related to motivation.* Certain personality traits can predispose a person to being well motivated. A study demonstrated that conscientiousness and extraversion were both associated with better sales performance. Cross-cultural factors typically influence which rewards or outcomes are likely to have the highest valence for a particular cultural group. A cross-cultural consideration in expectancy theory is that it depends on the extent to which workers believe they have control over the outcome of their efforts and how much faith they have in leaders to deliver rewards.

Key Terms and Phrases

Discussion Questions and Activities

1. Many of the sales associates at CarMax are recent college graduates. What would motivate a college graduate to pursue a career at CarMax?
2. Can you identify several factors about a job or company that would keep you engaged?
3. How does WIIFM explain the fact that many busy managers and professionals devote considerable amounts of their time to community activities and charities?
4. How would you know if a particular person had a strong need for power? For achievement? For affiliation?
5. Get together in a group and have each member give an example of how establishing a goal has been motivational for him or her.
6. How can a manager strengthen the expectancies of group members?
7. How does a person formulate an instrumentality for estimating the extent to which hard work will lead to a promotion?
8. Identify an outcome for which you have a strong negative valence. What type of motivated behavior would you engage in to avoid that outcome?
9. Identify a person who appears to have a high degree of grit, including yourself, if applicable. Ask that person if he or she is strictly pursuing a big reward or is also excited about the work involved in attaining the goal.
10. Based on your personal experiences, as well as listening to others and reading, identify one or two cultural groups that you think are strongly work motivated. What is the basis for your answer?

CASE PROBLEM: Motivating the Store Associates at Customer Haven

Customer Haven is a chain of 734 discount department stores located in 28 states as well as three Canadian provinces. CEO Beth frequently thinks about how store managers and department supervisors can motivate store associates to provide a better experience for customers. She recognizes that their customer base does not expect the same level of service they might receive at traditional department stores or at boutiques. Nevertheless, she sees room for improvement in the motivation of store associates to provide a better experience for customers.

At a recent meeting of her top-management team, Beth said, "As I tour a sampling of our stores, I see a lot of room for improvement in how we deal with customers directly and indirectly. I see a lot of merchandise thrown on the floor by customers and just left there by our associates. I see our associates walking around the store, carrying out their chores, who seem too busy to ever look at a customer. I hardly ever see a store associate look at a customer who seems confused and say to that customer, 'How can I help you?'"

Glenn, the director of merchandising, said to Beth, "What are you proposing Customer Haven do to motivate our store associates to a higher level of customer service?"

Beth responded, "Let's get modern. We will engage our workers by talking about advancement opportunities and how they can grow professionally. We will throw the occasional store party or picnic. As hundreds of studies on management and workplace behavior state, an engaged workforce is a motivated workforce."

With a concerned expression, Ashley, the HR director, responded, "Hold on, Beth, you are getting a little too fancy here. The majority of our store associates are paid the minimum wage or slightly higher. The ugly truth is that many of them need food stamps and other forms of public assistance just to survive financially. Many of our associates who own cars are way behind in their monthly car payments. I doubt that we can engage these associates who are struggling to meet basic needs."

Beth shook her head and said, "Ashley, you are too old-fashioned in your thinking. Making a decent living is important to our associates, but I think they could be made more concerned about bigger things, such as professional growth and providing a great customer experience."

Glenn said, "I'm not sure which one of you two is on the right track, but as an executive team, let's do something."

Case Questions

1. To what extent do you think the leadership at Customer Haven should concentrate on meeting the basic financial needs of store associates to motivate them to provide better customer service?
2. If you have ever shopped at Walmart, Kmart, or Target, to what extent do you think these popular discount stores face the same motivational problems as Customer Haven?
3. What do you recommend that management at Customer Haven do to enhance the motivation of its store associates to provide a better customer experience?

1. Original story created from facts and observations in the following sources: Michael C. Bush and Sarah Lewis-Kulin, "100 Best Companies to Work For 2018: Number 34, CarMax," *Fortune*, March 1, 2018, p. 60; Michael C. Bush and Sarah Lewis-Kulin, "The 100 Best Companies to Work For 2017: Number 77: CarMax," *Fortune*, March 15, 2017, p. 114; "CarMax Announces New Chief Human Resources Officer," CarMax, http://investors.carmax.com/news-releases, April 11, 2017, pp. 1–2; "CarMax: Nominate Your Workplace," www.reviews.greatplacetowork.com/carmax, September 12, 2017, pp. 1–8.

2. Michael S. Christian, Adela S. Garza, and Jerel E. Slaughter, "Work Engagement: A Quantitative Review and Test of Its Relation with Task Performance," *Personnel Psychology*, Number 1, 2011, p. 89.

3. Zinta S. Byrne, Janet M. Peters, and James W. Weston, "The Struggle with Employee Engagement: Measures and Construct Clarification Using Five Samples," *Journal of Applied Psychology*, September 2016, p. 122.

4. "2017 State of Employee Engagement Report," SABA, www1.saba.com/StateofEmployeeEngagementReport2017.html, © 2017Saba Software Inc.

5. Christian, Garza, and Slaughter, "Work Engagement," p. 94.

6. Susan Sorenson, "How Employee Engagement Drives Growth," *Gallup Business Journal*, June 20, 2013, p. 2.

7. Quoted in Sorenson, "How Employee Engagement Drives Growth," p. 2.

8. Data reported in W. Chan Kim and Renée Maubargne, "Blue Ocean Leadership," *Harvard Business Review*, May 2014, p. 62.

9. John Baldoni, "Employee Engagement Does More than Boost Productivity," *HBR Blog Network*, https://hbr.org/2013/07/employee-engagement-does-more, July 4, 2013, p. 1.

10. Tamar Lytle, "The Engagement Challenge," *HR Magazine*, October 2016.

11. Lewis Garrad and Tomas Chamorro-Premuzic, "The Dark Side of High Employee Engagement," *Harvard Business Review*, August 16, 2016, p. 3.

12. Abraham H. Maslow, "A Theory of Human Motivation," *Psychological Review*, July 1943, pp. 370–396; Abraham H. Maslow, *Motivation and Personality* (New York: Harper & Row, 1954), Chapter 5.

13. Lori Goler, Janelle Gale, Bryan Harrington, and Adam Grant, "The Three Things Employees Really Want: Career, Community, Cause," *Harvard Business Review*, February 20, 2018, p. 2.

14. Frederick Herzberg, Bernard Mausner, and Barbara Snyderman, *The Motivation to Work*, 2nd ed. (New York: John Wiley & Sons, 1959); Frederick Herzberg, *Work and the Nature of Man* (Cleveland: World Publishing, 1966).

15. David C. McClelland, "Business Drive and National Achievement," *Harvard Business Review*, July–August 1962, pp. 99–112; McClelland, *The Achieving Society* (New York: Van Nostrand, 1961).

16. David C. McClelland and David H. Burnam, "Power Is the Great Motivator," *Harvard Business Review*, January 2003, pp. 117–126, 142 (reprint of 1976 article plus *HBR* editor update).

17. Jane Churchouse and Chris Churchouse, *Managing People* (Hamshire, England: Gower Publishing Ltd., 1998); "Recognizing Workers' Needs," *Manager's Edge*, March 1999, p. 1.

18. Gary P. Latham, "Goal Setting: A Five-Step Approach to Behavior Change," *Organizational Dynamics*, Number 3, 2003, p. 311.

19. Edwin A. Locke and Gary P. Latham, *A Theory of Goal Setting and Task Performance* (Upper Saddle River, NJ: Prentice-Hall, 1990); Edwin A. Locke and Gary P. Latham (Eds.), *New Developments in Goal Setting and Task Performance* (New York: Routledge, 2013).

20. Latham, "Goal Setting: A Five-Step Approach to Behavior Change," p. 309.

21. John J. Donavan and David J. Radosevich, "The Moderating Role of Goal Commitment on the Goal Difficulty–Performance Relationship: A Meta-Analytic Review and Critical Reanalysis," *Journal of Applied Psychology*, April 1998, pp. 308–315; Howard J. Klein, Michael J. Wesson, John R. Hollenbeck, and Bradley J. Alge, "Goal Commitment and the Goal-Setting Process: Conceptual Clarification and Empirical Synthesis," *Journal of Applied Psychology*, December 1999, pp. 885–896.

22. Yitzhak Fried and Linda Haynes Slowik, "Enriching Goal-Setting Theory with Time: An Integrated Approach," *Academy of Management Review*, July 2004, p. 407.

23. Gary P. Latham, "The Motivational Benefits of Goal Setting," *Academy of Management Executive*, November 2004, p. 129; Lisa D. Ordóñez, Maurice E. Schweitzer, Adam D. Galinsky, and Max H. Bazerman, "Goals Gone Wild: The Systematic Side Effects of Overprescribing Goal Setting," *Academy of Management Perspective*, February 2009, p. 14.

24. B. F. Skinner, *Science and Human Behavior* (New York: Macmillan, 1953).

25. Victor H. Vroom, *Work and Motivation* (New York: John Wiley & Sons, 1964); Lynn E. Miller and Joseph E. Grush, "Improving Predictions in Expectancy Theory Research: Effects of Personality, Expectancies, and Norms," *Academy of Management Journal*, March 1988, pp. 107–122.

26. Alexander D. Stajkovic and Fred Luthans, "Social Cognitive Theory and Self-Efficacy: Going Beyond Traditional Motivational and Behavioral Approaches," *Organizational Dynamics*, Spring 1998, p. 66.

27. Amir Erez and Alice M. Isen, "The Influence of Positive Affect on the Components of Expectancy Motivation," *Journal of Applied Psychology*, December 2002, pp. 1055–1067.

28. J. Stacy Adams, "Toward an Understanding of Inequality," *Journal of Abnormal and Social Psychology*, Vol. 67, 1963, pp. 422–436; M. R. Carrell and J. E. Dettrich, "Equity Theory: The Recent Literature, Methodological Considerations,

and New Directions," *Academy of Management Review*, April 1978, pp. 202–210.

29. Robert Wood and Albert Bandura, "Social Cognitive Theory of Organizational Management," *Academy of Management Review*, July 1989, pp. 361–384.

30. Kenneth W. Thomas, *Intrinsic Motivation at Work: Building Energy and Commitment* (San Francisco: Berrett-Koehler Publishers, 2000).

31. Kevin W. Rockman and Gary A. Ballinger, "Intrinsic Motivation and Organizational Identification among On-Demand Workers," *Journal of Applied Psychology*, September 2017, pp. 1305–1316.

32. Gregory Moorehead and Ricky W. Griffin, *Organizational Behavior: Managing People and Organizations*, 4th ed. (Boston: Houghton Mifflin, 1995), pp. 147–148; Robert P. Vecchio, *Organizational Behavior*, 2nd ed. (Mason, OH: South-Western/ Thomson Learning, 1991), p. 193.

33. Thomas, *Intrinsic Motivation at Work*. (These comments are still relevant 15 years later.)

34. The research findings and most of the ideas in this section are based on the following sources: Angela Duckworth, Christopher Peterson, Michael D. Matthews, and Dennis B. Kelly, "Grit: Perseverance and Passion for Long-Term Goals," *Journal of Personality and Social Psychology*, No. 6, 2007, pp. 1087–1101; Angela Duckworth, *Grit: The Power of Passion and Perseverance* (New York: Scribner, 2016); Angela Duckworth and Lauren Eskreis-Winkler, "True Grit," *Observer*, Vol. 26, No. 4, April 2013, pp. 1–3.

35. Richard M. Ryan and Edward L. Deci, "Self-Determination Theory and the Facilitation of Intrinsic Motivation, Social Development, and Well-Being," *American Psychologist*, January 2000, pp. 68–78; Jeffrey Pfeffer, *Human Equation: Building Profits by Putting People First* (Boston: Harvard Business School Press, 1998), pp. 213–217.

36. Murray R. Barrick, Greg L. Stewart, and Mike Piotrowski, "Personality and Job Performance: Test of Mediating Effects of Motivation among Sales Representatives," *Journal of Applied Psychology*, February 2002, pp. 43–51.

37. These studies and observations are reported in "Managing Cross-Cultural Workforce" (http://home.skif.net/%7Etodorov/036.htm).

38. Jan Wieseke, Florian Kraus, Sascha Alavi, and Tino Kessler-Thönes, "How Leaders' Motivation Transfers to Customer Service Representatives," *Journal of Service Research*, Number 2, 2011, pp. 214–233.

Motivational Methods and Programs

CHAPTER 7

Africa Studio/Shutterstock.com

Chapter Outline

Motivation through Job Design

Motivation through Positive
Reinforcement Programs

Motivation through Recognition
and Pride

Motivation through Financial
Incentives

Choosing an Appropriate
Motivational Model

Implications for Managerial
Practice

Learning Objectives

**After reading and studying this chapter and doing the exercises, you
should be able to:**

1. Explain how to enhance motivation through job enrichment, the job
   characteristics model, and job crafting.

2. Summarize the basics of a positive reinforcement program in the
   workplace.

3. Identify rules and suggestions for motivating group members through
   positive reinforcement.

4. Explain why recognition and pride are good motivators, as well as the
   nature of reward and recognition programs in the workplace.

5. Describe how to effectively use financial incentives to motivate others,
   including the use of employee stock ownership plans and stock options.

6. Choose an appropriate motivational model for a given situation.

The telecommunications giant Huawei is a Chinese company owned by its employees. Huawei employs over 170,000 employees, including more than 40,000 non-Chinese, and serves more than 3 billion customers worldwide. Huawei is the ninth-largest information technology company in the world and the fourth-largest manufacturer of smartphones.

When Ren Zhengfei founded the company in 1987, he sought a way to decrease income inequality between the wealthy and average workers and also to develop a highly motivated workforce.

His solution was to implement an employee stock ownership plan (ESOP). Zhengfei owns 1.4 percent of the privately owned company's shares, with the rest owned by company employees.

The ESOP at Huawei is based on two key premises. First are the Confucian values of equality and harmony, thereby preventing large income gaps among employees. Zhengfei reasoned that if employees are company owners, they will be motivated to act as if they were entrepreneurs. With this mind-set, employees would initiate projects that could help each other earn more money and reduce income inequality. At the same time, the higher-performing employees could earn higher income. The second premise centers on the idea of equity. Hard work is rewarded by higher compensation, with the exception that overtime projects that do not help customers are not rewarded.

The ESOP means that Huawei is owned by its employees and that Zhengfei expects every employee to act like an owner, demonstrating dedication and commitment. The entrepreneurial spirit enables Huawei to learn and innovate. Workers care about belonging to and being proud of a collective, yet they also want to differentiate themselves from other workers by performing at their best.

During April and May of each year, department heads determine the number of shares, if any, each employee can purchase for the current year. An employee's position, work experience, and performance evaluation results from the previous year influence the ESOP shares the employee is offered. The use of performance evaluation data is important because employees who perform better will be rewarded with a bigger stake in the company. The company decides on the dividend amount per share at the shareholders' meeting based on the profitability of Huawei in the just-ended fiscal year. If the employees collectively helped improve company profits, they will earn bigger dividends.

Owning stock in the company encourages employees to work hard for long-term benefits. The ability of the ESOP to allocate and withdraw stock options based on performance helps improve productivity, as well as ensuring that the shares are allocated to the most productive and responsible employees.

Zhengfei sums up the motivational effect of the ESOP in these words: "Huawei belongs to its employees. If Huawei becomes bigger and creates more profit, employees will acquire benefits more from its ESOP and they will get huge motivation to work hard to enhance productivity."[1]

As the stock ownership program at Huawei illustrates, a standard practice for increasing employee motivation and productivity is to offer financial rewards for good performance. Motivational programs continue in importance because many employees are not fully engaged in their work, as described in Chapter 6. In this chapter, we describe motivational programs based on recognition, but we also examine motivation through job design, behavior modification, and reward and financial incentives. In addition, we describe choosing an appropriate motivational model, a topic that relates to both the present and previous chapter.

LEARNING OBJECTIVE 1
Explain how to enhance motivation through job enrichment, the job characteristics model, and job crafting.

Motivation through Job Design

A major strategy for enhancing motivation is to make the job so challenging and the worker so responsible that he or she is motivated just by performing the job. We will approach motivation through job design by explaining job enrichment, the job characteristics model, and job crafting. The self-managed work teams to be described in Chapter 10 are also a method of motivation through job design. Research and practice with motivation through job design has its roots in the two-factor theory described in Chapter 6.

Job Enrichment

Job enrichment refers to making a job more motivational and satisfying by adding variety, responsibility, and managerial decision making. At its best, job enrichment gives workers a sense of ownership, responsibility, and accountability for their work. Because job enrichment leads to a more exciting job, it often increases employee job satisfaction and motivation. People are usually willing to work harder at tasks they find enjoyable and rewarding, just as they will put effort into a favorite hobby. Managers and professionals in organizations typically have enriched jobs. Professional-level workers at the beginning of their career are particularly eager for job enrichment because they see it as a vehicle to professional growth.

Having enriched work to perform is motivational.

michaeljung/Shutterstock.com

job enrichment The process of making a job more motivational and satisfying by adding variety, responsibility, and managerial decision making.

Characteristics of an Enriched Job

According to the late Frederick Herzberg, the way to design an enriched job is to include as many of the characteristics described next as possible.[2] Figure 7-1 summarizes an updated version of the characteristics and consequences of enriched jobs.

1. *Direct feedback.* Employees should receive immediate evaluation of their work. Feedback can be built into the job (e.g., the feedback that closing a sale gives a sales representative) or provided by the manager.
2. *Client relationships.* A job is automatically enriched when a worker has a client or customer to serve, whether that client is internal or external. Serving a client is more satisfying to most people than performing work solely for a manager. An information systems specialist at a bank who interacts with loan officers is said to have a client relationship. However, interacting with hostile and verbally abusive customers is de-motivational and stressful rather than enriching.
3. *New learning.* An enriched job allows its holder to acquire new knowledge. The learning can stem from job experiences themselves or from training programs associated with the job.
4. *Control over method.* When a worker has some control over which method to choose to accomplish a task, his or her task motivation generally increases. An office manager, for example, might be told to decrease energy costs by 10 percent in the building. He or she would have control over the method if empowered to decide

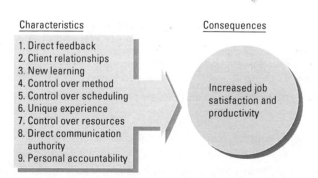

FIGURE 7-1 **Characteristics and Consequences of an Enriched Job**

New learning contributes to job enrichment.

how to decrease costs, such as adjusting the thermostat or finding a lower-cost energy supplier.

5. *Control over scheduling.* The ability to schedule one's work contributes to job enrichment. Scheduling includes the authority to decide when to tackle which assignments and to have some say in setting working hours, such as flexible working hours.

6. *Unique experience.* An enriched job has unique qualities or features. A business communications assistant, for example, has the opportunity to interact with visiting celebrities.

7. *Control over resources.* Another contributor to enrichment is having some control over resources, such as money, material, or people.

8. *Direct communication authority.* An enriched job provides workers the opportunity to communicate directly with other people who use their output. A software engineer with an enriched job, for example, handles complaints about the software he or she developed. The advantages of this dimension of an enriched job are similar to those derived from maintaining client relationships.

9. *Personal accountability.* In an enriched job, workers are responsible for their results. They accept credit for a job well done and blame for a job done poorly.

A highly enriched job has all nine of the preceding characteristics and gives the job holder an opportunity to satisfy growth needs such as self-fulfillment. A job with some of these characteristics would be moderately enriched. An impoverished job has none.

Meaningful Work as an Application of Job Enrichment

The current emphasis on meaningful work can be considered an application of job enrichment, particularly with respect to the dimensions of unique experiences and personal accountability. Helping employees find meaning in their work is a major component of employee engagement. Furthermore, helping employees find meaning in their work is a more widely used program of motivation than well-structured programs such as job enrichment, the job characteristics model, or the systematic use of positive reinforcement.

Work is meaningful when people feel they are doing work that matters or makes a difference. A Target store manager might think, "Every day what I do makes a difference because my mission is to help reduce the cost of living for people in my area. By shopping at Target, our customers can better provide for their families."

Areas of Impact

Research by the venerable consulting firm, McKinsey & Company, indicates that the opportunity to make an impact in the following four areas will most likely increase the meaningfulness of work for employees:

- *On society*—including making a better society, building the community, or managing resources carefully
- *On the customer*—for example, making life easier and providing a superior service or product
- *On the workgroup or team*—for example, having a sense of belonging, a caring environment, or working collectively in an efficient and effective manner
- *On themselves*—including personal development, higher financial compensation, and a sense of empowerment

A representative way in which leaders can make work highly meaningful is to give others the opportunity to lead projects or task forces. Such leadership opportunities enhance engagement and work meaningfulness for the heads of the project or task forces. Being given the opportunity to lead others also adds empowerment to the job.[3]

Feedback for Meaningful Work

Another way in which job enrichment is related to meaningfulness of work is that giving useful feedback makes work more meaningful. Harvard Business School professors Teresa Amabile and Steven Kramer gathered and analyzed diary reports from 238 professional-level workers in 26 project teams from seven companies across three different industries. The diaries were e-mailed by the researchers to participants, and asked a few questions about the day, including what stood out in relation to work.

Based on 12,000 diary entries, the authors discovered that a feeling of making progress was key to employee engagement and the feeling of performing meaningful work among these workers.[4] An example of a leader providing feedback to a worker on progress would be, "It looks like you found a way to reduce manufacturing costs by 1 percent toward our goal of a 15 percent reduction."

Self-Assessment 7-1 gives you an opportunity to think about how meaningful work applies to you.

Cause as Part of Meaningful Work

An analysis of hundreds of thousands of survey responses found that a major bucket (category) of motivators was *cause*. The term refers to purpose, or the feeling that you can make a meaningful impact, identifying with the organization's mission, and believing the mission is doing some good. If the mission is performing a social good, the worker is likely to experience pride. The concepts of impact and doing good are based on values and are therefore subjective. Assume that manufacturing engineer Conor helps produce a line of successful pickup trucks. He believes that pickup trucks help get important work done in society and also bring joy to thousands of their owners. Conor therefore believes that his work has an important cause. In contrast, manufacturing engineer Fatima, who also helps produce pickup trucks, believes that they waste resources and pollute the environment because of their relatively low gas mileage. She therefore feels that her work lacks a meaningful cause.[5]

Finding Meaning in Mundane Tasks

A sensible way of motivating others, as well as yourself, through meaningful work is to find a sense of purpose in mundane, or everyday, tasks. A brief moment of reflection about why you are performing a task can help boost your motivation and performance.[6] Ask yourself questions that help you see the big picture, such as a logistics specialist asking, "Why is it important that we ship these gloves in time for the winter season?" A business analyst might ask, "If I get this spreadsheet done, what bigger aspiration or value of mine will it support?" Perhaps the spreadsheet will help the CEO make better financial decisions that will create jobs for deserving families.

Empowerment and Involvement as a Type of Job Enrichment

A managerial practice that leads to job enrichment is to empower employees, as implied in characteristic 7 of job enrichment. Empowerment is the process of sharing power with group members, thereby enhancing their feelings of self-efficacy. Empowering workers usually enhances their motivation because having more power is intrinsically motivating. Involving employees in decisions that affect them is a form of empowerment, and is also motivational. Involvement leads to greater commitment and therefore facilitates being able to facilitate a change such as a new work method.[7] An example of empowerment and involvement follows:

> A construction company received a huge contract to rebuild a hotel in downtown New Orleans, 1 month after Hurricane Katrina struck. The project manager who was assigned the task said that it would be almost impossible to get the project completed on time because of the shortage of laborers and skilled workers in the Gulf Coast area. The project manager was then told by a company executive, "This job is your baby. If it were easy

empowerment The process of sharing power with group members, thereby enhancing their feelings of self-efficacy.

How Meaningful Is My Work?

Instructions: Indicate whether the following statements are mostly true or mostly false as they apply to your present, or a previous, job. If relating to a job you hold or have held is not relevant, relate each of the statements to school or volunteer work.

Statement about the Work and/or Job	Mostly True	Mostly False
1. When I am at work, the time goes by very slowly.		X
2. I feel totally absorbed in my work.		X
3. The excitement in my job fills me with energy.	X	
4. The work I do really has an impact on society.	X	
5. My job gives me as much pleasure as participating in my favorite pastime.	X	X
6. My job leaves me emotionally flat.		X
7. I discover something new and interesting about my job almost every week.	X	
8. The work I do really helps other people.	X	
9. It would make me sad to let my coworkers down.	X	X
10. I put a minimum of mental energy into my job.		X
11. I am a little embarrassed telling other people what I actually do for a living.		X
12. My work contributes to my purpose in life.	X	
13. I don't care if many celebrities earn much more money than I because my work is very important.	X	
14. I sometimes wonder: What is the purpose of my job and work?	X	
15. I would feel guilty if I took a sick day from work even if I really were sick.	X	

Scoring and interpretation: Give yourself 1 point for answering *Mostly True* to the following statements: 2, 3, 4, 5, 7, 8, 9, 12, 13, and 15. Give yourself 1 point for answering *Mostly False* to the following statements: 1, 6, 10, 11, and 14.

12–15: Your work is quite meaningful, and if your attitudes persist, you should have a long and rewarding career.

5–11: You have an average degree of meaningfulness in your work and job.

1–4: Your work may not be meaningful enough to bring you long-term satisfaction. You are advised to look for ways to make your work more meaningful, such as looking for new tasks that you perceive as more meaningful.

Source: A few of the statements in the quiz are based on questionnaire items presented in Michael S. Christian, Adela S. Garza, and Jerel E. Slaughter, "Work Engagement: A Quantitative Review and Test of Its Relation with Task Performance," *Personnel Psychology*, Number 1, 2011, pp. 108–109.

to accomplish, we would not have given you the assignment. Do whatever it takes to find the people you need to put the hotel back in shape. Spend all the money you want so long as we make a profit."

The project manager wound up renting a fleet of recreational vehicles that served as temporary housing for the project. Workers were recruited from as far north as Wisconsin and Vermont, in addition to whatever workers were available locally. The hotel opened on time for a key convention.

Before implementing a program of job enrichment, a manager must ask if the workers need or want more responsibility, variety, and growth in the first place. And not every worker cares about working for a grand purpose. Some employees' jobs are already enriched enough. Other employees do not want an enriched job because they prefer to avoid the challenge and stress of responsibility. A study conducted in a government service organization indicated that employees with a strong need for growth were more likely to respond to an opportunity for performing enriched work. The independent variable studied was the manager offering a case-processing specialist the opportunity to collaborate with him or her on a case.[8]

The Job Characteristics Model

The concept of job enrichment was expanded years ago to the **job characteristics model**, a method of job design that focuses on the task and interpersonal demands of a job.[9] The model is based on both needs theory and expectancy theory, with its emphasis on workers looking to satisfy needs through the job. To illustrate, a basic proposition of the model is that workers value outcomes to the extent that the outcomes can help satisfy their deficiency and growth needs. An outline of the job characteristics model is shown in Figure 7-2. According to the model, five measurable characteristics of a job can improve employee motivation, satisfaction, and performance. These characteristics are:

job characteristics model A method of job design that focuses on the task and interpersonal demands of a job.

1. *Skill variety*, the degree to which there are many skills needed to perform the job.
2. *Task identity*, the degree to which one worker is able to do a complete job, from beginning to end, with a tangible and possible outcome.
3. *Task significance*, the degree to which work has a heavy impact on others in the immediate organization or the external environment. Task significance is the building block of meaningful work. Furthermore, research evidence indicates that this characteristic has the biggest impact of the five in this list on work motivation.[10]
4. *Autonomy*, the degree to which a job offers freedom, independence, and discretion in scheduling and in determining procedures involved in its implementation.
5. *Feedback*, the degree to which a job provides direct information about performance.

These core job characteristics relate to critical psychological states or key mental attitudes. Skill variety, task identity, and task significance lead to a feeling that the work is meaningful. The task significance characteristic can be a potent motivator at all job

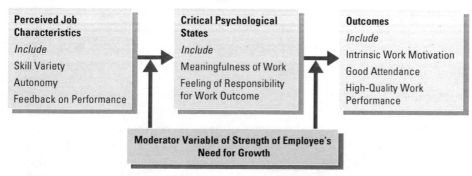

FIGURE 7-2 Key Components of the Job Characteristics Model of Job Enrichment

levels because it is the key part of the meaningfulness of work. The task dimension of autonomy leads logically to a feeling that one is responsible for work outcomes. The feedback dimension leads to knowledge of results. According to the model, a redesigned job must lead to these three psychological states for workers to achieve the outcomes of internal motivation, job satisfaction, growth satisfaction, low turnover and absenteeism, and high-quality performance.

The job characteristics model combines the five characteristics into a single index that reflects the overall potential of a job to trigger high internal work motivation. Called the Motivating Potential Score (MPS), the index is computed as follows:

$$MPS = \frac{\text{Skill Variety} + \text{Task Identity} + \text{Task Significance}}{3} \times \text{Autonomy} \times \text{Feedback}$$

Numeric values for each of the five job characteristics are obtained by tabulating the job holder's answers to the Job Diagnostic Survey, a written questionnaire. After computing the MPS, a researcher can evaluate whether redesigning a job actually changed employees' perceptions of its motivational value. It is much more likely that a researcher rather than a manager or human resources specialist would use the Job Diagnostic Survey.

A potential problem in implementing the job characteristics model, as well as job enrichment in general, is that supervisors and group members may not agree on what constitutes an enriched job. A study conducted in a university office setting with a variety of jobs found that supervisors and subordinates perceived their job characteristics differently. (The dimensions studied were the same as those contained in the job characteristics model.)

The most notable difference was found in task significance, with the supervisors rating this dimension higher than group members. A possible interpretation was that the supervisors had a clearer view of the "big picture," and thereby had a better understanding of the potential impact of a task. Another finding was that the group members perceived the enriched quality to have a bigger impact on job outcomes than did the supervisory level. An implication of these findings is that employees should play a major role in job redesign, since their perceptions of enrichment differ from their supervisors' perceptions.[11]

Job Crafting

The traditional view of a job is that a competent worker carefully follows a job description, and good performance means that the person accomplishes what is specified in the job description. A contemporary view is that a job description is only a guideline: The competent worker is not confined by the constraints of a job description. He or she takes on many constructive activities not mentioned in the job description.

One way workers frequently deviate from their job descriptions is to modify their job to fit their personal preferences and capabilities. According to the research of Amy Wrzesniewski and Jane E. Dutton, employees craft their jobs by changing the tasks they perform and their contacts with others to make their jobs more meaningful.[12] To add variety to her job, for example, a team leader might make nutritional recommendations to team members. The team leader has altered her task of coaching about strictly work-related issues to also coaching about personal health. She has also broadened her role in terms of her impact on the lives of work associates.

job crafting The physical and mental changes workers make in the task or relationships aspects of their job.

Job crafting refers to the physical and mental changes workers make in the task or in the relationship aspects of their jobs. Three common types of job crafting involve changing: (1) the number and type of job tasks; (2) the interaction with others on the job; and (3) one's view of the job. The most frequent purpose of crafting is to make the job more meaningful or enriched. A supermarket store manager, for example, might initiate a program to give surplus food to the homeless as a way of having a bigger impact on society. Examples of the three most frequent forms of job crafting follow with each one requiring worker initiative.

1. *Changing number, scope, and type of job tasks.* A product development engineer might change the quality or amount of interactions with people as a way of gaining acceptance for his or her ideas and moving the project to completion.
2. *Changing quality and/or amount of interaction with others encountered on the job.* Custodial workers in an office might interact with office workers to better understand their needs for office cleanliness.
3. *Changing the view of the job.* A customer-care worker in a call center might decide to perceive every customer demand for help or complaint as an important problem to be resolved, even one as mundane as a customer having forgotten to plug the desktop computer into an electrical outlet.

Fresh insights into job crafting stem from an experiment conducted with 140 employees in different departments of a Dutch health insurance company. The study involved crafting toward both personal strengths and interests. An item measuring crafting toward strengths was "I look for possibilities to do my tasks in such a way that it matches my strengths." A job interest item was "I make sure that I take on tasks that I like." The study found that job crafting through strengths led to a better fit between the person and the job, particularly for older workers. A better fit for the job might then lead to the incumbent being more highly motivated. A possible explanation for the age factor is that as employees age, they gain more insight into their strengths and develop a tendency to make work fit their identity.[13]

Motivation through Positive Reinforcement Programs

One of the most well-established approaches to motivating employees is based upon reinforcement theory. A **positive reinforcement program** is the application of reinforcement theory for motivating people in work settings. Although this type of program heavily emphasizes the use of positive reinforcement, punishment is used occasionally to motivate workers to improve their performance. Linking behavior with positive consequences is more effective than using negative motivators, and positive consequences arouse less controversy. Here we present an example of how positive reinforcement is used in organizations, followed by suggestions for everyday managerial application of positive reinforcement.

LEARNING OBJECTIVE 2
Summarize the basics of a positive reinforcement program in the workplace.

Positive reinforcement program The application of reinforcement theory for motivating people in work settings.

Positive Reinforcement Programs to Strengthen Employee Wellness Programs

The purpose of employee wellness programs is to help employees maintain good health for life and lower health insurance costs at the same time. Maintaining good health could mean curing an existing condition or preventing health problems. Although these goals are laudable, not every employee is eager to actively participate in a wellness program. For example, a heavy smoker might not participate in a smoking cessation program, and an obese person might not care about participating in a weight control program.

Many companies now make use of reinforcement principles to encourage effective use of wellness programs even if the application of positive reinforcement is not highly systematic and structured. Approximately one-half of employers offering wellness incentives tied rewards to completion of lifestyle modification programs, including weight loss, smoking cessation, and physical fitness.[14]

Tobacco use and obesity have been frequent targets of wellness programs, with employers prompting workers to stop smoking and lose weight through such means as the following:

■ Adopting no-smoking and/or no tobacco chewing on and off the job (e-cigarettes are still being pondered);

■ Offering cash incentive payments and gift cards for stopping smoking or losing weight;

■ Providing free health coaching about smoking and attaining a safe body mass index.[15]

Behavior modification is often used to help workers stop smoking.

Steve Aldana, the director of a wellness institute, advises us: "All the water bottles, squeeze balls, gift cards, T-shirts, and other external rewards won't have much of an effect on people who are already physically active." But the rewards will have an impact on those who wish to take action to improve their health or those who are beginning to experiment with a new lifestyle.[16]

A survey of 800 large and midsize employers conducted by a human resources consulting firm found that 79 percent of companies use incentives such as lower insurance premiums to attempt to nudge employees to improve their health. Twenty-four percent of the companies tied incentives to progress on measures such as a person's blood pressure or body mass index (a measure that takes into account weight in relation to height).

The positive reinforcement aspect of wellness programs emphasizes that employees should not be heavily rewarded simply for participating in the program. Jim Winkler, the chief innovation officer for health and benefits at the human resources consulting firm, Aon Hewitt, said, "To truly impact employee behavioral change, more and more organizations realize they need to closely tie rewards to outcomes and better results rather than just enrollment."[17]

Wellness programs that systematically use incentives have been criticized in several ways. One criticism is that forcing people to lose weight or quit smoking may be an invasion of their civil liberties. Another criticism is that when these programs penalize workers for unhealthy behavior, they may be unfairly singling out the very people who strongly need lower healthcare costs.[18] A related criticism is that wellness incentive programs could be used by employers to transfer the higher costs of healthcare to employees in poor health. Furthermore, an employer has to be careful not to violate the Americans with Disabilities Act by offering an incentive to overcome a condition caused by a genetic problem or an emotional disorder.

Rules for the Application of Positive Reinforcement

LEARNING OBJECTIVE 3
Identify rules and suggestions for motivating group members through behavior modification.

Principles of positive reinforcement can also be applied outside of a structured company program. Our focus here is on managers' day-by-day application of positive reinforcement, with the occasional use of punishment. An individual contributor attempting to motivate somebody else can also apply these rules. Following these eight rules increases the probability that a positive reinforcement program will achieve its intended result of increasing the motivation and productivity of individuals and groups. Although the rules have generally been developed with individuals, they also apply to rewarding group performance.

Rule 1: Choose an appropriate reward or punishment. An appropriate reward or punishment is one that is effective in motivating a worker or group and is feasible from the company standpoint. Rewards should have a high positive attraction and punishments a negative one. (Attraction is the same idea as valence.) If one reward does not work, another should be tried. Some rewards are ineffective because the worker does not want the reward, such as giving tickets to a football game to a worker who dislikes football. Feasible rewards include money, company stock, recognition, challenging new assignments, and status symbols such as a private work area.

Often the most basic type of reward, such as an expression of appreciation, has the strongest effect in achieving higher productivity and employee retention.[19] It is generally best to use the mildest form of punishment that will motivate a person, such as verbally expressing disappointment. Although widely used, fear is a generally ineffective form of punishment because it may cause resentment, revenge, and a degree of immobilization.

Rule 2: Reinforce the behaviors you really want to encourage. An axiom of positive reinforcement is that you get what you reinforce. If you give rewards to customer service representatives based on the number of requests for help they process, you will increase the number of calls. Customer service may not improve, however, because the representatives will feel compelled to quickly process the calls for help. Rewards for resolving customer problems have a greater probability of enhancing customer service. (It takes time and patience to resolve some problems received at a call center.)

Rule 3: Supply ample feedback. Positive reinforcement tactics cannot work without frequent feedback to individuals. Feedback can take the form of simply telling people they have done something right or wrong. Brief e-mail messages or handwritten notes are another common form of feedback. Be aware, however, that many employees resent seeing a message with negative feedback on their computer screen or smartphone.

Despite the motivational value of giving positive feedback, many managers and other workers avoid this action. In a self-assessment survey of 7,800 people, 37 percent conceded that they do not give positive reinforcement. The researchers who conducted the survey concluded that many managers think it is part of their job to tell direct reports bad news and correct their mistakes. Yet the managers think that taking the time to provide positive feedback is optional.[20]

Rule 4: Rewards should be commensurate with the good deed. Average performance is encouraged when all forms of accomplishment receive the same reward. Suppose one employee made substantial progress in reducing customer complaints. That person should receive more recognition (or a more valuable reward) than a group member who makes only a minor contribution to solving the problem.

Rule 5: Schedule rewards intermittently. Intermittent rewards sustain desired behavior longer and slow the process of desired behavior fading away when it is not rewarded. A reward that is given continuously may lose its impact. A practical value of intermittent reinforcement is that it saves time. Few managers have enough time to administer rewards for every appropriate response forthcoming from group members.

Rule 6: Rewards and punishments should follow the observed behavior closely in time. For maximum effectiveness, workers should be rewarded shortly after doing something right and punished shortly after doing something wrong. A built-in feedback system capitalizes on this principle. An example would be a computer procedure. If you do it correctly, you are rewarded because it works. Conversely, if you do the procedure incorrectly, it does not work, which acts as a mild punishment. If you administer rewards and punishments, strive to administer them the same day they are earned.

Rule 7: Make rewards visible to the recipient and to others. The person who receives the reward should be aware that it has been received. A person might receive a small bonus for good performance with the payment being virtually hidden in the paycheck. Because the reward is not noticed, it has a negligible impact on behavior.[21] Ideally, rewards should also be made visible to other employees besides the recipient. Rewards that are made public increase the status of the recipient and also let other employees know what kinds of behavior get rewarded.

Rule 8: Change the reward periodically. Rewards do not retain their effectiveness indefinitely. A major criticism of positive reinforcement as a motivational technique is that rewards go stale. Employees and customers lose interest in striving for a reward they have received many times previously. This is particularly true with a repetitive statement such as "Nice job" or "Fantastic." It is helpful for the manager to formulate a list of feasible rewards and try different ones from time to time.

Now do the Skill-Development Exercise to practice several of these rules for using positive reinforcement.

Motivation through Recognition and Pride

LEARNING OBJECTIVE 4
Explain why recognition and pride are good motivators, as well as the nature of reward and recognition programs in the workplace.

Motivating workers by giving them praise and recognition can be considered a direct application of positive reinforcement. Nevertheless, recognition is such a potentially powerful motivator that it merits separate attention. Also, reward and recognition programs are a standard practice in business and nonprofit firms. An example would be rewarding high-performing employees with gift cards or designating them "employees of the month." A reward and recognition program essentially focuses on rewards as a form of recognition. The gift card just mentioned might have a commercial value of $100, but its main value is to recognize a job well done. Pride is a motive that makes recognition an effective motivator.

Recognition as a Motivator

Recognition is a strong motivator because there is a normal human need to crave recognition. At the same time, recognition is effective because most workers feel they do not receive enough recognition. A survey, Stress in America, conducted by the American Psychological Association, indicated that only 46 percent of employees are satisfied with the recognition practices of their employer.[22] Workers, including your coworkers, want to know that their output is useful to somebody.

To appeal to the recognition need of others, identify a meritorious behavior and then recognize that behavior with an oral, written, or material reward. The rules for the use of positive reinforcement are directly applicable. An example of employee recognition is as follows. As the team leader of a production unit, you observe that Janice, one of the manufacturing technicians, has the best safety record in the plant—zero accidents in 5 years. You post a message on the company website notifying every company employee of Janice's accomplishment. A social recognition tool, The Recognition Wall, enables peers to congratulate each other on career milestones as well as other accomplishments. You may recall that the Spotlight awards at Intuit are a form of peer recognition.

An outstanding advantage of using recognition, including praise, as a motivator is that a person can give it with little or no cost, yet it can still be powerful. Recognition thus has an enormous return on investment in comparison to a cash bonus. A key purpose of recognition programs in organizations today is to drive engagement in the workforce. Recognition ranks close to compensation and career opportunities as contributing to engagement, particularly for millennials.[23] The following are several more points to consider to better understand and implement reward and recognition programs:

1. *Praise is one of the most powerful forms of recognition.* Praise works well because it enhances self-esteem if the praise is genuine. As indicated previously, praise is a supplement to other rewards such as compensation. Research conducted by the Gallup Organization indicates that lack of recognition or praise for performing good work is responsible for a 10 to 20 percent difference in revenue and productivity. Limited praise also drives involuntary turnover. A revealing study with teams found that the factor that accounted for the greatest difference between the most successful and least successful teams was the ratio of positive comments (or praise) to negative ones. The highest-performing teams gave each other more than five positive comments for each criticism. In contrast, the lowest-performing teams gave each other three negative comments for every positive one.[24]

   A challenge in using praise as a form of recognition is that not everybody responds well to the same form of praise. A germane example is that highly technical people tend not to like general praise like "Great job." Instead, they prefer a laid-back yet factual statement about how their output made a contribution.[25] Another difference in preferences for receiving praise is that some workers prefer public praise, such as during a face-to-face or virtual meeting. Other workers might prefer to receive praise in private. The differences just mentioned could be attributed to personality traits or cultural preferences.

2. *Feedback is an essential part of recognition.* Specific feedback about what the worker did right makes recognition more meaningful. For example, "The clever cartoon you inserted on our website increased sales by 22 percent for replacement keyboards." As just implied, the feedback should point to specific results and behaviors.

3. *Reward and recognition programs should be linked to organizational goals.* Many organizations understand that the biggest return on reward and recognition programs takes place when the rewards and recognition are linked to a business strategy. For example, if the company strategy is to develop a more culturally diverse workforce at all levels, an employee should be recognized for recruiting a Latina computer scientist.

4. *Employee input into what types of rewards and recognition are valued is useful.* A company might spend a lot of money giving away grandfather clocks to employees, only to find that they would prefer gift certificates to movies as a form of reward and recognition. Many employees enjoy having a meal with coworkers to celebrate accomplishments, while at the same time building team spirit. Yet here also individual differences are important. Some workers do not want to take time away from family responsibilities or social activities to participate in an after-hours meal.

   Cross-cultural factors can have a strong impact on what form of reward or recognition is motivational. In China, for example, a clock can backfire as a recognition symbol because the word for clock can suggest funeral or death. Instead of being a symbol of appreciation for good service, the clock's message could be interpreted as "Drop dead."[26]

5. *It is important to evaluate the effectiveness of the reward and recognition program.* As with all organizational behavior and human resources interventions, it is useful to assess how well the reward and recognition program is working. For example, the company could establish baseline measures of performance, administer the reward and recognition program, and then measure performance again. (Review the section about research methods in Chapter 1.)

6. *Peer recognition can be motivational.* Being recognized by peers is reassuring and motivational. In many offices this reality is acted upon

Recognition awards can be effective motivators.

by software-driven forms of peer recognition. Coworkers are given the opportunity to praise each other publicly with complimentary messages. At the same time, each worker who participates can see how many compliments others are receiving, thereby prompting competition to be recognized.[27] An example of a complimentary message would be, "Cathy, you were terrific in explaining to me how interest rates and bond prices are inversely related. Thanks so much." If a company does not use peer-recognition software, a simple text or e-mail message works equally well.

Peer-recognition programs are particularly useful for making recognition easy and frequent, assuming that workers are in contact with each other frequently, either face-to-face or electronically. When coworkers recognize each other on a shared board, the recognition value is boosted because it becomes visible.

The Organizational Behavior in Action box illustrates how recognition can be used to motivate workers in a basic industry.

Pride as a Motivator

Wanting to feel proud motivates many workers. Workers who are proud of their accomplishments are eager to receive recognition for what they have achieved. Striving to experience the emotion of pride most likely stems from the desire to satisfy the needs for self-esteem and self-fulfillment. Being proud of what you accomplish is more of an intrinsic motivator than an extrinsic motivator such as receiving a gift. Giving workers an opportunity to experience pride can therefore be a strong internal motivator.

Imagine that you are the assistant service manager at a company that customizes corporate jets to meet the requirements of individual clients. Your manager asks you to prepare a PowerPoint presentation of trends in equipment problems. You make your presentation to top management, the group applauds, executives shake your hand, and later you receive several congratulatory e-mail messages. One of the many emotions you experience is likely to be pride in having performed well. You are motivated to keep up the good work.

Pride is a strong motivator.

Workers can also experience pride in relation to recognition awards. For example, a worker might receive a crystal vase for having saved the company thousands of dollars in shipping costs. The vase might be more valuable to the worker as recognition for accomplishment than as a household decoration. The feeling of pride stems from having accomplished a worthwhile activity (saving the company money) rather than from being awarded a vase.

A new twist on pride in the workplace stems from sports, in the form of trash talk. A psychological definition of *trash talk* is "boastful remarks about oneself or insulting remarks about one's opponent delivered during competition." For example, a cost accountant might say to a coworker, "I just saved the company $100,000 on shipping costs. Do you think you're sharp enough to match that? I doubt it." The link between trash talk and pride is dual-sided, with the trash talker doing so because of pride in his or her own prowess. In turn, the recipient of the trash talk is prompted by pride to perform better than the giver.

Experiments conducted at the Wharton School of the University of Pennsylvania suggest that trash talk can motivate the recipient to perform better. An exception is that the recipient of trash talk often performs more poorly on creative tasks and on those requiring cooperation. The anger built into trash talk can be distracting![28]

According to consultant Jon R. Katzenbach, managers can take steps to motivate through pride. A key tactic is for the manager to set his or her compass on pride, not money. It is more important for workers to be proud of what they are doing day by day, than for them to be proud of reaching a major goal. The manager should celebrate "steps" (or attaining small goals) as much as the "landings" (the major goal). The most effective pride builders are masters at identifying and recognizing the small achievements that will instill pride in their people.[29]

Texas Pride Disposal CEO Pumps Up Workers through Recognition and Pride

Kevin Atkinson's love of garbage trucks began during his youth, when he followed garbage trucks on his bicycle and collected toy garbage trucks. Today, Atkinson is the CEO and co-owner of Texas Pride Disposal in Houston, a waste management enterprise with 54 employees and a fleet of 18 trucks that serves over 40,000 customers. The company grosses about $5 million annually. Pride means a lot to Atkinson, and he works hard to install this quality in his workforce. At the same time, the CEO recognizes that being a garbage worker is hard physical work and is usually dirty and smelly. Each crew picks up trash from about 1,200 houses per day.

"My employees do a job that is widely disrespected," says Atkinson. "People assume that if you work on a garbage truck you're a felon that can't do any better. The customers don't realize these are hard-working guys who are trying to do right by their families. They don't get recognition from the customers, so recognition has to come from the management team."

Atkinson begins his program of employee recognition in the hiring process when he dissuades people from working for Texas Pride. He describes how difficult the job is, such as being chewed by spider ants, enduring foul odors, and being exhausted from hauling tons of refuse in the form of picking up waste containers. The misery is then repeated the next working day. By discouraging job applicants, Atkinson believes that he can find workers who are truly committed to the job and know what they are getting into.

Atkinson attempts to win the loyalty of newly hired workers by jumping on the back of the truck and hauling garbage at least once a month. "I have a massive ant bite on the back of my arm right now," he says. "But that shows the crews I'd never ask them to do anything I won't do myself. It matters, and whenever I work on the truck, employees come into my office and comment on it."

Atkinson builds team spirit by emphasizing to his employees that Texas Pride Disposal is a team game. Although each employee is part of a three-person crew, employees are expected to familiarize themselves with the routes of the 16 other crews. Workers can earn extra compensation after they complete their regular responsibilities by joining another route or washing a truck. The workers regard the extra work as a financial bonus. Atkinson combines the additional compensation with a form of recognition by shaking the hands of the workers and thanking them for helping out. To trigger excellence, Atkinson showers his team with recognition and praise. The workers rarely receive positive feedback from customers, so he seeks ways to make them feel special.

Atkinson instills in the garbage workers the importance of taking pride in their work. He conducts safety meetings with his crews, explaining the importance of closing the lid on trash containers, following instructions given by the supervisor, and listening to customer comments. Atkinson does regular unannounced observations, in which he follows a truck to ensure that the crew is performing safely and correctly. He will stop a crew on the route, go through a safety checklist, and have each crew member sign the list. Atkinson's actions put the crew on notice that he considers their work important, and they should too. "We don't want an employee to ever think that they don't need to respect their job because it's trash," says Atkinson.

Atkinson holds a bachelor of science degree in business from Louisiana State University. During the summers of his college years, he worked on a garbage truck, which contributed to his passion for the role garbage hauling plays in society.

QUESTIONS

1. How might this story about giving recognition and instilling pride in the trash-removal industry apply to other work settings involving basic, manual work?

2. What about motivating the garbage workers by explaining to them that their grand purpose is to help create a sustainable planet through the company's recycling and safe disposal of waste?

3. Is Kevin Atkinson making good use of his degree in business?

Source: Original story based on facts and observations in the following sources: "How a CEO Motivates Employees in a Dirty, Sweaty Industry," Windstream View, www.inc.com/windstream/how-a-ceo-motivates-employees-in-a-dirty-sweaty-industry.html, November 2, 2016, pp. 1–2; Sandra Bretting, "Trash Entrepreneur Mines What Others Discard," *Houston Chronicle*, January 7, 2016, pp. 1–4; Texas Pride Disposal, www.texaspridedisposal.com.

Motivation through Financial Incentives

LEARNING OBJECTIVE 5
Describe how to effectively use financial incentives to motivate others, including the use of employee stock ownership plans and stock options.

A natural reinforcer for workers at any level is to offer them financial incentives for good performance. Using financial incentives as a motivator is another application of positive reinforcement. Financial incentives, however, predate formal positive reinforcement programs in the workplace and are also an application of common sense. The following sections describe three issues about the extensive subject of money as a reinforcer: linking pay to performance, stock ownership and options, and problems associated with financial incentives.

Linking Pay to Performance

Financial incentives are usually more effective when they are linked to (or contingent upon) good performance. Linking pay to performance generally motivates people to work harder because the link acts as a reinforcer. The recommended approach is to tie employee pay to specific performance criteria and link it directly to value-enhancing business results. The variable pay must be re-earned each year and does not permanently increase base salary. Based on a survey of 1,062 employers, a current trend is to keep salary increases relatively flat while continuing to invest more dollars in performance-based pay.[30]

A representative example of variable pay is the system at MetLife. One reason that variable pay is important at MetLife is that salaries are about average for the industry. The company measures the performance of employees and managers by comparing each person to others who are on the same level. Performance is measured on a 1-to-5 scale. The company then calculates which employees are categorized as top, middle, or bottom. Employees in the top category receive about 65 percent more in bonuses than those in the middle. Employees in the bottom category might receive no bonus.[31] This gives poor performers no salary increase, thereby having more money in the merit pool to pay to performers. At the same time, the company that gives no raise for poor results sends a message about the importance of good performance.[32]

Pay for performance is not based on achieving financial goals exclusively. Other performance factors may include providing good customer service, on-time delivery, ratings from client satisfaction surveys, being a good team player, and sharing knowledge with other workers. Merit (or variable) pay for both individuals and the team is based on actual results. Merit pay runs from 3 percent to over 15 percent of total compensation.

Individual and group differences often influence the type of pay for performance that is most likely to be an effective motivator. For example, a person with high risk-taking tendencies might be willing to accept a higher proportion of pay based on performance. Marketing professors Thomas Steenburgh and Michael Ahearne studied how industrial (as opposed to retail) sales representatives at different levels of sales performance reacted to financial incentives. The general finding from their research was that laggards, core performers, and stars who make up a sales force are motivated by different facets of the compensation plan. Several of the different responses to the compensation plan are summarized next.

- *Laggards* respond well to quarterly bonuses, and less well to annual bonuses. The study found that removing quarterly bonuses, and keeping only annual bonuses, would decrease performance in terms of revenue generated by 10 percent. It was also found that when companies have a supply of new salespeople in waiting, the social pressure enhances the low performers to boost their performance.

- *Core performers* respond well to multitiered targets, meaning that they are motivated by the prospects of achieving sales quotas set at three different levels (e.g., average, good, and outstanding). Contests that award noncash prizes, such as a company-paid weekend vacation for the family, are appealing to core performers. The reason is that the noncash prize may have some appeal that is lacking in the highest compensation award, such as a regional weekend vacation not being as disruptive to family life as a week-long overseas vacation.

- *Star performers* perform best when there is no cap on commissions because, with commission caps, they tend to slow down their sales efforts once they have earned the maximum commission possible. Overachievement bonuses in which higher rates kick in after quotas are met spur star performers to higher levels of sales. Star performers also respond well to sales contests in which multiple winners are possible instead of "one winner takes all."[33] Several other studies also indicate that companies sell more products and services when they remove caps on commissions.[34]

Cash bonuses are often used to motivate employees.

Although many employers believe they link pay to performance, research suggests that merit pay may not be so closely linked to performance. A team of researchers meta-analyzed the results of 39 studies about the relationship between pay and performance. A striking conclusion was that pay had little relationship to the quality of work but did show a moderately positive relationship with the *quantity* of work. However, managers are not completely to blame. It is often easier to measure how much work employees are performing (quantity) than how well they are performing (quality). The meta-analysis in question also confirms the obvious: People will produce more work when money is at stake.[35]

Employee Stock Ownership and Stock Options

A widely used method of motivating workers through financial means is to make them part owners of the business through stock purchases, as described in the chapter opener about Huawei. Two variations of the same idea of giving workers equity in the business are stock ownership and stock option plans. Stock ownership can be motivational because employees participate in the financial success of the firm as measured by its stock price. If employees work hard, the company may become more successful, and the value of the stock may increase.

Under an employee stock ownership plan (ESOP), employees at all levels in the organization are given stock. The employer either contributes shares of its stock or the money to purchase stock in the open market. Stock shares are usually deposited in employee retirement accounts. Upon retirement, employees can choose to receive company stock instead of cash. Employee stock ownership plans are popular because they are easy to understand and contribute to an ownership culture. However, an employee who invests too heavily in company stock may neglect other investments and lack a diversified portfolio.

Employee stock options are more complicated than straightforward stock ownership. **Stock options** give employees the right to purchase a certain number of company shares in the future at a specified price, generally the market price on the day the option is granted. If the stock rises in value, it can be purchased at a discount. If the stock sinks below the designated purchase price, the option is worthless (or "under water"). Stock options also have other goals related to organizational effectiveness including attracting and retaining talent, focusing employee attention on organizational performance, and creating a culture of ownership.[36]

stock option A financial incentive that gives employees the right to purchase a certain number of company shares at a specified price, generally the market price of the stock on the day the option is granted.

A major potential problem with stock options as a motivational tool is that they become worthless if a stock plunges because the employees left with the option to purchase stock at above the market value! However, some companies attempt to compensate for fallen stock price by increasing cash compensation or granting additional options at a more favorable price. The employee suffers from disappointed expectations, and the company looks foolish.

Problems Associated with Financial Incentives

Although financial incentives are widely used as motivators, they can create problems. For example, workers may not agree with managers about the value of their contributions. Financial incentives can also pit individuals and groups against each other. The result may be unhealthy competition rather than cooperation and teamwork. A problem noted with pay for performance is that the method typically rewards immediate, short-term actions. For example, executives can cut or postpone long-term investments to produce higher earnings today in order to earn a bonus based on profits this year. Expenses that might be defrayed to boost short-term profits include investing in research and development or purchasing new enterprise software.[37] Also, if employees focus on immediate results to earn bonuses, they will sometimes not invest effort in working on long-range ideas and exploratory tasks that could lead to innovation.[38] When a company moves too much of compensation into variable pay, many workers will feel more insecure about money. They might worry, for example, if they will earn enough to meet all their expenses.[39]

A major concern about pay-for-performance plans is that the ratings assigned to people (e.g., the high, medium, and low categories at MetLife) are too subjective. Another concern is that individual accomplishment is difficult to measure because most of a worker's contribution in an organization is partially attributed to the work of others, or the organizational system.

The most researched argument against financial rewards is that they focus the attention of workers too much on rewards such as money or stocks. (This follows the logic of the opposition to extrinsic motivation in general.) In the process, the workers lose out on intrinsic rewards such as joy in accomplishment. Instead of being passionate about the work they are doing, people become overly concerned with the size of their reward. One argument is that external rewards do not create a lasting commitment. Instead, they create temporary compliance, such as working hard in the short run to earn a bonus. A frequent problem with merit pay systems is that a person who does not receive a merit increase one pay period often feels that he or she has been punished. Another argument against financial incentives is that the rewards manipulate people in the same manner as bribes.

In reality, workers at all levels want a combination of internal rewards and financial rewards, along with other external rewards such as praise. The ideal combination is to offer exciting (internally rewarding) work to people and simultaneously pay them enough money so they are not preoccupied with matters such as salary and bonuses. Money is the strongest motivator when people have financial problems or heavy expenses. Imagine a worker needing to replace a roof or having two teenagers who both need orthodontia. He or she will be highly motivated to earn a bonus or a salary increase. Another reality is that even if a firm offers exciting work, great benefits, and wonderful coworkers, it usually needs to offer strong financial incentives to attract quality workers.

Choosing an Appropriate Motivational Model

LEARNING OBJECTIVE 6
Choose an appropriate motivational model for a given situation.

In this and the previous chapter, 13 approaches to understanding and enhancing motivation have been presented. Although these approaches have different labels, most of them have elements in common. In quick review, the thirteen approaches are: (1) the needs hierarchy, (2) the two-factor theory, (3) the achievement–power–affiliation triad, (4) goal theory, (5) reinforcement theory, (6) expectancy theory, (7) equity theory, (8) social learning theory, (9) intrinsic versus extrinsic motivation, (10) job design, (11) positive reinforcement programs, (12) recognition, and (13) financial incentives.

A fruitful approach to choosing an effective motivation theory or program for a given situation is for the manager (or other would-be motivator) to carefully diagnose the situation. Choose a motivational approach that best fits the deficiency or neglected opportunity in a given situation. Observe the people who need motivation, and also interview them about their interests and concerns. Then apply a motivational approach that appears to match the interests, concerns, deficits, or missed opportunity. Four examples will help clarify the diagnostic approach:

1. The manager observes that group members perform their jobs well enough to meet standards, but they are not excited about their work. Introducing job enrichment and intrinsic motivation could be just what the organizational behavioral specialist ordered.

2. The manager observes that group members appear interested in their work and that they like the company and their coworkers. Yet they spend too much time grumbling about personal financial problems. The most direct approach to enhancing motivation in this situation would be to introduce a program of financial incentives. To be effective, the financial payouts should be large enough to make a difference in the financial welfare of the workers.

3. The manager attempts to use recognition to motivate workers at different occupational levels. He or she should choose recognition methods that are likely to have the highest valence for the particular level of worker. Symbolic forms of recognition such as company hats, ties, and desk clocks are likely to have the highest valence for people at lower occupational levels, such as clerical and production workers. Professional-level workers are likely to be more motivated by written forms of recognition, including letters to their personal files documenting their contributions.

4. The manager attempts to motivate members of the contingent workforce such as temporary workers and part-time workers. Recognizing these workers' needs for security, company benefits might prove to have high valence, since many contingent workers lack a good benefits package.

Implications for Managerial Practice

1. Although motivation through job design is complex, time consuming, and expensive, it must be given careful consideration in any strategic attempt to enhance motivation and productivity. This is especially true because so many newcomers to the professional workforce seek to grow and develop on the job.

2. A helpful starting point in motivating workers is to ask them to describe in writing what they think would be effective motivators for them, including rewards and type of work. Recognize, however, that not everybody is aware of his or her true motivators. Some workers, for example, will say that the opportunity to make a difference is their biggest motivator, yet they respond better to token rewards such as a gift certificate. Observing what motivates workers should supplement the self-description of motivators. Despite this concern, the default tactic for motivating career-oriented people is to provide them the opportunity to perform work that they consider meaningful.

3. Recognizing workers is an important motivational tool, and is usually given only after a task or accomplishment is completed. In situations where it takes a long time to complete a task or assignment, such as in selling a large commercial truck or developing a system, the worker or team might therefore go without recognition for a long time. A solution is to recognize these workers for progress toward the larger goal. These interim acts of recognition are likely to be motivational for the worker acting diligently to accomplish a long-term goal.[40]

4. No motivational program is a substitute for adequate compensation, including pay and benefits. One of the many reasons that money remains an all-important reinforcer is that most people have financial worries. One problem is that family income has not kept up with the high cost of housing, creating financial pressures for many wage earners.

5. Managers and leaders do not always provide as much feedback as desired. To deal with this problem, soliciting feedback on your own could also enhance the meaningfulness of your work. A good feedback question is, "How am I doing in terms of meeting the goals you have set for my role?"

Summary of Key Points

1. *Explain how to enhance motivation through job enrichment, the job characteristics model, and job crafting.* A major strategy for enhancing motivation is to increase the challenge and responsibility in a job. An enriched, and therefore motivational, job includes some of the following characteristics: direct feedback, client relationships, new learning, control over method, control over scheduling, unique experience,

control over resources, direct communication authority, and personal accountability. Job enrichment works best when workers want or need more responsibility, variety, and growth, which is not a given.

The current emphasis on meaningful work can be considered an application of job enrichment particularly with respect to the dimensions of unique experience and personal accountability. Giving useful feedback makes work more meaningful. A managerial practice that leads to job enrichment is to empower employees. Empowering workers usually enhances their motivation because having more power is intrinsically motivating, thereby leading to job enrichment.

Job enrichment has been expanded to create the job characteristics model, which focuses on the task and interpersonal dimensions of a job. Five characteristics of a job can improve employee motivation, satisfaction, and performance: skill variety, task identity, task significance, autonomy, and feedback. These characteristics relate to critical psychological states, which in turn lead to outcomes such as internal motivation, satisfaction, low absenteeism, and high-quality performance.

Workers often enrich their own jobs by modifying their job descriptions themselves through crafting, or adapting their jobs in terms of (1) the number and types of tasks, (2) interactions with others, and (3) their view of the job. Choosing to perform tasks related to strengths and interests is another form of job crafting.

2. *Summarize the basics of a positive reinforcement program in the workplace.* Positive reinforcement programs are an application of reinforcement theory. Such programs have been used to strengthen employee wellness programs, with wellness incentives for completion of lifestyle modification programs, including weight control and smoking cessation.

3. *Identify rules and suggestions for motivating group members through positive reinforcement.* Positive reinforcement can also be applied outside of a formal program by the manager following these rules: choosing an appropriate reward or punishment, reinforcing the behaviors he or she wants to encourage, supplying ample feedback, making rewards commensurate with the good deed, scheduling rewards intermittently, giving rewards and punishments promptly, making the rewards visible to the recipient and others, and changing the reward periodically.

4. *Explain why recognition and pride are good motivators, as well as the nature of reward and recognition programs in the workplace.* Recognition is a strong motivator because there is a normal human need to crave recognition; most workers feel they do not receive enough recognition. To appeal to the recognition need of others, identify a meritorious behavior and then recognize that behavior with an oral, written, or material reward. Praise is a powerful form of recognition. Reward and recognition programs should be linked to organizational goals.

Employee input into what types of rewards and recognition are valued is useful. Peer recognition programs are particularly useful for making recognition easy and frequent. Wanting to feel proud motivates many workers, and workers who are proud of their accomplishments are eager to receive recognition for what they have achieved.

5. *Describe how to effectively use financial incentives to motivate others, including the use of employee stock ownership plans and stock options.* Financial incentives are a widely used motivator at all worker levels. Such incentives are more effective when they are linked to performance. Pay for performance is not based on achieving financial goals exclusively, and may include customer service and team player goals.

A widely used way of motivating workers with financial incentives is to make them part owners of the business through stock ownership. Under an employee stock ownership plan (ESOP), employees at all levels are given stock. Stock options give employees the right to purchase a certain number of company shares in the future at a specified price. If the stock price drops, the option is worthless.

Individual and group differences often influence the type of pay for performance that is most likely to be an effective motivator. Financial incentives can create problems such as poor cooperation and focusing too much attention on external rewards such as money or stocks. Instead of being passionate about the work they are doing, people become overly concerned with the size of the reward. In reality, workers at all levels want a combination of internal rewards and financial rewards, along with other external rewards such as praise.

6. *Choose an appropriate motivational model for a given situation.* A fruitful approach to choose an effective motivation theory or program for a given situation is for the manager to carefully diagnose the situation. A motivational approach is then chosen that best fits the deficiency or neglected opportunity in the situation. An example would be to understand that part-time workers might be strongly motivated by good benefits.

Key Terms and Phrases

Discussion Questions and Activities

1. Of the various characteristics of an enriched job mentioned in the chapter, which one or two factors would make a job highly meaningful to you? Explain why.
2. Give an example of how a technical support representative for an Internet service provider might craft his or her job.
3. In what way might the job of a CEO be considered enriched?
4. Give your own example of how rewarding one type of work behavior might result in behavior that the company really does not want to occur.
5. In what way does an ESOP require that employees have a long-range perspective in order for the method to be an effective motivator?
6. Which of the motivational programs and methods described in this chapter do you think would be particularly useful in motivating convenience store cashiers to perform at a high level?
7. What forms of recognition would be the most effective in motivating you? How do you know?
8. Why might trash talk be a more effective motivator when directed toward a coworker rather than your manager?
9. What do you think of being permitted to take a selfie with the company CEO as an effective reward in the company recognition program?
10. Ask a classmate whether he or she would prefer to take a new position that offered (a) below-average pay but some stock options, or (b) above-average pay but no stock options. What might the answer tell you about your classmate's personality?

CASE PROBLEM: Helping Amanda Find Her Purpose

Twenty-seven-year-old Amanda is the digital marketing manager for Calorie Containment, a company that provides a weight-loss program for women and men. Customers purchase 14 frozen meals a week on a subscription basis. The food is delivered to the home or picked up at a retail outlet. Customers also receive instructions about engaging in physical exercise and avoiding high-calorie snacks to supplement the food they receive from Calorie Containment. Another service Calorie Containment provides is customer support through a toll-free number and Internet chat. The customer support technicians are knowledgeable about dieting and weight loss but are not necessarily professionals in nutrition or physical health.

Brett, the marketing manager at Calorie Containment and Amanda's immediate manager, is satisfied with Amanda's performance as the digital marketing manager. Yet he has concerns about whether she is passionate about her work and also whether she has found the true purpose in her career. At times Brett thinks that Amanda accepted her position with Calorie Containment simply because she wanted experience in digital marketing.

Believing that passion and purpose are the keys to worker motivation, Brett decides to interview Amanda along these lines. An edited transcript of the interview follows:

Brett: Amanda, what inspires you about your position in our company?

Amanda: Getting a regular paycheck is inspirational when you have bills to pay. [Laughs] Seriously, I enjoy digging deep into digital marketing. I am learning so much—the technology keeps changing, and the competition gets tougher every few months. The fact that we do help some customers achieve their goal of losing weight is pretty decent.

Brett: What did you enjoy working on the most in recent months, and why?

Amanda: I worked very hard to put together a Facebook ad in conjunction with Katrina and Max [two members of the marketing team]. We got a whole bunch of likes and smiley faces.

Brett: What was especially good about that accomplishment?

Amanda: People are so blitzed with ads these days about weight loss that it's tough to get noticed. And we did, so that's terrific.

Brett: How is your work today getting you closer to what you want to achieve in your career?

Amanda: The experience I am accumulating is getting me closer to getting your job. [Laughs] I hope to become a big-company marketing executive in a consumer-products company. I feel I am on the right track here at Calorie Containment.

Brett: What is the purpose of your work at Calorie Containment?

Amanda: Face it, Brett, the company needs to make a profit to survive. My purpose is to add to the top line and the bottom line. In today's world, advertising in print, radio, or TV is losing its impact. That's where I fit in. Digital marketing has multiplied in importance.

Brett: I have enjoyed our candid conversation. But I recommend that you do some soul searching to find out why you are working in this industry and what you are doing to help the world.

Amanda: Don't get me wrong. I think that our diet program helps some people who think they need to lose weight and cannot do it on their own.

Case Questions

1. To what extent do you think that Amanda has found a purpose that will keep her highly motivated?
2. What would you recommend Amanda do to find a way to make her work more meaningful and purposeful?

3. What is your opinion as to whether or not Brett is invading Amanda's privacy with his line of questioning?

Source: The manager in this case based a couple of his questions on the following sources: Kristi Hedges, "5 Questions to Help Your Employees Find Their Inner Purpose," *Harvard Business Review*, August 17, 2017, pp. 3–4; Amy Jen Su, "How to Help Someone to Discover Work That Excites Them," *Harvard Business Review*, September 12, 2017, pp. 1–5.

Endnotes

1. Original story created from facts and observations in the following sources: Alexander Peng and John Hoffmire, "Huawei's Employee Stock Ownership Plan and Its Effect on Productivity: A Comparative Analysis of the 2010–2014 Financial Data of Huawei and ZTE," http://cleo.rutgers.edu/assets/articles, 2015, pp. 1–12; David De Cremer and Tian Tao, "Huawei: A Case Study of When Profit Sharing Works," *Harvard Business Review*, September 24, 2015, pp. 1–4; Zhibiao Zhu, James Hoffmire, John Hoffmire, and Fusheng Wang, "Employee Stock Ownership Plans and Their Effect on Productivity: The Case of Huawei," *International Journal of Business and Management Invention*, August 2013, pp. 17–22.

2. Frederick Herzberg, "The Wise Old Turk," *Harvard Business Review*, September–October 1974, pp. 70–80; Nico W. Van Yperen and Mariët Hagedoom, "Do High Job Demands Increase Motivation or Fatigue or Both? The Role of Job Control and Social Support," *Academy of Management Journal*, June 2003, pp. 339–348.

3. Susie Cranston and Scott Keller, "Increasing the 'Meaning Quotient' of Work," *McKinsey Quarterly*, January 2013, pp. 4–5.

4. Teresa Amabile and Steven Kramer, *The Progress Principle: Using Small Wins to Ignite Joy, Engagement, and Creativity at Work* (Boston, MA: Harvard Business School Press, 2011).

5. Lori Goler, Janelle Gale, and Adam Grant, "The Three Things Employees Really Want: Career, Community, Cause," *Harvard Business Review*, February 20, 2018, pp. 2–3.

6. Valerie Keller and Caroline Webb, "Find Purpose in Even Your Most Mundane Tasks at Work," *Harvard Business Review*, March 8, 2017, pp. 1–4.

7. Bob Nelson, "The Power of the I's: No-Cost Ways to Motivate Employees," *Success in Recruiting and Retaining* (National Institute of Business Management, 2000).

8. George B. Graen, Terri A. Scandura, and Michael R. Graen, "A Field Experimental Test of the Moderating Effects of Growth Need Strength on Productivity," *Journal of Applied Psychology*, August 1986, pp. 484–491.

9. John Richard Hackman and Greg R. Oldham, *Work Redesign* (Reading, MA: Addison-Wesley, 1980).

10. Ruth Kanfer, Michael Frese, and Russell E. Johnson, "Motivation Related to Work: A Century of Progress," *Journal of Applied Psychology*, March 2017, p. 342.

11. Marc C. Marchese and Robert P. Delprino, "Do Supervisors and Subordinates See Eye-to-Eye on Job Enrichment?" *Journal of Business and Psychology*, Winter 1998, pp. 179–191.

12. Amy Wrzesnierski and Jane E. Dutton, "Crafting a Job: Revisioning Employees as Active Crafters of Their Work," *The Academy of Management Review*, April 2001, pp. 179–201.

13. Dorien T. A. M. Kooij, M. van Woerkom, J. Wilkenloh, L. Dorenbosch, and J. J. Denissen, "Job Crafting towards Strengths and Interests: The Effects of a Job Crafting Intervention on Person-Job Fit and the Role of Age," *Journal of Applied Psychology*, June 2017, pp. 971–981.

14. Katie Thomas, "Companies Get Strict on Health of Workers," *The New York Times*, March 25, 2013, pp. 1–3; Matt Dunning, "More Companies Linking Rewards, Penalties to Wellness Program Results," *Workforce*, www.workforce.com/2012/08/09/more-companies-linking-rewards-penalties-to-wellness-program-results/, August 9, 2012, pp. 1–2.

15. "Employee Wellness Programs Prod Workers to Adopt Healthy Lifestyles," *Harvard School of Public Health*, Winter 2009, pp. 1–9. Updated 2014.

16. Steve Aldana, "Wellness Program Incentives: The Complete Guide," WellSteps, www.wellsteps.com/blog/2018/01/03/wellness-program-incentives/, January 10, 2018, p. 3.

17. Thomas, "Companies Get Strict on Health of Workers," p. 1.

18. Thomas, "Companies Get Strict on Health of Workers," p. 2.

19. Gregory Smith, "Simple Rewards Are Powerful Motivators," *HRfocus*, August 2001, p. 10.

20. Jack Zenger and Joseph Folkman, "Why Do So Many Managers Avoid Giving Praise?" *Harvard Business Review*, May 2, 2017, p. 2.

21. Stephen Kerr, "Practical, Cost-Neutral Alternatives that You May Know, but Don't Practice," *Organizational Dynamics*, Summer 1999, p. 65.

22. Survey cited in "Employees Want More Recognition, Growth Opportunity," *Monitor on Psychology*, May 2011, p. 12.

23. Susan Ladika, "Companies Recognizing Importance of Recognition." *Workforce*, December 2013, p. 52.

24. Research cited in Ken Blanchard, Vicki Stanford, and David Witt, "Singing the Praises of Praises," *Workforce*, April 2014, p. 38.

25. Andrew J. DuBrin, "Self-Perceived Technical Orientation and Attitudes toward Being Flattered," *Psychological Reports*, Vol. 96, 2005, pp. 852–854.

26. Irwin Speizer, "Incentives Catch on Overseas, but Value of Awards Can Too Easily Get Lost in Translation," *Workforce Management*, November 21, 2005, p. 46.

27. Yuliya Chernova, "When Peer Recognition Comes at the Push of a Button," *The Wall Street Journal*, March 13, 2017, p. R4.

28. Elizabeth Bernstein, "When Trash Talk Motivates," *The Wall Street Journal*, July 6, 2017, p. A11.

29. Cited in John A. Byrne, "How to Lead Now," *Fast Company*, August 2003, p. 66.

30. John Simons, "Bosses Reward Best and Forget the Rest as Merit Pay Gains," *The Wall Street Journal*, September 18, 2017, p. B2.

31. Janet Wiscombe, "Can Pay for Performance Really Work?" *Workforce*, August 2001, p. 29; "MetLife Salaries," Glassdoor, www.glassdoor.com/Salary/MetLife-Salaries-E2899.htm, March 22, 2018, p. 1.

32. Susan J. Wells, "No Results, No Raise," *HR Magazine*, May 2005, pp. 76–80.

33. Thomas Steenbuyrgh and Michael Ahearne, "Motivating Salespeople: What Really Works," *Harvard Business Review*, July–August 2012, pp. 70–79.

34. Doug J. Chung, "How to *Really* Motivate Salespeople," *Harvard Business Review*, April 2015, p. 57.

35. G. Douglas Jenkins, Jr., "Are Financial Incentives Related to Performance? A Meta-Analytic Review of Empirical Research," *Journal of Applied Psychology*, October 1998, pp. 777–787.

36. "How Stock Options Are Changing," *HRfocus*, October 2002, p. 7.

37. Radhakrishnan Gopalan, John Horn, and Todd Milbourn, "Comp Targets That Work," *Harvard Business Review*, September–October 2017, p. 104.

38. "Has Usefulness of Pay for Performance Run Its Course?" *Ioma's Report on Salary Surveys®*, January 2003, pp. 1, 14.

39. Fay Hansen, "The New Way to Pay," *Workforce Management*, October 24, 2005, p. 36.

40. "Recognize Staff for Small Achievements," *Manager's Edge*, December 2005, p. 4.

Interpersonal Communication

CHAPTER 8

Chapter Outline

The Communication Process

Communication and Information Technology

Nonverbal Communication

Organizational Channels of Communication

Barriers to Interpersonal Communication

Overcoming Communication Barriers

Persuasive and Power-Oriented Language

Implications for Managerial Practice

Africa Studio/Shutterstock.com

Learning Objectives

After reading and studying this chapter and doing the exercises, you should be able to:

1. Describe the communication process.

2. Describe the impact of communication technology on interpersonal communication in organizations.

3. Explain how nonverbal communication can be used to enhance communication.

4. Present details about the various channels of communication in organizations.

5. Summarize barriers to effective communication and how to overcome them.

6. Explain how to overcome potential cross-gender and cross-cultural communication problems.

7. Recognize the basics for becoming a more persuasive and power-oriented communicator.

In-N-Out Burger is a successful fast-food chain with 324 stores in six states. Corporate headquarters are in Irvine, California. The company president is Kynsi Snyder, who inherited the business. Because of a series of family tragedies, Snyder became the sole heir to the fortune her grandfather started when he opened the first In-N-Out drive-through restaurant in 1948. When Snyder took over leadership of the company, she became one of the youngest billionaires in the country.

With respect to wages and benefits, In-N-Out is the leading fast-food chain. Entry-level salaries are higher than the prevailing minimum wage in each state in which the company operates. Restaurant managers are paid, on average, more than $160,000 per year. Store managers are granted company-paid international trips if they attain target goals. Although high wages contribute to the success of In-N-Out Burger, company management and many associates believe that effective communication is the major contributor to company success.

The job-placement firm Glassdoor says that the secret ingredient to In-N-Out's speedy service is good communication between workers and management. According to reviews submitted to Glassdoor, the hamburger chain does well in keeping associates up to date: "The managers are great communicators and try to make scheduling work for you and run smooth shifts."

At In-N-Out Burger, open communication between associates and management is actively promoted. Company management believes that good communication is essential to the well-being of the organization. Furthermore, problems, concerns, or complaints that are left unresolved have a negative impact on the company's work and work environment.

Any employee who has a question, concern, or complaint related to his or her employment relationship is encouraged to bring it to the attention of his or her supervisor immediately. Among these concerns and complaints might be disciplinary action, unfair treatment, discrimination, or retaliation relating to wages, hours, or working conditions. This open-door policy is an integral part of In-N-Out management's practice of open communication. Making appropriate use of the policy is encouraged without the associate having to fear reprisal.

A customer-service representative working for In-N-Out Burger submitted a company review to Glassdoor that included the comment that part of the job was to communicate clearly with coworkers and management.[1]

The In-N-Out Burger story illustrates how effective communication can improve morale and productivity, and that effective communication comes about by design. Communication is the basic process by which managers and professionals accomplish their tasks. People in positions of authority consistently rank communication skills as one of those vital for success. At times, a newsletter can be the communication medium of choice. But communication is enhanced by interacting with employees at all levels about issues large and small.

The purpose of this chapter is to explain key aspects of interpersonal communication in organizations and to make suggestions for improved communication. To achieve this purpose, we include information about the communication process, the impact of information technology on communication, overcoming various barriers to communication, and how to develop a more power-oriented communication style.

The Communication Process

LEARNING OBJECTIVE 1
Describe the communication process.

Interpersonal communication takes place through a series of steps, as illustrated in Figure 8-1. For effective communication to take place, six components must be present: a communication source or sender, a message, a channel, a receiver, feedback, and the environment. "Noise" can also have an impact on communication. As you study this model,

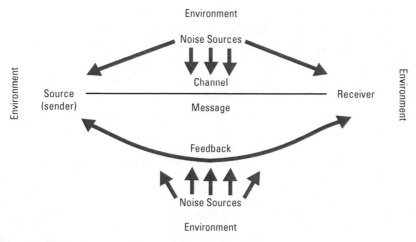

FIGURE 8-1 The Communication Process

Various sources of interference can prevent a message getting from sender to receiver as intended.

you will observe that perception and communication are closely linked. To help explain the communication process, assume that a production manager wants to inform a team leader that productivity in his department slipped last month.

1. *Source (the sender).* The source of a communication event is usually a person attempting to send a spoken, written, sign language, or nonverbal message to another person or persons. The perceived authority and experience of the sender are important factors influencing how much attention the message will receive.

2. *Message.* The heart of a communication event is the **message**, which is a purpose or an idea to be conveyed. Many factors influence how a message is received. Among them are clarity, the alertness of the receiver, the complexity and length of the message, and how the information is organized. The production manager's message will most likely get across if she says directly, "I need to talk to you about last month's below-average productivity figures."

3. *Channel (medium).* Several communication channels, or media, are usually available for sending messages in organizations. Typically, messages are written, spoken, or a combination of written and spoken. Some kind of nonverbal cue, such as a smile or hand gesture, accompanies most spoken messages. In the production manager's case, she has chosen to drop by the team leader's office and deliver her message in a serious tone instead of sending an electronic message.

4. *Receiver.* A communication event can be complete only when another party receives the message and understands it properly. In the example under examination, the team leader is the receiver. Perceptual distortions of various types (as described in Chapter 3) act as filters that can prevent a message from being received as intended by the sender. If the team leader is worried that his job is at stake, he might get defensive when he hears the production manager's message.

5. *Feedback.* Without feedback, it is difficult to know whether a message has been received and understood. The feedback step also includes the reactions of the receiver. If the receiver takes action as intended by the sender, the message has been received satisfactorily. The production manager will know her message got across if the team leader says, "OK, when would you like to review last month's production figures?" Effective interpersonal communication therefore involves an exchange of messages between two people. The two communicators take turns being receiver and sender. Feedback is necessary to make communication an interactional encounter in which the people participate in the process of conversing.[2]

6. *Environment.* A full understanding of communication requires knowledge of the environment in which messages are transmitted and received. The organizational

message A purpose or an idea to be conveyed in a communication event.

culture is a key environmental factor that influences communication. It is easier to transmit controversial messages when trust and respect are high than when they are low. Also, in some organizations, workers hesitate to bring negative results to the attention of management for fear of being reprimanded.

7. *Noise.* Distractions such as noise have a pervasive influence on the components of the communication process. In this context, noise is anything that disrupts communication, including the attitudes and emotions of the receiver. Noise includes work stress, fear, ambivalence, and strong advocacy for an opposing position. In a more literal sense, the whir of machinery, piped-in music, and the chatting of coworkers with each other and on cell phones are also examples of noise in the workplace.

noise Anything that disrupts communication, including the attitude and emotions of the receiver.

Communication and Information Technology

LEARNING OBJECTIVE 2
Describe the impact of communication technology on interpersonal communication in organizations.

Communication technology has influenced the quantity and quality of interpersonal communications in the workplace. Quite often the influence has been positive, but at other times communication effectiveness has decreased. Four developments that illustrate the impact of information technology on interpersonal communication are e-mail, blogging, presentation technology, and remote working.

E-Mail and Related Technologies

E-mail has had two major impacts on interpersonal communication and has become a standard form of communication within and across organizations. First, written messages have replaced many telephone and in-person interchanges, with virtually all office workers being connected by e-mail networks. Group members often keep in regular contact with one another without having lengthy meetings or telephone conversations. Second, people receive many more messages than they did by paper and telephone. Many managers and professionals process over 300 e-mail messages per day.

E-mail facilitates communication in many ways, including people in various parts of the world exchanging information without worrying about trying to connect through different time zones. A more subtle consequence of e-mail is that it enhances industrial democracy. Today, messages are no longer filtered through layers of management.

A widespread problem with e-mail is that it encourages the indiscriminate sending of messages, including trivial information, mass distribution of information of interest to a limited number of people, the exchange of jokes and sports news, attachments not related to work, and requests for seemingly unimportant information. The blitz of messages requires many people to work extra hours just to sort through their mail on matters that do not add value to the organization. E-mail senders can reduce the confusion created by receiving large numbers of e-mails by using a specific subject line, such as, "Possible Major Sale," or "Potential Sexual Harassment Lawsuit."

Some business firms have counterattacked the problems associated with e-mail by shifting to related technologies. A frequently used method is to place information to be shared with others on an intranet (company internet) or company blog, such as used at the company Wordpress.com. There is no mandated list of blogs that workers have to follow. Instead workers choose to access blogs with information about projects important to them.[3] A problem with using blogs to replace e-mail is that you might want to communicate with a person who has not chosen to open the project-related blog and does not receive the information you want to provide. Also, you may want to communicate with a coworker about something that is unrelated to any project he or she is working on. As a result, if you use the blog system, you do not reach that person.

Other e-mail alternatives are texting, instant messaging and more elaborate forms of groupware that allow workers to create websites for the team's use on a specific project. *Texting* is a smartphone service limited to 160 characters. *Instant messaging* is usually a message sent by computer that allows for longer messages, although instant messages are typically brief. E-mail will probably remain strong for one-to-one communication, but the tools just mentioned will be relied on more heavily for collaboration.[4] For many workers, it is easier to open an e-mail attachment than bother going to another site, such as Dropbox, to download a file.

Most readers are familiar with the business use of chat for resolving customer-service problems. Group chat is now widely used to enhance collaboration on problem solving. Chat can be both immediate and synchronous, as in a meeting, or asynchronous (people can wait to respond) like e-mail. Chat is therefore useful as collaboration software or for message exchange between two people. The 1,300-member design team at IBM uses the chat feature of Slack to discuss and quickly vote on proposed designs.[5]

Despite the sophisticated new techniques to replace e-mail, it has become a standard method of communicating within and across organizations that is rapid and efficient if used with common sense and courtesy. E-mail provides the opportunity to communicate directly with one or more people without involving hundreds of others with your posts. Ted Schalder, a technology analyst with Forrester Research Inc., puts it this way: "People use e-mail because it's the best, most reliable way to get to anybody on the planet, and none of these other tools let you do that; none of them."[6]

Although processing e-mail overwhelms many people, the situation has been more manageable for many workers as the technology has matured. They dedicate certain times of the day to e-mail exchanges to avoid being distracted from other important work. (For some workers, however, responding to e-mail *is* their job, and being away from e-mail is a distraction.) Constantly checking e-mail can impair concentration and lower your productivity, especially if you are doing analytical work. A recent analysis of many studies suggests that for most workers, the technique of turning off e-mail alerts but still checking e-mail approximately every 45 minutes helps reduce stress by giving workers a feeling of control.[7]

It is also important to ignore e-mail messages that do not apply to you, or delete them immediately. Furthermore, company e-mail systems receive less spam than home systems, partially because the company is more likely to use powerful spam filters. Also, the sophisticated e-mail user deletes spam after about a 2-second glance.

Another way of coping successfully with e-mail is to respond to complicated e-mails that require a complex answer at the start of the workday. Research suggests that decision-making capacity declines throughout the day, so the longer you wait to respond to that demanding e-mail, the more difficult it will be.[8]

Company Blogs

As just implied, the company blog is a standard form of electronic communication, paralleling the use of blogs in private life. Blogs originated by consumers are often used to complain about products or services, and less often to compliment a company. Blogs were first used by business to communicate with customers in a personal, direct manner, and perhaps form a bond with them.[9]

The blog communicates business information, but with a soft, human touch. For example, a product manager for home generators might say, "We recently heard from a homeowner in Vermont. The town was hit with an overwhelming flood, and thousands of homes had no electricity. His wife was 8 months pregnant and frightened to be without electricity. The husband got our generator started right way, and the house then had enough power for them to stay warm and even watch TV. He said thanks to everybody who helps make our nifty generator."

A company might also use a blog to communicate its side of the story in response to outside criticism, such as the company explaining that rumors of its selling dated meat were completely unfounded. The company blog can also be used to communicate with employees in a relaxed, casual tone. Employees, as well as customers, can interact with the blog by providing comments that can be a source of valuable feedback to management as well as a communication directly to other visitors to the site.

Presentation Technology

Virtually every reader of this textbook has witnessed or given a talk using presentation technology, especially PowerPoint, which has been installed on well over 1 billion computers. Speakers in all types of organizations supplement their talk with computer slides and often organize their presentation around them. Some speakers sit slumped in a chair, narrating the slides. Many people want presentations reduced to bulleted items and eye-catching graphics. (Have you noticed this tendency among students?) The ability to prepare a slide presentation has become an indispensable corporate survival skill. Audiences have become accustomed to watching an array of impressive graphics during oral presentations.

The communication challenge here is that, during an oral presentation, the predominant means of connection between sender and receiver is eye contact. When an audience is constantly distracted from the presenter by movement on the screen, sounds from the computer, or lavish colors, eye contact suffers and so does the message. Another problem is that the speaker who relies on multimedia to the exclusion of person-to-person contact may be communicating the subtle message, "I am not really necessary."[10] The implication for presenters is to find a way to integrate speaking skills with presentation technology. Following are a few sensible suggestions:

- *Reveal points only as needed.* Project the computer slides only when needed, and use a cursor, laser pointer, or metal pointer for emphasis.

- *Talk to the audience and not the screen.* A major problem with computer slides is that the presenter as well as the audience is likely to focus continually on the slide. If the presenter minimizes looking at the slide, and spends considerable time looking at the audience, it will be easier to maintain contact with the audience.

- *Tell a story and show some slides to support that story.* Unless your role is to strictly present some data, keep in mind that the most effective corporate presenters present a story in an interesting narrative. The PowerPoint slides are used to supplement the story.

- *Keep the slide in view until the audience gets the point.* A presenter will often flash a slide or transparency without giving the audience enough time to comprehend the meaning of the slide. It is also important for presenters to synchronize the slides with their comments.[11]

- *Project the key points of your presentation as headlines, using a large font.* Most audiences appreciate seeing an outline of your presentation flashed on the screen, a sentence or two (or a small amount of data) at a time using a large font. In this way, the slides become headlines that help the audience follow your oral presentation.

Following the suggestions just presented can help overcome the many criticisms of PowerPoint presentations, such as the animations and cartoons being irrelevant, the role of the speaker being diminished because the slides become the presentation, and bullet points being the enemy of thought.

Remote Working

A major deviation from the traditional work schedule is having a full-time or part-time schedule working away from company premises. An estimated 20 to 30 million people in the United States work at home, out of their cars, or from customer premises as corporate employees, at least 1 day per week. Approximately 3.7 million employees (2.8 percent of the U.S. workforce) work from home at least one-half the time.[12] Collectively, they are referred to as *remote workers*. Technology companies rely the most heavily on remote workers.

In recent years several major companies, including Yahoo, Bank of America, Aetna, and IBM, have reduced or completely eliminated their telecommuting programs.[13] A major reason for cutting back on remote work programs is that many managers believe that face-to-face interactions in the office enhance creativity and collaboration. Another advantage of people being together in one physical location is that they can help other workers when their own workload is light.

The majority of people who work at home do so only a day or two per week. Mobile technology has facilitated people working from a variety of locations, including cafés, parks, and beaches. Concerns about terrorist threats, contagious diseases, and the high cost of gasoline have made working at home appear even more desirable for many workers in recent years.

Telecommuting is an arrangement in which employees use computers to perform their regular work responsibilities at home or in a satellite office. Employees who telecommute usually use computers tied to the company's main office. People who work at home are referred to as *telecommuters* or *teleworkers*. People who work at home are either assigned a computer by the company or possess their own computer and related equipment. In addition to using computers to communicate with their employer's office, telecommuters may attend meetings on company premises and stay in contact by telephone and teleconferences. The output of distributed workers is measured frequently by computer.

Many reports suggest that remote workers are more productive, in general, than their counterparts who work in a traditional office. One example is a study conducted at CTrip, a travel agency in Shanghai, China, with 16,000 employees. The study found that employees working from home experienced a 13 percent increase in performance. About 9 percent of the improvement was from working 5 more minutes per shift because of fewer breaks and sick days. Four percent of the productivity increase stemmed from more telephone calls per minute attributed to a quieter working environment.[14]

A major communication challenge to telecommuters is that they rely very heavily on e-mail and groupware and therefore lose out on the social interaction of work, which is so important to many people. Another challenge for remote workers is that they are expected to respond to company requests outside of typical working hours, partially because there is no standard work week for a professional working away from the office. Teleworkers are also encouraged to spend some time in the traditional office in face-to-face communication with other workers. Avoiding such contact can lead to feelings of isolation, that one is not a part of the office communication network. People who are successful at telecommuting are usually those with relatively low affiliation needs.

telecommuting Working at home and sending output to the office electronically.

The Impact of Computer-Mediated Communication on Behavior

As alluded to previously, digital communication has had a major impact, both positive and negative, on behavior in organizations. In this section we look at both sides and related issues.

Positive Impact

On the positive side, communication has become more widespread and immediate than previously with most workers probably wondering what the world of work was like previous to the digital era. With computer-mediated communication, information can be exchanged at a rapid pace, keeping large numbers of people informed and alert. More people have a voice because e-mail, and sometimes instant messaging, is possible with senior managers. For example, it is much easier for an entry-level worker to send an e-mail to the division president than to telephone, send a letter to, or have a meeting with the executive.

Negative Impact

Digital information has also had substantial negative impacts on behavior in organizations. Many workers suffer from the lack of a human touch—they want to relate to a person rather than engage in so many electronic exchanges. It is more difficult to motivate, listen to, or encourage a worker electronically than in person. An emoticon smiley is not as warm as a face-to-face smile. Many workers suffer from substantial productivity losses as they become enticed into excessive Internet surfing during company time. As a result, these workers may suffer from lower performance evaluations and even job loss. Similarly, reading e-mail messages and searching the Internet becomes so time-consuming that the worker neglects the human interaction aspects of the job, such as dealing with coworker and customer problems.

Excessive use of computers often leads to repetitive motion disorder, leaving the worker discouraged and pained. Customer service often deteriorates as a result of information technology. Many banks, for example, force customers with a service problem to call a toll-free number rather than allowing them to deal with a branch representative. A voice-response system instructs the customer to punch in a lengthy account number and make choices from a complicated menu. The process is time consuming and difficult for customers not familiar with information technology. The result can be resentment, frustration, and the loss of a customer.

Computer-mediated communication often results in *wired managerial workers*. Being electronically connected to the office at all times leads many managers and professionals to complain that their employers expect them to be always available for consultation. Wi-Fi–enabled small computers enable workers to stay connected to company data even more readily than with the traditional systems.

Multitasking Problems

Decades of research indicate that the quality of mental output and depth of thought deteriorates as a person attends to more than one task simultaneously. One of the problems is that the brain does not handle multitasking well. The brain rapidly toggles (an on-and-off switch effect) among tasks, rather than performing true simultaneous processing. For example, a man might be preparing a department budget while talking to a coworker about the upcoming office party. Yet he is not technically doing two things at once: For about 5 seconds he might be looking at budget entries, and then listening to the coworker talk about the party.

According to brain research, few people can concentrate on more than one task at once. The more workers switch back and forth between tasks, the less they accomplish, particularly with respect to professional and technical tasks. Thousands of computer users tracked their actions for periods of time using the software tool RescueTime. The results painted a sobering portrait of frenzied workers who switch tasks an average of hundreds of times daily, not including accessing smartphones. The more the workers switched, the less they accomplished. A lesson drawn from the logging activities of the workers in the study was that by sticking to one task at a time, you will be more productive.[15]

Multitasking also has enormous negative consequences for organizations. According to Basex, a business research firm, the estimated annual cost to the U.S. economy from multitasking is $997 billion and a minimum of 28 billion hours of wasted time.[16] Multitasking is inherently rude when dealing with another person. Many complaints have been made about customer-contact workers who deal with one customer while talking to another on a smartphone. The opposite problem is also true—some customers talk on their smartphone or send and receive text messages while being served by a store associate, thereby marginalizing the associate.

The Human Touch

To capitalize on the benefits of computer-mediated communication devices, it is important to keep in mind that the human touch is still important. The capability to send and receive messages electronically should not mean that human contact has become undesirable or unnecessary. Robbie Briggs, president and CEO of Briggs Freeman Sotheby's International Realty, offers this thought:

> There's not an emoticon in the world that can replicate a light touch on the shoulder, warm smile or the authenticity of a laugh with a colleague. Particularly when his or her desk is only a few feet away.[17]

A revealing perspective on the importance of maintaining the human touch in a digitized workplace comes from a study of 4,000 full-time workers in 10 countries conducted by Future Workplace and Randstad. A key finding was that although digital natives have drastically different values than previous generations, 39 percent prefer in-person communication over digital modes, including e-mail, social networking, and video conferencing. Another finding was that 41 percent of gen Z (22 years or younger) and millennial workers prefer working in a traditional office as opposed to a co-working space or working from home.[18]

Nonverbal Communication

The most obvious modes of communication are speaking, writing, and sign language. (Many business meetings today include an interpreter who signs for deaf members of the audience.) A substantial amount of interpersonal communication also occurs through **nonverbal communication**, the transmission of messages by means other than words. *Body language* refers to those aspects of nonverbal communication directly related to movements of the body, such as gestures and posture. Nonverbal communication usually supplements rather than substitutes for writing, speaking, and sign language.

The general purpose of nonverbal communication is to express the feeling behind a message. Suppose that a sales representative stands tall when saying, "Our payroll processing service is devoid of bugs and glitches." The representative's posture reveals confidence in making this pitch. The same message delivered in a slouched position with one hand over the mouth would communicate a feeling of limited confidence.

Nonverbal communication incorporates a wide range of behaviors. Nevertheless, it can be divided into the following nine categories.[19]

LEARNING OBJECTIVE 3
Explain how nonverbal communication can be used to enhance communication.

nonverbal communication The transmission of messages by means other than words.

Teleworking you don't see non verbal communication

1. *Environment.* The physical setting in which the message takes place communicates meaning. This would include office décor, a type of automobile, and the type of restaurant or hotel chosen for a business meeting. Bigger deals are typically negotiated and consummated in more luxurious restaurants, whereas discussions about work assignments might be held in a family-style restaurant.
2. *Body placement.* The placement of one's body in relation to someone else is widely used to transmit messages. Facing a person in a casual, relaxed style indicates acceptance. Moving close to another person is also a general indicator of acceptance. However, moving too close may be perceived as a violation of personal space, and the message sender will be rejected.

Hand gestures are an important aspect of nonverbal communication.

Direct eye contact enhances interpersonal communication.

3. *Posture.* Another widely used clue to a person's attitude is his or her posture. Leaning toward another person suggests a favorable attitude toward the message one is trying to communicate. Leaning backward communicates the opposite. Standing up straight is generally interpreted as an indicator of self-confidence, while slouching is usually a sign of low self-confidence.

4. *Hand gestures.* Gestures of the hand, such as frequent movements to express approval and palms spread outward to indicate perplexity, provide meaningful hints in communication. Making a steeple with your hands in the presence of others connotes deep thought, and hints at being powerful.

5. *Facial expressions and movement.* The particular look on a person's face and movements of the person's head provide reliable cues as to approval, disapproval, or disbelief. Observing these expressions is particularly valuable when receiving feedback from superiors, coworkers, or customers. Assume that you ask about the effectiveness of your idea for improving a work process. The other person says, "Pretty good" but looks down and avoids eye contact with you. You might mention in a positive way that you would like to know more because he or she does not appear enthusiastic.

6. *Voice tone.* Aspects of the voice such as pitch, volume, quality, and speech rate may communicate confidence, nervousness, or enthusiasm. Intelligence is often judged by how people sound, with people speaking quite slowly or quite rapidly (as in slurred speech) appearing less intelligent.

7. *Clothing, dress, and appearance.* The image a person conveys communicates such messages as "I feel powerful" and "I think this meeting is important." For example, wearing one's best business attire to a performance evaluation interview would communicate the idea that "I think this meeting is very important." Even different types of business casual clothing can send a message, with people wearing stylish and fresh-appearing casual clothing appearing to be the more powerful.

8. *Mirroring.* To mirror is to build rapport with another person by imitating his or her voice tone, breathing rate, body movement, and language. Mirroring relies 10 percent on verbal means, 60 percent on voice tone, and 30 percent on body physiology. A specific application of mirroring is to conform to the other person's posture, eye movements, and hand movements. The person feels more relaxed with you as a result of your imitation.

9. *Touching.* Touch is a powerful vehicle for conveying such emotions as warmth, comfort, agreement, approval, reassurance, and physical attraction. Yet, behavior involving touching in the workplace is governed by cultural attitudes and status.[20] Touching among people who are at approximately the same organizational rank is frequently used to convey agreement and reassurance. Touching between people of different ranks often indicates power and status differences, with the higher-ranking person more likely to initiate the touching. Concerns about sexual harassment and sexism have greatly limited the use of touching in the office. If professional sporting events are considered part of the workplace, then

Touching others on the job can be perceived positively or negatively.

same-sex touching and hugging to express enthusiasm and approval are rampantly practiced!

One of many practical applications of nonverbal communication is to project enthusiasm and confidence with body language. Here are a few recommendations:[21]

- *Smiling is essential.* A smile connotes warmth and is an effective way of conveying trust.

- *Loosen your facial expression.* A tight, grim look gives the appearance of being unapproachable. Relax your muscles, and look for opportunities to smile and offer encouraging nods.

- *Move closer to message senders.* Work associates feel you are listening intently when you lean slightly toward them when they speak. It is a subtle way of showing that you want to hear every word.

- *Gesture to reinforce a point.* If you are excited or pleased with an idea, do not rely exclusively on words to communicate these feelings. Pump a fist, clap your hands, or point approvingly at the speaker. Use the gesture that feels the most natural to you.

Being mindful of nonverbal communication has increased in importance as more organizations rely on videoconferencing and its advanced version, telepresence. The latter technology is aligned with the eyes of the person on the screen and delivers superb audio quality.[22]

Despite the recommendations and implications of the information about nonverbal communication, keep in mind that many nonverbal signals are ambiguous. For example, a smile usually indicates agreement and warmth, but can also indicate nervousness.

Organizational Channels of Communication

Messages in organizations travel through many different channels, or paths. Communication channels can be formal or informal and can be categorized by the direction they follow.

LEARNING OBJECTIVE 4
Present details about the various channels of communication in organizations.

Formal Communication Channels

Formal communication channels are the official pathways for sending information inside and outside an organization. The primary source of information about formal channels is the organizational chart. It indicates the channels the messages are supposed to follow. By carefully following an organizational chart, an entry-level worker would know how to transmit a message to the CEO. Formal communication channels are often bypassed using communication technology. Using e-mail, anybody can send a message to anybody else in the organization. During an emergency, workers are also likely to bypass formal channels, such as a technician telephoning the plant manager directly about a chemical spill.

Many companies have developed formal communication channels for managing crises such as fires and explosions, hurricanes, massive product recalls, financial scandals, and terrorist attacks. One of the most crucial parts of a disaster plan is how to communicate with the company's workforce during a crisis. A key part of the challenge is to locate and reestablish contact with employees who may be scattered in the streets or stranded in airports around the world. Websites have now become the premier formal crisis communication channel. Formal channels during a crisis are necessary for informing employees about a disaster, work assignments, health services and grief counseling, and assistance in returning to work.

The formal communication channels are precisely specified in a traditional bureaucratic organization with its many layers. Communication channels are more difficult to follow in the modern **network organization,** a spherical structure that can rotate self-managing teams and other resources around a common knowledge base. The key purpose of the network organization is to enter into temporary alliances with other firms in order to capitalize on the combined talents. *Strategic alliance* is the term often used to describe these temporary, multifirm ventures. An example of a successful strategic alliance is Starbucks

formal communication channels The official pathways for sending information inside and outside an organization.

if not on site
one worker might
not know who to
contact (teleworking) 1/2 time

network organization A spherical structure that can rotate self-managing teams and other resources around a common knowledge base.

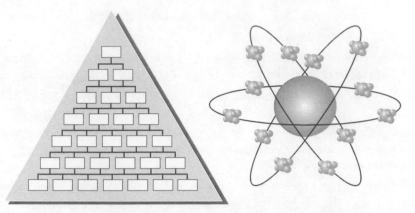

FIGURE 8-2 Communication Pathways in a Hierarchical Organization and a Spherical Organization

Communication pathways are more complex in a spherical organization than in a hierarchical organization.

and bookseller Barnes & Noble. Having a well-known coffee shop in many of its stores helps Barnes & Noble keep customers happy and browsing for books.

Figure 8-2 shows the contrast between a bureaucracy (pyramid shape) and a network organization (spherical shape). The connecting lines can be considered formal communication channels.

Meetings, both physical and virtual, are a formal communication channel in almost all but very small organizations. A meeting is formal when it is called for by a person in a position of authority, usually a manager. Although virtual meetings (conducted electronically) have gained in popularity, C-level executives still spend at least half of their time in face-to-face meetings. Middle managers are in meetings about one-third of their time at work.[23]

Informal Communication Channels

An **informal communication channel** is the unofficial network of channels that supplements the formal channels. Most of these informal channels arise out of necessity. For example, people will sometimes depart from the official communication channels to consult with a person with specialized knowledge. Suppose an administrative professional in the inventory-control department spoke and wrote fluent German. Employees from other departments would regularly consult him or her when they were dealing with a customer from Germany.

Informal communication channels help explain why changes in organizational structure (one which specifies the formal communication channels) sometimes do not change the quantity and quality of work that gets accomplished. The same pattern of networks that workers use to accomplish their tasks may not change despite the changes on the organizational chart.[24]

The Grapevine

The **grapevine** is the major informal communication channel in organizations. The *grapevine* refers to the tangled pathways that can distort information. The term referred originally to the snarled telegraph lines on the battlefield during the U.S. Civil War. The grapevine is often thought to be used primarily for passing along negative rumors and negative gossip. Gossips sometimes use the Internet and e-mail as channels for transmitting negative gossip. When left to fester, gossip can cause individuals chagrin, and also lead to turnover, conflict, and lawsuits. Gossip often increases when workers are bored or lack ample information about company events. Managers can often stop negative gossip by confronting the source of the gossip, demanding that he or she stop. Positive gossip, however, makes a contribution to the organization because trading information strengthens ties among workers and humanizes the workplace.[25]

Rumors

Rumors are an important communication force within organizations, and they tend to thrive in organizations with poor corporate communication, such as a penitentiary. Furthermore, an active grapevine is correlated with higher levels of stress, threat, and insecurity. Respondents to a worldwide survey agreed that rumors are an important early source of information. To ensure that rumors are more helpful than harmful, management might do the following:

- Be wary of vague communication, which fosters misinterpretation and anxiety.
- Promote healthy, accurate communication. Encourage employees to discuss rumors with their manager.
- Avoid concealing bad news. Promise employees that they will receive accurate information as soon as it becomes available.
- Correct erroneous communications that relate to organizational policies, practices, and strategic plans.[26]

A problem with inaccurate rumors is that they can distract workers, create anxiety, and decrease productivity. A frequent by-product of false rumors about company relocation or a pending merger is that some of the more talented workers leave in the hopes of more stable employment.

Chance Encounters and Management by Walking Around

Another informal channel of significance is *chance encounters*. Unscheduled informal contact between managers and employees can be an efficient and effective communication channel. John P. Kotter found that effective managers do not confine their communication to formal meetings.[27] Instead, they collect valuable information during chance encounters. Spontaneous communication events may occur in the cafeteria, near the water fountain, in the halls, and on the elevator. In just 2 minutes, the manager might obtain the information that would typically be solicited in a 30-minute meeting or through a series of e-mail exchanges.

One important communication channel can be classified as either formal or informal. **Management by walking around** involves managers intermingling freely with workers on the shop floor or in the office, as well as with customers. By spending time in personal contact with employees, the manager enhances open communication. During contacts with employees, the manager will often ask questions such as, "How are you enjoying your work?" or "What bottlenecks have you encountered today?" Because management by walking around is systematic, it could be considered formal. However, a manager who circulates throughout the company is not following the formal paths prescribed by the organizational chart. Management by walking around differs from chance encounters in that the latter are unplanned events; the former occurs intentionally.

management by walking around The process of managers intermingling freely with workers on the shop floor and in the office, and with customers.

Communication Directions

Messages in organizations travel in five directions: downward, upward, horizontally, diagonally, and spherically. *Downward communication* is the flow of messages from one level to a lower level. It is typified by a middle manager giving orders to a lower-level supervisor or by top management sending announcements to employees. Information is sometimes transmitted from a higher level to a lower one without the sender inviting a response. When this occurs, the feedback built into two-way communication is lost. In-N-Out Burger, as described in the chapter opener, emphasizes downward communication to ensure that all employees know what is expected of them.

Upward communication is the transmission of messages from lower to higher levels in an organization. It is the most important channel for keeping management informed about problems within the organization. Management by walking around, chance encounters, and simply talking regularly to employees are factors that improve upward communication. An **open-door policy** is a more formal upward communication channel that allows

open-door policy An understanding in which any employee can bring a gripe to the attention of upper-level management without checking with his or her immediate manager.

employees to bring a gripe to top management's attention without first checking with their manager. Upward communication is more widely used in less bureaucratic firms than in highly bureaucratic firms. Almost all executives contend that they value upward communication, whether or not the majority of employees agree.

An example of the importance of upward communication took place in 2014 when GM initiated a "Speak Up for Safety Program." The program's purpose was to eliminate perceived and real barriers to candid communication between employees and their leaders. Workers were to be recognized for contributing ideas, and high-level managers would be held accountable for acting promptly on the ideas. The program was triggered by ignition switch failure linked to the recall of more than 2 million automobiles and a minimum of 13 people killed.[28]

Horizontal communication is sending messages among people at the same organizational level. It often takes the form of coworkers from the same department talking to one another. Horizontal communication is the basis for cooperation. When coworkers are not sharing information with and responding to one another, they are likely to fall behind schedule. Also, efforts are duplicated and quality suffers. Another type of horizontal communication takes place when managers communicate with other managers at the same level.

Diagonal communication is the transmission of messages to higher or lower organizational levels in different units. A typical diagonal communication event occurs when a manager from one department contacts a lower-ranking person from a department outside of his or her chain of command.

Spherical communication is communication among members from different teams in the network organization. The communication events take place with team members from the same or different organizations. Visualize a team member from Nike Corporation communicating directly with a team member from Samsung Corporation. He wants to talk about a strategic alliance to develop a basketball shoe with a built-in smartphone!

Barriers to Interpersonal Communication

LEARNING OBJECTIVE 5
Summarize barriers to effective communication and how to overcome them.

The information presented so far has been helpful in understanding how communication takes place in organizations. Here we explore further why messages sent from one person to another are often not received exactly as intended. As was shown in Figure 8-1, barriers (or noises) exist at every step in the communication process. Interference is most likely to occur when a message is complex, arouses emotion, or clashes with a receiver's mental set. An emotionally arousing message may deal with topics such as money or personal inconvenience. A message that clashes with a mental set challenges the receiver to make a radical shift in thinking. For example, a human resources manager had difficulty getting across the message that managers could no longer make a specific request for a woman to fill an administrative assistant position.

Eight communication barriers are described here. The first four relate primarily to the sending of messages; the next three relate more to receiving them, and the last one could relate to sending or receiving. Figure 8-3 lists barriers to communication, as well as the means for overcoming them, which will be described in the next section of the chapter.

semantics The varying meanings people attach to words.

1. *Semantics.* Many communication problems are created by **semantics**, the varying meanings people attach to words. The symbols (both words and nonverbal behavior) used in communication can take on different meanings for different people. Consequently, it is possible for a person to misinterpret the intended meaning of the sender. One phrase fraught with varying interpretations is "essential personnel." When a CEO announces before a downsizing that only essential personnel will be retained, many people are left wondering about their status. Few people can accept the message that they are "nonessential."

filtering The coloring and altering of information to make it more acceptable to the receiver.

2. *Filtering of negative information.* A formidable upward communication barrier is **filtering**, the coloring and altering of information to make it more acceptable to the receiver. Many managers and individual workers filter information to avoid displeasing their superiors, such as when describing a revenue shortfall. Filtering is

FIGURE 8-3 Barriers to Communication and Means for Overcoming Them

Understanding barriers to communication should be followed up with effective tactics for overcoming them. The techniques for overcoming barriers listed on the right do not necessarily correspond to the barriers listed on the left.

Barriers	Overcoming Barriers
1. Semantics	1. Clarify ideas before sending.
2. Filtering of negative information	2. Motivate the receiver.
3. Lack of credibility of the sender	3. Discuss differences in frames of reference.
4. Mixed signals	4. Foster informal communication.
5. Different frames of reference	5. Communicate feelings behind the facts.
6. Value judgments	6. Be aware of nonverbal communication.
7. Information overload	7. Repeat the message and obtain feedback.
8. Poor communication skills	8. Adapt to the other person's communication style.
	9. Engage in meta-communication.
	10. Send a handwritten note to the receiver.

most likely to take place when top-level management has a history of punishing the bearer of bad news.

3. *Lack of credibility of the sender.* The more trustworthy the source or sender of a message, the greater the probability that the message will get through clearly. In contrast, when the sender of the message has low credibility, many times it will be ignored. Credibility in sending messages is so important that it is a major contributor to effective leadership.

4. *Mixed signals and mixed messages.* Communications can break down with a subtle variation of low credibility. The disconnect occurs from **mixed signals**—sending different messages about the same topic to different audiences. For example, a company might brag about the high quality of its products in public statements. Yet on the shop floor and in the office, the company tells its employees to cut corners whenever possible to lower costs. A *mixed message* occurs when you send one message to a person about desired behavior, yet behave in another way yourself. A mixed message of this type would occur when an executive preaches the importance of social responsibility, yet practices blatant job discrimination.

mixed signals Communication breakdown resulting from the sending of different messages about the same topic to different audiences.

5. *Different frames of reference.* People perceive words and concepts differently depending on their **frame of reference**, a perspective and vantage point based on past experience. A typical example of the frame-of-reference problem took place in a financial service company that was instituting work-streamlining teams to improve productivity. The vice president of operations announced the program with great enthusiasm, only to find that the message was received in a distorted, negative fashion. The problem was that the vice president perceived productivity improvement as a vehicle for ensuring increased profits and survival. Lower-ranking employees, however, perceived productivity improvement as a way for the company to maintain output while laying off workers.

frame of reference A perspective and vantage point based on past experience.

6. *Value judgments.* Making value judgments prior to receiving an entire message interferes with the communication of its intended meaning. A **value judgment** is an overall opinion of something based on a quick perception of its merit. When value judgments are made too hastily, the receiver hears only the part of the message that he or she wishes to hear. A manager might begin to read an announcement about a dependent-care center to be sponsored by the company. The manager might make a

value judgment An overall opinion of something based on a quick perception of its merit.

quick value judgment that this program is "just another human resources initiative to keep people happy." By so doing, the manager will block out the information that dependent-care facilities often increase productivity by reducing absenteeism and turnover. It is also possible that a hasty value judgment will prompt a person to discount a message despite listening to it fully.

7. *Information (or communication) overload.* Electronic communication has contributed to the problem of too much information being disseminated throughout most private and public firms. **Information (or communication) overload** occurs when people are so overloaded with information that they cannot respond effectively to messages, resulting in stress. As a result, they experience work stress. Managers and staff professionals alike are exposed to so much printed, electronic, and spoken information that their capacity to absorb it all is taxed. The human mind is capable of processing only a limited quantity of information at a time. The receiver and sender both contribute to communication overload. The receiver's "circuits are jammed," yet many senders contribute to the problem by disseminating too much information to the same person.

8. *Poor communication skills.* A comprehensive communication barrier is a limited ability to send or receive a message clearly. The sender might garble a written or spoken message so severely that the receiver cannot understand it, or the sender may deliver the message so poorly that the receiver does not take it seriously. The inability or unwillingness to listen is also a poor communication skill. A frequently displayed poor communication skill is to rely too heavily on clichés and standard expressions that can give the impression that a person is not giving much careful attention to what he or she is saying and is also unimaginative. Businesspeople and athletic coaches are particularly guilty of repetitively using such expressions as "at the end of the day," "scale," and "incentivize," often several times in the same paragraph. Such expressions also suggest that the sender cannot be bothered to express himself or herself on the topic without relying on worn-out phrases that he or she has heard countless times before.[29]

Overcoming Communication Barriers

An effective strategy for improving communication in organizations is to overcome communication barriers. The following sections provide an overview of tactics and techniques for improving the sending and receiving of messages. In addition, they describe methods of overcoming problems in communicating with people of the opposite sex and from different cultures.

Improving the Sending of Messages

Improving the way messages are sent will help overcome communication barriers. Implementing the following suggestions will improve the chances that messages are received as intended.

1. *Clarify ideas before communicating.* Many communications fail because of inadequate planning and lack of understanding of the true nature of the message to be communicated. To plan effectively, managers and professionals must consider the goals and attitudes of those who will receive the message and those who will be affected by it. Part of clarifying ideas is to present them in a clear, exciting manner, at a level appropriate for the audience. Not presenting ideas clearly, such as in a baffling written performance evaluation, can have legal consequences. If the employee was fired for poor performance, the performance evaluation should have been unambiguous about the poor performance.[30]

2. *Motivate the receiver.* The recipient of the message has to be motivated to attend to the message. This is best accomplished by appealing to the receiver's interests or needs. In sending a message to higher-level management, it is important to frame it in terms of how it contributes to earning money, saving money, or productivity.

information (or communication) overload A situation that occurs when people are so overloaded with information that they cannot respond effectively to messages, resulting in stress.

3. *Discuss differences in frames of reference.* A method for understanding and dealing with differences in frames of reference is to recognize that people have different frames of reference, or perspectives, that influence how they interpret events. When two people look at a situation with different frames of reference, a communication problem may occur. For instance, a business owner might say, "We should be able to get this order ready for shipment by Monday morning if we work all day Saturday and Sunday." The employee may respond, "How horrible. Nobody works on Saturday and Sunday; those are family days." From the perspective of the business owner, you work as much as necessary to meet a business goal. But from the standpoint of this worker in particular, a person works a limited number of hours, and reserves other times for personal activities.

The solution to this communication clash is to discuss the frames of reference. The two people live by different rules or guidelines (a major contributor to a frame of reference). If they can recognize that they are operating with different perspectives, the chances for agreement are improved. People can change their frames of reference when the reasons are convincing. For example, the worker in the preceding situation may never have thought about investing time on weekends to help the employer succeed.

4. *Foster informal communication.* An abundance of informal, open communication enhances trust within an organization. Negative rumors are less likely to appear on the grapevine when talking about sensitive topics comes naturally. Ample casual meeting areas such as lounges and conference rooms also contribute to informal communication. Management by walking around and chance encounters are other contributors to the flow of informal communication. Informal communication also fosters gossip, yet when the trust level is high, the gossip is more likely to be positive, such as buzzing about who is going to receive a major promotion.

5. *Communicate feelings behind the facts.* The facts in a message should be accompanied by the appropriate feelings. Feelings add power and conviction to the message. The sender of the message should explain his or her personal feelings and encourage the receiver to do the same. For example, a manager who is disappointed with the quality of a finished product might say, "The product has a cheap look. I'm disappointed with the attention you paid to product design. How do you feel about my criticism?" A less-effective approach would be to simply criticize the poor design without mentioning feelings. Expressing feelings is part of *speaking directly*.

6. *Be aware of nonverbal communication.* A speaker's tone of voice, expression, and apparent receptiveness to the responses of others have an impact on the receiver. These subtle nonverbal aspects of communication often affect the listener's reaction to a message even more than the content of the communication. When sending messages to others, it is important to keep in mind all the aspects of nonverbal behavior described previously.

7. *Repeat the message and obtain feedback.* People frequently do not process a message when first heard, so it is best to repeat the message, perhaps using more than one channel such as an in-person comment backed up by a text message. A study conducted with project managers in six companies found that managers who are deliberately redundant get their projects completed more quickly and deliberately than those who send the same message less frequently.[31]

After a message has been delivered more than once, it is still advisable to ask for feedback on how well the message has been received. Asking questions, encouraging the receiver to express reactions, following up on contacts, and subsequently reviewing performance are

Communicating the feelings behind the facts helps overcome communication barriers.

ways of obtaining feedback. A powerful method of obtaining feedback is to request, "Could you please summarize what you heard me say?"

8. *Adapt to the other person's communication style.* People communicate more freely with those who match their communication style. If you want to assume the burden for decreasing communication barriers with another person, then make some adaptations to his or her style. If your communication target prefers e-mail or text messages to telephone calls, use e-mail or text messages rather than phone calls, except for highly sensitive matters. If your manager prefers brief, bulleted summaries rather than well-developed narrative reports, prepare such brief reports for him or her. If your target responds best to anecdotes, develop anecdotes to support your major points. In contrast, if the receiver prefers statistics to anecdotes, prepare statistics to support major points. It is usually possible to learn the other person's style by careful observation, and by posing a question such as, "How do you like your information presented?"

9. *Engage in metacommunication.* When having a difficult time getting through to another person, it helps to talk about your communication difficulty. To **metacommunicate** is to communicate about your communication to help overcome barriers or to resolve a problem. If, as a manager, you are trying to get through to a group member with an angry facial expression, you might say, "You look upset about our conversation. Is this a bad time to talk with you about something important?" The group member might counter, "I think I'm carrying too big a workload, so I'm not very happy." With the air cleared, communication might now flow more smoothly.

10. *Send a handwritten note to the receiver.* Part of overcoming communication barriers is to get the receiver's attention, as suggested in suggestion 2. In today's world of digitized communication, an effective attention-grabbing tactic is to write a handwritten note to the receiver of your message. The effectiveness of handwritten thank-you notes is well acknowledged, and a study conducted on house purchases provides convincing evidence of the power of the pen. An analysis of 14,000 purchase offers for houses revealed that sending a handwritten note to the seller increased the buyer's odds of making the winning bid by 54.2 percent. Effective letters mention that the prospective purchaser will take good care of the house, and they also reflect serious intent to purchase.[32] (The handwritten-note tactic is probably only necessary when the seller has competitive bids for his or her house.)

> **metacommunicate** To communicate about your communication to help overcome barriers or resolve a problem.

Improving the Receiving of Messages

Listening is a basic part of communication, and many communication problems stem from the intended receiver not listening carefully. An extensive analysis of the type of oral communication needed to succeed in the workplace found that listening is more important than conversing or presenting.[33] This finding is counterintuitive because many people believe that making sparkling oral presentations is the key to success in the workplace.

Reducing communication barriers requires a special type of listening. **Active listening** means listening for full meaning without making premature judgments or interpretations. The active listener listens intently, with the goal of empathizing with the speaker. As a result of listening actively, the listener can feed back to the speaker what he or she thinks the speaker meant. Feeding back the content is referred to as *paraphrasing*, such as "You say you are unhappy with progress in enhancing our customer satisfaction ratings." Too much paraphrasing, however, can be disruptive and annoying. Paraphrasing should focus on key points in the conversation.

> **active listening** Listening for full meaning without making premature judgments or interpretations.

The empathy aspect of active listening is recognized as a vital skill for a wide variety of workers. Geoff Colvin, an established business writer, observes that there is a mushrooming demand for employees with affective, nonlogical abilities that cut across the economy. Empathy, viewed as sensing at a deep level the feelings and thoughts of others, is the foundation. In this regard, a retailing CEO from Germany said his biggest hiring challenge is to find people who are empathetic and collaborative.[34] Some of the leadership success of Microsoft CEO Satya Nadella is attributed to his ability to empathize with employees and customers. Nadella believes that it is his mission to teach, listen, and absorb new ideas rather than thinking he has all the answers.[35] As with other effective leaders and managers, Nadella uses listening to help build relationships with people.

Observing nonverbal cues is another facet of active listening. For example, if an employee laughs slightly whenever he mentions a deadline, dig for more information. The laughter may signal that he thinks the deadline is unrealistic.

An active listener also avoids traps such as reacting too quickly to a word or phrase that stirs emotion. Instead he or she carefully interprets the word and analyzes what the word or phrase might mean to the sender. The active listener might hear a speaker say, "People with a weak work ethic have no place in this company." Before getting angry or accepting the entire message, the active listener would wait to find out what the sender really means by a "weak work ethic."

An active listener will postpone presenting his or her viewpoint, particularly in conflict situations. By holding back on presenting your side of the story, the other person will feel fully heard, and then will be more likely to listen to your viewpoint. When people feel shut off, they are unlikely to listen carefully.

A foundational skill for the active listener is to ask open-ended questions because these questions invite an explanation rather than a one-word response. Open-ended questions begin with words such as: "Tell me about," "Explain to me," "How are you doing with our project?" and "Where are you headed?" Two examples of closed-ended questions are, "Will you make your deadline?" and "Do you like your job?"

Listening can be an important factor in business success. Many companies invest considerable time and energy to better understand the thinking, values, and behavioral patterns of their customers. Quite often the same processes the companies use to gain insights into their customers can be used to learn more about their own employees, such as asking about job satisfaction and morale. Improving listening skills can also improve teamwork. Anne Hardy is the leader of a 20-person team at SAP that includes 14 nationalities. She said that this diversity makes it difficult sometimes to get team members to listen carefully to each other. After a seminar on improving listening skills, team members listened better to each other as well as paid attention to emotion and calming down before responding to a colleague.[36]

The Organizational Behavior in Action insert illustrates the importance executives often place on listening to stakeholders.

Do the Skill-Development Exercise to build your ability to listen actively.

Dealing with Gender Differences in Communication Style

Despite the trend toward equality in organizations, substantial interest has arisen in identifying differences in communication styles between men and women. People who are aware of these differences will face fewer communication barriers between themselves and members of the opposite sex. As we describe these differences, recognize them as group stereotypes, reflecting how the average man or woman is likely to behave. Individual differences in communication style are usually more important than group (men vs. women) differences. Key differences in gender-related communication styles are as follows:[37]

- Women prefer to use communication for building rapport and social connections.
- Men prefer to use talk primarily as a means of preserving independence and status by displaying knowledge and skill, and women tend to downplay their status.
- Men prefer to work out their problems by themselves, whereas women prefer to talk out solutions with another person.
- Women want empathy, not solutions. When women share feelings of being stressed out, they seek empathy and understanding.
- Women are more likely to compliment the work of a coworker, while men are more likely to be critical.
- Men tend to be more direct in their conversation, while women emphasize politeness.

Nasdaq CEO Adena Friedman Went on a Listening Tour

Adena Friedman became president and chief executive officer (CEO) of the stock exchange Nasdaq on January 1, 2017, thereby becoming the first woman to head a major global stock exchange. She is also a member of the Board of Directors. Friedman brought to the position more than 20 years of industry expertise. She is credited with contributions that helped transform Nasdaq into a leading global exchange as well as a technology solutions company that operates on six continents. Prior to assuming the CEO role, Friedman served as president and chief operating officer (COO) of Nasdaq during 2016. As the COO, she was responsible for all of the company's business segments.

From March 2011 until June 2014, Friedman served as the chief financial officer and managing director of the Carlyle Group. She then rejoined Nasdaq as president to oversee the technology, information, and corporate businesses that made up two-thirds of company revenues at Nasdaq. Prior to joining Carlyle, Friedman was a member of the Nasdaq management team for over 10 years.

Friedman believes strongly that human emotion is responsible for much of the volatility in the price of stocks, mutual funds, and bonds. She also believes that to manage and lead effectively, you have to understand human emotion, and that listening carefully to people is essential for such understanding.

When Friedman returned to Nasdaq, one of her initial steps was to embark on a global listening tour. "I met with clients and employees in every single one of our divisions across the world," notes Friedman. She traveled to 22 cities in her first 18 months in her new role. During this extensive trip, Friedman gained many insights into the business that helped prepare her for the CEO position. One such insight was that clients and employees are an excellent source of ideas for improving the functioning of a major global stock exchange.

Friedman graduated with an MBA from the Owen Graduate School of Management of Vanderbilt University. She also holds a BA in political science from Williams College. Friedman attributes some of her business success to the lessons she learned in the taekwondo studio where she earned a black belt. Friedman says that this Korean martial art was useful in building her leadership skills.

QUESTIONS

1. Why did Friedman spend so much time and money visiting employees and clients across the globe when she could have used e-mail, chat, text messaging, or Internet surveys to gather information?

2. Any thoughts on how a martial art such as taekwondo could help a person become successful as a manager and a leader?

Source: Original story created from facts and observations in the following sources: Bradley Hope, "Friedman to Be Nasdaq Operating Chief," *The Wall Street Journal*, December 16, 2015, p. C4; Susie Gharib, "Nasdaq CEO Adena Friedman Talks Confidence, Leadership, and Taekwondo," *Fortune*, February 7, 2018, p. 1; "CNBC Interview with Adena Friedman, Nasdaq CEO at the World Government Summit in Dubai," CNBC, www.cnbc.com/2018/02/13/cnbc-interview-with-adena-friedman-nasdaq-ceo-at-the-world-government-summit-in-dubai.html, February 13, 2018, pp. 1–4; "Nasdaq Leadership: Adena T. Friedman, Nasdaq, http://business.nasdaq.com/discover/nasdaq-leadership/adena-friedman/index.html, 2018, p. 1.

Actively Listening to a Coworker

Before conducting the following role-playing, review the keys to effective listening presented in the text. The suggestion about paraphrasing is particularly important when listening to a person who is talking about an emotional topic.

One student plays the role of a coworker who has just been offered the position of manager of another department. He or she will be receiving 10 percent higher pay and be able to travel overseas twice a year for the company. The person is eager to describe full details of this good fortune to a coworker but, at the same time, has some concerns about the promotion. The person is concerned that his or her spouse might not appreciate the idea of overseas travel.

Another student plays the role of the coworker to whom the first worker wants to describe his or her good fortune. The second worker wants to listen intently to the first worker. At the same time, the listener is facing some urgent work problems and therefore may have to fight being distracted.

Other class members will rate the second person on his or her listening ability.

- Women tend to be more conciliatory when facing differences, while men become more intimidating.
- Men are more interested than women in calling attention to their accomplishments or hogging recognition.
- Women tend to downplay their certainty about a subject, while men are more likely to minimize their doubts. As a result, women tend to appear less confident than men, even when their confidence levels are equal.
- Women are more likely to use a gentle expletive, whereas men tend to be harsher. (Do you think this difference really exists?)
- Women use "I," "me," and "mine" more than do men. This difference reflects the fact that

Recognizing gender differences in communication can facilitate good communication.

women are more self-attentive and aware of their internal state. Men make more frequent use of "a," "an," and "the" because men talk more about objects and things. Women also make more frequent use of the third-party pronouns "he," "she," and "they" because women talk more about people and relationships.[38]

Men tend to interrupt women during meetings. Academic studies and observations have found that being interrupted, talked over, or penalized for speaking out is widely experienced by women when they are outnumbered by men.[39]

Understanding these differences can help you interpret the behavior of people, thus avoiding a communication block. For example, if a male team member is not as effusive with praise as you would like, remember that he is simply engaging in gender-typical behavior. (Again, this is a gender stereotype that is not universally applicable.) Factor in this gender difference before taking the shortfall personally.

A potential dysfunction of stereotypes about gender differences in communication is that it can lead to a disconnect between men and women in the workplace. Men might talk over women, not giving them a chance to speak or ignoring them. Women, in contrast, might think men are being needlessly aggressive, and not take them seriously.

Overcoming Cross-Cultural Communication Barriers

LEARNING OBJECTIVE 6
Explain how to overcome potential cross-gender and cross-cultural communication problems.

The modern workforce has become more culturally diverse in two major ways. Many subgroups within our own culture have been assimilated into the workforce, and there is increasing interaction with people from other countries. Cultural differences within a diverse country, such as the United States or Canada, can be as pronounced as differences between two countries. Managers therefore face the challenge of preventing and overcoming communication barriers created by differences in language and customs. Sensitivity to cultural differences goes a long way toward overcoming these potential communication barriers. If you are aware that these barriers exist, you will be ready to deal with them. In addition, communicators should keep in mind several suggestions:

1. *Show respect for all workers.* The same behavior that promotes good cross-cultural relations in general helps overcome communication barriers. A widely used comment that implies disrespect is to say to a person from another culture, "You have an accent." If you were in that person's culture, you, too, might have an accent.
2. *Use straightforward language and speak slowly and clearly.* When working with people who do not speak your language fluently, speak in an easy-to-understand manner. Face-to-face communication is particularly helpful to check for comprehension. Minimize the use of idioms and analogies specific to your language. Particularly difficult for foreigners to interpret are sports analogies such as "This should be a slam dunk." Also perplexing are general idioms such as "My manager

FIGURE 8-4 Cross-Cultural Differences in Communication

- Members of Asian and some Middle-Eastern cultures consider direct eye contact rude.

- Japanese people rarely use the word "no." When they say "yes" ("hai"), it acknowledges only that they have heard what was said.

- When Japanese people nod, they are indicating that you have been heard and understood, not necessarily that they agree with you.

- Korean people are hesitant to say "no," even when they have rejected a proposal. Koreans feel it is important to have visitors leave with good feelings.

- British people understate their feelings. If a British person says "Your report does raise a few questions," the real meaning is probably "Your report is atrocious."

- People from Latin America are very conscious of rank, and they expect the manager to be the voice of authority. Consequently, Latin Americans may be hesitant to make suggestions to a superior.

- Americans are eager to get down to business quickly and will therefore spend less time than people from other cultures in building a relationship.

- Americans value time much more than do people from other cultures. They are therefore more likely than people from other cultures to appear perturbed when a person shows up late for a meeting.

- In the North American culture, the hands up emoji symbolizes praise. In China, the same emoji means "stay away from me."[40]

passed the buck," or "Our competitor is over the hill." Slang can be difficult for non-native speakers to interpret also because its literal meaning can be quite different from the thought it is intended to convey. A good example is "Shut up!" which literally means "Stop talking." Depending on the intonation of the voice, "Shut up" can mean "I don't believe you," "Really?" or "That's difficult to believe."[41]

3. *Be alert to cultural differences in customs and behavior.* To minimize cross-cultural communication barriers, recognize that many, subtle, job-related differences in customs and behavior may exist. For example, Asians may feel uncomfortable when asked to brag about themselves in the presence of others. From their perspective, calling attention to oneself at the expense of another person is rude and unprofessional. Figure 8-4 presents a sampling of cross-cultural differences in customs and behavior that relate to communications.

4. *Be sensitive to differences in nonverbal communication.* All cultures use nonverbal communication, but the specific cues differ across cultures. To receive messages accurately when working with people from diverse cultures, one must be sensitive to these differences. For example, in some cultures, maintaining eye contact with a person in a position of authority is frowned upon, and does not reflect disinterest.

5. *Do not be diverted by style, accent, grammar, or personal appearance.* Although these superficial factors all relate to business success, they are difficult to interpret when judging a person from another culture. It is therefore better to judge the merits of the behavior.[42] (This is also good advice in dealing with people from your own culture.) A brilliant individual from another culture may be still learning your language and thus make basic mistakes when speaking in your tongue. Or he or she might also not have yet developed a sensitivity to dress style in your culture.

6. *Be attentive to individual differences in appearance.* A major cross-cultural insult is to confuse the identity of people because they are members of the same race or ethnic group. Research experiments suggest that people have difficulty seeing individual differences among people of another race because they react to race first, such as thinking, "He has the lips of an African American." However, people can learn to search for more distinguishing features, such as a dimple or eye color.[43]

7. *Recognize that contributing ideas during meetings might be influenced by the participant's culture.* Team members from more egalitarian (democratic) cultures such as the United States and Canada may be accustomed to voicing their unfiltered ideas and opinions, including disagreeing with the meeting leader. In contrast, meeting participants from hierarchical cultures such as Japan and China tend to voice their opinion only after more senior colleagues have expressed their views, partly out of respect for authority.[44] It may therefore be necessary for the leader of the meeting to encourage highly respectful meeting participants to speak up.

Do the Skill-Development Exercise to improve your cross-cultural effectiveness when communicating.

Cross-cultural differences can influence communication.

Persuasive and Power-Oriented Language

A major part of being persuasive involves choosing the right linguistic style, which is a person's characteristic speaking pattern. Deborah Tannen explains that **linguistic style** involves such behaviors as the amount of directness used, pacing and pausing, word choice, and the use of such communication devices as jokes, figures of speech, anecdotes, questions, and apologies.[45] A linguistic style is complex because it includes the culturally learned signals by which people communicate what they mean, along with how they interpret what others say and how they evaluate others. The complexity of linguistic style makes it difficult to offer specific prescriptions for using a power-oriented style. Nevertheless, here are many components of a linguistic style that would give power and authority to the message sender, and simultaneously would enhance his or her persuasiveness:[46]

LEARNING OBJECTIVE 7
Recognize the basics for becoming a more persuasive and power-oriented communicator.

linguistic style A person's characteristic speaking pattern, involving the amount of directness used, pacing and pausing, word choice, and the use of jokes, figures of speech, questions, and apologies.

- Choose words that show conviction, such as "I'm convinced," or "I'm confident that. . . ." Similarly, avoid expressions that convey doubt or hesitancy, such as "I think," or "I hope." Be bold in expressing ideas, yet do not attack people. Intensify your writing with action verbs such as "spearheaded," "expanded," "created," and "decimated." Avoid wimpy words and expressions, such as "To tell you the truth," "I could be wrong," "I'm just saying," and "I'm no expert."

- Emphasize direct rather than indirect talk, such as saying, "I need your report by 3 tomorrow afternoon," rather than, "I'm wondering if your report will be available by noon tomorrow." Also, do not leave people to guess what you really mean, hoping that the person will pick up on your hint. For example, if as the manager, you are concerned about a team member's frequent lateness, indirect talk would be, "You are rarely in your cubicle at 9 a.m." Direct talk would be, "You are frequently late to work."

- Frame your comments in a way that increases your listener's receptivity. The frame is built around the best context for responding to the needs of others. An example would be to use the frame "Let's dig a little deeper" when the other people in the room know something is wrong, but find pinpointing the problem to be elusive. Your purpose is to enlist the help of others in finding the underlying nature of the problem.

- Speak with a big picture or strategic perspective as you begin the conversation. People respond well to abstract ideas, such as "Let's improve the health of our employees." A less abstract idea would be going into detail at first about the workings and cost of an employee wellness center.

- Speak at length, set the agenda for a conversation, make jokes, and laugh. Be ready to offer solutions to problems, as well as suggest a program or plan. All of these points are more likely to create a sense of confidence in listeners.

- Apologize infrequently, and particularly minimize saying, "I'm sorry."

- Take deep breaths to project a firm voice. People associate a firm voice with power and conviction.

- Occupy as much space as possible when speaking before a group. Stand with your feet approximately 18 inches apart and place your hands on the top of your hips occasionally. The triangles you create with arms occupy space, and the hand-on-hip gesture symbolizes power to most people.

- Let others know of your expertise because people tend to defer to experts. Mention how much experience you have had in a particular phase of the business to get people to take your message more seriously. An executive might say, "I've brought two companies out of crises before, and I can do it for us right now."

- Put people in a receptive mood before asking them for something (pre-suasion). Persuasion is likely to be the most effective when you get others to agree with a message before it is even sent. You attempt to get the other person in a receptive mood before asking him or her for something. A practical approach to pre-suasion is to solicit other people's advice before proposing a key initiative. For example, you might ask for advice on your idea of consolidating three office locations into one. Asking for their advice makes the other people more favorable toward your idea.

- Use the pronoun "I" to receive more credit for your ideas. (Of course, this could backfire in a team-based organization.) Furthermore, research by psychologist James W. Pennebaker suggests that higher-status people use "I" less frequently than those of lower status. The higher-status person is thinking of what the other person needs to do. The lower-status person is more humble and thinking, "I should do this."[47]

Despite these suggestions for developing a power-oriented linguistic style, Tannen cautions that there is no one best way to communicate. How to project your power and authority is often dependent on the people involved, the organizational culture, the relative rank of the speakers, and other situational factors. The power-oriented linguistic style should be interpreted as a general guideline. Another consideration is that you may not want to project a powerful, imposing image. Some managers and professionals prefer to play a more laid-back, behind-the-scenes role. Keep in mind that the purpose of persuasive communication is to get other people to act in the way you think is desirable. A little trial and error might be necessary to see what works best for you.

Implications for Managerial Practice

1. Interpersonal communication is the basic process by which managers and professionals carry out their functions. It is therefore critical to work toward unclogging communication channels in all directions. Part of unclogging these channels is to overcome communication barriers following some of the guidelines presented in this chapter. It is particularly important to be aware of communication barriers and to recognize the receiver's frame of reference.

2. Two-way communication is usually superior to one-way communication. Interact with the receiver to foster understanding. While delivering your message, ask for verbal feedback and be sensitive to nonverbal signals about how your message is getting across. Look for signs of agreement such as smiling or nodding, or signs of disagreement such as sideways shaking of the head or a frown. By so doing, many communication barriers (e.g., value judgments) will be overcome.

3. Spoken and written communication in organizations, as well as in the world outside, has become increasingly informal, with even managers and professionals making grammatical errors and overusing abbreviations in e-mail and text messages. Nevertheless, committing too many language errors can hold a person back from being promoted into higher-level positions. Executives tend to use language more formally and commit fewer major errors in grammar, such as double negatives and the confusion of plural and singular.

4. A significant part of communication takes place in meetings, both face-to-face and virtual, and people's effectiveness is often judged by their behavior in meetings. Although the suggestion may be obvious, meetings are therefore an opportunity to display your effectiveness by contributing to the meeting and using your best communication skills.

Summary of Key Points

1. *Describe the communication process.* Interpersonal communication takes place through the following steps: source (the sender), message, channel (medium), receiver, and feedback. The environment in which the message is sent and noise are also part of the communication process.

2. *Describe the impact of information technology on interpersonal communication in organizations.* Advances in information technology have influenced the quantity and quality of interpersonal communications in the workplace. Four such advances are e-mail, telecommuting, blogging, and presentation technology. E-mail facilitates communication but contributes to information overload. Some business firms have counterattacked the problems associated with e-mail by shifting to related technologies such as intranets and company blogs. Chat is useful as collaboration software or for message exchange between two people. The company blog communicates business information with a soft, human touch, and can also be used to communicate similarly with employees.

   Telecommuters can lose out on face-to-face human interaction. People who make extensive use of presentation technology sometimes neglect to connect with the audience. Computer-mediated communication can enhance communication by being more widespread and rapid. Yet, many negative impacts are possible, including communication without the human touch, stress from repetitive motion disorder, the existence of wired managerial workers, and the encouragement of multitasking that leads to errors.

3. *Explain how nonverbal communication can be used to enhance communication.* Nonverbal communication helps express the feeling behind a message and includes the following forms: environment (physical setting), body placement, posture, hand gestures, facial expressions and movements, voice tone, dress and appearance, mirroring (to establish rapport), and touching. One of the many practical applications of nonverbal communication is to project enthusiasm and confidence with body language, such as when a person loosens his or her facial expression.

4. *Present details about the various channels of communication in organizations.* Formal communication channels are specified precisely in bureaucratic organizations. These channels are more difficult to follow in a network organization because of its spherical structure of teams. Informal communication channels supplement the formal channels, with the grapevine being the major informal communication channel. Rumors are an important communication force within organizations and provide information early. Management by walking around can be classified as both a formal and an informal channel. Messages in organization travel in five directions: downward, upward, horizontally, diagonally, and spherically (in the network organization). An open-door policy is an example of a formal upward communication channel.

5. *Summarize barriers to effective communication and how to overcome them.* Key barriers to communication include: semantics, filtering of negative information, lack of credibility of the sender, mixed signals, different frames of reference, value judgments, information overload, and poor communication skills. Overcoming these barriers can involve activities such as clarifying ideas before sending, motivating the

receiver, discussing differences in frames of reference, fostering informal communication, and communicating the feelings behind the facts. Also important are being aware of nonverbal behavior, repeating messages and obtaining feedback, adapting to the other person's communication style, engaging in metacommunications, and occasionally writing a handwritten note. Active listening facilitates receiving messages more accurately.

6. *Explain how to overcome potential cross-gender and cross-cultural communication problems.* Sensitivity to gender differences in style is important for overcoming communication barriers. For example, men tend to be more direct in their conversation, whereas women emphasize politeness. Cross-cultural communication barriers can be overcome in general by sensitivity to cultural differences. Two specific tactics are to show respect for all workers and to use straightforward language and speak slowly and clearly.

7. *Recognize the basics for becoming a more persuasive and power-oriented communicator.* To become a more power-oriented communicator, it is important to choose the right linguistic style. Among the features of a power-oriented linguistic style are choosing words that show conviction, emphasizing direct talk, and apologizing infrequently. Pre-suasion is also helpful.

Key Terms and Phrases

message, p. 163

noise, p. 164

telecommuting, p. 167

nonverbal communication, p. 169

formal communication channels, p. 171

network organization, p. 171

informal communication channels, p. 172

grapevine, p. 172

management by walking around, p. 173

open-door policy, p. 173

semantics, p. 174

filtering, p. 174

mixed signals, p. 175

frame of reference, p. 175

value judgment, p. 175

information (or communication) overload, p. 176

metacommunicate, p. 178

active listening, p. 178

linguistic style, p. 183

Discussion Questions and Activities

1. Describe a problem you have observed or heard about in the workplace that illustrates how poor communication among people can create a problem.

2. When a large number of job applicants are available to fill technical positions, hiring managers and human resource professionals are even more insistent about finding technical workers who have good communication skills. What might be the reasoning of these people hiring the technical workers?

3. Watch a business executive on television and evaluate how effectively the person uses nonverbal communication. Be ready to report your findings back to class.

4. In this era of widespread and extensive use of mobile devices, why do you think being able to maintain eye contact with other people might give a person a slight competitive edge in terms of consideration for jobs involving extensive contact with people?

5. If electronic communication has become so dominant in organizations, why do even information-technology firms such as IBM, Cisco Systems, and Dell still use sales representatives to meet with customers and prospective customers?

6. Write a sample Facebook or Twitter post that you think would impress your present or future employer.

7. How can an organization benefit from good upward communication?

8. A business analyst from the Dominican Republic, working in the United States, said to her manager, "I am having a problem in meetings. When my coworkers are laughing, I do not know what they are laughing about. They all speak English too fast for me." What should the manager do in this situation?

9. From what you have observed at school or on the job, is it true that when men outnumber women in the room, women tend to get talked over or interrupted frequently?

10. Ask a successful person his or her impression of the importance of being a persuasive, power-oriented communicator. Be prepared to share your observations with classmates.

CASE PROBLEM: HR Director Blake Wants to Persuade Company Leadership

Blake is the HR director of Dunbar Holdings, an industrial firm that manufactures aluminum components for other companies. Among its many products arc body frames for automobile companies and door frames for commercial buildings. Blake has been trying to come up with a new HR initiative for Dunbar that would strengthen the importance of his department and also do some good for the company. At the same time, one of his long-term concerns has been food insecurity suffered by children, even those whose parents work full time.

Blake therefore decides to write a persuasive e-mail to company management about an idea for eliminating any food insecurity in the families of the 1,100 Dunbar employees. The e-mail message he sent follows:

From: Blake Magnolia
Sent: May 1, 2019
To: (Names of management team)
Subject: Dunbar Hunger Initiative

Hello, Top Management of Dunbar,

Do I have your attention? Now, I'M GOING TO TELL YOU ABOUT AN IDEA THAT WILL MAKE DUNBAR A WORLD LEADER IN CARING FOR EMPLOYEES. Did you know that many of the families of our employees worry about having enough food to eat? Did you know that some of the children of our employees actually go to bed hungry? Did you know that some of the children of Dunbar employees experience FOOD SHAME IN SCHOOL? This means that their parents did not provide them with lunch or pay the school for the lunch. So the teacher calls out their names in front of the class for NOT HAVING ENOUGH MONEY TO PAY FOR LUNCH.

Think about my idea carefully before rejecting it immediately. I am proposing that we do a confidential survey of all our employees. We find out who doesn't have enough money to buy enough food to keep their family from food insecurity. We also LOOK FOR ANY INSTANCES OF FOOD SHAMING EXPERIENCED BY THE CHILDREN IN DUNBAR FAMILIES!!!!

We then provide supplementary pay of about $400 per month for any Dunbar employee whose family does not have enough food to eat or suffers from food insecurity. AS A RESULT OF THIS FOOD INSECURITY INITIATIVE, DUNBAR WILL BECOME A WORLD LEADER IN TAKING CARE OF THE FOOD NEEDS OF ITS EMPLOYEES. (☺) (☺) Instead of applying for food stamps paid for by taxpayers, Dunbar will be the benefactor.

Let me know what you think within five days so we can start this fantastic initiative.

Blake

Case Questions

1. How persuasive is this e-mail sent to the management team?

2. What recommendations do you have for Blake to make his message more persuasive?

3. What might be any unintended negative consequences of giving subsidies of $400 per month to Dunbar employees who are experiencing food insecurity?

Endnotes

1. Original story based on facts and observations in the following sources: "In-N-Out Burger Open Door Policy," EthicsPoint, https://secure.ethicspoint.com/domain/media/en/gui/28954/, July 2013; Lily Martis, "Top 10 Companies for Great Communicators," Monster, www.monster.com/career-advice/article/communication-companies-1017, 2017; Rob Wile, "This 35-Year-Old Woman Just Inherited In-N-Out Burger. She's Now a Billionaire," *Money*, http://time.com/money/4770527/in-n-out-lynsi-snyder-fortune-ownership/, May 8, 2016; Madison Flager and Lyndsey Matthews, "In-N-Out Managers Make $160,000 a Year Now," Delish, www.delish.com/food-news/news/a55528/in-n-out-managers-salary/, January 24, 2018, pp. 1–2; "In-N-Out Burger Management Reviews: Customer Service Representative," Indeed, www.indeed.com/cmp/In--n--out-Burger/reviews?fjobtitle=Customer+Service+Representative&fcountry=ALL, pp. 1–3, 2018.

2. Marty Stanley, "Focus on Communication Interactions," *Communication Briefings*, April 2011, p. 5.

3. Mike Prokopeak, "What If E-mail Got Pantsed?" *Workforce*, October 2013, p. 14.

4. Leena Rao, "Email: Unloved. Unbreakable," *Fortune*, May 1, 2015, pp. 54, 56.

5. Christopher Mims, "Chat Emerges as the Hottest Thing in IT," *The Wall Street Journal*, November 7, 2016, pp. B1, B5.

6. Quoted in Rachel Feintzeig, "A Company without E-mail? Not So Fast," *The Wall Street Journal*, June 18, 2014, p. B7.

7. Research reported in Andrew Blackman, "The Smartest Way to Use Email at Work," *The Wall Street Journal*, March 12, 2018, p. R1.

8. Dorie Clark, "Actually You Should Check Email First Thing in the Morning," *Harvard Business Review*, pp. 2–3.

9. Michelle Conlin and Andrew Park, "Blogging with the Boss's Blessing," *Business Week*, June 28, 2004, p. 102.

10. Jean Mausehund and R. Neil Dortch, "Presentation Skills in the Digital Age," *Business Education Forum*, April 1999, pp. 30–32.

11. Mausehund and Dortch, "Presentation Skills," pp. 31–32. "Death to PowerPoint," *Bloomberg Businessweek*, September 3–9, 2012, p. 84.

12. "The State of Telecommuting in the U.S. in 2017," www.workflexibility.org/state-of-telecommuting-us-2017, January 15, 2018, pp. 1–6.

13. Nicole Spector, "Why Are Big Companies Calling Their Remote Workers Back into the Office?" *NBC Business News*, July 27, 2017, p. 1.

14. "Telecommuters vs. Office Workers: Who's More Productive?" *SiliconANGLE* (http://siliconangle.com), October 14, 2013, pp. 2–3.

15. "Vision Statement: The Multitasking Paradox," *Harvard Business Review*, March 2013, pp. 30–31.

16. Cited in Susan G. Hauser, "'Mindfulness' over Matter of Multitasking," *Workforce Management*, December 2012, p. 10.

17. Robbie Briggs, "Real Estate Trends: The Thing about Technology," The Robbie Report, www.therobbiereport.com/2016/06/robbies-real-estate-trends-the-thing-about-technology/, July 15, 2016.

18. Jared Lindzon, "Communicating In-Person at Work Isn't Dead Yet, Says Gen Z," *Fast Company*, www.fastcompany.com/3063473/digitally-native-gen-z-still-wants-to-communicate-in-person-at-work, September 7, 2016, pp. 1–6.

19. Many of these ideas were first synthesized by Michael Argyle, *Bodily Communication*, 2nd ed. (Madison, CT: International Universities Press, 1990).

20. John V. Thrill and Courtland L. Bovée, *Excellence in Business Communication*, 5th ed. (Upper Saddle River, NJ: Prentice-Hall, 2002), p. 38.

21. Eric Barker, "How to Get People to Like You: 7 Ways from an FBI Behavior Expert," Ladders.com, May 29, 2017, p. 4; "Use Body Language and Gain Their Trust," *Manager's Edge*, April 2000, p. 5.

22. Steve McNelley and Jeff Machtig, "What Is Telepresence?" www.dvetelepresence.com/files/whatIsTelepresence.pdf, 2014, pp. 1–10.

23. Scott Dockweiler, "How Much Time Do We Spend in Meetings? (Hint: It's Scary)," The Muse, www.themuse.com/advice/how-much-time-do-we-spend-in-meetings-hint-its-scary, 2018, p. 3.

24. Interview by Bob Rosner, "Studying the World beneath the Org Chart," *Workforce*, September 2001, p. 65.

25. Cited in Mildred L. Culp, "Rumor Important, Say Managers Worldwide," WorkWise® syndicated column, March 28, 1999; "Make the Rumor Mill Work for You," *Executive Leadership*, May 2003, p. 7.

26. Samuel Greengard, "Gossip Poisons Business: HR Can Stop It," *Workforce*, July 2001, pp. 26–27; Jeremy Smerd, "Gossip's Toll on the Workplace," *Workforce Management*, March 2010, p. 3.

27. John P. Kotter, *The General Managers* (New York: Free Press, 1991).

28. "Getting GM Employees to Speak Up about Safety," *The Washington Post*, April 14, 2014, pp. 103.

29. Barton Swain, "All Worn Out," *The Wall Street Journal*, August 11, 2014, p. A11; "Which Buzzwords Would You Ban?" *The Wall Street Journal*, January 2, 2014, p. B4.

30. Carroll Lachnit, "Tongue-Tied," *Workforce Management*, August 2003, p. 10.

31. Paul Leonardi, Tsedal Neeley, and Elizabeth M. Gerber, "How Managers Use Multiple Media: Discrepant Events, Power and Timing in Redundant Communication," *Organization Science*, January–February 2012, pp. 98–117.

32. Leigh Kamping-Garder, 'Want the House? Write a Letter," *The Wall Street Journal*, January 19, 2018, pp. M1, M8.

33. Kyle Brink and Robert D. Costigan, "Oral Communication Skills: Are the Priorities of the Workplace and AACSB-Accredited Programs Aligned?" *Academy of Management Learning & Education*, June 2015, pp. 205–221.

34. Geoff Colvin, "Employers Are Looking for New Hires with Something Extra: Empathy," *Fortune*, September 27, 2014, p. 55.

35. Harry McCraken, "Satya Nadella Rewrites Microsoft's Code," *Fast Company*, September 18, 2017, pp. 52–53.

36. Sue Shallenbarger, "Tuning Out: Listening Becomes a Rare Skill," *The Wall Street Journal*, July 23, 2014, p. D3.

37. Deborah Tannen, *Talking from 9 to 5* (New York: William Morrow, 1994); Tannen, "The Power of Talk: Who Gets Heard and Why?" *Harvard Business Review*, September–October 1995, pp. 138–148; Daniel J. Canary and Kathryn Dindia, *Sex Differences and Similarities in Communication* (Mahwah, NJ: Erlbaum, 1998), p. 318.

38. "Cracking the Communication Code between Men and Women in the Workplace" (www.advancingwomen.com/workplace/crack_communcode.html).

39. Susan Chira, "Women Interrupted," *The Wall Street Journal*, June 15, 2017, p. B1.

40. Alina Dizik, "Mastering the Finer Points of American Slang," *The Wall Street Journal*, May 30, 2012, p. D3.

41. Max Mihelich, "Harassment by Emojis," *Workforce*, January–February 2018, p. 32.

42. Roger E. Axtell, *Gestures: The Do's and Taboos of Body Language around the World* (New York: Wiley, 1990).

43. Siri Carpenter, "Why Do They All Look Alike?" *Monitor on Psychology*, December 2000, p.

44. Ginka Toegel and Jean Louis Barsoux, "3 Situations Where Cross-Cultural Communication Breaks Down," *Harvard Business Review*, June 6, 2016, p. 2.

45. Deborah Tannen, "The Power of Talk: Who Gets Heard and Why?" *Harvard Business Review*, September–October 1995, pp. 138–148.

46. Tannen, "The Power of Talk," pp. 138–158; Robert B. Cialdini, "Harnessing the Science of Persuasion," *Harvard Business Review*, October 2001, p. 77; Cialdini, *Pre-suasion: A Revolutionary Way to Influence and Persuade* (New York: Simon & Schuster, 2016); Joel Stein, "Could You Explain It Less Clearly?" *Bloomberg Businessweek*, July 1–27, 2014, p. 63; Elizabeth Bernstein, "What Verbal Tics May Be Saying about Us," *The Wall Street Journal*, January 21, 2014, p. D3; "Be Direct When You Communicate," *Communication Briefings*, June 2011, p. 5.

47. Research reported in Elizabeth Bernstein, "A Tiny Pronoun Says a Lot about You and Your Status," *The Wall Street Journal*, October 8, 2013, pp. D1, D2.

Group Dynamics

nd3000/Shutterstock.com

Learning Objectives

After reading and studying this chapter and doing the exercises, you should be able to:

1. Describe the various types of groups and teams in organizations.

2. Summarize the stages of group development and key roles members occupy within a work group.

3. Identify the characteristics of an effective work group.

4. Understand group decision-making styles, and know how to implement the nominal group technique.

5. Pinpoint several potential problems with group effort, and know how to prevent them.

Casper is a global sleep company founded in 2014 that became one of the world's fastest-growing companies. The company sells mattresses directly to the customer shipped in a box measuring 41-by-21-by-20 inches. The mattresses come in six sizes weighing between 44 and 91 pounds. When released from the box, the mattress expands slowly with a gentle hissing sound. Casper now also sells pillows and sheets, along with a few other sleep products.

Casper sales reached $1 million in the first month, and within a few years, sales exceeded $200 million annually. The magazine *Fast Company* named Casper as one of the Most Innovative Companies in the World, and the Casper Mattress was crowned as one of *Time* magazine's best inventions of 2015.

Casper was launched by an effective work group and continues to rely heavily on carefully designed groups and teams for its success. In early 2013, five friends—Philip Krim, Neil Parikh, Luke Sherwin, Gabriel Flatemen, and Jeff Chapin—huddled together in a co-working space in Manhattan. All five had been part of startups that flopped. The friends held a couple of brainstorming sessions to think of a disruptive product in a traditional industry. The group wanted to follow the model of how Uber transformed the taxi business and how Craigslist moved a big chunk of the classified business online.

One product that seemed to fit was mattresses because Krim had sold mail-order bedding from his dorm room at the University of Texas 10 years previously. Parikh contributed the thought that purchasing a mattress was a terrible experience, being pressured by people working on commission. Casper was designed to ease customer discomfort in shopping and delivery and provide sleep comfort.

Each group member contributed different skills and had different backgrounds and experiences. Krim had expertise in mattresses. Sherwin had advertising experience that enabled him to build a brand that could resonate with the public. Flateman, a former music student, was a specialist in web design, so he took charge of presenting Casper online. Chapin was a stylist with nine years of experience in a leading design firm. Parikh had solid experience in physical science and technology, including working at two startups. A major challenge facing the group was how to fit big mattresses into small spaces, but the newly designed mattresses, which have a latex layer over memory foam, did the job.

Casper continues to focus on the effective work-group approach to building and sustaining the business. For example, Bekah, a member of a cross-functional team within the company, says, "Brainstorming sessions at Casper are always fun! We're big on working collaboratively where people quickly build on ideas and inspire each other towards new approaches."[1]

Effective work groups and collaboration are two of the topics covered in this chapter, and teamwork is covered more explicitly in the following chapter. The heavy emphasis on teams and group decision making in today's organizations only increases the importance of understanding teams and groups for tomorrow's managers. In modern organizations, standard practice is to organize all sorts of work around groups and teams. Under ideal conditions, group and team members agree to be accountable to each other, and they recognize that the work they are doing is a joint effort.[2]

Types of Groups and Teams

A **group** is a collection of people who interact with one another, work toward some common purpose, and perceive themselves as a group. The head of a customer service team and her staff would be a group. In contrast, 12 people in an office elevator would not be a group because they are not engaged in a collective effort. According to Jon R. Katzenbach and Douglas K. Smith, groups and teams function differently.[3] A **team** is a special type of group. Team members have complementary skills and are committed to a common purpose, a set of performance goals, and an approach to the task. An important part of team functioning is **teamwork**—an understanding of and commitment to group goals on the part of all team members.

Groups and teams can also be differentiated in other ways. A working group has a strong, clearly focused leader, while a team leader shares leadership roles. A group is characterized by individual accountability, while a team has individual and mutual accountability. Speaking informally, a team might be regarded as a supergroup.

A major factor in understanding both groups and teams is that they are governed to some extent by **group norms**, the guidelines for acceptable and unacceptable behaviors that are informally agreed on by group members. Norms include behaviors such as (a) praising a group member who has just given a presentation at a meeting, (b) not flaunting the use of a competitive product or service, (c) assisting a coworker who needs your expertise, and (d) working on weekends to finish a project if necessary. Any punishment for not complying with norms comes from the group rather than formal systems established by the organization.[4] For example, the offender might be excluded from a group lunch or not consulted on a work problem.

Being a good organizational citizen stems from both individual attitudes and group norms. One of the ways in which organizational citizenship behavior (OCB) and group norms are related is that when enough individuals in the group demonstrate OCB, the behavior becomes normative.[5] In one company, several members of the group took the initiative to welcome student interns and share work experiences with them, even when the interns worked in another department. Within a few years, helping interns became a group norm.

A study in a South Korea manufacturing setting suggests that when group members tend to be extraverted, they are more likely to engage in helping behaviors. A contributing factor to the helping behavior is the presence of cooperative group norms.[6] As a result, it would be easier for a norm of OCB to take hold.

Groups and teams have been classified in many different ways. Here we describe the distinctions between formal and informal groups and among four different types of work teams. In Chapter 10, more information is presented about work teams.

Formal versus Informal Groups

Some groups are formally sanctioned by management and the organization itself, while others are not. A **formal group** is one deliberately formed by the organization to accomplish specific tasks and achieve goals. Examples of formal or work groups include departments, projects, task forces, committees, and search teams to find a new executive. In contrast, **informal groups** emerge over time through the interaction of workers. Many informal groups arise from workers who interact with others over intranets or social media networks, such as workers discussing how to reduce the company's carbon emissions. Although the goals of these groups are not explicitly stated, informal groups typically satisfy a social or recreational purpose. Members of a department who dine together occasionally would constitute an informal group. Yet the same group might also meet an important work purpose of discussing technical problems of mutual interest.

Types of Work Teams

All workplace teams have the common elements of people who possess a mix of skills working together cooperatively. Four representative work teams are cross-functional teams, top management teams, crews, and virtual teams. Self-managing work teams are described in Chapter 10.

Projects, task forces, and committees are quite similar in design to cross-functional teams, so they do not receive separate mention here. No matter what label the team carries, its broad purpose is to contribute to a collaborative workplace in which people help one another achieve constructive goals. The idea is for workers to collaborate (a high level of cooperation) rather than compete with or prevent others from getting their work done.

As teams have become an integral part of the workplace, much effort has been directed toward specifying the skills and knowledge needed to function effectively on a team.

teamwork A situation in which there is understanding and commitment to group goals on the part of all team members.

group norms The guidelines for acceptable and unacceptable behaviors that are informally agreed on by group members.

formal group A group deliberately formed by the organization to accomplish specific tasks and achieve goals.

informal group A group that emerges over time through the interaction of workers, typically to satisfy a social or recreational purpose.

Cross-Functional Teams

cross-functional team A work group, composed of workers with different specialties but from about the same organizational level, who come together to accomplish a task.

It is common practice for teams to be composed of workers from different specialties. A **cross-functional team** is a work group composed of workers from different specialties, but at about the same organizational level, coming together to accomplish a task. The purpose of the cross-functional team is to get workers from different specialties to blend their talents toward a task that requires such a mix. Product development is the most frequent purpose of a cross-functional team. In addition, cross-functional teams are used for purposes such as improving quality, reducing costs, and in improving work processes.

A key success factor for cross-functional teams is that the team leader has both technical and process skills. The leader needs the technical background to understand the group task and to recognize the potential contribution of members from diverse specialties. At the same time, the leader must have the interpersonal skills to facilitate a diverse group of people with limited, zero, or even negative experiences working collectively.[7]

A major advantage of cross-functional teams is that they enhance communication across groups, thereby saving time. The cross-functional team also offers the advantage of a strong customer focus because the team orients itself toward satisfying a specific internal or external customer or group of customers. A challenge with these teams, however, is that they often breed conflict because of the different points of view.

To perform well on a cross-functional team, a person has to think in terms of the good of the larger organization rather than in terms of his or her own specialty. For example, a manufacturing technician might say, "If I propose using expensive components for the LED screen for television sets, would the product cost too much for its intended market?"

Virtual Teams

virtual team A group that conducts almost all of its collaborative work via electronic communication rather than face-to-face meetings.

A **virtual team** is a small group of people who conduct almost all of their collaborative work by electronic communication rather than face-to-face meetings. The team members are typically dispersed physically, but could also work in the same organization and contribute input at different times. Teleworkers are often part of a virtual team. E-mail and collaborative software (mentioned in Chapter 8 and later in this chapter) are the usual media for sharing information and conducting meetings. Videoconferencing and telepresence can contribute strongly to the workings of a virtual team.

Virtual teams are well suited for international business.

Use of Virtual Teams and Challenges Most high-tech companies make some use of virtual teams. Strategic alliances, in which geographically dispersed companies work with one another, are a natural fit for virtual teams. It's less expensive for the field technician in Iceland to hold a virtual meeting with his or her counterparts in South Africa, Mexico, and California than to bring them all together in one physical location. If simultaneous input is desired, finding a time that fits all time zones can be a struggle. Virtual teams are also an effective way of responding to new workforce demographics, in which the most talented employees may be located anywhere in the world, and may demand personal flexibility in terms of when and where to perform work.[8]

Global virtual teams face some unique opportunities and challenges. One advantage of team members from different time zones working together is that a project can be worked on 24 hours per day without anybody working an extended day. For example, workers in India can provide input to a project, pass it along to workers in England, who in turn pass it along to workers in New York. Yet global virtual teams also face the challenge of differences in perception of time and different nonwork days. July 4th may be a holiday for Americans, but not for Europeans. A project manager in Japan might need input from his or her counterparts in the United States and Europe on December 25, only to realize that most Americans and Europeans have a day off from work on Christmas Day.

Some members of the global virtual team might regard time as a precious commodity, while others might not be concerned about deadlines. The lead member of the global virtual team has to be aware of different perceptions of time and take actions such as building time-related norms.[9] For example, "Responding to client time demands transcends our personal convenience or cultural beliefs about time."

Another challenge with virtual teams is that some members press the mute button and do other work during the meeting. One way around this problem is for the virtual team leader to ask questions or request input from members periodically. Another approach is for the leader to greet people at the beginning of the meeting so that the members feel more involved in the meeting.[10]

Leadership and Management of Virtual Teams Although members of a virtual team have limited or minimum face-to-face contact with each other, they still need guidance and direction. In many firms, members of the virtual team participate in face-to-face team training before beginning the formal work of the team. After the team is established, it is essential to make sure that all team members understand their roles and responsibilities. Short, frequent, informal check-ups each day are useful, particularly a conference call to update each other on who is doing what. It is also helpful to assign roles or tasks to team members in advance of the meeting. For example, if meeting member Tanya is easily distracted, she might be asked to record each budget request that surfaces during the meeting.

A major responsibility in managing a virtual team is to foster a feeling of community. John McLaughlin, an entrepreneur who has built and sold two software companies composed entirely of remote workers, recommends encouraging communication among team members. It is helpful for team members to introduce themselves to each other, perhaps through an instant-messaging exchange. Encouraging communication could encompass getting them involved in local events and getting on location whenever feasible. Also, being respectful of time zones and preferences for work-life balance is important. Frequent interaction by phone and written messages helps build a sense of community.[11]

Shared Team Leadership and Performance Shared team leadership is a mutual influence process in which team members collaborate on decision making, share responsibility, and lead each other toward the attainment of goals. A study was conducted with 565 team members and team leaders on 101 research and development virtual teams from global manufacturing industries. Shared leadership was measured by a questionnaire, and team leaders rated team performance on the dimensions of work quantity, quality, keeping projects on schedule, and staying within budget. The results indicated that shared leadership was positively associated with team performance.[12]

shared team leadership A mutual influence process in which team members collaborate on decision making, share responsibility, and lead each other toward the attainment of goals.

Worker Suitability for Virtual Team Membership Employees best suited for virtual team membership are those who like, or at least do not mind, ambiguity in their work assignments. In contrast, people who like regimented schedules and concrete instructions are not well-suited for virtual work. A willingness to think independently and take the initiative is also helpful.[13] Being an effective virtual team member requires considerable self-discipline, as does being any type of remote worker. A major reason is that you often have to set your own work schedule, and a supervisor is not physically present. Self-Assessment 9-1 provides you an opportunity to think through your tendencies toward being self-disciplined.

Despite the efficiency of virtual teams, there are times when face-to-face interaction is necessary to deal with complex and emotional issues. Negotiating a new contract between management and a labor union, for example, is not well suited to a virtual meeting.

My Self-Discipline Tendencies

Indicate the extent to which each of the following statements describes your behavior or attitude by circling one number. The numbers refer to Disagree Strongly (DS), Disagree (D), Neither agree nor disagree (N), Agree (A), and Agree Strongly (AS). Consider enlisting the help of someone who knows your behavior and attitudes well to help you respond accurately to the statements.

Statement Related to Self-Discipline	DS	D	N	A	AS
1. I usually stay focused on whatever goal I am pursuing.	1	2	3	4	5
2. I have a mission or purpose in life.	1	2	3	4	5
3. Saving or investing for the future makes little sense when you can have fun with the money in the present.	5	4	3	2	1
4. If a person is highly talented, he or she does not have to invest much time in practicing the skill related to that talent.	5	4	3	2	1
5. I am able to work on my job for an entire hour without checking to see if I have a phone message, text message, or e-mail message.	1	2	3	4	5
6. I have developed a new skill in the last 12 months without being forced to by my employer or an instructor.	1	2	3	4	5
7. I almost never bother retaining facts any longer because I can find whatever facts I need on the Internet.	5	4	3	2	1
8. My days rarely turn out the way I hope.	5	4	3	2	1
9. Given a choice between receiving a gift of $1,000 today versus receiving a gift of $3,000 3 months from today, I would wait for the $3,000.	1	2	3	4	5
10. I would be willing to devote 15 minutes per day for 2 years to learn another language.	1	2	3	4	5
11. Working 60 hours per week for even a short period of time is something that I would never do.	5	4	3	2	1
12. I tend to daydream a lot, even on the job, during quiet moments with family and friends.	5	4	3	2	1
13. I usually read the owner's manual before I spend much time operating a new vehicle or complicated piece of electronic equipment.	1	2	3	4	5
14. When I'm involved in an important work project, I can enjoy myself fully at a recreational event after hours.	1	2	3	4	5
15. I feel that I'm moving forward a little bit each day toward achieving my goals.	1	2	3	4	5
16. I accomplish very little unless I am closely supervised.	5	4	3	2	1
17. Several people have described me as being conscientious.	1	2	3	4	5
18. My work area is neat, clean, and well organized.	1	2	3	4	5
19. I become bored easily.	5	4	3	2	1

My Self-Discipline Tendencies *(Continued)*

Statement Related to Self-Discipline	DS	D	N	A	AS
20. I am willing to work hard and long at a task even if the payoff is uncertain.	1	2	3	4	5
21. It makes sense for a marathon runner to keep going even when it appears that he or she has almost no chance of being among the top group of finishers.	1	2	3	4	5
22. I frequently misplace or lose items such as my keys, wallet, smartphone, or glasses.	5	4	3	2	1
23. Planning is difficult because life is so unpredictable.	5	4	3	2	1
24. I am able to concentrate on an entire news story if the subject interests me.	1	2	3	4	5
25. I'm terrible at remembering names of people I meet only once or twice.	5	4	3	2	1

Scoring and Interpretation: Calculate your score by adding up the numbers circled:

110–125: You are a highly self-disciplined person who should be able to capitalize on your skills and talents.

61–109: You have an average degree of self-discipline.

1–60: You appear to have a below-average degree of self-discipline that could be interfering with accomplishing goals and achieving satisfaction.

Crews

We are all familiar with the common usage of the term *crew* in relation to such groups as those who operate airplanes, boats, and firefighting equipment. The technical definition of the term means virtually the same thing. A **crew** is a group of specialists, each of whom has specific roles, performs brief events that are closely synchronized with the work of other specialists, and repeats these events under different environmental conditions. A crew is identified by the technology it handles, such as an aircraft crew or a deep-sea salvage operation. The crew members rarely rotate specialties, such as the flight attendant

crew A group of specialists, each of whom has specific roles, performs brief events that are closely synchronized with the work of other specialists, and repeats these events under different environmental conditions.

Rawpixel/Shutterstock.com

Crews are necessary for operating large-scale, complex equipment.

taking over for the chief pilot. (Special training and licensing would be required.) The following are several criteria of a group qualifying as a crew:[14]

- There are clear roles and responsibilities.
- The workflow is well established before anyone joins the team.
- Careful coordination is required with other members in order to perform the task.
- The group needs to be in a specific environment to complete its task.
- Different people can join the group without interfering with its operation or mission.

Because of the specialized roles they play, and the essential tasks they perform, much is expected of crews. The future of crews is promising. For example, computer-virus-fighting crews and crews fighting infectious diseases would be a welcome addition to business and society.

Top management teams usually take great pride in their company.

Top Management Teams

The group of managers at the top of most organizations is referred to as a team—the management team, or the top management team. Yet, few groups of top managers function as a team in the sense of the definition presented in this chapter. The CEO gets most of the publicity, along with credit and blame for what goes wrong. Nevertheless, groups of managers are teams in the sense that most major decisions are made collaboratively with all members of the top management group included. Tim Cook (Apple Inc.) and Michael Dell (Dell, Inc.) are examples of highly visible and intelligent CEOs who regularly consult with their trusted advisors before making major decisions.

The term *top management team* has another, less frequent meaning. A handful of companies are actually run by a committee of two or more top executives who claim to share power equally. The executives agree among themselves as to which type of decisions each one makes independently and which decisions they make collaboratively. In this way, they are like a husband-and-wife team running a household. An example of a two-person team sharing power at the top is Safra Catz and Mark Hurd, the co-CEOS at Oracle Inc., each with different major responsibilities. Some observers, however, are skeptical that a company can really be run well without one key executive having the final decision. Can you imagine your favorite athletic team having two head coaches?

Stages of Group Development

Key to understanding the nature of work groups is to know what the group does (the content) and how it proceeds (the process). A key group process is the group's development over time. To make this information more meaningful, relate it to any group to which you have belonged for at least 1 month. Understanding the stages of group development can lead to more effective group leadership or membership. The five group stages are shown in Figure 9-1, and described next:[15]

Stage 1: Forming. At the outset, members are eager to learn what tasks they will be performing, how they can benefit from group membership, and what constitutes acceptable behavior. Members often inquire about rules they must follow. Confusion, caution, and communality are typical during the initial phase of group development.

Stage 2: Storming. During this "shakedown" period, individual styles often come into conflict. Hostility, infighting, tension, and confrontation are typical. Members may argue to clarify expectations of their contributions. Coalitions and cliques may form within the

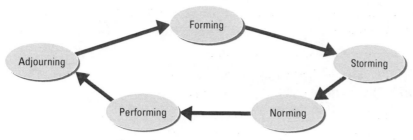

FIGURE 9-1 The Stages of Group Development

Most groups follow a predictable sequence of stages.

group, and one or two members may be targeted for exclusion. Subgroups may form to push for an agenda of interest to them. (Despite the frequency of storming, many workplace groups work willingly with one another from the outset, thus skipping stage 2.)

Stage 3: Norming. After storming comes the quieter stage of overcoming resistance and establishing group standards of conduct (norms). Cohesiveness and commitment begin to develop. The group starts to come together as a coordinated unit, and harmony prevails. Norms stem from three sources. The group itself quickly establishes limits for members, often by the effective use of glares and nods. For example, the team member who swears at the leader might receive angry glances from other members. Norms may also be imposed that are derived from the larger organization and from professional codes of conduct. A third source of norms might be an influential team member who inspires the group to elevate its performance or behavior. The head of an audit team might say, "Let's develop the reputation of an audit team that is the most professional and objective in the industry."

Stage 4: Performing. When the group reaches the performing stage, it is ready to focus on accomplishing its key tasks. Issues concerning interpersonal relations and task assignment are put aside as the group becomes a well-functioning unit. Intrinsic motivation and creativity are likely to emerge as the group performs. At their best, members feel they are working "for the cause," much like a political campaign team or a team bringing a breakthrough product to market.

Stage 5: Adjourning. Temporary work groups are abandoned after their task has been accomplished, much like a project team formed to erect an office tower. The same group members, however, have developed important relationships and understandings they can bring with them should they be part of the same team in the future. The link between adjourning and forming shown in Figure 9-1 is that many groups do reassemble after one project is completed. The link between stages 1 and 5 would not apply for a group that disbanded and never worked together again.

A key managerial challenge is to help the group move past the first three stages into performing. At times, group members may have to be confronted about the fact that they are spending too much time on process issues and not enough on the task at hand.

Roles within Groups

Another perspective on group process is to identify team members' roles.[16] Positive roles are described here to help you identify areas of possible contribution in group efforts:

1. *Knowledge contributor.* Being technically proficient, the knowledge contributor provides the group with useful and valid information. He or she is intent on helping with task accomplishment, and values sharing technical expertise with team members.
2. *Process observer.* A person occupying this role forces the group to look at how it functions, with statements such as, "We've been at it for two and a half hours, and we have taken care of only one agenda item. Shouldn't we be doing better?" The process observer might also point to excellent team progress.

Team Member Roles

Form small teams to conduct a 20-minute meeting on a significant topic. Possibilities include (1) a management team deciding whether to lay off one-third of the workforce in order to increase profits and (2) a group of fans who have volunteered to find a new team-mascot name to replace "Redskins." While team members conduct their heated discussions, other class members should make notes of which team members carry out which roles. Watching for the eight different roles can be divided among class members, such as people in the first row looking for examples of a knowledge contributor. Use the following role worksheet to help you make your observations. Summarize the comments indicative of the role.

Knowledge contributor: _____

Process observer: _____

People supporter: _____

Challenger: _____

Listener: _____

Mediator: _____

Gatekeeper: _____

Take-charge leader: _____

3. *People supporter.* A person occupying this role assumes some of the leader's responsibility for providing emotional support to teammates and resolving conflict. He or she serves as a model of active listening while others make presentations. The people supporter helps others relax by smiling, making humorous comments, and appearing relaxed. He or she supports and encourages team members even when disagreeing with them.

4. *Challenger.* To prevent complacency and noncritical thinking, a team needs one or more members who confront and challenge bad ideas. A challenger will criticize any decision or preliminary thinking that is deficient in any way, including being ethically unsound. Effective interpersonal skills are required to be a challenger. Antagonistic, attack-oriented people who attempt the challenger role lose their credibility quickly because they appear more interested in attacking than solving problems.

5. *Listener.* Listening contributes so substantially to team success that it constitutes a separate role, even though other roles involve listening. If other people are not heard, the full contribution of team effort cannot be realized. As a result of being a listener, a team member or team leader is able to summarize discussion and progress for the team.

6. *Mediator.* Disputes within the group may become so intense and prolonged that two people no longer listen or respond to each other. The two antagonists develop such polarized viewpoints that they are unwilling to move toward each other's point of view. Furthermore, they have moved beyond the point at which conciliation is possible. At this point, the team leader or a team member must mediate the dispute.

7. *Gatekeeper.* A recurring problem in group effort is that some members may fail to contribute because other team members dominate the discussion. Even when the viewpoints of the timid team members have been expressed, they may not be remembered because one or two other members contribute so frequently to discussion. When the opportunity gate is closed to several members, the gatekeeper pries it open. He or she requests that a specific team member be allowed to contribute or that the member's past contribution be recognized.

8. *Take-charge leader.* Some teams cry out for direction because either a formal leader has not been appointed or the appointed leader is unusually laid back. In such situations, a team member can assume the role of the take-charge leader. The problem could be that team members are hesitant to make even simple decisions or take a stand on controversial matters. A starting point for the take-charge leader is to encourage the team to define its mission and list its three main objectives.

According to the team-role theory developed by R. Meredith Belbin, it is important for group members to understand the roles that others play, when and how to let another group member take over, and how to compensate for the shortcomings of others in the group. Roles tend to be based on the psychological makeup of individuals, who adopt them naturally.[17] For example, a person who has developed good listening skills will gravitate toward the listener role, and a knowledgeable, bright person will naturally assume the knowledge-contributor role.

The Skill-Development Exercise gives you an opportunity to identify and observe the roles just described. Recognize, however, that these roles may overlap; they are not entirely independent of each other.

Characteristics of Effective Work Groups

Groups, like individuals, have characteristics that contribute to their uniqueness and effectiveness. As shown in Figure 9-2, these characteristics can be grouped into 11 categories. Our description of work-group effectiveness follows this framework.[18]

LEARNING OBJECTIVE 3
Identify the characteristics of an effective work group.

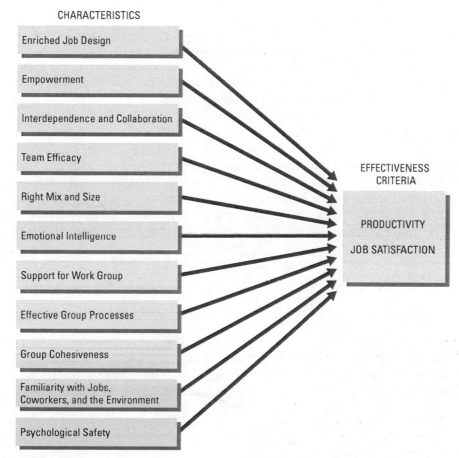

FIGURE 9-2 Work-Group Characteristics Related to Effectiveness

All of the characteristics to the left contribute to group effectiveness in terms of productivity and satisfaction.

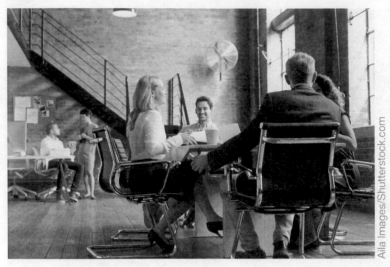
Open office space facilitates the exchange of ideas.

Job Design

Effective work groups follow the principles of job design embodied in job enrichment and the job characteristics model described in Chapter 7. For example, both task significance and task identity should be strong. Group members therefore perceive their work as having high intrinsic motivation.

A Feeling of Empowerment

An effective group or team believes that it has the authority to solve a variety of problems without first obtaining approval from management. Empowered teams share four experiences: potency, meaningfulness, autonomy, and impact. *Potency* refers to team members believing in themselves and exhibiting a confident, can-do attitude. Teams with a sense of *meaningfulness* have a strong collective commitment to their mission and see their goals as valuable and worthwhile. *Autonomy* refers to the freedom, discretion, and control the teams experience (the same as in job enrichment). A team experiences *impact* when members see the effect of their work on other interested parties such as customers and coworkers.[19]

Interdependence and Collaboration

Several types of interdependence characterize effective work groups. Such groups show task interdependence in the sense that members interact and depend on one another to accomplish work. *Task interdependence* is valuable because it increases motivation and enhances the sense of responsibility for the work of other group members. *Goal interdependence* refers to the linking of individual goals to the group's goals. For example, a member of a sales team might establish a personal compensation goal but realize this goal is possible only if the other team members achieve similar success. Aside from the reality of interdependence, clearly defined goals are a major requirement for group effectiveness. Interdependent feedback and rewards also contribute to group effectiveness. Individual feedback and rewards should be linked to group performance to encourage good team play.

Interdependence is also important because it facilitates collaboration among group members. Despite all that is said about the value of collaboration, it may not be frequently achieved at a high level. Chief information officers who attended *The Wall Street Journal* CIO Network conference were asked to grade their company on collaboration, and responded as follows: A, 5%; B, 34%; C, 45%; D, 16%; and F, 0%.[20] As will be mentioned later in the chapter, collaboration can reach a point of diminishing returns and become a drain on productivity.

Team Efficacy

team efficacy A team's belief that it can successfully perform a specific task.

As with self-efficacy at the individual level, a productive group believes in itself. **Team efficacy** refers to a team's belief that it can successfully perform a specific task. A meta-analysis of 259 different samples indicated that team efficacy had a statistically significant relationship with the job performance of teams. The relationship between team efficacy and performance was stronger when task interdependence was high rather than low. In other words, when group cohesiveness was more important, group self-confidence made a bigger contribution.[21]

Right Mix and Size

A variety of factors relating to the mix of group members is associated with effective work groups. A diverse group of members—in terms of experience, knowledge, and education—generally improves problem solving. Cultural diversity tends to enhance creativity because various viewpoints are brought into play. A study cautions, however, that only when each member of the group enjoys high-quality interactions can the full benefits of diversity be realized. The interactions relate to both the task itself (e.g., talking about improving a motorcycle starter) and social interactions (e.g., chatting about children during a break).[22] A problem with functional (technical specialty) diversity is that it can decrease the tendency of the group to stick together, as illustrated in a study of 93 research and new product development groups.[23]

A general statement about work-group diversity is that any one dimension of diversity can have positive or negative effects, depending on the circumstances. For example, when group motivation and task ability are high, diversity will most likely benefit group performance. Imagine an auto design team composed of motivated and talented members. Cultural and educational diversity is likely to help the team produce a winning auto design.[24]

Groups should be large enough to accomplish the work, but when groups become too large, confusion and poor coordination may result. Also, larger groups tend to be less cohesive. Research indicates that group effectiveness begins to diminish with more than 10 group members. Sub-teams are likely to form, encouraging divisive behavior.[25]

Cross-functional teams, work teams, committees, and task forces tend to be most productive with seven, eight, or nine members. Another important composition factor is the quality of the group or team members. Bright people with constructive personality characteristics contribute the most to team effectiveness. A study involving 652 employees composing 51 work teams found that teams with members higher in mental ability, conscientiousness, extraversion, and emotional stability received higher supervisor ratings for team performance.[26] (Put winners on your team, and you are more likely to have a winning team.)

Emotional Intelligence

As described in Chapter 2, emotional intelligence makes a major contribution to individual effectiveness. Teams also benefit from having members with high emotional intelligence in such ways as building relationships both inside and outside the team and understanding the subtle human aspects of their environment. An emotionally intelligent group, for example, would not propose a costly, elaborate program during a period of corporate downsizing.

For a group to be emotionally intelligent, it must do more than assemble a handful of emotionally intelligent members. High group emotional intelligence requires creating norms that establish mutual trust among members, a sense of group identity, and team efficacy. A potential problem, however, is that when group members trust one another too much, they neglect to monitor one another's work and may not catch errors and unethical behavior. The emotionally intelligent group deals constructively with emotion within the group, such as recognizing that the group is sad because a likable member has been downsized out of a job, or that the group is ecstatic because it has surpassed its annual productivity goal.[27]

A finding related to group emotional intelligence stems from a problem-solving experiment. It was found that groups with a larger number of women tended to perform better on several tasks, including brainstorming, decision making, visual puzzles, and solving a complex problem. The underlying factor is that women are more likely to have high social sensitivity—a key component of emotional intelligence.[28] A reasonable interpretation is that teams containing men with high social sensitivity would perform as well as teams with a higher number of women.

Support for the Work Group

The resources available to support the group and the context (environment) influence effectiveness. Key support factors include giving the group the information it needs, coaching group members, providing the right technology, and receiving recognition and other rewards. Training quite often facilitates work-group effectiveness. The training content typically includes group decision making, interpersonal skills, technical knowledge, and the team philosophy. Managerial support in the form of investing resources and believing in group effort fosters effectiveness. Communication and cooperation among groups improve group effectiveness, although management must help create an environment in which communication and cooperation can occur.

Effective Processes within the Group

Many processes (activities) that influence effectiveness take place within the group. One is the belief that the group can do the job (team efficacy), reflecting high team spirit. Effectiveness is also enhanced when workers provide *social support* to one another through such means as helping one another have positive interactions. *Workload sharing* is another process characteristic related to effectiveness. *Communication and cooperation* within the work group also contribute to effectiveness.

A group process that has a considerable impact is high-quality interaction among group members. Such interaction is characterized by trust, open communication, and a willingness to deal with conflict. A healthy type of conflict would be dealing with differences of opinion about work methods, processes, and equipment rather than having personality clashes. Clyde, a member of a construction group, might say, "I know about a hydraulic drill that will get the job done faster and also cost less." His comments are more effective than insulting another group member because of that person's opinion about the best drill for the job.

Interpersonal processes are important, and so are work processes. Teams that can be trusted to follow work processes and procedures tend to perform better. Adhering to such processes and procedures is also associated with high-quality output. Although following processes and procedures might appear to be a routine expectation, many problems are created by workers who fail to do so. For example, a group might show a dip in productivity if workers on a project fail to avoid downloading attachments from unknown sources that might contain a virus.

Group Cohesiveness

group cohesiveness A situation that takes place when members work closely with each other, in a unified, cooperative manner.

Group cohesiveness takes place when members work closely with each other, in a unified, cooperative manner. A cohesive group is likely to be effective. Cohesiveness is closely linked to several other dimensions of an effective work group. Collectively, the process characteristics described previously contribute to a group that pulls together. Without cohesiveness, a group will fail to achieve synergy. The right size and mix within a group will also foster group cohesiveness.

As with many organizational behavior concepts, group cohesiveness is composed of several components. *Interpersonal attraction* is a shared liking or emotional attachment to other members of the group. *Task commitment* is the extent to which there is a shared commitment to the group task. *Group pride* is the shared importance of being a member of the group. All three components are related to group efficiency in terms of making good use of resources, such as producing a website in a short period of time at a low cost. The components are also related to constructive behaviors, such as putting in the time required to produce a good proposal for a contract.[29]

Familiarity with Jobs, Coworkers, and the Environment

Another important factor related to work-group effectiveness is familiarity. *Familiarity* refers to the specific knowledge group members have of their jobs, coworkers, and the environment. If you are familiar with your

Group cohesiveness is important for high performance.

fizkes/Shutterstock.com

job, such as being an experienced market analyst, you have the knowledge base to make a better contribution to the group. If you know your group members well, there is more likely to be mutual trust, which facilitates group accomplishment. Knowing your coworkers also makes it easier to know whom to ask for certain types of assistance, which leads to higher productivity. Knowing the environment, or culture, contributes to group effectiveness in ways such as knowing the kind of initiatives management will or will not accept. For example, in some companies, suggesting that more money should be invested in the manufacture of a product is doomed to failure.

Psychological Safety

A final characteristic of an effective work group or team described here is for members to feel comfort and trust in dealing with each other, as mentioned in relation to emotional intelligence. The People Operations (the HR department) group at Google conducted research involving 200 interviews focused on 250 attributes of 180 active teams. The study concluded that how people interact with each other is the major contributor to team effectiveness and that psychological safety is the most important interaction factor. **Psychological safety** is the belief that you will not be punished or humiliated for speaking up with ideas, questions, concerns, or mistakes.

You feel psychologically safe with other group members when they are willing to both challenge you and support you in a positive manner. Other contributors to a feeling of psychological safety are when you believe that the other members of the group will listen to your ideas in a nonjudgmental way and that you can admit your mistakes.[30]

The characteristics of an effective work group or team should be supplemented by effective leadership. Team leaders must emphasize coaching more than controlling. Instead of being a supervisor, the leader should become a team developer.

Psychological safety The belief that you will not be punished or humiliated for speaking up with ideas, questions, concerns, or mistakes.

Group Problem Solving and Decision Making

Almost all but the very smallest organizations use some types of groups. A major activity of many of these groups, including teams, is to make decisions. Furthermore, groups make most major decisions in organizations. In general, decision making by groups has proven superior to individual decision making. An exception is that people working alone generate a greater number of creative alternative solutions to a problem than they do during group brainstorming.[31] One reason might be that if you spend your time thinking of solutions rather than listening to other group members, you produce more ideas.

One method of group problem solving, brainstorming, was described in Chapter 5. Here we describe group decision-making styles, along with two other methods of group decision making and problem solving—the nominal group technique and using collaborative software to make decisions.

LEARNING OBJECTIVE 4
Understand group decision-making styles, and know how to implement the nominal group technique.

crowdsourcing The gathering of input or information relevant to a particular task by enlisting the services of many people either paid or unpaid, typically via the Internet.

Group Decision-Making Styles

The term *group decision making* refers to a group playing a role in making a decision. Group decision making takes place in different degrees. One extreme is *consultative* decision making, in which the group leader consults with members before making a decision. The other extreme is *democratic* decision making, in which the problem at hand is turned over to the group, and group members are empowered to make the decision themselves.

Democratic decision making today often includes **crowdsourcing**, the gathering of input or information relevant to a particular task by enlisting the

Group decision making is widely used among knowledge workers.

services of many people either paid or unpaid, typically via the Internet. An electrical products manufacturer seeking to expand its traditional customer base gathered input through crowdsourcing. The company created an online portal where electricians, contractors, and inventors could submit new-product ideas. Toymaker Mattel used crowdsourcing to decide what should be the career of the next Barbie doll.[32] A useful feature of crowdsourcing is that it takes advantage of distant search, or seeking opinions from many people, at low cost.[33]

Midway between the two is *consensus* decision making, in which the manager shares the problem with group members. Together they generate and evaluate alternatives and attempt to reach agreement on a solution. Consensus is achieved when every member can say, "I have had an opportunity to express my views fully, and they have been thoughtfully considered by the group. Even though this solution is not the one I believe is optimal, it is acceptable and I will support it. I endorse the validity of the process we have undertaken."[34]

Whichever style of group decision is used, it is important to get all group members involved. If not, the most vocal, or opinionated, group members will dominate. When the group decision is being made in person or digitally, it is often necessary for the head of the group to ask a noncontributing member a polite question such as, "Lucy, we haven't received your input yet. What is your suggestion about the problem we are working on?" It is also helpful to encourage decision-making participants to share their diverse knowledge rather than suppress it.[35] A relevant statement by the group leader would be, "I know that we have different areas of expertise in the group, so I want us to use that information."

The Nominal Group Technique

The opposite of an interacting group is a nominal group whose distinguishing characteristic is silent effort during part of group problem solving. Brainstorming by computer allows for the same noninteractive input by group members. A version of the steps in the **nominal group technique (NGT)** used by the Centers for Disease Control of the U.S. Department of Health and Human Services proceeds as follows:

> **nominal group technique (NGT)** An approach to developing creative alternatives that requires group members to generate different solutions independently.

1. *Generating ideas.* The moderator presents the question or problem to the group in written form and reads the question to the group. The moderator directs everyone to write ideas in brief phrases or statements and to work silently and independently. Each person silently generates ideas and writes them down.
2. *Recording ideas.* Group members engage in a round-robin feedback session to concisely record each idea, without discussion or debate at this point. The moderator writes an idea from a group member on a flip chart, or a computerized equivalent, that is visible to the entire group. He or she proceeds to ask for another idea from the next group member, and so on. There is no need to repeat ideas; however, if group members believe that an idea provides a different emphasis or variation, it can be included. The moderator proceeds until all members' ideas have been documented.
3. *Discussing ideas.* Each recorded idea is then discussed to determine clarity and importance. For each idea, the moderator asks, "Are there any questions or comments group members would like to make about the item?" This step provides an opportunity for members to express their understanding of the logic and the relative importance of the item. The creator of the idea need not feel obliged to clarify or explain the item. Any member of the group can play that role.
4. *Voting on ideas.* Group members vote privately to prioritize the ideas. The votes are tallied to identify the ideas that are rated highest by the group as a whole. The moderator establishes what criteria are used to prioritize the ideas. To start, each group member selects the five most important or valuable ideas from the group list and writes one idea on each index card. Next, each member ranks the five ideas selected, with the most important or valuable receiving a rank of 5, and the least important or valuable receiving a rank of 1.
5. *Selecting the highest-ranking alternative.* After members rank their responses in order of priority, the moderator creates a tally sheet on a flip chart, or computerized

equivalent, with numbers down the left-hand side of the chart, which correspond to the ideas from the round robin. The moderator collects all the cards from the participants and asks one group member to read the idea number and number of points allocated to each one while the moderator records and then adds the scores on the tally sheet. The ideas that are the most highly rated by the group are the most favored actions or ideas in response to the question posed or problem presented by the moderator.[36]

The NGT has met with acceptance because it results in a disciplined decision. An advantage of this technique is that it combines the merits of individual reflection with the scrutiny of collective thought. One study demonstrated that the NGT overwhelmingly outperformed a standard brainstorming group.[37] Also, the NGT helps introverted people become actively involved in group activity.

The Organizational Behavior in Action box illustrates the voting and tallying aspects of the nominal group technique.

Using Collaboration Software and Social Platforms to Facilitate Group Problem Solving

The purpose of collaborative software is to help group members communicate with each other through computers of any type. Electronic brainstorming relies on collaborative software (or groupware) because software is applied to facilitate group decision making. Using electronic brainstorming, as well as the other electronic approaches to group problem solving, participants are free to comment on, or suggest a modification of, the ideas of other contributors. Assume that Ashley, a marketing assistant at a bicycle company, enters the following comment on her e-mail or website post: "I say, let's push for selling more adult tricycles in Florida because of the many seniors down there." Engineering technician Jason then adds to Ashley's's comment, "I love Ashley's idea. But why limit the marketing push to Florida? Let's follow the senior crowd right into Arizona and the Carolinas."

The various electronic approaches to group decision making have been labeled *social platforms* because they function in the same manner as social-networking websites. At the same time, because the group members can interact with each other frequently and comment on the posts placed by other group members, social platforms encourage collaboration.

At its best, collaborative software offers certain advantages over single-user systems. Some of the most common reasons people use collaborative software are as follows:[38]

- To facilitate communication by making it faster, clearer, and more persuasive
- To communicate when it would not otherwise be possible
- To enable telecommuting (working from home)
- To reduce travel costs
- To bring together multiple perspectives and expertise
- To assemble groups with common interests where it would not be possible to gather a sufficient number of people face-to-face
- To facilitate group problem solving and collaboration

Another example of collaborative software is a *shared whiteboard* that allows two or more people to view and draw on a common drawing surface even when they are at a distance. The link to group decision making is that drawing sketches and diagrams might be an important part of the decision making. An example would be a sales team suggesting ways of dividing a geographic territory for selling.

Collaboration software is often cloud based rather than kept within the company information system. A representative use of this type of cloud-based software is to facilitate project management. Among the types of information calling for collaboration are document repositories, tasks, assignment of responsibility for tasks, project milestones and deadlines, and project updates. Centralizing all this information in one place enables

Timber Oak Construction Uses the Nominal Group Technique

Based on an excellent year, Timber Oak Construction Company had $50,000 available to invest in a constructive purpose. Founder and CEO Luke brought the group together to decide what to do with the funds. Luke had used the NGT previously when he was a project manager at a larger construction company. He was impressed with the fact that the method tends to reduce bickering about reaching a decision. Each member of the group presented a preferred alternative, followed by some explanation and discussion.

Luke presented the five alternatives chosen by the group as follows:

A. Purchase solar panels for the warehouse.

B. Paint and refurbish the office and reception area.

C. Donate the funds to a shelter for homeless children in the city.

D. Purchase a high-end pickup truck.

E. Build a new locker room for the construction workers.

The alternatives were presented in an e-mail attachment, and voting was as shown in the table that follows. The table lists the alternatives, the rankings of 1 to 5 made by the top management team, and the tallying of the ranks.

Alternative C (donate the funds to a shelter for homeless children in the city) was ranked highest. After the decision was reached, Maria and Lauren clapped, and each of the other four managers said that they were pleased with the decision. Luke concluded, "We had five good alternatives. As a construction company, we will be proud of our effort to help build new lives."

Nominal Group Worksheet: Ranks (5 is highest) by Members and Tallying

Choice	Luke	Maria	Ron	Janine	Tom	Lauren	Sum of Ranks
A	2	4	3	5	2	2	18
B	1	2	5	2	5	4	19
C	3	5	4	4	3	5	24
D	5	1	2	3	1	1	13
E	4	3	1	1	4	3	16
Row and Column Sums	15	15	15	15	15	15	90

QUESTIONS

1. To what extent do you think Timber Oak Construction made effective use of the nominal group technique?

2. Would a better decision have been for Luke to divide the $50,000 equally among the five alternatives just to please all members of the group?

everyone on the team to have access to a repository of information. The cloud makes this access relatively simple and secure at the same time.[39]

An advantage of virtual problem solving is that it avoids the problem of a couple of people dominating the meeting, and some people making no contribution because they are timid. In-person meetings are useful for a final discussion or vote because of the exchange of ideas possible. Another problem with anonymity in problem solving is that many workers want to receive credit for their good ideas.

Despite all these potential applications and benefits of collaborative software and social platforms, the system will break down unless almost all the parties involved use the software as designed and intended. For example, all members of the virtual team must be willing to get online at the same time to have a productive meeting.

Potential Problems within Groups

LEARNING OBJECTIVE 5
Pinpoint several potential problems with group effort, and know how to prevent them.

Group activity, including group decision making, does not always lead to superior results. Failure to attain outstanding results typically stems from lacking the characteristics of effective work groups, as summarized in Figure 9-2. For example, a work group might fail if it was not empowered, the group was low on emotional intelligence, and the members were poorly trained. Furthermore, similar results would occur if the group lacked the support of management, members did not support one another, and members were quite unfamiliar with the task and with one another. Work-group failures also stem from dysfunctional processes. Here we look at three major processes within groups that can hamper their effectiveness: group polarization, social loafing, groupthink, and excessive collaboration.

Group Polarization

During group problem solving, or group discussion in general, members often shift their attitudes. Sometimes the group moves toward taking greater risks; this is called the *risky shift*. At other times, the group moves toward a more conservative position. The general term for moving in either direction is **group polarization**, a situation in which post-discussion attitudes tend to be more extreme than pre-discussion attitudes.[40] For example, as a result of group discussion, members of an executive team become more cautious about entering a new market.

group polarization A situation in which post-discussion attitudes tend to be more extreme than pre-discussion attitudes.

Group discussion facilitates polarization for several reasons. Discovering that others share our opinions may reinforce and strengthen our position. Listening to persuasive arguments may also strengthen our convictions. The "it's not my fault" attitude is another contributor to polarization. If responsibility is diffused, a person will feel less responsible—and guilty—about taking an extreme position.

Group polarization has a practical implication for managers who rely on group decision making. Workers who enter into group decision making with a stand on an issue may develop more extreme post-decision positions. For example, a group of employees who were seeking more generous benefits may decide as a group that the company should become an industry leader in employee benefits even in an era when benefits are being reduced.

Social Loafing

An unfortunate by-product of group effort is that an undermotivated person can often squeeze by without contributing a fair share. **Social loafing** is freeloading, or shirking individual responsibility, when a person is placed in a group setting and removed from individual accountability. If you have worked on group projects for courses, you may have encountered this widely observed dysfunction of collective effort.

social loafing Freeloading, or shirking individual responsibility, when placed in a group setting and removed from individual accountability.

The faulty ignition switch problem that plagued GM several years ago has been attributed in part to a form of social loafing in which people did not take responsibility for the problem. According to an internal GM report, the switch had so many problems that the engineer who designed it labeled it "the switch from hell." Yet no action was taken amid GM's committee culture in which people talk a lot about problems but do not fix them.[41]

Two motivational explanations of social loafing have been offered. First, some people believe that because they are part of a team, they can "hide in the crowd." Second, group members typically believe that others are likely to withhold effort when working in a group. As a consequence, they withhold effort themselves to avoid being taken advantage of. Their attitude is, "Why should I work so hard when the others are goofing off?" In contrast, a good organizational citizen would not succumb to social loafing.

Groupthink

A potential disadvantage of group decision making is **groupthink**, a deterioration of mental efficiency, reality testing, and moral judgment in the interest of group cohesiveness.

groupthink A deterioration of mental efficiency, reality testing, and moral judgment in the interest of group cohesiveness.

Simply put, groupthink is an extreme form of consensus. Those in this group atmosphere value getting along more than getting things done.[42] The group thinks as a unit, believes it is impervious to outside criticism, and begins to have illusions about its own invincibility. As a consequence, the group loses its powers of critical analysis. An example of groupthink that has taken place several times in recent years is investment banks selling securities that are based on the value of high-risk loans such as subprime mortgages and car loans. Members of the group making the decision to sell the securities probably know that the risks are too high, but neglect to express dissent. (Or, maybe they simply had low ethics.)

Groupthink is most likely to take place under certain conditions. A highly cohesive group favors groupthink because members identify strongly with the group. Other contributing factors include directive leadership, high stress, group insulation, and a lack of built-in mechanisms for evaluating decisions. Having to choose between two unfavorable alternatives can lead to groupthink. An example would be an executive group deciding whether to recall a potentially unsafe product (and taking a huge loss) or leaving the product in distribution (and risking human suffering and negative publicity). Having limited time to make a major decision is another contributor to groupthink because the contributors may rush through the decision-making process.

A negative implication of groupthink is that it interferes with effective decision making. The emotional factors of wanting to achieve consensus and not wanting to be perceived as an irritant by other group members interfere with a person making an optimal decision. You might think that the alternative chosen by the group is terrible, yet you suppress your dissent to avoid being perceived as a dissident.

Groupthink can often be prevented if the group leader or member encourages all group members to express doubts and criticism of proposed solutions to the problem. It is also helpful to periodically invite qualified outsiders to meet with the group and provide suggestions. A specific technique proposed for combating groupthink is having the group leader in advance of the meeting ask group members to write down their views anonymously on the decision in question. The leader then aggregates the individual statements into one list and distributes it to the group before the meeting. This kind of pre-commitment decreases group members' tendency to conform, even though the views remain anonymous.[43]

Excessive Collaboration

Collaboration is necessary for all types of groups to function effectively, but excessive collaboration can be dysfunctional. For many workers, particularly introverts, time working alone can be critical for recharging and creative problem solving. In the zeal to foster collaboration within groups, the value of people doing outstanding work by themselves is often forgotten.[44] If you are interrupted incessantly by text messages or alerts from collaboration software, concentration can suffer.

At many companies, workers assigned to groups spend about 80 percent of their time in meetings, on the phone, and responding to meetings. All this time spent on collaboration leaves little time for all the analytical work they must perform on their own. The excessive collaboration often leads to workflow bottlenecks and employee burnout. The latter stems from the long-term stress associated with the feeling of being behind on individual work because of the time spent in interacting with others.[45] (Recognize, however, that some workers want to avoid thinking alone and prefer continuous interaction with others in person or digitally.)

Implications for Managerial Practice

1. Be aware of group norms and the extent to which they facilitate or inhibit reaching organizational objectives. Reward systems must be developed that encourage high group performance. For example, if a group performs well on a given task and management then elevates performance standards, a norm toward lowered productivity may result.

2. When forming a new work group or team, recognize that time is needed before the group will be able to achieve maximum performance. Be alert to somewhat predictable stages of group formation and development: forming, storming, norming, and performing.

3. Be aware that group effectiveness is not a random occurrence. Strive to incorporate into the group many of the characteristics associated with work-group effectiveness, such as proper job design, the right composition, and workload sharing. At the same time, if the task to be performed does not really require interdependent work, a group is not likely to make a better contribution than individuals working independently.

4. Collaboration within the group has many positive features, but an overemphasis on collaboration can drain productivity and suppress individual problem solving. As a group or team leader, you should therefore strive for a balanced approach to collaboration and individual problem solving. Many workers need time alone to perform analytical work, such as providing input to a budget or preparing a schedule.

Summary of Key Points

1. *Describe the various types of groups and teams in organizations.* Groups and teams can be classified in various ways. They are governed to some extent by group norms, and organizational citizenship behavior stems from both individual attitudes and group norms. Formal groups are deliberately formed by the organization, whereas informal groups emerge over time through worker interaction. Four types of work teams described here are cross-functional teams, virtual teams (ones that meet digitally), crews, and top management teams. Virtual teams still need guidance and direction, and they also benefit from shared leadership.

2. *Summarize the stages of group development and key roles members occupy within a work group.* Groups are thought to go through five predictable stages of development: forming, storming, norming, performing, and adjourning. Group member roles include knowledge contributor, process observer, people supporter, challenger, listener, mediator, gatekeeper (letting others into the discussion), and take-charge leader.

3. *Identify the characteristics of an effective work group.* Effective work-group characteristics are well documented. The jobs should be enriched, and the members should have a feeling of empowerment. Group members should be interdependent in terms of tasks, goals, and feedback and rewards. Interdependence facilitates collaboration. Team efficacy, the feeling of being able to accomplish the task, is important. The group should be a heterogeneous mix of members who are flexible and have a preference for group work. Group emotional intelligence—especially in terms of developing trust—is useful.

   The group should have support, including giving the group the information it needs, coaching group members, providing the right technology, and receiving recognition and other rewards. The group process should include team spirit, social support, and workload sharing, and following work processes and procedures enhances performance. Group cohesiveness contributes to performance and satisfaction and is composed of interpersonal attraction, task commitment, and group pride. Group members should be familiar with their jobs, coworkers, and the work environment, and there should be psychological safety within the group.

4. *Understand group decision-making styles, and know how to implement the nominal group technique.* Group decision-making styles follow a continuum from being consultative, through being based on consensus, to being democratic. When consensus is reached, all group members are at least willing to support the decision. The nominal group technique capitalizes on the value of collective thought, yet minimizes some of the problems that occur in interacting groups. Using the NGT, each person writes down ideas separately and later shares ideas with the group before all the ideas are ranked by group members. Collaborative software is widely used for group problem solving and decision making. Two key advantages of collaborative software are reducing travel costs and bringing together multiple perspectives and expertise.

5. *Pinpoint several potential problems with group effort, and know how to prevent them.* Group effectiveness can be hampered in several ways. Polarization, or taking extreme positions, can result. Members may engage in social loafing, or freeloading. Groupthink, an extreme form of consensus and lack of critical reasoning, may occur as members strive for solidarity. An overemphasis on collaboration can leave no time for individual problem solving and might lead to burnout.

Key Terms and Phrases

group, p. 192

team, p. 192

teamwork, p. 193

group norms, p. 193

formal group, p. 193

informal group, p. 193

cross-functional team, p. 194

virtual team, p. 194

shared team leadership, p. 195

crew, p. 197

team efficacy, p. 202

group cohesiveness, p. 204

psychological safety, p. 205

crowdsourcing, p. 205

nominal group technique (NGT), p. 206

group polarization, p. 209

social loafing, p. 209

groupthink, p. 209

Discussion Questions and Activities

1. Explain the meaning of this sentence: "All teams are groups, but not all groups are teams."
2. As you join a new work group, how will you learn the norms in order to fit in well with the group?
3. Why is membership on a cross-functional team such good experience for becoming an executive?
4. What relevance do the activities of a crew, such as a firefighting team, have for a professional group in the office?
5. What is it about the nominal group technique that might make it particularly appealing to introverts?
6. What is the difference between group decision making and groupthink?
7. Suppose a person prefers texting over talking to people. How might this affect his or her ability to be an effective member of a work group?
8. What has been your experience regarding an effective size for a work group?
9. Explain whether you have observed any evidence of collaboration overload on the job or at school.
10. Ask an experienced worker what he or she thinks is the best aspect of working with a group. How does the person's response fit in with any of the information presented in this chapter?

CASE PROBLEM: The Mountain of Hope Isolate

The Mountain of Hope is a nonprofit agency in Louisville, Kentucky, whose mission is to find suitable foster homes for children who lack a family. Many of the children are from homes in which child protective services has deemed the parent or parents unfit to raise a child. Many of the children have been subject to physical abuse. Mountain of Hope is run by a group of five people with different professional specialties: Doreen is the agency head, Matt is the chief fundraiser, Addison is responsible for child placement, Alonzo is the director of finance and accounting, and Brooklyn is the coordinator of external contacts. In her key role, Brooklyn, a social worker, coordinates the services of Mountain of Hope with other agencies, such as law enforcement agencies and psychiatric hospitals.

Although the five staff members have different responsibilities, much of their work involves group decision making, including Monday-morning reviews of foster-care cases. On yet another Monday-morning case-review session, Brooklyn did not show up. Her excuse, as many times in the past, is that she sent her input to the group by e-mail as a substitute for her physical presence. During the meeting, Doreen said to the group, "Brooklyn is such a vital part of our agency. She's a highly professional social worker, and she is so good at working with the agencies in the community that we need to accomplish our work. I wish she would get more involved with us here in the office."

Matt added, "Brooklyn has such rich experience that I know she can be dynamite when we are trying to solve problems as a group. I have told her a few times that if she would get more involved in our placement decisions, Mountain of Hope would be more effective. Brooklyn told me that we would make equally good decisions and save a lot of time if we simply posted our ideas to each other."

Addison said that she agreed with Matt: "Every decision about placing a child in a foster home is a major decision. No one of us is as smart as the collective thinking of the five of us. I mentioned this to Brooklyn once over lunch, and she told me that I was underestimating the problem-solving ability of each staff member."

Doreen said, "I appreciate the candid talk we have had about Brooklyn. The consensus thinking is that she is a vital part of our agency. The problem is that we want her to be more of an integral part of our group, particularly in making decisions. I'm going to work on the problem of getting Brooklyn more involved with us."

Case Questions

1. How appropriate is it for several other members of Mountain of Hope to discuss Brooklyn's performance?

2. What do you recommend that Doreen do to get Brooklyn more involved in working with the group?

3. Explain whether Doreen should make a group decision about getting Brooklyn more involved in group decision making at Mountain of Hope.

Endnotes

1. Original story based on facts and observations in the following sources: Jim Motavalli, "5 Inspiring Companies That Rely on Teamwork to Be Successful," www.success.com, February 16, 2016, pp. 1–3; Lindsay Friedman, "Behind a $100 Million Mattress Startup, Casper Co-Founder Shares Advice on Finding Success as an Entrepreneur," entrepreneur.com, June 8, 2016, pp. 1–6; "Join the Dream Team/Casper®," casper.com.jobs; Richard Feloni, "The CEO of Casper Shares the Biggest Lessons He's Learned from Growing His Mattress Company to $750 Million in 5 Years," Business Insider (www.businessinsider.com), pp. 1–3.

2. Donna M. Owens, "Is Management Obsolete?" *HR Magazine*, May 2012, p. 28.

3. Jon R. Katzenbach and Douglas K. Smith, "The Discipline of Teams," *Harvard Business Review*, March–April 1993, p. 113.

4. Mark G. Ehrhart and Stefanie E. Naumann, "Organizational Citizenship Behavior in Work Groups: A Group Norm Approach," *Journal of Applied Psychology*, December 2004, p. 961.

5. Ehrhart and Naumann, "Organizational Citizenship Behavior," p. 964.

6. Erik Gonzales-Mulé et al., "Can We Get Some Cooperation around Here? The Mediating Role of Group Norms on the Relationship between Team Personality and Individual Helping Behaviors," *Journal of Applied Psychology*, September 2014, pp. 988–999.

7. Glenn Parker, "Team with Strangers: Success Strategies for Cross-Functional Teams" (www.glennparker.com/Freebees/teaming-with-strangers.html). Material copyright © 1998 Glen Parker.

8. Anthony M. Townsend, Samuel M. DeMarie, and Anthony R. Hendrickson, "Virtual Teams: Technology and the Workplace of the Future," *Academy of Management Executive*, August 1998, p. 17.

9. Carol Saunders, Craig Van Slyke, and Douglas R. Vogel, "My Time or Yours? Managing Time Visions in Global Virtual Teams," *Academy of Management Executive*, February 2004, pp. 19–31.

10. *Running Virtual Meetings* (HBR 20-Minute Manager Series) (Boston, MA: Harvard Business Review Press, 2016).

11. Susan Ricker, "3 Essentials to Managing Virtual Teams," *CareerBuilder* (*Democrat and Chronicle*), June 22, 2014,

p. 2F; Yael Zofi, *A Manager's Guide to Virtual Teams* (New York: AMACOM, 2011).

12. Julia E. Hoch and Steve W. J. Kozlowski, "Leading Virtual Teams: Hierarchical Leadership, Structural Supports, and Shared Team Leadership," *Journal of Applied Psychology*, May 2014, pp. 390–403.

13. Bill Leonard, "Managing Virtual Teams," *HR Magazine*, June 2011, p. 40.

14. Shelia Simsarian Webber and Richard J. Kimoski, "Crews: A Distinct Type of Work Team," *Journal of Business and Psychology*, Spring 2004, pp. 261–279.

15. J. Steven Heinen and Eugene Jacobsen, "A Model of Task Group Development in Complex Organizations and a Strategy of Implementation," *Academy of Management Review*, October 1976, pp. 98–111; Bruce W. Tuckman and Mary Ann C. Jensen, "Stages of Small Group Development Revisited," *Group & Organization Studies*, 2(1977), pp. 419–427.

16. Glen M. Parker, *Team Players and Teamwork: The New Competitive Business Strategy* (San Francisco: Jossey-Bass, 1990); Thomas L. Quick, *Successful Team Building* (New York: AMACOM, 1992), pp. 40–52; "Lead or Lay Back? How to Play the Right Role on a Team," *Executive Strategies*, November 1999, p. 2.

17. R. Meredith Belbin, "Team Builder," in *Business: The Ultimate Resource Business* (Cambridge, MA: Perseus Books, 2002), p. 966.

18. Based on literature reviews and original material in the following sources: Scott Keller and Mary Meaney, "High-Performing Teams: A Timeless Leadership Topic," *McKinsey Quarterly*, June 2017, pp. 1–7; Stanley M. Gulley, Kara A. Incalcaterra, Aparna Joshi, and J. Matthew Beaubien, "A Meta-Analysis of Team Efficacy, Potency, and Performance: Interdependence and Level of Analysis as Moderators of Observed Relationships," *Journal of Applied Psychology*, October 2002, pp. 819–832; Bob Sutton, "Why Big Teams Suck: Seven (Plus or Minus Two) Is the Magical Number Once Again," http://bobsutton.typepad.com, March 2014, pp. 1–4; Vanessa Urch Druskat and Steven B. Wolff, "Building the Emotional Intelligence of Groups," *Harvard Business Review*, March 2001, pp. 80–90; Anita Wooley and Thomas Malone, "What Makes a Team Smarter? More Women," *Harvard Business Review*, June 2011, pp. 32–33; Claus W. Langred, "Too Much of a Good Thing? Negative Effects of High Trust and Individual Autonomy in Self-Managing Work Teams,"

Academy of Management Journal, June 2004, pp. 385–399; David Spungin, "Google's Surprising Insights on Team Effectiveness," www.linkedin.com, April 1, 2016, pp. 1–4.

19. Bradley L. Kirkman and Benson Rosen, "Powering Up Teams," *Organizational Dynamics*, Winter 2000, pp. 48–52.

20. "What They're Thinking," *The Wall Street Journal*, February 11, 2014, p. R1

21. Stanley M. Gulley, Kara A. Incalcaterra, Aparna Joshi, and J. Matthew Beaubien, "A Meta-Analysis of Team Efficacy, Potency, and Performance: Interdependence and Level of Analysis as Moderators of Observed Relationships," *Journal of Applied Psychology*, October 2002, pp. 819–832.

22. Priscilla M. Elsass and Laura M. Graves, "Demographic Diversity in Decision-Making Groups: The Experiences of Women and People of Color," *Academy of Management Review*, October 1997, p. 968.

23. Robert T. Keller, "Cross-Functional Project Groups in Research and New Product Development: Diversity, Communications, Job Stress, and Outcomes," *Academy of Management Journal*, June 2001, pp. 547–555.

24. Daan van Knippenberg, Carsten K. W. De Dreu, and Astrid C. Homan, "Work Group Diversity and Group Performance: An Integrative Model and Research Agenda," *Journal of Applied Psychology*, December 2004, p. 1012.

25. Scott Keller and Mary Meaney, "High-Performing Teams: A Timeless Leadership Topic," www.mckinsey.com, June 2017, p. 2.

26. Murray R. Barrick, Greg L. Stewart, Mitchell J. Neubert, and Michael K. Mount, "Relating Member Ability and Personality to Work-Team Processes and Team Effectiveness," *Journal of Applied Psychology*, June 1998, pp. 377–391.

27. Vanessa Urch Druskat and Steven B. Wolff, "Building the Emotional Intelligence of Groups," *Harvard Business Review*, March 2001, pp. 80–90; Claus W. Langred, "Too Much of a Good Thing? Negative Effects of High Trust and Individual Autonomy in Self-Managing Work Teams," *Academy of Management Journal*, June 2004, pp. 385–399.

28. Anita Wooley and Thomas Malone, "What Makes a Team Smarter? More Women," *Harvard Business Review*, June 2011, pp. 32–33.

29. Daniel J. Beal, Robin R. Cohen, Michael J. Burke, and Christy L. McLendon, "Cohesion and Performance in Groups: A Meta-Analytic Clarification of Construct Relations," *Journal of Applied Psychology*, December 2003, pp. 989–1004.

30. Spungin, "Google's Surprising Insights on Team Effectiveness."

31. Larry K. Michaelsen, Warren E. Watson, and Robert H. Black, "A Realistic Test of Individual versus Group Decision Making," *Journal of Applied Psychology*, October 1989, pp. 834–839; Leigh Thompson, "Improving the Creativity of Organizational Work Groups," *Academy of Management Executive*, February 2003, p. 99.

32. Hollis Thomases, "How to Crowdsource Anything," *Inc* (www.inc.com), pp. 1–2.

33. Allan Afuah and Christopher L. Tucci, "Crowdsourcing as a Solution to Distant Search," *Academy of Management Review*, July 2012, pp. 355–375.

34. Cass R. Sunstein and Reid Hastie, "Making Dumb Groups Smarter," *Harvard Business Review*, December 2014, pp. 90–98.

35. William B. Eddy, *The Manager and the Working Group* (New York: Praeger, 1985), pp. 150–151.

36. Adapted from "Gaining Consensus among Stakeholders through the Nominal Group Technique," *Evaluation Briefs*, No. 17, 2006. Department of Health and Human Services, Centers for Disease Control and Prevention.

37. The evidence is reviewed in Thompson, "Improving the Creativity of Organizational Work Groups," p. 104.

38. "Making Internal Collaboration Work: An Interview with Don Tapscott," *McKinsey Quarterly*, January 2013, p. 2.

39. "Five Cloud Based Collaboration Use Cases," Ingram Micro Advisor, www.ingrammicroadvisor.com/unified-communications-and-collaboration/five-cloud-based-collaboration-use-cases, 2018, p. 2.

40. Our discussion is based on Gregory Moorhead and Ricky W. Griffin, *Organizational Behavior: Managing People and Organizations*, 4th ed. (Boston: Houghton Mifflin, 1995), pp. 278–279.

41. James R. Healey and Fred Meier, "GM: Ignorance Left 'Switch from Hell' Unfixed," *USA Today Money*, June 6, 2014, p. 5B.

42. Irving L. Janis, *Victims of Groupthink: A Study of Foreign Policy Decisions and Fiascoes* (Boston: Houghton Mifflin, 1972), pp. 39–40; Glenn Whyte, "Groupthink Reconsidered," *Academy of Management Review*, January 1989, pp. 40–56.

43. Research reported in "Avoid 'Groupthink,'" *Manager's Edge*, March 2003, p. 2.

44. Jennifer Kahnweiller, "Have We Gone Too Far in Promoting Collaboration?" *HR Magazine*, March 2018, pp. 26–27.

45. Rob Cross, Reb Rebele, and Adam Grant, "Collaborative Overload," *Harvard Business Review*, January–February 2016, pp. 74–79.

Teams and Teamwork

Chapter Outline

Mauricio Graiki/Shutterstock.com

Learning Objectives

After reading and studying this chapter and doing the exercises, you should be able to:

1. Explain the nature of a self-managed work team and characteristics associated with team-member success.

2. Explain several mechanisms by which continuous learning takes place in teams.

3. Explain how to foster teamwork.

4. Develop insight into managing on-site teams as well as virtual teams.

Caterpillar Inc. is the world's leading manufacturer of construction and mining equipment, diesel and natural gas engines, industrial gas turbines, and diesel-electric locomotives. Although Caterpillar is an industrial company, millions of consumers are familiar with "Cat." Many consumers who are not Caterpillar employees wear T-shirts with the Caterpillar trademark emblem. Caterpillar leadership and management emphasize that employees help each other succeed. As a team, workers share their unique talents to help those with whom they work, live, and serve.

Caterpillar management explains that the diverse thinking and decision making of its workforce strengthens the team, both domestically and globally. The company respects and values people with different opinions, experiences, and educational and cultural backgrounds. Management points out that by working together, the company can produce better results than any of the individual workers could achieve acting alone.

A specific example of the use of teams at Caterpillar is the implementation of quality-improvement teams following Six Sigma methodology. Among the many program participants are production technicians and group presidents. There are approximately 2,000 Black Belts (Six Sigma advanced specialists) at Caterpillar. A specific example of what Caterpillar does with Six Sigma is a project that improved the threaded joint design in the assembly process. The team project focused on continuous improvement in Caterpillar's quality culture.[1]

The story about the teams at Caterpillar illustrates that teams can play a central role in creating an effective organization. In this chapter, we extend the discussion of workplace groups by focusing on teams. Teams, as a special type of group, are part of the collaborative organization. Workers within teams collaborate with each other, and teams also collaborate with other groups and teams throughout the organization. In a collaborative workplace, workers pay attention to superordinate goals, in which the needs of customers, investors, and other stakeholders (parties at interest) are as important as the self-interest of the team and its members.[2]

The importance of teams in organizations is highlighted by the fact that a growing number of companies hire teams of workers instead of one individual. Also, several high-tech companies engage in "acqui-hiring" through buying startups with the purpose of hiring their talented teams. Furthermore, within a short period of time, newly appointed CEOs often recruit several colleagues from the same company they worked for previously because they know that the teamwork will be effective.[3]

Our study of teams encompasses self-managing work teams, the selection of members for teams, how teams emphasize continuous learning, how teamwork is faster, and ideas about managing on-site (physical) teams and virtual teams. The study of teams increases in importance when you recognize that the majority of knowledge workers in a wide range of occupations and industries are members of more than one project team at a time. In some companies, workers might be members of five, ten, or twelve teams at a time, thereby not working full time on any one team. Many teams therefore have overlapping membership.[4]

LEARNING OBJECTIVE 1
Explain the nature of a self-managed work team and characteristics associated with team-member success.

self-managed work team A formally recognized group of employees responsible for an entire work process or segment that delivers a product or service to an internal or external customer.

Self-Managed Work Teams

A dominant trend in job design is to organize workers into teams with considerable authority to direct and supervise themselves. A majority of U.S. corporations incorporate team structures, using some form of self-management, in their organizations. Team structures are also prevalent in European and Asian industry, particularly in manufacturing. A **self-managed work team** is a formally recognized group of employees responsible for an entire work process or segment that delivers a product or service to an internal or external customer.[5]

Self-managed (or self-managing) work groups originated as an outgrowth of job enrichment. Working in teams broadens the responsibility of team members. Implementing self-managed work teams requires that managers focus on empowering and motivating, rather than on controlling. Self-managing teams are considered ideal for collaboration.[6] A manager who uses a command-and-control style would not be comfortable with self-managed teams.

Small as well as large companies make use of this form of job design. The key purposes for establishing self-managed teams are to increase productivity, enhance quality, reduce cycle time (the amount of time required to complete a transaction), and respond more rapidly to a changing workplace. Next we describe the method of operation of these teams and take a brief look at the results.

Self-managed work teams solve many problems on their own.

Method of Operation

Members of a self-managed work team typically work together on an ongoing, day-by-day basis, thus differentiating a work team from a task force or committee. The work team is often given total responsibility or "ownership" of a product or service. A work team might be assigned the responsibility for preparing an online merchandise catalog. At other times, the team is given responsibility for a major chunk of a job, such as building a jet engine or an algorithm for assessing credit risk. The self-managed work team is often taught to think in terms of customer requirements. The team members might ask, "How easy would it be for a left-handed person to use this can opener?"

To promote the sense of ownership, workers are taught to become generalists rather than specialists. Each team member learns a broad range of skills and switches job assignments periodically. Members of the self-directed work team also receive training in team skills. Cross-training in different organizational functions is also important to help members develop an overall perspective of how the firm operates. As compiled by a team of experts,[7] the distinguishing characteristics of a self-directed work team are presented in Figure 10-1. Studying these characteristics will provide insight into work teams. As a result of having so much responsibility for a product or service, team members usually develop pride in their work and team. At best, the team members feel as if they are operating a small business, with the profits (or losses) directly attributable to their efforts. An entry-level worker, such as a data-entry specialist in a market research firm, is less likely to have such feelings.

Although self-managing work teams may have an internal team leader or work without one member being appointed as a leader, an external leader, such as a middle manager,

FIGURE 10-1 Characteristics of a Self-Managed Work Team

1. Team members are empowered to share many management and leadership functions, such as making job assignments and giving pep talks.
2. Members plan, control, and improve their own work processes.
3. Members set their own goals and inspect their own work.
4. Members create their own schedules and review their group performance.
5. Members often prepare their own budgets and coordinate their work with other departments.
6. Members typically order materials, keep inventories, and deal with suppliers.
7. Members are sometimes responsible for obtaining any new training they might need. (The organization, however, usually mandates the startup training.)
8. Members are authorized to hire their own replacements or assume responsibility for disciplining their own members.
9. Members assume responsibility for the quality of their products and services, whether provided to internal or external customers.

still makes a contribution. One study showed that self-managing work teams were more effective when the external leader coached the team and prepared the team for challenges. One such challenge would be a heavy workload in the near future. To prepare the team, the leader could analyze what resources would be needed to cope with the workload, and provide these resources, such as hiring a new team member.[8]

Their method of operation points to the importance of having certain personal characteristics to be an effective member of a self-managing work team. The general idea is that to be a successful team member you need the right personality and cognitive characteristics. For example, an effective team member in most settings would need to be extraverted, conscientious, and mentally quick enough to adapt to changing circumstances. A key characteristic of a self-managing team member is having a high level of interpersonal skill because of all the collaboration required.[9]

A study of self-managed teams illustrates how peers exerting control over each other enhance team and individual performance. Peer control in this study refers to peer assessments being linked to incentives. Data were collected from 587 factory production workers organized into 45 self-managed teams at three manufacturing plants in the midwestern United States. The plants were at three different companies and produced a variety of goods, including electronic equipment, small appliances, and rubber.

A statement used to measure peer control over incentives was "My chances for a pay raise depend on recommendations given by my team." It was found that when team members perceive that the distribution of financial rewards is dependent on input from teammates, they tend to perform better individually and collectively. The positive effect of peer control over rewards was more noticeable when team cohesion was low.[10] It could be that, in a highly cohesive team, there is more equality in the distribution of rewards.

Teamwork on the Fly as a Form of Self-Managing Team

Another application of self-managing teams is to use them as temporary project groups to tackle unexpected problems and to identify emerging opportunities. The process is referred to as *teamwork on the fly* because the teams are gathered so quickly and do not last for a long time. Experts are gathered from different divisions and disciplines to work on a major challenge. The typical application of these temporary self-managing teams is to accomplish something that hasn't been done before, and might not be repeated. A traditional self-managed team might not work well. Also, teamwork on the fly requires the gathering of high-level experts from various disciplines.

The best-known example of teamwork on the fly was the building of the Water Cube for the 2008 Beijing Olympics. The Water Cube was a 340,000-square-foot box framed in steel, covered in semi-transparent blue bubbles that were energy efficient. The structure was the joint effort of representatives from several design and engineering companies, and dozens of contractors and consultants.[11]

A key behavioral aspect of teamwork on the fly is for the person assembling the team to emphasize the purpose of the team—also important for almost all teams and groups. Purpose deals heavily with shared values that help answer why the project exists. For the Beijing Olympics, the purpose may have been to create unusual excitement about and recognition for their particular Olympics.

Self-Managed Work Team Effectiveness

Self-managed work teams demonstrate a reasonably good record of improving productivity, quality, and customer service. Corporate executives and

Self-managing teams have a high rate of success.

Dean Drobot/Shutterstock.com

Whole Foods Market Emphasizes Self-Managed Teams

Whole Foods Markets Inc. is the largest organic and natural foods grocer in the United States, although most grocery chains now have substantial organic food sections. The grocery sections of Walmart and Target also compete directly with Whole Foods. Shortly after its opening in 1980, CEO John Mackey developed an organizational structure built on interlocking teams. Employees are referred to as "team members," and teams are the building block of the organization.

Each Whole Foods store is organized around 8 to 10 teams for traditional departments such as produce, meats, and checkout. The size of teams ranges from 6 to 100, but the larger teams are divided into sub-teams. Each team is granted considerable autonomy in such areas as ordering food and merchandise, pricing, and running promotions. Team leaders are also members of the store leadership team, and the store team leaders are members of the regional leadership team. The regional presidents also constitute a team.

The self-directed teams at Whole Foods meet regularly to discuss and solve problems and show appreciation for each other's contributions. Every team plays a role in company improvement and innovation. Store leaders screen candidates and recommend them for a position on a specific team, but only the teams have the authority to approve candidates for a full-time position.

Competition across teams is encouraged, with teams competing against different teams in their own store and against similar teams in different stores and regions. The competition metrics include sales growth and productivity.

Each team is committed to the company's mission, as stated in these terms: "Whole Foods Market is passionate about helping people to eat well, improve the quality of their lives, and increase their lifespan."

In August 2017, Amazon purchased Whole Foods to strengthen its presence in the grocery business, including home deliveries. Immediately, Amazon Echo and Dot devices were being sold in Whole Food stores. Prices on many food products were marked down substantially in keeping with the Amazon strategy of low prices for consumers. For example, organic, responsibly farmed salmon was marked down 33 percent.

QUESTIONS

1. If you have ever shopped at or visited a Whole Foods store, have you noticed whether the self-managed team structure has any impact on customer service?

2. Should management and leadership at Whole Foods be concerned that their new owner, Amazon, sells many food products that are not natural or organic? Why or why not?

Source: Original story based on facts and observations in the following sources: David Burkus, "Why Whole Foods Builds Its Entire Business on Teams," *Forbes* (www.forbes.com), June 8, 2016, pp. 1–2; Arturo Cuenllas, "Whole Foods Market Management Case Study: A Benchmark Model for Hospitality," Conscious Hospitality (www.Conscious-Hospitality.com), March 2014, pp. 2–4; Lauren Thomas, "Amazon Officially Owns Whole Foods; Here Are the Products That Are Getting Marked Down," CNBC, (www.cnbc.com), August 28, 2017, pp. 1–2.

small-business owners have found that self-managed work teams are a highly effective form of work-group design. About 50 percent of the time, they result in at least some productivity gains, and effective teams can produce remarkable results. When self-management works, productivity gains of 10 to 20 percent are typical.[12]

The Organizational Behavior in Action box illustrates how a well-known, upscale grocery chain makes effective use of self-managed teams.

A major contributor to work-team effectiveness is the suitability of its members to a team operation. Self-Assessment 10-1 gives you a chance to think about your mental readiness to work on a team.

Despite their potential contribution, self-managed work teams create challenges for managers. High-caliber employees are required for the team because they must be able to solve problems on their own and rely less on a supervisor. Many of the personal qualities required for team effectiveness are outlined in Figure 10-1. Effective contributors to a self-managed team must be multiskilled, and not all employees are willing or able to develop new skills. Another challenge for the manager, particularly the team leader, is being left with relatively little to do because the team is self-managing. In some firms, however, a middle-level manager might have overall responsibility for several teams. The team leaders become the direct reports, and the manager acts as a facilitator.

Mental Readiness for Assignment to a Work Team

Respond to each statement using the following scale: Strongly Disagree (SD); Disagree (D); Neutral (N); Agree (A); Strongly Agree (SA).

	Amount of Agreement
1. Employees should make the majority of decisions related to their work.	SD D N A SA
2. It is possible for corporate employees to take as much pride in their work as if it were their own business.	SD D N A SA
3. Workers who lack advanced training and education are capable of making useful work improvements.	SD D N A SA
4. Groups can work effectively without a clear-cut center of authority.	SD D N A SA
5. It is worth sacrificing some specialization of labor to give workers a chance to develop multiple skills.	SD D N A SA
6. Competent workers do not require too much supervision.	SD D N A SA
7. Having authority over people is not as important as being part of a smoothly working team.	SD D N A SA
8. Given the opportunity, many workers could manage themselves without much supervision.	SD D N A SA
9. Cordial relationships are important even in a factory setting.	SD D N A SA
10. The more power workers are given, the more likely they are to behave responsibly.	SD D N A SA

Scoring and Interpretation: Score the answers 1 through 5, with SD being 1 and SA being 5. Add the numerical value you assigned to each statement and total your score. The closer your score is to 50, the higher is your degree of mental readiness to lead or participate on a work team. If your score is 30 or less, attempt to develop a more optimistic view of the capabilities and attitudes of workers. Start by looking for evidence of good accomplishments by skilled and semiskilled workers.

Continuous Learning by Teams

LEARNING OBJECTIVE 2
Explain several mechanisms by which continuous learning takes place in teams.

As teams of various types have evolved in recent years, increasing emphasis has been placed on continuous learning by members and by the team itself as an entity. The general belief is that continuous learning leads to individual development and higher team performance. A meta-analysis of 129 studies of training health-care teams produced encouraging results. The study indicated that team training can make the organization, such as a hospital, more effective and also lead to better patient care.[13]

Here we look at four important factors related to continuous learning by teams: team learning orientation, unusual problems and crises leading to rapid learning, collective problem solving, and team coaching, as depicted in Figure 10-2.

Team Learning Orientation

Research has suggested that an appropriate emphasis on team learning will enhance performance, but too much emphasis on learning might lower performance. Data for the study

KEY MECHANISMS

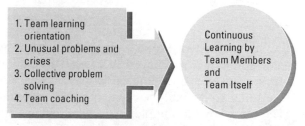

FIGURE 10-2 Key Mechanisms for Continuous Learning by Teams

Certain external factors as well as processes can foster continuous learning by teams.

were collected from the management team members of business units in a *Fortune* 100 consumer products company. Each business unit is responsible for marketing, producing, selling, and distributing the company's product line in the business unit's geographic market area. Performance was measured in terms of profitability relative to plan (or goals), and profitability relative to the number of units sold. The strength of team-learning orientation was measured by a questionnaire. Team members were asked to assess, on a 7-point scale, the extent to which their team: (a) looks for opportunities to develop new skills and knowledge, (b) likes challenging and difficult assignments, (c) is willing to take risks on new ideas in order to find out what works, (d) likes to work on things that require a lot of skill and ability, and (e) sees learning and developing skills as very important.

Performance data were collected 1 year after the measurement of team learning to provide a more precise understanding of how learning orientation is related to performance. For control purposes, factors such as team size, experience, and the functional (or professional discipline) composition of the teams were taken into account when investigating the relationship between team-learning orientation and performance. Controls were important for the experiment because a factor such as team experience might influence how much attention is paid to learning, with more-experienced teams emphasizing learning.

A major conclusion was that a team-learning orientation did help groups improve business unit performance up to a point, particularly when the team had been performing well. Another conclusion reached was that, if the organizational climate encourages learning, the team is more likely to engage in continuous learning.[14]

Unusual Problems and Crises Facing the Team

A workplace team can learn in a hurry when faced with an unusual problem or a crisis. D. Christopher Kayes describes the extreme example of September 11, 2001, when two pilots, five flight attendants, and 33 passengers responded to armed hijackers in midflight. In slightly over 30 minutes, a collection of passengers and crew formed a team, quickly analyzed the situation, asked around for additional information, wrote down a plan, and

Effective teams engage in continuous learning.

then took decisive action. The temporary team did not prevent the hijacking or a crash, but the plane was diverted from attacking a highly populated area by the team physically combating the hijackers.[15]

The relevance of fighting the hijackers to continuous team learning is that a team can learn from dealing with the unexpected. Faced with a crisis, a team will skip the usual stages of group development described in Chapter 9. Instead, the team will learn immediately how to deal with the unexpected, including a crisis. Team members learn from each other and perform at levels that go beyond the capacity of the individual learning alone. Much of the learning is prompted by the complexity of the problem. A recurring example is that of an office totally damaged by a fire, explosion, hurricane, or flood. The team assigned to the project gets the company, or unit, back up and running faster than anybody believed possible. Among the complex tasks is the retrieval of customer or patient information when both paper and computer files have been destroyed. (One team pleaded with customers to provide any records of transactions with the firm they might have.)

According to Kayes, much of team learning under unusual conditions stems from conversations among team members about specific and pressing problems. Conversation becomes the mechanism to shift individual knowledge into team learning. In the example of destroyed files, one team member said, "My aunt had a hardware store that catered to contractors. Her files were destroyed by a fire. She asked her customers to search their files to tell her what they owed. However crude it was, the system worked, and we can learn from her story."

Team learning from conversation has four elements. First is the generation phase—the team talks through the problem. Second is the gathering phase, consisting of asking around about ways of dealing with the problem. Third is the organizing phase—writing it down. Fourth is the acting phase—trying it out.[16] For example, a manufacturing firm was faced with a critical shortage of production technicians. Orders were being turned down because of being short-staffed. The HR director developed a plan to advertise directly to retail workers who had been laid off and offer them company-paid training in manufacturing techniques. The recruiting and training worked well enough to ease the shortage of production technicians.

Collective Problem Solving

One of the mechanisms for team learning is collective problem solving. Members freely share information and opinions with one another to facilitate problem solving.[17] The team learning can take place in several ways. The basic approach is to use group problem solving throughout the firm. As members solve problems together, they continue to learn. A clothing firm in the United States struggled with the challenge of exporting goods to China, as Chinese-made clothing was dominating the market. A team assigned to the project learned to find a few high-end niches in the market not now being served by Chinese manufacturers in China. The solution was profitable, leading to new team learning about exports and imports.

Another collective-problem-solving approach to team learning is to bring people together at a retreat, where they work in teams to reflect on ways of improving the organization. At one manufacturing company, a team-based revelation was that too many employee suggestions were too superficial, resulting in minor modifications of procedures or products. Supervisors were instructed to encourage workers to make suggestions that made dramatic improvements in how a product was manufactured, such as skipping a step or even questioning whether a part was needed at all. The continuous learning here is that the team learned how to bring about organizational improvement. In addition,

Collective problem solving is part of working on a team.

many individual employees learned to make suggestions of greater substance.

Team Coaching

A direct way for a team to engage in continuous learning is to be coached as a team, in contrast to individual members being coached. As it relates to assisting teams, **coaching** is a direct interaction with the team with the intention of improving team processes to enhance performance. Both managers and professional coaches engage in coaching. A manager might coach a product-development team toward becoming more adventuresome and risk prone by asking the question, "Have you folks ever thought of going beyond the state of the art? What blocks you from thinking of a revolutionary product?" The team as a whole might then reflect on the level of its creativity. Individual coaching on this issue would take the form of asking team members one at a time the same questions.

Effective teams share information among members.

Here, we briefly describe three aspects of team coaching: negative versus positive coaching, coaching functions, and leadership team coaching by an outside professional.

coaching A direct interaction with the team with the intention of improving team processes to enhance performance.

Negative versus Positive Coaching

The manager/coach can emphasize the positive or the negative. Positive coaching involves being supportive and reinforcing, such as pointing out where the product-development team has approached being revolutionary. In the process, the coach encourages self-management. Negative coaching emphasizes active intervention in the team instead of encouraging self-management by the team. An intervention in the product-development situation would be for the manager/coach to join the team for a few product-development brainstorming sessions so he or she could contribute a couple of revolutionary ideas.

Frederick P. Morgeson conducted a study in three organizations and found that supportive coaching was perceived as effective by team members. However, negative coaching in the form of the manager intervening was associated with effectiveness when the team was facing disruptive events.[18] (An axiom of leadership is that being direct with the group is important during an urgent problem.)

Coaching Functions

Another perspective on team coaching is that it consists of three primary functions, and each function works best at a particular point in the life cycle of the team.[19] *Motivational coaching* focuses on effort, and its functions are to minimize social loafing and to build shared commitment to the group and its tasks. Coaching aimed at motivation tends to be the most helpful when provided at the beginning of a performance period.

Motivational coaching can also take the form of applying pressure on the team.[20] Assume that the team leader has been told by upper management to get her team to submit constructive suggestions for cost reduction across the company. One month after the team has agreed to take on the assignment, no useful suggestions have been submitted. To increase pressure, the team leader might say, "Thirty days and no decent cost-reduction suggestions. I know that we can do better than this."

Consultative coaching focuses on performance strategy, and its functions are to point the way toward avoiding the wrong approach to the task, and to encourage proceeding with the task in ways that are aligned with task requirements. For example, a market research team might be encouraged to avoid using face-to-face focus groups to study whether a new method of storing image (photos and drawings) memories through an Internet service would have much of a market. Instead, the group might be coached to use an Internet survey technique because the respondents are the people who would most likely use the memory-storage service. Consultative coaching is most helpful when provided at the midpoint of a performance period, most likely because the team becomes aware of what type of task assistance it needs.

Educational coaching addresses knowledge and skills, and its main function is to encourage the best use of team-member talents, and to foster the development of members' knowledge and skills. A problem that sometimes arises in a team is that the ideas of an outspoken member are given more weight than his or her talent merits. Educational coaching is most helpful when provided after performance activities have been completed, so the team can perform even better in the future.

The time at which these coaching interventions are made influences their effectiveness, yet two other conditions are also influential. The first of these conditions is the extent to which key performance processes are constrained by external forces. With fewer constraints, coaching will have a more positive effect. For example, a cockpit-assembly team at an aircraft company can enhance its effectiveness in response to coaching only if there is an airplane awaiting construction.

The second of these conditions is the degree to which the group is a well-designed performing unit, following the characteristics of an effective work group described in Chapter 9. For example, if the mix of the team includes members who have considerable task-relevant knowledge and are conscientious, coaching will be more effective. As is generally recognized, it is much easier to coach talented people or groups!

Leadership Team Coaching by an Outside Professional

The team of organizational leaders is sometimes coached as an entity by an outside coach, often referred to as an *executive coach*. The subjects for coaching might include interpersonal or task issues. Interpersonal issues could include the executives having too much conflict among themselves, or having poor relationships with company insiders and outsiders. Task issues could include making hasty decisions, stonewalling against criticism, procrastinating, and behaving unethically. The role of the coach would not be to tell the leadership what to do, but to help leaders examine their own behavior and understand where improvement is needed. Often the focus is on individual members of the team, but the coaching is done with other team members present.

According to Manfred F. R. Ket de Vries, executive team coaching has become more in demand because managers realize that managing interpersonal relationships differentiates mediocre from high-performing organizations. The reason is that good interpersonal relationships help capitalize on talent and human capital. Many executives also realize that without continuous learning about dealing with people and making decisions, they will be left behind in an ever-changing global environment.[21]

The coaching session with the top management team might take different forms, but a basic approach would be to frame the activity as team building (improvement in working as a team). The session might include team members completing questionnaires about their own leadership effectiveness and that of the other team members. Some of the feedback is personal, and some is shared with other members of the group. For sharing, each member of the team receives feedback on how others perceived him or her, such as "Janet makes some creative decisions, but she sometimes makes bad decisions because she doesn't listen to other members of the team." The written feedback is supposed to be a starting point for discussions about how the team members work with each other, and how interpersonal relationships and decision making might be improved. During a coaching session, the coach might ask the participants to share the feedback they received.

In one session, the coach read feedback to the group about John, one of the executives present. The coach talked about John's need for details, his problems in delegation because of being a micromanager, his inclination to take over for less-capable subordinates, his occasional moodiness, and his tendency to work too hard and to become overstressed. Being confronted with such feedback can sometimes lead to change, but may require a few individual coaching sessions to supplement the team coaching. During the session, the coach brought John's strengths to the attention of the other team members, to help boost the executive's confidence.

Team members were also asked what advice they could give John to help him become even more effective. One member said John should stop protecting the incompetents in his department, and avoid doing their work in addition to his own. Another participant complained how difficult it was to approach John and the people who report to him.

The expectation of team coaching is that interactions like those just described will lead to changes in behavior and style that will enable the team to be more productive. As you have probably observed in working in teams, it is often people problems that prevent the group from excelling. The same is true of the executive suite.

Building Teamwork

Building teamwork is important for the obvious reason that so many organizations depend on teamwork. What is less obvious is the variety of work that requires effective teamwork. For example, Chris Theisen, a veterinary assistant, explains that a lot of teamwork is required in his position; he works with doctors, technicians, customer service representatives, and kennel staff daily.[22]

LEARNING OBJECTIVE 3
Explain how to foster teamwork.

The team player roles described in Chapter 9 point to actions the individual can take to become a team player. Self-Assessment 10-2 gives you the opportunity to gauge your current mental readiness to be a contributing team member. Here we highlight managerial actions and organizational practices that facilitate teamwork.[23] Good teamwork enhances but does not guarantee, a successful team. For example, a movie studio team might work smoothly and cooperatively together on a movie that is a box-office flop.

An all-encompassing way of developing teamwork is to encourage team members to develop **prosocial motivation**, the desire to expend effort to help others. Prosocial motivation enhances teamwork because it propels individuals to look for ways to cooperate with others, such as providing input into solving a difficult problem without looking for credit or recognition.

Prosocial motivation The desire to expend effort to help others.

A robust strategy for building teamwork is to *share leadership among team members*, rather than the traditional practice of one person being in charge of leading his or her subordinates. In some teams, for example, the position of team leader is rotated among team members for a 1-year term. Leadership sharing can help develop the abilities of other team members, resulting in higher performance of the team as a whole.

The manager can begin by helping team members believe that they have an *urgent constructive purpose*. A demanding performance challenge helps create and sustain the team. Early in the history of the group, the manager should establish trust by *empowering the group to determine how to meet the objectives*. Teamwork is fostered when the team leader establishes the direction, then steps aside to allow the group to work out the details of getting the job done.

A major strategy for teamwork is to promote the attitude that *working together effectively is the established norm*. Developing such a culture of teamwork will be difficult when a strong culture of individualism exists within the firm. Along these lines, it is helpful to divide up the workload evenly when possible. In this way, team members do not perceive some members as being overworked while a few others are social loafers.

The team leader can communicate the norm of teamwork by *making frequent use of words and phrases that support teamwork*. Emphasizing the words *team members* or *teammates* and de-emphasizing the words *subordinates* and *employees* helps communicate the teamwork norm.

A comprehensive tactic for building teamwork is to create a code of conduct for teamwork that functions much like a norm of teamwork, except that the code is

Positive attitudes contribute to effective teamwork.

Adisorn Saovadee/Shutterstock.com

Team Player Attitudes

Describe how well you agree with each of the following statements, using this scale: Disagree Strongly (DS); Disagree (D); Neutral (N); Agree (A); Agree Strongly (AS).

	DS	D	N	A	AS
1. I am at my best working alone.	5	4	3	2	1
2. I have belonged to clubs and teams ever since I was a child.	1	2	3	4	5
3. It takes far too long to get work accomplished with a group.	5	4	3	2	1
4. I like the friendship of working in a group.	1	2	3	4	5
5. I would prefer to run a one-person business than to be a member of a large firm.	5	4	3	2	1
6. It's difficult to trust others in a group on key assignments.	5	4	3	2	1
7. Encouraging others comes naturally to me.	1	2	3	4	5
8. I like the give and take of ideas that is possible in a group.	1	2	3	4	5
9. It is fun for me to share responsibility with other group members.	1	2	3	4	5
10. Much more can be accomplished by a team than by the same number of people working alone.	1	2	3	4	5
	Total Score _____				

Scoring and interpretation: Add the numbers you have circled to obtain your total score.

41–50 You have strong positive attitudes toward being a team member and working cooperatively with other members.

30–40 You have moderately favorable attitudes toward being a team member and working cooperatively with other members.

10–29 You much prefer working by yourself than being a team member. To work effectively in a company that emphasizes teamwork, you may need to develop more positive attitudes about working jointly with others.

written. The team creates a code that achieves consensus, and all members sign a copy of the code. To build the code, the manager or team leader identifies recurring issues that inhibit team performance and sets rules to govern that behavior. A few examples follow:

- Never abandon a teammate.
- Be on time.
- Keep all agreements. When necessary, clarify and commit to new agreements.
- Deal directly. If you have a problem with someone, go directly to that person with it or let it go.
- Be responsible. No laying blame on others, no justifications.
- Never humiliate anyone. No yelling or name-calling.
- Be loyal.

To enforce the code, thereby enhancing teamwork, if someone breaks the code, the manager or team leader says something such as, "This is what the code says and we all agreed to follow it."[24] A code of conduct also helps improve teamwork because the code facilitates *mutual trust among team members*. For example, if team members believe that their teammates will be responsible, deal directly with problems, and be loyal, mutual trust is enhanced.

Using the *consensus decision-making style* is another way to reinforce teamwork. By sharing in decision making, the leader communicates a sense of trust. As members collaborate in decision making, they are likely to develop more trust in each other's judgment. A sophisticated approach to enhancing teamwork is to *feed team members valid facts and information that motivate them to work together*. New information prompts the team to redefine and enrich its understanding of the challenge it is facing, thereby allowing team members to focus on a common purpose. A subtle yet potent method of building teamwork is for the team to *use language that fosters cohesion and commitment*. In-group jargon bonds a team and sets the group apart from others. An example is a team of information technology specialists saying "Send me a deck" to mean "Send me a PowerPoint presentation."

To foster teamwork, the manager should avoid **micromanagement**, or supervising group members too closely and second-guessing their decisions. Micromanagement can hamper a spirit of teamwork because team members do not feel in control of their own work. Yet, the team leader should also avoid a style of management so laid back that team members receive too little feedback and guidance (often referred to as *macromanagement*). A practical initiative that gets at the heart of teamwork is for team members to *learn what other members of the team are working on*. In this way, team members can fill in for each other, thereby fostering a spirit of teamwork.

Creating physical structures suited for teams, such as tables that can be rolled readily into a circle, is an effective organizational intervention to support teamwork. Group cohesiveness, and therefore teamwork, is enhanced when teammates are located close together and can interact frequently and easily. Frequent interaction often leads to camaraderie and a feeling of belonging. A useful method for getting people to exchange ideas is to establish a shared physical facility, such as a conference room, research library, or break lounge. Recognize, however, that workers still need private space so they can concentrate on work without interruption.

A key strategy for encouraging teamwork is to *reward the team as well as individuals*. The most convincing team incentive is to calculate compensation partially on the basis of team results. Team-based pay is useful for motivating employees to work more cooperatively, as long as the corporate culture emphasizes collaboration rather than individualism. A related approach to building teamwork is to avoid disincentives to teamwork, such as creating too wide a spread in compensation between the highest and lowest performers.[25] One problem is that the team members who feel that they are regarded as low performers might hesitate to cooperate with the highest performers to help prevent the latter from getting too much of the incentive pie.

Another option available to organizations for enhancing teamwork is to *send members to outdoor (or off-site) training*, a form of experiential learning. Participants acquire leadership and teamwork skills by confronting physical challenges and exceeding their self-imposed limitations. Rope activities are typical of outdoor training. Participants attached to a secure pulley with ropes will climb up a ladder and jump off to another spot. Walking over white-hot coals to promote bonding is another team-building activity. (Yes, some participants have been hospitalized.) All of these challenges are faced in teams rather than individually, which fosters the development of teamwork. Outdoor training is likely to have the most favorable outcomes when the trainer helps the team members comprehend the link between such training and on-the-job behavior.

The leader who looks to team-building exercises as a way of building teamwork should be aware that some of these exercises can waste time, cause physical injury,

micromanagement
Supervising group members too closely and second-guessing their decisions.

Housing for the Homeless

Organize the class into teams of about six people. Each team takes on the assignment of formulating plans for building temporary shelters for the homeless. The task will take about 1 hour and can be done inside or outside of class. The dwellings you plan to build, for example, might be two-room cottages with electricity and indoor plumbing.

During the time allotted to the task, formulate plans for going ahead with Housing for the Homeless. Consider dividing up work by assigning certain roles to each team member. Sketch out tentative answers to the following questions:

1. How will you obtain funding for your venture?
2. Which homeless people will you help?
3. Where will your shelters be located?
4. Who will do the actual construction?

After your plan is completed, evaluate the quality of the teamwork that took place within the group. Specify which teamwork skills were evident and which ones did not surface. Search the chapter for techniques you might use to improve teamwork. Here is a sampling of the many different skills that might be relevant in this exercise:

- Speaks effectively
- Listens to others
- Innovates solutions to problems
- Thinks outside the box
- Displays a high level of cooperation and collaboration
- Provides knowledge of the task
- Sees the big picture
- Focuses on deadlines

and/or create embarrassment. Kate Mercer, co-founder of the Leaders Lab, a British consultancy, wrote that for some people, participating in team-building exercises is more like forced fun, stirring up "ghastly visions of kneeling on the floor playing bongo drums in a conference room or building Lego constructions against the clock in competition with other departments."[26]

Some companies use off-site style team-building exercises on their own, without going to the time and expense of consultant-directed team building. Many companies organize team-building activities around rehabilitating the home of a lower-income person or building a playground in a poor area of the city. A creative approach to do-it-yourself team building is having a team take a tour bus instead of an airplane to meetings. Jarrod Moses, the founder and chief executive of the United Entertainment Group, a marketing agency, reports that his company takes a bus at least 25 times a year to different meetings throughout the country. He says, "There's an amazing culture that develops on the bus. You can learn so much about one another, and you develop this candor and trust that you don't get in the office."[27]

As the team develops, it is important for the team leader to pay attention to subgroups that might have formed.[28] Members of the subgroups might soon feel more loyal to each other rather than to the total team. The team leader might therefore continue to emphasize that a few of the members might be working more closely with each other but that "We are all part of the larger team."

The Skill-Development Exercise will give you additional experience in developing team skills. (We assume that most readers have had many opportunities to build team skills, in or outside of school.)

Managing On-Site Teams and Virtual Teams

LEARNING OBJECTIVE 4
Develop insight into managing on-site teams as well as virtual teams.

Many other topics in this textbook deal with managing people, including motivation, communication, leadership, encouraging creativity, and resolving conflict. Building teamwork, as just described, is also an essential part of team management. Managing teams involves a few considerations additional to those of managing people in general. Here we describe a few special considerations about managing both on-site (or physical) teams and virtual teams.

On-Site Teams

The long-term research of J. R. Hackman suggests there are five conditions that foster a team's effectiveness.[29] An *effective* team according to Hackman meets or exceeds the expectations of the user of its output (the client). Also, the group works well interdependently, and the group experience contributes to the learning and personal well-being of its members.

The first condition for fostering effectiveness is that the team be a real team in terms of working together interdependently and understanding what authority it has in managing its work processes. Stability of membership is also important. A team that met the definition of a team presented at the beginning of this chapter would constitute a real team. The second condition is that the team has a compelling direction. If the team does not have a clear idea of where it is headed, it could flounder. One recommendation is to express the overall team task as a single short statement. Subtasks can be assigned later.[30] A compelling direction for a team of financial planners might be, "Our portfolio of investments must have a return 4 percentage points better than the S&P 500 this year."

The third condition is for the team manager to provide an enabling structure, including the design of the work, the norms of conduct, and the mix of people in the team. The characteristics of an effective work group presented in Chapter 9 could be interpreted as factors that lead to an enabling structure. The fourth condition is a supportive organizational environment. Included here would be reward systems, information systems, and education systems to handle the complexity of teamwork. Few managers would have the authority to modify the total organization to provide support, but at least the manager can make organizational executives aware of this condition. The fifth condition is that to manage a team toward effectiveness, the leader needs to be an expert coach. Keep in mind the previous discussion of team coaching. In addition, recognize that an effective coach listens, gives encouragement, and rewards good performance.

As mentioned many times in this book so far, a dominant theme about group and team effectiveness is that shared leadership is essential. An additional perspective on the role of shared leadership is that over time such leadership results in more trust within the group. In turn, growth in group trust is related positively to performance improvement. Evidence about the importance of shared leadership stems from a meta-analysis of 42 samples. Among the findings was that shared leadership has its strongest impact when the work of team members is more complex.[31] This finding makes sense because shared leadership focuses on sharing responsibility with team members who have the expertise needed at the moment. As tasks become more complex, more expertise is required.

A practical way of enhancing work team effectiveness is to hold debriefing sessions after a project is completed to review what went well and what did not go well, to serve as a guide to future performance. During a debriefing, team members reflect on recent experiences, such as solving a complex problem, discuss what happened, and identify opportunities for improvement. The same approach is used by sports teams when they review the game video to look for areas of improvement. Experimental evidence for the usefulness of debriefing was gathered from students doing case analyses for a course in strategic management. Debriefing was much more effective when it was carefully guided, such as making sure that each team member provides input.[32]

Attaining Collaboration in Virtual Teams

A major challenge in managing virtual teams is to ensure that collaboration and a spirit of teamwork exist among the geographically dispersed members. Virtual team members may work in different time zones and even different companies. The suggestions for achieving virtual teamwork presented in Chapter 9 are aimed at the successful management of virtual teams. Here are some additional suggestions for enhancing collaboration, communication, and group cohesion.[33]

To begin, work agreements should be formal and signed. A written pact should outline the team's job responsibilities, expectations, and deadlines. The role of the team leader or facilitator should also be made clear, such as indicating that the leader will carefully review all output and make suggestions for revision. Agreement should also be reached about which network technology will be used for the group members to communicate with each other. The technology could be as basic as e-mail or as advanced as online workspace, where team members can store and edit documents and have access to a shared database. The shared document is helpful in making sure that team members are working on the latest version of the project.

The leader should provide an organizational chart that specifies whom to contact for every part of a project. In this way, each team member knows who is responsible for which phase of the project, thereby minimizing communicating to everyone on the team in search of information.

Although some virtual teams are far-flung, it is helpful to supplement virtual interaction with an occasional face-to-face meeting. Face-to-face meetings bring energy to collaboration that is difficult to attain electronically. The face-to-face meetings should focus on big issues facing the group, including major plans and brainstorming. If the entire group cannot meet together face to face, the manager or a delegate should make an occasional visit to team members in their various locations. A caution is that if meetings are too frequent, the advantages of being a virtual team disappear. Team members can work faster when they do not have to wait for meetings to make decisions. Also, timid members of the group are more likely to offer criticisms when done online rather than face to face.

A powerful technique for enhancing collaboration in a virtual team is to encourage trust among team members. Findings from 52 studies representing 12, 615 workers in 1,850 teams found that team trust facilitated coordination and cooperation in teams.[34] As mentioned in Chapter 9, emotional intelligence within the group facilitates trust. A trustworthy leader might have the spillover effect of virtual team members trusting each other, and the leader trusting team members might also enhance trust.

Implications for Managerial Practice

1. Employees chosen for self-managed work teams should be those who show pride in their work and enjoy working cooperatively with others. Self-nomination or asking for volunteers for the self-directed work team will decrease selection errors. After employees are selected, they must be trained thoroughly to become productive members of work teams. Essential training areas include problem-solving techniques, technical skills, and interpersonal and leadership skills.
2. Managers can remove themselves as impediments to self-management of teams, while retaining the role of adviser and resource person, by asking these questions of team members: (a) What is the cause of the problem? (b) What are you doing to fix it? (c) How will you know when it is accomplished? (d) How can I help? and (d) What are your contingency plans?[35]
3. Even well-motivated teams tend to function best when given deadlines for certain tasks. To help build commitment to the deadline, it is helpful to discuss its feasibility when the team receives the assignment. The discussion will sometimes point to impediments to reaching the deadline, such as needing another team member to carry out a specialized task. For example, a manufacturing team might need a robotics specialist part time to accomplish its mission.
4. Keep in mind the *team halo effect*, the curious phenomenon that teams are rarely blamed for their failures. Instead, the finger points to individual team members when the team does not accomplish its mission. Two studies conducted with business graduate students found that individuals were more likely to be identified as the cause of failure than the team as a whole.[36] It might therefore be valuable to recognize that the team as an entity could have problems that contribute to failure, rather than immediately blaming one or two individuals for poor performance.

Summary of Key Points

1. *Explain the nature of a self-managed work team and characteristics associated with team-member success.* A dominant trend in job design is to organize workers into self-managed work teams in order to increase productivity and quality and reduce cycle time. The team is given total responsibility for a product or service in dealing with an external or internal customer. Each team member learns a broad range of skills and switches job assignments periodically. Team members plan, control, and improve their own work processes. They usually order materials, keep inventories, and deal with suppliers. Self-managed work team members have to be mentally flexible and alert and possess at least average interpersonal skills. They must take pride in their work and enjoy working cooperatively.

2. *Explain several mechanisms by which continuous learning takes place in teams.* Continuous learning in teams is most likely to take place when the team has a moderate learning orientation, is faced with an unusual problem or crisis, engages in collective problem solving, and receives coaching as a team from the team leader or an outside professional coach.

3. *Explain how to foster teamwork.* Managers and leaders can enhance teamwork through many behaviors, attitudes, and organizational actions, including the following: Encourage team members to develop prosocial motivation; share leadership among members; give the team an urgent, constructive purpose; em-

power the group to determine how to meet the objectives; develop a norm for teamwork, and use words and phrases that support teamwork. It is also helpful to create a code of conduct for teamwork that facilitates mutual trust, use a consensus decision-making style, feed team members valid facts and information that motivate them to work together, and use language that fosters cohesion and commitment. In addition, refrain from micromanagement, ensure that team members learn what other team members are working on, create physical structures suited for teams, reward the team as well as individuals, and support outdoor (or off-site) training.

4. *Develop insight into managing on-site teams as well as virtual teams.* Building teamwork is a key part of managing teams. In managing on-site, or physical, teams, keep these conditions in mind: Make sure the group is a real team; give the team a compelling direction; provide an enabling structure for the team, such as the right size; provide a supportive organizational environment; and be an expert coach. To better attain collaboration, good communication, and group cohesion in virtual teams, follow these points: Have formal work agreements; clarify the team leader's role; agree on the network technology to be used; use an organizational chart to specify who is responsible for what; and have occasional face-to-face interaction.

Key Terms and Phrases

self-managed work team, p. 216

coaching (in relation to teams), p. 223

prosocial motivation, p. 225

micromanagement, p. 227

Discussion Questions and Activities

1. Do you see any ethical problems with the practice of companies hiring teams rather than individuals?

2. Why do so many workers believe that belonging to a team contributes to their job satisfaction?

3. Many managers believe that experience on a sports team is good preparation for performing well as a member of a workplace team. As a result, these managers often give preference in hiring to people with experience in team sports. What is your reaction to the thinking and behavior of these managers?

4. Visualize a work team manufacturing a luxury sports car. What would be the alternative way of manufacturing such a vehicle?

5. To build teamwork, one team leader at a manufacturing company encouraged the members of the team to all get the same small tattoo on their wrists. How do you like this idea?

6. Imagine yourself as a virtual team member, working with teammates geographically dispersed, whom you have never met in person. Explain whether you would feel like you were really working on a team.

7. Outdoor (or off-site) training has achieved enormous popularity as a method of developing teamwork, even without research substantiation. What factors do you think account for its popularity?

8. Observe directly or visualize the operations of a fast-food restaurant in which the workers are visible to the public, such as McDonald's or Burger King. To what extent are the workers functioning as a true team?

9. In what way can a micromanager sometimes be helpful to a team member?

10. Speak to a manager in a retail setting such as a supermarket or restaurant. Get his or her impression of the importance of teamwork in that work setting. Be prepared to share your findings with classmates.

CASE PROBLEM: Baxter Wants to Strengthen Teamwork

Baxter considers himself fortunate to be chosen as the team leader of one of the newly formed teams in the automobile-financing division of the bank where he works. The purpose of forming the team was to improve customer service. Each team now has the authority to lend money to individuals and automobile dealers, and to deal with delinquent loans, for specific geographic regions. Before the shift into teams, separate departments existed for sales, analysis of creditworthiness, and dealing with delinquent loans.

Although the auto-financing division was profitable, it received too many criticisms about poor service, particularly regarding the time required to process a loan, and poor results in loan collection. Sales representatives within the company said that it took too long to approve loans, particularly large loans to dealers who used the money to purchase inventory.

One of Baxter's first initiatives was to hold frequent in-person meetings to discuss how service was going to be improved. He emphasized to the team that the company had adopted the popular team concept and that teams were empowered to look for ways to improve efficiency and productivity. Baxter also emphasized that each team member had more responsibility than under the department structure. Each team member would be doing some sales, credit evaluation, and loan collection.

Team member Larry commented during one of the meetings, "Just think of it: three jobs in one, and being paid just as before."

During the same meeting, team member Maria asked, "What's so special about calling us a team? I had a nice job in the credit evaluation department before these teams were formed. I enjoyed the work. Now my job is more confusing."

Baxter responded, "The company decided this was the way to go. Trust me—everything will work out fine. Just go along with the idea for now."

Four months after the teams were formed, Baxter's boss, Beverly, met with him to discuss progress. Beverly said, "Your team isn't making as much progress as I would like. Loans to dealers are not being issued any faster, and neither are approvals for customers. Dealer complaints about delays and red tape are at about the same level as before we converted into teams. Loan collections aren't any better either. The other teams are making more progress. Does your team have a problem?"

"We do have a problem," said Baxter. "Everyone comes to work just as in the days before teams. They do most of the work alone, but they send e-mail messages to each other as needed. It seems to be business as usual. So far, the idea of a high-producing team hasn't caught on."

"Are you an effective team leader?" asked Beverly.

"I think I am," said Baxter. "I do everything I'm supposed to. I hold meetings. I post messages. I answer all questions asked of me. I try to settle problems."

Beverly replied, "I'll be back to you in two months to discuss your team's progress. I want to see some improved results in terms of better customer service."

Case Questions

1. How can Baxter become a more effective team leader?
2. What can Baxter do to get his team members more interested in functioning as a team?
3. What might Beverly do to help Baxter improve teamwork in his unit?

Endnotes

1. Original story created from facts and observations in the following sources: Andrew Tangel, "Caterpillar Comment Spooks Investors," *The Wall Street Journal*, April 25, 2018, p. B1; "Caterpillar's Global Purchasing Demonstrates the Power of Teamwork," Caterpillar News (www.caterpillar.com), pp. 1–2. Caterpillar © 2018; "6 Examples of Teamwork in Business,"

Ferguson Values (http://fergusonvalues.com), January 13, 2014, p. 2; "Continuous Product Improvement," (www.caterpillar.com), p 1. Caterpillar © 2018

2. Michael M. Beyerlein, Sue Freedman, Craig McGee, and Linda Moran, *Beyond Teams: Building the Collaborative Organization* (San Francisco: Jossey-Bass/Pfeiffer, 2003).

3. Sydney Finkelstein, "Companies Should Hire Teams, Not Individuals," *The Wall Street Journal*, October 30, 2017, p. B1.

4. Mark Mortensen and Heidi K. Gardner, "The Overcommitted Organization," *Harvard Business Review*, September–October 2017, pp. 58–65.

5. Richard S. Wellings, William C. Byham, and Jeanne M. Wilson, *Empowered Teams: Creating Self-Directed Work Groups That Improve Quality, Productivity, and Participation* (San Francisco: Jossey-Bass, 1991), p. 3.

6. "Let Self-Managing Groups Thrive," *Executive Leadership*, October 2013, p. 4.

7. This list is paraphrased from Wellings, Byham, and Wilson, *Empowered Teams*, p. 4.

8. Frederick P. Morgeson, "The External Leadership of Self-Managing Teams: Intervening in the Context of Novel and Disruptive Events," *Journal of Applied Psychology*, May 2005, pp. 497–508.

9. Frederick P. Morgeson, Matthew H. Reider, and Michael A. Campion, "Selecting Individuals in Team Settings: The Importance of Social Skills, Personality Characteristics, and Teamwork Knowledge," *Personnel Psychology*, Autumn 2005, pp. 583–611.

10. Greg L. Stewart, Stephen H. Courtright, and Murray R. Barrick, "Peer-Based Control in Self-Managing Teams: Linking Rational and Normative Influence with Individual and Group Performance," *Journal of Applied Psychology*, March 2012, pp. 435–447.

11. Amy C. Edmonson, "Teamwork on the Fly," *Harvard Business Review*, April 2012, pp. 72–80.

12. The evidence is reviewed in Roy A. Cook and J. Larry Goff, "Coming of Age with Self-Managed Teams: Dealing with a Problem Employee," *Journal of Business and Psychology*, Spring 2002, pp. 487–488; Leigh and Maynard, "Self-Managed Teams," p. 202.

13. Ashley M. Hughes et al., "Saving Lives: A Meta-Analysis of Team Training in Healthcare," *Journal of Applied Psychology*, September 2016, pp. 1266–1304.

14. J. Stuart Bunderson and Kathleen M. Sutcliffe, "Management Team-Learning Orientation and Business Unit Performance," *Journal of Applied Psychology*, June 2003, pp. 552–560.

15. D. Christopher Kayes, "Proximal Team Learning: Lessons from United Flight 93 on 9/11," *Organizational Dynamics*, *1*(2003), pp. 80–91.

16. Kayes, "Proximal Team Learning," p. 84.

17. Ruth Wageman, "How Leaders Foster Self-Managing Team Effectiveness: Design Choices versus Hands-On Coaching," *Organization Science*, *12*(2001), p. 561.

18. Morgeson, "The External Leadership of Self-Managing Teams," p. 505.

19. J. Richard Hackman and Ruth Wageman, "A Theory of Team Coaching," *Academy of Management Review*, April 2005, pp. 269–287.

20. Liane Davey, "How to Put the Right Amount of Pressure on Your Team," *Harvard Business Review*, July 1, 2016, pp. 1–4.

21. Manfred F. R. Ket de Vries, "Leadership Group Coaching in Action: The Zen of Creating High-Performance Teams," *Academy of Management Executive*, February 2005, pp. 61–76.

22. Cited in Robin L. Flanigan, "Teamwork, Says Veterinary Assistant, Always Saves the Day," *Democrat and Chronicle*, March 2, 2016, p. 2E.

23. Many of the ideas in this section come from "Teamwork in a Shock Trauma Unit: New Lessons in Leadership," *Leadership and Change*, www.Knowledge@Wharton.com, October 2004, pp. 1–6; Ruth Wageman, "Critical Success Factors for Creating Superb Self-Managing Teams," *Organizational Dynamics*, Summer 1997, p. 57; Jon R. Katzenbach and Douglas K. Smith, "The Discipline of Teams," *Harvard Business Review*, March–April 1993, pp. 118–119; Charlotte Garvey, "Steer Teams with the Right Pay," *HR Magazine*, May 2002, pp. 70–78; Christine Congdon, Donna Flynn, and Melanie Redman, "Balancing 'We' and 'Me,'" *Harvard Business Review*, October 2014, pp. 50–57; Ha Hu and Robert C. Liden, "Making a Difference in the Teamwork: Linking Team Prosocial Motivation to Team Processes and Effectiveness," *Academy of Management Journal*, August 2015, pp. 1102–1127.

24. "Improve Teamwork with a 'Code of Conduct,'" *Manager's Edge*, February 2005, p. 1; Blair Singer, *Rich Dad's Advisor: The ABC's of Building a Business Team That Wins*, Warner Business Books, www.twbookmark.com. (Audio book, 2005.)

25. Michael Mankins, Alan Bird, and James Root, "Making Star Teams Out of Star Players," *Harvard Business Review*, January–February 2013, p. 77.

26. Quoted in Kathleen Driscoll, "What to Do When Corporate Team Building Turns Embarrassing," *Rochester Business Journal*, December 1, 2017, p. 26.

27. Cited in Adam Bryant, "Take the Bus, and Watch the New Ideas Flow," *The New York Times* (www.nytimes.com), September 15, 2012, p. 2.

28. Andrew M. Carton and Jonathon N. Cummings, "A Theory of Subgroups in Work Teams," *Academy of Management Review*, July 2012, p. 441.

29. J. R. Hackman, *Leading Teams: Setting the Stage for Great Performances* (Boston: Harvard Business School Press, 2002).

30. "Clarify Team Roles to Ensure Success," *Manager's Edge*, August 2005, p. 6.

31. Danni Wang, David A. Waldman, and Zhen Zhang, "A Meta-Analysis of Shared Leadership and Team Effectiveness," *Journal of Applied Psychology*, March 2014, pp. 181–198.

32. Erik R. Eddy, Scott I. Tannenbaum, and John E. Mathieu, "Helping Teams to Help Themselves: Comparing Two Team-Led Debriefing Methods," *Personnel Psychology*, Number 4, 2013, pp. 975–1008.

33. "Seven Tactics to Build Cohesion," *Flexible Workplace Management*, sample issue, 2001 (Chicago: Lawrence Ragan Communications); Rachael King, "All Together Now: How Collaboration Software Can Make Your Company More Efficient," *Business Week SmallBiz*, Winter 2005, pp. 68–70.

34. Christina Breuer, Joachim Huffmeir, and Guido Hertel, "Does Trust Matter in Virtual Teams? A Meta-Analysis of Trust

and Team Effectiveness Considering Virtuality and Documentation as Moderators," *Journal of Applied Psychology*, August 2016, pp. 1151–1177.

35. Ann Majchrzak, Arvind Malhotra, Jeffery Stamps, and Jessica Lipnack, "Can Absence Make a Team Grow Stronger?" *Harvard Business Review*, May 2004, pp. 131–137; "Let Self-Managing Groups Thrive," *Executive Leadership*, October 2013, p. 4.

36. Charles E. Naquin and Renee O. Tynan, "The Team Halo Effect: Why Teams Are Not Blamed for Their Failures," *Journal of Applied Psychology*, April 2003, pp. 332–340.

Leadership in Organizations

ASDF_MEDIA/Shutterstock.com

Learning Objectives

After reading and studying this chapter and doing the exercises, you should be able to:

1. Describe key leadership traits, styles, and behaviors.

2. Explain the basics of three different contingency theories of leadership.

3. Present an overview of transformational and charismatic leadership.

4. Understand several ways of developing your leadership potential.

Marc Benioff is the cofounder and CEO of Salesforce, the firm that holds the biggest share of the market for software that helps salespeople track their interactions with customers and prospective customers. Salesforce was the first company to offer software as a service, later known as cloud computing.

At a Dreamforce conference held in San Francisco in 2016 with 170,000 attendees, Benioff introduced the product that he said would spur new growth for the company, Salesforce Einstein. "If this is not the next big thing, "I do not know what is," said Benioff. Einstein integrates artificial intelligence (AI) into almost all of Salesforce's products. Einstein provides predictive suggestions and insights into service, marketing, and sales, along with tools for collaboration. Einstein is also intended to serve as a new "nervous system" across the entire business.

Benioff achieves his highest job satisfaction from showing off the company's products and pitching his company to investors. Salesforce is regarded by business analysts as one of the world's most innovative big companies, and they attribute much of the company success to Benioff's forward-looking leadership. He describes three ways in which Salesforce has been in trailblazer in these words: "I think our top three are a technology model which is now known as the cloud, the subscription business model, and our 1-1-1 model." The latter refers to the company's philanthropic commitment to donate 1 percent each of equity, products, and employee hours to worthwhile causes. Salesforce has given away hundreds of millions of dollars to fund hospitals, schools, and a variety of charitable causes.

Although Salesforce has a deep management bench, Benioff makes all the major decisions, and the entire 28,000-person workforce follows his directives. Benioff relies heavily on intuition in making product decisions. For example, he asked company engineers to develop Chatter, an in-house messaging tool for Salesforce's application, a product that gave the company a consumer-oriented edge. Benioff's intuition also prompted him to acquire about one dozen AI companies and make Einstein the company's artificial intelligence brand.

Benioff believes an effective leader should be inspired by what he or she does. His enthusiasm permeates Salesforce and is said to inspire the many employees, partners, and customers to take on challenges year after year. Company insiders believe that Benioff's enthusiasm creates the energy that is behind Salesforce's success. *Forbes* wrote that "Benioff can still get excited about his own products like a kid who's found a new toy."

Benioff's primary non-work and non-family activity is helping charitable causes and supporting candidates for political office. He graduated with a BS degree in business administration from the University of Southern California.[1]

The story about Marc Benioff illustrates how a bold and charismatic leader can build an organization and inspire its members to attain extraordinary goals. Leadership has always been a topic of major importance to scholars and practitioners, and current interest is intense as organizations struggle to survive in a hyper-competitive world. Executives themselves think that knowledge of leadership is important for organizational success, as reflected in the wide variety of leadership development programs sponsored by companies.

Leadership is not just the domain of a few members of top management. Today, leadership is often thought of as being distributed among all group members, so one person is not responsible for all the leadership activities. Take-charge ability is important at all levels of management. Employees who are in direct contact with customers and clients often require stronger leadership than do higher-level workers. Entry-level workers often lack experience, direction, and a strong work ethic. Furthermore, the emphasis on teams means that effective team leaders are needed throughout the organization.

Another perspective on how leadership is implemented in the modern organization stems from an analysis of 7,400 leaders by 67,300 bosses, peers, subordinates, and themselves. A major finding was that senior executives should pay attention to exerting influence on their bosses as wells as colleagues.[2]

The discussion of leadership in this chapter centers on several topics of interest to managers and professionals: leadership traits, styles, and behaviors; contingency theories of leadership; transformational and charismatic leadership; substitutes for leadership; and the development of leadership skills. The following chapter deals with other topics closely associated with leaders, such as power and influence. First, however, we look at the nature of leadership.

The Nature of Leadership

Leadership involves influencing others to achieve objectives important to them and the organization. With effective leadership, people want to contribute to the organization's success. A representative definition is that **leadership** is the ability to inspire confidence and support among the people on whose competence and commitment performance depends.[3] The term *leadership* generally refers to leadership exercised at any organizational level, whereas *strategic leadership* refers to leadership activity among the top-level executives.

Although leadership is a major function of management, it is not the same thing *as* management. Management copes with complexity, which requires preserving order and consistency. Leadership, in comparison, copes with change in a competitive, rapidly evolving world. Effective leaders deal with change by formulating a vision of the future and setting a direction for that vision. Leaders focus on inspiration, vision, and human passion. Leadership is focused more on people, whereas management is focused more on results.[4] Leaders are also heavily involved in persuading and motivating others and spearheading useful changes.

Effective leadership and management are both required in the modern workplace. Managers must be leaders, but leaders must also be good managers. Workers need to be inspired and persuaded, but they also need assistance in developing and maintaining a smoothly functioning workplace.

Considerable evidence supports the commonsense belief that leadership contributes to organizational effectiveness. For example, a survey of 205 executives from public and private companies concluded that leadership actions can affect performance, but only if the leader is seen as responsible and inspirational. Leader behaviors that were positively related to company performance included only those related to inspiring others and to leader responsibility.[5]

Leadership Traits and Characteristics

A logical approach to understanding leadership is to study the traits and characteristics of effective leaders. For many years, scholars downplayed the study of leadership characteristics, but an interest in the inner qualities of leaders has reawakened, particularly with respect to ethical qualities and charisma, including vision. The traits of leaders relate closely to the degree to which others perceive these people to be leaders. For example, a person who exudes self-confidence would generally be perceived as having leadership qualities.

Evidence collected years ago confirms that effective leaders are different from other people—they have the "right stuff." The differences relate to the traits and characteristics described in this section.[6] A current model of leadership confirms the idea that traits of leaders influence their behaviors, which in turn influence how subordinates will respond.[7] A basic example is that a leader with natural warmth will be considerate of team members, which will facilitate their job satisfaction and productivity.

Hundreds of traits and personal characteristics of leaders have been researched over the years, dating back to the early 1900s. Here we discuss illustrative leadership qualities under the categories of cognitive skills and personality traits that research and careful observation support.

leadership The ability to inspire confidence and support among the people on whose competence and commitment performance depends.

LEARNING OBJECTIVE 1
Describe key leadership traits, styles, and behaviors.

Cognitive Skills

cognitive skills Mental ability and knowledge.

An effective leader must have appropriate **cognitive skills**, or mental ability and knowledge. Organizational leaders possess effective problem-solving ability. They anticipate problems before they occur and persevere until the problems are solved. In the process, they demonstrate imagination, creativity, and a willingness to experiment with unproven methods. Leadership positions place a continuously increasing demand on problem-solving ability. For example, managers are pressured to perform tasks in a shorter time with a smaller staff and contribute to developing a business strategy that will point the firm in the right direction. A meta-analysis of the relationship between leadership and intelligence concluded that intelligence contributes more to leadership performance when the leader is more directive (makes decisions on his or her own).[8] In such situations, the leader can use his or her problem-solving ability to good advantage instead of relying so heavily on the input of others.

It has been long believed that effective leaders are somewhat more intelligent than the average group member, but not to a major extent. A recent study conducted with 379 leaders supports this idea. Leader cognitive ability was measured with the Wonderlic Personnel Test of general intelligence, and leadership effectiveness was rated by questionnaire data from subordinates. The leaders perceived to be the most effective had higher but not outstanding Wonderlic scores, ranking slightly above the mental ability of the average group member (an IQ equivalent of 120).[9] One explanation for these findings is that group members expect the leader to be intelligent but not to the extent that the leader "loses" them.

A high-level cognitive skill is for an executive to be able to understand changing business conditions that could affect the organization, and then make appropriate adjustments. For example, in recent years, leaders at major technology firms such as Microsoft and IBM recognized that more users of both software and hardware were shifting to cloud services. As a result, these leaders had to quickly develop their cloud services.

Technical and professional competence, or knowledge of a particular business, is another cognitive requirement for effective leadership. When outsiders are brought into a company to fill senior management positions, they usually need a specialty to complement their leadership and administrative skills, such as being skilled in finance, marketing, operations, or industry knowledge. For example, Nestlé, the world's largest packaged food company, wanted to diversify away from slower-growing food and beverage products and move more into health care. Part of Nestlé's solution was to bring in Mark Schneider, who previously headed the German health-care giant Fresenius, as CEO.[10] In lesser leadership positions, technical competence is important because it is difficult to establish rapport with group members when the leader does not understand the technical details of the work.

Considering that a key cognitive skill for leaders is the ability to think strategically, you might find Self-Assessment 11-1 of value.

Personality Traits

Personality traits and characteristics have an important influence on leadership effectiveness. Which traits and characteristics are the most relevant varies with the situation. For example, enthusiasm may be more important for a sales manager for mortgage refinancing than for an inventory control manager. The sales manager's enthusiasm may be needed to help sales representatives cope with rejection by customers, particularly when telemarketing the refinancing of homes. A listing and description of some of the most important personality traits related to leadership effectiveness are presented next.

self-awareness Understanding oneself and insightfully processing feedback about oneself to improve personal effectiveness.

1. *Self-awareness.* A foundational trait for leadership effectiveness is **self-awareness**, understanding oneself and insightfully processing feedback about oneself to improve personal effectiveness. Self-awareness therefore has two components: seeing yourself clearly and also knowing how other people see you and how they are influenced by you.[11] (Self-awareness is considered by some researchers to be a component of emotional

How Strategic Is My Thinking?

Indicate your strength of agreement with each of the following statements: SD—strongly disagree; D—disagree; N—neutral, A—agree; SA—strongly agree.

	SD	D	N	A	SA
1. I often think about how world events will affect me personally.	1	2	3	4	5
2. I sometimes think about what could be done to save a well-known company that is failing.	1	2	3	4	5
3. A C-level executive should spend a part of each day just thinking about what the organization should be doing.	1	2	3	4	5
4. It's a poor use of money for an organization to invest in employee training when the company is not doing well financially.	5	4	3	2	1
5. Before accepting a new position, I would first evaluate how it fits into my long-term career goals.	1	2	3	4	5
6. I sometimes wonder if the work I do will still be relevant five years from now.	1	2	3	4	5
7. Taking care of day-by-day responsibilities is the best way to create a good future for an organization.	5	4	3	2	1
8. The most successful people in most fields are visionaries.	1	2	3	4	5
9. I am a "big-picture" thinker.	1	2	3	4	5
10. It is mostly a waste of time and money for a group of executives to go on a retreat to contemplate the future of their company.	5	4	3	2	1
11. Once a company hits a certain size, such as $50 million in annual sales, it does not have to worry much about competition.	5	4	3	2	1
12. An organization cannot become great without an exciting vision.	1	2	3	4	5
13. I sometimes think about the true purpose of my job.	1	2	3	4	5
14. Planning for the future is an exercise in fantasy.	5	4	3	2	1
15. If a company has a strategy department, other people in the company do not have to worry about thinking strategically.	5	4	3	2	1

Scoring and interpretation: Find your total score by summing the point values for each question.

66–75: You probably already think strategically, which should help you as a top-level manager as well as a strategic thinker in personal life.

45–65: You probably have a neutral, detached attitude toward thinking strategically.

15–44: Your thinking probably emphasizes the here and now and the short term. People in this category are usually not ready to provide strategic leadership to group members. They also do not worry much about the future.

intelligence.) The leader must be able to benefit from feedback that is sometimes obvious and at other times subtle. For example, a leader might notice a blank stare (a form of non-verbal feedback) while explaining a new initiative to group members. The leader could profitably use this feedback to use another approach to describe the initiative.

2. *Self-confidence.* A realistic degree of *self-confidence* is frequently associated with leadership effectiveness. A leader who is self-confident without being overbearing instills confidence among group members. Being self-confident also contributes to a leader being decisive, which is particularly important when the group is facing a major problem, such as a product recall. Self-confident leaders are also typically optimistic, which is helpful in motivating others.

Self-confidence contributes to leadership effectiveness.

The concept of self-confidence is useful in studying leadership because it illustrates the relationship between traits and behavior. A manager who is inwardly self-confident will behave confidently and will be perceived as acting cool under pressure. George P. Hollenbeck and Douglas T. Hall propose that leaders with high self-confidence are likely to stay motivated. They will work harder in approaching a task and exert more effort. The motivation propelled by self-confidence will also facilitate the leader staying with the task longer without positive feedback, and not becoming discouraged when faced with problems and difficulties.[12]

Self-confidence is also important because it contributes to being courageous. The leader must sometimes have the courage to make a decision even though others may think he or she is wrong, foolish, or both. It is easy to find advisors who recommend that you not take action, so courage is required to make a bold decision.[13] For example, a benevolent business owner might decide to hire a convicted felon to help the individual become a productive member of society. A key advisor says, "Don't take such a crazy risk." The business owner has the courage to take the risk, and the person with the prison record becomes an above-average performer.

A leader with low self-confidence will exhibit behavior at one of two extremes. At one extreme, an insecure boss will obsessively check on every detail to avoid mistakes that reflect poorly on his or her leadership. At the other extreme, a leader who lacks confidence in his or her own abilities will overly rely on others to accomplish tasks.

The trait of self-confidence contributes more to leadership effectiveness when it is combined with humility to prevent the leader from being overbearing. This is particularly true if the self-confident leader is also narcissistic. A study conducted in the health insurance industry found that leader narcissism (which has a strong component of self-confidence) can have a positive effect on follower perception and motivation when it is tempered by humility.[14]

3. *Proactivity.* Leadership is almost synonymous with taking the initiative, and being proactive includes taking the initiative to work on problems. A person with a **proactive personality** has a relatively stable tendency to effect environmental change. He or she makes things happen as part of his or her work role.[15] As a result, the leader with a proactive personality is more likely to be able to influence people and bring about constructive change. A study conducted in a large, consumer, packaged-goods company found that proactive senior managers establish more challenging goals for their business units. The higher goals were in turn associated with higher sales.[16] Self-Assessment 11-2 gives you an opportunity to think through your own tendencies toward being a proactive personality.

proactive personality A relatively stable tendency to effect environmental change.

4. *Trustworthiness and authenticity.* Trustworthiness contributes to leadership effectiveness in most situations. Being perceived as trustworthy involves many different behaviors. At the top of the list, however, are behavioral consistency and integrity. Consistency refers to reliability and predictability, such as when a manager conducts performance evaluations and reimburses for expenses as agreed. Integrity centers on telling the truth and keeping promises. Anand Mahindra is the managing director of an Indian indus-

trial and services conglomerate, the Mahindra Group. He notes, "The number 1 reason people come and stay is the atmosphere of integrity. The number 2 reason is empowerment and trust."[17]

Authenticity is a cluster of traits, related to trustworthiness. Authentic leadership is defined as being self-aware, confident, open, optimistic, resilient, and honest, and being more concerned about the welfare of others than personal welfare. For leaders to display authentic moral behavior, they must perceive their roles as including an ethical responsibility to all of their stakeholders, such as employees, subcontractors, and customers.[18] An example of such behavior would be establishing a scholarship fund for the teenage workers in an overseas clothing factory operated by a subcontractor.

To become more authentic, the leader has to consistently match words and deeds, as with being trustworthy. At the same time, the leader must establish good relationships with others, which could mean emphasizing different aspects of the self with different groups.[19] An example would be a financial manager acting reserved among bosses and colleagues, yet quite jovial and outgoing when collecting data in the factory. So long as being reserved and jovial were true parts of the manager's self, he or she would be authentic. So, trust pays!

Appearing trustworthy contributes to a person's leadership effectiveness.

Authentic leadership pays dividends for the leader as well as group members. An in-depth study of 44 executives found that authentic leadership reduced stress for leaders and increased their work engagement. Also of note, authentic leaders tended to experience less mental depletion when they interacted more with subordinates.[20]

The study mentioned earlier about business-unit performance and proactivity also found that when employees trust their district manager, they are more likely to perform well when facing challenging goals set by the manager.[21]

Self-Assessment 11-3 pinpoints the type of behaviors that prompt people to trust a leader.

5. *Emotional intelligence.* Emotional intelligence is a major contributor to leadership effectiveness.[22] As described in Chapter 2, the concept refers to managing ourselves and our relationships effectively. A newer conception of emotional intelligence is so broad that it encompasses many traits and behaviors related to leadership effectiveness, including self-confidence, empathy, and visionary leadership. Executives with a high level of emotional intelligence promote teamwork and exercise effective leadership because they are aware of how their reactions affect others.[23] For example, an emotionally intelligent leader would sense whether expressing anger would be helpful or harmful in a given situation.

Passion for the work and the people is a particularly important aspect of emotional intelligence for leadership effectiveness. It is difficult to inspire others if you are not passionate about your major work activities. Entrepreneurial leaders are frequently passionate about their work because they developed the concept behind their business, such as a new social media site for sharing images. Making connections with people is another aspect of emotional intelligence vital for effective leadership.

The empathy aspect of emotional intelligence has been emphasized recently as a contributor to effective leadership. Employees are more likely to be enthused and engaged if they feel that their leaders appreciate their concerns, understand their points of view, and welcome their feedback.[24] Empathy is also important when the leader coaches employees because he or she can better understand why the person being coached needs improvement. For example, an empathic leader might understand that a worker's personal problems are affecting his or her performance. Many leaders have failed because of glaring deficits in the self-control aspect of emotional intelligence. Such behaviors include sexually harassing a subordinate, insulting an ethnic group, storing child pornography on their desktop or tablet computers, or being drunk and disorderly in public.

My Tendencies toward Being a Proactive Personality

Indicate on a 1-to-5 scale the extent of your agreement with the statements below: Agree Strongly (AS), Agree (A), Neutral (N), Disagree (D), Disagree Strongly (DS).

	AS	A	N	D	DS
1. I plan carefully for things that might go wrong.	5	4	3	2	1
2. I don't worry about problems until after they have taken place.	1	2	3	4	5
3. If I see something that is broken, I fix it.	5	4	3	2	1
4. I have been told several times that I am good at taking the initiative.	5	4	3	2	1
5. I often let things like a computer password expire without making the necessary changes.	1	2	3	4	5
6. When something important needs doing, I wait for somebody else to take the initiative.	1	2	3	4	5
7. I think that having a home security system is a good investment in money.	5	4	3	2	1
8. I look around for good opportunities that would help me in my career or personal life.	5	4	3	2	1
9. I don't give much thought to the future because there is not much I can do about it.	1	2	3	4	5
10. It is a good idea to start saving or investing for retirement at the beginning of your career.	5	4	3	2	1
11. I begin projects and tasks by myself, without requiring prompting from somebody else.	5	4	3	2	1
12. The old saying, "The early bird gets the worm," doesn't make much sense in real life.	1	2	3	4	5
13. I let the future take care of itself without giving it much thought.	1	2	3	4	5
14. I set my own goals rather than have others set them for me.	5	4	3	2	1
15. I create a lot of change both in work and personal life.	5	4	3	2	1
16. I have often asked for feedback on my job performance.	5	4	3	2	1
17. If your job is going well, it is a bad idea to explore new job possibilities from time to time.	1	2	3	4	5
18. Once you have chosen a satisfactory career, it is a bad idea to explore the possibilities of another career from time to time.	1	2	3	4	5
19. I readily express my opinion about the effectiveness of a work process.	5	4	3	2	1
20. It is best to stick carefully to your job description rather than create responsibilities for yourself.	1	2	3	4	5
21. I regularly take positive steps to increase the chances that I will stay healthy and physically fit.	5	4	3	2	1
22. I am quite innovative both in work and personal life.	5	4	3	2	1

My Tendencies toward Being a Proactive Personality (Continued)

Scoring and Interpretation: Total the numbers corresponding to your answers.

100–110 Scores in this range suggest that you have strong tendencies toward being a proactive personality. Such proactivity should be (or already is) an asset to you in your career and personal life. Yet scoring 100 points or more could suggest that you sometimes annoy people with your constant need for taking on new responsibility and creating change.

Source: The idea for this scale and several of its statements stem from Thomas S. Bateman and J. Michael Grant, "The Proactive Component of Organizational Behavior: A Measure and Correlates," *Journal of Organizational Behavior*, March 1993, p. 112.

A concluding note about personality traits is that, even if one understands the dispositions of the leader, the situation in which the leader functions is also enormously important. Consultant Larraine Segil explains: "My research revealed that you can be a wonderful manager or leader, but if you have an organization that doesn't support or enable you, you're either going to leave the company or put on the cloaks and clothes of a nondynamic leader to protect your position."[25]

Leadership Behaviors and Styles

A focus on the activities carried out by leaders to enhance productivity and morale followed the trait approach. The **behavioral approach to leadership** attempts to specify how the behavior of effective leaders differs from their less effective counterparts. Dozens of leadership behaviors are mentioned in this chapter and throughout the text. A key concept here is **leadership style**, which is the relatively consistent pattern of behavior that characterizes a leader. Much of this consistency occurs because a leadership style is based somewhat on an individual's personality. Despite this consistency, some managers can modify their style as the situation requires.

Our presentation of leadership styles and behaviors consists of three parts: the pioneering Ohio State University and University of Michigan studies, servant leadership, and mindfulness as a leadership behavior.

behavioral approach to leadership An attempt to specify how the behavior of effective leaders differs from their less effective counterparts.

leadership style The relatively consistent pattern of behavior that characterizes a leader.

Leaders often rely on the group's judgment when making decisions.

Behaviors and Attitudes of a Trustworthy Leader

Listed here are behaviors and attitudes of leaders who are generally trusted by their group members and other constituents. After you read each characteristic, indicate on the right whether this is a behavior or attitude that you appear to have developed already, or whether it does not fit you at present.

	Fits Me	Does Not Fit Me
1. Tells people he or she is going to do something, and then always follows through and gets it done	☐	☐
2. Described by others as being reliable	☐	☐
3. Good at keeping secrets and confidences	☐	☐
4. Tells the truth consistently	☐	☐
5. Minimizes telling people what they want to hear	☐	☐
6. Described by others as "walking the talk"	☐	☐
7. Delivers consistent messages to others in terms of matching words and deeds	☐	☐
8. Does what he or she expects others to do	☐	☐
9. Minimizes hypocrisy by not engaging in activities he or she tells others are wrong	☐	☐
10. Readily accepts feedback on behavior from others	☐	☐
11. Maintains eye contact with people when talking to them	☐	☐
12. Appears relaxed and confident when explaining his or her side of a story	☐	☐
13. Individualizes compliments to others rather than saying something like "You look great" to a large number of people	☐	☐
14. Doesn't expect lavish perks for himself or herself while expecting others to go on an austerity diet	☐	☐
15. Does not tell others a crisis is pending when it isn't just to gain their cooperation	☐	☐
16. Collaborates with others to make creative decisions	☐	☐
17. Communicates information to people at all organizational levels	☐	☐
18. Readily shares financial information with others	☐	☐
19. Listens to people and then acts on many of their suggestions	☐	☐
20. Generally engages in predictable behavior	☐	☐

Scoring and Interpretation: These statements are mostly for self-reflection, so no specific scoring key exists. However, the more statements that fit you, the more trustworthy you are—assuming you are answering truthfully. The usefulness of this self-assessment quiz increases if somebody who knows you well answers it for you to supplement your self-perceptions. Your ability and willingness to carry out some of the behaviors specified in this quiz could have an enormous impact on your career because so many business leaders in recent years have not been perceived as trustworthy. Being trustworthy is therefore a career asset.

QUESTION

Suppose you think you are not as trustworthy as you could be to advance your leadership ability. What could you do about your too-low level of trustworthiness?

Pioneering Studies on Leadership Dimensions

Much of the theory underlying leadership styles can be traced back to studies conducted at Ohio State University and the University of Michigan beginning in the late 1940s. A major output of the Ohio State studies was the emphasis placed on two leadership dimensions: initiating structure and consideration.

Initiating structure describes the degree to which the leader establishes structure for group members. Structure is initiated by activities such as assigning specific tasks, specifying procedures to be followed, scheduling work, and clarifying expectations. A heavy emphasis on initiating structure often translates into an emphasis on attaining good results. Leadership authority Sydney Finkelstein writes, "Some of the best leaders I've seen, whether in research or coaching, come to work with a razor-sharp focus on results. These immensely successful bosses don't care much about being liked."[26] (Many leadership experts would disagree with the comment about being liked. Apple Inc. CEO Tim Cook is an example of a leader who achieves extraordinary results and is well liked for his humanistic approach to dealing with people.)

Consideration describes the degree to which the leader creates an environment of emotional support, warmth, friendliness, and trust. He or she does so by engaging in such behaviors as being friendly and approachable, looking out for the personal welfare of the group, keeping the group informed of new developments, and doing small favors for group members.[27] Figure 11-1 shows how leadership style can be based on a combination of these two key dimensions.

Many of the Ohio State studies were conducted with first-level supervisors and therefore may not apply well to executive leadership. It was discovered that employee turnover was lowest and job satisfaction highest under leaders who were rated highest in consideration. Research also indicated that leaders high on initiating structure were generally rated highly by superiors and had higher-producing work groups.

Researchers at the University of Michigan also investigated the differences in results obtained by production-centered and employee-centered managers (about the same idea as initiating structure versus consideration). Production-centered managers set tight work standards, organized tasks carefully, prescribed the work methods to be followed, and supervised closely. Employee-centered managers encouraged group members to participate in goal setting and other work decisions, and helped to ensure high performance by engendering trust and mutual respect.

initiating structure The degree to which the leader establishes structure for group members.

consideration The degree to which the leader creates an environment of emotional support, warmth, friendliness, and trust.

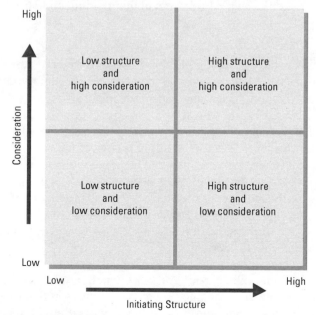

FIGURE 11-1 Leadership Styles Based on a Combination of Initiating Structure and Consideration

Giving clear instructions is part of initiating structure.

A dominant finding of the Michigan studies was that the most productive work groups tended to have leaders who were employee centered rather than production centered. Also, the most effective leaders were those who had supportive relationships with group members. They also tended to use group rather than individual decision making and encouraged subordinates to set and achieve high-performance goals. Despite this dominant finding, exceptions were found. A study conducted with 20,000 employees at a heavy-equipment manufacturer indicated that supervisors with the best production records were both production and employee centered.[28]

A meta-analysis indicates that the pioneering studies under discussion are still relevant to understanding leadership. The results revealed that both consideration and initiating structure are related to leadership outcomes. Consideration is more strongly related to satisfaction with the leader and job satisfaction in general. Initiating structure is slightly more strongly related to the job performance of leaders, as well as group and organization performance. An implication for leaders and managers is that to attain job satisfaction and production, attention must be paid to consideration and initiating structure.[29]

A study conducted online found that when workers perceived that they were getting the amount of consideration and initiating structure they needed, they tended to engage in more organizational citizenship behavior.[30] An explanatory point here is that there are individual differences in how much consideration and initiating structure workers feel they need.

In practice, effective leaders exhibit a wide range of behaviors in addition to the key behaviors mentioned here. The behaviors associated with trustworthiness are relevant here. A key leadership behavior is to understand the strengths and weaknesses of group members, and capitalize on each person's strengths. Rather than encourage employees to follow tight job descriptions that may include tasks they dislike or at which they are not good, the leader develops positions for group members based on their unique abilities. For example, if a store clerk is good at stocking and organizing shelves, yet poor in dealing with customers, he or she is assigned full time to maintaining and replenishing shelves.[31]

Servant Leadership

Some effective leaders believe that their primary mission is to serve the needs of their constituents. They measure their effectiveness in terms of their ability to help others. Instead of seeking individual recognition, servant leaders see themselves as working for the group members. A **servant leader** is one who serves constituents by working on their behalf to help them achieve their goals, not the leader's own goals. Such a leader is self-sacrificing and humble. A servant leader, for example, might take over the responsibilities of a team member on a given day so the team member can be home with an ailing spouse.

servant leader A leader who serves constituents by working on their behalf to help them achieve their goals, not the leader's own goals.

Servant leaders also focus on developing people, such as giving them an opportunity to acquire new skills and become leaders. A key behavior of the servant leader is to gain compliance through persuasion rather than demand compliance through edict.[32] The humanistic approach of the servant leader also helps build community, or a sense of togetherness, among the stakeholders.

Servant leadership is more accurately categorized as a related set of behaviors than a pure style. The servant leader uses his or her talents to help group members. For example, if the leader happens to be a good planner, he or she engages in planning because it will help the group attain its goals. Servant leadership has gained in popularity as companies attempt to establish harmony between executives and workforce members who dislike all-knowing and powerful leaders.[33]

Many academic administrators see themselves as servant leaders; they take care of administrative work so instructors can devote more time to teaching and scholarship. To be an effective servant leader, a person needs the many leadership traits and behaviors described in this chapter. CEOs can also be servant leaders, as revealed in a study of 126 CEOs in the software and hardware technology industries. Among the findings were that CEOs who are narcissistic are less likely to be servant leaders (as you would suspect), whereas being a company founder was positively associated with servant leadership. The firms with CEOs who acted as servant leaders tended to perform better in the long run, measured by return on assets.[34]

A servant leader is a careful listener.

A study about servant leadership was conducted in 224 stores of a U.S. retail organization, including 425 subordinates, 110 store managers, and 40 regional managers. Among the findings was that personality traits are related to being a servant leader. Leader agreeableness was positively related to servant leadership, but extraversion was negatively related. (Perhaps extraverted leaders do not listen enough to subordinates and tend to be self-centered.) Another finding of note was that servant leadership was associated with a higher degree of employee engagement and a lower degree of intention to quit.[35]

A study in a Quebec, Canada, company that makes high-technology products helps explain why servant leadership might lead to improved job performance and organizational citizenship behavior. It was found that the servant leader's focus on employee development helps him or her satisfy the psychological needs for autonomy (working independently), competence, and relatedness (relating to other people). The satisfaction of these three needs fuels employees to perform better and be good organizational citizens.[36]

Mindfulness as a Leadership Behavior

Leaders are frequently encouraged to concentrate on the present moment when dealing with others or performing analytical work. **Mindfulness** is concentrating on the present moment without making judgments about what is happening. Although mindfulness might be classified as a trait, we regard it more as a behavior because of its emphasis on what the leader does or how he or she acts. For example, you are being mindful when you listen to a group member's suggestion and concentrate intensely on the idea. Furthermore, you make no immediate judgments about the value of the idea and do not think about its past or future.[37] The reality that so many leaders are distracted by electronic devices has contributed to the importance of mindfulness.

mindfulness Concentrating on the present moment without making judgments about what is happening.

The mindful leader has traits and engages in behaviors that have long been associated with successful leadership, such as being observant, self-disciplined, and attentive to details that could affect important outcomes. An effective leader is supposed to look at the big picture, yet key details contribute to the big picture. Visualize Katerina, the director of human resources at a pharmaceutical company. Part of the big picture for her is for the company to have a committed, engaged workforce. On a recent tour of the company, Katerina is mindful enough to recognize that very few workers are smiling. To Katerina, this limited amount of smiling could indicate that employee morale is too low to contribute to an engaged workforce. Katerina now takes action by conferring with her supervisors about what can be done to elevate morale.

Several behaviors of a mindful leader are presented next:[38]

- The mindful leader is usually calm and has clarity and focus. He or he can help the group see the way out of a setback, such as having introduced a new product that flopped by suggesting how the group can develop a better product.

- As part of being observant, the mindful leader listens carefully and attempts to extract meaning from what people are saying. As the leader interacts with subordinates both in formal meetings and casual interactions, he or she looks for directly expressed and implied meanings. Assume that the leader asks a store manager how things are going, and the manager responds, "Not too bad." The mindful leader might respond, "In what way could things be better?"

- The mindful leader has a better memory, particularly if he or she has engaged in mindfulness training. An improved memory strengthens the leader's ability to perform the complex thinking needed for developing strategy, employing day-to-day problem solving, and engaging in complex interactions with others.

- The mindful leader is open to new ideas and multiple perspectives. Being mindful, the leader stays alert to what could be new and significant. As one executive described the risk of having poor focus (not being mindful), "When my mind wanders in a meeting, I wonder what business opportunity I've just missed."

Contingency Theories of Leadership

LEARNING OBJECTIVE 2
Explain the basics of three different contingency theories of leadership.

contingency theory of leadership The position that the best style of leadership depends on factors relating to group members and the work setting.

The behavioral theories of leadership provide general guidelines for leadership effectiveness, emphasizing both production and people. After the development of behavioral theories came an attempt to specify the conditions under which various leadership styles would lead to the best results. The intent was to make explanations of leadership precise and scientific. According to the **contingency theory of leadership**, the best style of leadership depends on factors relating to group members and the work setting. Contingent, or flexible, leadership can be thought of in terms of doing the right thing at the right time.[39]

A major contingency factor involves the needs of the group. For example, a leader might want to push ahead immediately with the implementation of a new technology, but if the group needs more training before implementation, the leader must first help the group develop the necessary skills. Here we present three contingency theories, or explanations, of leadership: Fiedler's contingency theory, the leader–member exchange model, and crisis leadership.

Fiedler's Contingency Theory of Leadership

Fred E. Fiedler developed an elaborate contingency model that holds that the best style of leadership is determined by the leader's work situation. Although historically important, studies and observations related to Fiedler's contingency theory have vanished. Fiedler's model specifies the conditions under which leaders should use task- and relationship-motivated styles.[40] (Observe again the two key leadership dimensions of initiating structure and consideration.) To implement Fiedler's theory, leadership style and the situation are measured through questionnaires.

Fiedler measures the leader's style by means of the least-preferred coworker scale (LPC). Whether the leader is primarily task or relationship motivated is measured by how favorably the leader describes his or her least-preferred coworker. The LPC is defined as the coworker with whom he or she would least like to work. Ratings of coworkers are made on a scale of polar-opposite adjectives such as "pleasant" versus "unpleasant." The logic is that people who describe their least-preferred coworker in relatively positive terms are relationship oriented. In contrast, people who describe their least-preferred coworker in very negative terms are task oriented.

situational control The degree to which the leader can control and influence the outcomes of group effort.

Situational control is the degree to which the leader can control and influence the outcomes of group effort. Measurements of situational control (or favorableness to the leader) are based on three factors, listed in order of importance:

1. *Leader–member relations.* The extent to which group members accept and support their leader.
2. *Task structure.* The extent to which the leader knows exactly what to do, and how well and in what detail the tasks to be completed are defined.

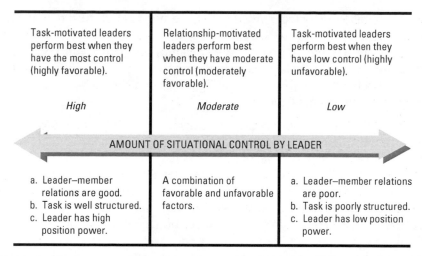

Task-motivated leaders perform best when they have the most control (highly favorable).	Relationship-motivated leaders perform best when they have moderate control (moderately favorable).	Task-motivated leaders perform best when they have low control (highly unfavorable).
High	*Moderate*	*Low*

AMOUNT OF SITUATIONAL CONTROL BY LEADER

a. Leader–member relations are good. b. Task is well structured. c. Leader has high position power.	A combination of favorable and unfavorable factors.	a. Leader–member relations are poor. b. Task is poorly structured. c. Leader has low position power.

FIGURE 11-2 **Summary of Findings from Fiedler's Contingency Theory**

3. *Position power.* The extent to which the organization provides the leader with: (a) the means of rewarding and punishing group members, and (b) appropriate formal authority to get the job done.

Numerous studies have investigated the relationship between leadership-style situational control by the leader and leadership effectiveness. Figure 11-2 summarizes the major findings of these studies of over 800 groups in various settings. The task-motivated style generally produces the best results when the leader has very high or very low control of the situation. The relationship-motivated style is best when the situation is under moderate or intermediate control.

A practical implication of Fiedler's theory would be for the leader to understand how to make the situation more favorable by: (a) improving relationships with group members, (b) enhancing task structure by providing more guidelines and instructions, and (c) requesting more position power from the organization.

The Leader–Member Exchange Model

The behavioral models presented so far assume that the leader relates in approximately the same manner toward all group members. George Graen and his associates have developed a leadership model that challenges the reality of such consistency in behavior. The **leader–member exchange (LMX) model** recognizes that leaders develop unique working relationships with each group member.[41] The LMX approach to understanding leadership is extensively researched and written about by scholars. Practicing managers might use LMX intuitively without recognizing that their actions follow the model.

A leader might be considerate and compassionate toward one team member yet rigid and unfeeling toward another. The different approaches to subordinates that depend on subordinates' characteristics classify the leader–member exchange model as a contingency theory.

Each relationship between the leader/manager and group member differs in quality. One subset of employees, the in-group, is given additional rewards, responsibility, and trust in exchange for their loyalty and performance. In contrast, another subset of employees (the out-group) is treated in accordance with a more formal understanding of supervisor–subordinate relations. The leader's first impression of a group member's competency heavily influences whether the group member becomes a member of the in-group or out-group.

In-group members have attitudes and values similar to the leader and interact frequently with the leader. Out-group members have less in common with the leader and operate somewhat detached from the leader. The one-to-one relationships have a major influence on the subordinate's behavior in the group. Members of the in-group become

leader–member exchange (LMX) model The model that recognizes that leaders develop unique working relationships with each group member.

part of a smoothly functioning team headed by the formal leader. Out-group members are less likely to experience good teamwork.

A contributing factor to the current heavy stream of research about LMX is that it is sensible: The quality of your relationship with your manager has a big impact on your job behavior and performance. Here we highlight research findings with the most direct implications for organizational behavior:

1. Being a member of the in-group facilitates achieving high productivity and satisfaction. Out-group members receive less challenging assignments and are more likely to quit because of job dissatisfaction.[42]

2. Despite the many consequences of positive leader–member exchanges, most supervisors are not overly influenced by them in making performance evaluations. Supervisors may have their "pets," but research has shown that supervisors can overcome these biases to make objective performance evaluations.[43]

3. Communication frequency between the leader and group member moderates (influences) the relationship between leader–member exchanges and performance evaluations. In a study of 188 private-sector workers, it was found that LMX was more strongly related to performance-evaluation results when the group members communicated more frequently with the manager. A second study with 153 public-sector workers found similar results. One implication of these studies is that the importance of LMX depends on how frequently supervisors and subordinates interact. LMX has the biggest impact when interactions are frequent.[44] Frequent interaction with the supervisor is probably important even to develop and maintain a positive leader–member exchange.

4. A study of 375 employees in 82 different teams in a large commercial bank in China found that building high-quality relationships with subordinates facilitated employees being engaged in their work roles (jobs). As a result of the enhanced engagement, employees tended to deliver superior performance. The study also found that the different quality relationships the leader established within the teams can negatively impact coordination within the teams, resulting in lowered team performance.[45] (Again, we see that the leader having "pets" within the team can backfire.)

5. The positive effects of LMX can extend beyond the present organization in which the relationship with the leader takes place and may persist after the worker leaves the current employer. A study conducted at a global technology organization in India found that employees with high-quality relationships with managers benefit from stronger professional development, which can pay off in finding jobs with more responsibility and higher pay in other companies. Furthermore, employees who enjoyed a favorable LMX at a previous job are likely to have goodwill toward their former employer.[46] (This finding is similar to the observation that students who enjoy high-quality relationships with their professors tend to form stronger bonds with their college or university.)

An important implication of the leader–member exchange is that the quality of the relationship between the leader/manager and each group member has important job consequences. A meta-analysis of 282 studies about the impact of LMX on task performance and behavior included these findings: LMX has a positive relationship with task performance, yet it has a negative relationship with counterproductive performance. (If you have a good-quality relationship with your leader, you are less likely to be counterproductive.) When the leader was trusted, a good-quality relationship was the most likely to result in high task performance and increased citizenship behavior. Another key finding of the meta-analysis was that LMX tended to prompt high task performance, but high task performance did not appear to trigger a better relationship with the leader.[47]

Crisis Leadership

Organizational leaders have to deal with crises frequently, including pending bankruptcies, scandalous or criminal behavior by executives, natural disasters such as floods and hurricanes, and an airplane crash experienced by an airline. Leading during a crisis can be classified as contingency leadership because the situation demands that the leader emphasize certain behaviors, attitudes, and traits. **Crisis leadership** is the process of leading group members through a sudden, largely unanticipated, extremely negative, and emotionally upsetting circumstance. Six key components of crisis leadership are described next.[48]

1. *Provide directive leadership.* The best-accepted principle of crisis leadership is that the leader should take decisive action to remedy the situation. The graver the crisis, the less time the leader has to consult a wide array of people. After the plan is formulated, it should be widely communicated to help reassure group members and other stakeholders that something concrete is being done about the predicament. For example, assume that the personal data of hundreds of thousands of consumers are stolen from a company's computer files. Company leadership has to quickly assure the public that steps are being taken to prevent such a breach from happening again and explain how the company will aid the victims of the pirating of personal data.

2. *Project self-confidence and trustworthiness.* Projecting self-confidence is especially important when leading an organization or a group out of a crisis because most people need to rely on a strong person when faced with turmoil. Displaying self-confidence also contributes directly to directive leadership. A financial executive observed that a confident boss finds the right balance between micromanaging (looking over every possible detail) versus delegating so much that his or her authority is diluted.[49] Displaying trustworthiness is helpful because many group members may be skeptical that the organization or organizational unit will survive.

3. *Exert emotional intelligence.* Continuing research into emotional intelligence suggests another reason for its contribution to effective leadership. When a company faces a sudden crisis, how leaders handle their emotions can determine whether the company survives. The emotionally intelligent leader is able to articulate a group's shared yet unexpressed feelings and develop a mission that inspires others. An example of a sudden crisis facing a company would be if it did not win a major government contract that could ensure its short-term survival.[50] A leader would talk about the grief the group was feeling and then point toward other areas of profitable activity for the group.

4. *Engage in sensemaking.* During a crisis, leaders play a major role when searching for answers to make sense of what is happening.[51] Imagine the situation of a supermarket chain declaring bankruptcy and closing 50 unprofitable stores. Employees, suppliers, and customers are confused, and many are frightened. Company leadership has to explain what the bankruptcy means, and does not mean, in terms of the present and the future of the company. For example, the CEO might explain, if true, that the remaining stores will continue to operate as in the past and that the company plans to emerge from bankruptcy as soon as feasible.

5. *Lead with compassion.* Displaying compassion for the concerns, anxieties, and frustrations of group members is a key interpersonal skill for crisis leadership. The type of compassionate leadership that brings about organizational healing involves taking some form of public action that eases pain and inspires others to act as well. Compassionate leadership encompasses two related sets of actions. The first is to create an environment in which the workers who experience or witness pain can freely discuss how they feel, such as a group meeting to talk about the crisis. The second is to create an environment in which the workers who experience or witness pain can find a method to alleviate their own suffering and that of others. The leader might establish a special fund to help the families of workers who were victims of the disaster or give workers the opportunity to receive grief counseling.

6. *Divide major problems into smaller chunks.* Here the leader acts as a skilled manager by giving workers bits of the major problem to work on so that they feel less overwhelmed by the crisis. When an obstacle is perceived as being too large, too complex, or too challenging, workers might feel overwhelmed and freeze in their

crisis leadership The process of leading group members through a sudden, largely unanticipated, extremely negative, and emotionally upsetting circumstance.

tracks. Visualize that a business firm is facing a cash-flow crisis. One group of employees might search for items in the office or factory that could be sold on an auction website. Another group might look for ways to consolidate space so that a company-owned building could be sold.

Transformational and Charismatic Leadership

LEARNING OBJECTIVE 3
Present an overview of transformational and charismatic leadership.

transformational leader One who helps organizations and people make positive changes in the way they conduct their activities.

charisma The ability to lead others based on personal charm, magnetism, inspiration, and emotion.

Considerable attention is paid to the type of leader who goes beyond merely conducting transactions with people, such as rewarding and disciplining them. The **transformational leader** is one who helps organizations and people make positive changes in the way they conduct their activities. Transformational leadership is closely linked to strategic leadership, which provides direction and inspiration to an organization. However, the emphasis in transformational leadership is on sweeping, positive changes. A major contributing factor to transformational leadership is **charisma**, the ability to lead others based on personal charm, magnetism, inspiration, and emotion. However, not all transformational leaders are charismatic, and not all charismatic leaders are transformational.

Transformational Leaders

Transformational leadership occurs when one or more persons engage with others in such a way that leaders and followers raise one another to higher levels of motivation and morality. The purposes of leaders and followers become fused, and the power bases are linked as mutual support for a common purpose.[52] In its pure form, transformational leadership is moral and uplifting and is concerned with engaging the hearts and minds of many people. The responsibility for leadership is thereby shared with many people.

The transformational leader exerts a higher level of influence than does a transactional (routine) leader and thereby motivates people to do more than expected. Transformational leadership is key to revitalizing large organizations of many types. A transformational leader can develop new visions for a firm and mobilize employees to accept and work toward attaining these visions. At their best, transformational leaders make a difference in the lives of others, such as creating jobs, saving jobs, giving people an opportunity for personal development, or engaging in philanthropy.[53]

Transformations take place in one or more of the following ways, with not every transformational leader accomplishing all of them:

1. By using culture change to bring about the changes in attitudes and behaviors necessary to move the organization forward. A major shift of this kind to is move an organization way from being risk-averse to a culture of risk taking and exploration.[54]
2. By getting people to transcend their self-interests for the sake of the work group and the firm.
3. By helping workers to adopt a long-range, broad perspective and focus less on day-by-day concerns.
4. By helping people understand the need for both emotional, intellectual, and often urgent change. A transformational leader recognizes the emotional component to resisting change and deals with it openly.
5. By committing to greatness. Greatness encompasses striving for business effectiveness such as profits and high stock value, as well as impeccable ethics.[55]
6. By encouraging high performance through engaging in worthwhile exchanges with group members. A high-quality LMX relationship leads to an unstated emotional bonding that facilitates subordinates wanting to perform better.[56]
7. By finding the work environment pleasant and expressing happiness, leaders are more likely to be perceived as transformational—and therefore able to bring about transformations.[57]

Few leaders can qualify as meeting all the behavioral and moral criteria of transformational leadership, yet if we focus on achieving a business turnaround while still treating workers humanely, many executives qualify. A representative example is Marc Lore, the

U.S. e-commerce chief at Wal-Mart. Early in his tenure, he acquired five companies, including brands that "resonate with millennial shoppers." He has also spearheaded dramatic growth in Walmart.com.[58] Lore is a well-liked executive who shows an interest in the well-being of company employees. Some turnaround leaders, however, use brutal tactics to restore profitability to a firm, including slashing the payroll by as much as 50 percent, selling off assets, and delaying payments to suppliers. The positive turnaround artist works closely with people to restore a healthy psychological climate.

An example of the research evidence that transformational leadership can help improve organizational performance comes from data collected from middle managers in a large Brazilian company in the energy sector. Transformational leadership was measured by responses of subordinates to a questionnaire, and managerial performance was measured by annual performance evaluations. The results of the study demonstrated that leadership effectiveness, as measured by the achievement of organizational outcomes such as productivity and profit, is a direct function of the leader's transformational behavior. Another aspect of the study found that intelligence and conscientiousness were associated with transformational leadership.[59] (Here again, we see the importance of individual differences in understanding organizational behavior.)

The accompanying Organizational Behavior in Action box provides an example of the type of changes a transformational business leader brings about, and the type of results she attempts to attain.

Charismatic Leadership

Charisma in a leader generally inspires group members and facilitates transformations. Charisma, to a large extent, lies in the eye of the beholder and involves a relationship between the leader and the follower. A good example is Jack Ma, the founder of Alibaba, the giant e-commerce company and related businesses, considered by many to be one of the greatest Chinese entrepreneurs of all time, as well as a warm and friendly person. Yet some people consider him to be power-hungry and indifferent to the plight of the poor. When a charismatic leader has good ethics, the transformations will be beneficial to society.

A key characteristic of charismatic leaders is their *vision*. They offer a vision (or lofty goal) of where the organization is headed and how it can get there (a plan). A vision is multifaceted, extending beyond organizational goals. It also involves a way of identifying with the organization, aligning with the organization's actions and strategies, and even building a collective identity for the firm.[60] A sense of vision inspires employees to perform well. Charismatic leaders often use input from workers to craft their visions so that the vision will appear more realistic. As an example of a vision statement, here is the one from Caterpillar:

> Our vision is a world in which all people's basic needs—such as shelter, clean water sanitation, food, and reliable power—are fulfilled in an environmentally sustainable and a company that improves the quality of the environment and the communities in which we live.

A survey of 2,000 workers found that the most inspiring leaders are those who use their unique combinations of strengths, including charisma, to motivate individuals and teams to take on bold missions. Equally important, these leaders hold workers responsible for results.[61]

Charismatic leaders are *masterful communicators*. They formulate believable dreams and portray their vision of the future as the only path to follow. Charismatics also use metaphors to inspire people. An example is a favorite aphorism of Richard Marcus, the president of Neiman-Marcus stores: "If you follow in someone else's footsteps, you never get ahead." Another aspect of the communication style of charismatic leaders is that they inspire stakeholders with stories that tell an important message. (See Skill-Development Exercise 11-1.) Almost by definition, leaders perceived as charismatic by group members score high on *extraversion*.[62] Quite often leaders, as well as others, are labeled as charismatic because they are friendly and outgoing.

Glaxo CEO Emma Walmsley Shakes Up the Organization to Spur Growth

Emma Walmsley is the chief executive officer of GlaxoSmithKline (also referred to as Glaxo or GSK), the largest drugmaker in the United Kingdom, a position she has held since April 2017. Prior to becoming CEO, Walmsley was the CEO of GSK Consumer Healthcare. She joined GSK in 2010 as head of Consumer Healthcare, Europe. Before joining GSK, she worked for the beauty products firm L'Oréal for 17 years, where she occupied a variety of general management roles in Paris, London, and New York.

Walmsley's elevation to CEO underlined Glaxo's shift to higher-volume, lower-margin drugstore staples, including toothpaste and painkillers. Although Walmsley lacked direct pharmaceutical experience, her knowledge of consumer-focused products fit Glaxo's shifting emphasis on product mix. A key investor said this about Walmsley's appointment as CEO: "The positive is anybody coming from the outside of pharmaceuticals brings a fresh set of eyes." Walmsley's consumer expertise fit Glaxo's strategic shift to focus on consumer health-care products and vaccines.

Soon after being appointed CEO, Walmsley began her change initiatives. She recruited from the outside a new head of pharmaceuticals and a new chief scientific officer. She then replaced 50 top managers, or 40 percent of Glaxo's top management team. Walmsley attracted new executives from some of the world's leading companies, including Google and Novartis. She said she wanted to bring new ideas and skills and increase diversity within the team.

During a CNBC interview, Walmsley said, "Beyond the operational execution short-term, it's going to be all about R&D [research and development] and preparing for the next wave of growth for GSK in the 2020s and beyond." Walmsley reasoned that Glaxo had spread itself too broadly, yet she also wanted to concentrate on a handful of new pharmaceuticals. As a consequence of this planning, Walmsley canceled 30 drug-development programs and invested 80 percent of GSK's research dollars in therapies to treat respiratory disorders, HIV, infectious disease, cancer, and inflammatory disease.

While Walmsley was CEO of Consumer Healthcare at the company, her colleagues were reported to have described her as a strong and dynamic leader who combines a personable style with a steely focus. She was known to set clear objectives and pay close attention to meeting key performance indicators (KPIs). Walmsley was also observed as focusing heavily on talent development, but it was also noted that she can be ruthless with underperformers.

Walmsley obtained a Master of Arts in classic and modern languages from Oxford University.

QUESTIONS

1. In what way is Emma Walmsley a transformational leader?

2. How surprising is it that a CEO who holds a master's degree in classic and modern languages would make such harsh changes as firing 50 executives and dumping 30 drug-development programs?

Source: Original story based on facts and observations in the following sources: James Paton, "Glaxo CEO Replaced 50 Top Managers in Shakeup to Spur Growth," *Bloomberg* (www.bloomberg.com), January 8, 2018, pp. 1–2; Arlene Weintraub, "GlaxoSmithKline CEO Reshuffles 40% of Management Team in Bid to Bring in New Ideas," *Pharma* (www.fiercepharma.com), January 9, 2018, pp. 1–3; Denise Rolard and Joann S. Lublin, "Glaxo Taps Consumer Chief," *The Wall Street Journal*, September 21, 2016, p. B1; "Emma Walmsley, CEO GlaxoSmithKline," www.gsk.com; "Profile: Emma Walmsley, GSK's New Chief Executive," *Financial Times*, September 2016.

Charismatic leaders at their best *inspire trust*. Quite often their followers are willing to gamble with their careers to follow their chief's vision, such as accepting a low starting salary with stock options based on the start-up's vision of great success. Charismatic leaders are *energetic* and use an action-oriented leadership style. They exude energy, serving as a model for getting things done well and on time.

Charismatic leaders are adept at *managing their impression well*, which helps them to be perceived as charismatic.[63] Impression management can take place at the physical level, such as an appealing appearance, yet can also take place at an intellectual level. An intellectual example would be a person indicating he or she has powerful contacts, such as by saying, "Mark Zuckerberg and I were discussing the future of social media just last week."

Being at the center of an advice network (refers to leaders who are socially active in terms of giving and receiving advice) helps a person to be perceived as charismatic, and this perception has been shown to enhance team performance.[64] The studies that reached this conclusion measured in-person interactions, yet social media networks might attain the same result.

Creating an Organizational Story with an Underlying Meaning

This exercise about organizational stories to communicate an underlying meaning proceeds in two stages, and involves a group in role-playing.

Stage 1: Visualize one of your favorite companies, with you being a highly placed manager in that company. Your job is to create a story that tells an important message about the company and its values. An example would be the story about how Mark Zuckerberg started the foundational concept for Facebook while still a college student. This story has helped communicate the idea that youthful curiosity is valued at Facebook. Your story may be just 1 or 2 minutes in length, but it should communicate a strong message.

Stage 2: Each manager/storyteller meets with four other classmates, who play the roles of new employees during a company orientation. All five members of the group will have their turn at being (a) a storyteller and (b) an employee going through the orientation. When you are the storyteller, communicate your story with passion and commitment. The four other employees can be as cooperative (gullible) or as skeptical as they would like.

After the role-playing is completed, think through whether, if the stories were true, they might have had an impact on how the people who heard the stories might have behaved in the organization.

Charisma has become a huge field of study in itself, with both positive and negative commentaries about its effectiveness. A recent meta-analysis on the subject found that charismatic leadership has many positive outcomes, including improved performance of individuals (including organizational citizenship; behavior), groups, and the organization.[65]

Charisma is not necessarily a mystical, inborn set of characteristics and behaviors. As Skill-Development Exercise 11-2 shows, charisma is an attainable skill if you have the discipline to practice the techniques the exercise outlines. Observe that several of the suggestions are geared toward impression management. Two studies conducted at the University of Lausanne demonstrated that business students can be taught to behave more charismatically. Charismatic behavior of the participants was measured by trained observers. The skills taught resembled a few of those described in Skill-Development Exercise 11-2.[66]

A major concern about the heavy emphasis on charisma for leadership is that too many CEOs are evil charismatics who win the support of thousands and then plunder the organization for personal gain.[67] Another potential problem is that when the charismatic leader is also highly narcissistic, he or she tends to abuse power and take advantage of followers.[68] As a backlash to relying so heavily on charismatic executives, major corporations in recent years have sought hard-working, ethical individuals as CEOs, even if they are less flamboyant. The ideal executive leader would be an ethical, hard-working, and charismatic person. One of many possible examples is Emma Walmsley of Glaxo.

Charisma helps influence subordinates.

Developing Your Leadership Potential

How to develop one's leadership potential is a subject almost without limits because so many personal attributes, types of information, behaviors, and experiences contribute to leadership effectiveness. Almost every topic in organizational behavior might contribute to a leader's effectiveness, such as understanding individual differences, teamwork, and organizational culture. A valuable piece of advice about developing your leadership potential is to recognize that self-development plays a major role. Here we mention in passing four major contributors to developing one's potential as a leader.

LEARNING OBJECTIVE 4
Understand several ways of developing your leadership potential.

Developing Charisma

Establishing the goal of becoming more charismatic is the starting point for developing charisma. In addition, you can then discipline yourself to develop some of the traits and characteristics described in the text. Here are a dozen suggestions for skill development:[69]

1. *Use visioning.* If you are the leader of an organizational unit, develop a dream about its future. Discuss your vision with others in the unit and your immediate superior.

2. *Make frequent use of metaphors.* Develop metaphors to inspire people around you. A commonly used one after a group has suffered a substantial setback is, "Like the phoenix, we will rise from the ashes of defeat."

3. *Inspire trust and confidence.* Make your deeds consistent with your promises. Get people to believe in your competence by making your accomplishments known in a polite, tactful way.

4. *Make others feel capable.* Give out assignments on which others can succeed, and lavishly praise their success.

5. *Be highly energetic and goal oriented.* Impress others with your energy and resourcefulness. To increase your energy level, exercise frequently, eat well, and get ample rest.

6. *Express your emotions frequently.* Freely express warmth, joy, happiness, and enthusiasm.

7. *Develop and display a sense of humor.* Appropriate use of humor helps build workplace relationships because people feel more comfortable with people who make them feel good, and humor often puts people in a good mood. Self-effacing humor is often effective, whereas humor that pokes fun at others is usually highly ineffective.

8. *Smile frequently, even if you are not in a happy mood.* A warm smile seems to indicate a confident, caring person, which contributes to a perception of charisma.

9. *Make everybody you meet feel that he or she is quite important.* For example, at a company meeting, shake the hand of every person you meet. Be generous in your recognition of the accomplishments of others.

10. *Focus on the positive.* Charismatic people are optimists who minimize complaints and emphasize what positive steps can be taken to overcome a problem.

11. *Maintain positive body language.* To radiate authenticity and confidence, stand and sit up straight, and make eye contact. When standing, keep your feet about 12 inches apart. When sitting, do not tap your feet nervously. Look polished and wrinkle-free. Use a low and clear voice tone.

12. *Lead by example.* A subtle part of being perceived as charismatic is to be a positive model for others, such as demonstrating how committed you are to the mission of the group, department, or organization.

A starting point in developing leadership potential is to *acquire a good education, both formal and informal.* Education includes schooling at all levels and regular acquisition of information. Both help develop critical-thinking skills and provide the knowledge needed to make decisions as a leader. Most leaders have knowledge, and when asked a question do not consistently respond, "Wait, I'll google it." Furthermore, to be creative, one needs to combine bits of knowledge. Leadership development programs sponsored by employers should be considered part of education. Thousands of possibilities exist, including both cognitive and experiential content. Two examples are "becoming a strategic thinker" and "helping counterproductive workers."

Broad experience is also a major contributor to the development of leadership potential because work experience in a variety of settings helps one develop a broad perspective. Supervising entry-level workers is an excellent starting point in a leadership career because it provides the opportunity to motivate and inspire workers who are not well paid and often lack many job skills. Another valuable aspect of experience is to model effective bosses, and not model ineffective bosses. Broad experience increases in value for leadership development if new assignments are more complex, such as being assigned the supervision of a department that is threatened with being eliminated.

Another experience-based way to develop one's leadership capability is to be *guided by a mentor.* A mentor often provides tutoring, coaching, guidance, and emotional sup-

My Leadership Journal

A potentially important aid in your development as a leader is to maintain a journal or diary of your experiences. Make a journal entry within 24 hours after you carried out a significant leadership action, or failed to do so when the opportunity arose. You therefore will have entries dealing with leadership opportunities both capitalized upon and missed. An example: "A few of my neighbors were complaining about all the vandalism in the neighborhood. Cars were getting dented and scratched, and lamplights were being smashed. A few bricks were thrown into home windows. I volunteered to organize a neighborhood patrol. The patrol actually helped cut back on the vandalism." Or, in contrast: "A few of my neighbors . . . windows. I thought to myself that someone else should take care of the problem. My time is too valuable."

Also include in your journal such entries as feedback you receive on your leadership ability, leadership traits you appear to be developing, and key leadership ideas you read about. Review your journal monthly and make note of any progress you think you have made in developing your leadership skills. Also consider preparing a graph of your leadership-skill development. The vertical axis can represent skill level on a 1 to 100 scale, and the horizontal axis might be divided into time intervals, such as calendar quarters.

port. Common practice today is to have several mentors, and also to be mentored online. For example, a text message, e-mail, or tweet from a mentor can provide quick guidance, such as, "I loved the way you closed that sale, but you need to make fewer errors in reporting the details of the sale to the home office."

The actions of a mentor point to another major way of developing leadership potential—*obtaining feedback on your performance*. Feedback can come from a boss, a mentor, a coworker, a customer, or subordinate. Not all feedback can be taken seriously, but when there is consistency in feedback from several people, it might serve as a call to action. For example, if three different people told you that you are too laid back in meetings, it might be time to become a more active participant during meetings. Many organizations offer the opportunity for managers, as well as other workers, to obtain 360-degree feedback. Such feedback is an assessment based on data collected from colleagues, subordinates, and clients. The feedback helps illuminate how well workers are performing and which behaviors individuals might change to be more effective leaders and have a more productive workplace.[70]

Skill-Development Exercise 11-3 will give you the opportunity now and in the future to further develop your leadership skills.

Implications for Managerial Practice

1. Technically competent and well-motivated employees require less guidance and control than do their less competent and poorly motivated counterparts.
2. Exhibiting charisma can benefit the vast majority of leaders. Although charisma is somewhat dependent on long-standing personality characteristics, it can be enhanced through such means as suggested in Skill-Development Exercise 11-2 on page 256.
3. Although the modern organization emphasizes team-oriented, collaborative leadership, organizations still need decisive, creative, and independent-thinking leaders.
4. A fruitful approach to choosing an effective leadership theory, model, or explanation is for the manager to carefully diagnose the situation. Choose a leadership approach that best fits the deficiency or neglected opportunity in a given situation. Observe the people to be led, and also interview them about their interests, goals, and concerns. Then apply a leadership approach that appears to match the interests, concerns, deficits, or missed opportunities. The following example will help clarify this diagnostic approach:

A manager observes that the group is accomplishing its job, and morale is satisfactory. Yet something is missing; a sense of urgency and excitement does not pervade the atmosphere. In this situation, the leader is advised to take the steps in his or her power to behave like a transformational and charismatic leader.

5. Be skeptical about simplistic approaches to understanding leadership that point to one concept as the "secret to effective leadership" or "the one trait that defines leadership." Instead, use the approach just described in point 4.

Summary of Key Points

1. *Describe key leadership traits, styles, and behaviors.* Certain traits and characteristics contribute to leadership effectiveness in many situations. These personal attributes fall into the general categories of cognitive skills and personality characteristics, including emotional intelligence. Self-awareness, self-confidence, proactivity, trustworthiness, and good problem-solving ability are examples of key traits.

    A foundational concept of the behavioral approach to leadership includes the two dimensions of initiating structure and consideration. Similarly, production-centered and employee-centered leadership include the same. Mindfulness is another key leadership behavior.

2. *Explain the basics of three different contingency theories of leadership.* Fiedler's contingency theory specifies the conditions under which leaders need to use task-motivated and relationship-motivated styles. In situations of high control and low control, the task-motivated style is better. Relationship-motivated leaders have the highest-producing groups under situations of moderate control. The leader–member exchange model emphasizes that leaders have unique relationships with group members. In-group members

have good relationships with the leader, whereas out-group members have poor relationships. Being part of the in-group enhances productivity and satisfaction.

Suggestions for effective crisis leadership include (a) provide directive leadership, (b) project self-confidence and trustworthiness, (c) exert emotional intelligence, (d) engage in sensemaking, (e) lead with compassion, and (f) divide major problems into smaller chunks.

3. *Present an overview of transformational and charismatic leadership.* The transformational leader is a charismatic person who helps bring about profound changes in people and the organization, often transforming the culture. Charismatic leaders are known to have vision, be masterful communicators, and inspire trust. They are also adept at managing their impression well. Charisma can be developed to some extent.

4. *Understand several ways of developing your leadership potential.* Leadership potential can be developed in many ways, including studying organizational behavior. Four approaches to leadership development are: acquiring formal and informal education, obtaining broad experience, being mentored, and obtaining feedback on your performance.

Key Terms and Phrases

leadership, p. 237

cognitive skills, p. 238

self-awareness, p. 238

proactive personality, p. 240

behavioral approach to leadership, p. 243

leadership style, p. 243

initiating structure, p. 245

consideration, p. 245

servant leader, p. 246

mindfulness, p. 247

contingency theory of leadership, p. 248

situational control, p. 248

leader–member exchange (LMX) model, p. 249

crisis leadership, p. 251

transformational leader, p. 252

charisma, p. 252

Discussion Questions and Activities

1. Describe how a person might be a good leader but a poor manager.
2. With shared leadership, teamwork, and group decision making being so popular, why bother attempting to become a charismatic and highly intelligent leader?
3. What would a manager of yours have to do before you considered him or her to be trustworthy?

4. Provide an example of how being proactive helps a leader be successful, based on your personal observations or an incident from the news, a movie, or a television show.
5. Assuming you believe that the leader–member exchange theory is valid, how would you go about becoming part of a leader's in-group?

6. What would be an example of a crisis a leader might have to deal with at the first level in an organization, such as a department or team?
7. In your opinion, how charismatic is the president of the United States? What is the basis for your conclusion?
8. Describe a scenario in which a team leader or first-level supervisor can be a transformational leader.
9. Assume that you have a 6-year-old in the family. Based on what you have studied in this chapter about leadership, how do you think you could help that child become a leader in later life?
10. Identify several ways in which being a college graduate enhances a person's chances of becoming a leader in business, in the nonprofit sector, or in public life.

CASE PROBLEM: Division President Dennis Individualizes His Approach to Team Members

Dennis is the president of the kitchen and bathroom supplies division of a manufacturing company. His division manufactures and sells to retailers and wholesalers such items as sinks, refrigerators, ovens, ranges, bathtubs, showers, toilets, and associated plumbing. The company products are sold through home supplies stores, department stores, and large hardware stores, as well as directly to consumers online.

One day Dennis was discussing how well he was performing as a leader with Kristen, the vice president of human resources. Kristen said, "We will review some of the multirater feedback with you. It appears to be consistent with some of the informal comments I have heard about your leadership as the division president. Your top-management team likes the strong leadership you bring to the division, but they think you play favorites."

"What do you mean by that?" said Dennis.

Kristen replied, "I want to show you some of the written comments on the anonymous forms completed online. You will most likely find it helps explain the comments about you playing favorites.

"Manager A says that you are a kind and caring leader who always takes her needs into account. When she needed time off to take care of a parent who was moving to a nursing home, you gave her three days off with pay. When she wanted some experience with analytics, you found the right project for her.

"Manager B says that you can be harsh and indifferent. One time he told you that if you could hire one more online sales support representative, he could boost sales by 10 percent. He said that you flatly rejected his request, saying there was no money in the budget for an additional hire.

"Manager C says that you talk too much in meetings, both face-to-face and virtual meetings, about our director of marketing. You talk as if that person were single-handedly responsible for the success of our division.

"Manager D says that you practically ignore her. If she tries to tell you something funny, you don't even smile. She thinks that you are a good strategic leader but that you act like a zombie toward her."

Dennis said to Kristen, "It's good to know that I am viewed as an effective leader. Yet I find some of this feedback troubling. I thought that an effective leader was supposed to have different relationships with different subordinates. How else can you deal with the reality that each subordinate is different?"

Case Questions

1. In what way does this case illustrate the LMX model of leadership?
2. To what extent do you think the feedback presented by the members of the top-management team will help Dennis hone his leadership style?
3. If Dennis does not want to be perceived as playing favorites, what should he do differently in his leadership approach?

Endnotes

1. Original story created from facts and observations in the following sources: Adam Lashinsky, "Benioff in Bloom," *Fortune*, November 1, 2017, pp. 64–72; Alexa, Schirtzinger, "7 Lessons from Salesforce CEO Marc Benioff, the Decade's Top Innovator," www.salesfroce.com/blog, pp. 1–2; Rachel King, "Salesforce's Ambitions Face Test," *The Wall Street Journal*, December 10, 2016, p. B1; Alex Konrad, "Nonstop Benioff," *Forbes*, September 13, 2016, pp. 84, 88–98.

2. Thomas Bartz and Patrick Barwise, "Why Effective Leaders Must Manage Up, Down, and Sideways," McKinsey & Company (www.mckinsey.com), April 2017, pp. 1–6.

3. W. Chan Kim and Renee A. Mauborgne, "Parables of Leadership," *Harvard Business Review*, July–August 1992, p. 123.

4. John P. Kotter, "What Leaders Really Do," *Harvard Business Review*, May–June 1990, pp. 103–11; John O'Leary, "Do Managers and Leaders Really Do Different Things?" *Harvard Business Review*, June 20, 2016, pp. 1–6.

5. "Duke University Executive Leadership Survey," March 2009, p. 2.

6. Shelly A. Kirkpatrick and Edwin A. Locke, "Leadership: Do Traits Matter?" *Academy of Management Executive*, May

1991, pp. 48–60; Edwin A. Locke and Associates, *The Essence of Leadership: The Four Keys to Leading Successfully* (New York: Lexington/ Macmillan, 1991), pp. 13–34.

7. John Antonakis, David W. Day, and Birgit Schyns, "Leadership and Individual Differences: At the Cusp of a Renaissance," *The Leadership Quarterly*, August 2012, p. 647.

8. Timothy A. Judge, Amy E. Colbert, and Remus Ilies, "Intelligence and Leadership: A Quantitative Review and Test of Theoretical Propositions," *Journal of Applied Psychology*, June 2004, p. 548.

9. John Antonakis, Robert J. House, and Dean Keith Simonton, "Can Super Smart Leaders Suffer from Too Much of a Good Thing?" *Journal of Applied Psychology*, July 2017, pp. 1003–1021.

10. Saabira Chaudhuri, "Nestlé Turns to New CEO for Health Push," *The Wall Street Journal*, January 3, 2017, p. B3.

11. "Are You a Self-aware Leader?" *Knowledge@Wharton* (interview with Tasha Eurich) (http://knowledge.wharton.upenn.edu), June 14, 2017, p. 2.

12. George P. Hollenbeck and Douglas T. Hall, "Self-Confidence and Leadership Performance," *Organizational Dynamics*, Issue 3, 2004, p. 259.

13. "What Is Courage?" (Interview with Warren Bennis), *Fast Company*, September 2004, p. 99.

14. Bradley P. Owens, Angela S. Wallace, and David A. Waldman, "Leader Narcissism and Follower Outcomes: The Counterbalancing Effect of Leader Humility," *Journal of Applied Psychology*, July 2015, p. 1201.

15. Thomas S. Bateman and J. Michael Grant, "The Proactive Component of Organizational Behavior: A Measure and Correlates," *Journal of Organizational Behavior*, March 1993, p. 103; Antonakis, Day, and Schyns, "Leadership and Individual Differences," p. 645.

16. Craig D. Crossley, Cecily D. Cooper, and Tara S. Wernsing, "Making Things Happen through Challenging Goals: Leader Proactivity Trust, and Business-Unit Performance," *Journal of Applied Psychology*, May 2013, pp. 540–549.

17. Quoted in Geoff Colvin, "Ignore These Leadership Lessons at Your Peril," *Fortune*, October 20, 2013, p. 85.

18. Douglas R. May, Adrian Y. L. Chan, Timothy D. Hodges, and Bruce J. Avolio, "Developing the Moral Component of Authentic Leadership," *Organizational Dynamics*, Number 3, 2003, p. 248.

19. Rob Goffee and Gareth Jones, "Managing Authenticity: The Paradox of Great Leadership," *Harvard Business Review*, December 2005, pp. 86–94.

20. Crossley, Cooper, and Wernsing, "Making Things Happen through Challenging Goals: Leader Proactivity Trust, and Business-Unit Performance," p. 545.

21. Matthias Weiss, Stefan Razinskas, Julia Backmann, and Martin Hagel, "Authentic Leadership and Leaders' Well-Being: An Experience Sampling Study," *The Leadership Quarterly*, April 2018, pp. 209–231.

22. Travis Bradberry, "Is Emotional Intelligence a Good Measure of Leadership Ability?" *HR Magazine*, November 2015, p. 22.

23. Daniel Goleman, "Leadership That Gets Results," *Harvard Business Review*, March–April 2000, p. 80; Gabrielle Wirth and Gary Gansle, "Jump toward Emotional Intelligence," *HR Magazine*, October 2012, p. 87.

24. Prudy Gourguechon, "Empathy Is an Essential Leadership Skill—And There's Nothing Soft about It," *Forbes* (www.forbes.com), December 26, 2017, pp. 1–3.

25. Quoted in Shari Caudron, "Where Have All the Leaders Gone?" *Workforce*, December 2002, p. 31.

26. Sydney Finkelstein, "Why You Don't Want a Nice Boss," BBC (www.bbc.com), August 26, 2016, p. 2.

27. The concepts of initiating structure and consideration stem from Ralph M. Stogdill and Alvin E. Coons (eds.), *Leader Behavior: Its Description and Measurement* (Columbus: Ohio State University Bureau of Business Research, 1957); Carroll L. Shartle, *Executive Performance and Leadership* (Upper Saddle River, NJ: Prentice-Hall, 1956).

28. Arnold S. Tannenbaum, *Social Psychology of the Work Organization* (Monterey, CA: Wadsworth, 1966), p. 74; Robert Dubin, "Supervision and Productivity: Empirical Findings and Theoretical Considerations," in Walter Nord (ed.), *Concepts and Controversies in Organizational Behavior* (Glenview, IL: Scott, Foresman and Company, 1972), pp. 524–525.

29. Timothy A. Judge, Ronald F. Piccolo, and Remus Ilies, "The Forgotten Ones? The Validity of Consideration and Initiating Structure in Leadership Research," *Journal of Applied Psychology*, February 2004, pp. 36–51.

30. Lisa Schurer et al., "Forgotten Not Gone: An Examination of Fit between Leader Consideration and Initiating Structure Needed and Received," *Journal of Applied Psychology*, September 2012, pp. 913–930.

31. Marcus Buckingham, "What Great Managers Do," *Harvard Business Review*, March 2005, pp. 70–79.

32. The persuasion reference is "6 Humble Traits of Servant Leaders," *Executive Leadership*, June 2013, p. 8.

33. Robert K. Greenleaf, *The Power of Servant Leadership* (San Francisco: Berrett-Koehler, 1998); James C. Hunter, *The World's Most Powerful Leadership Principle: How to Become a Servant Leader* (New York: Crown Business, 2004).

34. Suzanne J. Peterson, Benjamin M. Galvin, and Donald Lange, "CEO Servant Leadership: Exploring Executive Characteristics and Firm Performance," *Personnel Psychology*, Number 3, 2012, pp. 569–596.

35. Emily M. Hunter et al., "Servant Leaders Inspire Servant Followers: Antecedents and Outcomes for Employees and the Organization," *The Leadership Quarterly*, April 2013, pp. 316–331.

36. Myriam Chiniara and Kathleen Bentein, "Linking Servant Leadership to Individual Performance: Differentiating the Mediating Role of Autonomy, Competence and Relatedness Need Satisfaction," *The Leadership Quarterly*, February 2016, pp. 124–141.

37. Ute R. Hülsheger, "Benefits of Mindfulness at Work: The Role of Mindfulness in Emotion Regulation, Emotional Exhaustion, and Job Satisfaction," *Journal of Applied Psychology*, March 2013, p. 310.

38. Daniel Goleman, "Here's What Mindfulness Is (and Isn't) Good For," *Harvard Business Review*, September 28, 2017, pp. 1–6; Manish Chopra, "Want to Be a Better Leader? Observe More and React Less," *McKinsey Quarterly* (www.mckinsey.com), February 2016, pp. 1–6; Christy Cassia, "The Truly Mindful Workplace: A Reality Whose Moment Is Arriving," UCSD Center for Mindfulness (http://ucsdefm), December 11, 2012, pp. 1–4: Erika Garms, "Practicing Mindful Leadership," www.td.org, March 08, 2013, pp. 1–5.

39. Gary Yukl and Richard Lepsinger, *Flexible Leadership: Creating Value by Balancing Multiple Challenges and Choices* (San Francisco: Jossey-Bass, 2004).

40. Fred E. Fiedler, Martin M. Chemers, and Linda Mahar, *Improving Leadership Effectiveness: The Leader-Match Concept*, 2nd ed. (New York: John Wiley & Sons, 1984); Martin M. Chemers, *An Integrative Theory of Leadership* (Mahwah, NJ: Lawrence Erlbaum Associates, 1997), pp. 28–38.

41. George Graen and J. F. Cashman, "A Role-Making Model of Leadership in Formal Organizations: A Developmental Approach," in J. G. Hunt and L. I. Larson (eds.), *Leadership Frontiers* (Kent, OH: Kent State University Press, 1975), pp. 143–165; Robert P. Vecchio, "Leader–Member Exchange, Objective Performance, Employment Duration, and Supervisor Ratings: Testing for Moderation and Mediation," *Journal of Business and Psychology*, Spring 1998, pp. 327–341.

42. Robert P. Vecchio, "Are You In or OUT with Your Boss?" *Business Horizons*, vol. 29, 1987, pp. 76–78.

43. Vecchio, "Leader-Member Exchange," p. 340.

44. K. Michele Kacmar, L. A. Witt, Suzanne Zivnuska, and Stanley M. Gulley, "The Interactive Effect of Leader–Member Exchange and Communication Frequency on Performance Ratings," *Journal of Applied Psychology*, August 2003, pp. 764–772.

45. Alex Ning Li and Hui Liao, "How Do Leader–Member Exchange Quality and Differentiation Affect Performance in Teams? An Integrated Multilevel Dual Process Model," *Journal of Applied Psychology*, September 2014, pp. 847–866.

46. Sumita Raghuram, Ravi Shanker Gajendran, Xiangmin Liu, and Deepak Somaya, "Boundaryless LMX: Examining LMX's Impact on External Career Outcomes and Alumni Goodwill," *Personnel Psychology*, No. 2, 2017, pp. 399–428.

47. Robin Martin, et al., "Leader-Member Exchange (LMX) and Performance: A Meta-Analytic Review," *Personnel Psychology*, No. 1, 2016, pp. 67–121.

48. Several of the ideas here are based on Andrew J. DuBrin, "Personal Attitudes and Behaviors of Effective Crisis Leaders," in Andrew J. DuBrin (ed.), *Handbook of Research on Crisis Leadership in Organizations* (Cheltenham, UK: Edward Elgar, 2013), pp. 1–19.

49. "What Is Courage?" (interview with Warren Bennis), *Fast Company*, September 2004, p. 99.

50. Galit Meisler, Era Vigoda-Gadot, and Amos Drory, "Leadership beyond Rationality: Emotional Leadership in Times of Organizational Crisis," in Andrew J. DuBrin (ed.), *Handbook of Research on Crisis Leadership in Organizations* (Northampton, MA: Edward Elgar, 2013), pp. 127–148.

51. Ian A. Combe and David J. Carrington, "Leaders' Sensemaking under Crises: Emerging Cognitive Consensus over Time with Management Teams," *The Leadership Quarterly*, June 2015, p. 207.

52. "Leadership," in *Business: The Ultimate Resource Business* (Cambridge, MA: Perseus Books Group, 2002), p. 916; James McGregor Burns, *Leadership* (New York: Harper & Row, 1978).

53. Marshall Sashkin and Molly G. Sashkin, *Leadership That Matters* (San Francisco: Berrett-Koehler, 2003).

54. Scott Anthony and Evan I. Schwartz, "What the Best Transformational Leaders Do," *Harvard Business Review*, May 8, 2017, p. 7.

55. John J. Hater and Bernard M. Bass, "Supervisors' Evaluations and Subordinates' Perceptions of Transformational and Transactional Leadership," *Journal of Applied Psychology*, November 1988, p. 695; Noel M. Tichy and Mary Anne Devanna, *The Transformational Leader* (New York: Wiley, 1990).

56. Hui Wang, Kenneth S. Law, Rick D. Hackett, Duanxu Wang, and Zhen Xiong Chen, "Leader–Member Exchange as Mediator of the Relationship between Transformational Leadership and Followers' Performance and Organizational Citizenship Behavior," *Academy of Management Journal*, June 2005, p. 430.

57. Sirkwoo Jin, Myeong-Gu Seo, and Debra L. Shapiro, "Do Happy Leaders Lead Better? Affective and Attitudinal Antecedents of Transformational Leadership," *The Leadership Quarterly*, February 2016, pp. 64–84.

58. Alexandra Wolfe, "Marc Lore: Wal-Mart's U.S. e-Commerce Chief Looks to the Future of Shipping," *The Wall Street Journal*, January 27–28, 2018, p. C11.

59. Flavia Cavazotte, Valter Moreneo, and Meteus Hickman, "Effects of Leader Intelligence, Personality and Emotional Intelligence on Transformational Leadership and Managerial Performance," *The Leadership Quarterly*, June 2012, pp. 433–455.

60. Jay A. Conger and Rabindra N. Kanungo, *Charismatic Leadership in Organizations* (Thousand Oaks, CA: Sage, 1998).

61. Eric Garton, "How to Be an Inspiring Leader," *Harvard Business Review*, April 25, 2017, p. 2.

62. Joyce E. Bono and Timothy A. Judge, "Personality and Transformational and Transactional Leadership: A Meta-Analysis," *Journal of Applied Psychology*, October 2004, pp. 901–910.

63. William L. Gardner and Bruce J. Avolio, "The Charismatic Relationship: A Dramaturgical Perspective," *Academy of Management Review*, January 1998, p. 33.

64. Prasad Balkundi, Martin Kilduff, and David A. Harrison, "Centrality and Charisma: Conquering How Leader Networks *and* Attributions Affect Team Performance," *Journal of Applied Psychology*, November 2011, pp. 1209–1222.

65. George C. Banks, et al., "A Meta-Analytic Review and Future Research Agenda of Charismatic Leadership," *The Leadership Quarterly*, August 2017, pp. 508–529.

66. John Antonakis, Marika Fenley, and Suie Liechti, "Can Charisma Be Taught? Tests of Two Interventions," *Academy of Management Learning and Education*, September 2011, pp. 374–396; Antonakis, Fenley, and Liechti, "Learning Charisma," *Harvard Business Review*, June 2012, pp. 127–130.

67. Rakesh Khurana, *Searching for a Corporate Savior* (Princeton, NJ: Princeton University Press, 2002).

68. Margarita Mayo, "If Humble People Make the Best Leaders, Why Do We Fall for Charismatic Narcissists?" *Harvard Business Review*, April 7, 2017, p. 3; Emily Grijalva et al., "Narcissism and Leadership: A Meta-Analytic Review of Linear and Nonlinear Relationships," *Personnel Psychology*, No. 1, 2015, pp. 1–47.

67. Several of the suggestions are from Roger Dawson, *Secrets of Power Persuasion: Everything You'll Need to Get Anything You'll Ever Want* (Upper Saddle River, NJ: Prentice Hall, 1992), pp. 179–194: Robert A. Eckert, "The Two Most Important Words," *Harvard Business Review*, April 2013, p. 3; "Life's Work: Lorne Michaels," *Harvard Business Review*, September 2013, p. 144; Elizabeth Holmes, "The Charisma Boot Camp," *The Wall Street Journal*, August 6, 2014, p. D1.

70. Harriet Edleson, "Do 360 Evaluations Work?" *Monitor on Psychology*, November 2012, p. 59.

Power, Politics, and Influence

El Nariz/Shutterstock.com

Chapter Outline

Learning Objectives

After reading and studying this chapter and doing the exercises, you should be able to:

1. Identify sources of power for individuals and subunits within organizations.

2. Describe the essence of empowerment.

3. Pinpoint factors contributing to, and examples of, organizational politics.

4. Differentiate between the ethical and unethical use of power, politics, and influence.

5. Identify and describe a variety of influence tactics.

6. Explain how managers can control dysfunctional politics.

Satya Nadella became the third chief executive officer (CEO) in the history of Microsoft Corp. in 2014. His previous position with the company was executive vice president (EVP) of the cloud and enterprise group. He had been with the company for 22 years, beginning as an electrical engineer. Nadella has steered the company away from a mobile strategy that was not going as well as planned, instead focusing on other segments, including cloud computing and artificial intelligence (AI). During Nadella's first four years with Microsoft, the company's market value increased 130 percent. In 2018, he was included in *Time* magazine's 100 most influential people in the world list.

Nadella began his CEO position by establishing a new mission and vision for Microsoft. His primary focus was to make the company more innovative because the company was losing some of its dominance in software for business and personal use. A new mission and vision were also needed because, throughout the industry, software as a product was being replaced by software as a service. Many companies now run their information technology (IT) infrastructure on cloud-based services.

Nadella's record of accomplishment as CEO of Microsoft has been widely lauded. Under his leadership, Microsoft has reversed its fortune and returned to being a growth stock after being stagnant for nearly a decade. Nadella has turned long-entrenched competitors such as Apple and Google into partners, an approach that appears to be paying off.

Nadella says that he tries to avoid the hubris that can damage companies and people. Yet he does believe in having confidence, as long as he understands the line between self-confidence and having the ability to learn. In addition to having confidence, Nadella believes that a CEO must have empathy. In Nadella's view, empathy is, among other things, a key source of business innovation because innovation stems from one's ability to grasp customers' unmet, unarticulated needs.

Nadella's vision has helped inspire Microsoft's work with AI, holograms, and virtual reality for various professional fields. On the medical front, InnerEye is an AI product intended to help doctors efficiently demarcate cancerous tumors, a process that is notoriously lengthy and difficult to perform manually. HoloLens is a holographic headset that enables virtual and augmented reality experiences. Boeing is using this device to train engineers and to improve information-gathering processes for pilots fighting wildfires. Nadella fundamentally believes that AI can empower humans to do and achieve more.

One aspect the culture shift has focused on is changing Microsoft from a "know-it-all" to a "learn-it-all" company. Nadella observed that when a company has enjoyed great success and has invented many crucial concepts, it has a temptation to believe it has mastered everything. That temptation needs to be resisted. "We aren't trying to be the cool kid or the cool company," said Nadella. "Our sole purpose is to build technology so that others can create more technology."

Nadella received a bachelor's degree in electrical engineering from the Manipal Institute of Technology (India), an MS degree in computer science for the University of Wisconsin–Milwaukee, and an MBA from the University of Chicago, Booth School of Business.[1]

This story about the CEO of a dominant IT company illustrates how influential and powerful a business executive can be in terms of impact on the organization and outside world. A hidden message is that it takes political skill to rise to the top of an organization with so many talented people.

Power, politics, and influence are such major parts of the workplace that they have become standard topics of organizational behavior. In this chapter, we approach power, politics, and influence from multiple perspectives. We describe the meaning of these concepts, how power is obtained, and how it is shared (empowerment). We examine why organizational politics is so prevalent, and then describe the tactics of politics and influence. In addition, we describe the control of dysfunctional politics, and ethical considerations about the use of power, politics, and influence. As you read the chapter, you will learn that some tactics of power, politics, and influence violate ethical codes and therefore should be avoided.

The Meaning of Power, Politics, and Influence

A challenge in understanding power, politics, and influence in organizations is that the terms appear close in meaning. Here we present meanings of these terms aimed at providing useful distinctions. **Power** is the potential or ability to influence decisions and control resources. The predominant view of power is that it is the influence over others' actions, thoughts, and outcomes.[2] Realize that, like gravity, power cannot be observed directly. Yet you can observe its effects, such as when the corporate name is used as a verb.[3] For example, "Have you 'googled' that job applicant yet?" Or, "Have you 'Scotch Taped' the envelope?"

Many definitions of *power* center on the ability of a person to overcome resistance in achieving a result. Some researchers suggest that power lies in the potential, while others focus on use.[4] As a hedge, our definition includes both potential and use. If you have a powerful battery in your car, isn't it still powerful whether or not it is in use?

Politics is a way of achieving power. As used here, **organizational politics** refers to informal approaches to gaining power through means other than merit or luck. In recent years, scholars have recognized that being skilled in organizational politics is a positive force for individuals and can help the organization. **Political skill** is a combination of social astuteness with the capacity to adjust and adapt behavior to different situational demands. As a result, the person with political skill inspires trust and support, controls and influences the responses of others, and appears genuine and sincere.[5]

Influence is close in meaning to *power*. *Influence* is also the ability to change behavior, but it tends to be more subtle and indirect than *power*. *Power* indicates the ability to affect outcomes with greater facility and ease than *influence*.[6] A person who has political skill is able to use influence behaviors in organizations, such as building strong relationships with key people.

Managers and professionals often need to use political tactics to achieve the power and influence they need to accomplish their work. An example would be a human resources manager cultivating the support of a top executive so he or she can proceed with a program of employee wellness. Cultivating support is a political tactic.

power The potential or ability to influence decisions and control resources.

organizational politics Informal approaches to gaining power through means other than merit or luck.

political skill A combination of social astuteness with the capacity to adjust and adapt behavior to different situational demands.

Sources of Individual and Subunit Power

An encouraging note about the study of power is that the basic ideas behind power have remained stable over time, no matter how much technological change takes place. Part of the reason, explains Jeffrey Pfeffer, is that the use of power can be linked to survival advantages. For example, most people have a self-enhancement motive, and they have a desire to be identified and associated with success and winners.[7]

The sources or bases of power in organizations can be classified in different ways. A useful starting point is to recognize that power can be used to forward either the interests of the organization or personal interests. **Socialized power** is the use of power to achieve constructive ends. An example would be the manager who attempted to gain power to spearhead a program of employee wellness. **Personalized power** is the use of power primarily for the sake of personal aggrandizement and gain.[8] An example would be a new CEO using his power to insist that company headquarters be moved to a location near his home or that his family members be allowed to use a company jet.

Here we classify the sources (and also the bases and origins) of power that stem from the organization, from the individual, and from providing resources.[9]

LEARNING OBJECTIVE 1 Identify sources of power for individuals and subunits within organizations.

socialized power The use of power to achieve constructive ends.

personalized power The use of power primarily for the sake of personal aggrandizement and gain.

Power Granted by the Organization (Position Power)

Managers and professionals often have power because of the authority, or right, granted by their positions. The power of a manager's position stems from three sources: legitimate power, coercive power, and reward power. **Legitimate power** is based on the manager's

legitimate power Power based on one's formal position within the hierarchy of the organization.

Your appearance can contribute to your personal power.

coercive power Controlling others through fear or threat of punishment.

reward power Controlling others through rewards or the promise of rewards.

expert power The ability to influence others because of one's specialized knowledge, skills, or abilities.

referent power The ability to influence others that stems from one's desirable traits and characteristics; it is the basis for charisma.

formal position within the hierarchy. A government agency head, for example, has much more position power than a unit supervisor in the same agency. Managers can enhance their position power by formulating policies and procedures. For example, a manager might establish a requirement that he or she must approve all new hires, thus exercising authority over hiring.

Founding a company grants considerable power to the individual because it is expected that he or she "call all the shots." Steve Blank, a specialist in high-tech startups, points out the founders often have so much power that it can lead to abuse.[10] For example, the founder might demand personal favors from employees or allocate too much company revenue for personal use, such as exotic family vacations.

Coercive power comes from controlling others through fear or threat of punishment. Typical organizational punishments include bypassing an employee for promotion, terminating employment, and giving damaging performance evaluations to people who do not support initiatives, even if the initiatives are unethical or illegal. The threat of a lawsuit by an employee who is treated unjustly serves as a constraint on legitimate power and is referred to as *subordinate power*. Another source of power for employees stems from being a shareholder, such as an employee who owns company stock criticizing the CEO during a shareholder meeting and being listened to.[11] **Reward power** involves controlling others through rewards or the promise of rewards. Examples of this include promotions, challenging assignments, and recognition given to employees.

The effectiveness of coercive power and reward power depends on the perceptions and needs of group members. For coercive power to be effective, the employee must fear punishment and care about being a member of the firm. Conversely, an employee who does not care much for recognition or power would not be strongly influenced by the prospect of a promotion.

Power Stemming from the Individual (Personal Power)

Managers and other categories of workers also derive power from two separate personal characteristics: knowledge and personality. **Expert power** is the ability to influence others because of one's specialized knowledge, skills, or abilities. For expertise to be an effective source of power, group members must respect that expertise.

Exercising expert power is the logical starting point for building one's power base. Powerful people in business, government, and education almost invariably launched their careers by developing expertise in a specialty of value to their employers. Furthermore, expert power keeps a person in demand for executive positions. A representative example is Hugo Barra, who was the vice president of Android product management at Google Inc. when he left the company for a Chinese smartphone maker, Xiaomi. After successfully expanding Xiaomi's reach beyond China, four years later, Barra moved back to Silicon Valley to embark on a new venture, unnamed at the time. Barra began at Google after the company bought the voice-recognition company Nuance Communications Inc. Barra launched his career as a software engineer and has been an in-demand manager since early in his career.[12]

Referent power is the ability to influence others that stems from one's desirable traits and characteristics. It is based on the desire of others to be led by or to identify with an inspiring person. Having referent power contributes to a perception of being charismatic, but expert power also makes a contribution. For example, being perceived as highly creative contributes to a person's charisma.

Expert power is a key source of power.

Power from Providing Resources

Another way of understanding the sources of power is through the **resource dependence** perspective. According to this perspective, the organization requires a continuing flow of human resources, money, customers, technological inputs, and material to continue to function. Subunits or individuals within the organization who can provide these resources derive power from this ability.[13]

A variation on power from providing resources is the derivation of power from gossip, which is an important resource in many organizations. Most people know that an influential member of the grapevine can accrue a small degree of power, and a scientific analysis supports this idea. The authors of the analysis define *gossip* as "informal and evaluative talk in an organization, usually among no more than a few individuals, about another member of that organization who is not present."[14] According to the model developed, a supplier of gossip will develop the sources of power already described, such as reward, expert, and coercive power. However, if the person provides mostly negative gossip, his or her referent power will decrease.

resource dependence perspective The need of the organization for a continuing flow of human resources, money, customers, technological inputs, and material to continue to function.

Power from Meeting the Expectations of Group Members: Implicit Leadership Theory

Another perspective on leadership power is that a leader can accrue power by behaving and acting in the way group members expect. For example, a team leader who is intelligent and dedicated when team members want an intelligent and dedicated leader will have some power based on meeting these expectations. According to **implicit leadership theory,** group members develop prototypes specifying the traits and abilities that characterize an ideal business leader. People are characterized as true leaders on the basis of the perceived match between their behavior and character and the leader category they have in their minds. Implicit leadership theories (or expectations) are the benchmarks group members use to form an impression of their leader/manager. Group members have both prototypes and antiprototypes (what they want the leader not to be).

In organizational settings, the leadership prototypes (desirable characteristics and traits) are as follows: sensitivity, intelligence, dedication, charisma, strength, and attractiveness. The antiprototypes are tyranny and masculinity (a sexist term for being cold and nonrelationship oriented). A study of 439 employees indicated that the closer the

implicit leadership theory An explanation of leadership contending that group members develop prototypes specifying the traits and abilities that characterize an ideal business leader.

Movie Actress Jessica Alba Becomes Powerful Business Entrepreneur

Jessica Albert first experienced fame as an A-list movie actress. She then founded The Honest Company in 2012, as an online consumer-products company that pairs cool design with organic and ecologically safe products. A major thrust of the company is to supply the marketplace for ethical consumerism. The company has more than 100 products and over $300 million in annual sales and is a 400-person company. About 25 percent of The Honest Company's merchandise is now sold in physical retail stores, including Target and Nordstrom. *Forbes* has named Alba as one of the richest entrepreneurs under age 40, with a net worth estimated at $350 million. She has also been ranked by *Forbes* as one of America's Richest Self-Made Women.

The idea for The Honest Company brand arose in 2008 when Alba was pregnant and became concerned about the safety of all the baby shower gifts she was receiving. (As a child, Alba experienced an allergic reaction to a laundry detergent marketed toward babies.) She then started researching the chemicals found in everyday products and even lobbied Congress to reform the use of harmful chemicals. "Enough people have to get sick or die from a certain ingredient or chemical before it's pulled from the marketplace," said Alba.

Today, The Honest Company offers a range of products, including eco-friendly diapers, bug sprays, dish soap, kitchen cleaner, and multivitamins. Diapers and baby wipes constitute a major part of the business. The majority of online revenue comes from a monthly subscription service for diapers and wipes.

Alba spends a major portion of her work time overseeing marketing and brand development. In 2017, the company underwent a major reorganization, laying off 80 people and bringing on board a new CEO, Nicholas Vlahos, a former Clorox executive. The purpose of hiring a new CEO was to broaden beyond an e-commerce model to an omnichannel one.

A few years ago, The Honest Company experienced problems that contradicted its mission. The company agreed to pay $1.55 million to settle a class-action lawsuit contending that it misled buyers about ingredients in its laundry detergent and dish soap. The Honest Company was also sued by a customer who said its sunscreen does not work and is not a natural product. The company has also had to recall some baby wipes and baby powder because of potentially toxic ingredients. The Honest Company outsources the manufacturing of many of its products and therefore does not have total control over quality.

Alba and her company deny all wrongdoing in the lawsuits it has faced. She touts the value of learning from your mistakes. Alba said, "I think the most valuable lessons actually come from making mistakes and going down the wrong path. Now, making the same mistake three times, that's where you have some problems."

QUESTIONS

1. Which types of power does Alba display?
2. In what way might the lawsuits that The Honest Company has faced erode some of Alba's power?
3. How ethical are Alba and her executive team in denying all wrongdoing in the charges the company has faced?

Source: Original story created from facts and observations in the following sources: Sarah Berger, "Jessica Alba Felt 'So Alone' in the Early Days of Her Company," CNBC (www.cnbc.com), February 6, 2018, pp. 1–4; Clare O'Connor, "Natural Woman," *Forbes*, June 15, 2015, pp. 66–74; Ruth Reader, Jessica Alba on The Honest Company's Evolution," *Fast Company* (www.fastcompany.com), April 18, 2017, pp. 1–2; Julia Horowitz, "Jessica Alba's The Honest Company Can't Catch a Break," CNN Money (www.money.cnn.com), June 12, 2017, pp. 1–3.

employees perceived their manager's profile to fit the implicit leadership theory they endorsed, the better the quality of the leader–member exchange.[15] It can be inferred that, as a result of these high-quality exchanges, the leader has a little more power.

The Organizational Behavior in Action box describes an executive who has made intelligent use of a variety of types of power.

As mentioned earlier in relation to company founders, having too much power can corrupt a leader. David Owen, a British physician and parliamentarian, labels this abuse of power the *hubris syndrome*, defined as a "disorder of the possession of power, particularly power which has been associated with overwhelming success for a period of years." Taking on greater responsibility and pressure can lead to a rewiring of the brain in which caring about other people diminishes.

The way out of this trap is for the powerful person to develop compassion. A recommended approach is to seek opportunities to show compassion. For example, John

Chambers, the former CEO of Cisco Systems, established a system to inform him within 48 hours of any employee, anywhere in the world, who was experiencing a severe loss, accident, or illness. After being notified, Chambers would write a letter and extend his support to that employee.[16]

Empowerment of Group Members

Distributing power throughout the organization has become a major strategy for improving productivity, quality, satisfaction, and motivation. Employees experience a greater sense of self-efficacy (self-confidence for a particular task) and ownership in their jobs when they share power. **Empowerment** is the process of sharing power with group members, thereby enhancing their feelings of self-efficacy.[17] A few basic points about empowerment are shown in Figure 12-1.

Participative management or leadership is the general strategy for empowering workers. The techniques of participative management, such as goal setting, modeling, and job enrichment, have been described in previous chapters. The information about empowering teams presented in Chapter 10 is also relevant here. To link empowerment directly to leadership, empowerment can be regarded as shared leadership as opposed to vertical leadership. Such shared leadership is particularly necessary when the work within the group is interdependent, creative, and complex. The typical work of cross-functional teams and virtual teams calls for shared leadership or empowerment.[18]

LEARNING OBJECTIVE 2
Describe the essence of empowerment.

empowerment The process of sharing power with group members, thereby enhancing their feelings of self-efficacy.

A study of 35 sales and service virtual teams showed that team empowerment was related to two measures of team performance—process improvement and customer satisfaction. Empowerment was measured by a questionnaire with statements such as, "My team makes its own choices without being told by management." Empowerment was even more effective for the virtual teams with fewer face-to-face meetings, suggesting that the less virtual team members meet with a manager, the more empowerment they need.[19]

An empowered group is often productive and satisfied.

To bring about empowerment, managers must remove conditions that keep employees powerless, such as authoritarian supervision or a job over which they have little control. An example of a person in a low-control job would be a manager who cannot shut off interruptions even to prepare budgets or to plan. Employees must also receive information that increases their feelings of self-efficacy. When employees are empowered, they will take the initiative to solve problems and strive hard to reach objectives.

Empowerment may not proceed smoothly unless certain conditions are met. A major consideration is that the potentially empowered workers must be competent and interested in assuming more responsibility. Otherwise the work will not get accomplished. W. Alan Randolph observed 10 companies that made the transition to empowerment.[20]

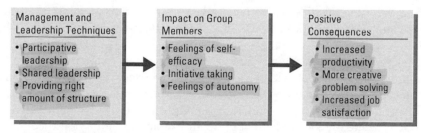

Management and Leadership Techniques	Impact on Group Members	Positive Consequences
• Participative leadership • Shared leadership • Providing right amount of structure	• Feelings of self-efficacy • Initiative taking • Feelings of autonomy	• Increased productivity • More creative problem solving • Increased job satisfaction

FIGURE 12-1 The Basics of Empowerment

The first key to effective empowerment is *information sharing*. Lacking information, it is difficult for workers to act with responsibility.

Another critical factor for successful empowerment is for management to *provide more structure* as teams move into self-management. To initiate empowerment, managers must teach people new skills and make the parameters clear. Workers need to know, for example, "What are the limits to my empowerment?" The third critical factor is that *teams must gradually replace the traditional organizational hierarchy*. Empowered teams not only make recommendations, but they also make and implement decisions and are held accountable. A major contributing factor to successful empowerment, found in a study of a large food company, was that teams acted as managers. They hired and fired people, appraised performance, scheduled work, and managed a budget.

Empowerment is also more effective when the empowered individuals and teams are told what needs to be done but are *free to determine how to achieve the objectives*. Allowing people to determine the most efficient and effective work techniques is the essence of empowerment. A final consideration for successful empowerment is implied in the other conditions. *Unless managers trust employees*, empowerment will not be effective or even take place. For example, when employees are trusted, they are more likely to be given the information they need and be granted the freedom to choose an appropriate method.

Another way of looking at the contribution of empowerment is that, when the leader has too much power, team performance might decline. This conclusion was reached on the basis of a series of three studies conducted with students participating in simulation exercises, including solving a homicide investigation. Team performance was linked to finding the correct solution to the problems. Among the findings was that leaders who felt they had a high degree of power spent more time talking (or verbally dominating) during the team meetings than did leaders who felt they had less power. High-power leadership also was associated with lower levels of open communication in teams, and consequently led to diminished team performance.[21] The take-away from this study for the workplace is that group leaders who feel they have a lot of power might tend to dominate the discussion during meetings and therefore not make good use of talent within the team.

As with many techniques related to leadership and management, empowerment can be overdone to the point that it becomes a burden. For example, the manager might expect the group to take on an additional responsibility, such as recruiting and hiring another group member, that interferes with the conduct of their regular work. A study conducted at six research centers in the Republic of Korea found that too many empowering practices by the leader can result in job-induced tension for group members. In turn, the tension diminished the positive impact of empowerment on work-role performance.[22] Similarly, a meta-analysis suggests that empowering leadership can motivate employees and fuel their creativity. Yet empowerment can create additional burdens and stress that may diminish their routine performance.[23]

Now that we have described the sources of power and empowerment, we shift focus to more details about political behavior and influence tactics.

Organizational Politics

LEARNING OBJECTIVE 3
Pinpoint factors contributing to, and examples of, organizational politics.

leader political support The concept refers to tactics of organizational politics and influence engaged in by leaders to provide followers with necessary resources to advance individual, group, or organizational objectives.

Our study of organizational politics includes the reasons behind political behavior in the workplace, as well as ethical and unethical tactics We emphasize again that the effective use of organizational politics can enhance leader effectiveness and the well-being of subordinates. A relatively new concept, **leader political support** points to the positive effects just mentioned. The concept refers to tactics of organizational politics and influence engaged in by leaders to provide followers with necessary resources to advance individual, group, or organizational objectives.[24] An information technology manager might build into his or her network a good relationship with the vice president of finance. The goal would be to make the vice president more amenable to funding a project that would develop mobile apps for a wide range of the company's services.

Factors Contributing to Political Behavior

The most fundamental reason for organizational politics is the political nature of organizations. Coalitions of interests and demands arise both within and outside organizations. Similarly, organizations can be viewed as loose structures of interests and demands in competition with one another for attention and resources. The interaction among different coalitions results in an undercurrent of political tactics, such as when one group tries to promote itself and discredit another.

Another contributor to political activity is the pyramid structure of organizations—a reality despite all the emphasis on shared leadership and empowerment. The people at the top of the organization hold most of the power, while people at each successive level down the hierarchy hold less power. The amount of power that can be distributed in a hierarchy is limited. Power-oriented managers sometimes cope with the limited amount of power available by expanding their sphere of influence sideways. For example, the director of the food-stamp program in a government agency might attempt to gain control over the housing assistance program, which is at the same level.

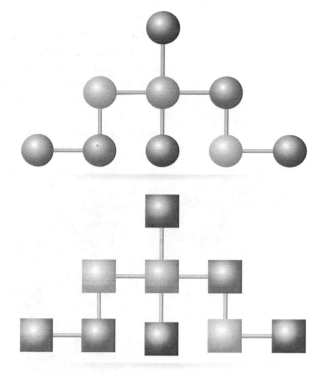

A pyramid-shaped organization is a source of organizational politics.

Executive coach Marshall Goldsmith observes a major reason for "kissing up" (a form of organizational politics) to people in power. Without meaning to, many managers create an environment in which people learn to reward others with accolades that are not really warranted. People who are kind, courteous, and complimentary toward their managers are most likely to receive the most recognition—assuming their job performance is at least in the acceptable range.[25] In support of this observation, a recent survey of 1,000 office employees found that 43 percent of them say acting interested in their boss's "dumb story" is at least moderately important in getting promoted.[26]

Political behavior by senior management helps establish a climate for such behavior. When C-level executives are highly political, it contributes to a climate of acceptance for organizational politics. One of the most visible aspects of political behavior is favoritism in its many forms. When lower-ranking managers perceive that the practice exists among senior management of placing poorly qualified friends into high-paying positions, the lower-ranking managers are likely to follow suit.

Downsizings and team structures create even less opportunity for climbing the hierarchy, thus intensifying political behavior for the few remaining powerful positions. Worried about layoffs themselves, many workers attempt to discredit others so that the latter would be the first to go. Internal politics generally increase as good jobs, promotions, and bonuses become scarcer. Organizational politics is also fostered by the need for power. Executives have much stronger power needs than others and thus propel themselves toward frequent episodes of political behavior. Because executives are responsible for controlling resources, their inner desire to do so helps them in their jobs. A personalized power need is more likely to trigger political behavior than a socialized power need.

Finally, a devious reason for the existence of politicking is **Machiavellianism**, a tendency to manipulate others for personal gain. (Niccolo Machiavelli was a 15th-century political philosopher whose book, *The Prince*, describes how leaders may acquire and maintain power by placing expediency above morality.) One analysis suggests that many ambitious and successful corporate executives have strong Machiavellian tendencies, such as acquiring other companies just to give the appearance of true corporate growth.[27]

Machiavellianism A tendency to manipulate others for personal gain.

To make effective use of organizational politics, managerial workers must be aware of specific political strategies and tactics. To identify and explain the majority of political behaviors would require years of study and observation. Managers so frequently need support for their programs that they search for innovative political maneuvers. Furthermore, new tactics continue to emerge as the workplace becomes increasingly competitive.

Self-Assessment 12-1 gives you an opportunity to think through your tendencies to engage in organizational politics. In the two following sections we describe mostly ethical, followed by unethical, political tactics.

Mostly Ethical and Positive Political Tactics

LEARNING OBJECTIVE 4
Differentiate between the ethical and unethical use of power, politics, and influence.

Here we describe political tactics that many people would consider to be ethical and positive. Nevertheless, some managers and management scholars regard all political tactics as being ethically tainted. The relevance of being able to use political tactics effectively was demonstrated in an analysis of 130 studies of political skill, as measured by a questionnaire similar to the one presented here. Positive relationships were found between political skill and the following outcomes: self-efficacy, job satisfaction, organizational commitment, work productivity, organizational citizenship behavior, career success, and personal reputation. Equally impressive, it was found that political skill was negatively related to experiencing physiological strain (the negative effects of stress). The positive outcomes of political skill went beyond those that could be attributed to positive personality traits or high mental ability.[28]

1. *Develop power contacts through networking.* A fundamental principle of success is to identify powerful people and then establish alliances with them. Cultivating friendly, cooperative relationships with powerful organizational members and outsiders can make the managerial worker's cause much easier to advance. These contacts can support a person's ideas and recommend him or her for promotions and visible temporary assignments. The social networks within an organization can be as important as the networks revealed by the organizational chart. For example, someone who does not have much formal authority, such as a financial analyst, might have considerable clout with the CEO.

   A challenge in the era of electronic communications is that face time, or in-person contact, is helpful for building contacts. It is important to converse with powerful people in person in addition to sending them electronic messages. Although still electronic, an occasional telephone call is a useful supplement to e-mail or text messages for purposes of building a network.

2. *Manage your impression.* You will recall that charismatic leaders rely heavily on impression management, and the same technique is important for other success-oriented people. An example of an ethical impression-management tactic would be to contribute outstanding performance and then make sure key people know of your accomplishments. Making others aware of what you accomplish is often referred to as *achieving visibility.* When tactics of impression management appear insincere, they are likely to create a negative impression and thus be self-defeating. A key person to impress is your immediate superior. Many firms send professionals to etiquette training because displaying proper etiquette makes a positive impression on customers and clients.[29]

3. *Make your boss look good.* A bedrock principle of organizational politics is to help your boss perform well, which is one of the reasons you probably were hired. Positioning yourself as a supporting player for your boss will help your performance evaluation and therefore your career. Consultant Karl Bimshas suggests that a good starting point is to ask questions of this nature: "What do you think should be my highest priority right now?" Then turn in a good performance with respect to the priority.[30]

Managing your impression is a necessary political tactic.

The Positive Organizational Politics Questionnaire

Answer each question "mostly agree" or "mostly disagree," even if it is difficult for you to decide which alternative best describes your opinion.

	Mostly Agree	Mostly Disagree
1. Pleasing my boss is a major goal of mine.	___	___
2. I go out of my way to flatter important people.	___	___
3. I am most likely to do favors for people who can help me in return.	___	___
4. Given the opportunity, I would cultivate friendships with powerful people.	___	___
5. I will compliment a coworker even if I have to think hard about what might be praiseworthy.	___	___
6. If I thought my boss needed the help, and I had the expertise, I would show him or her how to use an electronic gadget for personal life.	___	___
7. I laugh heartily at my boss's humor, so long as I think he or she is at least a little funny.	___	___
8. I would not be too concerned about following a company dress code, so long as I looked neat.	___	___
9. If a customer sent me a compliment through e-mail, I would forward a copy to my boss and another influential person.	___	___
10. I smile only at people in the workplace whom I genuinely like.	___	___
11. An effective way to impress people is to tell them what they want to hear.	___	___
12. I would never publicly correct mistakes made by the boss.	___	___
13. I would be willing to use my personal contacts to gain a promotion or desirable transfer.	___	___
14. I think it is a good idea to send a congratulatory note to someone in the company who receives a promotion to an executive position.	___	___
15. I think "office politics" is only for losers.	___	___

Scoring and Interpretation: Give yourself a plus 1 for each answer that agrees with the keyed answer. Each question that receives a score of plus 1 shows a tendency toward playing positive organizational politics. The scoring key is as follows:

1. Mostly agree
2. Mostly agree
3. Mostly agree
4. Mostly agree
5. Mostly agree
6. Mostly agree
7. Mostly agree
8. Mostly disagree
9. Mostly agree
10. Mostly disagree
11. Mostly agree
12. Mostly agree
13. Mostly agree
14. Mostly agree
15. Mostly disagree

1–6, Below-average tendency to play office politics

7–11, Average tendency to play office politics

12 and above, Above-average tendency to play office politics; strong need for power

Thinking about your political tendencies in the workplace is important for your career because most successful leaders are moderately political. The ability to use politics effectively and ethically increases with importance in the executive suite. Most top executives are effective office politicians. Yet being overly and blatantly political can lead to distrust, thereby damaging your career.

4. *Keep informed.* In addition to controlling vital information, it is politically important to keep informed. Successful managers and professionals develop a pipeline to help them keep abreast, or even ahead, of developments within the firm. For example, a politically astute individual might befriend a major executive's assistant.

5. *Be courteous, pleasant, and positive.* Courteous, pleasant, and positive people are the first to be hired and the last to be fired (assuming they are also technically qualified).[31] A key part of being courteous, pleasant, and positive is to socialize with coworkers, including having meals and drinks with them. Executive coach Leslie Williams observes: "Socialization has everything to do with influence. It's not enough to just be good at your job." In addition to doing a good job, you have to be somebody that people know and know well enough to trust.[32]

6. *Ask satisfied customers to contact your manager.* A favorable comment by a customer receives considerable weight because customer satisfaction is a top corporate priority. If a customer says something nice, the comment will carry more weight than one from a coworker or subordinate. The reason is that insiders might praise you for political reasons, whereas a customer's motivation is thought to be pure.

7. *Bring forth solutions rather than problems.* A strongly meritorious political tactic is to focus on bringing solutions rather than problems to the attention of your direct manager. The basic approach is to say something to the effect of, "Here is a problem I have identified, and here is what I would like to do about it with your approval." According to business writer Matt Rosoff, managers hate to hear a direct report say, "Somebody should…" In other words, the subordinate is identifying a problem and thinks that the manager or somebody else should work on its resolution. The boss hears, "I'd like to add another task to your to-do list."[33]

8. *Avoid political blunders.* A strategy for retaining power is to refrain from making power-eroding blunders. Committing these politically insensitive acts can also prevent you from attaining power. Leading blunders include: strong criticism of a superior in a public forum; going around your manager with a complaint; and making a negative social media post about your employer. Another blunder is burning your bridges by creating ill will with former employees. The Organizational Behavior Checklist will serve as a reminder of the types of political blunders (gaffes) to avoid in order to preserve a positive image.

9. *Use sincere flattery.* A powerful tactic for ingratiating yourself to others is to flatter them honestly and sincerely. Although one meaning of the term *flattery* is insincere praise, another meaning refers to a legitimate compliment. Charismatic people use flattery regularly. Skill-Development Exercise 12-1 will help you develop flattery skills.

Political skill can be developed through careful observation and experience, coupled with improving one's emotional intelligence. Research with 260 business graduate students showed that mentoring can be an effective way of developing political skill. Ninety percent of the students were employed, and those who had a mentor or mentors responded to a questionnaire about the quality of their mentoring. Results indicated that participants who had a mentor showed significantly better political skill than participants who did not have a mentor.[34]

Mostly Unethical and Negative Political Tactics

In this section we describe tactics of organizational politics that most people would consider to be unethical and negative. The majority of people who use these tactics would not admit to their use.

1. *Backstabbing.* The ubiquitous backstab requires that you pretend to be nice but all the while plan someone's demise. A frequent form of backstabbing is to inform your rival's immediate superior that he or she is faltering under the pressure of job responsibilities. The recommended approach to dealing with a backstabber is

to confront the person directly, ask for an explanation of his or her behavior, and demand that he or she stop. Threaten to complain to the person's superior.[35]

2. *Embrace-or-demolish.* The ancient strategy of embrace-or-demolish suggests that you remove from the premises rivals who suffered past hurts through your efforts. (The same tactic is called "take no prisoners.") Otherwise the wounded rivals might retaliate at a vulnerable moment. An illustration of embrace-or-demolish is when, after a hostile takeover, many executives lose their jobs because they opposed the takeover.

3. *Stealing credit.* For many workers, the most detestable form of office politics is for their boss, or other worker, to take credit for their ideas without acknowledging the source of the idea. The credit stealing breeds distrust, damages motivation, and is sometimes misperceived as a perk of power.[36] A good starting point in stopping idea thieves is to hold a one-on-one session with the thief, and confront the issue. If the issue is not resolved, tell key decision makers about the idea theft.[37]

4. *Territorial games.* Also referred to as *turf wars*, **territorial games** involve protecting and hoarding resources that give a person power, such as information, relationships, and decision-making authority. The purpose of territorial games is to compete for three kinds of territory in the modern corporate survival game: information, relationships, and authority. A relationship is "hoarded" in such ways as not encouraging others to visit a key customer, or blocking a higher performer from getting a promotion or transfer by informing other managers that he or she is mediocre.[38] Other examples of territorial games include monopolizing time with clients, scheduling meetings so someone cannot attend, and shutting out coworkers on an important assignment.

territorial games Also known as *turf wars*, territorial games refer to behaviors involving the hoarding of information and other resources.

If you and your colleague are in a dispute over who owns a project or task or who gets to decide how to use a part of the team budget, getting angry will rarely lead to a resolution. Conflict specialist Amy Gallo recommends that you ditch the win-lose framework and instead focus on a common goal. Demonstrate to the other person that you are open-minded and want to do what is best for the organization.[39] You might say, for example, "Perhaps I misinterpreted who should be the lead person on this project. Let's just get the job done, and I can be the lead person on the next project."

A Short Course in Effective Flattery

Flattering others is an effective way of building personal relationships (or engaging in organizational politics), if done properly. Suggestions for effective flattery are presented here. *Flattery* here refers to pleasing others through complimentary remarks or attention; we are not referring to *flattery* in the sense of giving insincere or excessive compliments. To build your skills in flattering others, practice these suggestions as the opportunity presents itself. Rehearse your flattery approaches until they feel natural. If your first attempt at flattery does not work well, analyze what went wrong the best you can.

■ *Use sensible flattery.* Effective flattery has at least a spoonful of credibility, implying that you say something positive about the target person that is quite plausible. Credibility is also increased when you point to a person's tangible accomplishment. Technical people in particular expect flattery to be specific and aimed at genuine accomplishment.

■ *Compliment what is of major importance to the flattery target.* You might find out what is important to the person by observing what he or she talks about with the most enthusiasm.

■ *Flatter others by listening intently.* Listening intently to another person is a powerful form of flattery. Use active listening (see Chapter 8) for best results.

■ *Flatter by referring to or quoting the other person.* By referring to or quoting (including paraphrasing) another person, you are paying that person a substantial compliment.

■ *Use confirmation behaviors.* Use behaviors that have a positive or therapeutic effect on other people, such as praise and courtesy. Because confirmation behaviors have such a positive effect on others, they are likely to be perceived as a form of flattery.

■ *Give positive feedback.* A mild form of flattering others is to give them positive feedback about their statements, actions, and results. The type of feedback referred to here is a straightforward and specific declaration of what the person did right.

■ *Remember names.* Remembering the names of people with whom you have infrequent contact makes them feel important. To help remember the person's name, study the name carefully when you first hear it and repeat it immediately.

■ *Explain the impact on you.* Tell the person how his or her actions or behavior positively affect you. An example: "I tried your suggestion about avoiding multitasking on important tasks, and my error rate has gone down dramatically."

■ *Avoid flattery that has a built-in insult or barb.* The positive effect of flattery is eradicated when it is accompanied by a hurtful comment, such as "You have good people skills for an engineer" or "You look good. I bet you were really beautiful when you were younger."

To build your skills in flattering others, you must try some of the previous techniques. For starters, within the next few days flatter a classmate, coworker, boss, or friend for something laudable the person accomplished. Or, flatter a customer-contact worker for a service well delivered. Observe carefully the results of your flattery.

Sources: Andrew J. DuBrin, "Political Blunders in Organizations," in Eran Vigoda-Gadot and Amos Drory (eds.), *Handbook of Organizational Politics*, 2nd ed. (Cheltenham, UK: Edward Elgar, 2016), pp. 179–186; Karen Judson, "The Fine Art of Flattery," *Kiwanis*, March 1998, pp. 34–36, 43; Elizabeth Bernstein, "Why Do Compliments Cause So Much Grief?" *The Wall Street Journal*, May 4, 2010, pp. D1, D6; Andrew J. DuBrin, "Self-Perceived Technical Orientation and Attitudes toward Being Flattered," *Psychological Reports*, Vol. 96, 2005, pp. 852–854.

5. *Good-mouthing an incompetent to make him or her transferable.* A long-entrenched devious political maneuver in large firms is for a manager to give outstanding performance evaluations to an incompetent worker or troublemaker within the group. By good-mouthing the undesired worker, he or she becomes more marketable within the company. Although this technique can sometimes work, most experienced human resource professionals are aware of this tactic. An HR director noted, "We look for a certain pattern when a manager is puffing up a worker for transfer. Typically the problem worker received low evaluations for a long time, then starts getting outstanding evaluations. When this happens, we really grill the manager about the worker who has been offered for transfer."

6. *Placing a weak manager under you to help secure your position.* A negative political tactic practiced mostly in the executive suite is for a high-level manager to

recruit a lame person to a managerial position reporting to him or her. The lame person is valued because he or she is unlikely to become a candidate as a successor to the first executive—who would not have pulled this stunt if he or she were highly competent and secure.

E-mail, including instant messaging and text messaging, has become a major vehicle for conducting both ethical and unethical organizational politics. To help manage their impressions, many people distribute e-mails regarding their positive contribution to a project to many key people. E-networking is a convenient way to maintain minimum contact with many people, until the in-person meeting can be arranged. People flatter their target person via e-mail and send copies to key people. On the downside, some people reprimand others by e-mail and let others know of the target's mistakes. Sometimes managers who are haggling with each other will send a copy to a common boss, hoping that the boss will intervene in the dispute.[40] A productivity problem with so many people being copied for political purposes is that in-boxes can become overloaded.

Organizational Influence Tactics

In addition to using power and political tactics to win people over to their way of thinking, managerial workers use a variety of influence tactics. Extensive research has been conducted on social influence tactics aimed at upward, horizontal, and downward relations.[41] The person doing the influencing chooses which tactic seems most appropriate for a given situation. Nine of the most frequently used influence tactics are described here.

LEARNING OBJECTIVE 5
Identify and describe a variety of influence tactics.

1. *Leading by example* means that the manager influences group members by serving as a positive model of desirable behavior. A manager who leads by example shows consistency between actions and words. For example, suppose a firm has a strict policy on punctuality. The manager explains the policy and is always punctual. The manager's words and actions provide a consistent model. Leading by example is also considered quite useful as a way of encouraging ethical behavior.

2. *Assertiveness* refers to being forthright in making demands without violating the rights of others. It involves a person expressing what he or she wants done and how he or she feels about it. A manager might say, for example, "Your report is late, and that makes me angry. I want you to get it done by noon tomorrow." Assertiveness, as this example shows, also refers to making orders clear.

3. *Rational persuasion* means appealing to reason and logic. Strong managers and leaders frequently use this influence tactic. Pointing out the facts of a situation to group members to get them to do something exemplifies rationality. Intelligent people respond the best to rational appeals.

4. *Ingratiation* refers to getting someone else to like you, often through the use of flattery and doing favors. A typical ingratiating tactic would be to act in a friendly manner just before making a demand. Effective managerial workers treat people well consistently to get cooperation when it is needed. Ingratiation, or simply being likable, is an effective way of gaining the cooperation of others. A study of 133 managers found that, if an auditor is likable and gives a well-organized argument, managers tend to comply with his or her suggestions even when they disagree and the auditor has insufficient supporting evidence.[42]

   A theoretical analysis of the subject concluded that humor is an effective type of ingratiatory behavior. One reason humor leads to ingratiation is because it makes the person with the sense of humor more attractive to the target. Humor may also be seen as more acceptable than an ingratiation tactic such as doing a favor for another person.[43]

5. *Projecting warmth before emphasizing competence* is a major workplace influence tactic. Considerable research about human behavior indicates that, by first focusing on displaying warmth and then blending in shows of competence, leaders will be more influential. For example, before presenting facts about the value of using

High-Quality Exchanges with Coworkers

Groups of about six people get together to simulate an ongoing work team.

A suggestion would be to visualize the group as a product-development team at General Motors (GM) to develop a product (that is not a vehicle). Imagine that top-level management is applying heavy pressure on the product-development team to arrive at an innovative idea today. (If you dislike the GM scenario, invent another group problem.) At the same time, your group believes strongly that high-quality exchanges will help you accomplish your task. As you discuss your potential innovative ideas, engage in high-quality exchanges (including flattery) without going to the extreme of being a sickening office politician.

After you have completed the group role-playing, hold a debriefing session in which you analyze what some of the best high-quality exchanges among group members were. Also, make any observations you can about how the high-quality exchanges affected group creativity.

Warmth and friendliness are important sources of influence.

cloud technology, the leader might smile and wave gently. Two specific ways of being perceived as warm are (a) to speak with lower pitch and volume, as if comforting a friend, and (b) to express agreement with something the influence target says.[44] (Projecting warmth might be classified as an ingratiating tactic.)

6. *Exchange* is a method of influencing others by offering to reciprocate if they meet your demands. When asking favors in a busy workplace, it is best to specify the amount of time the task will take, such as by saying "I will need 10 minutes of your time sometime between now and next Wednesday." Be aware of what skills or capabilities you have that you can barter with others. Perhaps you are good at removing a computer virus or explaining the tax code. You can then offer to perform these tasks in exchange for favors granted to you. Skill-Development Exercise 12-2 will help you personalize the use of exchange as an influence tactic.

7. *Inspirational appeal and emotional display* is an influence method centering on the affective (as opposed to the cognitive) domain. Given that leaders are supposed to inspire others, such an influence tactic is important. An inspirational appeal usually involves an emotional display by the person seeking to influence. It also involves appealing to group members' emotions.

8. *Joking and kidding*, according to one survey, are widely used to influence others on the job.[45] Good-natured ribbing is especially effective when a straightforward statement might be interpreted as harsh criticism. A manager concerned about the number of errors in a group member's report might say, "Now I know what you are up to. You planted all those errors just to see if I really read your reports."

9. *Strategic sexual performance* has been recognized by a group of scholars as a positive influence tactic if used properly. The authors of the research refer to sexuality outside the realm of disruptive behavior such as an office romance or sexual harassment. They define *strategic sexual performance* as "behavior that is imbued with sexual intent, content, or meaning by its performers, observers, or both, and that is intended to influence a target person or persons in some way." Such a behavior would include lightly touching an influence target to capture his or her attention about a work-related suggestion, or simply winking. Other examples include smiling, giving long gazes or intense eye contact, and compliments about the target's physical features. An everyday example would be for a restaurant server to wear provocative clothing in order to receive higher tips.[46] (The strategic use of sexual performance can also be framed as ingratiation.)

A meta-analysis of 49 studies involving close to 9,000 people sheds light on which influence tactics are the most effective in getting work accomplished and establishing good relationships with work associates. Among the tactics mentioned previously, rational persuasion, inspirational appeal, and ingratiation were the most effective. The meta-analysis also suggested that rational persuasion is the most effective tactic across a wide variety of conditions and situations.[47]

Which influence tactic should you choose? Managers are unlikely to use all the influence tactics in a given situation. Instead, they tend to choose an influence tactic that fits the demands of the circumstance. The outcome of a specific influence attempt is also determined by factors such as the target's motivation and organizational culture. For example, strategic sexual performance is likely to be more acceptable in a restaurant or manufacturing plant than in a research laboratory. Also, any influence tactic can trigger target resistance if it is inappropriate for the situation or is applied unskillfully. Tact, diplomacy, and insight are required for effective application of influence (and political) tactics.

Influence tactics are more effective when they are combined with political skill, such as using joking and kidding without being offensive. A study conducted with college students who were interning at retail stores demonstrated the importance of combining political skill with the influence tactic of ingratiation. The study found that when interns ingratiated themselves toward supervisors, it resulted in higher performance ratings when coupled with high levels of political skill. In contrast, ingratiation led to lower performance ratings when the interns using ingratiation had low levels of political skill.[48]

The Control of Dysfunctional Politics and Ethical Considerations

Carried to excess, organizational politics and influence tactics can hurt an organization and its members. One consequence is that when political factors far outweigh merit, competent employees may become unhappy and quit. Another problem is that politicking takes time away from tasks that could contribute directly to achieving the firm's goals. Many managers spend more time developing political allies (including "kissing up") than coaching group members or doing analytical work.

LEARNING OBJECTIVE 6
Explain how managers can control dysfunctional politics.

The most comprehensive antidote to improper, excessive, and unethical organizational politics is to rely on objective measures of performance. This is true because people have less need to behave politically when their contributions can be measured directly. With a formal system of goal setting and review, the results a person attains should be much more important than the impression the person creates. However, even a goal-setting program is not immune to politics. Sometimes the goals are designed to impress key people in the organization. As such, they may not be the most important goals for getting work accomplished. Another political problem with goal setting is that some people will set relatively easy goals so they can look good by attaining all their goals.

Meshing individual and organizational objectives would be the ideal method of controlling excessive, negative political behavior. If their objectives, needs, and interests can be met through their jobs, employees will tend to engage in behavior that fosters the growth, longevity, and productivity of the firm. L. A. Witt investigated how goal congruence between the individual and the organization affected political behavior. When employees perceived considerable politics in the workplace, their commitment to the organization and job performance both suffered. However, when employees and their superiors shared the same goals, commitment and performance were less negatively affected by politics.[49]

Jay Parikh, the global head of engineering and infrastructure at Facebook, writes that the company has worked hard to prevent office politics. One suggestion of note is to "Look for empire builders, self-servers, and whiners in the hiring process—and don't hire them." A key purpose of candidate-screening questions is to find candidates who minimize organizational politics and fit into a team environment. Two of the screening questions Facebook interviewers use are as follows:

■ Describe a few of your peers at your company and what type of relationship you have with each of them.

■ What does office politics mean to you, and do you see politics as your job?[50]

Finally, open communication can also constrain the impact of political behavior. For instance, open communication can let everyone know the basis for allocating resources, thus reducing the amount of politicking. Organizational politics can also be curtailed by threatening to discuss questionable information in a public forum. If one employee engages in backstabbing of another, the manager might ask her or him to repeat the anecdote in a staff meeting. It has been said that sunlight is the best disinfectant to deviousness.

Our discussion of sources of power, political tactics, and influence tactics should not imply an endorsement of all of these methods to gain an advantage in the workplace. Each strategy and tactic must be evaluated on its merit by an ethical test, such as those described in Chapter 4. One guiding principle is to turn the strategy or tactic inward. Assume that you believe that a particular tactic (e.g., ingratiation) would be ethical in working against you. It would then be fair and ethical for you to use this tactic in attempting to influence others.

Another guiding principle is that it is generally ethical to use power and influence to help attain organizational goals. In contrast, it is generally unethical to use the same tactics to achieve a personal agenda and goals not sanctioned by the organization. Yet even this guideline involves enough "grayness" to be open for interpretation. Skill-Development Exercise 12-3 provides an opportunity to evaluate the ethics of influence tactics.

Recognize also that both the means and the ends of political behavior must be considered. A study of the subject cautioned, "Instead of determining whether human rights or standards of justice are violated, we are often content to judge political behavior according to its outcomes."[51] The authors of the study suggest that when it comes to the ethics of organizational politics, respect for justice and human rights should prevail for its own sake.

Implications for Managerial Practice

1. Embrace rather than avoid organizational politics. Extend yourself to help coworkers and colleagues, and they might reciprocate. A quid-pro-quo arrangement can move your career forward faster than only hard work, talent, and loyalty.[52]
2. Recognize that a significant portion of the efforts of organizational members will be directed toward gaining power for themselves or their group. At times, some of

this behavior will be directed more toward self-interest than organizational interest. It is therefore often necessary to ask, "Is this action being taken to help this person or is it being done to help the organization?" Your answer to this question should influence your willingness to submit to that person's demands.

3. If you want to establish a power base for yourself, a good starting point is to develop expert power. Most powerful people began their climb to power by demonstrating their expertise in a particular area, such as being outstanding in sales or a niche within information technology. (This tactic is referred to as becoming a subject-matter expert.)

4. In determining if a particular behavior is motivated by political or merit considerations, evaluate the intent of the actor. The same action might be based on self-interest or concern for others. For instance, a team member might praise you because he believed that you accomplished something of merit. On the other hand, that same individual might praise you to attain a favorable work assignment or salary increase.

Summary of Key Points

1. *Identify sources of power for individuals and subunits within organizations.* Power, politics, and influence are needed by managers to accomplish their work. In the model presented here, managers and professionals use organizational politics to achieve power and influence, thus attaining desired outcomes.

   Socialized power is used to forward organizational interests, whereas personalized power is used to forward personal interests. Power granted by the organization consists of legitimate power, coercive power, and reward power. Power stemming from the individual consists of expert power and referent power (the basis for charisma). According to the resource dependence perspective, subunits or individuals who can provide key resources to the organization accrue power. At times, gossip can be a power-giving source. Power can also be derived from meeting the group members' expectations of how a leader should behave (implicit leadership theory).

2. *Describe the essence of empowerment.* Managers must act in specific ways to empower employees, including removing conditions that keep employees powerless and giving information that enhances employee feelings of self-efficacy. Five critical conditions for empowerment are for an organization to share information with employees, provide them with structure, use teams to replace the traditional hierarchy, grant employees the freedom to determine how to achieve objectives, and trust employees. When the leader has too much power, team performance might decline.

3. *Pinpoint factors contributing to, and examples of, organizational politics.* Contributors to organizational politics include the political nature of organizations, the pyramid structure of organizations, encouragement of unwarranted accolades from subordinates, political behavior by senior management, less opportunity for vertical advancement, the need for power, and Machiavellianism.

   Among the ethical tactics of organizational politics are the following: developing power contacts; managing your impression; making your boss look good; keeping informed; being courteous, pleasant, and positive; asking satisfied customers to contact your manager; bringing forth solutions rather than problems; avoiding political blunders; and using sincere flattery. Among the unethical tactics are the following: backstabbing, embracing-or-demolishing, stealing credit, playing territorial games, good-mouthing incompetents, and choosing a weak manager as an underling.

4. *Differentiate between the ethical and unethical use of power, politics, and influence.* Political behaviors chosen by an individual or organizational unit must rest on ethical considerations. A guiding principle is to use only those tactics you would consider fair and ethical if used against you. Also recognize that both the means and the ends of political behavior must be considered.

5. *Identify and describe a variety of influence tactics.* Influence tactics frequently used by managerial workers include leading by example, assertiveness, rational persuasion, ingratiation, projecting warmth before emphasizing competence, exchange, inspirational appeal and emotional display, joking and kidding, and strategic sexual performance.

6. *Explain how managers can control dysfunctional politics.* Approaches to controlling dysfunctional politics include relying on objective performance measures, meshing individual and organizational objectives, minimizing political behavior by top management, screening job candidates for political tendencies, and implementing open communication, including threatening to discuss politicking publicly.

Key Terms and Phrases

power, p. 265

organizational politics, p. 265

political skill, p. 265

socialized power, p. 265

personalized power, p. 265

legitimate power, p. 265

coercive power, p. 266

reward power, p. 266

expert power, p. 266

referent power, p. 266

resource dependence perspective, p. 267

implicit leadership theory, p. 267

empowerment, p. 269

leader political support, p. 270

Machiavellianism, p. 271

territorial games, p. 275

Discussion Questions and Activities

1. Jeff Bezos, the founder and CEO of Amazon, is widely regarded as one of the most powerful people in business. What are a few sources of his power?

2. What might be the negative consequences to a manager if he or she ignored power, politics, and influence tactics?

3. How might having a lot of power help a person achieve ethical ends within an organization?

4. What type of power might a worker acquire to help prevent his or her job being outsourced?

5. Why does empowering workers often motivate them to work harder?

6. What differences do you see between being skilled at organizational politics and simply being nice to people?

7. What can a person do to become more effective at using the influence tactic of rational persuasion?

8. Imagine yourself as a business student interning in a retail store. What would be a good example of an ingratiating statement you might make to your manager?

9. What do you think of the ethics of using "strategic sexual performance" to influence others on the job?

10. What can you do today to start increasing your power? Compare your observations with those of your classmates.

CASE PROBLEM: The Lands' End Fashionista Fades from Glory

Frederica Marchionni was appointed as CEO of Lands' End, the catalogue retailer that featured durable and basic-fashion clothing, in February 2015. She had previously been the president of the high-fashion company Dolce & Gabanna USA and was a senior vice president of Ferrari before that. Her hiring was a heavy departure for the Wisconsin maker of practical clothing. Lands' End was trying to enhance its brand and appeal to the fashion-conscious consumer. The company had been acquired by Sears in 2002 before becoming an independent company again 12 years later.

After 19 months on the job, Marchionni was forced out as chief executive. During her brief tenure, she tried to bring about major changes at Lands' End that angered employees and turned away shoppers. Marchionni pushed to inject high style into the maker of outdoor-type and casual clothes by adding slimmer fits, stiletto heels, and a fresh line of active wear. She revamped the catalog, hired celebrity photographers, and paid for input from a Vogue stylist.

The focus on high fashion did not appear to be a good fit for Lands' End. The company had found a niche in high-waist jeans and practical outwear and specialized in cold-weather clothing. With sales declining during a difficult period for most retailers, the board at Lands' End had to try something different. But featuring many slim-fit styles and SoHo pop-up stores seemed destined to displease the brand's core demographic group. Marchionni had reduced catalog expenditures to invest in the pop-up stores.

Company insiders said that Marchionni spent only about one week per month at the company headquarters in Dodgeville, Wisconsin. She spent the rest of her working days at an office in the garment district of New York City. When Marchionni was hired, the board wrote into her contract that she could remain in New York. As losses were increasing, the company board thought that Marchionni was trying to make too many changes too quickly. One of the changes she proposed was to make Lands' End less dependent on weather by focusing on clothing that can be worn year-round. The company had been deriving a big chunk of its revenue from coats and bathing suits.

Marchionni made one mistake that cast doubt on her ability to empathize with the typical Lands' End customer. In a new catalog, she tried to illustrate the idea of Lands' End being an American icon by interviewing another American icon, Gloria Steinem, who was known for her strong liberal views, including a pro-abortion-rights agenda. A swift negative reaction surfaced to the interview from many of the company's conservative customers. Many customers and Catholic schools, a large number of which had purchased school uniforms from Lands' End, said they would boycott the company because of Steinem's active pro-choice position. (The interview in the catalog did not mention abortion.)

Not all opinions of Marchionni's performance were negative. Steven Marotta, a retailing analyst, applauded her efforts and described her as "an effective brand manager and operator." He also noted that Marchionni's progress was stymied by the worst consumer-goods market in eight years.

Marchionni also believed that she made a positive contribution to Lands' End, saying: "I am honored to have led this extraordinary company and proud to have succeeded in providing a vision to expand its position in the industry with a multi-dimensional strategy. However, the board of directors and I have agreed it is time for others to bring Lands' End into the future."

Case Questions

1. To what extent did Frederica Marchionni bring the right expertise to her position as CEO of Lands' End?

2. Identify at least one mistake in organizational politics made by Marchionni.

3. Based on your knowledge of Lands' End merchandise, how well do you think Marchionni's vision was a good fit for the company?

Source: Original story based on facts and observations in the following sources: Krystina Gustafson, "Lands' End High-Fashion CEO Is Out," CNBC (www.cnbsc.com), September 26, 2016, pp. 1–2; Suzanne Kapner and Joann S. Lublin, "Lands' End CEO Is Pushed Out after 19 Months," *The Wall Street Journal*, September 27, 2016, p. B1: Jennifer Reingold, "Why Lands' End Ousted Its Change Agent," *Fortune* (www.fortune.com), October 6, 2016, 1–8; Phil Wahba, "Lands' End CEO Marchionni Out after Failing to Take Brand Upscale," *Fortune* (www.fortune.com), September 26, 2016, pp. 1–3; John Grgurich, "Why Land's End Fashionista CEO Failed," *The Fiscal Times* (www.thefiscaltimes.com), September 29, 2016, pp. 1–3.

Full disclosure: The author owns a Lands' End sweater and enjoys its comfort and style.

Endnotes

1. Original story based on facts and observations in the following sources: "Microsoft CEO Satya Nadella: How Empathy Sparks Innovation" (interview with Adam Grant), *Knowledge@Wharton* (www.knowledge.wharton.upenn.edu), February 12, 2018, pp. 1–5; "Satya Nadella: CEO, Microsoft," *Forbes/Profile* (www.forbes.com); Walter Isaacson, "Satya Nadella," *Time* (http://time.com/collection/most-influential-people-2018; "Satya Nadella: CEO, Microsoft," *Bloomberg Businessweek*, December 25, 2017, pp. 46–50; Marco della Cava, "Nadella Counts on Culture Shock to Drive Microsoft Growth, *USA Today*, February 20, 2017, p. 4B.

2. Book review in *Personnel Psychology*, Summer 2002, p. 502.

3. Jerry Useem, "Power," *Fortune*, August 11, 2003, p. 58.

4. Daniel J. Brass and Marlene E. Burkhardt, "Potential Power and Power Use: An Integration of Structure and Behavior," *Academy of Management Journal*, June 1993, pp. 441–442.

5. Christian Ewen et al., "Further Specification of the Leader Political Skill-Leadership Effectiveness Relationships: Transformational and Transactional Leader Behaviors as Moderators," *The Leadership Quarterly*, August 2013, p. 517.

6. Robert P. Vecchio, *Organizational Behavior: Core Concepts*, 4th ed. (Mason, OH: South-Western/Thomson Learning, 2000), p. 126.

7. Jeffrey Pfeffer, "You're Still the Same: Why Theories of Power Hold over Time and across Countries," *Academy of Management Perspectives*, November 2013, pp. 269–280.

8. Leonard H. Chusmir, "Personalized vs. Socialized Power Needs among Working Men and Women," *Human Relations*, February 1986, p. 149.

9. John R. P. French and Bertram Raven, "The Basis of Social Power," in Dorwin Cartwright and Alvin Zander, eds., *Group Dynamics: Research and Theory* (Evanston, IL: Row, Peterson and Company, 1962), pp. 607–623.

10. Steve Blank, "When Founders Go Too Far," *Harvard Business Review*, November–December 2017, pp. 94–101.

11. Lydia Depillis, "Rank-and-File Workers Have a Lot More Power over Corporations Than They Think," (www.washingtonpost.com), June 13, 2014, pp. 1–5.

12. Paul Mozur and Evelyn M. Rusli, "Google Executive Leaves for Startup," *The Wall Street Journal*, August 30, 2013, p. B3; Vlad Savov, "Hugo Barra Is Leaving Xiaomi," *The Verge* (www.theverege.com), January 23, 2017, pp. 1–2.

13. Jeffrey Pfeffer, *Managing with Power* (Boston: Harvard Business Review Publications, 1990), pp. 100–101.

14. Nancy B. Kurland and Lisa Hope Pelled, "Passing the Word: Toward a Model of Gossip and Power in the Workplace," *Academy of Management Review*, April 2000, p. 429.

15. Olga Epitropaki and Robin Martin, "Implicit Leadership Theories in Applied Settings: Factor Structure, Generalizability, and Stability Over Time," *Journal of Applied Psychology*, April 2004, pp. 293–310; Epitropaki and Martin, "From Ideal to Real: A Longitudinal Study of the Role of Implicit Leadership Theories on Leader-Member Exchanges and Employee Outcomes," *Journal of Applied Psychology*, July 2005, pp. 659–676.

16. Rasmus Hougaard, Jacqueline Carter, and Louise Chester, "Power Can Corrupt Leaders, Compassion Can Save Them," *Harvard Business Review*, February 15, 2018, pp. 2–4.

17. Jay A. Conger and Rabindra N. Kanungo, "The Empowerment Process: Integrating Theory and Practice," *Academy of Management Review*, July 1988, pp. 473–474.

18. Craig L. Pearce, "The Future of Leadership: Combining Vertical and Shared Leadership to Transform Knowledge Work," *Academy of Management Executive*, February 2004, pp. 47–57.

19. Braley L. Kirkman, Benson Rosen, Paul E. Tesluk, and Cristina B. Gibson, "The Impact of Team Empowerment on Virtual Team Performance: The Moderating Role of Face-to-Face Interaction, *Academy of Management Journal*, April 2004, pp. 175–192.

20. W. Alan Randolph, "Navigating the Journey to Empowerment," *Organizational Dynamics*, Spring 1995, pp. 19–31.

21. Leigh Plunkett Tost, Francesca Gino, and Richard P. Larrick, "When Power Makes Others Speechless: The Negative Impact of Leader Power on Team Performance," *Academy of Management Journal*, October 2013, pp. 1465–1486.

22. Minyoung Cheong, et al., "Two Faces of Empowering Leadership: Enabling and Burdening," *The Leadership Quarterly*, August 2016, pp. 602–616.

23. Allan Lee, Sara Willis, and Amy Wei Tian, "Empowering Leadership: A Meta-Analytic Examination of Incremental Contribution, and Moderation," *Journal of Organizational Behavior*, August 2017, pp. 306–325.

24. B. Parker Ellen III, Gerald R. Ferris, and M. Ronald Buckley, "Leader Political Support: Reconsidering Leader Political Behavior," *The Leadership Quarterly*, December 2013, pp. 842–857.

25. Marshall Goldsmith, "All of Us Are Stuck on Suck-Ups," *Fast Company*, December 2003, p. 117.

26. Mike B. Smith and Veronica Bravo, "USA Snapshots," *USA Today*, April 26, 2018, Section B, p. 1.

27. Stanley Bing, *What Would Machiavelli Do?* (New York: HarperCollins, 2000).

28. Timothy P. Munyon, James K. Summers, Katina M. Thompson, and Gerald R. Ferris, "Political Skill and Work Outcomes: A Theoretical Extension, Meta-Analytic Investigation, and Agenda for the Future," *Personnel Psychology*, No. 1, 2015, pp. 143–184.

29. Susan Ricker, "Manners Make for Good Business," CareerBuilder.com, April 13, 2014, p. 1; "Etiquette for the Young—with Bite," *The Associated Press*, June 8, 2002.

30. Cited in Susan Ricker, "Make Your Boss, Yourself Look Good," CareerBuilder.com, October 26, 2014, p. 1.

31. "'Career Insurance' Protects DP Professionals from Setbacks, Encourages Growth," *Data Management*, June 1986, p. 33. The same principle is equally valid today.

32. Quoted in Amy Joyce, "Schmoozing on the Job Pays Dividends," *The Washington Post*, November 13, 2005.

33. Matt Rosoff, "The Two Words Your Boss Never Wants to Hear from You," CNBC (www.cnbc.com), May 27, 2013, p. 1.

34. Suzzette M. Chopin, Steven J. Danish, Anson Seers, and Joshua N. Hook, "Effects of Mentoring on the Development of Leadership Self-Efficacy and Political Skill," *Journal of Leadership Studies*, Issue 3, 2013, pp. 17–32.

35. "Face Cowardly Backstabbers in the Workplace," *Knight Ridder* story, February 13, 2000.

36. Jared Sandberg, "Some Bosses Never Meet a Success That Isn't Theirs," *The Wall Street Journal*, April 23, 2003, p. B1.

37. "Stopping Idea Thieves: Strike Back When Rivals Steal Credit," *Executive Leadership Extra!* April 2003, p. 3.

38. Annette Simmons, *Territorial Games: Understanding & Ending Turf Wars at Work* (New York: AMACOM, 1998).

39. Amy Gallo, "How to Negotiate a Turf War at Work," *Harvard Business Review*, September 27, 2017, pp. 1–5.

40. Jeffrey Zaslow, "The Politics of the 'CC' Line," *The Wall Street Journal*, May 28, 2003, p. D2.

41. Several of the tactics are from Gary Yukl and Cecilia M. Falbe, "Influence Tactics and Objectives in Upward, Downward, and Lateral Influence Attempts," *Journal of Applied Psychology*, April 1990, pp. 132–140; Soojin Lee, et al., "How Do I Get My Way? A Meta-Analytic Review of Research on Influence Tactics," *The Leadership Quarterly*, February 2017, pp. 210–228. Part of the definitions of assertiveness and ingratiation stem from Pamela L. Perrewé and Debra L. Nelson, "Gender and Career Success: The Facilitative Role of Political Skill, *Organizational Dynamics*, Vol. 4, 2004, pp. 372–373.

42. Research reported in Sue Shellenbarger, "Why Likability Matters More Than Ever at Work," *The Wall Street Journal*, March 26, 2014, p. D3.

43. Cecily D. Cooper, "Just Joking Around? Employee Humor Expression as Ingratiatory Behavior," *Academy of Management Review*, October 2005, pp. 765–776.

44. Amy J. C. Cuddy, Matthew Kohut, and John Neffinger, "Connect, Then Lead: To Exert Influence, You Must Balance Competence with Warmth," *Harvard Business Review*, July–August 2013, pp. 54–61.

45. Andrew J. DuBrin, "Sex Differences in the Use and Effectiveness of Tactics of Impression Management," *Psychological Reports*, *74* (1994), pp. 531–544.

46. Marla Baskerville Watkins, Alexis Nicole Smith, and Karl Aquino, "The Use and Consequences of Strategic Sexual Performances," *Academy of Management Perspective*, August 2013, pp. 173–186.

47. Lee et al., "How Do I Get My Way?" p. 224.

48. Yongmei Liu, et al., "When Ingratiation Backfires: The Role of Political Skill in the Ingratiation-Internship Performance Relationship," *Academy of Management Learning & Education*, December 2014, pp. 569–586.

49. L. A. Witt, "Enhancing Organizational Goal Congruence: A Solution to Organizational Politics," *Journal of Applied Psychology*, August 1998, pp. 666–674.

50. Jay Parikh, "How Facebook Tries to Prevent Office Politics," *Harvard Business Review*, June 29, 2016, p. 2.

51. Gerald F. Cavanagh, Dennis J. Moberg, and Manuel Velasquez, "The Ethics of Organizational Politics," *Academy of Management Review*, July 1981, p. 372.

52. Tamara Lytle, "In It to Win It," *HR Magazine*, July/August 2016, p. 43.

Conflict and Stress

CHAPTER 13

Antonio Guillem/Shutterstock.com

Chapter Outline

Learning Objectives

After reading and studying this chapter and doing the exercises, you should be able to:

1. Understand the nature of conflict in organizations and its leading causes.

2. Have the necessary information to resolve many workplace conflicts, including dealing with difficult people.

3. Be aware of basic negotiating and bargaining techniques to resolve conflict.

4. Understand the nature, causes, and consequences of work stress.

5. Explain what organizations can do to manage and reduce stress.

6. Do a more effective job of managing your own stress.

Based in Dallas, Texas, Ryan, LLC is a leading global tax services firm that has become highly acclaimed as a professional workplace. The company employs 2,200 people worldwide, divided into 450 teams. An award from *Fortune* recognizes Ryan's pioneering work culture within the professional services industry, particularly with respect to its flexible work schedules. Ryan's flexible work program was triggered in 2007 by a team leader, Kristi Bryant, whose 60-hour-plus work weeks were creating conflict in balancing work and family life.

With her wedding approaching the following year, Bryant had enough and submitted her resignation. Instead of accepting her resignation, G. Brint Ryan, the chief executive officer (CEO), asked that she stay and be part of an effort to change the organizational culture with respect to work flexibility. Ryan called for a team to figure out quickly a company-wide work flexibility policy. The result was "myRyan," a policy that changed the firm's culture drastically. Today, instead of tracking time spent in the office, the professional staff tracks only client billable and project hours, along with internal project hours. Employees are now rewarded for results, including profitability, rather than the number of hours worked.

Except for certain groups, work time is flexible. For example, some workers might spend 70 percent of their time in the office and 30 percent working remotely. Other workers might use a 60–40 split between work in the office and remote work. Employees who hold positions not easily adaptable to remote work are encouraged to develop their own plans for work flexibility. A group of receptionists, for example, set their own schedules so that they included a half-day off from work while still staffing office reception.

An internal task force developed ways to measure results under myRyan. Metrics such as client satisfaction scores, revenue generation, and goal achievement are recorded on a dashboard to provide managers with the objective results employees produce. When an employee is not attaining goals, there is an option to pull his or her flexibility benefit, yet this rarely happens. As the flex policy has progressed, voluntary turnover has been reduced to single digits, and client satisfaction has increased. As a recruiting tool, myRyan has been an outstanding success in drawing job seekers to the firm.

The myRyan program was not easy to implement at first, but with extensive discussion and workshops, most managers learn to implement work flexibility successfully. Ryan explained that "You have to go through the process of 'de-guilting' working from home, working on the road, and working at times that are convenient for you."

In reflecting on the flexible-work program, Ryan said, "The most important thing we learned throughout this whole exercise is that myRyan, in our view, enables people to achieve not just success at work, but success in life."[1]

The story about the tax services firm illustrates how many companies seek to reduce a major source of workplace conflict: balancing the demands of work and family and personal life. The same type of conflict can be stressful for many workers.

The purpose of this chapter is to present information that will help the reader understand two closely related processes: conflict and stress.

Conflict in Organizations

LEARNING OBJECTIVE 1
Understand the nature of conflict in organizations and its leading causes.

conflict The opposition of persons or forces giving rise to some tension, or a disagreement between two or more parties who are interdependent.

Conflict refers to the opposition of persons or forces giving rise to some tension, or to a disagreement between two or more parties who are interdependent.[2] A conflict occurs when two or more parties pursue mutually exclusive goals, values, or events. Each side believes that what it wants is incompatible with what the other wants, such as two groups wanting to use the same conference room at the same time. Conflict can also take place at the individual level when a person has to decide between two incompatible choices. For example, a person might have to choose between accepting a job transfer and remaining in town with family and friends. Refusing to transfer could mean a job loss, whereas accepting the transfer would mean less contact with family and friends.

Conflict has enough emotional content to lead to stress for the individuals involved. Similarly, factors that create conflict, such as abusive supervision, are also sources of job stress. Conflict and stress can be studied as part of group behavior because so much conflict and stress is generated by interactions among two or more people. Our study of conflict concentrates on sources of conflict; task versus relationship conflict; the consequences of conflict; and various methods, including negotiation, for resolving conflict.

Dealing with conflict is a regular part of a manager's job.

Sources and Antecedents of Conflict

Conflict is pervasive in organizations. Managers allegedly spend between 20 and 30 percent of their work activities directly or indirectly resolving conflict. The sources, antecedents, or outright causes of conflict are numerous, and the list is dynamic. At any given time, a new and potent source of conflict might emerge, such as management's current emphasis on hiring freelance workers rather than offering full-time employment and paying full benefits. Here we describe six illustrative sources of workplace conflict.

Perceived Adverse Changes

A high-impact source of conflict is a change in work methods, conditions of work, or employment opportunities that the people involved perceive negatively. **Downsizing**, the laying off of workers to reduce costs and increase efficiency, is one such change. An aspect of downsizing that continues to gain momentum is the automation of jobs, such as replacing rapid-service restaurant workers with tablet computers that customers can use to order food. People who want the jobs are in conflict, as are the workers who see their coworkers dismissed.

downsizing The laying off of workers to reduce costs and increase efficiency.

Continuous downsizing, even when business conditions improve, can precipitate labor versus management conflict. Management wants to eliminate as many jobs as possible, whereas the labor union values job security for its members. Despite these conditions, all parties do not perceive downsizing as an adverse change. Company executives may believe that downsizing is rightsizing, leading to an efficient, competitive firm that will attract investors.

Line versus Staff Differentiation

A major form of conflict takes place between line and staff units. Line units deal with the primary purposes of the firm, such as the sales group in a business firm. Staff units deal with the secondary purposes of the firm, such as the environmental protection unit in a business firm. They also deal with the activities necessary to make the line activities more efficient and effective. Staff units might do the hiring and the labor-contract interpretations, and verify that the line group complies with environmental laws. Yet they would not manufacture or sell the product or service. Although some researchers regard the line versus staff dichotomy as outdated, most managers and professionals in organizations still find this distinction useful.

Staff managers and professionals advise managers but cannot make certain decisions about themselves. A human resources professional, for example, might advise top management about the adverse consequences of downsizing following a merger. Nevertheless, this professional does not have the authority to halt the downsizing. Line and staff workers may conflict when the line manager perceives that the staff professional is attempting to heavily influence his or her decisions.

Sexual Harassment

sexual harassment Unwanted sexually oriented behavior in the workplace that results in discomfort and/or interference with the job.

Many employees experience conflict because of sexual harassment by a manager, coworker, customer, or vendor. **Sexual harassment** is unwanted sexually oriented behavior in the workplace that results in discomfort and/or interference with the job. High-profile cases of sexual harassment have received extensive formal media and social media attention in recent years in many fields, including traditional business, show business, politics, civil service, the military, labor unions, and professional and amateur athletics.

Types and Frequency Sexual harassment is divided into two types. In *quid pro quo* harassment, the employee's submission to or rejection of unwelcome sexual advances is used as the basis for a tangible employment action about the employee. An example of a tangible employment action is hiring, firing, or failing to promote a person. The demands of a harasser can be explicit or implied. Sexual harassment is considered illegal when it takes place so frequently or is so severe that it creates a hostile work environment or adversely affects the victim's job.

Hostile working environment harassment occurs when someone in the workplace creates an intimidating, hostile, or offensive working environment. A tangible employment advantage or adverse economic consequence does not have to exist. The hostile-environment type of harassment is subject to considerable variation in perception and interpretation. A company executive might hang a French impressionist painting of a partially nude woman in the lobby. Some people would find this offensive and intimidating and complain that they were harassed. Others might compliment the executive for being a patron of the arts.

The meanings and interpretations of what constitutes sexual harassment continue to evolve with judicial rulings. For example, having a pornographic site open on a desktop computer will usually be interpreted as hostile environment harassment. At the extreme, a sexist comment might result in a sexual harassment complaint. A sexist comment to a woman might be, "I doubt you are good at mechanics." A sexist comment to a man might be, "I doubt you are good at dealing with customer feelings." Unwanted hugging might be interpreted as sexual harassment.

Sexual harassment in the workplace was first recognized as the behavior of males directed against females. Over the years, many more claims have been made by males against females, males against males, and females against females. Complaints of transgender workers about sexual harassment have surfaced recently. With respect to the sexual harassment of women, a recent poll indicated that 30 percent of women had experienced unwanted sexual advances from male coworkers. Earlier polls have suggested much higher rates of harassment against women. Twenty-three percent reported they were harassed by men who had influence over their jobs, and 95 percent said male harassers usually go unpunished. In a Quinnipiac University national poll, one in five males reported that he had been sexually harassed.[3] Estimates of the frequency of sexual harassment might be underreported because many workers are concerned about retaliation, such as being blocked from promotion or being fired undeservedly.

Industries with large numbers of female low-wage workers have much higher rates of sexual harassment that receive little publicity. During a recent 10-year period, more than 41,000 charges of sexual harassment were filed with the Equal Employment Opportunity Commission (EEOC), with the hotel and food industries and the retail sector having the most charges at approximately 13 percent each. The media and entertainment industries accounted for less than 3 percent of complaints about sexual harassment.[4]

Role of Perception A group of researchers provided useful insights into the role of perception in deciding which behaviors of supervisors and coworkers constituted either type of harassment. Typical harassment behaviors include physical contact, inappropriate remarks, a sexual proposition, a threat or promise associated with a job, comments on the other person's physical appearance, or a glaring stare at the person being harassed. The setting for the survey was a manufacturing plant that had a strict policy against sexual harassment. Furthermore, the supervisory and professional personnel had had training in dealing with sexual harassment. Employee perceptions were compared with U.S. federal guidelines on sexual harassment—the basis for a "correct" response.

The responses indicated that the majority of workers can accurately identify behaviors frequently associated with quid pro quo harassment. However, the same workers had difficulty identifying behaviors used to establish evidence of a hostile work environment. Male workers had a slight edge in the accuracy of their perceptions about what constitutes harassment, and women in white-collar jobs were more accurate than women in blue-collar jobs.[5] More recent research suggests that some men and women underestimate the discomfort their unwanted overtures cause recipients.[6] For example, "I didn't know that sending her 10 text messages asking her to out to dinner was so intimidating. What's the big deal about saying no to my requests?"

Aside from creating legal problems, sexual harassment is serious because it can create extensive damage to its victims, including such effects as anxiety, depression, eating disorders, drug abuse, voluntary job turnover, and post-traumatic stress.[7]

Eliminating and Decreasing Harassment The EEOC identified eliminating sexual harassment among its key priorities in its Strategic Enforcement Plan and increased its class-action suits to achieve this goal. The EEOC recommends that a policy against sexual harassment include racial and ethnic harassment, as well as that directed at people with disabilities. Another strong EEOC recommendation is that employees who believe they have been harassed should have multiple ways of filing a complaint. Examples include complaining to the immediate supervisor or to the human resources department or sending an e-mail to top-level management. The EEOC also specifies that the antiharassment policy must have a strong nonretaliation section.[8]

Company policy that emphasizes the illegality of sexual harassment is helpful in minimizing harassment on the job. The policy should be supported by an organizational culture that promotes just treatment of employees by managers and coworkers. A highly effective preventive measure is for individual workers to assert their rights at the first instance or hint of harassment. An example would be a woman explaining to a supervisor who hugged her suggestively that she will not tolerate such behavior and that she will file a report to upper management should the incident be repeated. The policy is an important first step, but a U.S. federal court ruling specified that proof merely of the existence of an antiharassment policy is insufficient. The court wants to see that the policy was effective in practice in reasonably preventing and correcting any harassing behavior.[9]

Many more complaints about sexual harassment are filed than courts can possibly handle. Furthermore, employers can defeat Title VII of the federal Civil Rights Act of 1964 by demonstrating that they have an internal mechanism in place to report harassment and that the plaintiff neglected to use the mechanisms.[10]

Many recommendations to managers have been advanced to help prevent sexual harassment in the workplace. A particularly useful one is offered by attorney Jonathan A. Segal, who suggests that managers detail what constitutes prohibited conduct. Three key points should be made by management:

- Offensive conduct can occur not only in the workplace but also at company-sponsored business and social events and can even include pursuing a romantic relationship with a coworker by calling or texting him or her during nonworking hours.

- Harassing behavior beyond that of other employees can be reported, including the behavior of customers, vendors, and suppliers.

- Harassment taking place through social media, e-mail, and text messages is within the scope of prohibited conduct.[11]

The combination of EEOC dictates and company policies against harassment helps reduce conflict over sexual harassment because the source of the conflict is reduced or eliminated. For example, not feeling forced to listen to lewd comments by a supervisor, coworker, or customer makes for a less conflictual and more peaceful work environment.

Despite all the efforts to prevent and control sexual harassment, complaints about and formal charges of sexual harassment continue to surge. One possible reason for the surge is that those who have been sexually harassed feel freer to report the incidents. For example, the #MeToo movement has encouraged thousands of women, and several men, to report on past incidents of being sexually harassed. Another possibility is that the publicity about such behavior entices many people to harass others, much like a "copycat crime."

Management must carefully evaluate all accusations of sexual harassment and not assume that the accused person is guilty. A person accused of sexual harassment deserves to present his or her side of the story and should receive due process from the organization.

One of the reasons that sexual harassment is difficult to prevent and decrease is that it is about power as well as sex. James Campbell, a professor of leadership and management at the University of Texas at Arlington, says that sexual harassment is about power, aggression, and manipulation and is an abuse of power.[12]

Factional Groups and Intragroup Conflict

Interpersonal conflict often takes place because there are different factions (subgroups) within groups with different points of view and different loyalties. The factions often take place because of a merger, and groups are formed to balance the representatives from the two merged companies, such as two merged banks. Factional groups may also arise when a joint venture takes place, such as two companies working together to produce top-of-the-line home-entertainment centers. Each of the two parent companies assigns a few of its own managers to be on the new, joint-venture's management team. Often the factional group consists of two subgroups, each with several representatives, such as a cost-cutting task force consisting of three representatives each from marketing, operations, and finance. The potential for conflict within factional groups increases when the subgroups differ substantially in demographic characteristics, such as age, gender, and educational level.

Factional group conflict is often referred to as *intragroup conflict* because the problems exist inside the group among its members. Intragroup conflict can arise from various sources, such as diverse opinions and perspectives, and generational conflicts. Incivility, personality clashes, and bullying (described later) also contribute to intragroup conflict.

Competing Work and Family Demands

Balancing the demands of career and family has become a major challenge facing today's workforce. The challenge is particularly intense for employees who are part of a two-wage-earning family. **Work–family conflict** occurs when the individual has to perform multiple roles: worker, spouse, and often, parent or guardian of a dependent parent. (Work–family conflict is usually referred to as *work–life* conflict, but that term overlooks the idea that work is a big part of life.) This type of conflict is frequent because the multiple roles are often incompatible. Imagine having planned to attend your child's championship soccer game and then being ordered at the last minute to attend a late-afternoon meeting. Men as well as women experience considerable work–family conflict because of the desire to be successful at work and also spend a lot of time engaged in family activities, including being a good parent.[13]

Work–family conflict works in two directions: Work can interfere with the family, and the family can interfere with work. An example of the latter would be when a person's partner says, "If you don't work fewer hours and spend more time at home, I'm going to leave you." A substantial source of work–family conflict is workers responding to digital messages from employers while participating in family activities, even during dinners and children's sporting events. A survey conducted by the American Psychological Association Center for Organizational Excellence found that more than 50 percent of employed adults check work messages at least once a day over the weekend, before or after work, and while home sick. Furthermore, it was found that 44 percent of workers responded to e-mails and text messages from work during vacation.[14]

Impact on Individual Work–family conflict is significant for the individual. A survey of 513 employees in a *Fortune 500* company supports the plausible finding that working

work–family conflict Conflict that ensues when the individual has to perform multiple roles: worker, spouse, and often, parent.

long hours interferes with family life. The long hours, in turn, lead to depression for some individuals and stress-related health problems, such as ulcers.[15] Work–family conflict is also a problem for employers because stressed-out workers are often less productive due to a reduced ability to concentrate on work. Furthermore, a study revealed that dual-earner couples who experienced work–family conflict were more likely to experience family interruptions at work, tardiness, and absenteeism.[16]

The complexity of work–family conflict with respect to individuals was demonstrated in a study about family-to-work conflict conducted at five information technology (IT) companies in southern China. A sample survey item measuring family-to-work conflict was, "In the morning, my home life interferes with my responsibilities at work." The study found that on days when employees experienced more morning family-to-work conflict, they reported a high degree of emotional exhaustion in the afternoon. Increased afternoon exhaustion, in turn, was linked to more displaced aggression toward supervisors in the afternoon and more displaced aggression toward family members in the evening. (A basic example of displaced aggression would be yelling at a child because of being frustrated at work.) The problem of misplaced aggression was lessened when the manager appeared to be understanding of the worker's family-to-work problem.[17]

Reducing Work–Family Conflict The general solution to work–family conflict is to have workplaces where employees have a choice of when, where, and how they do their work, as described in the chapter opener. Organizational programs to help reduce work–family conflict include flexible working hours, work-at-home programs, dependent-care centers, and parental leave programs. Time off to take care of urgent family demands, including parent-teacher conferences, is another potent approach to alleviating work–family conflict.

A meta-analysis of work–family conflict studies found that organizational support is more important for reducing work–family conflict than are flexible work arrangements.[18] Support includes communicating relevant information, emotional empathy, and tangible assistance. An example of support would be a supervisor granting a person an afternoon off from work to take a child to a pediatrician. The most effective type of support is not necessarily part of a formal program but an individual case-by-case arrangement with a worker who needs flexibility. For example, team member Carlos might need three days off from work because his partner suddenly needs heart surgery.

A positive outcome of flexible work arrangements is that they lead to enhanced job satisfaction for the participants, as revealed in a study of 700 workers from the IT department of a large company. Half the employees were included in the pilot flexibility program. These workers received training that explained how they could control where and when they worked, providing they met their work goals, and the arrangement worked for their teams. The control group consisted of the 350 employees who worked under existing rules that included a work-from-home option that employees could request, but was not always granted. A survey indicated that the flex-work group members were more likely to feel they had control over their schedules, received more support from their supervisors for their personal lives, and had sufficient time to spend with their families.[19]

A note of caution for career-minded people is that a conflict-free balance between work and home life may be difficult to attain because significant career accomplishments require so much commitment. In the words of business writer Keith H. Hammonds, "Simply cutting back on work inevitably fails, because in real life, success in work is predicated on achievement. In a competitive business environment—which is to say, every business environment—leadership requires commitment, passion, and to be blunt, a lot of time."[20]

Incivility, Personality Clashes, Bullying, and Abusive Supervision

Many instances of workplace conflict stem from individuals' dispositions as well as personality clashes. (A *disposition* is a characteristic attitude, similar to a personality trait.) People who are rude and uncivil or engage in bullying readily enter into conflict. Incivility (or employees' lack of regard for one another) has gained attention as a cause of workplace conflict.

Incivility researcher Christine Porath says that left unchecked, rampant incivility makes our days tenser. Incivility also leads to a loss of focus, a decline in productivity, a deliberate slacking off among disgruntled employees, and sometimes serious health problems. Another problem is that an organizational climate characterized by rudeness can result in aggressive behavior, high turnover, and lost customers. Being treated uncivilly by others often results in reciprocating by treating others in an uncivil manner. ("Act nasty to me, and I'll act nasty to somebody else.") Incivility can create divisiveness in a team, destroy collaboration, and diminish a sense of psychological safety. As a result, team effectiveness suffers. Incivility often stems from a person experiencing heavy work pressure, but communication technology is another key factor. It is much easier to have misunderstandings when communication does not include tone of voice or facial expression.[21]

Many other workplace conflicts arise because of people simply disliking each other. A **personality clash** is an antagonistic relationship between two people based on differences in personal attributes, preferences, interests, values, and styles. People involved in personality clashes often have difficulty in specifying why they dislike each other. Generational differences can result in personality clashes based on differences in values. As described in Chapter 4, members of different generations often have different values, and these differences can lead to workplace conflict.

Bullying behavior contributes to substantial interpersonal conflict in the workplace. One reason the problem of bullying has attracted so much attention in recent years is that parents who deal with school bullying recognize that the same problem can happen in the workplace. A bully is one who tries to control his or her victim through fear and intimidation. Among the typical behaviors of bullies are interrupting others, ranting in a loud voice, excessive teasing, hostile glares, and making threats. A typical attitude of a bullying boss is "My way or the highway," sending the message that the employee's suggestions are unwelcome. Research suggests that the most likely victims of supervisory bullying are those workers with less power, especially those working in personal service roles, such as housekeepers, nannies, and office assistants.[22] Bullying is often triggered by a person being under considerable pressure, such as a sales manager frantically attempting to attain a sales goal.

As with sexual harassment, bullying behavior leads to conflict because a worker's demands for tranquility on the job are incompatible with the demands of the harasser or bully. Bullied workers complain of a range of psychological ailments, such as anxiety, sleeplessness, panic attacks, and low self-esteem. The verbal abuse aspect of bullying leads to a hostile environment and can drive many people to leave an employer.[23] Bullying is also associated with racial discrimination because the bully will often insult another worker based on his or her race or ethnicity.

Abusive supervision has received considerable research attention as a form of workplace bullying. A study with working adults suggests that supervisors are the most likely to be abusive in response to poor performance by the subordinate. Supervisors with a tendency toward being hostile combined with limited self-control are the most likely to be abusive. The study also suggested that supervisors who were mindful of their feelings of hostility were less likely to have hostile outbursts.[24] Using surface acting to deal with angry customers is another factor that appears to trigger abusive supervision. A study found that this type of surface acting weakened a supervisor's self-control, leading to incidents of abusing subordinates.[25]

Task versus Relationship Conflict

Another way of examining conflict is to look at its source. Does it arise because of work or personal issues? Some conflicts within the group deal mostly with disagreements over how work should be done. They are referred to as *task* (or *cognitive*) conflicts because they deal mostly with the work itself rather than with emotions and relationships. Two group members, for example, might argue over whether it is better to use their limited advertising budget to buy space on the outside of a bus versus air time on the radio. **Task conflict** focuses on substantive, issue-related differences pertaining to the work itself.

---

personality clash An antagonistic relationship between two people based on differences in personal attributes, preferences, interests, values, and styles.

task conflict Conflict that focuses on substantive, issue-related differences pertaining to the work itself.

These issues are tangible and concrete and can be dealt with more by intellect than by emotion. Other conflicts within the group are more people oriented. They occur because people have personality clashes, are rude to each other, or simply view many problems and situations from different frames of reference.

Relationship conflict focuses on personal, individual-oriented issues. The conflict relates to subjective issues that are dealt with more by emotion than by intellect.[26] One symptom that relationship conflict exists within the group is when, during a meeting, two people say to each other frequently, "Please let me finish. I'm still speaking."

Task conflict in moderate doses can be functional because it requires teams to engage in activities that foster team effectiveness. Team members engaged in moderate task conflict critically examine alternative solutions and incorporate different points of view into their goals or mission statement. Because frank communication and different points of view are encouraged, task conflict can encourage innovative thinking. In contrast, relationship (or affective) conflict undermines group effectiveness by blocking constructive activities and processes. By means such as directing anger toward individuals and blaming each other for mistakes, relationship conflict leads to cynicism and distrust.

Task versus relationship conflict is a form of intragroup conflict. As with most aspects of organizational behavior, this type of conflict is influenced by the psychological needs of group members. A study of 145 teams found that, when group members had strong needs for achievement, more task conflict took place. When the need for affiliation of the group members was relatively high, relationship conflict was more likely to surface.[27]

An analysis of many studies cautions that task conflict and relationship conflict can be equally disruptive. A little conflict may be beneficial, but this advantage quickly decreases as conflict intensifies.[28] The underlying explanation is that most people take differences of opinion personally, whether the issue is strictly the task or one of personal characteristics.

When task conflict spews out of control and leads to relationship conflict, the benefits of task conflict are quickly lost.[29] Assume that a mortgage team is debating whether to use artificial intelligence (AI) to evaluate mortgage risks, and the discussion continues for a week. Soon each side starts to accuse the other of not understanding the mortgage business, and insults are exchanged. The team becomes temporarily dysfunctional, and the benefits of task conflict are lost.

Consequences of Conflict

Conflict results in both positive and negative consequences. The right amount of conflict may enhance job performance, but too much or too little conflict lowers performance. If the manager observes that job performance is suffering because of too much conflict, he or she should reduce it. If performance is low because employees are too placid, the manager might profitably increase conflict. For example, the manager might establish a prize for top performance in the group.

Positive Consequences of Conflict

Many managers and scholars believe that job conflict can have positive consequences. As described previously, recent evidence indicates that the right amount of conflict is usually quite low—somewhat like fat in your diet. When the right amount of conflict is present in the workplace, one or more of the following outcomes can be anticipated.

1. *Increased creativity.* Talents and abilities surface in response to conflict. People become inventive when they are placed in intense competition with others. The anger that often stems from conflict can lead to imaginative problem solving, such as being so angry about being passed over for promotion that the individual finds a way of becoming more promotable. A surprising finding is that anger helps people calm down and get ready to address a problem, not run from it.[30]

2. *Increased effort.* Constructive amounts of conflict spur people to new heights of performance. People become so motivated to win the conflict that they may surprise themselves and their superiors with their work output. A study conducted in a

long-term health-care organization found that mild task conflict prompted employees to feel more active, energized, interested, and excited about work.[31]

3. *Increased diagnostic information.* Conflict can provide valuable information about problem areas in the department or organization. When leaders learn of conflict, they may conduct investigations that will lead to the prevention of similar problems.

4. *Increased group cohesion.* When one group in a firm is in conflict with another, group members may become more cohesive. They perceive themselves to be facing a common enemy.

Negative Consequences of Conflict

When the wrong amount or type of conflict exists, job performance may suffer. Some types of conflict have worse consequences than others. A particularly bad form of conflict is one that forces a person to choose between two undesirable alternatives. Negative consequences of conflict include the following:

1. *Poor physical and mental health.* Intense conflict is a source of stress. A person under prolonged and intense conflict may suffer stress-related disorders. Many acts of workplace violence stem from highly stressed employees or former employees who experienced conflict with supervisors or coworkers.

2. *Wasted resources.* Employees and groups in conflict frequently waste time, money, and other resources while fighting their battles. One executive took a personal dislike to one of his managers and therefore ignored his cost-saving recommendations.

3. *Poor performance and sidetracked goals.* When emotional conflict is too strong, the team performance may suffer because not enough attention is paid to the task. Emotions may run so high in the group that the members may be unable to discuss their differences in a rational way. This problem has been found to be prevalent in multicultural groups.[32]

4. *Heightened self-interest.* Conflict within the group often results in extreme demonstrations of self-interest at the expense of the group and the larger organization. Individuals or groups place their personal interests over those of the rest of the firm or customers. One common result of this type of self-interest is hogging resources. A team member might attempt to convince the team leader to place him on an important customer-troubleshooting assignment even though he knows his rival on the team is better qualified.

5. *Workplace violence.* A disastrous consequence of intense conflict on the job is that it may result in workplace violence. Employees who are angry with their supervisor, or who think they may be terminated, or who argue intensely with coworkers, may become so enraged that they go on a shooting rampage. One terrifying example is that in 2015, two TV journalists in Virginia were shot to death by a disgruntled former colleague before he fatally shot himself. The assassin had been fired by the station two years previously because of anger issues.[33]

Conflict-Management Styles

Before describing specific methods of resolving conflict, it is useful to understand five styles of handling conflict. As shown in Figure 13-1, the five styles are based on a combination of satisfying one's own concerns (assertiveness) and satisfying the concerns of others (cooperativeness).[34]

1. *Competitive.* The competitive style is a desire to achieve one's own concerns or goals at the expense of the other party, or to dominate. A person with a competitive orientation is likely to engage in win-lose power struggles.

2. *Accommodative.* The accommodative style favors appeasement, or satisfying the other's concerns without taking care of one's own. People with this orientation may be generous or self-sacrificing just to maintain a relationship. A dissatisfied employee might be accommodated with a larger-than-average pay raise just to calm the person down and obtain his or her loyalty.

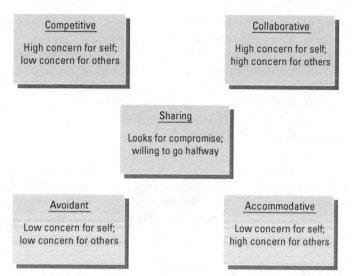

FIGURE 13-1 The Five Classical Conflict-Management Styles

3. *Sharing.* The sharing style is halfway between domination and appeasement. Sharers prefer moderate but incomplete satisfaction for both parties, which results in a compromise. The phrase "splitting the difference" reflects this orientation and is commonly used in activities such as negotiating a budget or purchasing equipment.

4. *Collaborative.* In contrast to the other styles, the collaborative style reflects a desire to fully satisfy the desires of both parties. It is based on an underlying philosophy of win-win, the belief that, after conflict has been resolved, both sides should gain something of value. A win-win approach is genuinely concerned with arriving at a settlement that meets the needs of both parties, or at least one that does not badly damage the welfare of either side. When a collaborative approach is used, the relationship between the parties improves. An example of a win-win approach would be for a manager to permit a call-center employee to work from home provided that his or her productivity increased enough to pay for the equipment needed to set up a work station at home.

5. *Avoidant.* The avoider is both uncooperative and unassertive. He or she is indifferent to the concerns of either party. The person may actually withdraw from the conflict or rely on fate. A manager sometimes uses the avoidant style to stay out of a conflict between two team members, who are left to resolve their own differences.

> **win-win** The belief that, after conflict has been resolved, both sides should gain something of value.

Conflict-Resolution Methods

Styles of dealing with conflict are closely related to methods of resolving conflict. For example, a collaborative style is a way of managing and resolving conflict. Here we present a sampling of conflict-resolution methods by describing confrontation and problem solving, as well as several structural methods.

Confrontation and Problem Solving

A widely applicable approach to resolving conflict is **confrontation and problem solving**, a method of identifying the true source of conflict and resolving it systematically. The confrontation approach is gentle and tactful rather than combative and abusive. Reasonableness is important because the person who takes the initiative in resolving the conflict wants to maintain a harmonious working relationship with the other party. Resolving a conflict often involves emotion, such as being angry with the other side. The best results will be attained if the emotion is expressed in a reasonable, assertive manner rather than being explosive. A reasonable expression of emotion might be, "I am upset that this problem has lingered so long. I want to resolve it today."

During the confrontation, one person decides to work cooperatively and confronts the second person. At this point, the person confronted may indicate a willingness to accept

> **confrontation and problem solving** A method of identifying the true source of conflict and resolving it systematically.

the confrontation or may decide to gloss over its seriousness. Often the conflict is resolved at this step, particularly if it is not serious or complicated.

After the confrontation, the two parties discuss their own opinions, attitudes, and feelings in relation to the conflict, attempting to identify the real issue. For example, the real cause of conflict between a manager and a team member might be that they have a different concept of what constitutes a fair day's work. After understanding the real issue, the parties attempt to develop specific means of reducing or eliminating the cause of the conflict. If the cause cannot be changed (such as changing one's opinion of a fair day's work), a way of working around the cause is devised. If both parties agree on a solution, then the confrontation has been successful. After the solution has been implemented, both parties should check periodically to ensure that their agreements are being kept.

The collaborative style of conflict resolution meshes together confrontation and problem solving. A major outcome is that trust is built between two parties as they search for the real reason for conflict.

Confront, Contain, and Connect for Anger

A variation of confrontation and problem solving has been developed specifically to resolve conflict with angry people, and it involves confronting, containing, and connecting. You *confront* by jumping right in and getting agitated workers talking to prevent future blowups. The confrontation, however, is not aimed at arguing with the angry person. If the other person yells, you talk more softly. You *contain* by moving an angry worker out of sight and out of earshot. At the same time, you remain impartial. The supervisor is advised not to choose sides or appear to be a friend. Finally, you *connect* by asking open-ended questions such as "What would you like us to do about your concern?" to get at the real reasons behind an outburst. Using this approach, one worker revealed he was upset because a female coworker got to leave early to pick up her daughter at day care. The man also needed to leave early 1 day a week for personal reasons but felt awkward making the request. So instead of asserting himself in explicit and direct fashion about his needs, he flared up.

An important feature of the confront, contain, and connect technique is that it provides angry workers a place where they can vent their frustrations and report the outbursts of others. Mediator Nina Meierding says: "Workers need a safe outlet to talk through anger and not feel they will be minimized or put their job in jeopardy."[35]

Structural Methods

A structural method of resolving conflict emphasizes juggling work assignments and reporting relationships so that disputes are minimized. One structural method for resolving conflict is for a manager to have direct control over all the resources he or she needs to get the job done. In this way, the manager is less likely to experience conflict when attempting to get the cooperation of people who do not report directly to him or her.

Conflict can often be reduced or prevented by one or more members from one organizational unit exchanging places with those of another unit; for example, shifting from purchasing to manufacturing. Working in another unit can foster empathy. Reassigning people in this way can also encourage people to develop different viewpoints in the affected groups. As the group members get to know one another better, they tend to reduce some of their distorted perceptions of one another. (Cross-functional teams accomplish the same purpose.) Exchanging members works best when the personnel exchanged have the technical competence to perform well in the new environment.

open-door policy An understanding in which any employee can bring a gripe to the attention of upper-level management without checking with his or her immediate manager.

In some firms, top management maintains an **open-door policy**, in which any employee can bring a gripe to its attention without checking with his or her immediate manager. The open-door policy is a popular grievance procedure because it allows problems to be settled quickly.

A long-standing structural approach to conflict resolution is an appeals procedure. When the person cannot resolve a problem with his or her manager, the person appeals to a higher authority. The higher authority is ordinarily the next level of management or a member of the human resources department. When a dispute (conflict) involves a union worker, the higher authority would be a union representative. The ability to help two group members in a dispute resolve their conflicts is considered a high-level management skill. Listening to the disputants and helping them to understand the true problem facing them is a useful start in resolving the conflict. Facilitating communication between the two parties, such as asking good questions, is also helpful.

Having an effective method for resolving disputes between workers and managers minimizes the number of instances in which a company is served with a complaint or a notice of a claim from a state or federal agency. Most top-level managers would prefer to learn about an employee dispute themselves early in the dispute so the problem can be resolved, rather than from a lawyer representing the individual.[36]

A manager sometimes has to help coworkers resolve their conflict.

Dealing with Difficult People

A challenge all workers face from time to time is dealing constructively with workers who appear intent on creating problems and thereby creating conflict. For a variety of reasons, these difficult or counterproductive people perform poorly themselves or interfere with the job performance of others. A **difficult person** is an individual who creates problems for others, yet has the skill and mental ability to do otherwise. The number of difficult employees appears to be increasing in recent years, as indicated by the number of managers referring such individuals to employee assistance programs. Counselors who specialize in dealing with behavioral problems are affiliated with employee assistance programs. Plausible reasons for the increased number of difficult people in the workplace are that job stress has increased or that society is breeding more narcissistic personalities.[37]

The bully mentioned earlier is an example of a difficult person. Another of many examples is the "yes-person" who will agree to any commitment and promise any deadline, but will rarely deliver. Some well-known executives are sometimes difficult people in their interactions with work associates. Another type of difficult or toxic coworker is the person who is quick to "throw others under the bus." These individuals are quick to assign blame to others when problems arise.[38] Psychiatrist Jody Foster (not the actress!) notes that, when workers act in inappropriate ways (e.g., bullying, excessive micromanaging, displaying narcissistic tendencies), the results can be devastating to the entire workplace.[39]

The techniques described next have wide applicability for helping difficult people change to more constructive behavioral patterns.

1. *Use tact and diplomacy in dealing with annoying behavior.* Coworkers who irritate you rarely do annoying things on purpose. Tactful actions on your part can sometimes take care of these annoyances without having to confront the problem. For example, point to the phone in your hand if noisy coworkers are gathered outside your cubicle. Tact and diplomacy are useful for dealing with a variety of disrupters, such as those coworkers who consistently talk about their personal interests, such as sports and favorite restaurants, while you are trying to focus on work. When subtlety does not work, it may be necessary to proceed to the confrontational tactics described earlier. Tact and diplomacy can also be incorporated into confrontation. In addition to confronting a person, you might point out the individual's good qualities.

2. *Hold an honest and candid conversation with the toxic coworker.* You cannot assume that a person who is annoying you continually will suddenly change for the

LEARNING OBJECTIVE 2
Have the necessary information to resolve many workplace conflicts, including dealing with difficult people.

difficult person An individual who creates problems for others yet has the skill and mental ability to do otherwise.

good. Make an honest attempt to provide productive feedback to the individual, and perhaps ask for feedback in return about what you might be doing wrong in the work relationship.[40] For example, you might say: "It is difficult for me to get my point across when you talk over my voice every time we work on a problem together. Is there anything I am doing wrong that makes work difficult for you?"

3. *Use nonhostile humor.* Nonhostile humor can often be used to help a difficult person understand how his or her behavior has affected others. Also, the humor will help defuse conflict between you and that person. The humor should point to the person's unacceptable behavior, yet not belittle the person. Assume that you and a coworker are working jointly on a report. Whenever you turn over a portion of your work for review, the person finds some fault. You point out lightly that striving for perfection is admirable but the striving is creating stress for you.

4. *Give recognition and attention.* Counterproductive or difficult people, like misbehaving children, are sometimes crying out for attention. By giving them recognition and attention, their counterproductive behavior will sometimes cease. If their negative behavior is a product of a more deeply rooted problem, recognition and attention alone will not work. Other actions will need to be taken, such as referring such persons for counseling.

5. *Reinforce civil behavior and good moods.* In the spirit of positive reinforcement, when a generally difficult person behaves acceptably, recognize the behavior in some way. Reinforcing statements would include, "It's enjoyable working with you today," and "I appreciate your professional attitude."

Negotiating and Bargaining

LEARNING OBJECTIVE 3
Be aware of basic negotiating and bargaining techniques to resolve conflict.

negotiating and bargaining
Conferring with another person in order to resolve a problem.

Conflicts can be considered situations calling for **negotiating and bargaining**, conferring with another person in order to resolve a problem. For example, when you are trying to negotiate a fair salary for yourself, you are simultaneously trying to resolve a conflict between yourself and your employer. At first, the demands of the two parties may seem incompatible, but through mutual-gains negotiation, a salary may emerge that satisfies both parties. The term *mutual gains* refers to the idea that both parties win. Self-Assessment 13-1 (pp. 300–301) provides you an opportunity to think through your own tendencies toward mutual-gains bargaining.

Harvard Business School professor Alison Wood Brooks offers a suggestion for effective negotiation that supports all the tactics described next. She recommends that you deal with the anxiety that often precedes entering negotiations by reframing anxiety as excitement; think of yourself as being excited rather than nervous about the upcoming negotiation. Also, build your confidence by practicing negotiation when the opportunity presents itself, such as negotiating for more time to complete an important project.[41]

Compromise

In compromise, one party agrees to do one thing if the other party agrees to do something else. Compromise is a realistic approach to resolving conflict and is almost inescapable in our culture. People enter into negotiation and bargaining sessions expecting a compromise solution. Assume, for example, that a company is negotiating to have a custom-designed machine built for a certain price. The buyer does not expect to get all the features desired at that price, while the seller anticipates throwing in more features than he or she first offered in order to close the deal.

The major problem with compromise is that the two parties may wind up with a solution that pacifies both but does not solve the problem. One example would be buying only half of the equipment that each of two department heads requests. As a result, neither department really shows the productivity gain that would have been possible if the full request had been granted to both sides.

Allow Room for Negotiation, but Be Plausible

The basic tactic of compromise is to begin with a demand that allows you room for compromise and concession. Anyone who has ever negotiated for the price of an automobile or house recognizes this basic approach. If you think your 10-speed bicycle is worth $400, you might put it on sale for $500. A potential buyer makes an initial offer of $300. After negotiation you wind up with an offer of $400, precisely what you wanted. However, be prepared to go beyond common sense. Most people believe that allowing room for negotiation includes beginning with an extreme demand or offer. (An example would be the seller asking $850 for the bicycle, or the potential buyer offering $150.) Law firm chairman David Boies recommends that you do not stake out a position so high that the other side concludes that is your walk-away point, and the negotiation ends right there.[42] A plausible demand is better because it shows you are bargaining in good faith. Also, if a third party has to resolve the conflict, a plausible demand or offer will receive more sympathy than an implausible one.

Use Facts More than Threats

During negotiation, both sides often become emotional, sometimes to the point of one party threatening the other, such as saying, "If you don't change that feature on your website that you copied from us, I will sue you so heavily that your company will go bankrupt." It is a better negotiating tactic to stick with the facts, rather than threatening the other side. In this example, the executive might say, "We want you to remove that feature because the legal interpretation we received is that the feature is our intellectual property."

Joseph Grenny, a social science writer, notes that people want psychological safety within a negotiating session. You should therefore do everything you can to share your understanding of the situation without triggering a perception of hostility or malicious intent on your part. Frame your statement as a natural consequence, not planned revenge. Rather than threatening the other side in the website example, the executive would state, "I have an obligation to protect our company's intellectual property."[43]

Focus on Interests, Not Positions

Rather than clinging to specific negotiating points, keep your overall interests in mind and try to satisfy them. Remember that the true object of negotiation is to satisfy the underlying interests of both sides. Here is how this strategy works:

> While job hunting, you are made an offer for a position you really want. You have a certain starting salary in mind, which is $5,000 more per year than the job offers. Your real interests are probably to be able to live a particular lifestyle with your salary, whereas your position is to attain a particular starting salary. Your interests are best served by examining the total compensation package, including employee benefits, along with the cost of living in the area. Agreeing to a starting salary lower than you had planned might serve your true interests best.

A key benefit of focusing on interests rather than positions is that it helps to place the emphasis away from winning and toward what you really want to achieve. If you focus on mutual interests, your intent will be to solve a problem rather than to outmaneuver the other side. For example, if a customer makes an unrealistic demand, your best interest is to somehow satisfy that demand without losing money and retain the customer.

Make Small Concessions Gradually

Making steady concessions leads to more satisfactory agreements in most situations. Gradually, you concede little things to the other side, such as throwing in an air pump and a backpack if the person agrees to move up the offer for the 10-speed bike. The small-concession tactic is described as a *soft approach* to bargaining. The hardline approach is

My Approach to Negotiation

The following quiz is designed to give you tentative insight into your major approach to negotiation. Check whether each statement is mostly true or mostly false as it applies to you now or would apply to you if you were negotiating something important.

Statement about Negotiation	Mostly True	Mostly False
1. I look at negotiations as a time to do battle.	☐	☐
2. During negotiation, I like to see the other side smile.	☐	☐
3. The first person to grant a concession in negotiation is acting foolishly.	☐	☐
4. I like to see the other side squirm during negotiation.	☐	☐
5. Negotiation is the time to find workable compromises.	☐	☐
6. An ideal result of negotiation would be for me to get exactly what I want and the other side to get nothing.	☐	☐
7. To intimidate the other side during negotiation, I like to shout and scream.	☐	☐
8. A little kindness toward the other side goes a long way in negotiation.	☐	☐
9. An effective negotiation tactic is to show respect for the other side.	☐	☐
10. An effective negotiation tactic is to grant a series of small concessions to the other side.	☐	☐
11. I know that I have been successful when the other side walks away from the negotiation with nothing.	☐	☐
12. I know that I have been successful when the other side walks away from the negotiation thinking that he or she got a good deal.	☐	☐
13. When the negotiation session is over, there is one winner and one loser.	☐	☐
14. As the old saying goes, "The winner takes all."	☐	☐
15. When negotiations are complete, both sides should walk away with something valuable.	☐	☐
16. For one side to win in negotiation, the other side has to lose.	☐	☐
17. If you smile during a negotiation session, the other side will try to take advantage of you.	☐	☐
18. After both sides have agreed on major issues during a negotiation, it is a good idea for one side to try to grab a last-minute concession.	☐	☐
19. Negotiation is only fun for me when I win big.	☐	☐
20. Negotiation is not very complicated: one side wins, and the other side loses.	☐	☐
21. I like to begin negotiations with an outrageous demand or offer.	☐	☐

My Approach to Negotiation *(Continued)*

Statement about Negotiation	Mostly True	Mostly False
22. An effective negotiator bargains in good faith.	☐	☐
23. It would make me feel cheap if I offered somebody only one-half of his or her asking price.	☐	☐
24. Being tactful and diplomatic helps you be a successful negotiator.	☐	☐
25. After negotiations are complete, I would be willing to shake hands (or exchange fist bumps) with the other side and say, "It was a pleasure doing business with you."	☐	☐

Scoring and interpretation: Give yourself 1 point, indicating a tendency toward being a mutual-gains negotiator, for each question you answered as follows:

1. Mostly False	6. Mostly False	11. Mostly False	16. Mostly False	21. Mostly False
2. Mostly True	7. Mostly False	12. Mostly True	17. Mostly False	22. Mostly True
3. Mostly False	8. Mostly True	13. Mostly False	18. Mostly False	23. Mostly True
4. Mostly False	9. Mostly True	14. Mostly False	19. Mostly False	24. Mostly True
5. Mostly True	10. Mostly True	15. Mostly True	20. Mostly False	25. Mostly True

If you scored 19 or more points for the 25 statements just listed, you have a strong tendency toward being a negotiator who attempts to find solutions that benefit both sides. You show genuine concern for the welfare of the other side. This is the nontraditional approach to negotiation, but it goes a long way toward establishing constructive relationships within organizations.

to make your total concession early in the negotiation and grant no further concessions. In our example, "My bike is for sale at $400 including an air pump and a backpack. I will keep the bike rather than let it go for less."

Use Deadlines

Giving the other side a deadline is often helpful in winning a negotiation or resolving a conflict. Deadlines often force people into action because they require some type of external control or motivation. Here is an example of how you might be able to use deadlines to gain advantage in your negotiation: "Will I be receiving a promotion to project leader by December 31? If not, I will be forced to accept employment at another company that has offered me such a promotion."

Ask the Other Side, "What Do You Want Me to Do?"

An effective tactic for both negotiation and other forms of conflict resolution is to ask the other side what he or she would like you to do in order to reach an agreement. If you do what the other side wants, you will often have reached an agreement. The underlying psychology is that, having suggested the solution, the other side will feel committed. Here is an example:

Your teammates and you are dividing up the work for a large task. It appears that several of your teammates do not think you are making an equitable contribution. After negotiating your contribution for about 30 minutes, you find that negotiations are stalled. You then ask, "What would you people like me to do?" Because you are so cooperative, the other team members will probably not make an outrageous demand. Also, they will probably regard your contribution as equitable because they formulated it.

Make a Final Offer

In many instances, presenting a final offer will break a deadlock. You might frame your message something like this: "I am willing to set up your Web page for $450. Call me when you are willing to pay that much for this specialized piece of work." Sometimes the tactic will be countered by a final offer from the other side. "Thanks for your interest in helping me set up a Web page. But the maximum price I am willing to pay is $250. Call me or text me if that price is acceptable to you." One of you will probably give in and accept the other person's final offer.

After having studied negotiating and bargaining tactics, along with other techniques of conflict resolution, now do Skill-Development Exercise 13-1. It deals with the most important goal of negotiation.

Work Stress

LEARNING OBJECTIVE 4
Understand the nature, causes, and consequences of work stress.

stress The mental and physical condition that results from a perceived threat that cannot be dealt with readily.

As used here, **stress** is the mental and physical condition that results from a perceived threat that cannot be dealt with readily. Stress is therefore an internal response to a state of activation. The stressed person is physically and mentally aroused. Stress will ordinarily occur in a threatening or negative situation, such as worrying about losing one's job or being reprimanded. However, stress can also be caused by a positive situation, such as receiving a large cash bonus. The topic of work stress is of enormous interest to managers and other professionals because of its impact on productivity and its legal and human consequences. Companies lose an estimated $300 billion annually because of stress, taking into account below-standard job performance, turnover, and psychological depression. Furthermore, job stress can lead to physical problems that kill about 120,000 people in the United States each year.[44]

Our study of work stress centers on its consequences and sources, along with individual and organizational methods for managing stress. Because stress deals heavily with personal perceptions, you are invited to take Self-Assessment 13-2 (pp. 304–305).

Symptoms and Consequences of Work Stress

stressor Any force creating the stress reaction.

A person experiencing stress displays certain symptoms indicating that he or she is trying to cope with a **stressor**, any force creating the stress reaction. These symptoms can include a host of physiological, emotional, and behavioral reactions. A problem with stress symptoms is that they lead to an adverse impact on employee health and well-being.

Symptoms of Stress

Physiological symptoms of stress include increased heart rate, blood pressure, breathing rate, pupil size, and perspiration. Men, in particular, who respond most intensely to mental stress, have a higher risk of blocked blood vessels, which increases their risk of heart attack and stroke. If stress symptoms are severe or persist over a prolonged period, the result can be additional stress-related disorders, such as migraine headaches, ulcers, colitis, and allergies. Stress also leads to a chemical imbalance that adversely affects the body's immune system. Thus, the overly stressed person becomes more susceptible to disease and suffers more intensely from existing health problems.

An overwhelming task can be a stressor.

Emotional symptoms of stress include anxiety, tension, depression, discouragement, feeling unable to cope, boredom, prolonged fatigue, feelings of hopelessness, and various kinds of defensive thinking. *Workplace anxiety* is a response to stressors that involves feelings of nervousness, uneasiness, and tension about job-related performance.[45]

Behavioral symptoms include nervous habits such as facial twitching, as well as sudden decreases in job performance due to forgetfulness and errors in concentration or judgment. If the stress is particularly uncomfortable or distasteful, it will lower job performance. The effect is greater for more-complex jobs. An example of a stressor that will lower job performance for all people is a bullying, abrasive boss who wants to see the employee fail.

Negative and Positive Consequences of Work Stress

Similar to conflict, not all stress is bad. People require the right amount of stress to keep themselves mentally and physically alert. The approximate relationship between stress (or anxiety) and performance is known as the Yerkes-Dodson law that has endured for over 100 years. As the task becomes more complex, less arousal or stress can be tolerated to achieve optimal performance, as illustrated in Figure 13-2. Yet, individual differences are important. For some people, a high amount of stress increases their ability to process information and get a complex task accomplished.

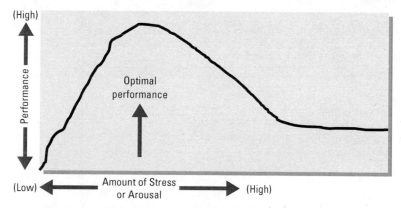

FIGURE 13-2 The Yerkes-Dodson Law for a Complex Task

A certain amount of stress is needed to perform well, but a very high stress level interferes with performance, particularly on a complex task such as preparing a budget.

Source: Developed by Robert M. Yerkes and John D. Dodson, Department of Psychology, Harvard University, 1908.

The Stress Questionnaire

Directions: Apply each of the following questions to the last 6 months of your life. Check the appropriate column.

Statement about Stress	Mostly Yes	Mostly No
1. Have you been feeling uncomfortably tense lately?	☐	☐
2. Are you engaged in frequent arguments with people close to you?	☐	☐
3. Is your social life very unsatisfactory?	☐	☐
4. Do you have trouble sleeping?	☐	☐
5. Do you feel apathetic about life?	☐	☐
6. Do many people annoy or irritate you?	☐	☐
7. Do you have constant cravings for candy and other sweets?	☐	☐
8. Is your cigarette, alcohol, or chocolate consumption substantially up?	☐	☐
9. Do you find yourself checking your e-mail or smartphone every few minutes even when not a business or social necessity?	☐	☐
10. Do you find it difficult to concentrate on your work?	☐	☐
11. Do you frequently grind your teeth?	☐	☐
12. Are you increasingly forgetful about little things, such as paying a bill or responding to an important e-mail or text message?	☐	☐
13. Are you increasingly forgetful about big things, such as appointments and major errands?	☐	☐
14. Are you making too many trips to the restroom?	☐	☐
15. Have people commented lately that you do not look well (or "good")?	☐	☐
16. Do you get into verbal fights with people too frequently?	☐	☐
17. Have you been involved in more than one physical fight lately?	☐	☐
18. Do you have a troublesome number of tension headaches?	☐	☐
19. Do you feel nauseated frequently?	☐	☐
20. Do you feel light-headed or dizzy almost every day?	☐	☐
21. Do you have churning sensations in your intestines too often?	☐	☐
22. Are you in a big hurry all the time?	☐	☐
23. Are far too many things bothering you?	☐	☐
24. Do you frequently feel exhausted for no particular reason?	☐	☐
25. Do you have difficulty shaking colds or other infections?	☐	☐

The Stress Questionnaire *(Continued)*

Scoring and Interpretation: The following guidelines are of value only if you answered the questions sincerely:

0–7, Mostly Yes answers: You seem to be experiencing a normal amount of stress.

8–17, Mostly Yes answers: Your stress level seems high. Become involved in some kind of stress-management activity, such as those described later in this chapter.

18–25, Mostly Yes answers: Your stress level appears much too high. Discuss your stress levels with a mental health professional or visit your family doctor (or both).

A person's perception of something or somebody usually determines whether that person or thing will be a positive or negative stressor. For example, one manager might perceive a quality audit by a corporate executive to be so frightening that he or she is irritable in dealing with team members. Another manager might welcome the visit as a chance to proudly display his or her department's high-quality performance.

A useful perspective on the positive consequences of stress is that gaining control over job demands, doing meaningful work, and receiving support and encouragement from supervisors and coworkers are closely linked to the potential benefits of stress.[46]

One explanation of why heavy stress decreases performance is that the associated anxiety creates cognitive interference that makes it difficult to give undivided attention to the task at hand. An example would be an anxious truck driver who cannot pay careful attention to road hazards.[47]

After prolonged exposure to job stress and anxiety, a person runs the risk of feeling burned out—a drained, used-up feeling. **Burnout** is a pattern of emotional, physical, and mental exhaustion in response to chronic job stressors. The same syndrome (collection of symptoms) is sometimes regarded as *work exhaustion*. Cynicism, apathy, and indifference are the major behavioral symptoms of the burned-out worker. Personal accomplishment finally diminishes as a result of burnout.[48] Continuous heavy work demands, such as many Wall Street research analysts and sales consultants working 60 hours per week plus having long commutes, are a major contributor to burnout.

> **burnout** A pattern of emotional, physical, and mental exhaustion in response to chronic job stressors.

Job burnout often leads to depression, and depression often leads to burnout. An encouraging note about this two-directional relationship was found in a study of over 2,000 adults who came to a medical center for three routine health exams over time. Strenuous physical activity, as reported by the participants in the study, tended to reduce both burnout and depression.[49]

Factors Contributing to Work Stress

A host of a person's internal factors, as well as adverse organizational conditions, can cause or contribute to job stress. As with sources of conflict, the list is dynamic. New sources of stress surface as the work environment changes. For example, today thousands of industrial and retail salespeople feel less job security because so much of the sales function has moved to the Internet.

Factors within the Individual

A general stressor that encompasses both individual and organizational factors is having to cope with significant change. The more significant the change you have to cope with in a short period of time, the greater the probability that you will experience a stress disorder.[50] Changes might include new living quarters, a new job, unemployment, getting married, or becoming a parent. Hostile, aggressive, and impatient people, labeled as having Type A personalities, find ways of turning almost any job into a stressful experience, in contrast to their more easygoing counterparts with Type B personalities. In addition to being angry, the outstanding trait of people with a Type A personality is their strong

Type A people are quite conscious of time.

sense of time urgency. A person with a Type A personality is prone to cardiovascular disorders, particularly when the individual is hostile.

Recognize, however, that not every hard-driving, impatient person is correctly classified as having a Type A personality. Managers and professionals who love their work and enjoy other people are not particularly prone to heart disease. These people experience more positive emotions than hostility and anger.

Having an external locus of control predisposes people to job stress because they do not believe they can control key stressors in their environment. Managers and professionals with a limited tolerance for ambiguity are prone to frustration and stress because high-level job responsibilities are often ambiguous. **Negative lifestyle factors** also predispose one to job stress. Among them are poor exercise and eating habits and heavy consumption of caffeine, alcohol, tobacco, and other drugs. Another factor predisposing a person to stress is a pessimistic attitude. Being optimistic, in contrast, helps a person ward off stress.

Another form of stress many workers bring on themselves is **nomophobia**, a form of anxiety stemming from having no access to a smartphone or the phone battery being dangerously low. (*Nomophobia* is short for non-mobile phobia and is also referred to as battery anxiety.) The same condition is characterized by the fear people can experience when they are out of mobile contact entirely.[51] A lost phone can result in a panic attack. You may have observed nomophobia among people who cannot still at a meeting, in a classroom, or at a restaurant table when they do not have a smartphone at hand.

Adverse Organizational Conditions

High stress levels created by adverse organizational conditions lead to many negative symptoms. According to the **job demands–job control model**, workers experience the most stress when the demands of the job are high, yet they have little control over the activity.[52] A customer service representative dealing with a major blooper by the firm would fit into this category. In contrast, when job demands are high and the worker has high control, the worker will be energized, motivated, and creative. An industrial sales representative who decides which customers to call on might fit here.

A major contributor to work stress is *role overload*. Demands on managers and professionals are at an all-time high as companies attempt to increase work output and decrease staffing at the same time. Better financial results are achieved by having fewer employees accomplish more work, thereby fostering role-overload stress.

A long-recognized contributor to work stress is **role conflict**—having to choose between competing demands or expectations. We have already touched on role conflict in the study of value conflicts in Chapter 4 and work–family conflicts in this chapter. If a person complies with one aspect of a role, compliance with the other is difficult. *Person–role* conflict occurs when the role(s) an employer expects a worker to perform conflict with the person's basic values. A vegan working as a purchasing agent at a meat-packing company would suffer this type of conflict.

Emotional labor, as described in Chapter 4, is a work-induced type of stress related to role conflict. The worker is stressed because of feeling obliged to act in a way that conflicts with his or her true feelings. Emotional labor also creates stress because it contributes to work–family conflict.[53]

Another role-related stressor is **role ambiguity**, a condition in which the jobholder receives confusing or poorly defined expectations. Role ambiguity involves several factors. First, there is insufficient information about the worker's expected performance. Second, there is unclear or confusing information about expected job behaviors. Third, there is uncertainty about the outcome (e.g., promotion or dismissal) of certain on-the-job behaviors.[54]

negative lifestyle factors Behavior patterns predisposing a person to job stress, including poor exercise and eating habits and heavy consumption of caffeine, alcohol, tobacco, and other drugs.

nomophobia A form of heavy anxiety stemming from having no access to a smartphone or the phone battery being dangerously low.

job demands–job control model An explanation of job stress contending that workers experience the most stress when the demands of the job are high, yet they have little control over the activity.

role conflict Having to choose between competing demands or expectations.

role ambiguity A condition in which the jobholder receives confused or poorly defined role expectations.

The relevance of the three role stressors just described has been magnified by a meta-analysis that found role overload, role conflict, and role ambiguity can all result in less organizational citizenship behavior. Part of the problem is that the stressors hinder the employees' ability to pursue their achievement goals.[55] The role-stressed employee might think, "I'm too stressed to bother going out of my way to help others."

A powerful stressor for knowledge workers is information overload. Workers often have to process so much information that their brain circuits become overloaded, leading to stress and lowered concentration. Many workers encourage overload by multitasking while receiving information. Attempting to accomplish more than one task at a time, such as keeping your eyes focused on three different monitors, can create anxiety for many—but not all—people.

Role overload is a frequent workplace stressor.

Organizational Approaches to Stress Management

Negative stress is disruptive to productivity and employee well-being, prompting organizations to engage in stress management. Here we look at several illustrative approaches to stress management.

LEARNING OBJECTIVE 5
Explain what organizations can do to manage and reduce stress.

Emotional support from an immediate superior can help group members cope better with job stress. One study compared the illness rate between two groups of employees who faced comparable heavy stressors. Employees who felt they had their manager's support suffered only half as much illness in 12 months as those who felt they lacked such support. Supportive behaviors that help employees feel more effective include (a) keeping communication channels open and (b) providing the right kind of help (such as verbal encouragement or time off from work to recover from a heavy stressor).[56]

To help combat negative stress, as well as to promote wellness, many employers offer programs that encourage employees to stay in good physical and mental shape. A **wellness program** is thus a formal organization-sponsored activity to help employees stay well and avoid illness. Workshops, seminars, activities, and medical procedures offered in a wellness program include the following: medical examinations, stress-management techniques, smoking-cessation programs, and preventive health care. (You will recall from Chapter 7 that positive reinforcement is often used to motivate employees to participate actively in a wellness program.)

wellness program A formal organization-sponsored activity to help employees stay well and avoid illness.

Many advocates say wellness programs are preventing health problems and helping workers reduce and prevent stress. The effectiveness of wellness programs, however, is controversial. Payoffs to the organization are difficult to measure because the programs have so many components.[57] Part of the problem is that not all individuals pushed by their employers to enter a wellness program are highly motivated to stay well and reduce stress. You should therefore not let group results discourage you from staying well and managing stress.

The accompanying Organizational Behavior in Action box describes a comprehensive wellness program offered by a well-known technology company.

Another approach to help employees combat stress is to give them the opportunity to nap on company premises. Napping is one of the most effective methods of treating and preventing stress. Everyday job stress can often be alleviated by taking a 15- to 20-minute nap to restore alertness and memory and to decrease the effects of fatigue. For career-minded people, the slogan "You snooze, you win" replaces "You snooze, you lose."

An example of a novel approach by an organization to managing stress is *walking meetings*, of approximately 20 minutes in length, conducted outside the building (weather permitting). The setting of the meeting provides a pleasant change of scenery from the

Cisco Systems Takes a Broad Approach to Employee Wellness

Cisco Systems Inc. is a multinational technology company with headquarters in San José, California. The company manufactures and sells Internet protocol–based networking products and services for the communications and information technology industry. It has been said that the company provides the infrastructure of the Internet. Cisco Systems has 73,000 employees and annual sales of approximately $49 billion.

Cisco has a comprehensive wellness program focused on improving and sustaining employee physical and mental health. Although a few aspects of the wellness program are aimed directly at dealing with job stress, all of its components are potentially useful in preventing or treating stress. For example, worrying about finances is a major stressor for many employees, and financial counseling helps deal with the problem. The company's traditional wellness offerings include access to seven high-tech U.S. fitness centers that provide cloud-based software to record their workouts, interact with trainers, and watch television during workouts. Employees can also connect their own fitness apps, such as a Fitbit, to the "wellness cloud."

The Cisco well-being platform consists of four pillars of health: physical, emotional, social, and financial. As a technology company, the four pillars have high-tech components, with the goal of "using the right technology at the right time to drive the right behaviors." Part of the emotional pillar, for example, is a mindfulness workshop that enables employees to practice mindfulness using mobile apps and computer games.

The financial health program includes webinars on a variety of topics, including how to manage a 401(k). Financial counseling is offered to employees that includes face-to-face meetings with financial planners. Workers are offered a personal money coach for 90 days. The social component of the well-being program includes giving employees a week of paid time off annually for volunteer work. Another feature of the social component is a generous paid parental-leave program.

The physical fitness component of the wellness program is enormous. A prime example is the 24,000-square-foot Life Connections Center located at company headquarters. The facility offers on-site primary medical care, fitness centers, outdoor sports courts, hiking and biking paths, and a child-care center. Acupuncture and physical therapy are also available to employees.

The Melbourne, Australia, Cisco facility sponsors the Cisco Run Club that offers both 5- and 10-km runs.

QUESTIONS

1. With a wellness program of this immensity, would you think that Cisco Systems employees are much healthier and less stressed than employees at most other companies?

2. What research method would you suggest to measure whether the Cisco wellness program is improving employee health, satisfaction, and productivity?

Source: Original story based on facts and observations in the following sources: Susan Milligan, "Wellness Blows Up: The Next Generation of Wellness Programs Define Health Much More Broadly," *HR Magazine*, September 2017, pp. 60–67; "Health and Wellness Program," Cisco Live! (www.Ciscolive.com), pp. 1–2; James A. Martin, "8 Easy Ways to Keep Employees Engaged in Wellness," *CIO* (www.cio.com), July 14, 2016, pp. 1–6; Sarah K. White, "5 Companies That Impress with Employee Benefits," *CIO* (www.cio.com), August 24, 2015, p. 7.

screens, desks, and walls and also offers physical exercise. The meeting leader makes sure the fresh-air break includes an agenda.[58]

Individual Approaches to Stress Management

LEARNING OBJECTIVE 6
Do a more effective job of managing your own stress.

Techniques individuals can use to manage stress can be divided into three categories: control, symptom management, and removal of the stressor.[59]

Control

Methods of controlling and reducing stress include getting the right emotional support. Receiving social support—encouragement, understanding, and friendship—from other people is a key strategy for coping with work and personal stress.

An equally important control technique is to practice good work habits and time management. By establishing priorities and minimizing procrastination, you can gain better control of your life. Gaining control is especially important because feeling out of control is a major stressor. Demanding less than perfection from yourself can also help prevent stress. Decreasing clutter in your life can also reduce stress by improving concentration and reducing the feeling of being overwhelmed. Periodically throwing out digital and printed information and physical possessions you do not need is an effective method of reducing clutter.

Symptom Management

Dozens of symptom-management techniques have been developed, and no stress-management program is complete without using at least one. Getting appropriate physical exercise is an excellent starting point for symptom management. Physical exercise helps dissipate some of the tension created by work stress and also helps the body ward off future stress-related disorders. One way in which exercise helps combat stress is by releasing endorphins. These are morphine-like chemicals produced in the brain that act as painkillers and antidepressants.

Another widely applicable symptom-management technique is the **relaxation response,** a general-purpose method of learning to relax on your own that is a form of meditation. The key ingredient of this technique is to get quiet and comfortable. At the same time, think of the word "one" (or any simple chant or prayer) with every breath for about 10 minutes. The technique slows you down both physiologically and emotionally and at the same time reduces the adverse effects of stress. A major contribution of the relaxation response is that it is a physical state of deep rest that counteracts the harmful effects of fighting stressors.[60] The relaxation response and meditation are quite similar to the more modern approach of *mindfulness* in which people learn to concentrate on the moment to reduce stress and sharpen their focus.

Much of the benefit of the relaxation response can also be achieved by napping or visualizing a pleasant fantasy for about 10 minutes. Yoga offers many of the benefits of the relaxation response; however, pushing yoga too far can be dangerous for people with high blood pressure or disorders of the joint. The stress busters listed in Figure 13-3 are aimed mostly at symptom management.

relaxation response A general-purpose method of learning to relax by oneself, which includes making oneself quiet and comfortable.

FIGURE 13-3 **Stress Busters**

- Take a nap when facing heavy pressures. Napping is one of the most effective techniques for reducing and preventing stress.
- Give in to your emotions. If you are angry, disgusted, or confused, admit your feelings. Suppressing your emotions adds to stress. Talk to a friend or counselor about your problems.
- Take a brief break from the stressful situation and do something small and constructive, such as washing your car, emptying a wastebasket, or cleaning out a drawer.
- Get a massage because it can loosen tight muscles, improve your blood circulation, and calm you down.
- Get help with your stressful task from a coworker, manager, or friend.
- Concentrate intensely on reading uninterrupted for a minimum of 30 minutes, and put away all electronic devices, however painful the experience might be at first.
- Have a quiet place at home and enjoy a brief idle period there every day.
- Take a leisurely day off from your routine, or at least take a brief walk during a particularly stressful day.
- Finish something you have started, however small. Accomplishing almost anything reduces some stress, particularly if you are goal oriented.
- Strive to do a good job, but not a perfect job.
- Work with your hands, doing a pleasant task.
- Find somebody or something that makes you laugh, and have a good laugh.
- Minimize drinking caffeinated or alcoholic beverages, and drink fruit juice or water instead.
- Eat fruits or vegetables for snacks rather than junk food.

Personal Stress-Management Action Plan

Most people face a few powerful stressors in their work and personal lives, but few people take the time to clearly identify these stressors or develop a plan for remedial action. The purpose of this exercise is to make you an exception. Here is an opportunity to develop an inventory of your stressors, think through the problems they may be causing you, and develop action plans you might take to remedy the situation. Use the form below or create one with a word-processing table or a spreadsheet.

Work or School Stressor	Symptoms This Stressor Is Creating for Me	My Action Plan to Manage This Stressor
1.		
2.		
3.		
Personal Life Stressor	Symptoms This Stressor Is Creating for Me	My Action Plan to Manage This Stressor
1.		
2.		
3.		

Seven days after preparing this worksheet, observe if any of your stress symptoms have diminished. Also, identify those stressors for which only a long-term solution is possible. One young man reported that a major work stressor he faced is that he wanted to work in international business, and emphasized doing business with Italian fashion companies. Yet he was experiencing stress because he had almost zero knowledge of the Italian language or culture. (By the way, can you offer this man any suggestions?)

A brief nap at the desk can reduce job stress.

Rehan Qureshi/Shutterstock.com

Removal of the Stressor

Removal-of-the-stressor methods of stress management are actions and reappraisals of situations that provide the stressed individual some escape from the stressor. Eliminating the stressor is the most effective escape technique. For example, if a manager experiences stress because of serious understaffing in his or her department, he or she should negotiate to receive authorization to hire additional staff. Mentally blocking out a stressful thought is another removal technique, but it may not work in the long run. Without constructive action about the problem, a stressor will usually return.

Skill-Development Exercise 13-2 provides you with a systematic approach to managing your stress.

Implications for Managerial Practice

1. A manager's goal should be to maintain optimal levels of conflict and stress in his or her unit. Sometimes this will involve the reduction of conflict; at other times, a modest amount of conflict stimulation may be necessary.

2. Approximately 20 to 30 percent of a manager's time involves resolving conflict. It is therefore important for a manager to develop effective conflict-resolution skills. A good starting point is to use confrontation and problem solving.

3. Given that an optimal amount of stress facilitates performance, a manager should strive to design the appropriate amount and kinds of stressors for both individuals and groups. Manipulating stressors is much like manipulating the challenge level of a job. Stress can be increased or decreased by manipulating the amount of job responsibility, goal difficulty, tightness of deadlines, amount of supervision, and critical feedback.

4. Managers should encourage team members to embark on a systematic program of stress management, considering today's turbulent work environment. Workers who are already managing stress well should be encouraged in their efforts.

Summary of Key Points

1. *Understand the nature of conflict in organizations and its leading causes.* Workplace conflict has many sources, including the following: perceived adverse changes; line versus staff differentiation; sexual harassment; factional groups and intragroup conflict; competing work and family demands; and incivility, personality clashes, bullying, and abusive supervision. Task conflict focuses on substantive, issue-related differences. Relationship conflict focuses on personal, individual-oriented issues that are dealt with more by emotion than by intellect. Conflict in small doses leads to positive outcomes, such as increased creativity. Negative consequences of conflict include wasted resources and workplace violence.

2. *Have the necessary information to resolve many workplace conflicts, including dealing with difficult people.* Five styles of handling conflict based on a combination of concern for oneself and concern for the other side have been identified: competitive, accommodative, sharing, collaborative (win-win), and avoidant. A widely applicable approach to resolving conflict is confrontation and problem solving, in which the true source of the conflict is identified and then resolved systematically. The recommended confrontational approach is a gentle and tactful one. To resolve conflict with an angry person, one might confront him or her, contain the angry situation, and connect with the person.

   A structural method of resolving conflict emphasizes juggling work assignments and reporting relationships so that disputes are minimized. An appeals procedure is a structural approach. Techniques for dealing with difficult people include using tact and diplomacy, using nonhostile humor, giving recognition and attention, and reinforcing civil behavior and good moods.

3. *Be aware of basic negotiating and bargaining techniques to resolve conflict.* Negotiating and bargaining techniques include the following: compromising, allowing room for negotiation but being plausible; focusing on interests, not positions; making small concessions gradually; using deadlines; asking the other side, "What do you want me to do?"; and making a final offer.

4. *Understand the nature, causes, and consequences of work stress.* Stress is an internal response to a state of activation, ordinarily occurring in a threatening or negative situation. Stress symptoms include a host of physiological, emotional, and behavioral reactions. Many of these symptoms can adversely affect job performance. After prolonged job stress, a person may experience burnout. A general stressor that encompasses both individual and organizational factors is having to cope with significant change. Factors within a person contributing to work stress include a Type A personality, an external locus of control, negative lifestyle factors, and a pessimistic attitude.

   Adverse organizational conditions are another set of stressors. According to the job demands–job control model, workers experience the most stress when the demands of the job are high yet they have little control over the activity. Other stressors include role overload and worry about potential job loss. Role conflict, role ambiguity, and information overload are other stressors of significance. Another potential stressor is being part of a culturally diverse group.

5. *Explain what organizations can do to manage and reduce stress.* Organizational approaches to stress management include providing emotional support to employees, establishing a wellness program, allowing for napping on the job, and the use of walking meetings.

6. *Do a more effective job of managing your own stress.* Individual methods of preventing and controlling stress can be divided into three categories: attempts to control stressful situations, symptom management, and removal of the stressful situation. Specific tactics include eliminating stressors, getting sufficient physical exercise, using relaxation techniques, getting emotional support from others, and improving work habits. Also see the stress-buster list in Figure 13-3.

conflict, p. 286

downsizing, p. 287

sexual harassment, p. 288

work–family conflict, p. 290

personality clash, p. 292

task conflict, p. 292

relationship conflict, p. 293

win-win, p. 295

confrontation and problem solving, p. 295

open-door policy, p. 296

difficult person, p. 297

negotiating and bargaining, p. 298

stress, p. 302

stressor, p. 302

burnout, p. 305

negative lifestyle factors, p. 306

nomophobia, p. 306

job demands–job control model, p. 306

role conflict, p. 306

role ambiguity, p. 306

wellness program, p. 307

relaxation response, p. 309

Discussion Questions and Activities

1. Get together in a small group to present evidence that being effective at resolving conflict is still a major problem in business and society.
2. In what way does the presence of junk-mail advertising in e-mail and pop-up ads on websites create conflict? Who are the parties in conflict?
3. Conflict is said to have some functional consequences. Describe an example of how conflict has ever improved your work or personal life.
4. Visualize yourself as the branch manager in Aspen, Colorado, and one of the team members wants a flexible work schedule so he can profit from the best days for skiing this ski season. How would you handle his request?
5. Why do so many workers at all organizational levels still commit sexual harassment despite all the information available about its illegality and immorality?
6. Visualize yourself as the parent of an 8-year-old daughter. You and the other parent have a parent-teacher conference scheduled for Thursday at 4 p.m. On Thursday morning, your boss calls for a 4 p.m. meeting. How would you deal with this conflict?
7. Do you experience nomophobia? How do you know?
8. Identify a job in any field of business that you think creates negative stress for most incumbents, and pinpoint the stressors.
9. How much authority should the director of a wellness program have in deciding which foods should be on the menu in the company cafeteria? (Her reasoning is that she wants employees to eat only healthy foods on company premises.)
10. What do you see as the advantages and disadvantages of using walking meetings to help reduce stress and burnout?

CASE PROBLEM: The Concerned Sales Trainee

Emma was thrilled about the position she just landed as a sales representative for a company that provides data backup and storage for small organizations throughout the country. She was assigned a sales territory in San Diego, California, where she lived with her husband and two preschool-aged children. Before working her territory, Emma was required to attend 10 days of training and onboarding at company headquarters in Cleveland, Ohio.

One of the key trainers in the program was Wesley, an energetic and successful man in his early fifties. During a beverage-and-food break at the first morning of the training and onboarding program, Wesley approached Emma and complimented her on her "great California tan," and "knockout appearance." Emma was not particularly comfortable with the comments, but she let them pass.

Before the dinner meeting on the second night of the program, Wesley approached Emma and engaged her in a conversation about how she was enjoying the sales training and onboarding. He then handed her a business card and said, "I thought perhaps that you might be a little lonely being away from home for 10 days, so here is my business card. Please get in touch with me if you would like to hang out with me a little."

Emma thought that Wesley was stepping over the line of good business judgment, but she smiled politely and said, "Thanks anyway, but I am so overwhelmed with all this important information I am receiving that I have no spare time. I'm not too lonely because I use Skype to stay in touch with my husband and children."

The following morning, Emma received a text message from Wesley that said, "You are totally charming and beautiful. Get back to me."

Emma later phoned her best friend Crystal and said, "Wesley is influential because he is the national sales manager. But I think that his behavior toward me might constitute sexual harassment. Yet, five days into my job, I guess I shouldn't attempt to lodge a complaint about a company executive."

Crystal replied, "You have got to do something. The national sales manager is a predator."

Questions

1. To what extent is Wesley sexually harassing Emma?
2. If Wesley is guilty, what type of sexual harassment is he committing?
3. What steps should Emma take so that she can stop Wesley's advances yet still maintain a good working relationship with him?
4. What would be the advantages and disadvantages of Emma filing a complaint about Wesley with the company?

Endnotes

1. Original story created from facts and observations in the following sources: Susan Milligan, "My Job Ate My Vacation," *HR Magazine*, April 2016, pp. 28–36; "Ryan Named a Best Workplace in Consulting and Professional Services by *Fortune*," Ryan (http://ryan.com), February 23, 2017, pp. 1–3; "Ryan LLC," When Work Works (www.whenworkworks.org); Lauren Dixon, "How Ryan Flipped to Flex," Talent Economy (www.talenteconomy.io), December 14, 2016, pp. 1–6; Dana Wilkie, "How One CEO Got 'Flextime' Religion," *SHRM* (www.shrm.org), June 25, 2014, pp. 12.

2. Yuhyung Shin, "Conflict Resolution in Virtual Teams," *Organizational Dynamics*, Vol. 4 (2005), p. 332.

3. Washington Post-ABC News poll, 2017, reported in Dori Meinert, "Indecent Behavior," *HR Magazine*, February 2018, p. 35; Brendan L. Smith, "What It Really Takes to Stop Sexual Harassment," *Monitor on Psychology*, February 2018, p. 39.

4. Smith, "What It Really Takes to Stop Sexual Harassment," pp. 41–42.

5. Marjorie L. Icenogle, Bruce W. Eagle, Sohel Ahman, and Lisa A. Hanks, "Assessing Perceptions of Sexual Harassment Behaviors in a Manufacturing Environment," *Journal of Business and Psychology*, Summer 2002, pp. 601–616.

6. Vanessa K. Bohns and Lauren DeVincent, "To Reduce Sexual Misconduct, Help People Understand How Their Advances Might Be Received," *Harvard Business Review*, April 26, 2018, pp. 1–6.

7. Smith, "What It Really Takes to Stop Sexual Harassment," p. 39.

8. Jonathan A. Segal, "Stamping Out Harassment," *HR Magazine*, June 2014, p. 111.

9. Andrew Slobodien and Elizabeth Peters, "Beyond Harassment Prohibitions: Don't Just 'Set and Forget' Anti-Harassment Policies," *HR Magazine*, November 2012, p. 76.

10. Sara Randazzo, "Sex Claims Face Hurdles," *The Wall Street Journal*, November 24, 2017, p. A3.

11. Jonathan A. Segal, "Strengthen Your Harassment Complaint Process," *HR Magazine*, April 2018, p. 65.

12. Cited in Smith, "What It Really Takes to Stop Sexual Harassment," p. 38.

13. Julie Bennett, "Balancing Work and Home Life Is Not Only a Woman's Issue," Society of Human Resource Management supplement appearing in *The Wall Street Journal*, June 20, 2012, p. B9.

14. Survey reported in Greg Keller, "NYC Bill Would Shield Workers from After-Hours Calls, Emails," *The Commercial Appeal*, May 20, 2018.

15. Virginia Smith Major, Katherine J. Klein, and Mark G. Ehrhart, "Work Time, Work Interference with Family, and Psychological Distress," *Journal of Applied Psychology*, June 2002, pp. 427–436.

16. Leslie B. Hammer, Talya N. Bauer, and Alicia A. Grandey, "Work–Family Conflict and Work-Related Withdrawal Behaviors," *Journal of Business and Psychology*, Spring 2003, pp. 419–436.

17. Yihao Liu, "Work–Family Conflict, Emotional Exhaustion, and Displaced Aggression Toward Others: The Moderating Roles of Workplace Interpersonal Conflict and Perceived Managerial Family Support," *Journal of Applied Psychology*, May 2015, pp. 793–808.

18. Tammy D. Allen, Ryan C. Johnson, Kaitlin M. Kirbuz, and Kristen M. Shockley, "Work–Family Conflict and Flexible Work Arrangements: Deconstructing Flexibility," *Personnel Psychology*, Number 2, 2013, pp. 345–376.

19. Jena McGrefor, "More Proof That Flexibility Programs Work," *The Washington Post* (www.washingtonpost.com), May 9, 2014, pp. 1–2.

20. Keith H. Hammonds, "Balance Is Bunk," *Fast Company*, October 2004, p. 72.

21. "Why We Need to Kick Incivility Out of the Office" (interview with Christine Porath), *Knowledge@Wharton* (*knowledgewharton.upenn.edu*), June 210, 2017; Christine Porath, "How Rudeness Stops People from Working Together," *Harvard Business Review*, January 20, 2017, p. 2; Christopher C. Rosen, Joel Koopman, Allison Gabriel, and Russell E. Johnson, "Who Strikes Back? A Daily Investigation of When and Why Incivility Begets Incivility," *Journal of Applied Psychology*, November 2016, pp. 1620–1634.

22. Vincent J. Roscingo, Steven H. Lopez, and Randy Hodson, "Supervisory Bullying, Status Inequalities, and Organizational Context," *Social Forces*, July 2009, pp. 1561–1589; Dana Wilkie, "Where the Bullies Are," *HR Magazine*, March 2016, p. 52,

23. Arthur H. Bell, *You Can't Talk to Me That Way* (Franklin Lakes, NJ: Career Press, 2005).

24. Lindie H. Liang, et al., "Why Are Abusive Supervisors Abusive? A Dual-System Self-Control Model," *Academy of Management Journal*, August 2016, pp. 1385–1406.

25. Kai Chi Yam, et al., "Out of Control: A Self-Control Perspective on the Link between Surface Acting and Abusive Supervision," *Journal of Applied Psychology*, February 2016, pp. 292–301.

26. Carlsen K. W. De Dreu and Laurie Weingart, "Task versus Relationship Conflict, Team Performance, and Team Member Satisfaction: A Meta-Analysis," *Journal of Applied Psychology*, August 2003, pp. 741–749.

27. Jinseok S. Chun and Jin Nam Choi, "Members' Needs, Intragroup Conflict, and Group Performance," *Journal of Applied Psychology*, May 2014, pp. 437–450.

28. De Dreu and Weingart, "Task versus Relationship Conflict," p. 746.

29. Ruchi Sinha, et al., "Skewed Task Conflicts in Teams: What Happens When a Few Members See More Conflict than the Rest?" *Journal of Applied Psychology*, July 2016, p. 1046.

30. Joann Ellison Rodgers, "Go Forth in Anger," *Psychology Today*, April 2014, p. 76.

31. Gergana Todorva, Julia B. Bear, and Laurie B. Weingart, "Can Conflict Be Energizing? A Study of Task Conflict, Positive Emotions and Job Satisfaction," *Journal of Applied Psychology*, May 2014, pp. 451–467.

32. Mary Ann Von Glinow, Debra L. Shapiro, and Jeanne M. Brett, "Can We *Talk*, and Should We? Managing Emotional Conflict in Multicultural Teams," *Academy of Management Review*, October 2004, pp. 578–592.

33. Charisse Jones, "Reporters' Killings Lead to Workplace Reviews," *USA Today*, August 30, 2015.

34. Kenneth Thomas, "Conflict and Conflict Management," in Marvin D. Dunnette (ed.), *Handbook of Industrial and Organizational Psychology* (Chicago: Rand McNally College Publishing, 1976), pp. 900–902.

35. The quote and technique are both from Kathleen Doheny, "It's a Mad, Mad Corporate World," *Working Woman*, April 2000, pp. 71–72.

36. F. Peter Philips, "Ten Ways to Sabotage Dispute Management," *HR Magazine*, September 2004, p. 163.

37. Jennifer Schramm, "The Rise of the Difficult Employee?" *HR Magazine*, June 2012, p. 144.

38. Eric Titner, "Signs Your Co-Worker Might Be Toxic," Career Opportunities, the Job Network (www.thejobnetwork.com), March 11, 2018, p. 1.

39. Cited in "How Disruptive Behavior by Employees Can Devastate a Workplace," *Knowledge@Wharton* (http://knowledge.wharton.upenn.edu), March 27, 2013, p. 1.

40. Abby Curnow-Chavez, "4 Ways to Deal with a Toxic Coworker," *Harvard Business Review*, April 10, 2018, p. 4.

41. Alison Wood Brooks, "Emotion and the Art of Negotiation," *Harvard Business Review*, December 2015, pp. 59–60.

42. David Boies, "How to Negotiate," *Bloomberg Businessweek*, April 16–22, 2012, p. 63.

43. Joseph Grenny, "How to Deal with the Irrational Parts of a Negotiation," *Harvard Business Review*, June 6, 2016, pp. 1–6.

44. "Transforming Stress through Awareness, Education, and Collaboration," American Institute of Stress (www.stress.org), January 12, 2018, p. 3; Rita Pyrillis, "Many Workplaces Failing Stress Test," *Workforce*, May 2015, p. 15.

45. Bonnie Hayden Cheng and Julie M. McCarthy, "Understanding the Dark and Bright Sides of Anxiety: A Theory of Workplace Anxiety," *Journal of Applied Psychology*, May 2018, pp. 537–560.

46. Research cited in Sue Shellenbarger, "Turn Bad Stress into Good," *The Wall Street Journal*, May 8, 2013, p. D1.

47. Cheng and McCarthy, "Understanding the Dark and Bright Sides of Anxiety," p. 553.

48. Cynthia L. Cordes and Thomas W. Dougherty, "A Review and Integration of Research on Job Burnout," *Academy of Management Review*, October 1993, p. 622.

49. Sharon Toker and Michal Biron, "Job Burnout and Depression: Unraveling Their Temporal Relationship and Considering the Role of Physical Activity," *Journal of Applied Psychology*, May 2012, pp. 699–710.

50. Rabi S. Bhagat, "Effects of Stressful Life Events on Individual Performance and Work Adjustment Processes within Organizational Settings: A Research Model," *Academy of Management Review*, October 1983, pp. 660–671.

51. Tripp Mickle, "Your Phone's Nearly Out of Power, Remain Calm, Call a Doctor," *The Wall Street Journal*, May 5–8, 2018, pp. A1, A10.

52. Marilyn L. Fox, Deborah J. Dwyer, and Daniel C. Ganster, "Effects of Stressful Job Demands and Control on Physiological and Attitudinal Outcomes in a Hospital Setting," *Academy of Management Journal*, April 1993, pp. 290–292.

53. David T. Wagner, Christopher M. Barnes, and Brent A. Scott, "Driving It Home: How Workplace Emotional Labor Harms Employee Home Life," *Personnel Psychology*, No. 2, 2014, pp. 487–516.

54. J. B. Teboul, "Facing and Coping with Uncertainty during Organizational Encounter," *Communication Quarterly*, 8 (1994), pp. 190–224.

55. Erin M. Eatough, Chu-Hsiang Chang, Stephanie A. Miloslavic, and Russell E. Johnson, "Relationships of Role Stressors with Organizational Citizenship Behavior: A Meta-Analysis," *Journal of Applied Psychology*, May 2011, pp. 619–632.

56. Sandra L. Kirmeyer and Thomas W. Dougherty, "Work Load, Tension, and Coping: Moderating Effects of Supervisor Support," *Personnel Psychology*, Spring 1988, pp. 125–139.

57. Rachel Emma Silverman, "Employers Pull Back on Wellness Benefits," June 20, 2016, p. B5.

58. Dori Meinert, "Relax, Recharge, Renew," *HR Magazine*, August 2017, p. 28.

59. The framework for this section is from Janina C. Latack, "Coping with Job Stress: Measures and Future Directions for Scale Development," *Journal of Applied Psychology*, August 1986, pp. 522–526.60. Reported in "Are You Working Too Hard? A Conversation with Mind/Body Researcher Herbert Benson," *Harvard Business Review*, November 2005, p. 54.

Organization Structure and Design

CHAPTER **14**

Production Perig/Shutterstock.com

Learning Objectives

After reading and studying this chapter and doing the exercises, you should be able to:

1. Identify and define the foundational concepts of organization structure, including the informal organization.

2. Specify the basic features of the bureaucratic form of organization structure, including how it is divided into departments.

3. Describe two key modifications of a bureaucratic structure: matrix and flat.

4. Describe the nature of outsourcing and how it influences organization structure.

5. Describe the organizational designs referred to as "horizontal structures" and "network structures."

General Electric Company was co-founded by Thomas Edison over 125 years ago and began by manufacturing electric light bulbs. Over the years, GE continued to invent devices and technologies, such as electric appliances, power stations, jet engines, and vacuum tubes for computers, that have or had a major impact on how people live and work. GE remains a conglomerate with over $100 billion in annual sales, yet in recent years it has experienced major setbacks.

In 2008 the company had to be bailed out by loan guarantees from the federal government and investor Warren Buffet. During the stock market boom of 2017, GE lost 46 percent of its value and was forced to cut it stock dividend in half because it was short on cash. At one time, the GE Capital division was the company's major profit source, but it ran into financial troubles, including a $6 billion charge related to a decade-old cost. At one point GE made a massive investment in natural gas power plants at the same time the market for gas turbines was plummeting. The company was left with loads of turbines it could not sell. Another challenge GE faced was a $31 billion pension shortfall, the biggest faced by any U.S. corporation.

In 2017, the GE board appointed company insider John Flannery as CEO to spearhead a company turnaround. Flannery was recognized for turning around GE Healthcare after spending most of his career at GE Capital. The turnaround plan Flannery developed focused on simplifying GE and its organization structure, as well as slashing costs wherever feasible. A major step was for GE to concentrate on four core businesses: power, aviation, health care, and renewables. The other GE businesses in 2018 were oil and gas, finance, transportation, and lighting. GE decided to dispose of these four divisions by 2020 through sales, spin-offs, and joint ventures. Flannery planned to make GE smaller and simpler. "Complexity hurts us," he said. Another goal was to reduce costs by $2 billion in 2018.

To help raise cash, GE merged its railroad business with Westinghouse Air Brake Technologies Corp. (Wabtec Corp.) and also planned to sell the light-bulb division. Flannery initiated a wide range of cost cuts: He grounded GE's fleet of six business jets; downsized thousands of corporate-level positions; shut down three research centers and moved some of the research and development work into business units; delayed part of a corporate relocation project; terminated a program of company cars for executives; and cancelled an annual three-day networking retreat in Boca Raton, Florida.

After one year of his turnaround efforts, Flannery said he was seeing progress in GE's performance in terms of earnings, cash flow, and profit margins. Costs were also reduced by $805 million.[1]

The story about the CEO of an iconic company shows how organization structure, including the downsizing of assets and personnel, can play a major role in the profitability and viability of a business enterprise. In this chapter, we describe organization structure because understanding structure is part of organizational behavior. Structure and behavior influence each other. For example, a loose organization structure, such as a collection of teams, requires employees to work productively without the benefit of close supervision. In contrast, some employees need careful guidelines for conducting their work and therefore need a tighter structure, such as a bureaucracy.

Another example of how structure influences behavior is that workers are shaped by their positions.[2] Some workers are seen as being mean and uncaring when it is really their position that dictates their behavior, such as a government caseworker refusing welfare payments to an applicant who has not submitted the necessary paperwork. Also, an executive who lays off 1,000 workers might seem heartless, yet his or her position demands taking extreme steps to earn a profit.

The purpose of this chapter is to understand the various types of organization structures and factors that influence the structure for a given purpose. Three terms need to be clarified first. An **organization** is a collection of people working together to achieve a

organization A collection of people working together to achieve a common purpose (or simply a big group).

common purpose (or simply a big group). **Organization structure** is the arrangement of people and tasks to accomplish organizational goals. The structure is usually indicated on the organizational chart, along with specifying who reports to whom. **Organizational design** is the process of creating a structure that best fits a purpose, strategy, and environment. For example, a giant motor company like General Motors emphasizes organization by product, such as having a separate division for Cadillac.

Another perspective about the relationship between organizational structure and behavior is that structure deals with the universal problems of division of labor and integration of effort.[3] For example, an appropriate structure must be chosen to allow people to carry out their specialty, yet encourage collaboration at the same time. Self-managing work teams, as described in Chapter 10, are an example of such an organization structure.

organization structure The arrangement of people and tasks to accomplish organizational goals.

organizational design The process of creating a structure that best fits a purpose, strategy, and environment.

Foundational Concepts of Organizational Structure

Organizations are so complex that many different variables are required to describe them, similar to describing people or machines. To get started understanding how organizations are structured, we look at five key concepts: formal versus informal, degree of formalization, degree of centralization, span of control, and complexity. You will observe that several concepts about organization structure overlap, thereby simplifying the understanding of organizations.

LEARNING OBJECTIVE 1
Identify and define the foundational concepts of organization structure, including the informal organization.

Formal versus Informal Structure

Understanding the difference between the formal and informal structure is akin to understanding the difference between formal and informal groups, as described in Chapter 9. The **formal organization structure** is an official statement of reporting relationships, rules, and regulations. The rules and regulations are designed to cover all the events and transactions that are likely to take place in conducting the business of the organization. For example, the formal organization structure tells managers how to respond to employee requests for an educational leave of absence or what to do with damaged parts from vendors.

formal organization structure An official statement of reporting relationships, rules, and regulations.

The **informal organization structure** is a set of unofficial working relationships that emerges to take care of the events and transactions not covered by the formal structure. The informal structure supplements the formal structure by adding a degree of flexibility and speed. A widespread application of the informal structure is the presence of "tech fixers" in most firms who supplement the technical support center. For example, marketing assistant Rick might be skilled at resolving website-related problems. As a consequence, many people call on Rick for some quick assistance, even though the formal organization indicates that they should use the tech support center for help with website problems.

informal organization structure A set of unofficial working relationships that emerges to take care of the events and transactions not covered by the formal structure.

Another perspective on the informal organization structure is that all companies have hidden shadow organizations where much of the real work gets accomplished. The shadow organization is revealed by social network analysis, which traces who talks to whom, who listens, and how most of the information and influence really flows. The nodes in the network are the people, and the links show relationships or flow between and among the nodes.

Social network analysis helps explain how work gets accomplished in a given unit, such as two people interacting with each other to figure out how to solve a baffling technical problem. The interrelationships among network members can become quite complicated because of the great number of people and the interactions among them.

Social network analysis reveals the informal social relationships and the unofficial communication channels, so it also helps to understand informal groups and informal communication channels. Tracking the informal relationships within an organization can help explain how and why new hires either succeed or fail to be assimilated into the corporate culture. Workers who connect to the right information flow will perform better because of the connections they make. Visualize Mia, a product designer for home appliances who needs some creative ideas about the design of a refrigerator exterior. Her network includes creative people throughout the organization, so she can tap them for ideas to accomplish her task.

Social network mappers begin by surveying company employees to find answers to several key questions. The basic one is: To whom do you go for information about what's going on? Other questions are asked about the frequency of interaction or are used to differentiate between requests for information and requests for influence. Based on the answers, the mappers draw diagrams that graphically show who is connected to whom.[4]

Social network analysis can benefit managers by revealing if people are getting the information they need to perform their jobs well. The same analysis can point to which employees are in the best position to disseminate useful information to other workers. Carried to the extreme, social network analysis could be used to identify whom team members communicate with and which team members rarely communicate with others.

Degree of Formalization

formalization The degree to which expectations regarding the methods of work are specified, committed to writing, and enforced.

The dimension of **formalization** is the degree to which expectations regarding the methods of work are specified, committed to writing, and enforced. The more policies, rules, and procedures there are specifying how people should behave, the more formalized the organization. An organization with a high degree of formalization is likely to have a high degree of specialization of labor and high delegation of authority. A more formal organization is more bureaucratic. A motor vehicle bureau usually has a high degree of formalization, especially in dealing with the public. (People cannot order vanity license plates without paying a fee, no matter how sweetly they ask!) An example of formalization would be a company allocating specific meal allowances rather than permitting business travelers to be reimbursed for whatever meal expenses they incurred.

Degree of Centralization

centralization The extent to which executives delegate authority to lower organizational units.

Centralization refers to the extent to which executives delegate authority to lower organizational units. The smaller the amount of delegation, the more centralized the organization. In a decentralized firm, however, some decisions are more centralized than others. Strategic decisions—those involving the overall functioning of the firm—are more likely to be centralized than operational decisions. An organization that relies heavily on functional (specialized) units will be more centralized because top management needs to coordinate the functions of the various units.

Domino's Pizza is a highly centralized firm. Company headquarters makes all the major decisions about matters such as the menu and décor of their establishments, the quality of their products, and the speed of their deliveries. An example of a highly decentralized firm is Lockheed Martin, organized around five core business areas: aeronautics, information systems and global solutions, missiles and fire control, missions systems and training, and space systems. CEOs of the companies affiliated with each business area have considerable latitude in running their businesses yet must meet financial targets set by headquarters.

Decentralization helps make large organizations more democratic because more managers throughout the company have more decision-making authority. Yet decentralization can lead to duplication of effort and high costs. For example, if all the automotive divisions of the Volkswagen Group, including Audi, Volkswagen, and Porsche, develop their own dashboard touchscreens, the costs would be excessive. In contrast, if the various automobiles use the same touchscreen, the savings would be substantial—especially because the Volkswagen Group is often ranked as one of the two largest automotive manufacturers in the world.

Span of Control

span of control The number of workers reporting directly to a manager.

A major characteristic of an organization is the average number of people each manager supervises. The **span of control** is the number of workers reporting directly to a manager. The larger the span of control, the more freedom and independence granted to subordinates. Correspondingly, the smaller the span of control, the more closely subordinates are supervised.

A large span of control works best with competent and efficient managers and group members. When group members do relatively similar work, the manager can supervise more people, such as one call-center manager supervising 30 call-center technicians.

As the movement toward granting more autonomy to people throughout the organization has taken hold, spans of control have increased. The trend is particularly noticeable at the executive level. According to research conducted by a management consultant and a business school professor, the CEO's average span of control has doubled in recent years. During the 1980s, the span of control for CEOs averaged about five; today the span is approximately ten.[5] The Microsoft Corporation organizational chart shown in Figure 14-2 (see p. 323) reflects this trend.

Complexity

Complexity refers to the number of different job titles and organizational units. Large organizations often have hundreds of departments and thousands of job titles. In a complex organization, many of the job titles are esoteric, such as "risk analyst," "data scientist," and "fleet manager." The more complex the organization, the more difficult it is to manage. Complexity typically increases in direct proportion to size. Small organizations have fewer job titles and departments.

complexity The number of different job titles and units within an organization.

The concept of *differentiation* is closely linked to complexity. A horizontally differentiated organization has many different job titles and many different departments doing separate work, whereas a vertically differentiated organization has many levels. A giant bureaucracy such as Citigroup has considerable horizontal and vertical differentiation.

Complexity can have a downside because, as an organization becomes more complex, getting tasks completed may take a lot of time. As described in the chapter opener, the giant corporation GE intends to become less complex. A few years ago, it was discovered that it took GM nearly 10 years to repair defective ignition switches that could cause cars to suddenly shut down as the switches turned off. (The problem was often created by drivers who used key rings weighted down by carrying many keys.) The picture that emerged from an internal investigation at GM of the events that led to the recall was a company burdened by bureaucratic complexity and unable to act decisively and swiftly.[6]

The Bureaucratic Form of Organization

As already implied, a **bureaucracy** is a rational, systematic, and precise form of organization in which rules, regulations, and techniques of control are precisely defined. *Bureau* is the French word for "office," indicating that a bureaucracy is a form of organization with many different offices. Also, *crat* derives from the Greek word for "rule." Figure 14-1 depicts the basic concept of the bureaucratic form of organization. A bureaucracy was conceived of by Max Weber to be the ideal organization, having the following characteristics:

LEARNING OBJECTIVE 2
Specify the basic features of the bureaucratic form of organization structure, including how it is divided into departments.

bureaucracy A rational, systematic, and precise form of organization in which rules, regulations, and techniques of control are precisely defined.

- Rules and procedures controlling organizational activities
- A high degree of differentiation among organizational functions
- A high degree of job specialization
- An organization of offices determined by hierarchy, with each unit reporting to a higher unit and no unit free-floating
- A heavy emphasis on rules and norms to regulate behavior
- Interpersonal relations characterized by impersonality in place of favoritism
- Selection and promotion based on merit
- All administrative actions recorded in writing[7]

Although many organizations have trimmed in size, the bureaucratic form of organization has not disappeared. Between 1983 and 2014, the number of managers, supervisors,

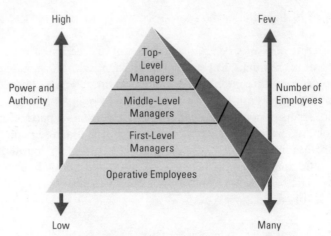

FIGURE 14-1 The Bureaucratic Form of Organization

In a bureaucracy, power is concentrated at the top. Note that team leaders are typically found at the first level or middle level of management.

and support staff in the U.S. workforce increased by 90 percent. Employment in other occupations grew by less than 40 percent. Other countries also experienced a growth in managerial workers.[8]

In visualizing a typical bureaucracy, it appears that one person is in charge of every function, including running the enterprise. In reality, authority is shared to some extent in top-level positions. You will recall the existence of top management teams as described in Chapter 10, in which major executives share responsibility for directing an enterprise. A dual-executive team was more frequent for a while in major corporations. A company founder would often divest day-to-day responsibilities to another executive, so the founder could concentrate more on strategy and building relationships with the outside world. In other words, the CEO delegates responsibilities for operations to a chief operations officer (COO). Yet in the last few years, many companies have eliminated the COO position, thereby enabling the CEO to have more contact with company operations.

Until a few years ago, several major corporations operated with two executives functioning as the CEO, or the *dual-CEO structure*. A notable example is Whole Foods Inc., which had co-CEOs for six years. The company board decided a more streamlined structure was necessary.[9] Kraft Foods Inc. gave up on the idea of sharing the CEO position and returned to relying on one CEO, partially because outstanding results were not forthcoming. Paying two executives to accomplish the same job is also a major financial investment unless they both agree on half-pay. Another problem is confusion among many organizational members as to which CEO is responsible for which decisions and who is really in charge of the company.

Before reading about the good and bad sides of bureaucracy, complete Self-Assessment 14-1. It will help you assess how well you might fit into a bureaucracy.

The Contribution of Bureaucracy

Bureaucratic forms of organization have persisted because, if used properly, they make possible large-scale accomplishments that cannot be achieved by small groups of people working independently. The basic defense of bureaucracies is that they perform large, needed tasks in a predictable fashion. The Social Security Administration is an example of a large bureaucracy that accomplishes an astonishing amount of work each month in paying benefits to approximately 64 million Americans. Elliot Jacques has aptly expressed the contribution of bureaucracy:

> Thirty-five years of research has convinced me that managerial hierarchy (or bureaucracy) is the most efficient, hardiest, and in fact the most natural structure ever devised for large corporations. Properly structured, hierarchy can release energy and creativity, rational productivity, and actually improve morale.[10]

The Attitude toward Bureaucracy Checklist

Indicate whether you Mostly Agree (MA) or Mostly Disagree (MD) with the following 10 statements.

Statement related to bureaucracy	MA	MD
1. I dislike having rules and regulations to guide me.	☐	☐
2. I enjoy working without the benefit of a carefully detailed job description.	☐	☐
3. I find it helpful to have a knowledgeable supervisor give me guidance and advice.	☐	☐
4. Regular working hours and regularly scheduled vacations are important to me.	☐	☐
5. I much prefer being expected to perform a variety of tasks than being assigned a job specialty.	☐	☐
6. I would much prefer working for a large, well-established organization than working for a startup company, even though the compensation was the same at both employers.	☐	☐
7. Having reasonably good job security is much more important to me than the opportunity to make much more money in an unknown company.	☐	☐
8. A person's rank in an organization should not bring him or her much respect.	☐	☐
9. I think that breaking company rules is fine, provided it is for a good purpose.	☐	☐
10. Major decisions should be made only after careful review by several layers of management.	☐	☐

Scoring and Interpretation: Give yourself one point for each question that you answered in the bureaucratic direction, as follows:

Mostly Agree, questions 2, 3, 4, 6, 7, and 10; Mostly Disagree, questions 1, 5, 8, and 9. The greater the number of statements that you answered in the bureaucratic direction, the more likely that your attitudes and personality are suited to working in a bureaucracy. If your score is zero, look for employment in a startup, or start your own business. If you scored 10, get a job in a nuclear power plant (and don't forget to wear your badge or security chip).

A similar argument is that dumping the policies and procedures characteristic of a bureaucracy can weaken an organization. In many cases, these procedures embody a vast organizational memory of best practices. Having tossed out the manuals, many organizations discover that their employees are frustrated because they have to improvise with little guidance. A lot of time is wasted in reinventing and redeveloping useful procedures that have been discarded. For example, a newly appointed credit manager might not have a policy for dealing with a long-term, reliable customer who suddenly becomes delinquent with payments.

The hierarchical form of organization called bureaucracy emerged from necessity. It is the only form of organization that enables a firm to employ large numbers of people and still hold them clearly accountable for their results. Bureaucracy is important also for the emotional reason that it fulfills our deep need for order

Some workers feel frustrated with the many rules and regulations in a bureaucracy.

Rusian Guzov/Shutterstock.com

and security.[11] As an employee, it is comforting to know that there is an efficient system in place to deposit your pay directly into your bank twice per month, and that if the fluorescent bulb in your office burns out, you know which office (bureau!) to call.

Another positive role played by a bureaucracy is to serve as a system of checks and balances, such as making sure that a new product or process is safe. A classic example is that, after BP loosened up on its many safety regulations and inspections, a few disasters came about. One was the Deepwater Horizon Well explosion in 2010, which leaked approximately 5 million gallons of oil into the Gulf of Mexico.[12]

Two management professors, Daisy E. Chung and Beth Bechky, conducted a study demonstrating how a bureaucratic structure facilitates task accomplishment. The two production settings chosen for the study were a film set and a semiconductor manufacturing firm, both of which had many bureaucratic elements. It was found that in both settings, workers were able to fulfill their bureaucratic expectations with a minimum of complaints or frustration. These expectations included adhering to a budget and tracking work across departments. The positive outcome took place because the specialists in both settings recognized that making bureaucracy work enabled them and their colleagues to maintain a sense of control of essential tasks.[13]

Potential Dysfunctions of a Bureaucracy

Not all bureaucracies work like Max Weber intended. The major problem is that members of the bureaucracy often carry out its characteristics to the extreme. Organizations that rely heavily on formal controls to direct people sometimes suppress initiative and decision making at lower levels of management. Too many controls and too many reviews of decisions can also lower productivity. A bureaucracy is subject to rigidity in handling people and problems. Although a bureaucratic design is supposed to hold people accountable for results, some people in large bureaucracies tend to "pass the buck," or claim that a particular problem is the responsibility of another department or person. A bureaucracy's well-intended rules and regulations sometimes create inconvenience and inefficiency.

A major problem within large bureaucracies is that they are clumsy and slow, often prompting companies to go outside when they need something done in a hurry, such as developing a prototype of a new product. (As described later, almost all bureaucracies have built-in structures to overcome the slowness problem.)

Even hugely successful business firms often fall victim to the problems associated with bureaucracy. Eamonn Kelly of Deloitte Consulting argues that the functional structure of large organizations is poorly matched for the current business climate. He points out that a structure in which functional specialists head up discrete teams enables the divisions of a company to operate in silos with insufficient integration or cohesion.[14]

As Microsoft Corp. hit 30 years of age, it transformed quite naturally into a large, complex organization. According to one analysis, the company's growing pains have delayed product introductions, leaving the door open for Microsoft to be beaten to market by younger, more nimble competitors like Google and Yahoo. Among the specific bureaucratic problems have been miscommunication and different units working on overlapping technology without adequate cooperation.[15] In 2013, a new functional structure, as shown in Figure 14-2, was developed to achieve better coordination across products and services. As described in Chapter 11, under the leadership of CEO Satya Nadella, Microsoft has overcome its previous problems and moved forward in exciting and profitable directions.

It is sometimes necessary to deal with red tape in a bureaucracy.

Jorgen mcleman/Shutterstock.com

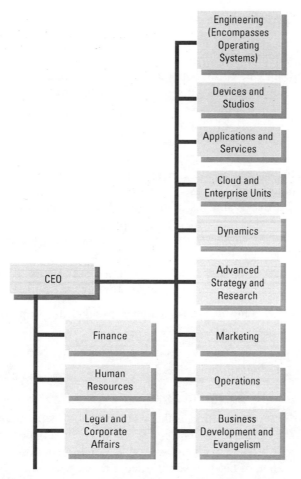

FIGURE 14-2 Functional Structure at Microsoft Corporation

Observe that each box below the level of chief executive officer (CEO) indicates an executive in charge of a specific function or activity, such as having responsibility for marketing. Note also that the Microsoft CEO, Sata Nadella, has a span of control of 12.

Another frequent problem in a bureaucracy is high frustration accompanied by low satisfaction. The sources of these negative feelings include red tape, slow decision making, and an individual's limited influence on how well the organization performs.

Most of the arguments about the potential problems of bureaucracy are based on observations of behavior. A study of 330 employees in 95 teams at the Taiwan Customs Bureau provides some empirical support for the negative consequences of bureaucracy. A major finding of the study was that team bureaucracy in terms of centralization and formalization can suppress the expression of individual differences that may engender creativity. For purposes of the study, team leaders rated the creativity of team members.[16]

Three Types of Departmentalization

In bureaucratic and other forms of organization, the work is subdivided into departments or other units. The departmentalization capitalizes upon the classic bureaucratic principle of specialization and also helps avoid confusion. Can you imagine the chaos if all the workers in an organization of more than 50 people worked in one large department? The process of subdividing work into departments is called **departmentalization**.

Here we will use charts to illustrate two frequently used forms of departmentalization: functional and product/service. Most organizational charts show a combination of these two types, along with other forms of departmentalization, such as division into geographic regions.

departmentalization The process of subdividing work into departments.

Functional Departmentalization

functional departmentalization
The grouping of people according to their expertise.

Functional departmentalization involves grouping people according to their expertise. Bureaucracies are almost always organized into functional departments. Within a given department, the work may be further subdivided. For instance, finance may include subunits for accounts receivable, accounts payable, and payroll. The names of functional departments vary widely with the nature of the business or enterprise. Figure 14-2 illustrates the functional structure of Microsoft Corporation. Under the Microsoft strategy developed in 2013, the company is organized into nine key groups based on essential business functions. Each function spans across and serves all business lines, such as mobile devices and the search engine. Finance, human resources, and legal and corporate affairs are also included in the Microsoft functional structure.

The advantages and disadvantages of functional departmentalization follow those of a bureaucracy. *Silo* is a term frequently used to point to the disadvantages of functional departmentalization. A silo implies that the people within one department remain isolated and shut off from the rest of the organization, instead of building working relationships with people in other departments. Leadership consultant Kevin Elkenberry gives two examples of how the silo mentality can be overcome for the good of the organization:

- A sales representative builds relationships with other departments as a way to better meet a customer need.
- A middle manager in information technology shares her budget with another department that is short on funds.[17]

Product and Service Departmentalization

product/service departmentalization The arrangement of departments according to the products or services they provide

Product/service departmentalization is the arrangement of departments according to the products or services they provide. When specific products or services are so important that they almost become independent companies, product departmentalization makes sense. Figure 14-3 presents a version of product/service departmentalization at Caterpillar Corp., the renowned manufacturer of construction equipment. One purpose of a product or service organization is to push decision making further down into the organization. Another purpose of the structure is to help a company be nimble, while at the same time encouraging cooperation among the various product divisions. For example, members of the construction industries, solar turbines, and excavation divisions might readily exchange technical ideas.

Line versus Staff Units

In Chapter 13, line and staff groups were mentioned in relation to conflict. Line and staff groups are present in most forms of departmentalization, yet the organizational

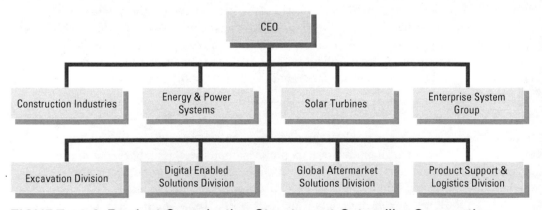

FIGURE 14-3 Product Organization Structure at Caterpillar Corporation

Notes: 1. The organization structure at Caterpillar is not a pure product structure because four functional groups also report to the CEO: legal & secretary, customer & dealer support, procurement, and human resources. 2. Organization structures are subject to frequent change, and the above structure might not be exactly the one used today.

chart rarely makes such designations. In Figure 14-2, the line units would be engineering, devices and studios, applications and services, cloud and enterprise units, dynamics, advanced strategy and research, marketing, operations, and business development and evangelism. The staff units would be finance, human resources, and legal and corporate affairs. Yet some observers classify finance as a line unit because of its major importance to the functioning of the organization.

The distinction between line and staff is often blurred. (Line groups are responsible for the primary purposes of the firm, whereas staff groups are responsible for the secondary purposes.) Members of some departments are not sure if they are perceived as line or staff by top management, leading to role ambiguity. A marketing executive said, "The key purpose of our firm is to provide goods to customers. Yet when cutbacks take place, marketing people get chopped first. It makes no sense to me."

Key Modifications of the Bureaucratic Structure

LEARNING OBJECTIVE 3
Describe two key modifications of a bureaucratic structure: matrix and flat.

To overcome several of the disadvantages of the bureaucratic and functional forms of organization, several other structures have developed. Typically, these less-bureaucratic structures are used to supplement or modify the bureaucratic structure. Teams, as described in Chapter 10 in the context of job design, have emerged as the most widely used supplement to the bureaucratic structure. Task forces and projects follow a similar departure from bureaucracy. Here we describe the matrix organization structure and the flat structure as organization arrangements.

Matrix Organization Structure

Traditional organizations can be slow to respond to change. A frequently used antidote to this problem is the **matrix organization structure** that consists of a project structure superimposed on a functional structure. A **project** is a temporary group of specialists working together under one manager to accomplish a fixed objective, such as launching a major new product. The word "matrix" refers to the feature of something contained within something else, similar to a grid with numbers in the cells (see Figure 14-4).

matrix organization structure An organization consisting of a project structure superimposed on a functional structure.

project A temporary group of specialists working together under one manager to accomplish a fixed objective.

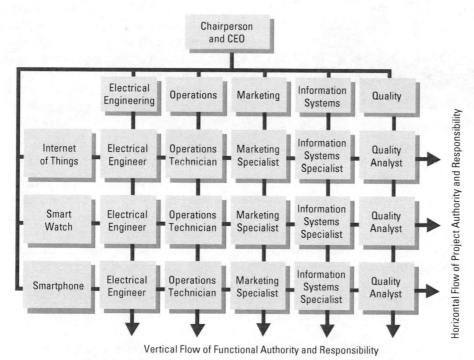

FIGURE 14-4 Matrix Organization in an Electronics Company

In a matrix organization, a project structure is superimposed on a functional structure.

Projects are a key part of a matrix structure.

The distinguishing feature of the matrix organization is the responsibility of the project or program manager to achieve results through employees who also report directly to another manager or have dual reporting responsibilities. For example, a person assigned to a project in a matrix organization might report to both the project manager and the manager in his or her regular department.

A major purpose of the matrix organization is to allow the firm to take advantage of new opportunities and solve special problems. Instead of developing a new organization containing functional departments, the firm leaves the original organization intact. The project or program managers within the matrix structure have access to the resources of the functional departments. A key advantage of the matrix organization is its ability to implement important projects that demand intense, sustained attention for a limited time. An investment bank, for example, might use a matrix structure to build a cryptocurrency capability. On the negative side, the matrix structure often creates problems because people assigned to projects within the matrix have a dual reporting relationship.

Project managers play a key role in organizations.

The matrix organization highlights the importance of project structures because projects are embedded in the matrix. Projects have high status because they are used to accomplish important goals, such as launching a new product or culturally diversifying a workforce. The position of project manager is also seen as excellent training and experience for growth into higher management.[18] To be an effective project manager, the individual must use a high level of interpersonal skill (e.g., the ability to resolve conflict) as well as technical skill to achieve goals. The project manager needs good technical skills because he or she interacts directly with skilled professionals and must also provide technical input to decisions.

The Organizational Behavior in Action box illustrates how a large business enterprise makes use of two different types of departmentalization at the same time.

Flat Organization Structures and Downsizing

flat organization structure An organization structure with relatively few layers.

A **flat organization structure** is one that has relatively few layers. A flat structure is less bureaucratic for two reasons. First, fewer managers in this form of organization are available to review the decisions of other people. As a by-product, customer service is often improved because many customer problems can be resolved without waiting for layers of approval. Second, because the chain of command is shorter, there is less concern about authority differences among people. Most large organizations have moved toward flatter structures, continuing a trend that began over 35 years ago. (You may recall the comment made earlier that the number of managerial workers has increased. Despite this fact, structures have still become flatter because many organizations have grown in terms of their workforce.)

Part of the success of Nike has been attributed to its flat structure. With Nike, each brand has a department, and each department makes decisions without requiring approval from the CEO. The product teams and product managers make decisions about product specifications and production.[19]

Mondelez Organizes Its Snacking Business by Category and Geography

Mondelez International Inc. is one of the world's biggest snack companies with annual revenues of approximately $26 billion, and 80,000 employees. The company's purpose and vision is to create moments of joy for consumers by building the world's best snacking company. Mondelez manufactures and markets food and beverage products for consumers in about 160 countries. The company is a world leader in biscuits, chocolate, gum and candy, and powdered beverages.

Mondelez was formed in 2012 after Kraft Foods split off its snack brands into a new company to encourage growth by concentrating on this enormous food category. The Mondelez name was suggested by Kraft employees and is derived from the words *mundus* ("world") and *delez*, an offshoot of the word meaning "delicious."

Approximately 85 percent of the company's annual revenue is generated in snacks, and nearly 75 percent of sales are generated outside of North America. Company leadership believes that snacking is a strong category considering long-term consumer trends and that Mondelez is positioned to win as a leader in the snack space. Among the company's leading global brands are Oreo, Cadbury, Ritz, and Trident.

To help focus the business and organize its many products and workers, Mondelez uses a variety of organization structures. Its geographic structure is organized as follows, with the percent of sales by region indicated in parentheses: North America (26%); Latin America (14%); AMEA (Asia Middle East Africa) (22 %); and Europe (38%). The breakdown of sales by category might also be considered a product structure within the geographic structure, as follows: Biscuits (42%); Chocolate (31%); Gum & Candy (14%); Beverages (5%); and Cheese and Grocery (8 %).

1. How helpful do you think the two types of organization structures presented in giving company insiders and outsiders an overview of the operations of Mondelez?

2. Should leadership at Mondelez become concerned about the consumer movement toward health foods and away from processed foods? If so, how should the product category be modified?

Source: Original story based on facts and observations reported in the following sources: "Mondelez International 2018 Fact Sheet," Mondelez International (www.mdlz.com); Gisselle Gaitan, "Mondelez International Announces Leadership Team Changes," dsn (www.drugstoresnews.com), October 25, 2017, pp. 1–2; Tim O'Connor, "Mondelez International," *Supply Chain World* (www.scw .mag.com), February 21, 2016, pp. 1–3.

Small- and medium-sized businesses have held onto their traditionally flat structures, which are usually imposed by not having enough money to build management depth. To minimize the number of managers needed to run a business, small businesses often rely on communication technology to supply workers with all the information they need instead of consulting with a supervisor. Yet, with organizations of all types, too little hierarchy may lead to decisions not getting made or to decisions made wrongly by employees who lack the appropriate experience, motivation, and accountability to do the work of missing managers.[20]

Flatter organization structures created by downsizing lead to greater organizational efficiency about half the time. A controversial aspect of flat structures created by downsizing is that they result in substantial human suffering. Even when jobs are plentiful, losing a job can result in considerable emotional turmoil for the individual. Survivors of the downsizing also experience problems, such as guilt. Another problem with downsizing is that it can leave an organization depleted and slow down a future recovery. For example, in 2016 many oil-field services companies were depleted after reducing prices and laying off workers. Two years of belt-tightening in the oil patch left them short on cash and human resources as demand for their services by energy companies picked up.[21] More will be said about the problems associated with downsizing as a change strategy in Chapter 16.

The most extreme form of nonbureaucratic organization is to eliminate managers, thereby creating a self-managing organization. Morning Star, the world's largest tomato ingredient processor, uses this extreme form of flat structure. During the tomato season, the company swells to 2,400 employees. The company has been managing without managers for about 25 years. No worker is assigned a boss; employees negotiate responsibilities with coworkers. Every worker can spend company money, and each worker is responsible for purchasing the tools needed to accomplish his or her work. The mission of the company is considered to be the boss, and workers are empowered to the extreme, resembling a giant, self-managing team. Morning Star workers therefore manage themselves.

A key feature of the Morning Star approach to running the organization is that annually each employee negotiates a Colleague Letter of Understanding (CLOU) with the other employees who are most affected by his or her work. At the same time, the letter describes the employee's contribution to the company's success. The CLOU functions as an operating plan for fulfilling each worker's mission. A detail of a CLOU might state that one agrees to load certain containers onto a truck or operate equipment in a certain way.

Among the advantages to Morning Star, the company without managers, are lower operating costs, better decision making because of pushing decisions down to the front line, and higher loyalty to the company. Among the disadvantages are difficult adjustments for workers accustomed to working in a hierarchy, less accountability for employees who fail to deliver, and no corporate ladder to climb for ambitious employees.[22]

Several medium-size companies have eliminated the CEO position in recent years, instead turning to committees and consensus to manage the organization. The leaders of these companies, including DPR Construction, say that these structures increase collaboration and enhance decision making at all levels. DPR's 4,000 employees feel empowered to suggest ideas and make decisions independently. To help compensate for the absence of a CEO, veteran company leaders rotate on and off its eight-member management committee. The input of the experienced leaders gives consistency to management. Decision making by committees at DPR, similar to other firms operating without a CEO, has the disadvantage of being slow and frustrating, including a lot of arguing.[23]

Outsourcing as an Organizational Arrangement

LEARNING OBJECTIVE 4
Describe the nature of outsourcing and how it influences organization structure.

outsource The practice of having work performed by groups outside the organization.

offshoring The practice of having work performed by a company in an overseas location.

A widespread practice among organizations of all types and sizes is to outsource, or have work performed for them by other organizations. When the work is performed by a company in an overseas location, the process is often referred to as offshoring. Outsourcing, including offshoring, is an integral part of the globalization of business. Instead of performing all the manufacturing or service work domestically, the global enterprise has some of the work performed in other countries. An overseas call-center is an example of the globalization of service.

Outsourcing is linked to organization structure because it is a method of dividing work: Certain activities are assigned to groups outside the organization. Another way of framing outsourcing is that it is a vast network of interconnected enterprises that depend on one another for services. By outsourcing, a company can reduce its need for employees and physical assets and reduce payroll costs. Many firms outsource the development and start-up phases of their e-commerce units to outside information-technology consultants.

Here we describe three aspects of outsourcing that impact human behavior in organizations: the scope of outsourcing, its time zone advantages, and using home-based workers.

The Scope of Outsourcing

Outsourcing has advanced so far that some companies do little more than develop an idea for a product, with product development, manufacturing, and marketing being done by other firms. Performing outsourced work for other companies has become an industry of its own, including companies that fulfill orders for online stores. United Parcel Service (UPS) exemplifies how far outsourcing has advanced. The world's largest delivery company provides a wide variety of services for other companies through its subsidiary, UPS Supply Chain Solutions. The services other companies outsource to UPS include emergency electronic repairs, fixing laptops, installing giant X-ray machines, operating customer-service hotlines, packaging consumer electronics, and issuing corporate credit cards. The type of work Supply Chain provides lends itself to domestic outsourcing because much of the work is needed urgently. UPS stores every conceivable part in its giant warehouse in Louisville, Kentucky, so it can perform repairs quickly. The highly regarded brand name UPS has facilitated the growth of the outsourcing business.

A third-party logistics provider (3PL) such as UPS is often hired because of its expertise in shipping products that are temperature-sensitive. Healthcare companies, for example, rely on UPS because it can safely ship drugs and medicines that must be kept cool. UPS offers a fully compliant cold-chain infrastructure that can ship cold-sensitive health products at a lower cost than the manufacturers of the drugs and medicine.[24]

Even activities as complex as the research and design of products are sometimes outsourced. A company might design its own core product and have noncore products designed by another firm. The purpose of outsourcing design is to have prod-

Considerable work from the United States and Canada is outsourced to China.

ucts designed at high speed and low cost by a smaller firm. Even the manufacture of luxury goods is sometimes outsourced; for example, part of the Giorgio Armani collection is constructed in Eastern Europe rather than Italy.

Much to the chagrin of labor unions and local workers, many companies outsource work to geographic areas where workers are paid lower wages. Among the many examples of outsourcing would be a small company hiring another company to manage its payroll and employee benefits, and a large manufacturing firm having certain components made by another firm. A recent thrust in outsourcing is for U.S. firms to send white-collar professional jobs overseas, including jobs in software development and financial services. Overall, the outsourcing movement has been a boon for small- and medium-sized firms that perform stable work for larger organizations.

Cloud computing has also facilitated outsourcing. A "human cloud" of workers domestically and around the globe can be assigned a variety of work tasks via an online platform. Staffing, or *talent engagement*, is done entirely online, from recruitment and assignment to payment, especially for contingent (part-time or temporary) workers. The human cloud is a growing part of the global outsourcing movement.[25]

A key implication of outsourcing as an organizational design strategy is that people over whom you have no direct control perform work for your company. Other managers are responsible for leading and managing employees who perform important functions for the organization. A frequent concern in the clothing, toy, and consumer electronics industries is that subcontractors sometimes engage in unsavory practices, such as violating wage and child-labor laws. Outsourcing has led to sweatshops as smaller firms compete to offer the lowest possible price for manufacturing goods. Outsourcing can therefore create ethical dilemmas.

Another key human aspect of outsourcing is that it breeds conflict over which functions should be outsourced. Labor unions vehemently oppose a company sending jobs to lower-wage countries in order to save money, thereby resulting in job loss for union members. Department heads within a company fight to defend themselves against being outsourced, such as outsourcing the training function of the human resources department. Another example would be the head of a software development unit in a U.S. company struggling against a plan to outsource software development to an Indian company. Proponents of global outsourcing argue that it enables the domestic company to remain competitive, thereby saving jobs. Also, many overseas companies, such as Toyota, export thousands of jobs to other countries including the United States.

The opponents of large-scale outsourcing are making gains in the form of **reshoring**, the bringing of jobs back to a country that outsourced these jobs previously. Henry Moser, a former manufacturing executive, founded the Reshoring Initiative, an industry-led effort

reshoring The bringing of jobs back to a country that outsourced these jobs previously.

to bring manufacturing jobs back to the United States. This initiative helps companies of different sizes calculate the true cost of manufacturing in other countries as well as understand the risks associated with offshoring. Among these risks are increased wages in many overseas countries, fluctuating currencies, higher transportation and fuel costs, and violations of intellectual property rights. In 2016, for the first time in decades, more manufacturing jobs returned to the United States than left, for a net gain of 25,000 manufacturing positions. Some of the gain was attributed to non-U.S. companies investing in U.S. factories.[26]

Time Zone Advantages of Outsourcing

When knowledge work needs to be performed in a sequence, with one person or group building on the output of the previous person, outsourcing offers a unique advantage. While one group is off duty, another group in a different time zone in a distant country prepares the input the first group will need by the morning. A more complex possibility is for work to be performed in sequence across three time zones. A group in one time zone collects the data for a key report and then transmits the data to a group in the next time zone that translates the data into PowerPoint slides. The slides and backup data are then transmitted to a third group in another time zone that prepares the final report. Instead of the project taking three work days, it is all accomplished within 24 hours.

As mysterious as this aspect of globalization appears, it is not much different in concept than nightshift workers handing over their input in the morning to dayshift workers. On an international level, here is an example: Sandra, a virtual team member in Boston, finishes her part of a project at 5 p.m. EST. She sends her output to Ben, a team member in Seoul, South Korea, and it arrives at 7 a.m. his time. Ben finishes his contribution to the project at 3 p.m. his time, and then sends his output to Claire, a team member in Paris, arriving at 7 a.m. her time. Claire finishes her work, and then at 5 p.m. her time sends it back to Sandra in Boston, where it arrives on Sandra's desktop at 11 a.m. EST so she can have the input before noon. (All this is very confusing, but international workers keep several clocks with different time zones going at the same time.) The general idea is that workers across the globe can collaborate 24/7, even if the time zones do not match precisely.

Outsourcing to Homes Instead of Offshoring

Offshoring has its problems, such as the language barrier of the call-center workers not speaking English in a manner comprehensible by all English-speaking people in the United States. A similar problem is not understanding the culture, such as the caller making reference to a major sporting event or an athletic team. Another challenge is coordinating and managing the work of people in another country. To deal with this problem, many firms, including Office Depot and Sears Holding, are outsourcing customer service work to people at home. Outsourcing to homes has been facilitated by expanded broadband Internet access, less expensive computer technology, and advanced call-routing systems. Home (or virtual) agents typically work for low pay and no benefits, and have to deal with many irate customers.

The work of home agents is carefully monitored, and background noise such as dogs barking and children playing is usually not allowed. Nevertheless, the appeal of working at home is so strong for so many people that the industry is expanding rapidly. Virtual agents have considerable flexibility in choice of when to work. About 70 percent to 80 per-

Outsourcing to homes enables virtual agents to work from their home.

Olly/Shutterstock.com

cent of home agents have college degrees in comparison to 30 percent to 40 percent of call-center workers. Turnover among home agents is much less than for their call-center counterparts.[27]

Leading-Edge Organization Structures

Spin-offs from traditional organization structures continue to emerge as organizations strive to improve their efficiency and effectiveness. A major reason for these changes is that a traditional hierarchical organization can be too cumbersome to respond to changes in the environment. Two leading-edge forms are the horizontal structure and the network organization.

LEARNING OBJECTIVE 5
Describe the organizational designs referred to as "horizontal structures" and "network structures."

The Horizontal Structure

A major current development in organizational design is to work horizontally rather than vertically. A **horizontal structure** is the arrangement of work by teams that are responsible for accomplishing a process. The virtual organization is thereby similar to the establishment of work teams. A major difference, however, is that team members are responsible for a process rather than a product or service. The difference is subtle; the team aims at delivering a product or service to a customer rather than focusing on the product or service itself. Instead of focusing on a specialized task, all team members focus on achieving the purpose of all the activity, such as getting a product in the hands of a customer. In a horizontal structure or process organization, employees take collective responsibility for customers.[28] Self-managing work teams typically have a horizontal structure.

One approach to switching from a task emphasis to a process emphasis in a horizontal structure is through **business process reengineering**, the radical redesign of work to achieve substantial improvements in performance. "Reengineering" searches for the most efficient way to perform a large task. The emphasis is on uncovering wasted steps, such as people handing off documents to one another to obtain approval. Eliminating workers who perform nonessential tasks is another goal of reengineering. E-commerce can be considered a way of reengineering the work of sales representatives. If goods are exchanged over the Internet, the need for industrial sales representatives shrinks considerably. Fewer purchasing agents are needed also because buying over the Internet is more efficient than speaking directly to sales representatives.

As a result of reengineering, work is usually organized horizontally rather than vertically. The people in charge of the process act as team leaders who guide the team toward the completion of an important core process, such as new product development or filling a complicated order. Key performance objectives for the team would include "reduce cycle time," "reduce costs," and "reduce throughput time." Figure 14-5 illustrates the horizontal structure, as do the projects embedded in the matrix organization shown in Figure 14-4.

A caution to managers and prospective managers is to recognize that the push toward the horizontal structures and reengineering should not be embraced without qualification.

horizontal structure The arrangement of work by teams that are responsible for accomplishing a process.

business process reengineering The radical redesign of work to achieve substantial improvements in performance.

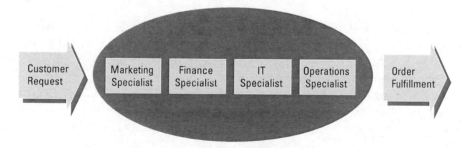

FIGURE 14-5 A Horizontal Structure

In a horizontal structure, even though specialists are assigned to the team, they are expected to understand one another's tasks and perform some of those tasks as needed.

Having a "task mentality" is still important because expertise is still crucial in many endeavors. A surgical team, for example, still relies on highly proficient specialists such as brain surgeons and anesthetists. Also, wouldn't you prefer that a specialist had designed the operating system on your smartphone when you need to call somebody to rescue you from a life-threatening situation?

The Network Structure

Another fast-growing development in organization structure is for organizations to affiliate with one another based on their need to share resources. Few companies have all the assets and resources in their firm to accomplish new endeavors. The best resources and talents are borrowed as needed. A **network structure (or virtual organization)** is a temporary association of otherwise independent firms that are linked by technology to share expenses, employee talents, and access to one another's markets.[29] Outsourcing is somewhat like forming a network structure, except that the relationship is more limited and contractual.

network structure (or virtual organization) A temporary association of otherwise independent firms linked by technology to share expenses, employee talents, and access to one another's markets.

A pure network structure would have neither corporate headquarters nor an organizational chart. Hierarchy would be sacrificed to speed of decision making, and vertical integration would be supplanted by horizontal integration across company boundaries. Each contributor to the network would stick to its core competency—what it does best, such as manufacturing a particular component, marketing the finished product, or developing a new product.

For most organizations, the network structure supplements the regular structure, much like a large project. Many large organizations have small units that use the network structure for forming strategic alliances with other companies. Smart television receivers, for example, are typically the product of a strategic alliance among several companies. Strategic alliances are also formed to market products. For example, IBM formed a strategic alliance with Apple Corp. to provide IBM business software on Apple mobile devices.

Proponents of the network structure see it as a fluid and flexible entity taking the form of a group of collaborators who link together to capitalize on a specific opportunity. After the opportunity has been met, the venture will typically disband. However, some alliances and partnerships are relatively permanent. An essential requirement is that members of the alliance must trust one another. One incompetent or dishonest member of the network can ruin or severely damage the multiple venture. It is not uncommon for an overseas member of a strategic alliance to steal the other's technology and become a direct competitor.

The horizontal and virtual structures place additional demands on the interpersonal skills of the workers involved. Relationships tend to be more stable in a functional structure, whereas horizontal and virtual structures involve more temporary relationships. A person has to get up to speed quickly in establishing working relationships. Furthermore, the authority structure is less clear, so the individual may have to rely more on informal influence tactics. Personal power becomes more important than positional power.

Implications for Managerial Practice

1. An overriding decision in organizational design is the choice between a bureaucratic or a more flexible structure. Bureaucratic structures are better suited to repetitive tasks in a stable environment, in which centralized control is desirable. High-technology firms such as aerospace companies make extensive use of flexible structures, such as project and matrix structures. Relatively low-technology firms such as lumber mills and refuse-collection firms rely more on bureaucratic structures.

2. As an organization grows and matures, it inevitably needs centralized controls and some degree of bureaucracy or formalization. Yet, when the firm becomes very large, it is necessary to develop smaller, more flexible units, such as projects and task forces. These units help the organization remain adaptive, and they are found in every large organization.

3. A design decision for a large organization is usually not an issue of hierarchical versus flexible, but instead, one of choosing which units should be hierarchical and which ones should be nonhierarchical or team-based.

4. Organization structure influences behavior in many ways. A key factor is that specialization can lead to job dissatisfaction and boredom for many workers. An exception is that some highly trained workers prefer to be superspecialists, such as package designers.

5. Leading-edge organizational designs are becoming increasingly popular. Managers and nonmanagers alike need high-level interpersonal skills to function effectively in such structures because they must often rely more on informal than formal authority.

Summary of Key Points

1. *Identify and describe the foundational concepts of organization structure, including the informal organization.* Organization structure is the arrangement of people and tasks to accomplish organizational goals, whereas organizational design is the process of creating an appropriate structure. An informal organization emerges to take care of the events and transactions not covered by the formal structure. Social network analysis is useful in depicting the informal structure. The more formalized an organization, the more it is bureaucratic. The more centralized an organization, the more extensively top managers delegate responsibility. The span of control is an important characteristic of an organization because it helps determine how closely workers are supervised. Organizations vary in their complexity, or differentiation, among subunits. Most organization have both line and staff units.

2. *Specify the basic features of the bureaucratic form of organization structure, including how it is divided into departments.* A bureaucracy is a rational, systematic, and precise form of organization. In it, rules, regulations, and techniques of control are defined precisely. Properly used, bureaucracy allows for large-scale accomplishments. Problems associated with bureaucracy include suppression of initiative through overcontrol, high job frustration, and low job satisfaction. A bureaucracy can also be clumsy and slow. Departmentalization is the division of work into manageable units. Two key forms of departmentalization are functional and product/service. Most firms use several types of departmentalization. The functional organization has both the advantages and disadvantages of a bureaucracy. Line and staff units are frequently built into a departmentalized structure.

3. *Describe two key modifications of a bureaucratic structure: matrix and flat.* Bureaucratic structures are commonly supplemented by organic, or highly adaptable, organizational units. A matrix structure consists of a project structure imposed on a functional structure. The matrix manager must achieve results through employees who are also responsible to another manager. A flat structure has relatively few layers, which speeds up decision making. Downsizing typically leads to a flatter structure. The most extreme form of nonbureaucratic organization is to eliminate managers, thereby creating a self-managing organization.

4. *Describe the nature of outsourcing and how it influences organization structure.* Outsourcing is an arrangement whereby one organization has work performed by another, including offshoring. Outsourcing is linked to structure because it is a method of dividing work. Outsourcing has advanced to the point that performing work for other industries has become an industry of its own, and complex activities like research and design are outsourced. Outsourcing leads to conflict over lost jobs and which jobs should be outsourced.

Outsourcing allows for completing segments of projects around the clock because of time zone differences among the countries where the work is performed. The movement of outsourcing to workers at home involves moving work into the homes of virtual agents. Although it is low-paid work, the demand for these jobs is high. The opponents of large-scale outsourcing are making gains in the form of reshoring, or bringing jobs back to the country that outsourced these jobs previously.

5. *Describe the organizational designs referred to as "horizontal structures" and "network structures."* Two leading-edge organization structures are the horizontal structure and the network structure. A horizontal structure arranges work by teams that are responsible for accomplishing a process. Business process reengineering is closely associated with horizontal structures. A network structure, or virtual corporation, is a temporary association of otherwise independent firms that join forces to exploit an opportunity. Each network member contributes its core competency.

Key Terms and Phrases

organization, p. 316

organization structure, p. 317

organizational design, p. 317

formal organization structure, p. 317

informal organization structure, p. 317

formalization, p. 318

centralization, p. 318

span of control, p. 318

complexity, p. 319

bureaucracy, p. 319

departmentalization, p. 323

functional departmentalization, p. 324

product/service departmentalization, p. 324

matrix organization structure, p. 325

project, p. 325

flat organization structure, p. 326

outsource, p. 328

offshoring, p. 328

reshoring, p. 329

horizontal structure, p. 331

business process reengineering, p. 331

network structure (or virtual organization), p. 332

Discussion Questions and Activities

1. Many readers of this text are not yet in a position to lay out an organization structure. How might they make use of information about organization structure and design?

2. Explain whether Starbucks (or choose Yum! Brands or McDonald's) has a bureaucratic form of organization.

3. What hints would you look for to analyze the degree of formalization in the company for which you were being interviewed?

4. What evidence could you present that having a "functional mindset" is natural for most people? (*Hint:* For example, when people visit a hospital or grocery store, in what way do they think in terms of departmentalization?)

5. Why is it that so many business owners who say they do not like bureaucracy nevertheless welcome large bureaucratic organizations, like Ford Motor Company, as customers?

6. Microsoft, as well as several other information-technology companies, advertise that their software systems make companies less bureaucratic. How might this claim be true?

7. Why would working in an organization that relied on wide spans of control be frustrating for many people?

8. If a company such as Morning Star is able to operate without managers, why don't well-known companies such as GM, Microsoft, and Facebook get rid of all their managers?

9. What impact do you think the widespread use of robots will have on the outsourcing of manufacturing jobs to other countries?

10. A friend of yours has a startup firm that manufactures solar panels and so far has 10 employees. Which type of organization structure do you recommend that your friend use, and why?

SKILL-DEVELOPMENT EXERCISE 14-1

Choosing an Organization Structure for Your Own Company

Imagine that you, along with three other investors, just purchased a consumer products company that has $24 million in annual sales and 80 employees. The six products the company manufactures and sells are radios, lamps for home and office, lawn mowers, snow blowers, hair dryers for beauty salons, and shopping carts for supermarkets. Work with your investors to design an organization structure for your company that you think will help the company prosper. Draw your design, and provide your rationale for the design. And how about a name for the company you just bought?

Designing an Office for a Virtual Customer Agent

Work in a team to design a home office for a virtual customer agent, a worker whose responsibilities are to fill orders for merchandise for three different companies. The agent receives calls through a toll-free number and then uses the computer to enter the order. He or she also processes online orders. The office in question will be placed somewhere in a three-bedroom house that also has a family room, kitchen, basement, and enclosed porch.

While designing the office, include such factors as the layout of the furniture and equipment, the equipment needed, and any decorations. Keep in mind ergonomic factors that focus on making the equipment easy to use and have low risk to physical problems such as carpal tunnel syndrome and backaches. Because the virtual agent will have to pay for the office setup, derive a tentative budget.

Draw your design on any convenient format, including a flip chart, whiteboard, blackboard, or computer screen. Your team leader might be asked to present the design to the rest of the class so class members can compare the effectiveness of each design.

CASE PROBLEM: Proposed Organizational Structure Change at Montana Vehicles

Carla, the CEO of Montana Vehicles Inc., is proud of her company's penetration across so many markets. Montana produces a variety of motorized vehicles, similar to John Deere, although Montana has a very small market share. The major product lines of Montana are motorcycles, motorized wheelchairs and shopping carts, trailers for vehicles, snow removal and lawn care machines, and forklift trucks. The Montana organizational chart is depicted in Exhibit 14-1.

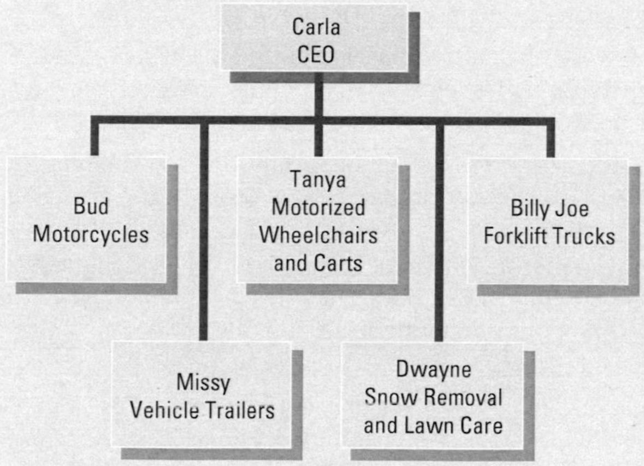

Carla has said on more than one occasion that the organization of Montana Vehicles has too much overlap and not enough cross-exchange of ideas. "We have loads of talented people in each division, but they work in silos. I would like to see more advances in manufacturing and technology shared across our product lines. To give you a small example, an engineer in our forklift truck division developed a great little gear made out of plastic. But no other division is using the same gear. And why is each group purchasing mobile devices from a different vendor?"

EXHIBIT 14-1 The Montana Vehicle Organizational Chart

Case Questions

1. What modifications to the Montana Vehicles organization structure could be made to bring about the coordination and cross-exchange of ideas that Carla would like to see happen?
2. Draw a new organizational chart for Montana Vehicles that would help bring about the improvements Carla is seeking.

Endnotes

1. Story based on facts and observations in the following sources: Thomas Gryta, "GE to Give Up Railroad Business," *The Wall Street Journal*, May 22, 2018, pp. B1, B2; "GE: The Turnaround Strengthens," *Seeking Alpha* (https://seekingalpha.com), April 23, 2018, pp. 1–2; Drake Bennett, "What the Hell Is Wrong with General Electric?" *Bloomberg Businessweek*, February 5, 2018, pp. 42–49; Glenn Surowiec, "General Electric: Turnaround Progressing Under 'Outsider CEO,'" *MOI Global* (https://moiglobal.com), March 5, 2018, pp. 1–2; Thomas Gryta and Joann S. Lublin, "New Chief at GE Starts Undoing the Costly Path," *The Wall Street Journal*, October 19, 2017, pp. A1, A9.

2. Interview by Shelia M. Puffer, "Changing Organizational Structures: An Interview with Rosabeth Moss Kanter," *Academy of Management Executive*, May 2004, p. 99.

3. Phanish Puranam, Oliver Alexy, and Markus Reitzig, "What's 'New' about Forms of Organizing?" *Academy of Management Review*, April 2014, p. 177.

4. Valdis Krebs, "Social Network Analysis: A Brief Introduction" (www.orghnet.com). Copyright © 2000–2011, Valdis Krebs.

5. Gary L. Neilson and Julie Wulf, "How Many Direct Reports?" *Harvard Business Review*, April 2012, pp. 112–119; "What's Your Ideal Span of Control?" *Pingboard* (https://pingboard.com), November 15, 2016, p. 2.

6. Joseph B. White, "At 'New' General Motors, the Old Red Tape Still Rules," *The Wall Street Journal*, March 7–8, 2014, p. B4.

7. Max Weber, *The Theory of Social and Economic Organization* (New York: Free Press, 1947).

8. Gary Hamel and Michele Zanini, "More of Us Are Working in Big Bureaucratic Organizations than Ever Before," *Harvard Business Review*, July 5, 2016, p. 2.

9. Annie Gasparro, "Grocer Eliminates Dual-CEO Structure," *The Wall Street Journal*, November 3, 2016, p. B1.

10. Elliot Jacques, "In Praise of Hierarchy," *Harvard Business Review*, January–February 1990, p. 127.

11. Harold J. Leavitt, "Why Hierarchies Thrive," *Harvard Business Review*, March 2003, p. 98.

12. Raymond Fisman and Tim Sullivan, "The Unsung Beauty of Bureaucracy: Companies Need to Achieve the Right Mix of Rules and Freedom," *The Wall Street Journal*, March 16–17, 2013, p. C2.

13. Daisy E. Chung and Beth Bechky, "When Bureaucracy Is Actually Helpful, According to Research," *Harvard Business Review*, January 3, 2018, pp. 1–5.

14. Cited in Sarah Halzack, "Why Today's C-Suite May Soon Be a Thing of the Past" (www.washingtonpost.com), April 10, 2014, pp. 1–2.

15. Allison Linn, "Internal Tapes Bog Down Microsoft," The Associated Press, October 10, 2005.

16. Giles Hirst, Daan Van Knippenberg, Chin-Hui Chen, and Claudia A. Sacramento, "How Does Bureaucracy Impact Individual Creativity? A Cross-Cultural Investigation of Team Contextual Influences on Goal-Orientation-Creativity Relationships," *Academy of Management Journal*, June 2011, pp. 624–641.

17. Kevin Elkenberry, "On Silos and Accountability," *Executive Leadership*, February 2015, p. 7.

18. Lori Wade, "7 Reasons Why Project Management Is a Good Career Move," KnowledgeHut (www.knowledgehut.com), May 29, 2018, pp. 1–6.

19. Dwight Chestnut, "Nike's Flat Organization Structure," *eHow*, August 26, 2014, p. 1.

20. Mark Henricks, "Falling Flat?" *Entrepreneur*, January 2005, p. 69.

21. Alison Sider, "Deep Job Cuts Slow Revival of Oil Fields," *The Wall Street Journal*, July 8, 2016, pp. B1, B2.

22. Gary Hamel, "First, Let's Fire All the Managers," *Harvard Business Review*, December 2011, pp. 48–60; Leigh Buchanan, "One Company's Audacious Org Chart: 400 Leaders, 0 Bosses," *Inc.* (www.inc.com), April 18, 2013, pp. 1–3; Jacob Morgan, "How Morning Star Farms Operates without Any Managers," *Forbes* (www.forbes.com), June 4, 2014, pp. 1–2.

23. Rachel Feintzeig, "Companies Are Managing with No CEO," *The Wall Street Journal*, December 14, 2016, p. B5.

24. Chuck Salter, "Surprise Package," *Fast Company*, February 2004, pp. 62–66; "Third-Party Logistics Providers Can Make All the Difference in Cost, Service," *The Washington Post* (www.thewashingtonpost.com), March 22, 2017, pp. 1–2.

25. "How the 'Human Cloud' Is Starting to Change the Way Enterprise Firms Develop Their Contingent Workforce," B2B News Network (www.b2bnn.com), February 2018, pp. 1–2.

26. April Glaser, "Why Manufacturing Jobs Are Coming Back to the U.S.—Even as Companies Buy More Robots," *Recode Daily* (www.recode.net), pp. 1–3; Candace Moody, "Work Wanted: Reshoring Initiative Is Meant to Bring Manufacturing Jobs Back to the United States, and It's Working," *The Florida Times-Union* (http://members.jacksonville.com), September 9, 2014, pp. 1–2.

27. Sue Shellenbarger, "Outsourcing Jobs to the Den: Call Centers Tap People Who Want to Work at Home," *The Wall Street Journal*, January 12, 2006, p. D1; Luke Arthur, "Disadvantages of Outsourcing Customer Service," *eHow* (www.ehow.com), August 31, 2014, pp. 1–3.

28. Ann Majchrzak and Qianwei Wang, "Breaking the Functional Mind-Set in Process Organizations," *Harvard Business Review*, September–October 1996, p. 93.

29. William H. Davidow and Michael S. Malone, *The Virtual Corporation: Structuring and Revitalizing the Corporation for the 21st Century* (Edward Burlingame Books/Harper Business, 1992).

Organizational Culture and Knowledge Management

wavebreakmedia/Shutterstock.com

Chapter Outline

Learning Objectives

After reading and studying this chapter and doing the exercises, you should be able to:

1. Describe three aspects of organizational culture: how it is determined, its dimensions, and how it is learned.

2. Explain some of the major consequences and implications of organizational culture.

3. Describe the 4I framework of a learning organization and components of the learning organization.

4. Pinpoint strategies and techniques for knowledge management.

5. Specify methods for sharing information within an organization.

Netflix, the dominant provider of video-watching services, is also highly regarded for its corporate culture that contributes to its success. The statement of culture was formulated by CEO Reed Hastings and Patty McCord, the former chief talent officer at Netflix, and other workers. The culture is a mixture of values, human resource policies, and generalities for leading a successful life. McCord perceives the culture to be the way people operate when no one is looking.

Hastings believes that the true secret to the success of Netflix has not been an innovative business model, but rather a high-performance culture that focuses on fostering freedom and responsibility. A public statement of Netflix's corporate culture was first made on a PowerPoint deck posted on a website. Sheryl Sandberg, the celebrity COO of Facebook, called the deck one of the most important documents ever to come out of Silicon Valley. The presentation of the culture went viral, with at least 7 million viewers on the Web so far.

The nucleus of Netflix's talent philosophy is that the best thing you can do for employees is to hire only "A" players as coworkers because excellent players trump everything else. Fully competent adults rely on common sense and logic to accomplish tasks and do not have to be guided by a long list of human resource policies. This foundational belief about talent makes it possible to implement the corporate culture. A few features of this culture are described in the next several paragraphs.

The Netflix culture is based on nine, clearly defined values: judgment, communication, impact, curiosity, innovation, courage, passion, honesty, and selflessness. Hastings states that he expects Netflix employees to question any actions they perceive to clash with the organization's declared values. A hard-hitting, cultural, value-related policy is that attaining only adequate performance will get any level of worker cut from the team with a good severance package. The purpose of this policy is to create room for a star in that role. Jerks are not tolerated, even if they are brilliant; they also will receive a severance package.

The culture deck is a collaborative document prepared by Reed, McCord, and other managers in the company. Preparing the document was a 10-year effort, and it has been used as an onboarding document internally. The deck includes a no-fixed-vacation policy, meaning that the employee takes as much vacation as he or she desires, so long as the person is doing a great job and covering assigned responsibilities. Freedom and responsibility, in contrast to command and control, are a key part of the culture (as stated earlier), meaning that good managers give employees the right context in which to make decisions and let the employees make the decisions.

"Values are what we value" states the Netflix culture, meaning that real values are represented by what a person does, not what he or she says. A resolution or goal is worthless unless the person works hard to bring about the end result stated in the resolution or goal. At the same time, hard work is much less important than results. Trying and failing repeatedly might mean that you should try something else instead. Another suggestion built into the culture is to never shy away from taking on big challenges. The Netflix employee is advised to dive into big challenges that are outside his or her comfort zone.

Although the Netflix culture captivates many of its best employees and loads of Web surfers, not every employee is so convinced that Netflix is the model employer. A former employee stated on a blog that everyone is so concerned about the firings that nobody will stick his or her neck out. Employees just fight fires and try to look good.[1]

The story about Netflix just presented illustrates the relevance of organizational (or corporate) culture. The concept of corporate culture is so well known and relevant that, according to a recent survey, highlighting the company culture is done by 73 percent of recruiters to compete against other employers. (Better benefits come in second at 54 percent.[2]) In this chapter we discuss organizational culture and how to understand it. The present chapter also emphasizes a topic closely related to culture—how an organization as an entity makes good use of knowledge, including getting workers to effectively share their knowledge with each other.

Organizational Culture

As implied in previous mentions of the term, **organizational culture** is a system of shared values and beliefs that influence worker behavior. Edgar Schein was the first management theorist to define the corporate culture and to explain how the culture is such a dominant force in organizations. Much of his original thinking has influenced these more recent ideas about organizational culture.[3] Organizational culture may be considered a soft concept, yet the culture itself is quite durable. Having the right organizational culture can bring a strategic advantage to a company.[4] Culture is considered to be among the primary levers at the disposal of organization leaders to maintain organizational viability and effectiveness. As illustrated in the Netflix story, a culture is unique to each business, difficult for rivals to copy, and leads to profits.

An entrenched culture might take 10 years to change, such as a smug and insular company becoming more open to ideas and new ways of doing things.[5] A specific example is the difficulty top management at the Coca-Cola company faced for years in getting people to believe that, for the company to continue to prosper in the long run, it must not rely so heavily on carbonated beverages for its revenues.

The term *organizational climate* is close in meaning to the organizational culture, and the study of climate predates the study of culture. Climate is about the measurable properties of the perceived work environment that influence the motivation and performance of workers.[6] For example, workers might perceive a company to have a good safety climate or a strong digital climate. (Both are measurable, whereas culture is usually more difficult to measure.) Organizational climate remains an important part of organizational behavior.

Our study of organizational culture focuses on its determinants, its dimensions, how it is learned, and its consequences.

The organizational culture at Netflix has contributed to its success.

organizational culture A system of shared values and beliefs that influence worker behavior.

Determinants of Organizational Culture

Many forces shape a firm's culture. Often its origin lies in the values, administrative practices, and personality of the founder or founders. Also, the leader's vision can have a heavy impact on culture. An example is John Chambers, the former CEO of Cisco Systems, who dreamed of Cisco becoming one of the world's greatest companies. A historically important example of the impact of a leader on culture is Herb Kelleher, the founder of Southwest Airlines, who is considered pivotal in shaping one of the most distinctive organizational cultures. Up until Kelleher's retirement about 12 years ago, Southwest was considered very dependent on his personality and character. After his retirement for health reasons, his personality could still be felt. At the core of Southwest are the values of humor and altruism. For example, Southwest employees have established a catastrophe fund to help workers who need more assistance than usual employee benefits cover. Also, flight attendants and pilots use jokes and games to put customers at ease (a practice now copied by several other airlines).[7]

Organizational culture responds to and mirrors the conscious and unconscious choices, behavior patterns, and prejudices of top-level managers. As the founders leave or become less active, other top-level managers help define the culture. One of the ways in which Lou Gerstner, the former CEO and chair of IBM, changed the IBM culture was to relax its dress standards. His intent was to create a more relaxed (and less rigid) atmosphere at IBM. His successors, Sam Palmisano and then Virginia Rometty, have continued the tradition.

The culture of the society in which a firm operates also helps determine its culture. Sooner or later, society's norms, beliefs, and values find their way into the firm. Societal values are communicated through means such as the media, conversations, and education. The emphasis on sexual and racial equality in U.S. society has become incorporated into the value culture of many employers. The emphasis on collegiality translates into harmony and cooperation in the workplace at many Scandinavian companies, including Ikea.

LEARNING OBJECTIVE 1
Describe three aspects of organizational culture: how it is determined, its dimensions, and how it is learned.

Another perspective on national culture is that the introduction of values from another society into a retail business can be a competitive advantage. For example, the Korean values of high quality and reliability, and spotless factories, have helped fuel the success of the Hyundai and Kia car brands in the United States.

The industry to which a firm belongs helps shape its culture; for example, the culture of a high-tech information technology firm is quite different from that of a meat-packing facility. A public utility will have a culture different from a food manufacturer of comparable size. Heavy competition and low profit margins may force the food manufacturer to operate at a faster pace than the utility, which has more limited competition. Because of deregulation, competition among utilities has increased in recent years even though they face a less competitive environment than many manufacturers.

Dimensions of Organizational Culture

The dimensions, or elements, of culture help explain the nature of the subtle forces that influence employee actions. For example, a culture that values risk taking encourages employees to try new ways of doing things. The employees will do so without concern that they will be punished for failed ideas. The following list describes 12 influential dimensions of culture. A subtle point is that a dimension of organizational culture links closely with its consequences. For example, if a culture has a dimension of innovation, it will succeed in a marketplace demanding innovative products and services.

1. *Values.* The foundation of any organizational culture is values. A firm's philosophy is expressed through values, and values guide behavior on a daily basis. Values also contribute directly to the ethical atmosphere within a firm. An ethical workplace starts at the top of the organization. HR professionals within organizations, however, are expected by the Society for Resource Management (SHRM) to influence others to behave in an ethical manner and also to perform as an ethical role model.[8]

   A positive value that contributes to a healthy organizational culture is a high regard for human welfare, exhibited in programs and policies that enhance employee health and well-being. The Cisco well-being platform described in Chapter 13 is an illustration of this value in practice.

2. *Organizational stories with underlying meanings and myths.* Stories are circulated in many organizations to reinforce principles that top management thinks are important. An oft-repeated story is how company officials or other workers inconvenienced themselves to satisfy a customer or client need, such as foraging through a salvage yard to find a replacement part for a customer's old machine. Myths are dramatic narratives or imagined events about the firm's history. (A myth is more exaggerated than an organizational story.) Myths contribute to corporate legends, help unify groups, and can build competitive advantage. At United Parcel Service (UPS), for example, stories are repeated about drivers overcoming severe obstacles or reaching inaccessible locations to deliver packages.

   According to Ron Storn, VP of People at the ride-sharing service Lyft, one of the company's key values is to uplift people. The following story reinforces this value and helps uplift company employees: During a meeting of all 500 Lyft employees, a woman stood on the stage and told the story of how a Lyft driver drove her daughter to safety from a vicious roommate and also helped her pack and unpack her belongings into a hotel room. A photo of the driver smiling appeared on the screen behind the choked-up mother as she recounted the impact the driver's kindness had on her, the daughter, and the rest of the family.[9]

3. *Degree of stability and rapidity of decision making.* A fast-paced, dynamic firm has a different culture from that of a slow-paced, stable one. Top-level managers send out signals by their own energetic or lethargic stance regarding how much they welcome innovation. The degree of stability also influences the strength of a culture and whether or not a culture can take root. In a relatively stable organization, decisions tend to be made deliberately, whereas in a less stable organization, decisions are

made more rapidly, often on the fly. Up until the last few years, General Motors was regarded as a stable organization in which decisions about new products were made deliberately and cautiously, at times leading to conservative risk taking.

4. *Resource allocations and rewards.* The ways in which money and other resources are allocated have a critical influence on culture. The investment of resources sends a message about what the firm values. A basic example is the allocation of bonuses at Jetco Delivery, a trucking firm with about 145 employees. Teamwork is a strong value at the company, so bonuses are based on team performance, not individual performance.[10]

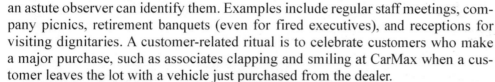
How quickly people make decisions is part of the organizational culture.

5. *Rites and rituals.* Part of a firm's culture is made up of its traditions, or its rites and rituals. Few companies think they have rites and rituals, yet an astute observer can identify them. Examples include regular staff meetings, company picnics, retirement banquets (even for fired executives), and receptions for visiting dignitaries. A customer-related ritual is to celebrate customers who make a major purchase, such as associates clapping and smiling at CarMax when a customer leaves the lot with a vehicle just purchased from the dealer.

6. *A sense of ownership.* The movement toward stock ownership for an increasing number of employees has created an ownership culture in many firms, in which workers are inspired to think and act like owners. An ownership culture includes increased loyalty, improved work effort, and the alignment of worker interests with those of the company. An ownership culture can be reflected in everyday actions, such as conserving electricity, making gradual improvements, and not tolerating sloppy work by coworkers. An ownership culture can backfire, however, if employee wealth stays flat or decreases as a result of stock ownership, or worse if the company goes under.[11]

7. *Belief in a higher purpose.* A dominant characteristic of many of the companies judged to be The 100 Best Companies to Work For is that employees have a sense of purpose. Employees derive deep satisfaction from feeling what they do is good and right. A belief in a higher purpose is easy to understand if one works for a pharmaceutical company. Employees of some financial services firms also believe that they are occupying a useful role in society. For example, at Edward Jones, the financial services giant, helping achieve financial security is part of the mission.[12]

Many firms are making a values shift to embody a sense of higher purpose in order to appeal to Millennials as workers and, by extension, as customers also. Josh Bersin, a Deloitte consultant who researchers trends in organizational cultures, says, "Young people are calling the shots, and they don't even know it."[13]

8. *Innovativeness and organizational ambidexterity.* A cultural dimension of significance in most fields is the innovative spirit of the workforce. As described in Chapter 5 about our study of creativity, an environment that encourages innovation contributes to individual creativity. The study of innovation will be introduced again in

Celebrations are a meaningful aspect of company rituals.

Owning company stock can contribute to a feeling of loyalty.

Chapter 16 about organizational change. Genentech, the biotech giant, is driven by a spirit of innovation, such as the development of a breast-cancer drug.[14]

Organizational ambidexterity is a flexible approach to innovation that is part of the culture. The term refers to the ability of an organization to efficiently take advantage of existing market opportunities while at the same time creating and innovating to meet the challenges of future markets.[15] The ambidextrous organization helps build excitement into the culture as the firm prospers in the present and has even better prospects for the future. Google Inc. is an ideal example as it prospers now and looks to future projects, such as a driverless automobile, wearable technology (including computer chips inserted in clothing), and a partnership in developing a longevity drug.

9. *Organizational justice.* A highly meaningful aspect of organizational culture for employees is what they perceive to be a climate of justice or fairness throughout the organization. Justice refers to how fairly employees are treated by organizational authorities. A climate of justice has three components: organizational decisions (distributive justice); decision-making procedures (procedural justice); and the quality of interpersonal treatment as part of these procedures (interpersonal justice). Visualize an employee who was accused of making private use of company equipment, such as using a company pickup truck to haul firewood for his house. He would look at the decision about any reprimands, the steps taken to decide on the punishment, and with how much dignity he was treated while being reprimanded for the rules infraction.

   An organizational climate perceived to be fair and just is likely to enhance job satisfaction, productivity, customer satisfaction, and organizational citizenship behavior.[16] (Of course, if the worker in question was simply advised to "not do it again," he would perceive the company to be highly just.)

10. *Orientation toward serving employees.* The presence of enough servant leaders in an organization helps foster a dimension of culture characterized by the desire to serve others. A person whose leader wants to serve him or her will often want to serve others. The cultural dimension of orientation toward service refers to behavioral norms and shared expectations of giving high priority to helping others. A study of 961 employees in 71 restaurants investigated how servant leadership contributed to a serving culture (serving each other, not customers). A serving culture was measured by such questionnaire statements as, "Managers and employees at our store put others' best interests ahead of their own." The study showed that servant leaders do create a culture of serving and that the serving culture enhanced restaurant performance and store performance.[17]

11. *Orientation toward serving customers.* Virtually every business organization, nonprofit organization, or government agency believes that providing good service to customers or clients is important. When a climate of good service toward customers is combined with an ethical climate, business performance tends to be strong. A study collected data from employees and managers at a major digital movie theater chain in China. Service climate was measured with managers' responses to such statements as, "Our employees are friendly and helpful to customers." It was found that the combination of a high service climate and ethical climate had a positive impact on business results. The results were measured in customer attendance rates and revenue per employee, including theater tickets and food and beverage sales.[18] A study with 16,862 medical sales representatives across 77 subsidiary companies

A Contrast between the Service Design of Starbucks and Dunkin' Donuts

Patricia O'Connell is the president of Aerten Consulting, a company that helps other companies design their service experience. She explains that "when you walk into a restaurant, you walk into a hotel, you interact with a company, you go into the lobby of a business, every step of that interaction between you and that company, that brand, that business, needs to be designed in order to give you a satisfactory experience."

O'Connell notes, "One of the classic examples we use to explain service design really quickly is Starbucks versus Dunkin' Donuts—who's a Starbucks person, who's a Dunkin' Donuts person? People usually have a very strong preference. Ostensibly both companies are selling the same thing, coffee. But that's not all they're selling. They're selling very different experiences. Dunkin' is grab and go—there's a reason the slogan is 'America runs on Dunkin.' The logo is very hot. Hot pink, hot green. Starbucks is much more about being relaxed and leisurely. It's not for the person who wants to get up and go."

O'Connell and her writing partner Thomas A. Stewart were talking to an audience in Seattle once and asked for a show of hands: Who's a Dunkin' person, and who's a Starbucks person? Stewart notes, "If you think about it, it's really interesting. At Starbucks, the seating is laid back, and at Dunkin' there are little stools if there's anything at all. [A little exaggerated

because some Dunkin' Donut stores have tables and chairs upstairs.] So these are examples of how you're selling coffee. You're selling better than average coffee. But what you're doing is creating two very different experiences, and people are in one camp or the other. There are not many people who say 'Whichever's closest.' They have a preference. And that preference is because the experience is different, and it's designed that way very consciously on both sides."

QUESTIONS

1. What differences, if any, do you think there are between people who would feel comfortable working as a barista at Starbucks versus a counter worker at Dunkin' Donuts?

2. What differences in organizational culture have you observed (or can you imagine) between Starbucks and Dunkin' Donuts?

3. Is it possible that O'Connell and Stewart are overlooking the fact that the tastiness of donuts and pastries also influences whether a consumer is a fan of Starbucks' versus Dunkin' Donuts?

Source: Excerpted and adapted from: An Interview with Thomas A. Stewart and Patricia O'Donnell, "'Woo, Wow, and Win': Designing a Captivating Customer Experience," *Knowledge@Wharton* (http://knowledgefe.wharton.upenn.edu), September 21, 2017, pp. 2–4.

---

of a multinational health-care enterprise found similar results. Profitability was enhanced in customer-service-oriented firms that also emphasized good ethics.[19]

12. *Joy and happiness.* An important dimension of organizational culture from the standpoint of employees is the extent of joy and happiness that pervades the organization. Joy and happiness are a component of the emotional culture. An outstanding example is Vail Resorts Inc., where management recognizes that cultivating joy among employees also facilitates customers having fun, which has a big impact in the hospitality business. (Vail, Colorado, is a world-famous ski resort, but the company also has 15 other locations.) CEO Bob Katz espouses "Have fun" as a corporate value. Resort managers model joy regularly and prescribe it for their teams. For example, ski-lift operators are often seen dancing, making jokes, and doing whatever is necessary to entertain guest while still emphasizing ski safety.[20]

In addition to the dominant culture of a firm, the subculture also influences behavior. A **subculture** is a pocket in which the organizational culture differs from the dominant culture, as well as other pockets of subculture. In a bank, the consumer loan division may have a culture different from that of the mortgage group because the consumer group has to work with much shorter time frames in processing loans.

Figure 15-1 presents key aspects of the organizational culture of business firms most likely to be familiar to you. Scanning Figure 15-1, combined with other references to culture in this chapter and elsewhere in the book, will add to your understanding of organizational culture.

subculture A pocket in which the organizational culture differs from the dominant culture, as well as other pockets of subculture.

FIGURE 15-1 A Sampling of Organizational Cultures of Well-Known Companies

Google (major division of Alphabet Inc.)—Has been designated as the tech company with the best corporate culture. Employees are inspired by Google's purpose: "To organize the world's information and to make it universally accessible and useful." High job satisfaction is emphasized through such perks as free meals, on-site massages and dry cleaning, and flexible work schedules. Employees are given the freedom to think creatively and innovatively and are encouraged to have fun at work, including bringing their dogs to work. Collaboration is encouraged. Employees label themselves "Googlers" and believe they are a superior group of people, with some saying that it is more difficult to be hired by Google than to be accepted into Harvard.

IKEA—Egalitarian values run deep in the company, including a de-emphasis on rank. The U.S. president carries the title "country manager." Very informal culture with roots in Swedish culture, yet the culture is quite strong in terms of worker commitment to the culture. Emphasis on informality, cost-consciousness, and a humble, down-to-earth approach. Simplicity, such as not having overly complicated work procedures, is also valued. Workers are allowed considerable responsibility.

Nike—Go-it-alone, insular culture characterized by a desire for growth within, rather than taking on the hassles of integrating a merger with another company. Very difficult for outside executives to be accepted by the inner circle. An attitude of secrecy and exclusivity around projects pervades the company. Employees are so loyal that many of them tattoo a Nike "swoosh" onto their legs.

Home Depot—Rowdy corporate culture, with the idea of growing big and fast. Workers used to drive forklift trucks through aisles with customers around. Dedication to helping customers by offering practical solutions to household problems. Cultural diversity is highly valued as reflected in the mix of their workforce. Customer diversity is highly valued as reflected in the posting of the languages spoken by store associates (especially in mixed ethnic neighborhoods).

Coca-Cola—Bureaucratic, slow-moving, with major changes taking a long time to implement. New CEO in 2017 wanted company to shake off culture of cautiousness that had gripped the company for more than a century. Continuing profits from beverages kept key employees in the past from seeing the need for change. For many years it had a bloated corporate staff. Gradually has shifted to a faster-moving culture, willing to experiment on new products, acquisitions, and new arrangements with suppliers. Employees tend to be loyal and are expected to drink Coke or other company beverages. Workers are geared toward professional behavior.

Southwest Airlines—Strong, trusting partnerships between managers and workers and unions that allow all concerned to execute the intricacies of an airline running smoothly. Strong emphasis on valuing human resources and intrinsic job satisfaction. Positive job attitude a key hiring factor. Emphasis on a relaxed work environment in which employees are regarded as even more important than Southwest customers. Three key corporate values are "a warrior spirit," "a servant's heart," and "a fun-luving (meaning loving) heart."

Apple Inc.—A strong cultural attitude of being winners who have changed and continue to change the world. Considerable emphasis on cognitive intelligence and creativity, combined with the smug attitude that people who work at lesser companies are less intelligent and imaginative. Very little tolerance for poor performance. The company emphasizes secrecy about its products and services and emphasizes obsessive attention to details.

Alibaba—This e-commerce giant has a cultish corporate culture that has touches of a video game. Company employees are referred to as "Alipeople" and are encouraged to choose nicknames from warriors in martial art novels. CEO Jack Ma uses the name Feng Qingyang, a sword master and kung fu guru. Job performance is measured in part by adherence to the company's core values, including integrity, teamwork, and strong customer focus.

Sources: Forbes Technology Council, "13 Reasons Google Deserves Its 'Best Company Culture' Award," *Forbes* (www.forbes.com), February 8, 2018, pp. 1–2; Will Leitch, "Isn't Google Awesome?" *Bloomberg Businessweek*, April 6–12, 2015, p. 64; Beth Kowitt, "At Ikea: No Ranks, No Rancor," *Fortune*, March 14, 2016, pp. 202–203; Jim Riley, "Would You Fit into the Organizational Culture at Ikea?" (www.tutor2U.net), May 22, 2013, pp. 1–4; Max Nisen, "At Nike, Workers Quote the Company's Maxims Like the Ten Commandments," *Business Insider* (www.businessinsider .com), February 15, 2013, pp. 1–2; "Living Our Values" (http://careershomedepot.com), 2014; Aixa M. Pascual, "Tidying Up at Home Depot," *Business Week*, November 26, 2001, pp. 102–104; Jennifer Maloney, "Shaking the 'New Coke Syndrome,'" *The Wall Street Journal*, May 10, 2017, p. B1; Albrecht Rothacher, "Coke Nation Embodying Corporate Culture" (www.globalspec.com), November 17, 2014, p. 1; Ken Makovsky, "Behind the Southwest Airline Culture" (www.forbes.com), November 21, 2013, pp. 1–3; "Culture Is the Key at Southwest Airlines," *Emerald for Managers*, 2014, pp. 1–2; Dylan Love, "Former Employee: 'At Apple, They Really Are After You'," *Business Insider* (www.businessinsider.com), January 9, 2013, pp. 1–2; Jessica Guynn and Calum MacLeod, "Jack Ma's e-Commerce Giant Prepares to Take On the World," *USA Today*, September 15, 2014, p. 2. Some of the observations are based on scattered comments from employees of the above companies.

How Workers Learn the Culture

Employees learn the organizational culture primarily through **socialization**, the process of coming to understand the values, norms, and customs essential for adapting to the organization. Socialization is therefore a method of indoctrinating employees into the organization in such a way that they perpetuate the culture. The socialization process takes place mostly by learning through imitation and observation.

Another important way in which workers learn the culture is through the teachings of leaders, as implied in the cultural dimension of resource allocations and rewards. Organizational members learn the culture to some extent by observing what leaders pay attention to, measure, and control.[21] Suppose a coworker of yours is praised publicly for doing community service. You are likely to conclude that an important part of the culture is to help people outside the company. Senior executives will sometimes publicly express expectations that help shape the culture of the firm. At Paychex Inc., the founder and former chairman, Tom Golisano, sets the tone for a practical-minded, action-oriented culture with dedicated managers. He reflects:

> We expect our senior management to be hands on. And I think when you talk to a lot of people who come from larger organizations, a lot of times they come from a different culture and it's hard for them to adapt. They expect in most cases a much healthier benefits and wage package, okay? They expect larger support staffs. They expect a little more freedom in their time and movement than we're willing to give them.[22]

socialization The process of coming to understand the values, norms, and customs essential for adapting to an organization.

The Consequences and Implications of Organizational Culture

Depending on its strength, a firm's organizational culture can have a pervasive impact on organizational effectiveness, as illustrated in the chapter-opening story about Netflix. Employees of a firm with a strong culture will follow its values with little questioning. A weaker culture provides only broad guidelines to members. Six major consequences and implications of organizational culture are outlined in Figure 15-2 and summarized next.

LEARNING OBJECTIVE 2
Explain some of the major consequences and implications of organizational culture.

1. *Competitive advantage and organizational effectiveness.* The right organizational culture contributes to gaining competitive advantage in several ways, including

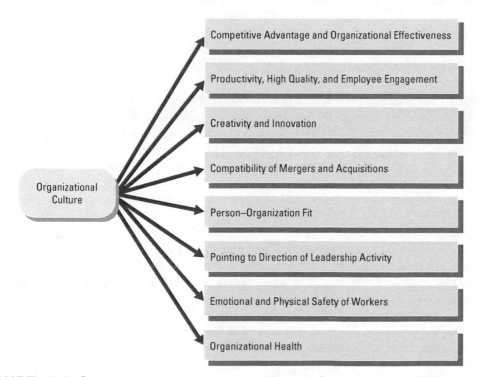

FIGURE 15-2 **Consequences and Implications of Organizational Culture**

increased market share, profit, and smooth functioning of the organization. You will recall that the CEO of Netflix attributes much of its success to its corporate culture.

2. *Productivity, quality, and engagement.* The consequence of competitive advantage and organizational effectiveness often happens because a culture that emphasizes productivity, including high quality, encourages workers to be productive and engaged.

   A culture that values the dignity of human beings fosters high morale, job satisfaction, and employee engagement. A human resource management specialist has observed that if corporate stewards tend the culture well, they will have an engaged and committed workforce for many years.[23] The consistently strong performance of Southwest Airlines is partially attributed to its humane and fun-loving culture that leads to high job satisfaction and motivation, often resulting in high productivity.

3. *Creativity* and *innovation.* A major contributor to innovation is a corporate culture that encourages creative behavior. Gary Hamel has identified specific features of a culture that inspire innovation, including setting very high expectations, creating a cause about which workers can be passionate, encouraging radical ideas, and allowing talented people in the company to easily transfer to different business areas within the firm. Also, innovators must be paid exceptionally well. As Hamel states, "Entrepreneurs won't work for peanuts, but they'll work for a share of the equity, a piece of the action."[24]

4. *Compatibility of mergers and acquisitions.* A reliable predictor of success in merging two or more firms is the compatibility of their respective cultures. When the cultures clash, such as a bureaucratic firm merging with a team-oriented one, the result can be negative synergy. Approximately 40 percent to 50 percent of mergers and acquisitions fail. Jennifer Vergilii, an attorney specializing in mergers and acquisitions, said, "There's a staggering percentage of mergers that fail, and the reason is that you can't get the two cultures to mesh."[25] A cultural clash between mergers is often manifested in such small items as the members of one company wearing sandals and tank tops to work, versus the members of the other company preferring more formal business attire.

5. *Person–organization fit.* An important success factor for the individual is finding an organization that fits his or her personality. Similarly, an organization will be more successful when the personalities of most members fit its culture. In one study, organizations were measured on dimensions such as stability, experimenting, risk taking, and an orientation toward rules. The preferences of professional employees regarding culture were measured and compared with the culture of their firms. Good person–organization fits result in more commitment and higher job satisfaction.[26]

6. *Pointing to direction of leadership activity.* Much of a top-level manager's time is spent working with the forces that shape the attitudes and values of employees at all levels. A key leadership role is to establish what type of culture is needed for the firm and then shape the existing culture to match that ideal. Charles D. Morgan, the former top executive at Acxiom Corp. and now an entrepreneur, sums up the link between culture and company leadership in these words: "Your culture should be everything you do as a business. It should be how you solve problems, build products, and work in teams. For the CEO and other leaders, it's about how you lead."[27]

7. *Emotional and physical safety of workers.* An organizational culture in which rudeness, incivility, and sexual harassment are discouraged and punished increases the probability of workers feeling safe emotionally and physically. In contrast, a culture that tolerates or ignores these negative behaviors leads to many workers feeling threatened and intimidated. In recent years, the cultures of numerous startups in Silicon Valley have been accused of improper conduct toward women or hostile work environments. One of the reasons that the founder and chief executive of Uber Technologies Inc. resigned was because many women employees complained of being mistreated and sexually harassed. Similarly, some executives at Social Finance Inc. (SoFi) were accused of engaging in or tolerating improper behavior toward women.[28]

8. *Organizational health.* A culture that facilitates attaining the previous seven consequences would result in a strong and healthy organization. As defined by the consultancy McKinsey & Company, organizational health is "The organization's ability to align around a commons vision, execute against that vision effectively, and renew itself through innovation and creative thinking." A healthy organization tends to perform well financially.[29] The concept of organizational health is so broad that it encompasses many different methods and techniques of organizational behavior, including creative problem solving and leadership among many others described in this book.

The Learning Organization

Closely related to organizational culture and change is the idea that an effective organization engages in continuous learning by proactively adapting to the external environment. A **learning organization** is one that is skilled at creating, acquiring, and transferring knowledge and at modifying behavior to reflect new knowledge and insights.[30] Although we speak of organizational learning, it is still individual people who create the conditions for such learning. Our approach to understanding the learning organization will be to first describe a framework of a learning organization, followed by a sampling of building blocks or components.

LEARNING OBJECTIVE 3
Describe the 4I framework of a learning organization and components of the learning organization.

learning organization An organization that is skilled at creating, acquiring, and transferring knowledge and at modifying behavior to reflect new knowledge and insights.

The 4I Framework of a Learning Organization

The 4I framework is instructive because it describes the processes involved in a firm making systematic use of information. A portion of the framework that appears most useful to practitioners is presented here and shown in Figure 15-3. A premise behind this framework is that organizational learning that results in organizational renewal encompasses the entire enterprise, not simply the individual or group. Another premise is that the organization operates in an open system, rather than having solely an individual focus. As is well known, an organization must satisfy the demands of the external world, or it will perish.

As explained by Mary M. Crossan, Henry W. Lane, and Roderick E. White, organizational learning is composed of four processes: intuiting, interpreting, integrating, and institutionalizing.[31] The four processes work together to link the individual, group, and organizational levels. The four processes are the glue that binds the structure together. The three learning levels (individual, group, and organization) define the structure through which organizational learning takes place (as does all of organizational behavior). The authors of the framework believe that, because so much research has built on and extended the framework, it is close to being a theory of organizational learning.

Individual level. Intuiting and *interpreting* take place at the individual level. *Intuiting* is the preconscious (not quite explicit or conscious) recognition of the pattern and/or possibilities inherent in a personal stream of experience. *Intuiting* is essentially intuition,

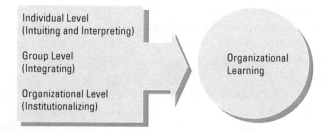

FIGURE 15-3 **The 4I Framework of Organizational Learning**

Organizational learning takes place at three levels and involves four processes.

Source: Original diagram based on information presented in Mary M. Crossan, Henry W. Lane, and Roderick E. White, "An Organizational Learning Framework: From Institution to Institution," *Academy of Management Review*, July 1999, p. 525.

Group learning is a key part of organizational learning.

and it relies on hunches about events taking place in the organization. *Interpreting* is explaining through words and/or actions an insight or idea to oneself and to others. A manager might develop the intuition that the company is not getting its fair share of repeat business. He might then say to coworkers, "Could we be facing some problem with our products that prompts many customers to forget about us after one try?"

Group level. Integration takes place at the group level. This is the process of developing shared understanding among individuals and of taking coordinated action. Dialogue about the problem and joint action is critical to the development of shared understanding. The group might bat around the problem by asking "What is it about us that prompts so many customers to try us once and not come back?"

Organization level. Institutionalization takes place at the organization level. This is the process of ensuring that routine actions occur. At first, the integrating taking place at the group level will be ad hoc and informal. However, if the coordinated action is recurring and substantial, it will become institutionalized. Tasks become defined, actions specified, and organizational mechanisms put in place to ensure that certain actions occur.

Institutionalizing can also be regarded as the process of embedding learning achieved by individuals and groups into the organization. In the example at hand, an institutionalized process might be to follow up with first-time customers regarding the reasons they intend to return or not return.

An implication of the 4I framework for managers is that, for organizational learning to take place, individuals should be encouraged to share their intuition and insights with other individuals and the group. In this way, the best insights will eventually become institutionalized. A more recent line of investigation emphasizes the importance of both transformational and transactional leadership in encouraging the institutionalization of learning. Transformational leadership might point the way for the new learning, while transactional leadership would help reinforce the institutional learning at the work-group level.[32] The supervisor, for example, might reward a worker for using recently acquired knowledge about better ways to handle inquiries.

A refinement of the 4I framework emphasizes that political tactics provide the social energy that translates the insights of individuals and groups into the institutions of an organization. Without a key player exerting influence, a useful idea might never become institutionalized. The idea becomes neglected in the press of everyday activities. Instead, if a champion of the idea keeps pushing for its acceptance, the idea may become institutionalized.[33] An example might be a business analyst in a large firm continually pushing the company to use ethanol fuel in more of its hundreds of vehicles to help reduce pollutants sent into the air. In addition to being smart, the innovation champion would need good connections in the company.

Building Blocks of a Learning Organization

To become and remain a learning organization, certain characteristics and behaviors are required of organizational members, as described next.[34] Although organizational theorists speak of a learning organization, the workers do the learning. The collective wisdom of the workers might then translate into a learning organization.

Double-Loop Learning

An in-depth, nondefensive type of learning takes place in a learning organization. **Double-loop learning** occurs when people use feedback to confront the validity of the goal or the values implicit in the situation. When you engage in double-loop learning, you change the governing values or assumptions themselves. As a result, you change your actions. A conventional-thinking manager (one who engages in single-loop learning) at a tire distributor observes that sales have been declining (feedback from the environment). The manager then asks, "How can we more effectively market retread tires for automobiles?" As a double-loop learner, the same manager might ask, "Why are we even selling retreads for the automotive market? The demand is declining, and they are not very safe." Note that the sales manager is being open and nondefensive about his or her product line, and is changing the assumption that retreaded tires even make a contribution to society.

double-loop learning A change in behavior that occurs when people use feedback to confront the validity of the goal or the values implicit in the situation.

Systems Thinking

In the learning organization, members regard the organization as a system in which everybody's work affects the activities of everybody else. Systems thinking also means keeping the big picture foremost in everybody's mind and being keenly aware of the external environment. This is true because the organization is part of a system that includes the outside world. A systems thinker at Brooks Brothers said over a decade ago, "The trend even among affluent businesspeople is away from our ultraconservative image. Our customer base is declining. If we don't want Brooks Brothers to be perceived as a museum of fashions past, we had better modify our product line." Brooks Brothers was able to modify its product image just enough to satisfy the modern conservative dresser without alienating its remaining die-hard ultraconservatives. Each store has elegant products to satisfy the conservative and ultraconservative dresser.

Team Learning

A learning organization emphasizes collective problem solving. Members freely share information and opinions with one another to facilitate problem solving. The team learning can take place in several ways. The basic approach is to use group problem solving throughout the firm. However, a large firm might bring people together at a retreat where they work in teams to reflect on ways of improving the organization.

Personal Mastery of the Job

Continuous learning usually is required to master a job in the modern organization. Two major examples are learning new information technology as it applies to the job and learning more about different cultures. For continuous learning to take place, each member must develop expertise. Quite often this detail is overlooked because of the emphasis on learning in groups. Collective learning is much more productive when every member of the group brings something valuable to the table.

Translation of New Knowledge into New Ways of Behaving

Given that learning involves a change in behavior, a true learning organization translates knowledge into action. Learning at a superficial level would occur if managers attended a seminar on expectancy theory and simply retained key principles. Members of a learning organization would *apply* expectancy theory.

Learning from Other Organizations

Some of the best insights an organization can acquire stem from studying competitors and other firms. Borrowing ideas from the competition, also known as "benchmarking," took place long before the concept of a learning organization arose. A learning organization systematizes the process while at the same time attempting to be ethical. "Learning from others" is most ethical when the learning does not directly capitalize on an idea a competitor spent considerable time and money developing.

Substantial learning can take place in copying the practices of firms not directly in your line of business. Suppose you would like to establish a worldwide method of distributing hard-to-get automobile parts, like a carburetor for a 1956 Edsel. You carefully study the marketing techniques of Amazon.com and Alibaba.com. You set up an elaborate system, copy the order and shipping process of these firms, and call yourself Oldautoparts.com. Because your benchmarking targets do not distribute hard-to-find auto parts, nobody gets hurt. You are a learning organization without directly copying another company's ideas.

An example of a company with a learning-obsessed culture is WD-40. The company produces WD-40, a powerful lubricant for metal parts that also aids in the removal of rust. Comparable brands exist, but WD-40 is used in four out of five American households and almost all factories, mines, and construction sites in the country. When Garry Ridge became CEO of WD-40 in 1987, he recognized that the company had become too dependent on its one, almost cult-like product. He decided to build an organizational culture that emphasized learning. Part of his solution was for everyone at the company to take the "WD-40 Maniac Pledge," a vow to become a "learning maniac."

Ridge demanded that his management team become more interested in possibilities for the organization, its products, and the brand. He placed a premium on learning, experimenting, and improvising, transforming an old business into a vibrant company. Today, WD-40 sells its products in 176 countries and has launched a collection of new brands and products. Two other well-known company products are 3-in-One Oil and Lava hand soap for heavy-duty cleaning.[35]

Knowledge Management

A major consequence of a learning organization is that knowledge is managed more effectively. **Knowledge management (KM)** is a systematic approach to documenting, applying, and transferring the know-how and experience of employees.[36] A major objective of knowledge management is to make effective use of the vast store of useful information and experience possessed by employees. Often this knowledge has to be transferred to affiliates in other countries and with different cultures.

Managing knowledge well achieves goals such as innovation, nonduplication of effort, and competitive advantage. When knowledge is managed effectively, information is shared as needed, whether it is printed or stored electronically or in the brains of workers. The justification for knowledge management is that intellectual capital is a resource that allows for survival and competitive advantage. **Intellectual capital** is knowledge that transforms raw materials and makes them more valuable. It is also a capital asset consisting of intellectual material.[37] The intellectual capital of many firms, consisting of the know-how and intelligence of the workers, is far more valuable than their physical assets, consisting mostly of a handful of machines and furniture. Firms high in intellectual capital and low in physical capital include software development companies, consulting firms, and advertising agencies. Knowledge management also helps deal with the problem of knowledge loss when competent employees leave the firm. If the employee's useful knowledge, including creative ideas, is documented by the firm, a knowledgeable employee's departure is a less serious problem.

Knowledge-Management Strategies and Techniques

Given that knowledge management can help an organization succeed, various strategies and techniques have been developed to foster the process. The building blocks of a learning organization are also closely tied in with the knowledge-management strategies and techniques to be described next.

Hire the Right Persons

Hiring people who are good at learning and teaching makes a substantial difference in the effectiveness of knowledge management (KM). Thomas H. Davenport explains: "Not enough companies have built into their competency models how well people learn and pass on their knowledge informally on the job. If you've got people who are hungry to learn and people who are good at transferring knowledge, the organization will be much more alive."[38] People with the right stuff for KM are most likely to be those who have demonstrated intelligence, accumulated knowledge, and displayed intellectual curiosity in the past.

Create Knowledge

Creating knowledge is an important first step for managing knowledge. The strategy is easily stated but not so easy to implement. First, you need intelligence to create the knowledge, and you also need the conditions favoring creativity and innovation described in Chapter 5. The 4I model of organizational learning provides a partial explanation of how knowledge is created. To understand the need for creating new knowledge, it is useful to perceive every product, service, and work process as a bundle of knowledge. For example, the Jeep Wrangler is the intelligence bundled in the ability to transform a 75-year-old design to fit modern tastes for the retro look, do the appropriate engineering and manufacturing, and market and distribute the product to customers.

A standard approach to creating knowledge is to scan the environment for information that might apply to one's situation. The Internet and paid-for databases have become standard techniques for environmental scanning. Executive scanning is often done to search for information that could affect the future of the firm.[39] Just a few years ago, residential real estate developers scanned the environment to help predict what type of structures might be in demand in the future. It became apparent that home ownership would be declining, so developers invested heavily in constructing multifamily dwellings, including apartment buildings. Because it can take at least two years from site location to completed apartment complex, environmental scanning is particularly necessary.

A successful organization creates knowledge.

Another perspective on knowledge creation is that servant leadership facilitates the process by sharing leadership responsibilities. Because leadership is shared, there is mutual influence and direction, as well as caring relationships. The mutual influence and caring stimulate greater exchange of ideas, experiences, and expertise among servant leaders and group members that results in the generation of new knowledge.[40]

Because the leader and the group members are functioning as partners, they tend to exchange ideas, thereby creating knowledge that did not exist previously. For example, suppose an authoritarian leader says to the sales group, "Increase the customer retention rate by 15 percent by the end of the quarter." A minimum of discussion is likely to take place within the group about why the customer retention rate is low. Instead, imagine the servant leader saying, "Our customer retention rate is far too low. How can we work together to improve our retention rate?" Discussion and idea sharing leading to new knowledge is more likely to take place.

Close the Gap between Knowing and Doing

Why don't companies accomplish more if they have so much knowledge and expertise? Jeffrey Pfeffer and Robert I. Sutton believe that companies have fallen into the knowing–doing gap because doing something requires the hard work of making something happen. Managing knowledge is not enough; it must be converted into action. It is easier and safer to have intellectual discussions, to gather large databases, and to invest in technical infrastructure than it is to actually execute. The challenge for companies and the people in them is to build a culture of action.[41] Often this means taking decisive action that results in repeat business, such as an airline having a high percentage of on-time flights or a retailer offering commissions to sales representatives in the stores.

A big gap between knowing and doing stems from the challenge of big data and analytics. Managers now have access to enormous amounts of complicated data about customers, employees, and operations, but these data do not translate readily into useful knowledge.[42] For example, artificial intelligence (AI) might inform WD-40 management that people who purchase WD-40 and 3-in-One oil purchase a lot of hand tools and garden tools. Translating this tidbit into profitable action might prove difficult.

Methods of Sharing Information

LEARNING OBJECTIVE 5
Specify methods for sharing information within an organization.

A major goal of the learning organization and knowledge management is for organizational members to share relevant information. Sharing can take place in all four organizational directions: downward, laterally, upward, and diagonally. Many of the strategies and techniques already described in this chapter contribute directly or indirectly to information sharing. Although knowledge management does not appear to be highly complicated, few organizations have figured out how to share knowledge among employees or how to pass it on when one employee transfers or quits.[43]

Here we briefly describe six focused methods for sharing information. Self-Assessment 15-1 provides you with an opportunity to reflect on your own tendencies toward information sharing.

1. *In-house Yellow Pages.* The basic idea of company Yellow Pages is to compile a directory of the skills, talents, and special knowledge of employees throughout the firm. To be useful, the Yellow Pages have to go far beyond basic information and job experience. The directory should indicate the specialized knowledge of the people listed and their level of expertise. When faced with a problem requiring specialized talent, employees can consult the Yellow Pages for a person who can help.

2. *Intranet communication systems.* Many firms use intranets and online forums to spread and share knowledge. Workers who need to share information log on to an internal collaboration network to access content posted by another worker within the company. Accessing the site saves the time of sending around numerous e-mails asking for information, as well as sending text messages or making phone calls. An example of the use of such a network is LifeSize Communications, a videoconferencing company in Austin, Texas. In one situation, the company wanted advice about how to sell a product against a competitor. The post-in question showed a detailed description of conversations the partner had with the customer and included iPhone photos of the competitor's product that pointed to key differences between the two videoconferencing systems. The sharing of information provided an effective way of selling against the competitor.[44]

   An analysis of problem solving conducted in an online discussion forum within a global engineering firm provides some clues as to which problems workers bother with—and therefore share information about. An influential factor was whether the recipient of the message thought the problem involved fit his or her expertise.

My Tendencies toward Sharing Knowledge

Directions: Indicate whether each of the following statements is mostly true or mostly false as it applies to your own attitudes and behaviors.

Statement about Knowledge Sharing	Mostly True	Mostly False
1. I am very secretive at work or school.	☐	☐
2. When I get a good idea in relation to work, I will usually describe it to a coworker as soon as possible.	☐	☐
3. I post loads of personal information about myself on social media sites.	☐	☐
4. Only a fool would tell coworkers about a great idea he or she had for a new business.	☐	☐
5. I try to make sure I get full credit for any useful new idea I have at work.	☐	☐
6. I am willing to let coworkers know about a good idea I have for improving work efficiency.	☐	☐
7. I think it is important that laws about intellectual property rights be strictly enforced.	☐	☐
8. Only a jerk would describe in great detail an idea he or she had for a new product, service, or book.	☐	☐
9. If I thought I had a money-making idea, I would share it with other people in a brainstorming activity for course such as this one.	☐	☐
10. I think that Coca-Cola is completely justified in keeping its secret receipt for its syrup in a vault.	☐	☐
11. I enjoy working as part of a team and sharing ideas.	☐	☐
12. If a student submits a paper to a professor, I like the idea of indicating that the ideas are copyrighted, such as stating "© Mary Ketchum. All rights reserved."	☐	☐
13. I would be comfortable posting my best ideas for work improvement or a new product on my company's intranet.	☐	☐
14. I worry a lot about a boss stealing my best ideas, even if he or she appears to be honest.	☐	☐
15. I enjoy providing a coworker with new information or teaching him or her a new skill.	☐	☐

Scoring and Interpretation: Give yourself 1 point for having answered Mostly True to the following statements: 2, 3, 6, 9, 11, 13, and 15. Give yourself 1 point for having answered Mostly False to the following statements: 1, 4, 5, 7, 8, 10, 12, and 14.

12 or higher: You have very positive attitudes toward sharing knowledge with others. However, you might be a little too trusting of people whose intentions you do not know.

5–11: You tend to have about-average attitudes toward information sharing.

0–4: You have negative attitudes toward information sharing, and you may need to become a little more open with your ideas to work well in a team setting.

Reciprocity also had an effect in the sense that the recipient of a request to help solve a problem kept in mind whether the sender had helped him or her in the past. Requests in relation to problems that were too long and too complex tended to receive less attention. Having several competing problems to work on also had a negative influence on information sharing.[45]

3. *Encouraging knowledge sharing in employee networks.* Networks, both those on the computer and face-to-face, are a major mechanism for knowledge sharing. For example, if a person has an extensive network within the organization, he or she is likely to receive tidbits of useful, work-related information. One recruiter in the network might say to another in his or her network, "I came across a small black college in Georgia that is a wonderful source of mechanical engineering candidates. Let me tell you about it."

   A study of 700 employees in an engineering, information technology, and management consultancy demonstrated that both the characteristics of the network and the individual influence the amount of information sharing that takes place. The main finding of the study was that knowledge sharing happens best when having a central position in a network, motivation, and ability are the highest. *Ability* in this context refers to the ability to learn from others as well as to understand how one's knowledge can be used by other workers.[46]

4. *Personal explanations of success factors.* An advanced method of information sharing is for key organizational members to teach others what they know through explanations of success factors. Noel Tichy refers to these stories as the "teachable point of view" because they help leaders become teachers. The teachable point of view is a written explanation of what a person knows and believes about what it takes to succeed in his or her own business, as well as in business in general. About two pages in length, the document focuses on critical success factors, such as: What would it take to knock out the competition? Tichy claims that this hard-hitting method of information sharing is used in hundreds of companies.[47]

5. *Fostering dialogue among organization members.* To promote the importance of information sharing, company leaders should converse about the importance of intellectual capital and the development of core competencies.[48] At the same time, workers throughout the firm should be encouraged to share useful suggestions, tidbits of knowledge, and success stories about problem solving. This type of information sharing can take place face-to-face, but e-mail exchanges also play a vital role. The most consistent observation about knowledge management and information sharing is that the human touch is more important than technology. David Gilmour, the president of a knowledge systems company, advises that technology should not flood people with information or take it from them. It is better to identify connections that are valuable to the people who are being connected.[49]

   When GM president Dan Ammann (he reports to the CEO) was first dealing with the problems created by the ignition-switch recall, one of his first moves was to look for ways information could be more effectively shared. He said, "We needed to break down internal silos, integrate, and require transparency across the business so that everyone is sharing information. We want what we are calling a 'zero-defect mentality.'"[50]

6. *Sharing physical facilities and informal learning.* An important method of fostering dialogue is to develop shared physical facilities, as described in Chapter 10 about teamwork development. Considerable information sharing is likely to take place in a snack lounge or company information resource center. At the same time, informal learning takes place, which is almost synonymous with information sharing.

Implications for Managerial Practice

1. To manage organizational culture, one must first understand the culture of the firm and then use that knowledge to guide one's own behavior and that of group mem-

bers. For example, an executive might resist downsizing as a way to reduce costs because laying off productive and loyal employees conflicts with the firm's values.

2. The most important and the most practical aspect of the learning organization and knowledge management is for workers to share useful information with one another. In your role as a manager, you should therefore make a systematic effort to ensure that information is shared in the total organization or your organizational unit. Establish both formal steps (e.g., an intranet) and informal methods (e.g., simply encouraging people to exchange good ideas) to accomplish information sharing.

3. To facilitate knowledge creation, managers should encourage more frequent formal and informal interactions and establish strong ties with employees. Furthermore, the availability and diffusion of knowledge occur when people have strong relationships with each other. Organizational leadership should therefore encourage stronger relational ties among employees in order to leverage knowledge creation.[51]

4. Several theorists have mentioned that a company's true competitive advantage derives from intellectual capital. If this observation is valid, then one of the highest organizational priorities is to recruit and retain knowledgeable and intelligent workers. Even during a downsizing, maximum effort should be invested in retaining the best thinkers and most knowledgeable people in the company.

5. In addition to encouraging the sharing of knowledge, managers should discourage the hiding of knowledge. A study conducted in Slovenia found that hiding knowledge prevents colleagues from generating creative ideas and also might have negative consequences for the creativity of a knowledge hider.[52] Another consideration is that hiding knowledge works against the spirit of knowledge management.

Summary of Key Points

1. *Describe three aspects of organizational culture: how it is determined, its dimensions, and how it is learned.* The origins of organizational culture often lie in the values, administrative practices, and personality of its founders. Other key influences are the societal culture, the industry, and the organization's code of conduct. Organizational culture has various dimensions, such as the values, stories, and myths maintained by the organization; the degree of stability and rapidity of decision making; resource allocation and rewards; rights and rituals; the sense of ownership within the firm; belief in a higher purpose; and innovativeness and organizational ambidexterity. The culture is taught primarily through socialization and the teaching of leaders.

2. *Explain some of the major consequences and implications of organizational culture.* The consequences and implications of organizational culture include competitive advantage and organizational effectiveness; productivity, quality, and employee engagement; creativity and innovation; compatibility of mergers and acquisitions; the person–organization fit; and the direction of leadership activity.

3. *Describe the 4I framework of a learning organization and components of the learning organization.* According to the 4I framework, organizational learning that results in organizational renewal encompasses the entire enterprise. Organizational learning is composed of

four processes: intuiting, interpreting, integrating, and institutionalizing. The four processes work together to link the individual, group, and organizational levels. Intuiting and interpreting take place at the individual level, integrating takes place at the group level, and institutionalizing takes place at the organizational level. Both transformational and transactional leadership can facilitate the institutionalization of knowledge. Political skill is also necessary to institutionalize knowledge. Components of the learning organization include (a) double-loop learning, (b) systems thinking, (c) team learning, (d) personal mastery of the job, (e) translation of new knowledge into new ways of behaving, and (f) learning from other organizations.

4. *Pinpoint strategies and techniques for knowledge management.* Strategies and techniques for knowledge management include (a) hiring the right persons, (b) creating knowledge, and (c) closing the gap between knowing and doing.

5. *Specify methods for sharing information within an organization.* Information sharing is at the heart of a learning organization and knowledge management. Six specific methods are (a) in-house Yellow Pages, (b) intranet communication systems, (c) encouraging knowledge sharing in employee networks, (d) personal explanations of success factors, (e) fostering dialogue among organizational members, and (f) sharing physical facilities and informal learning.

Key Terms and Phrases

organizational culture, p. 339

subculture, p. 343

socialization, p. 345

learning organization, p. 347

double-loop learning, p. 349

knowledge management (KM), p. 350

intellectual capital, p. 350

Discussion Questions and Activities

1. During the past two decades, the term *corporate culture* has become so widely used that it is almost as well known as a term such as *return on investment*. What do you think accounts for the popularity of the term *corporate culture*?

2. How would you describe the organizational culture of Walmart (or any other large retailer) based on whatever evidence you have? If necessary, visit your local Walmart (or other large retailer) to make firsthand observations.

3. Why do so many CEOs believe that their primary responsibility is managing organizational culture? What happened to making a profit?

4. Identify any organization you know about that you think would best fit your personality. Justify your reasoning.

5. What relevance does *organizational culture* have for members of the gig economy (essentially, freelance workers)?

6. What do you think of the assertion made by many business observers that corporate culture is more important than a company's strategy in determining its success?

7. How should a manager deal with professional workers who are hesitant to share information because they are concerned that a coworker will steal their best ideas and take credit for them?

8. Give an example of how a first-level manager might engage in systems thinking.

9. What do you think would happen in most companies if they implemented the Netflix approach to allowing employees to take as much vacation as they wanted so long as they got their work done?

10. Ask two experienced managers or corporate professionals what they think is the higher purpose of their employer and whether they care about the purpose.

CASE PROBLEM: Construction Manager Blake Wants to Size Up the Culture

Thirty-two-year-old Blake had worked for six years as a construction supervisor at a mid-size construction company. One of his major career goals was to move up to a senior management position in a commercial construction company. At his present employer, however, all the senior management positions went to family members by birth or marriage, and Blake was an outsider. As a result, Blake decided to conduct a job search. As he suspected, his skills and experience were in strong demand in the healthy construction economy at the time.

The second company Blake interviewed with for a construction manager position was a commercial builder in Chicago, only a thirty-minute commute from where he lives. After a series of telephone interviews, video interviews, and in-person interviews, Blake was made an attractive offer at 15 percent higher pay than he was receiving at the family business. The construction manager position was year-round because the company performed internal as well as external construction work. Blake said he was excited about the offer but wanted 10 days to reach a final decision.

Blake thought highly of the job offer and the company but believed that he should learn more about the company's culture to ensure that he would be a good fit. He thought to himself, "As they say, I should exercise due diligence." Blake's first step in checking out the corporate culture was to ask the construction company receptionist what she thought of the company. She responded, "Awesome. Anything else I can help you with?"

Next Blake went to one of the company's present construction jobs, the renovation of a 100-year-old office building. He explained to a few construction workers who were on break that he was considering working for the company, so he wanted their input on what it was like working there. One worker said, "Company management believes in a fair day's work for a fair day's pay. No complaints on my part." A second worker said, "If you're looking for an easy job, go someplace else. They expect a lot out of you here." A third worker said, "You have to put up with the heat, the cold, and a ton of work, but you get good pay and fair treatment in return." Blake thanked the workers for their willingness to speak with him.

Blake then asked about 12 people in his network if they knew anybody who worked for his prospective employer. He finally identified three people, an accountant, a project manager, and a sales representative, along with their contact information. When asked about the type of company atmosphere, the accountant replied, "Only the strong survive here. You have to produce to justify your compensation." The project manager said, "If you are serious about working for us as a construction manager, you could have a fine career. But you have to be ready to think on your feet, provide strong leadership, and get your hands dirty." The sales representative said, "I'm proud of what I am accomplishing here, but it's no picnic. I earn every commission dollar."

Blake thought he was learning a lot about the organizational culture, but he wanted one more vital input. Based on information on the construction company's website, he identified a recent customer and found a way to contact a building manager who worked for the cus-

tomer. When asked about what she thought of the construction company in question, she replied, "They are decent, hardworking people. They got the job done on time and within budget."

Blake concluded, "I have uncovered no skeletons in the closet, and what I hear impresses me. I'm going to phone in my acceptance at 8:30 tomorrow morning."

Case Questions

1. What do you think of Blake's approach to sizing up the organizational culture at his prospective employer?

2. What other approach would you recommend that Blake have taken to assess the organizational culture?

3. Based on the evidence that Blake collected, what is your size-up of the culture of Blake's new employer?

Endnotes

1. Original story created from facts and observations in the following sources: Interview with Patty McCord, "Learning from Netflix: How to Build a Culture of Freedom and Responsibility," *Knowledge@Wharton* (knowledge@wharton.upenn .edu), May 29, 2018, pp. 1–8; Patty McCord, "How Netflix Reinvented HR," *Harvard Business Review*, January–February 2014, pp. 70–76; "The Netflix Culture of Excellence," The Simple Dollar (www.thesimpledollar.com), September 17, 2014, pp. 1–14; Henry Blodgett and Dina Sector, "Revealed: The Secrets to Netflix's Success," *Business Insider* (www .thebusinessinsider.com), July 15, 2011, pp. 1–2.

2. Survey reported in Jae Yang and Paul Trap, "Recruiting as Marketing Tool," *USA Today*, November 17, 2014, p. 4B.

3. Edgar Schein, "Careers, Culture, and Organizational Learning," in *Business: The Ultimate Resource* (Cambridge, MA: Perseus Books Group, 2002), p. 1044.

4. Boris Groysberg, Jeremiah Lee, Jesse Price, and J. Yo-Jud Cheng, "The Leader's Guide to Corporate Culture," *Harvard Business Review*, January–February 2018, p. 45.

5. Interview of Heinrich von Pierer, "Transforming an Industrial Giant," *Harvard Business Review*, February 2005, p. 122.

6. "Organizational Climate Definition: Everything You Need to Know," www.hello.com/blog, February 4, 2016, p. 1.

7. Katrina Brooker, "Can Anyone Replace Herb?" *Fortune*, April 17, 2000, pp. 186–192; Tom Belden, "Will Fun Be Enough?" *The Inquirer* (www.philly.com), January 24, 2006.

8. "Point/Counterpoint: Is It HR's Job to Create an Ethical Culture?" *HR Magazine*, February 2018, pp. 22–23.

9. Erica Keswin, "Use Stories from Customers to Highlight Your Company's Purpose," *Harvard Business Review*, June 22, 2017, pp. 2–3.

10. Brian Fielkow, "Culture Is the Key Differentiator," *Executive Leadership*, September 2014, p. 3.

11. Falice Chin, "How Does an Employee-Owned Company Work?" Chron (http://smallbusiness.chron), November 16, 2014, p. 2.

12. Michael C. Bush and Sarah Lewis-Kulin, "The 100 Best Companies to Work For," *Fortune*, March 1, 2018 p. 56.

13. Quoted in Jeremy Bordend, "As Millennials Take Leadership Roles, It Spells Changes in Corporate Culture," *The Christian Science Monitor* (www.csmonitor.com), June 22, 2017, p. 2.

14. Bush and Lewis-Kulin, "The Best 100 Companies," p. 57.

15. Pankaj C. Patel, Jake G. Messersmith, and David P. Lepak, "Walking the Tightrope: An Assessment of the Relationship between High-Performance Work Systems and Organizational Ambidexterity," *Academy of Management Journal*, October 2013, p. 1421.

16. Daniel S. Whitman et al., "Fairness at the Collective Level: A Meta-Analytic Examination of the Consequences and Boundary Conditions of Organizational Justice Climate," *Journal of Applied Psychology*, July 2012, pp. 776–791.

17. Robert C. Liden, Sandy J. Wayne, Chenwci Liao, and Jeremy D. Meuser, "Servant Leadership and Serving Culture: Influence on Individual and Unit Performance," *Academy of Management Journal*, October 2014, pp. 1434–1452.

18. Kaifeng Jiang, et al., "Do It Well and Do It Right: The Impact of Service Climate and Ethical Climate on Business Performance and the Boundary Conditions," *Journal of Applied Psychology*, November 2016, pp. 1553–1568.

19. Adam T. Myer, Christian N. Thoroughgood, and Susan Mohammed, "Complementary of Competing Climates? Examining the Interactive Effects of Service and Ethical Climates on Company-Level Financial Performance," *Journal of Applied Psychology*, August 2016, pp. 1178–1190.

20. Sigal Barsade and Olivia A. O'Neill, "Managing Your Emotional Culture," *Harvard Business Review*, January–February 2016, p. 62.

21. Gerard George, Randall G. Sleeth, and Mark A. Siders, "Organizing Culture: Leader Roles, Behaviors, and Reinforcement Mechanisms," *Journal of Business and Psychology*, Summer 1999, p. 548.

22. Quoted in Andy Meisler, "Spare Him the Gurus," *Workforce*, June 2003, p. 36.

23. Ronald J. Alsop, "Cultural Awareness," *Workforce Management*, July 2011, p. 42

24. Gary Hamel, "Reinvent Your Company," *Fortune*, June 12, 2000, pp. 97–118. The quote is from page 118.

25. Quoted in Susan Milligan, "Culture Clash," *HR Magazine*, August 2014, p. 21.

26. Charles A. O'Reilly III, Jennifer A. Chatman, and David F. Caldwell, "People and Organizational Culture: A Profile Comparison Approach to Assessing Person–Organization Fit," *Academy of Management Journal*, September 1991, pp. 487–516.

27. Charles D. Morgan, "Culture Change/Culture Shock," *Management Review*, November 1998, p. 13; "Entrepreneur Charles Morgan in New Ventures," *The City Wire* (www.thecitywire.com), March 12, 2012, pp. 1–6.

28. Peter Rudegeair, "SoFi Staff Criticize Startup's Culture," *The Wall Street Journal*, September 11, 2017, pp. B1, B2; Katie Reilly, "Every Event That Led to Uber CEO Travis Kalanick's Resignation," *Fortune* (www.fortune.com), June 21, 2017, pp. 1–3.

29. Chris Gagnon, Elizabeth John, and Ron Theunisson, "Organizational Health: A Fast Track to Performance Improvement," *McKinsey Quarterly* (www.mckinsey.com), September 2017, p. 2.

30. David A. Garvin, "Building a Learning Organization," *Harvard Business Review*, July–August 1993, p. 80.

31. Mary M. Crossan, Henry W. Lane, and Roderick E. White, "An Organizational Learning Framework: From Intuition to Institution," *Academy of Management Review*, July 1999, pp. 522–537. The framework is updated in Mary M. Crossan, Henry W. Lane, and Roderick E. White, "Reflections on the 2009 *AMR* Decade Award: Do We Have a Theory of Organizational Learning?" *Academy of Management Review*, July 2011, pp. 446–460.

32. Vera Dusya and Mary Crossan, "Strategic Leadership and Organizational Learning," *The Academy of Management Review*, April 2004, p. 235.

33. Thomas B. Lawrence, Michael K. Mauws, Bruno Dyck, and Robert F. Kleysen, "The Politics of Organizational Learning: Integrating Power into the 4I Framework," *Academy of Management Review*, January 2005, pp. 180–191.

34. Robert M. Fulmer and Philip Gibbs, "The Second Generation Learning Organizations: New Tools for Sustaining Competitive Advantage," *Organizational Dynamics*, Autumn 1998, pp. 7–20; Chris Argyris, "Double-Loop Learning, Teaching and Research," *Academy of Management Learning & Education*, December 2002, pp. 206–218; "From the Editors: Honoring the Legacy of Chris Argyris by Devoting Attention to How Managers Learn," *Academy of Management Learning & Education*, March 14, 2014, pp. 1–4.

35. Bill Taylor, "How WD-40 Created a Learning-Obsessed Company Culture," *Harvard Business Review*, September 16, 2016, pp. 1–6.

36. Book review in *Academy of Management Executive*, February 2002, p. 161.

37. Thomas A. Stewart, "Intellectual Capital," in *Business: The Ultimate Resource*, p. 159.

38. Quoted in Louisa Wah, "Making Knowledge Stick," *Management Review*, May 1999, p. 27.

39. Rajiv Nag and Dennis Gioia, "From Common to Uncommon Knowledge: Foundations of a Firm-Specific Use of Knowledge as a Resource," *Academy of Management Journal*, April 2012, p. 424.

40. Rishabh Rai and Anand Prakash, "A Relational Perspective to Knowledge Creation: Role of Servant Leadership," *Journal of Leadership Studies*, Issue 2, 2012, pp. 61–85.

41. Cited in Alan Webber, "Why Can't We Get Anything Done?" *Fast Company*, June 2000, pp. 168–180.

42. Martin Ihrig and Ian MacMillan, "Managing Your Mission-Critical Knowledge," *Harvard Business Review*, January–February 2015, p. 82.

43. Scott Thurm, "Companies Struggle to Pass on Knowledge That Workers Acquire," *The Wall Street Journal*, January 23, 2006, p. B1.

44. Dave Zielinski, "Group Learning: Use Social Media to Engage Employees in Knowledge Sharing," *HR Magazine*, May 2012, p. 49.

45. Martine R. Haas, Paola Criscuolo, and Gerard George, "Which Problems to Solve? Knowledge Sharing and Attention Allocation in Organizations," *Academy of Management Journal*, June 2015, pp. 680–711.

46. Mia Reinholt, Torben Pedersen, and Nicolai J. Foss, "Why a Central Network Position Isn't Enough: The Role of Motivation and Ability for Knowledge Sharing in Employee Networks," *Academy of Management Journal*, December 2011, pp. 1277–1297.

47. Noel Tichy, "The Teachable Point of View," *Harvard Business Review*, March–April 1999, p. 82.

48. William Miller, "Building the Ultimate Resource," *Management Review*, January 1999, p. 45.

49. David Gilmour, "How to Fix Knowledge Management," *Harvard Business Review*, October 2003, pp. 16–17.

50. Jeff Bennett, "Would You Buy a Cadillac from This Man?" *The Wall Street Journal*, November 12, 2014, p. B8.

51. Rai and Prakash, "A Relational Perspective to Knowledge Creation," p. 77.

52. Matej Cerne, et al., "What Goes Around Comes Around: Knowledge Hiding, Perceived Motivational Climate, and Creativity," *Academy of Management Journal*, February 2014, pp. 172–192.

Organizational Change and Innovation

vectorfusionart/Shutterstock.com

Learning Objectives

After reading and studying this chapter and doing the exercises, you should be able to:

1. Describe the influence model of the change process in organizations.

2. Explain why people resist change and how to manage such resistance.

3. Describe four major factors that create organizational change.

4. Explain the nature of organization development.

5. Develop useful insights into managing change in your job and career.

6. Identify eight behavioral principles of innovation.

Crate & Barrel is a leader in the home furnishings specialty retailing industry. The retailer, with 120 stores, including its CB2 stores, is known for its exclusive designs, excellent values, and outstanding customer service. Working with European studios and manufacturers, Crate & Barrel was among the first to offer reasonably priced, stylish household goods and contemporary design to American consumers. Up until a few years ago, almost all the company merchandise was sold in stores. Crate & Barrel had very little social media presence and relied primarily on still photographs to showcase its furniture.

Neela Montgomery, chief executive and former chairman of the board, decided it was time to modernize the established furniture chain by decluttering the stores and investing heavily in social media and digital capabilities. A key goal was to make Crate & Barrel an omnichannel retailer. The company was not ready to give up on selling in physical stores but planned to use online sales to support in-store sales. Mike Relich, the chief operating officer (COO), said that offline and online sales have to work together: "If you cut stores, your e-commerce sales will go down."

The combination of a website, mobile app, and brick-and-mortar stores enables a customer to visit a store and actually touch and hold pillows to see if the feel is right; he or she can then go online to order the pillows in the preferred color or to avoid having to carry them around the mall or to a vehicle. Online sales now account for one-half of Crate & Barrel's sales revenues.

Crate & Barrel now has more than one million Instagram followers and uses more digital content than still photos by publishing videos on YouTube weekly. Under Montgomery's direction, the chain now invests more than one-half of its advertising budget on digital media.

In addition to expanding its digital footprint, Crate & Barrel continues to improve its physical stores. The store environments have become more experiential, more about design-related events and product partnerships that create excitement and disruption. Also, the digitalization of Crate & Barrel is designed to create improved shopping experiences by making interactions between employees and customers more fluid and devoid of frustration.

Another key information-technology-based improvement implemented by Crate & Barrel was to modify the supply chain to get merchandise to customers more quickly. For e-commerce business, shipping times have been reduced to an average of four days, with shorter times planned for the future.

Similar to other major retailers, Crate & Barrel is scrutinizing how Big Data, the cloud, and analytics can help the company better understand customers in terms of what products they want to buy, when they want to buy them, and where to warehouse the merchandise. Relich reasons that by tying together omnichannel capabilities, the retailer can collect more data about customers. Browsing behavior can be tied with transactional behavior.

To date, the organizational changes at Crate & Barrel appear to be working. Since the digital transformation began, sales have climbed steadily, with an 8 percent increase reported recently.[1] (A notable accomplishment in the present retail environment.)

The story about the retailer of fashionable furniture and home furnishings illustrates how many organizations have relied on information technology as a method of bringing about change that has an impact on the behavior of customers and employees. Although the Crate & Barrel experience may be positive, corporate transformations are difficult to execute. Recent data suggest that three-quarters of change efforts flop—either they fail to deliver the anticipated benefits or they are abandoned entirely.[2] Understanding the processes involved in organizational change is therefore important.

In this chapter, we present key aspects of organizational change: a model of the change process, an analysis of resistance to change and overcoming such resistance, forces that create change, organization development, and dealing with change at a personal level.

An Influence Model of the Change Process in Organizations

LEARNING OBJECTIVE 1
Describe the influence model of the change process in organizations.

"The only constant is change" is a frequently repeated cliché in the workplace. To meet their objectives, managers and professionals must manage change effectively almost daily. Even companies that appear from the outside to work in a stable environment are faced with change. A classic example is Hershey Foods Corporation, which has been making chocolate products since 1905, including the remarkably stable brands of Hershey's Milk Chocolate Bar and Reese's Peanut Butter Cups. However, the technology for distributing chocolate products, including Internet sales, has created enormous challenges for the chocolate maker.

A company executive said almost two decades ago, "Keeping up with the technology is probably the greatest challenge. Imagine how different it is to make chocolate now than when Milton Hershey was making his first caramel. From the time chocolate is made to the time it reaches the consumer, it's dealing with new technology the whole way."[3] Two years later, the vice president (VP) and chief information officer (CIO) said, "Hershey's information systems are providing the necessary data to support the transformation of the organization and business processes."[4]

Ten years later, Hershey announced the opening of a new facility featuring a $300 million investment in state-of-the-art technology never used before in the manufacture of confectionery. The plant's new information technology systems include automated diagnostics systems to help keep operations running smoothly 24 hours per day.[5] The point again is that even with a relatively stable product line, Hershey managers and employees have to deal with major changes in technology.

Competitive threats are a primary mover for changes within an organization, even for market leaders. For example, major packaged foods producers have been challenged by small food companies producing what the public perceives as healthier choices. In response, a few of the major producers have sold off poorly performing brands and also created new divisions to produce and market more natural foods. The many other types of change in organizations include changes in technology, organizational structure, and the people with whom one works, such as customers and company insiders.

A major observation about change is that the ability to change is somewhat related to size: Large organizations are more resistant to change than small- or medium-sized organizations. Part of the problem is that, in a large organization, many people are involved, so many layers of approval are needed for change to take place. Furthermore, because an organizational culture is composed of the attitudes of organizational members, the larger the number of employees, the larger the number of individual attitudes that have to be changed to bring about organizational change.

Organizational change has been studied from different perspectives. Here we present a model of organizational change based on years of research and practical experience by change specialists Tessa Bassford and Bill Schaninger. The model described next, and outlined in Figure 16-1, is referred to as the influence model of organizational change and has the following components: fostering understanding and conviction, reinforcing

FIGURE 16-1 The Influence Model of Organizational Change

Source: Based on information presented in Tessa Bassford and Bill Schanginger, "The Four Building Blocks of Change," McKinsey & Company (www.mckinsey.com), April 2016, pp. 1–8.

with formal mechanisms, developing talent and skills, and role modeling. The researchers found that successful transformations were almost eight times more likely to use all four components of the model as opposed to just one.[6] You will find the key ideas in the model built into other aspects of change presented in this chapter, particularly in reference to dealing with resistance to change.

Fostering Understanding and Conviction

Believing in the "why" behind a change can inspire people to change their behavior. Leaders therefore have to spend sufficient time communicating the rationale behind their change efforts. In times of transformations, it is recommended that leaders develop a change story that helps all stakeholders understand where the organization is headed, why it is changing, and why this change is important. Leaders at Crate & Barrel, as well as at other retailers, had to explain to employees that selling beautiful merchandise in stores was no longer enough to generate sufficient store visits from today's shoppers. Stores had to shift to creating exciting experiences, such as demonstrations by décor experts, to attract potential customers.

Reinforcing with Formal Mechanisms

The changes in behavior required by the organizational changes should be reinforced, following the principles of positive reinforcement described in Chapters 6 and 7. Rewards that are the most effective for the situation must be chosen carefully. A Middle Eastern telecommunications company examined performance drivers and found that collaboration and purpose were more important than compensation. The organizational change in question was moving the company to substantially higher levels of customer service. Company management therefore shifted from awarding minor individual bonuses for performance to celebrating how specific teams made a real difference in the lives of customers. The shift increased motivation and also saved the company millions of dollars.

Developing Talent and Skills

Organizational changes often require that organizational members develop talents and skills to fit the new thrust brought about by the changes. Assume that an organization is going through a change to become more culturally diverse with respect to employees and the customer base. Key talents and skills to develop include becoming more culturally sensitive and relating more effectively to people outside one's demographic group.

As will be described in Chapter 17, among the initiatives taken by the organization to develop such talent and skills are diversity training, anti-bias training, and workshops in developing cultural intelligence. Yet before such training is effective, many workers will need help in overcoming their self-serving bias in thinking they are already highly effective in cross-cultural relationships. Self-serving biases might also have to be dealt with as an organization is attempting a digital transformation: Most people who can operate a desktop computer or smartphone successfully think they have high-level information-technology skills.

Role Modeling

Organizations seeking employee support for major transformational efforts need to recognize that key opinion leaders throughout the organization may exert considerable influence. The point is that other workers will model the behavior of staff members they perceive to have sound opinions. Imagine that an organization decides it should transform into a paperless company—a difficult transition even in an increasingly digital work environment. Handfuls of influential people who talk positively about going paperless, and go paperless themselves, will facilitate the desired organizational change.

Why People Resist Change

Before a company's managers can gain support for change, they need to understand why people resist change. People resist change for reasons they think are important, the most common being the fear of an unfavorable outcome. This outcome could be less money, personal inconvenience, more work, or any other outcome viewed as negative. People also resist change for such varied reasons as not wanting to disrupt social relationships and not wanting to break well-established habits.

LEARNING OBJECTIVE 2
Explain why people resist change and how to manage such resistance.

A deep-level reason many employees resist change is that they face competing commitments. Even if the worker wants to go along with a workplace change, he or she might direct productive energy toward a hidden competing commitment. Organizational psychologists Robert Kegan and Lisa Laskow Lahey explain that an employee who moves slowly on a project may have an unrecognized competing commitment to avoid an even tougher assignment that might follow. If he performs well on the present project, he might be given an even greater challenge that he fears might be beyond his potential.[7] The competing commitment functions as an immunity to change. Another example of a competing commitment is that a worker might resist performing well in a new supervisory position; if she performs well as a supervisor, she might be perceived as being disloyal to members of the work group of which she was a well-accepted member.

Even when people do not view a change as potentially damaging, they may sometimes resist it because they fear the unknown. People will sometimes cling to a system they dislike rather than change. According to folk wisdom, "People would rather deal with the devil they know than the devil they don't know." Workers may also resist change because they are aware of weaknesses in the proposed changes that may have been overlooked or disregarded by management.[8]

A sales manager resisted her company's proposal to shift a key product to dealer distribution. She explained that dealers would give so little attention to the product that sales would plunge. Despite her protests, the firm shifted to dealer distribution. Sales of the product did plunge, and the company returned to direct selling.

Another subtle reason for resisting change is that the change might be perceived as damaging the person–environment (or organization) fit. This conclusion was based on a study of 34 separate work units experiencing 21 different organizational changes including reengineering projects, reorganization, and implementation of new technology.[9] Suppose an Avon representative has built a successful business, relying heavily on her network of personal contacts, including sending text messages to them. She particularly enjoys visiting the homes of customers and placing orders by hand on order forms. The representative now learns that customers should be encouraged to place their replacement orders on the Avon website. Although the representative will still receive commissions on these sales, she resists getting her customers to shift to placing their orders on the Internet. The Avon rep feels that the new work environment is not a good fit for her skills.

The reasons for resistance to change presented so far emphasize factors within the individual and, to some extent, the social context. Baruch Shimoni, a professor at the Bar-Ilan University in Israel, has developed a theory that resistance is more likely located within the individual's social dispositions (similar to a tendency). His reasoning is that resistance is a social practice built into the system, produced by people's social dispositions. The resistance develops over time in frequent interactions between people and social structures in a given social context.[10]

Although this theory may appear highly abstract, it has practical implications. The workplace environment, including the work group, influences how the individual will react to a proposed organizational change. For example, a worker might hear frequently from coworkers that management is often looking for ways to exploit them, leading to a high degree of skepticism about management initiatives. When management announces a new method of measuring worker productivity, the worker in question might think that the new method will result in him or her receiving a lower year-end productivity bonus.

Group discussion can help overcome resistance to change.

Gaining Support for Change

Gaining support for change, and therefore overcoming resistance, is an important managerial responsibility. Here we look at 11 of these techniques for gaining support for change.

1. *Allow for discussion and negotiation.* Support for change can be increased by discussing and negotiating the more sensitive aspects of the change. The two-way communication incorporated into the discussion helps reduce some employee concerns. Discussion often leads to negotiation, which further involves employees in the change process. Town-hall meetings between senior executives and workers in different locations of a company have become a popular vehicle for gaining acceptance to change. During the meetings, executives field questions from the local workers.

2. *Allow for participation.* The best documented way of overcoming resistance to change is to allow people to participate in the changes that will affect them. A powerful participation technique is to encourage people who already favor the change to help in planning and implementation. These active supporters of the change will be even more strongly motivated to enlist the support of others. A related approach is to grant responsibility for change to workers who have a capacity to find unique ways to look at problems that seem impossible to solve. Labeled "positive deviants," these individuals are able to see solutions where others do not.

3. *Point out the financial benefits.* Because so many employees are concerned about the financial effects of work changes, it is helpful to discuss these effects openly. If employees will earn more money as a result of the change, this fact can be used as a selling point. For example, the CEO of a small company told his employees, "I know you are inconvenienced and ticked off because we have cut way back on office support. But some of the savings will be invested in bigger bonuses for you." Much of the grumbling subsided.

4. *Avoid change overload.* Too much change in too short a time leads to negative stress. So it is helpful to avoid overloading employees with too many sweeping changes in a brief time period. Too much simultaneous change also causes confusion, leading to foot-dragging about the workplace innovation. The more far-reaching the innovation is, such as restructuring a firm, the greater is the reason for not attempting other innovations simultaneously. To avoid an overwhelming amount of change, a few organizations are taking a company-wide approach and coordinating all the changes taking place with the use of portfolio management techniques. It is helpful to stagger the rollouts of changes so that the same groups do not get hit with too many changes at the same time.[11]

5. *Gain political support for change.* Few changes get through organizations without the change agent forming alliances with people who will support his or her proposals. Often this means selling the proposed changes to members of top-level management before proceeding down the hierarchy. It is much more difficult to create change from the bottom up.

6. *Communicate relevant information.* A standard method of reducing resistance to change is through communication of relevant information. The method is likely to be the most effective when people resist change because they lack sufficient information. For example, workers may resist making the necessary preparations for outsourcing part of their work until they are informed about the scale of the outsourcing program and how it will affect their jobs.

Change overload can trigger resistance to change.

7. *Avoid citing poor performance as the reason for change.* Instead of criticizing, the change agent should accurately describe market challenges or budget restraints and show employees why change is necessary for survival. For example, do not say to employees, "If things hadn't become so sloppy around here, we wouldn't need to change." Instead, tell them, "Our competitors can deliver the finished product in half the time because of this new technology. If we don't make the change too, we'll lose all our key accounts."

8. *Incorporate the human touch.* Some changes are resisted because they are perceived to diminish valued human contact. Many workers and customers may be impressed with an information technology device that eliminates having to deal with a human to complete a transaction. The same workers, however, may resist the change because they enjoy human contact. Perhaps employees might be able to receive counseling about their benefits through an interactive computer program, or a voice recognition system, yet they would *prefer* to interact face-to-face with a benefits counselor.

9. *Pay attention to the emotional aspects of change.* Another aspect of behavior that must be dealt with in overcoming resistance to major change is emotion. Too often the manager attempting to sell the change focuses on cognitive aspects alone, such as making a rational presentation of the merits of the change. One example of paying attention to emotion would be to enable workers to express tension and anxiety they have about the change, such as worrying about whether a merger with another company will make them second-class citizens. Another way of paying attention to emotion is to formulate a metaphor that evokes positive feelings.[12] In the merger situation, the manager might talk about the group becoming part of a bigger family with room for everyone.

10. *Appoint coaches as facilitators of change.* Change can be so difficult for employees that receiving encouragement and factual assistance from a coach can be helpful. The coach can be a manager or other staff member who receives the proper training to act in that role. St. Vincent Charity Medical Center and Providence Hospitals saw the need to undergo "lead process improvement," a method of eliminating wasteful effort and maximizing efficiency in order to stay competitive in the new healthcare environment. To accomplish the process improvement, employees needed to be involved and engaged in problem solving. The director of organization development at St. Vincent spearheaded selecting and training a group of 40 coaches to help implement the process improvement initiatives. These individuals included the senior leadership team and supervisors who were effective at employee engagement. The coaches, in turn, helped other supervisors bring about the desired changes in process improvements.[13]

11. *Leaders must change also.* As explained in the discussion of the influence model of organizational change, the intended changes are more likely to work if the leaders are a model for the changes. Dean Anderson, a change consultant, provides this example: "If you're going to move toward more openness and collaboration, you better make sure that people are seeing that in your executives."[14]

To practice the concepts of managing change, do the Skill-Development Exercise that follows.

Four Major Factors That Create Organizational Change

Many forces can create change in organizations. Here we pinpoint three representative forces: downsizing, information technology, and a shift in work roles. A more subtle force is a value shift within the organization.

LEARNING OBJECTIVE 3
Describe four major factors that create organizational change.

Downsizing and Workforce Reduction as a Change Strategy

Downsizing has already been mentioned as a significant stressor and as a method of achieving a flat structure. Downsizing is also the most often used deliberate organizational

Gaining Support for Change

One student plays the role of a team leader who is to meet today with team members to sell them on the idea that the company plans to shift from a standard workweek to a 4/40 workweek (work 10 hours per day, 4 days per week). About six other students play the role of the team members, several of whom have mixed reactions to the proposed change. The team leader should use the techniques for gaining support for change described in this section or in the section on the influence model of organizational change. Team members who do not like the contemplated change should express what they consider valid reasons for resisting the change. Other class members should observe and then provide feedback.

change in the last 40 years, even during times of relative prosperity for companies. Governmental and educational institutions also downsize in response to financial pressures. The layoffs at Tesla in 2018 illustrate how financial pressures can prompt a high-profile company to downsize its workforce. Nine percent of the company's 40,000 employees were let go, with the majority being salaried. CEO Elon Musk explained that the reasons for the layoffs were that the company had many duplicate positions and that the reduction in staff would help with the goal of earning a profit. (Tesla had yet to report an annual profit.)[15]

The merger of companies is also a force for downsizing because of duplications in positions, such as having two human resource and information-technology departments in the merged firm. Many downsizings come about because many fields have consolidated, such as retail chains buying each other and a major retailer like Wal-Mart or Target driving other retailers to reduce their staffs to stay in business.

Cost reductions are often necessary because the survival of the firm is at stake. Laying off workers can sometimes make a firm more competitive by lowering costs, but, at the same time, this causes enormous confusion and resentment. Downsizing can also leave a firm so understaffed that it cannot capitalize on new opportunities. Another concern is that downsizing depletes human assets and interferes with organizational learning because so much information stored in people's memories leaves the firm.[16]

An important perspective on downsizing as a change strategy is to specify the conditions under which it has the best chance of contributing to organizational effectiveness.[17] To begin with, top management should ponder whether downsizing can be avoided. Instead of laying off employees, a way should be sought to better utilize their expertise. Some cost cutting can be achieved by involving employees in improving work methods and processes. Under ideal circumstances, key people can look to penetrate new markets. As a last-ditch maneuver to avoid downsizing, a company might reduce the salaries of all workers, or place workers on a 4-day workweek, thereby having enough money to pay a full workforce.

The first key to a successful restructuring is to integrate downsizing with the company's long-term strategies. The firm must determine where the business is headed and which employees are needed to ensure that future. The company must identify and protect high-potential individuals who are needed to carry the firm forward. After delayering, firms must decentralize and empower key individuals to conduct their jobs. The downsizing survivors must be revitalized by redefining their positions. (A problem is that survivors often have to assume the workload of several people.) It is therefore essential to eliminate low-value and non-value activities such as multiple reviews of other people's work and meetings without meaningful agendas.

Downsizing often disrupts the life of workers.

After restructuring, teamwork must be emphasized more than previously because much cooperation is required to accomplish the same amount of work with fewer human resources. The downsized organization may require a new structure. It should be redesigned to reflect the changed jobs, processes, and responsibilities. Horizontal as well as vertical relationships must be specified. Considerable attention must be paid to the human element before and after downsizing. A carefully implemented system of performance evaluation increases the chances that good work performance and the possession of vital skills should receive more weight than favoritism in retaining employees.

A progressive approach is to offer training to employees designated for downsizing so they might qualify for any vacant positions in the company. Downsizing survivors in all companies need an outlet to talk about their grief and guilt in relation to laid-off coworkers. As is often done, laid-off workers should be given assistance in finding new employment and redirecting their careers.

At times, a large and prosperous organization can implement a program that will decrease the need for future layoffs. In 2013, leadership at AT&T concluded that 100,000 of its 240,000 employees were working in jobs that would become irrelevant within a decade. Instead of eventually letting these workers go, the company decided to retrain all of these workers by 2020. The results of retraining have been favorable as measured by organizational outputs, such as how quickly new products generate revenue.[18]

Information Technology and Organizational Change

Advances in information technology have facilitated a variety of profound changes in organizations. The new term to cover the impact of information technology on organizations is *digital disruption*. Your knowledge of information systems and information technology will help you visualize many organizational changes created by digitalizing information. A major change is that electronic access to information has made much of the delayering of organizations possible. Many middle management and coordinator positions have been eliminated because there is less need for people to act as conduits of information. Instead, information seekers obtain information via computers. Information technology has forced hundreds of companies to change their product offerings. Two small examples are that people purchase fewer hard-copy roadmaps today, and fewer low-priced watches are sold because many people use their smartphones to tell time.

In the long range, the computerization of the workplace may create more jobs, such as a surge in the demand for software engineers and call-center technicians. Yet a profound change for many managers, sales representatives, and professionals is that their jobs have disappeared. A few examples: Automobile dealerships require fewer sales representatives because consumers do much of their shopping online. Fewer human resource professionals are needed because standard HR functions, such as speaking to a benefits counselor, are replaced by software. And cloud computing is replacing the need for large IT departments.

Experts predict that the "hollowing out" of the middle-class workforce is a continuing trend. They predict the loss of millions of more positions as information technology continues to advance.[19] Perhaps the net effect of job losses will be organizations with a smaller number of managers and professionals. Many of these people will have to accept lower-paying and lower-skill jobs or shift to positions in high demand.

Information technology has played a key role in making organizations more democratic. Democracy is enhanced because more people have access to information. E-mail and intranets make it easier for lower-ranking members to communicate directly with

Information technology has brought about profound changes in the workplace.

higher-ranking members. Before the surge in information technology, such direct interaction was rare in large firms.

Although information technology has made organizations more democratic, many communications are also more impersonal. E-mail messages and other communication software, such as shared Web pages, have replaced many conversations that might have profited from face-to-face interaction. Self-service systems for key functions, such as filing travel and expense reports and obtaining information about benefits, make it difficult to chat with someone about a problem. (At the same time, these impersonal systems save the organization time and money, such as through hiring fewer people to work on expense accounts.)

The Internet has substantially changed the nature of many businesses, such as companies interacting more directly with customers and suppliers. Many retail sales positions and industrial sales positions have been eliminated by e-commerce. The Internet has transformed some industries. A good example is the newspaper industry where changes mirror what is happening in other industries. To survive, the industry has had to rely on its traditional strength of offering detail and depth. Services must now also be offered in both hard copy and online. Newspapers were among the first commercial entities on the Internet. Information on the Internet is now offered free, pay-per-view, and by subscription. Similar to newspapers, advertising agencies have to cope with a major shift away from print ads toward advertising on the Internet. Advertising agency managers and professionals who lack advanced skills in digital marketing have been replaced in the thousands by the digitally savvy.

Enterprise software that links together the various functions of the enterprise to one another and to customers affects job behavior. A smaller number of managers is needed because fewer employees are needed when enterprise software is fully implemented. The remaining key workers must be skilled in information technology, problem solving, and interpersonal skills. Information technology has created substantial changes in how long and where people work. Accessing and responding to e-mail and text messages have added hours to the workweek of many employees. Another change is that managers and professionals feel obliged to stay in frequent contact with the office, even during nights, weekends, and vacations.

Artificial intelligence (AI) is a subset of information technology that has brought about substantial changes in organizations, particularly with respect to decision making, as described in Chapter 5. The effect, however, is not to replace human judgment but to give the decision maker more data on which to base a decision. A subprime auto lender, for example, might use AI to analyze thousands of facts about applicants to assess their creditworthiness even if they have poor credit. The manager makes the final decision using the data provided.

Artificial intelligence is likely to create some job losses, but how many is difficult to estimate. A report from Forester predicts that by 2021 intelligent agents and related robots will have eliminated a net of 6 percent of jobs, with *net* meaning that AI will also create many new positions.[20] If organizations have smaller workforces because of artificial intelligence, fewer managers will be needed. Artificial intelligence could also replace some corporate professional positions because its results might be used to replace human judgment. For example, less demand might exist for investment fund managers, real estate appraisers, and market researchers. A counterinfluence is that many new firms and divisions of larger firms might be formed using artificial intelligence as a platform, resulting in the employment of many managers and corporate professionals.

An indirect effect of artificial intelligence in organizations is that the managers least likely to be replaced are those who exercise good judgment in decision making and have outstanding interpersonal skills. Artificial intelligence is not a substitute for emotional intelligence.

The accompanying Organizational Behavior in Action insert illustrates how digitalization is used to transform a business enterprise in a basic industry.

How Kloeckner Metals Embraces Digital Disruption

Kloeckner & Co is a global steel service company with $8 billion in annual revenues. The U.S. affiliate Kloeckner Metal Corp. is headquartered in Roswell, Georgia, and has more than 50 locations in the country, with over 2,400 employees. Among the company's 200,000 products are hot roll products, structural steel, sheets, pipes, plates, and custom products such as steel housing for furnaces. The wide variety of Kloeckner services include laser cutting, plate processing, coil coating, metal roof manufacturing, finishing, and shipping and logistics.

The U.S. company's "Kloeckner & Co. 2022" strategy plans to disrupt the steel service industry through an aggressive, innovative digitalization initiative, supported by a team of 60 software engineers based in Berlin. Part of the goal of the disruption is to attract employees ranging from workers who understand complex equipment on the shop floor to a variety of business professionals in sales, purchasing, and finance. The company's efforts toward the digitalization of manufacturing are regarded by some as part of the next industrial revolution.

An internal analysis by the parent company several years ago concluded that the steel industry's supply and value chain remained highly inefficient, with transactions slowed down by communication technologies limited to telephones, faxes, and e-mails. The strategy of becoming more digital was first implemented in Europe through digitizing purchasing and logistics practices. Kloeckner Metals formed a digital innovation group that operates separately from the IT group.

The U.S. company is already benefiting from lower costs and greater efficiency, and customers are benefitting from an enhanced buying experience and smoother interactions with Kloeckner staff members. Customers are able to purchase products and services digitally, which streamlines the traditional sales channels and eliminates many antiquated processes, such as faxing product specifications to Kloeckner. Customers are already using digital contract portals, online shops, and order overviews.

In addition to spearheading the digitalization movement, Kloeckner also plans to make better use of the data that digitalization provides. Kloeckner has partnered with several artificial intelligence companies to predict steel demand and price trends more accurately, along with a more in-depth analysis of customer behavior.

John Ganem, head of the U.S. affiliate, said that he wants to build the Kloeckner management team of the future. "The industry as a whole has had a hard time attracting young people who have been looking to enter teach, pharma, or financial companies," he said. "We are asking ourselves how to attract young people into the industry, how do we train them, and how do we keep them motivated. The move to digital is part of the answer."

To help attract new employees to the company, including digital natives, Ganem is developing summer internships for students, more active recruitment of students, and formal management training. An example of the latter is the Emerging Leaders Program that brings employees from North America and Europe to Berlin so that they can learn more about the company and gain leadership experience. Ganem said, "We will want our employees to learn the business from top to bottom and from bottom to top."

QUESTIONS

1. Why would some manufacturing specialists consider the digitalization of manufacturing to be the next industrial revolution?

2. How would you fit into the transformed steel industry if you decided to pursue such a career path?

Source: Original story based on facts and observations in the following sources: Steven Nghe, "Industry 4.0: Digitalization of Manufacturing," Kloeckner Metals (www.kloecknermetals.com). July 21, 2017, pp. 1–10; Phil Bolton, "Kloeckner Metals Corp's New CEO to Aggressively Pursue Digital Strategy," Kloeckner Metals (www.kloecknermetals.com), December 7, 2017, pp. 1–7; "How a Steel Company Embraced Digital Disruption," *McKinsey Quarterly* (www.mckinsey.com), May 2016, p. 14.

The Transition from Carrying Out a Job to Performing Work

A subtle change in the workplace is that traditional job descriptions are becoming too rigid to fit the flexible work roles carried out by many workers. An emerging trend is for companies to hire people to "work" rather than to fill a specific job slot. Yet job descriptions, especially for specialized jobs such as data scientist, manufacturing engineer, and marketing coordinator, are still widely used.

Many people are hired because of their ability to solve new problems.

This sea of change in work design can be overwhelming for people whose paradigm is to think of work as occupying a particular job. A starting point in the shift is to think about how to accomplish work rather than fill a job. A company might look more for a good person–organization fit than for candidates to fill a particular job. This could mean hiring people with entrepreneurial drive who are customer focused.

To make this approach to work roles function well, the organization structure has to be flexible, and employees have to have access to different opportunities. Also, managers have to be willing to let employees experiment and work in different positions. A cornerstone idea is that workers' skills have to be matched to the project. For example, a creative person from anywhere in the firm might be assigned to a cross-functional product development team.

A related perspective about many modern workers having flexible roles rather than fixed positions is that the ability to learn is a major attribute for success, as mentioned in Chapter 3. The work environment changes so rapidly that a person needs to know how to learn. Think of a health administrator in a hospital in recent years. Insurance company and government regulations concerning payments and deductibles change so rapidly that the health administrator has to acquire new information rapidly. Even with the help of healthcare software, the administrator still has to make rapid adjustments.

The hiring criteria at Google Inc. illustrate how the ability to learn can be more useful to the corporation than previous job knowledge. Laszlo Bock, the former senior vice president of people operations at Google, says the least important attribute the company looks for in a candidate is expertise. Across the company, Google has five hiring attributes. "If it's a technical role," he explains, "we assess your coding ability, and half the roles in the company are technical roles. For every job though, the No. 1 thing we look for is . . . learning ability. It's the ability to process on the fly. It's the ability to pull together disparate bits of information."[21] Although Bock has left the company, Google has continued with his hiring criteria.

The implication for managers is that shifting away from relatively fixed job descriptions to emphasizing work roles is part of dealing with change in organizations. For many managers, this shift is difficult because job descriptions are the essence of bureaucracy.

Changing the Values of an Organization

A less tangible way in which an organization might change is to make a value shift. Workers who had different values must now change their values to prosper. A classic example is that banks had to learn to value customers more as regulations allowed a larger range of players into the mortgage business. Instead of doing customers a favor by granting them a mortgage, banks had to curry favor with potential mortgage customers. The value shift was from indifference toward high concern for customer service.

A more modern example is the value shift IBM underwent over a decade ago. The company's long-standing values grew out of traditions begun in 1914. The three principles known as *Basic Beliefs* at the time were (a) respect for the individual, (b) the best customer service, and (c) the pursuit of excellence. Over time, these values were changed into a sense of arrogance and entitlement throughout IBM. In later years, Sam Palmisano, CEO at the time, spearheaded a change in values using a computerized tool that collected employee input. Over a 72-hour period, thousands of IBM employees participated in an intranet discussion called "ValuesJam." A small team, with input from the CEO, arrived at a set of new corporate values:

- Dedication to every client's success
- Innovation that matters—for our company and the world
- Trust and personal responsibility in all relationships

These values are supposed to drive operational decisions made by IBM employees. Today, more than two-thirds of IBM's revenues stem from software and services (e.g., consulting). The values become so important because IBM customers are buying more knowledge in the form of services than hardware. IBM is therefore selling knowledge contained in the brains of employees.[22] A translation of a value into decision making would be for an IBM sales representative to think, "What service would best help my customer become more profitable?" rather than thinking, "How much IBM hardware can this customer possibly afford to buy?" Another example is that the new values would encourage IBM workers to develop innovations for such noble purposes as improving medical services and combating terrorism. The third value would translate into such behaviors as pricing products and services fairly.

Changing the values of an organization is often incorporated into changing the organizational culture because culture is linked so closely to values. Norm Sabapathy is the executive vice president of people and an owner and operator of commercial real estate in Toronto, Ontario.[23] He says that the first step in driving a culture change is to define desired values and behaviors. Workers need to understand how values relate to day-to-day behavior. The change agent needs to develop behavioral descriptors for each value he or she defines. Actionable behaviors for each value must be defined for people at all job levels. Assume that a real estate developer wants to change the corporate value of cautiousness to sensible risk taking. Here are actionable behaviors for two roles in the company:

Loan officer: Instead of using industry rules of thumbs and heuristics for creditworthiness, be willing to take on a higher level of risk when it appears prudent. Give a little more weight to your intuition than in the past.

Property investor: Do not be completely bound by standard property valuations. Imagine the possibilities in a distressed commercial property. Be willing to risk a decent amount of money on a property that might have a huge payoff in five years assuming that our renovation team does an outstanding job.

Organization Development as a Change Strategy

LEARNING OBJECTIVE 4
Explain the nature of organization development.

When it is necessary to bring about long-term, significant changes in a firm, a formal method of organizational change is sometimes used. **Organization development (OD)** is any strategy, method, or technique for making organizations more effective by bringing about constructive, planned change. You might think of an executive coach working with the individual to bring about change, whereas an organization development professional focuses on improving the entire organization. OD applies principles of human behavior to promote healing, growth, and constructive change in organizations.[24] In its pure form, organization development attempts to change the culture toward a more democratic and humanistic model and is therefore value driven. At other times, organization development aims to help change the technology or structure of the firm.

organization development (OD) Any strategy, method, or technique for making organizations more effective by bringing about constructive, planned change.

Here we describe a process model of organization development, followed by more information about three other OD approaches. The outdoor training approach to team development described in Chapter 10 can also be classified as organization development.

A Process Model of Organization Development

A process model of organization development was developed over 40 years ago that incorporates the important features of many different OD change efforts.[25] The model builds on earlier strategies for organization development and is flexible enough to diagnose problems in most organizations. A key feature is that the OD specialist and staff members are both involved in bringing about constructive change. The eight steps in the model are described next.

Step 1: Preliminary problem identification. The manager recognizes that a problem exists that interferes with work effectiveness. The problem could include the manager's behavior, such as the manager not making effective use of input by group members in his or her planning.

Step 2: Managerial commitment to change. The manager must commit to taking the necessary steps to implement the change program. The manager is warned that the change program could involve negative feedback about his or her behavior.

Step 3: Data collection and analysis. Before organization development can proceed, the climate must be assessed through interviews, observations, and a written survey. Information is obtained about such topics as the manager's alertness and open-mindedness, cooperation with other departments, problem-solving ability, and trust. This information is used to develop objectives for constructive changes. Collecting data is an important part of an effective change effort.[26] The alternative is for the change agent to simply use his or her judgment about what needs improvement. As implied above, the data can take the form of interview summaries and more objective data from questionnaires.

Step 4: Data feedback. Data collected in Step 3 are shared with the manager and staff members. In this way, staff members can compare their perceptions with those of others, and the manager shows ownership of the problem.

Step 5: Identification of specific problem areas. The OD specialist helps staff members give the manager feedback regarding strengths and weaknesses. Although the manager may not agree with the feedback, he or she must accept the perceptions. Problem areas among the staff members can also be identified in this step.

Step 6: Development of change strategies. The emphasis is on identifying root problems and developing action steps. A spirit of teamwork often develops as problems are identified that can be attributed to both the manager and staff members.

Step 7: Initiation of behavior. An action step(s) is selected and implemented that seems to be the best solution to the problem. The behavioral change strategy considers who, what, when, and where. For example, the manager (who) will make sure that the planning and priority setting (what) are accomplished during staff meetings (when) in the conference room (where).

Step 8: Evaluation. An attempt is made to evaluate whether the behavior changes made in Step 7 by both the manager and staff members have improved behavior and work results. Evaluation data may be collected through more interviews and observations, including speaking to the manager's superior.

Large-Scale Organizational Change

large-scale organizational change The method used to accomplish a major change in the firm's strategy and culture.

At best, organization development is a method of change aimed at breathing new life into a firm. **Large-scale organizational change** is the method used to accomplish a major change in the firm's strategy and culture. The process is sometimes referred to as "bending the frame," to indicate that the firm is changed in a significant way.[27] A company needs large-scale organizational change, or a turnaround, when it faces major internal or external problems. A high turnover rate suggests that the company is not a good place to work for a variety of possible reasons. When a company develops a reputation for high turnover, it will be difficult to attract talented, motivated replacements. Loss of established business and the failure to obtain new business is virtual proof that the company is in trouble. Shifting from an authoritarian (or command and control) style organization to a team-based organization would be a typical example of a large-scale change. Closely related is the shift from a slow-moving bureaucracy to a more nimble, entrepreneurial-style firm.

One of the most stunning turnarounds took place at Apple Inc. In 1997, Apple was a struggling manufacturer of computers used mostly in educational settings, and it almost folded. The shift to providing hardware plus services, particularly iTunes, triggered a forward momentum that enabled Apple to have the highest market valuation in the world.

Extensive survey data gathered by McKinsey & Company indicates that for a wide variety of business firms, most transformations involve the implementation of a digital solution, as illustrated with Crate & Barrel and Kloeckner Metals. To bring about effective change with respect to digitalization, it is important to communicate the desired outcome of the changes, such as enabling customers to use multiple channels when shopping. Implementation is more likely to be successful when the people with the most relevant expertise develop the business case. Successful digital transformations should also use key performance indicators (KPIs) to measure progress.[28] A KPI for the digital transformation at Kloeckner might be "number of digital natives hired for sales, marketing, and accounting positions."

Transformational Leadership and Organizational Change

A starting point in bringing about large-scale organizational change is to place a transformational leader in charge. Another important consideration, as advanced by the research and analysis of Larry Hirschhorn, is to organize the transformational effort into three campaigns: political, marketing, and military. Following these procedures will help bring order to the chaos often associated with a large-scale change initiative.[29]

The *political campaign* creates a coalition strong enough to support the initiative, and also to receive guidance from the people involved in the change. The change initiator may have to inspire others at first, and then build consensus at a later point. At other times, a change in organizational structure might be necessary to help build the coalition. For example, a layer of management might be eliminated so division heads can interact directly with the CEO who spearheads the large-scale organizational change.

The *marketing campaign* is designed to publicize and sell the benefits of the initiative. The campaign concentrates on listening to ideas that surface from the field as well as on working with lead customers to design the initiative. (A lead customer makes an advanced use of a product or service or uses it in an imaginative way—such as closing wounds with duct tape!) Another approach to receiving input is to directly observe what is happening in the field. For example, top management at a large insurance company wanted to enhance productivity throughout the organization. During field visits, organizational behavior specialists discovered that, in the most successful offices, managers held huddles rather than formal meetings at the beginning of each day, covering the same topics as would the meetings. The huddles were then recommended to all branch offices. The marketing campaign also includes giving a theme to the change initiative, such as "Getting It Done," meaning that executives would help lower-ranking managers resolve problems and eliminate unnecessary work.

The *military campaign* is aimed at deliberately engaging with others to overcome resistance, using many of the ideas just described for winning support for change. It is essential for the change initiator to stay closely involved with the change effort because many large-scale initiatives fail simply because they are neglected shortly after the kickoff.

A final consideration here about large-scale organizational change is to involve as many people as feasible. The efficient and effective implementation of change requires a critical mass of people through the organization who are committed to the outcomes; not just consultants and leaders, but everyone.[30] (Knowledge of individual differences suggests that such total commitment to improving the organization is highly unlikely, even though it's an ideal worth striving for.)

As with most forms of organization development, an external or internal consultant is usually required to bring about large-scale change. Line managers may be responsible for implementing the change, but advisors trained in organizational behavior help in the process.

The Role of Emotions and Influential Employees

Large-scale organizational change may appear to be a logical, step-by-step process that if followed carefully will lead to success. In reality, emotional reactions to the change will influence its success or failure, as implied in our discussion of resistance to change. A study of over 3,000 employees in a government agency dealing with transportation highlights the role of emotion in organizational change. The study found that employees' positive and negative affective experiences during the initial phases of organizational change influenced the success of the change. As you would suspect, positive attitudes facilitated success, and negative attitudes facilitated failure. The early attitudes also influenced later behavioral responses to the change. Behavioral responses included actions that supported the change, as well as resisted the change. A side finding was that transformational leadership was helpful in bringing about positive attitudes.[31]

A new theoretical perspective on employee response to organizational change emphasizes that four key behaviors are accompanied by affective states. In other words, there is emotion associated with the behavioral responses to change. When change recipients react with *change proactivity*, they are excited, elated, and enthusiastic—an excellent outcome for managers who are the change agents. When the response is *change acceptance*, the change recipients are calm, relaxed, and content—a satisfactory outcome for the change agent. Associated with *change disengagement* are despair and helplessness—most likely leading to a failed organizational change. When workers display *change resistance*, they are stressed, angry, and upset—leading to a clear failure of the organizational change.[32]

An example of an organizational change that would most likely trigger change proactivity would be moving to a spacious and comfortable new facility; increasing the workforce with talented, likable people; and revising compensation upward. An example of a change that might trigger resistance would be downsizing one-quarter of the workforce, moving into cramped quarters, and imposing mandatory pay cuts.

High-Performance Work Systems as Organization Development

high-performance work system (HPWS) A system of HR practices designed to enhance employees' skills, engagement, and productivity in such a way that the workforce becomes a source of sustainable competitive advantage.

A grouping of effective human resource programs can sometimes be an effective approach to organization development. A **high-performance work system (HPWS)** is a system of HR practices designed to enhance employees' skills, engagement, and productivity in such a way that the workforce becomes a source of sustainable competitive advantage.[33] (The term "high-performance work systems" also refers to granting more decision-making authority to manufacturing workers.) The general goal of an HPWS is to attract, retain, and motivate workers toward attaining organizational goals. This lofty goal is accomplished by creating a fit between the knowledge, skills, and abilities of a person and job tasks.[34]

A key difference between a high-performance human resource work system and simply having an assortment of HR practices is that the HPWS links the various programs in a coherent way. For example, the performance evaluation system might be used to follow up on how well the programs of recruitment and selection are working. Research might be conducted to see if job candidates who were strongly recommended later receive above-average performance evaluations.

The installation of a high-performance work system can be a positive force for organization development if individual and organizational performances truly improve. It would take considerable effort to ensure that the various HR initiatives are linked, such as using pay practices that improve motivation, engagement, and therefore enhance productivity.

The available evidence suggests that high-performance work systems contribute to organization development. A study of 22 local government authorities in Wales demonstrated that such a system was strongly and significantly related to unit performance. The high-performance work systems were associated with enhanced levels of job satisfaction, organizational commitment, and psychological empowerment. In turn, these positive attitudes led to enhanced organization citizenship behaviors which then led to better departmental performance. The performance metrics varied with the purpose of the agency, such as the housing authority finding homes for people.[35]

A study of 215 high-tech small- to medium-sized enterprises found that the use of an HPWS facilitated organizational ambidexterity.[36] A plausible explanation for this unusual finding is that, when workers are properly developed and motivated, the people can better accomplish high-level tasks such as attaining a focus on present and future innovation.

Managing Change Yourself

LEARNING OBJECTIVE 5
Develop useful insights into managing change in your job and career.

A major factor in managing change is coping well with change yourself. All the approaches to organizational change described in this chapter work more effectively with individuals predisposed to managing change well. According to research on the topic, individual

How Flexible Are You?

To succeed as a managerial worker, a person needs a flexible attitude, an ability to be open to others, and a willingness to listen. Where do you stand on being flexible? Assess yourself by answering "Often," "Sometimes," or "Rarely" to the following questions.

	Frequency		
	Often	Sometimes	Rarely
1. Do you tend to seek out only those people who agree with your analysis on issues?	☐	☐	☐
2. Do you ignore most of the advice from coworkers or other students about doing your work more efficiently?	☐	☐	☐
3. Do your team members go along with what you say just to avoid an argument?	☐	☐	☐
4. Have people referred to you as "rigid" or "close-minded" on several occasions?	☐	☐	☐
5. When presented with a new method, do you immediately look for a flaw?	☐	☐	☐
6. Do you make up your mind early with respect to an issue and then hold firmly to your opinion?	☐	☐	☐
7. When people disagree with you, do you tend to belittle them or become argumentative?	☐	☐	☐
8. Do you often feel you are the only person in the group who really understands the problem?	☐	☐	☐
9. Do you prefer to keep using old software even though more than one new update has been published?'	☐	☐	☐
10. Do you resist trying new foods?	☐	☐	☐

Scoring and Interpretation: If you answered "Rarely" to eight questions, you are unusually adaptable and therefore probably cope well with change. If you answered "Sometimes" to at least six questions, you are on the right track, but more flexibility would benefit your ability to deal with change. If you answered "Often" to five or more questions, you have a long way to go to improve your flexibility and adaptability to change. You are also brutally honest about your faults, which could be an asset.

adaptability to change at work refers to a person's response to new demands or ill-defined problems, including rapid changes on the job. A key factor in job and career success is adaptability.[37] Our approach to providing insight into self-managing change is divided into relevant research and personal suggestions. To help you think through your flexibility about dealing with change, do Self-Assessment 16-1.

Empirical Research about Coping with Organizational Change

A study involving over 500 employees in six organizations and five countries supported the well-accepted belief by practicing managers that some employees adapt better to organizational change than others. The ability to cope with change was measured both by self-reports and managerial assessments of how the workers coped with change. Seven personality factors presumed to be related to change were measured: locus of control, generalized self-efficacy, self-esteem, positive affectivity (similar to optimism), openness to experience, tolerance for ambiguity, and risk aversion. The seven traits were reduced to two factors: positive self-concept and risk tolerance.

A key result was that having a positive self-concept and a tolerance for risk were positively related to both measures of coping with change. The strongest and most consistent dispositional, or personality, variables among the seven traits in terms of their relationship to coping with change were tolerance for ambiguity and positive affectivity.[38] The implication supports what you probably suspected: People who can tolerate a lack of clarity and structure, and who are optimistic, cope well with change.

Suggestions for Coping with Change

The research just reported has a few implications for your ability to manage change well: Practice dealing with ambiguous tasks (such as unclear assignments) and work on having a positive general disposition. Consider also the following practical suggestions: *Look for the personal value that could be embedded in a forced change.*[39] If you are downsized, take the opportunity to assume responsibility for your own career rather than being dependent on the organization. Many downsizing victims find a new career for themselves that better fits their interests, or try self-employment in search of more job security.

When faced with a significant change, *ask What if? questions*, such as "What if my company is sold tomorrow?" "What if I went back to school for more education?" and "What if I did accept that one-year assignment in China?" When confronting major change, *force yourself to enjoy at least some small aspect of the change*. Suppose the edict comes through the organization that purchases can now be made only over the Internet. This means you will no longer be able to interact with a few of the sales reps you considered to be buddies. With the time you save, however, you will have spare hours each week for leisure activities.

You are less likely to resist change if you *recognize that change is inevitable*. Dealing with change is an integral part of life, so why fight it? Keep in mind also to *change before you have to, which can lead to a better deal*. If your manager announces a new plan, get on board as a volunteer before you are forced to accept a lesser role. If your company has made the decision to start a business-process-improvement program, study the subject early and ask for a role as a facilitator or team leader. Stop trying to be in control all the time because you cannot control everything. Many changes will occur that you cannot control, so relax and enjoy the ride. Finally, recognize that change has an emotional impact, which will most likely cause some inner turmoil and discomfort. Even if the change is for the better, you might remain emotionally attached to your old system—or neighborhood, car, or smartphone.

Continuous learning has been cited at several places in this text as a positive force in an individual's career. Continuing to acquire useful knowledge is also helpful in dealing with change because you have the new knowledge at hand to get past the change.[40] When digital photography became dominant, the operators of many portrait studios felt threatened and were too slow to offer digital services to their customers. Many of these photographers who waited too long were forced out of business. In contrast, many other portrait photographers were early learners of digital technology, and survived the transition well.

Behavioral Principles of Innovation

LEARNING OBJECTIVE 6
Identify eight behavioral principles of innovation.

innovation The process of creating new ideas and their implementation or commercialization.

Innovation often brings major changes to an organization as new products and services are offered by the firm. At the same time, many change efforts are aimed at building an organizational culture that fosters **innovation**—the process of creating new ideas and their implementation or commercialization. Innovation is one of the most widely discussed and researched topics in business. Our purposes are served here by describing briefly eight principles of innovation closely linked to organizational behavior.

1. *Question traditional beliefs or orthodoxies.* A bedrock principle of both creativity and innovation is to question the way something has been done traditionally. Searching for alternatives can lead to innovation. Tradition may block potential innovations because people are reluctant to abandon what already works.[41] Many entrepreneurs have spotted the possibilities of the sharing economy, in which people are willing to share their resources in order to earn income. A prime example is Brian Chesky, the CEO of Airbnb, a company that enables homeowners and renters of large dwellings to charge people to stay at their homes instead of renting hotel space. The innovation is that companies such as Airbnb act as digital clearinghouses to enable asset owners to monetize the unused capacity of assets they already own. At the same time, consumers can rent from other people rather than rent or purchase from a company.[42]

Innovation begins with a creative idea.

2. *Think positively and have a strong network.* A frustration for many workers with a creative idea is that the idea does not lead to innovation because they do not expect a positive outcome and lack the necessary contacts. Corporate innovators as well as entrepreneurs have to believe in their ideas, and they have to know the right people. A study conducted in a global agricultural processing firm with employees and their supervisors supported the conclusion just stated. It was found that individuals were able to improve the chances of their creative ideas being turned into innovations when they expected positive outcomes. It was also important to be a skilled networker or to have developed a set of strong relationships with people who would buy into their ideas.[43]

3. *Think in terms of transformations.* At the corporate level, the biggest returns on investment come from high-risk transformational initiatives. Although company leadership might invest only 10 percent of its innovation resources in a transforming idea, the biggest return is likely to stem from the new development.[44] Amazon.com has profited handsomely from enabling competitors to sell on its website. For example, you might order a book from Amazon but it is sold by another book distributor and this fact is indicated by Amazon. Because Amazon already had the infrastructure to sell online, inviting competitors to sell through Amazon was not an enormous expense.

4. *Embrace failures as the cost of risk taking.* An axiom of creativity is that it is a numbers game in which most ideas fail but a few are winners that become true innovations. As is well-known, most successful novelists first faced many rejection slips from publishers, and Thomas Edison tried hundreds of different filaments before he perfected the light bulb. Astro Teller is the scientist who directs work at Google's innovation lab (referred to as Google X). His job title is Captain of Moonshots, with moonshots referring to audacious innovations that have a tiny chance of succeeding but might revolutionize the world if they do. Teller explains that the toleration for setbacks at Google X is uncharacteristically high. Four major innovations that have emerged from X are driverless cars, Google Glass, high-altitude Wi-Fi balloons, and glucose-monitoring contact lenses.[45]

5. *Look to be disruptive.* A recurring theme in innovation is to discover ways to disrupt the business activities of other companies or to ward off being disrupted by new competitors. A disruptive innovation is aimed at serving a market of new or less demanding customers with a product that may be inferior or easier to use.[46] Among the many disruptive innovations in modern times have been sharing cars replacing

alphaspirit/Shutterstock

purchasing them, smartphones disrupting personal computers and expensive cameras, cell phones disrupting watches, and manufactured patio homes replacing larger, standard homes. A controversial disruption is a computer app that enables people to call private vehicles as a substitute for a taxi. The controversy comes from established cab companies and city regulators, as well as displaced drivers of traditional taxis.

New disruptive innovations emerge regularly as entrepreneurs and company employees try to find a new, inexpensive niche in an established market. An example is Cristina DeVito, the cofounder and CEO of Collective Hotels and Retreats, a company that builds pop-up luxury tent resorts in upscale locations such as Aspen and Vail in Colorado and Governor's Island in New York City. The approach is called *glamping*, referring to "glamor camping." The problem solved is finding a way to stay at famous locations without paying for an expensive hotel, and the disruption is to the hotel industry.

6. *Welcome entrepreneurial catalysts.* Innovation within the organization can often be stimulated by a select number of workers throughout the global organization with an entrepreneurial spirit who know how to pull together resources for a worthy purpose. Entrepreneurial catalysts are mission-driven leaders who round up corporate resources that are outside their traditional span of control in order to address major challenges. These individuals form strong networks and coalitions within and outside the company because they are driven to solve major problems.

7. *Change the culture.* As explained in Chapter 15, innovation is an important consequence of organizational culture. Many large-scale organizational-change efforts are aimed at producing a more innovative culture, and many newly appointed CEOs proclaim that one of their major goals is to produce a more innovative, less risk-averse culture. One example is John Donahoe, who was the CEO of eBay from 2008 until 2015. The company's core business was slipping, and the acquisition of Skype had gone wrong. Donahoe stated that he wanted to develop a culture of experimentation.[47] Today eBay is a prosperous company that does far more than conduct online auctions of used merchandise. eBay offerings now include being a business site for small businesses and selling new, fixed-price goods.

8. *Impose some constraints on innovation.* An organization cannot invest in the vast majority of innovative, or potentially innovative, ideas that surface. Instead, the company has to target its money toward those ideas for products or services holding the most promise. The dramatic turnaround of the toymaker LEGO in recent years has depended heavily on rejuvenating the company's core business through the injection of discipline into the company's new product development. Company management thinks that the discipline is more important than radical innovation. LEGO had been losing money because very few of its new products, including theme parks, were generating a profit, and most of the company's patents had expired. The company was also facing a breakup.[48]

A team composed of researchers and an experienced business executive conclude that the role of a leader of innovation is not to set a vision and motivate others to execute the vision. Instead, his or her role is to create a community that is willing and able to innovate.[49] (However, the leader's vision could be to create a community of innovators.) Procter & Gamble might be classified as a community of innovators because the company's product ideas stem not only from the research and development department but also from workers throughout the company. Furthermore, Procter & Gamble looks outside as well as inside the company for innovative ideas.

Implications for Managerial Practice

1. The biggest challenge in implementing workplace innovations is to bring about cultural change. Workers' attitudes and values have to change if the spirit of innovation is to keep smoldering. An effective vehicle for bringing about such change is for top-level managers and others to exchange ideas. Formal arrangements, such as

regularly scheduled staff meetings, facilitate exchanging ideas, reflecting on values, and learning what behavior is in vogue. Encouraging informal meetings can often achieve the same purpose with a higher degree of effectiveness.

2. Learning how to cope well with change yourself is a key part of managing change. An example of change would be dealing with an employer taking away your cubicle and expecting you to work in an open area with no privacy.

3. Although many organizations expect managers and professionals to adapt to flexible work roles, the importance of developing expertise in one or two specialties remains critical to long-term career success. For example, if you are a supply-chain specialist, it would be foolish to forget that expertise simply because your employer wanted you to take on a marketing role for a period of time.

Summary of Key Points

1. *Describe the influence model of the change process in organizations.* The influence model of organizational change is based on substantial research practice. Its four components are fostering understanding and conviction, reinforcing with formal mechanisms, developing talent and skills, and role modeling.

2. *Explain why people resist change and how to manage such resistance.* People resist change for a variety of reasons they think are important; the most common being the fear of an unfavorable outcome. Also, facing competing commitments may create immunity to change, and the change might be perceived as damaging the person–environment fit. Techniques for overcoming resistance include: (1) allowing for discussion and negotiation, (2) allowing for participation, (3) pointing out financial benefits of a change, (4) avoiding change overload, (5) gaining political support for change, (6) communicating relevant information, (7) avoiding citing poor performance as the reason for change, (8) incorporating the human touch, (9) paying attention to the emotional aspects of change, (10) appointing coaches as facilitators of change, and (11) having leaders change also.

3. *Describe four major factors that create organizational change.* Downsizing as a change strategy is most likely to be effective when it is integrated into the company's long-term strategies. Low-value work must be eliminated, teamwork must be emphasized, and considerable attention must be paid to the human element. Information technology has facilitated change in organizations, including making them more democratic because of the increased accessibility of information. The Internet is changing the nature of many businesses, such as allowing companies to interact more directly with customers and suppliers. Information technology has created substantial changes in how long and where people work. Artificial intelligence is creating organizational change in terms of decision making and also in some job losses and gains.

Another force for change in organizations is the transition from a jobholder meeting the demands of a job description to a person carrying out a variety of work roles, or different kinds of work. Changes in behavior of workers can also stem from a value shift in the organization, such as becoming more dedicated to every client's success. A culture shift also requires a major change in values,

4. *Explain the nature of organization development.* Organization development brings about constructive, planned change, including modifying the culture. Using the process model of organization development, both the OD consultant and staff members are involved in bringing about constructive change. Large-scale organization development is used to accomplish a major change in the firm's strategy and culture. The large-scale change effort should be organized into three campaigns: political, marketing, and military. As many people as feasible should be involved in the change effort.

Emotional reactions to change will influence its success or failure. It is helpful to start the change effort with the most connected and flexible employees because they will exert personal influence to help bring about change. Emotions are tied in with behavioral reactions to change, such as change proactivity being associated with excitement, elation, and enthusiasm.

A grouping of effective human resources programs can sometimes be an effective approach to organization development. The high-performance work system is such a grouping and can create a workforce that is a source of sustainable competitive advantage. Linkage analysis is a tool for translating gains in one part of the organization to the firm as a whole.

5. *Develop useful insights into managing change in your job and career.* People who score high on the personality factors of positive self-concept and risk tolerance adapt better to change. Two specific traits related to dealing well with change are tolerance for ambiguity and positive affectivity. Among the suggestions for managing change well are searching for the personal value that could be embedded in forced change, asking "What if?" questions, forcing yourself to enjoy at least some small aspect of the change, recognizing that

change is inevitable, and understanding that change has an emotional impact.

6. *Identify eight behavioral principles of innovation.* Behavioral principles of innovation include: (1) question traditional beliefs or orthodoxies, (2) think positively and have a strong network, (3) think in terms of transformations, (4) embrace failures as the cost of risk taking, (5) look to be disruptive, (6) welcome entrepreneurial catalysts, (7) change the culture, and (8) impose constraints on innovation.

Key Terms and Phrases

Discussion Questions and Activities

1. Approximately 45 years ago, many managers and scholars were concerned that the computerization of the workplace would lead to enormous resistance to change. Whatever happened to resistance to change to computers?

2. What do you predict will be a major change that employees will have to cope with in the upcoming years?

3. How can a manager tell if an employee is resisting change?

4. Why might the transition from "jobs" to "work" lead to resistance to change from many people?

5. How does change at the individual level contribute to organizational change?

6. Identify a major change you will have to cope with in the next several years and describe your plan of action for coping with it.

7. How is your program of studies helping you to learn how to adapt to change?

8. A frequent criticism of job résumés is that so many people use the word "innovative" to describe themselves. So what other term should the résumé writer use who considers himself or herself to be innovative?

9. So far, millions of people throughout the world still enjoy physical activities such as walking or jogging; bicycling; and playing softball, soccer, tennis, and golf. Can you visualize any technologies that will "disrupt" these activities?

10. For years, lists of innovative companies have included Apple Inc. and Google Inc. right at the top of the list. Why do you think these two companies are considered to be highly innovative?

CASE PROBLEM: Resisting Change at Car Destination

Doreen is the CEO of Car Destination Inc., a super-dealership that sells new cars, SUVs, and pickup trucks from five different manufacturers, and also has a large used-car lot. Car Destination has been profitable over the years, even eking out a profit during two different business recessions. Yet Doreen has the nagging thought that Destination is slipping a little behind the times. In talking with an outside advisor, Doreen said, "The vehicle-sales business is changing more rapidly than we are changing. Fewer consumers are influenced as much as they were in the past by the sales representative. Instead, they ferret out information on the Internet on what they think the price of a vehicle should be.

Also, they shop online to find the lowest possible price for what they want. When they arrive at the dealership, they even know what accessories and features they want, so they are less influenced by what our reps have to say. Another problem is that a greater number of customers who do come to the dealership to purchase a car or truck don't want to haggle with the rep."

Based on these concerns, plus some discussions with a few automobile executives, Doreen decides to change the business model at Destination. The new business model she wants to introduce to her management staff and to sales representatives requires that sales representatives no longer work on commission. They will now be salaried associates who try to satisfy the needs of customers. Furthermore, Destination will now offer fixed sticker prices on all new and used vehicles. No more negotiating with customers about price. Doreen calls a meeting for the following Monday morning with all of her managers and two of the senior sales representatives to discuss the new business model. She labels the new model "The no-hassle Destination."

Doreen describes the new business model, using a PowerPoint presentation to support her talk. She speaks for 15 minutes without accepting comments or questions, but she does notice a few grimaces and anxious expressions on the faces of the Destination staff. Doreen finally says, "Okay gang, I've talked enough for now. Let me know what you think of our new business model."

Tony, a veteran sales representative, speaks first: "Doreen, it's good to know that our CEO is up-to-date on the automotive sales business. But Saturn tried what you are talking about. The company lost tons of money and finally was eliminated by GM. The sales reps did everything but hug and kiss the customers who drove off the lot with a new Saturn." (The people present laugh nervously.)

Melody, the used-car sales manager, offered her opinion: "Doreen, with due respect to the wisdom of our CEO, 'The no-hassle Destination' may not work here. Maybe we could act like CarMax sales associates—we hire a bunch of good-looking sales reps, dress them in khakis and polo shirts, and teach them to keep a smile on their faces all the time. But when our clientele comes to Destination to purchase a used car, they like to negotiate. I love the look on the face of a customer who has just been given a discount. Buying a used car or truck is a sport. It's not like purchasing a six-pack of beer." (The group laughs loudly at the beer analogy.)

Sam, the new-vehicle sales manager, said with a concerned expression, "Doreen, I think the business model you propose probably works well in some situations. But we should think this through quite carefully. Our best reps are making a ton of money. If you put them on a fixed and modest salary, our stars would leave for the competition. A fixed salary is probably okay for the Car-Max associate, but I think experienced pros much prefer commission sales."

Kaleb, the director of finance, offered a suggestion: "Doreen, I say let us wait a bit before introducing this model. We need to study the potential impact of the new business model on our profitability. We are a consistently profitable super-dealership. A key factor is that the salaries we pay sales reps are quite low because they earn so much on commission. This helps lower our fixed costs. We could wind up with a handful of sales associates who produce very little in relation to their salary and benefits."

Feeling frustrated, Doreen said, "Let's break for now and return to this discussion tomorrow morning. You folks don't seem ready quite yet to shift to 'The no-hassle Destination.'" As she gathered her notes, Doreen thought, "For the new model to work well, I will have to change some of these negative attitudes."

Case Questions

1. How strong does the resistance to the new business model at Destination appear to be?
2. What advice can you offer Doreen for overcoming the resistance to change?
3. What is your opinion of the potential effectiveness of "The no-hassle Destination" business model? Explain your reasoning.

Endnotes

1. Original story based on facts and observations in the following sources: "Crate and Barrel to Transform Its Retail Experience in the Cloud with Infor," https://finance.yahoo.com, January 13, 2017, pp. 1-2; Khadeeja Safdar, "Crate and Barrel Refurbished," *The Wall Street Journal*, March 22, 2018, p. B8; Sharon Gaudin, "Crate and Barrel Workers to Balance Online and Offline Sales," www.computerworld.com, January 17, 2017, pp. 1–3; Andria Cheng, "For Retail, the Next Big Shakeup Is Organizational, "January 26. 2017, pp. 1–2.

2. N. Anand and Jean-Louis Barsoux, "What Everyone Gets Wrong about Change Management," *Harvard Business Review*, November–December 2017, p. 80.

3. "Hershey Thinks Its Delivery Problems Are Now Over," Associated Press, April 20, 2000.

4. Christopher Koch, "Supply Chain: Hershey's Bittersweet Lesson," *CIO News* (www.cio.com), November 15, 2002, pp. 1–3.

5. Adrienne Selko, "Hershey's New Plant Features New Technology for Industry," *Industry Week* (www.industryweek.com), September 25, 2012, pp. 1–4.

6. Tessa Bassford and Bill Schanginger, "The Four Building Blocks of Change," McKinsey & Company (www.mckinsey.com), April 2016, pp. 1–8.

7. Robert Kegan and Lisa Laskow Lahey, "The Real Reason People Won't Change," *Harvard Business Review*, November 2001, pp. 84–92.

8. James A. F. Stoner and R. Edward Freeman, *Management*, 4th ed. (Upper Saddle River, NJ: Prentice-Hall, 1989), p. 369.

9. Steven D. Caldwell, David M. Herold, and Donald B. Fedor, "Toward an Understanding of the Relationship among Organizational Change, Individual Differences, and Changes in Person–Environment Fit: A Cross-Level Study," *Journal of Applied Psychology*, October 2004, pp. 868–882.

10. Baruch Shimoni, "What Is Resistance to Change? A Habitus-Oriented Approach," *Academy of Management Perspectives*, November 2017, pp. 257–270.

11. Dori Meinert, "Why Change Efforts Fail," *HR Magazine*, February 2018, p. 17.

12. Shaul Fox and Yair Amichai-Hamburger, "The Power of Emotional Appeals in Promoting Organizational Change Programs," *Academy of Management Executive*, November 2001, pp. 84–93.

13. Robin Broadnax, "Changing Change Management," *HR Magazine*, April 2014, pp. 42–44.

14. Quoted in Meinert, "Why Change Efforts Fail," p. 17.

15. William White, "Tesla Layoffs 2018: Which Jobs Are on the Chopping Block?" Investor Place (https://finance.yahoo.com), June 13, 2018, p. 1.

16. Susan Reynolds Fisher and Margaret A. White, "Downsizing in a Learning Organization: Are There Hidden Costs?" *Academy of Management Review*, January 2000, pp. 244–251.

17. Sane Robertson, "Effective Downsizing Methods" (www .brighthub.com), July 13, 2011, pp. 1–3; Sherry Kuczynski, "Help! I Shrunk the Company," *HR Magazine*, June 1999, pp. 40–45; "Layoffs Are Not Inevitable," Associated Press, November 19, 2001.

18. Sandra J. Sucher and Shalene Gupta, "Layoffs That Don't Break Your Company: Better Approaches to Workforce Transitions," *Harvard Business Review*, May–June 2018, p. 125.

19. "Millions of Middle-Class Jobs Lost to Technology," Associated Press, January 23, 2013.

20. Callum McClelland, "The Impact of Artificial Intelligence—Widespread Job Losses," www.iotforall.com, December 31, 2016, p. 1.

21. Thomas L. Friedman, "How to Get a Job at Google," *The New York Times* (www.nytimes.com), February 22, 2014, p. 1.

22. Interview with Samuel J. Palmisano by Paul Hemp and Thomas A. Stewart, "Leading Change When Business Is Good," *Harvard Business Review*, December 2004, pp. 60–70; Larry Meyers, "Sell IBM: Moribund Business, Overvalued Stock" (www.sdeekingalpha.com), November 6, 2014, pp. 1–6.

23. Christina Folz, "Culture Change," *HR Magazine*, October 2016, p. 18.

24. Book review by Rick Tallarigo Sr., in *Personnel Psychology*, Winter 2002, p. 1033.

25. Joseph A. Young and Barbara Smith, "Organizational Change and the HR Professional," *Personnel*, October 1988, p. 46; Wendell L. French, "Organization Development, Objectives, Assumptions, and Strategy," *California Management Review*, Vol. 2, 1969, p. 26.

26. Janine Waclawski and Allan H. Church (eds.), *Organization Development: A Data-Driven Approach to Organization Change* (San Francisco, CA: Jossey-Bass, 2002).

27. Leonard D. Goodstein and W. Warner Burke, "Creating Successful Organizational Change," *Organizational Dynamics*, Spring 1991, p. 4.

28. Blake Lindsay, Eugene Smit, and Nick Waugh, "How the Implementation of Organizational Change Is Evolving," McKinsey & Company (www.mckinsey.com) February 2018, pp. 1–5.

29. Larry Hirschhorn, "Campaigning for Change," *Harvard Business Review*, July 2002, pp. 98–104.

30. Richard H. Axelrod, *Terms of Engagement: Changing the Way We Change Organizations* (Williston, VT: BK Publishers, 2000).

31. Myeong-gu Seo, et al., "The Role of Affect and Leadership during Organizational Change," *Personnel Psychology*, No. 1, 2012, pp. 121–165.

32. Shaul Orge, Jean M. Bartunek, Gasyong Lee, and Boram Do, "An Affect-Based Model of Recipients' Responses to Organizational Change Events," *Academy of Management Review*, January 2018, pp. 65–86.

33. Samuel Aryee et al., "Impact of High-Performance Work Systems on Individual- and Branch-Level Performance: Test of a Multilevel Model of Intermediate Linkages," *Journal of Applied Psychology*, March 2012, p. 287; Gaye Õzçelik, Meryem Aybas, and Cavide Uyargil, "High Performance Work Systems and Organizational Values: Resource-Based View Considerations," *Procedia—Social and Behavioral Sciences*, Vol. 235, November 2016, pp. 332–341.

34. Pankaj C. Patel, Jake G. Messersmith, and David P. Lepak, "Walking the Tightrope: An Assessment of the Relationship between High-Performance Work Systems and Organizational Ambidexterity," *Academy of Management Journal*, October 2013, p. 1421.

35. Jake G. Messersmith, Pankaj C. Patel, and David P. Lepak, "Unlock the Black Box: Exploring the Link between High-Performance Work Systems and Performance," *Journal of Applied Psychology*, November 2011, pp. 1105–1118.

36. Messersmith, Patel, and Lepak, "Walking the Tightrope," pp. 1420–1442.

37. David Chan (ed.), *Individual Adaptability to Changes at Work* (New York: Routledge, 2014), p. i.

38. Timothy A. Judge, Carl J. Thoresen, Victor Pucik, and Theresa M. Welbourne, "Managerial Coping with Organizational Change: A Dispositional Perspective," *Journal of Applied Psychology*, February 1999, pp. 107–122.

39. The first two items on the list are from Fred Pryor, "What Have You Learned from Change?" *Managers Edge*, September 1998, p. 2.

40. Al Siebert, *The Resiliency Advantage* (San Francisco, CA: Berrett-Koehler, 2005).

41. Mohanbir Sawhney and Sanjay Khosla, "Managing Yourself: Where to Look for Insight," *Harvard Business Review*, November 2014, p. 128.

42. Tomio Geron, "The Share Economy," *Forbes*, February 11, 2013, pp. 58–66.

43. Markus Baer, "Putting Creativity to Work: The Implementation of Creative Ideas in Organizations," *Academy of Management Journal*, October 2012, pp. 1102–1119.

44. Bansi Nagli and Geoff Tuff, "Managing Your Innovation Portfolio," *Harvard Business Review*, May 2012, pp. 66–74.

45. Jon Gertner, "The X Factor," *Fast Company*, May 2014, pp. 66–73.

46. Clayton Christensen and Michael E. Raynor, *The Innovator's Solution: Creating and Sustaining Successful Growth* (Boston: Harvard Business School Press, 2003); Maxwell Wessel and Clayton M. Christensen, "How to Manage Disruption," *Harvard Business Review*, December 2012, pp. 55–64.

47. Interview with John Donahoe, "How eBay Developed a Culture of Experimentation," *Harvard Business Review*, March 2011, p. 93.

48. Donald Sull, "The Simple Rules of Disciplined Innovation," McKinsey & Company (www.mckinsey.com), May 2015, p. 1; "A True Toy Story: LEGO's Incredible Turnaround Tale," www.theinfocenter.com, October 6, 2017, pp. 1–4.

49. Linda A. Hill, Greg Brandeau, Emily Truelove, and Kent Lineback, "Collective Genius," *Harvard Business Review*, June 2014, pp. 94–102.

Cultural Diversity and Cross-Cultural Organizational Behavior

Chapter Outline

Tyler Olson/Shutterstock.com

Learning Objectives

After reading and studying this chapter and doing the exercises, you should be able to:

1. Understand the scope, competitive advantages, and potential problems associated with cultural diversity.

2. Identify and explain key dimensions of cultural differences.

3. Explain what is required for managers and organizations to become multicultural.

4. Be more aware of barriers to good cross-cultural relations.

5. Explain how motivation, ethics, appropriate negotiation skills, conflict resolution, and empowerment practices can vary across cultures.

6. Appreciate the nature of diversity training and cultural training, including cultural intelligence and anti-bias training.

Capital One Financial regularly makes its way high on the list of *Fortune*'s 100 Best Companies to Work For. The company's approach to being inclusive and culturally diverse is cited as one reason for the high rank. Capital One has 43,700 employees, with 49 percent minorities. (Capital One is the company with the frequently placed television ad using the tagline, "What's in your wallet?") The credit card company is cited as "welcoming to all walks of life," with an unsurpassed focus on cultural diversity. Employees say that CEO Richard Fairbank is focused on ensuring that all employees know where the company is going.

Capital One has also been cited by *Fortune* as the 10th-best workplace for diversity, noting that many workplaces pay lip service to inclusion, but this finance company giant really delivers. To obtain the list of the best business firms, the Great Place to Work organization surveyed more than 400,000 employees who were either a racial or ethnic minority, female, LBGTQ (lesbian, bisexual, gay, transgender or queer, or questioning), physically disabled, or born before 1964. Capital One was included among the companies those surveyed enjoyed working for the most.

Lane S. Hopkins, the chief diversity and inclusion officer at Capital One, heads a team that is opening doors for every company employee to feel included, engaged, and empowered. "Our goal is to generate the broadest possible range of ideas, and create exactly what our customers need. Inclusion is how we'll succeed, for our customers and our business," Hopkins said. She also notes that inclusion refers to creating an environment in which all individuals are understood, valued, and respected. Capital One management has found that inclusion fosters collaboration, innovation, and excellence. As a result, employees are helped to reach their full potential and feel connected to other work associates. Lane emphasizes that Capital One wants to win in the marketplace and that the company's success depends on having a workforce that reflects its customer base.

Lane identifies allies and advocates as change agents on the path to inclusion. She observes that the company needs Hispanics in its Asian Network, heterosexuals in its LGBT Network, and men in its Women's Network. (An employee network is a group of workers with a shared demographic characteristic, such as being gay or African American.) "When we understand each other, we are more comfortable inviting diverse points of view," said Lane.

One of the ways in which Capital One has earned a strong reputation for inclusion and diversity is that management listens to employee concerns and complaints about feeling excluded. Several years back, a group of 19 women employees in the Capital One technology group put together a presentation that documented the challenges faced by women in the company. Among the problems cited were low representation on key teams, feelings of isolation, and micro-aggressions. In response to the presentation, company leadership explored a variety of initiatives to support diversity. Among them was a company-funded initiative that has become the Women in Tech Demo Days in New York. At the event, women develop tech tools to address such problems as helping male allies learn to support women in the workplace and in the tech community.[1]

We have already mentioned demographic and cultural diversity at several places in this text. Chapter 9 described cross-cultural communication barriers. Chapter 15 described how cross-cultural differences can hamper a merger, and cross-cultural issues were raised in relation to many other concepts throughout the text. One purpose of this chapter is to provide additional insights that managers and professionals can use to capitalize upon diversity within and across countries.

The fact that business has become increasingly global has elevated the importance of understanding cross-cultural and international organizational behavior. Furthermore, the U.S. workforce continues to become more culturally diverse. The demographic profile

Cross-Cultural Attitudes and Skills

Listed here are various skills and attitudes that employers and cross-cultural specialists think are important for relating effectively to coworkers in a culturally diverse environment. Check the appropriate column.

	Applies to Me Now	Not There Yet
1. I have spent some time in another country.	☑	☐
2. At least one of my friends is deaf, blind, or uses a wheelchair.	☐	☑
3. Currency from other countries is as real as the currency from my own country.	☑	☐
4. I can read in a language other than my own.	☑	☐
5. I can speak in a language other than my own.	☑	☐
6. I can write in a language other than my own.	☑	☐
7. I can understand people speaking in a language other than my own.	☑	☐
8. I would feel comfortable reporting to a physically disabled boss.	☑	☐
9. My friends include people of races different from my own.	☑	☐
10. My friends include people of different generations.	☑	☐
11. I feel (or would feel) comfortable having a friend with a sexual orientation different from mine.	☒	☑
12. My attitude is that, although another culture may be very different from mine, that culture is equally good.	☑	☐
13. I would be willing to (or already do) hang art from different countries in my home.	☑	☐
14. I would accept (or have already accepted) a work assignment of more than several months in another country.	☑	☐
15. I have a passport that has not expired.	☑	☑

Scoring and Interpretation: If you answered "Applies to Me Now" to 10 or more of these statements, you most likely function well in a multicultural work environment. If you answered "Not There Yet" to 10 or more of these statements, you need to develop more cross-cultural awareness and skills to work effectively in a multicultural work environment. You will notice that being bilingual gives you at least five points on this quiz.

of the United States is changing rapidly, with minorities forecast to reach majority status by 2044, attributed in part to the projected growth of Asian, Hispanic, and multiracial populations.[2]

Our description of cultural diversity and cross-cultural organizational behavior will include a presentation of key concepts, as well as ideas for developing diversity and cross-cultural skills. Before reading on, do Self-Assessment 17-1 about cross-cultural skills and attitudes. It will help you think through how multicultural you are now.

Cultural Diversity: Scope, Competitive Advantages, and Potential Problems

LEARNING OBJECTIVE 1
Understand the scope, competitive advantages, and potential problems associated with cultural diversity.

Cultural diversity can be approached from many different perspectives relating both to its interpersonal and business aspects. In this section, we describe the scope and goals of cultural diversity, how it affects business results, and potential problems with a culturally diverse workforce. Diversity training is given separate attention later.

The Scope and Goals of Cultural Diversity

Improving cross-cultural relations includes understanding the true meaning of appreciating demographic and cultural diversity. To appreciate diversity, a person must go beyond tolerating and treating people from different racial and ethnic groups fairly. Recognize, however, that some people criticize the diversity movement for being overinclusive instead of assisting people who have been held back or discriminated against because of demographic factors such as race or age. The true meaning of valuing diversity is to respect and enjoy a wide range of cultural and individual differences, thereby including everybody.

Many diversity specialists now prefer the term *inclusion* to *diversity* and also focus on the similarities among people rather than differences. You will recall the frequent use of the term *inclusion* in reference to the diversity initiatives at Capital One. Rosanna Durruthy, head of diversity, inclusion, and belongingness at LinkedIn, emphasizes that diversity is inclusive of each and every one of us. Diversity focuses on the uniqueness each person brings into the environment to create alchemy.[3]

To be diverse is to be different in some measurable way. Although the diversity factor is measurable in a scientific sense, it may not be visible on the surface. Upon meeting a team member, it may not be apparent that the person is diverse from the standpoint of being dyslexic, color-blind, gay, lesbian, or vegan. However, all of these factors are measurable.

As just implied, some people are more visibly diverse than others because of physical features or disabilities. Yet the diversity umbrella is supposed to include everybody in an organization. The goal of a diverse organization is for persons of all cultural backgrounds to achieve their full potential, not restrained by group identities such as sex, nationality, or race. In recent years, more attention has been paid to the full acceptance of transgender workers. "Transgender" refers to a person having a gender identity (or sex) different from the sex at birth.[4]

Culturally and demographically diverse groups are a way of life in modern organizations.

FIGURE 17-1 The Diversity Umbrella

Diversity has evolved into a wide range of group and individual characteristics.

- Race
- Sex or gender
- Religion
- Age (young, middle-aged, and old)
- Generational differences including attitudes (e.g., Baby Boomers vs. Generation X and Generation Y)
- Ethnicity (country of origin)
- Education
- Abilities
- Mental disabilities (including attention deficit disorder)
- Physical disabilities (including hearing status, visual status, able-bodied, wheelchair user)
- Values and motivation
- Sexual orientation (heterosexual, homosexual, bisexual, transgender, or transsexual)
- Marital status (married, single, divorced, cohabitating, widow, widower)
- Family status (children, no children, two-parent family, single parent, grandparent, opposite-sex parents, same-sex parents)
- Personality traits
- Cognitive differences (including levels of mental ability and big-picture vs. little-picture thinking)
- Functional background (area of specialization, e.g., marketing or HR)
- Technology interest (high tech, low tech, technophobe)
- Weight status (average, obese, underweight, anorexic)
- Hair status (full head of hair, bald, wild hair, tame hair, long hair, short hair)
- Style of clothing and appearance (dress up; dress down; professional appearance; casual appearance; tattoos; body piercing, including multiple earrings, nose rings, lip rings)
- Tobacco status (smoker vs. nonsmoker, chewer vs. nonchewer)
- Your addition(s) to the list

Another goal of the diversity movement is to celebrate differences rather than regard everybody as the same. Jilma Meneses, the chief executive officer of Catholic Charities, said earlier in her career that people of color are expecting not just to be stirred into the melting pot but to be acknowledged and celebrated for their cultural differences.[5]

Diversity is seen today as a mechanism for business success including generating more ideas and serving customers better. Another subtle indicator of how far diversity has proceeded in the United States is that, in recent years, an African American became the chairman of Microsoft, and another African American was appointed as CEO of JCPenney, then Home Depot. Yet, the race of both was not mentioned in most media accounts of the appointments.

Figure 17-1 presents a broad sampling of the ways in which work associates can differ from one another. Studying this list can help you anticipate the types of differences found culturally as well as individually. Individual factors are also important because people can be discriminated against for personal characteristics as well as group factors. Many people, for example, believe they are held back from promotion because of their weight-to-height ratio.

The Competitive Advantage of Diversity

Encouraging cultural and demographic diversity within an organization helps an organization achieve social responsibility goals. Also, diversity sometimes brings a competitive advantage to a firm. Before diversity can offer a competitive advantage to a firm, it must be woven into the fabric of the organization. This stands in contrast to simply having a "diversity program" offered periodically by the human resources department. Instead, the human resource efforts toward accomplishing diversity should be managed as part of organizational strategy. For example, many successful business firms publicly commit to an inclusion and diversity strategy and cascade this commitment to managers throughout the organization.[6]

The potential competitive (or bottom-line) benefits of cultural diversity, as revealed by research and observations, are described next.

1. *Managing diversity well offers a marketing advantage, including increased sales and profits.* A study of more than 1,000 companies covering 12 countries found that gender diversity in top-level management was associated with higher profits. Business firms in the top quartile in gender diversity in top management were 21 percent more likely to have above-average profits than companies in the fourth quartile. The same study found that companies with the most ethnically diverse executive teams are 33 percent more likely to outperform comparable companies on profitability.[7]

   Allstate Insurance Company invests considerable effort into being a culturally diverse business firm. More than coincidentally, Allstate is now recognized as the nation's leading insurer of African Americans and Hispanics. Appeals to specific cultural groups, including websites written in the language of the target group, enhanced sales substantially. (It is also possible that more profitable companies are more willing to invest in diversity.)

2. *Effective management of diversity can reduce costs.* More effective management of diversity may increase the job satisfaction of diverse groups, thus decreasing turnover and absenteeism and their associated costs. A diverse organization that welcomes and fosters the growth of a wide variety of employees will retain more of its minority and multicultural employees. Also, effective management of diversity helps avoid costly lawsuits over being charged with discrimination based on age, race, or sex.

3. *Companies with a favorable record in managing diversity are at a distinct advantage in recruiting talented people.* Those companies with a favorable reputation for welcoming diversity attract the strongest job candidates among women and minorities. The recruitment and retention of global talent have become an essential element of corporate success in today's economy. A shortage of workers gives extra impetus to cultural diversity. The driver-starved trucking industry has been recruiting in urban Latino communities, as well as other communities with a high minority population. The National Minority Trucking Association has been working closely with the trucking industry to help supply more drivers, including reaching out to community centers and churches.[8]

4. *Workforce diversity can provide a company with useful ideas for favorable publicity and advertising.* A culturally diverse workforce or its advertising agency can help a firm place itself in a favorable light to targeted cultural groups. During Kwanzaa, the late-December holiday celebrated by many African Americans, McDonald's Corp. has run ads aimed at showing its understanding of and respect for African Americans' sense of family and community. For such ads to be effective, however, the company must also have a customer-contact workforce that is culturally diverse. Otherwise, the ads would lack credibility.

Wheelchair users are included in the diversity umbrella.

Phovoir/Shutterstock.com

5. *Workforce heterogeneity may also offer a company a creativity advantage.* As mentioned in relation to effective groups (Chapter 9), creative solutions to problems are more likely when a diverse group attacks a problem. Diverse teams have a stronger tendency to frequently reexamine facts and remain objective, and culturally diverse leadership is associated with more new product development than is homogeneous leadership at the top of the organization.[9]

   A study, however, of management groups in banks found that the relationship between heterogeneity and productivity is complex. It was found that, in banks with more entrepreneurial strategies, both low- and high-management group heterogeneity were associated with higher productivity than was moderate heterogeneity.[10] Conceivably, moderate heterogeneity just created confusion within the group with respect to producing useful ideas.

6. *Avoiding cultural gaffes.* A culturally diverse staff can also offer the advantage of helping a company avoid publicity and advertising that is offensive to a cultural or demographic group. A Dunkin' Donuts franchise in Thailand launched an advertising campaign in 2013 that showed a smiling woman with bright pink lips in blackface makeup. Human Rights Watch called on Dunkin' Donuts to withdraw what they regarded as a "bizarre and racist" advertisement and one that would draw "howls of outrage" if released in the United States. The CEO for Dunkin' Donuts in Thailand said the criticism was "paranoid American thinking."[11]

   The culturally diverse staff still has to be hyper-alert to what might possibly offend a cultural or national group. In 2018, Gap Inc. sold T-shirts depicting a map of China that omitted Taiwan, disputed islands in the South China Sea, and disputed parts of the regions of Tibet and Xinjiang. Gap immediately was widely criticized on Chinese social media for the omission. In response, Gap apologized and withdrew the offending T-shirt from the Chinese market. (Gap Inc. has 27 stores in China.)[12]

Potential Problems Associated with Diversity

In addition to understanding the competitive advantages of diversity within an organization, a brief look at some of the potential problems is also helpful. Cultural diversity initiatives are usually successful in assembling heterogeneous groups, but the group members do not necessarily work harmoniously. The potential for conflict is high. In general, if the demographically different work-group members are supportive toward each other, the benefits of group diversity, such as more creative problem solving, will be forthcoming. Group members must also share knowledge with each other for the heterogeneous groups to be successful. Another problem is that diverse groups may be less cohesive than those groups with less cultural diversity among the members.

A study of 60 work units in New York State sheds light on the potential problems with work-group diversity. Most of the groups studied were composed of Caucasian and African American workers. It was found that the true benefits of diversity surface only when there are support-based relationships among dissimilar workers. Furthermore, it was found that heterogeneous peers supported each other more when the task was interdependent and when a high-support climate prevailed. However, there was a tendency for supportive relationships to decrease when the proportion of racially different others increased. For example, a group that was composed of 25 percent minority members would be likely to have more supportive relationships than a group with 50 percent minority members. Another curious finding was that when groups were composed of African Americans as well as other minority group members, relationships were more supportive.[13]

Culturally diverse groups sometimes might enter into conflict because of value differences related to their culture. The globalization taking place in Germany exemplifies the problem. German corporate culture emphasizes layers of worker protection, and these values may clash with those of American executives. Oliver Hecker, a district manager of a German industrial union, says that culture clashes are everywhere. "I would call it figures-focused American meets value-focused German," he said. His reference was to a focus on employees and the community as much as on shareholders.[14] (Hecker's stereotype of American managers holds some truth but also has many exceptions.)

Cross-Cultural Values

LEARNING OBJECTIVE 2
Identify and explain key dimensions of cultural differences.

Useful background information for understanding how to work well with people from different cultures can come from examining their values. We approach this task by looking at how cultures differ with respect to certain values. As described in Chapter 4, values are a major force underlying behavior on and off the job. Many years of research suggest that culture can be as important as personality traits in influencing how a person might behave on the job.[15] Imagine Helen, who was raised in China but now works in the United States. One of her strongly held values is to cooperate with group members and be positive toward them. When asked to provide negative feedback about a coworker in a peer-evaluation system, she therefore refuses.

One way to understand how national cultures differ is to examine their values. Here we examine 10 values and how selected nationalities relate to them, based on the work of several researchers.[16] Geert Hofstede conducted the original work in value dimensions in research spanning 18 years, involving over 160,000 people from over 60 countries. Some of his original work is presented here, along with updating and refinements by other researchers. Differences in cultural values are stereotypes, reflecting how an average person from a particular culture might behave. Cultural values follow a normal curve, as do personality traits. People within a culture are likely to vary considerably among themselves; for example, many Latin Americans have casual attitudes toward time, with others placing a high value on being punctual and making effective use of time. A summary of these cultural values is presented next.

individualism A mental set in which people see themselves first as individuals and believe that their own interests take priority.

collectivism A value emphasizing that the group and society receive top priority.

1. *Individualism versus collectivism.* At one end of the continuum is **individualism**, a mental set in which people see themselves first as individuals and believe that their own interests take priority. **Collectivism**, at the other end of the continuum, is a feeling that the group and society receive top priority. Members of a society that values individualism are more concerned with their careers than with the good of the firm. Members of a society that value collectivism, in contrast, are typically more concerned with the organization than with themselves. Highly individualistic cultures include the United States, Canada, Great Britain, Australia, and the Netherlands. Japan, Taiwan, Mexico, Greece, and Hong Kong are among the countries that strongly value collectivism. The current emphasis on teamwork, however, is softening individualism in individualistic cultures.

power distance The extent to which employees accept the idea that members of an organization have different levels of power.

2. *Power distance.* The extent to which employees accept the idea that members of an organization have different levels of power is referred to as **power distance**. In a high-power-distance culture, the boss makes many decisions simply because she or he is the boss. Group members readily comply because they have a positive orientation toward authority. In a low-power-distance culture, employees do not readily recognize a power hierarchy. They accept directions only when they think the boss is right or when they feel threatened. High-power-distance cultures include India, France, Spain, Japan, Mexico, and Brazil. Low-power-distance cultures include the United States, Israel, Germany, and Ireland. According to the GLOBE studies of 62 societies, organizational practices in most countries support a generally high level of power distance (as well as materialism as listed below).[17]

Power distance also has some impact on how much abuse from supervisors employees are willing to take, with high-power-distance workers being more tolerant of mistreatment by supervisors. A study supporting this finding was conducted by recruiting participants both online and through printed advertisements. One of the study's findings was that high-power-distance individuals (those who believe that managers are more powerful) are less likely to regard abusive supervisors as being unjust.[18]

uncertainty avoidance The extent to which people accept the unknown and tolerate risk and unconventional behavior.

3. *Uncertainty avoidance.* People who accept the unknown and tolerate risk and unconventional behavior are said to have low **uncertainty avoidance**. In other words,

these people are not afraid to face the unknown. A society ranked high in uncertainty avoidance contains a majority of people who want predictable and certain futures. Low uncertainty-avoidance cultures include the United States, Canada, Australia, and Singapore. Workers in Israel, Japan, Italy, and Argentina are more motivated to avoid uncertainty in their careers.

Concern for others is a key cultural value.

4. *Materialism versus concern for others.* In this context, **materialism** refers to an emphasis on assertiveness and the acquisition of money or material objects. It also means a de-emphasis on caring for others. At the other end of the continuum is **concern for others**, an emphasis on personal relationships, and a concern for the welfare of others. Materialistic countries include Japan, Austria, and Italy. The United States is considered to be moderately materialistic. Scandinavian nations all emphasize caring as a national value.

5. *Long-term orientation versus short-term orientation.* Workers from a culture with a **long-term orientation** maintain a long-range perspective, and thus are thrifty and do not demand quick returns on their investments. A **short-term orientation** is characterized by a demand for immediate results and a propensity not to save. Pacific Rim countries are noted for their long-term orientation. In contrast, the cultures of the United States and Canada are characterized by a more short-term orientation.

6. *Formality versus informality.* A country that values **formality** attaches considerable importance to tradition, ceremony, social rules, and rank. At the other extreme, **informality** refers to a casual attitude toward tradition, ceremony, social rules, and rank. Workers in Latin American countries highly value formality, such as lavish public receptions and processions. Americans, Canadians, and Scandinavians are much more informal. The workplace across the world is becoming much more informal, with workers at all levels making less use of titles and last names. The informality of communication by Internet has fostered informality.

7. *Urgent time orientation versus casual time orientation.* Individuals and nations hold different views regarding the importance of time. People with an **urgent time orientation** perceive time as a scarce resource and tend to be impatient. People with a **casual time orientation** view time as an unlimited and unending resource and tend to be patient. Americans are noted for their urgent time orientation. They frequently impose deadlines and are eager to get started doing business. Asians and Middle Easterners, in contrast, are patient negotiators.

8. *High-context versus low-context cultures.* Cultures differ in how much importance they attach to the surrounding circumstances, or context, of an event. **High-context cultures** make more extensive use of body language. Some cultures, such as the Asian, Hispanic, and African American cultures, are high context. In contrast, northern European cultures are **low context** and make less use of body language. The American culture is considered to be medium-low context. People in low-context cultures seldom take time in business dealings to build relationships and establish trust.

9. *Work orientation/leisure orientation.* A major cultural-value difference is the number of hours per week people expect to invest in work instead of leisure or other nonwork activities. American corporate professionals typically work about 55 hours per week, take 45-minute lunch breaks, and 2 weeks of vacation. According to the International Labor Organization (ILO), Americans work 137 more hours per year than do their Japanese counterparts, 260 more hours per year than British workers, and 499 more hours than French workers.[19]

materialism An emphasis on assertiveness and the acquisition of money and material objects. Usually measured along a continuum, with concern for others at the opposite end.

concern for others An emphasis on personal relationships and a concern for the welfare of others. Usually measured along a continuum, with materialism at the opposite end.

long-term orientation In describing national culture, taking a long-range perspective.

short-term orientation In describing a national culture, a demand for immediate results.

formality Attaching considerable importance to tradition, ceremony, social rules, and rank.

informality A casual attitude toward tradition, ceremony, social rules, and rank.

urgent time orientation The perception of time as a scarce resource, therefore leading to impatience.

casual time orientation The perception of time as an unlimited and unending resource, leading to patience.

high-context culture A culture that makes more extensive use of body language.

low-context culture A culture that makes less use of body language.

10. *Performance orientation.* A difference stemming from the GLOBE study of 62 cultures is the degree to which a cultural value encourages and rewards group members for performance improvement and excellence. The value is imposed on school children, university students, and workers. Many Asian countries, including China, Hong Kong, Japan, Korea, Singapore, and Taiwan rank high on performance orientation.[20]

Although the dimensions of cultural values just described are broad national stereotypes, they still relate to meaningful aspects of organizational behavior. A study on the impact of cultural values investigated how similarity to peers and supervisors influences career advancement in an individualistic versus collectivistic society. The participants in the study were bank tellers working for the same multinational bank in Hong Kong and the United States. Both personality and individualism versus collectivism were measured by questionnaires. The researchers did not assume that work units in Hong Kong banks were collectivistic, or that work units in the United States were individualistic.

One major finding was that having a personality similar to peers was positively associated with promotion in units with high individualism. In units with high collectivism, having a personality similar to the boss was instead positively associated with advancement.[21] (The lesson here is that if you find yourself in an individualistic work group, emphasize your personality traits that match your coworkers. In a collectivistic work group, do what you can to emphasize personality traits similar to your supervisor.)

How might a person use information about cultural differences to enhance interpersonal effectiveness? A starting point would be to recognize that a person's national values might influence his or her behavior. Assume that the managerial worker wanted to establish a good working relationship with a person from a high-context culture. To begin, he or she might emphasize body language when communicating with the individual.

Another application would be to recognize that many Asian Americans may need to be encouraged to talk in meetings because they have been taught to respect authority and to defer to elders. Consultant Jane Hyun observes, "Unfortunately this reticence gets mistaken for aloofness or arrogance or inattention, when it is usually just the Asian habit of respecting authority. We wait for our turn to speak—and often our turn just never comes."[22]

Multicultural Workers and Organizations

A major message from the study of international and cross-cultural organizational behavior is that managers, other workers, and their organizations need to respond positively to cultural diversity. Here we look separately at the multicultural worker and the multicultural organization.

The Multicultural Worker

The **multicultural worker** has the skills and attitudes to relate effectively to and motivate people with little regard to race, gender, age, social attitudes, and lifestyles. A multicultural worker has the ability to conduct business in a diverse, international environment. Achieving such competence is a combination of many factors, including some of the traits associated with effective leadership described in Chapter 11. A few skills and attitudes are especially relevant for achieving the status of a multicultural manager or worker.

Being able to deal effectively with people from other cultures, whether they are in another country or your own country, is a career asset. The Society for Human Resource Management (SHRM) Competency Model states that global and cultural effectiveness is "the ability to value and consider the perspectives and backgrounds of all parties."[23] This type of competency is required for HR professionals but applies to managers and workers from many disciplines.

Cultural Integration

A major requirement for attaining multiculturalism is cultural integration—the ability to reconcile another culture with one's home culture. Research conducted by three professors from different countries found that being able to integrate diverse perspectives contributes to greater creativity and professional achievement. A major driver of such integration is the ability to make psychological connections among multiple cultures. Particularly important for workers on assignment in another country is to adapt to the local environment, embracing new perspectives and behaviors yet still staying connected to the home environment.[24]

To make this abstract idea a little more concrete, think of Ashley, a mechanical engineer and windmill specialist, on a six-month assignment in France. While in France, she must adapt to ceremonial dinners and show considerable respect for French executives. Ashley adapts to these behaviors but recognizes that, when she returns to the United States, she will have less business ceremony and will work in a more egalitarian environment.

A good starting point is to make strides toward becoming bilingual. International businesspeople respect the fact that a managerial worker is bilingual even if the second language is not their primary language. For example, if an American speaks French, the American can relate well to Italians and Spanish people. The tortuous reasoning is that many Italians and Spanish speak French as a third language, and respect the American who speaks a little French. Yet the importance of developing a second language has become confusing. Most high-level workers around the world speak English because it has become the language of business. If the person from another country speaks English and detects that you can speak English, he or she will want to converse with you in English. A moderating factor, however, is that, if you are fluent in that person's language, he or she will usually be willing to converse with you in his or her native language.

Cultural Sensitivity

A major requirement for becoming a multicultural worker is to develop **cultural sensitivity**, an awareness of and a willingness to investigate the reasons why people of another culture act as they do.[25] Persons with cultural sensitivity will recognize certain nuances in customs that will help build better relationships with people from different cultural backgrounds than their own. A positive example is that for an executive to conduct business successfully in China, he or she must build a *guanxi* (a network of relationships or connections among parties). The *guanxi* must be built internally with subordinates, peers, and superiors as well as externally with clients, suppliers, and government officials. Relationship building of this type takes time, but it is a cultural imperative in China.[26]

cultural sensitivity An awareness of and a willingness to investigate the reasons why people of another culture act as they do.

In addition to being culturally sensitive, the multicultural manager or worker also must avoid cultural insensitivity. An example of cultural insensitivity follows:

> A manager in a telecommunications firm in Washington, DC, wanted to recognize the outstanding accomplishments of a worker, who was born and raised in India, on a major project. The manager offered the worker guest coupons to a steakhouse, not stopping to think that an Indian raised in India probably does not eat steak. The worker appreciated the recognition but laughed to his coworkers in describing the incident.

Figure 17-2 provides specific examples of nuances to consider. In addition, the information in Chapter 8 about overcoming cross-cultural communication barriers is directly relevant. Being able to deal effectively with cultural differences can be a make-or-break factor (or mediating variable) in the success of overseas ventures. Applying the information in Figure 17-2 will be the most effective when you understand the cultural values driving the behavior. For example, the information about the importance of business cards in Japan is generated in part because Japanese people value power distance, and the company a person works for helps determine his or her status. The value of collectivism also fosters the exchange of cards.[27]

An effective strategy for becoming a multicultural worker is to simply respect others in the workplace. To respect another culture is to recognize that, although the other culture is different, it is equally good. A person from one culture might therefore say, "Eating rattlesnakes for dinner is certainly different from my culture, yet I can see that eating rattlesnakes is as good as eating cows." (Which living organisms constitute palatable

FIGURE 17-2 Protocol Dos and Don'ts in Several Countries

Several specialists in cross-culture etiquette suggest adhering to the following dos and don'ts in the countries indicated. Remember, however, that these suggestions are not absolute rules.

Great Britain

DO say "please" and "thank you" often.

DO arrive promptly for dinner.

DON'T ask personal questions because the British protect their privacy.

DON'T gossip about British royalty. Allow the British to take the initiative with respect to gossiping about royalty, such as mentioning juicy stories in the tabloids.

France

DO shake hands when greeting. Only close friends give light, brushing kisses on cheeks.

DO dress more formally than in the United States. Elegant dress is highly valued.

DON'T expect to complete any work during the French 2-hour lunch.

DON'T chew gum in a work setting.

Italy

DO write business correspondence in Italian for priority attention.

DO make appointments between 10:00 a.m. and 11:00 a.m. or after 3:00 p.m.

DON'T eat too much pasta, as it is not the main course.

DON'T hand out business cards freely. Italians use them infrequently.

Greece

DO distribute business cards freely so people will know how to spell your name.

DO be prompt even if your hosts are not.

DON'T expect to meet deadlines. A project takes as long as the Greeks think is necessary.

DON'T address people by formal or professional titles. The Greeks want more informality.

Japan

DO present your business cards with both hands and a slight bow as a gesture of respect.

DO present gifts, American-made and wrapped.

DON'T knock competitors.

DON'T present the same gift to everyone, unless all members are the same organizational rank.

DON'T attempt to kiss or hug work associates.

China

DO reach for your Chinese boss's hand first. A high-ranking person in the company should never initiate a handshake. A limp grip connotes humility and respect.

DO be impressed by a business card from a Chinese businessperson. Place the card on a table in front of you so you can continue to admire it.

DON'T point with one finger because it is considered very rude.

DON'T give clocks as gifts because the pronunciation of the Chinese phrase "to give clocks" could also mean "to attend to a dying relative."

Most Asian Countries

DO be polite and respect authority. Most Asian cultures emphasize polite gestures such as gentle bowing and smiling to indicate acceptance or agreement.

DON'T emphasize the number 4, such as giving a pack of four bottles of cologne or cigars as a gift, and do not rent a conference room on the fourth floor of a hotel. The number 4 connotes death in many Asian cultures.

Sources: TWA Ambassador, October 1990, p. 69; Inc. Magazine's Going Global; Japan Inc., January 1994; Rita Pyrillis, "Just a Token of Your Appreciation?" Workforce Management, September 2011, pp. 3, 6; Christina Larson, "The Chinese Take Their Etiquette Seriously," Bloomberg BusinessWeek, June 3–9, 2013, pp. 15–16; Eric Spitznagal, "Impress Your Chinese Boss," Bloomberg Businessweek, January 9–15, 2012, pp. 80–81; "How to Research Culture before Moving Abroad," Personal Business (onlinefx.westernunion.com) © 2016 Western Union Holdings Inc.

food is a major day-by-day cultural difference.) Respect comes from valuing differences. Respecting other people's customs can translate into specific attitudes, such as respecting one group member for wearing a yarmulke on Friday or another for wearing an African costume to celebrate Kwanzaa.

Cultural Agility

According to Paula Caligiuri, the multicultural worker who achieves all the competencies just mentioned would attain cultural agility. She defines cultural agility as "Mega competency that enables professionals to perform successfully in cross-cultural situations. It is a combination of natural abilities, motivation to succeed, guided training, coaching, and development over time."[28] A key implication here is that it takes considerable time, effort, and ability to become a high-level multicultural worker.

Multiple Cultural Identities

The term *multicultural worker* also refers to employees who have more than one cultural identity, thereby belonging to multiple worlds. Take the example of Hugo, a manufacturing engineer who was raised and educated in Mexico. He now lives in the United States and works in a Toyota manufacturing plant. Hugo speaks Spanish and English fluently and has strong ties to both Mexico and the United States. His girlfriend is Chinese American, so Hugo also feels part of the Chinese culture. Organizations are experiencing an increasing number of employees who have internalized more than one culture. These multicultural workers find it relatively easy to be the kind of multicultural person who can conduct business in a diverse environment.[29]

Positive Indifference

Another useful dimension of being able to work well across cultures is to embrace *positive indifference*. The term refers to being able to overlook a variety of cultural differences that are not especially important yet still remaining optimistic about engaging another culture. For example, it is usually not worth being frustrated about having to wear an identification badge or having to file frequent key performance indicators.[30] Instead, the difference might be overlooked, and you are then free to concentrate on important matters, such as working jointly to make the project a success.

The Multicultural Organization

As more workers in a firm develop multicultural skills, the organization itself can achieve the same skill level. A **multicultural organization** values cultural diversity and is willing to encourage and even capitalize on such diversity. Developing a multicultural organization helps achieve the potential benefits that come with valuing diversity. In addition, the multicultural organization helps avoid problems that crop up when managing diversity, such as increased turnover, interpersonal conflicts, and communication breakdowns.

multicultural organization An organization that values cultural diversity and is willing to encourage and even capitalize on such diversity.

To move toward being a multicultural organization, business firms take a variety of diversity initiatives. A leading example is MGM Resorts, which consistently wins national diversity honors, including being named in DiversityInc's list of Top Companies for Diversity. DiversityInc tracks the nation's top companies in terms of hiring, retaining, and promoting women, minorities, people with disabilities, LGBTQ individuals, and veterans. Close to 70 percent of the company's employees are minorities. Forty-four percent of the management staff are women, and minorities comprise 43 percent of MGM Resorts' members of management.[31]

Since 2001, MGM Resorts has invested a total of $1.8 billion with Minority- and Women-Owned Business Development Enterprises suppliers, representing 11 percent of MGM's total spending on biddable projects for goods and services. An example of a specific resort diversity initiative is the MGM Mirage Bellagio in Las Vegas. The hotel and resort runs a 9-month executive-mentoring program to ready high-potential minority workers in management positions for advancement into the executive suite. The hotel also offers a 6-month Management Associate Program—6 months of training to prepare recent minority graduates for careers in management through mentoring, classroom instruction, job shadowing, and hands-on experience.[32]

SAP America Inc. is another example of a multicultural organization. In an industry underrepresented by women workers, SAP received a seal of approval for its commitment to gender diversity from Economics Dividends for Gender Equality (EDGE). SAP America is the first U.S. tech company to receive EDGE certification. "We have a holistic diversity and inclusion strategy," said Anka Wittenberg, chief diversity and inclusion officer at SAP headquarters in Germany. "It's not about filling a quota. At SAP, we are very committed to finding sustainable solutions."

SAP's gender diversity initiatives include a yearlong leadership development program. Also included is a monthly webinar series covering organizational behavior topics such as negotiation, effective communication, and political savvy. Women constitute more than 30 percent of SAP's global workforce and occupy about 25 percent of all leadership positions.[33]

Barriers to Good Cross-Cultural Relations

LEARNING OBJECTIVE 4
Be more aware of barriers to good cross-cultural relations.

An important part of achieving a multicultural organization and good cross-cultural relationships in general is to understand barriers to such harmony. Major barriers of this type are described as follows:[34]

1. *Perceptual expectations.* Achieving good cross-cultural relationships is hampered by people's predisposition to discriminate. They do so as a perceptual shortcut, much like stereotyping. An example would be a sales representative encountering an important customer, a man apparently in his 80s. The sales rep begins to patronize the old man, talking to him in a childlike manner. The rep is then informed that the person he is patronizing is the chairman of the board, who is still quite active. (Oops, a lost sale!) Because people are not naturally nondiscriminatory, a firm has to put considerable effort into becoming multicultural.

2. *Ethnocentrism.* The multicultural worker avoids **ethnocentrism**, the assumption that the ways of one's own culture are the best ways of doing things. Many cultures consider themselves to be the center of the world. One consequence of this attitude is that people from one culture prefer that people from other cultures be more similar to themselves. English people would therefore have more positive attitudes toward the Scottish than they would toward Brazilians. Despite this generalization, some countries that appear to have similar cultures are intense rivals. Many Japanese dislike Korean people, and vice versa; another example would be French and Belgians.

3. *Intergroup rather than interpersonal relations.* In intergroup relations, we pay attention only to the group of which a person is a member. In interpersonal relations, we pay attention to a person's characteristics. An interpersonal relationship requires more effort because we have to attend to details about the other person. Automobile manufacturers have implemented extensive training programs to help sales representatives develop interpersonal rather than intergroup relations with women buyers. In the past, many sales reps would lose valuable sales prospects because they assumed that women were not the decision makers about an automobile purchase.

4. *Stereotypes in intergroup relations.* As a result of stereotypes, people overestimate the probability that a given member of a group will have an attribute of that group. People tend to select information that fits the stereotype and reject inconsistent information. As a consequence, they readily draw conclusions about people from other cultural groups without carefully listening and observing. As a Chinese American woman reported, "I'm tired of people assuming that I like math and science and that I'm good with details. I'm a people person with a creative bent. I actually hate math." (A problem here is that the woman may be excluded from job assignments that fit her true capabilities.)

5. *Language differences.* A major barrier to good cross-cultural relationships is language differences. When people do not understand each other's language, the possibility for misunderstanding multiplies. A team member who was a native of France on assignment in the United States said the boss was "retarded," so the meeting would have to wait. The other team members thought this was an insult, but *en retard* in French refers to being late. On a more somber note, language barriers cause many industrial accidents in the United States. Hispanics in the United States are frequently employed in dangerous industries, particularly construction. Language barriers between workers and supervisors make safety training exceptionally difficult.

6. *Cultural assumptions.* A **cultural assumption** is a form of stereotype in which we attribute attitudes and behaviors to members of a group without verifying our in-

ethnocentrism The assumption that the ways of one's own culture are the best ways of doing things.

cultural assumption A form of stereotype in which we attribute attitudes and behaviors to members of a group, without verifying our information.

formation. Making this assumption could create a communication and personal barrier between individuals. A naïve assumption is that an Italian visitor to your company would like to dine at an Italian restaurant. A more serious assumption is that all African Americans are liberal (or all blacks think alike). In reality, many blacks are quite conservative both politically and socially.

7. *Biases against another demographic group.* Few people admit to being biased against members of another demographic group, but these biases continue to exist both at the conscious and preconscious levels. A bias is similar to a negative cultural assumption but often stronger. Research conducted by Joan C. Williams and her daughter, Rachel Dempsey, suggests that subtle biases against women have held them back from many promotions and pay increases in the information-technology industry. (These biases may exist despite a notable exception, such as a woman, Sheryl Sandberg, being the COO and number two in command at Facebook Inc.) One of the biases against women cited by Williams is called "prove it again," referring to the idea that women have to provide more evidence of competence than men do to be seen as equally capable.[35] More will be said about biases in the section later in the chapter about anti-bias training, as well as in the end-of-chapter case.

Many companies have overcome gender stereotypes about workers.

wavebreakmedia/Shutterstock.com

Cross-Cultural Processes

Another approach to understanding international and cross-cultural organizational behavior is to examine similarities and differences in important processes. Five such areas in which cross-cultural differences may surface are motivation, ethics, negotiations, conflict resolution methods, and empowerment practices.

LEARNING OBJECTIVE 5
Explain how motivation, ethics, appropriate negotiation skills, conflict resolution, and empowerment practices can vary across cultures.

Cross-Cultural Motivation

For managers to effectively lead and influence workers from another culture, they must use a motivational approach that fits the culture in question. Motivational concepts apply across cultures providing that the manager has relevant information about two key factors. The manager must know which needs the people are attempting to satisfy and which rewards will satisfy those needs. A case in point is reinforcement theory. All human beings are motivated by rewards, yet which rewards have high valence varies across cultures. An American worker might respond well to individual recognition, while a South Korean worker might respond better to sharing a reward with the group.

A two-country study found that cultural factors influence the effectiveness of participative management as a motivational technique. The participants in the study were junior workers in the Hong Kong and U.S. branches of a large multinational bank. A major finding was that for employees who saw themselves as inseparable from the group, a strong positive relationship was found between an opportunity to participate and group performance—assuming the participants felt competent about participating.[36] In short, when people believe in collective effort, it helps them benefit from participative decision making.

Cross-Cultural Ethics

Coping with cross-cultural ethical codes challenges many international managers. When faced with an ethical dilemma, should managers abide by ethical codes of their own country or those of the country they are visiting? A recurring ethical dilemma is that, in many countries like Pakistan and Mexico, government officials demand payments to expedite certain transactions. In the United States, direct payments to government officials to win contracts are illegal and unethical. The Foreign Corrupt Practices Act does not outlaw payment to foreign government officials, providing such payoffs are part of the country's business practices. To get around the direct payment prohibitions, some countries demand that large American companies donate technology to the foreign country, with China being a leading example. Money is not exchanged, but the foreign country receives side benefits from dealing with a U.S. company.

One questionable way in which managers cope with cross-cultural differences in ethics is to outsource work to another country that would be unethical, or illegal, in their own countries. A lethal example is the recycling of automobile and truck batteries. During recycling, acid leaks from these batteries and the fumes are extraordinarily toxic. Several countries, including Australia, contract with small firms in India to recycle these batteries. The small Indian firms take virtually no safety precautions for the workers.

Cross-Cultural Negotiations

Negotiation is one of the single most important skills for the international manager or specialist. A major challenge in skill development is that negotiation styles vary from one culture to another. Managers should negotiate when the value of the exchange and the relationship is important. Managerial negotiation requires significant adaptation when conducted in a foreign culture. A do-or-die attitude is often self-defeating. A list of suggestions for negotiation abroad follows. Each of the first five points includes the American attitude that could be self-defeating and explains how it can be improved.[37]

1. *Use a team approach.* Most American managers are convinced they can handle any negotiation by themselves, while other countries rely on negotiation teams. Bringing several Americans to the negotiating table may convey a seriousness of purpose and commitment.

2. *Be patient.* A striking difference between American negotiations and those in many foreign cultures concerns time. Japanese, Chinese, and Arab negotiators, for example, are willing to spend many days negotiating a deal. Much of their negotiating activity seems to be ceremonial (including elaborate dining) and unrelated to the task. This often frustrates the "strictly business" American.

3. *Learn to tolerate less than full disclosure of information.* Many Americans believe that "laying one's cards on the table" is a valuable negotiating tactic. As a consequence, they expect honest information and are frustrated when it is not forthcoming. Because many foreign negotiators routinely practice small deceptions at the negotiating table, less than full disclosure must be tolerated.

4. *Accept silence as part of negotiating.* Unlike Asian negotiators, Americans often become uncomfortable when more than 10 seconds elapses without somebody making a task-related comment. It is sometimes fruitful to remain silent and wait for the other side to make an offer or reveal the nature of its thinking.

5. *Take no for an answer sometimes.* Americans are highly competitive in a negotiating session and take each loss personally. Foreign customers and suppliers, in contrast, are often willing to lose one negotiating session to build a solid long-term relationship with people and firms.

6. *Learn about the other culture's negotiating style in advance.* Part of doing your homework for negotiating in another culture involves having an awareness of negotiating stereotypes for the other culture. A few possibilities: Japanese prefer an exchange of information to confrontation; Russians love combat; Spanish negotiators are individualistic; Koreans are team players; Asians are high in context, so you have to watch the body language and what is *not* said.[38]

7. *A starting point in cross-cultural negotiations is whether members of the culture tend to seek integrative or distributed outcomes.* An integrative outcome focuses on both sides walking away from negotiation with something of value, whereas a distributed outcome looks for one side to win as much as possible. A synthesis of

Effective negotiation tactics can vary across cultures.

many studies suggests that negotiators for Western nations (e.g., Germany, Israel, Norway, Sweden, and the United States) are more likely to use an integrative bargaining approach. In contrast, East Asian nations (e.g., China, Hong Kong, Japan, and Thailand) are more likely to favor distributive bargaining. Negotiators from Middle Eastern/South Asian nations (e.g., India and Qatar) are also more likely to favor distributive bargaining.[39]

8. *Vary your negotiation approach according to whether you trust or distrust the other side.* Trust is often an issue in cross-cultural negotiations, such as one side fearing that the other side will steal the company's technology. Three illustrative tactics to use when you trust the other side are: (a) get to know your counterpart personally, (b) engage in reciprocal questions and answers, and (c) keep agreements tentative until the end. Three illustrative tactics to use when you distrust the other side are: (a) look for hidden patterns and cues in your counterpart's offers and responses, (b) make reciprocal concessions, and (c) express sympathy, apologize, or compliment your counterpart.[40]

A useful perspective on these suggestions is that a person is rarely on a level playing field when negotiating in another country. Adapting to the other side's negotiating tactics may help to place negotiations on an equal footing. However, Americans should not necessarily be the only group adapting their negotiating tactics to fit different cultures. Businesspeople from around the world may have to develop a cross-cultural negotiating style.

Conflict Resolution Models across Cultures

Research provides some quantitative evidence that national culture influences which method of conflict resolution a manager chooses. Catherine Tinsley sorted conflict resolution models into three types: resolving conflict by (a) deferring to status power, (b) applying regulations, and (c) integrating interests. According to her observations, preference for a model, or method, is influenced by culture that filters information and guides members toward a particular model. The 396 participants in the study were managers from Japanese, German, and American cultures. All participants had been educated by business programs in their cultures and were currently working for companies in their cultures. Participants completed surveys about resolving conflict over different approaches to solving a business problem.

A major finding was that Japanese, German, and American managers tended to use different models when resolving workplace conflict. Half the variance (reasons for something taking place) in choosing a conflict model could be accounted for by a manager's cultural group membership. Japanese preferred a status power model (using their authority). Germans preferred a regulations model (appealing to rules and regulations), and Americans preferred an interests (win–win) model. Tinsley cautions that these cross-cultural differences may complicate the work life for expatriate managers who find themselves trying to manage conflict in a foreign cultural system. A particular concern is that American managers may be surprised to learn that colleagues from Japanese and German cultures do not favor the interests model.[41]

Empowerment and Continuous Improvement across Cultures

A team of researchers investigated how well the management practices of empowerment and continuous improvement fit different cultures. Data were collected from employees from a United States–based multinational corporation with operations in the United States, Mexico, Poland, and India. The major findings were as follows:

- Continuous improvement was related to high levels of satisfaction with coworkers and the work itself in all four countries. No negative findings were associated with continuous improvement in any country, suggesting that continuous improvement and self-development are a good fit in all the cultures studied.

- The outcomes associated with empowerment varied with the country and culture. Workers in the United States, Mexico, and Poland had favorable views of their supervisors when they used a high degree of empowerment. Indian employees, however, rated their supervisors low when empowerment was high. (Indians value high power distance, and therefore expect the supervisor to retain most of the power.)

- In the United States and Mexico, empowerment was unrelated to coworker satisfaction, yet in Poland, empowerment was positively related to coworker satisfaction. In India, empowerment was shown to have a negative impact on coworker satisfaction.[42]

- A meta-analysis of 105 studies conducted in 30 countries found that empowering leadership practices had a more beneficial impact on the performance of routine tasks in Eastern rather than in Western cultures. The authors of the study suggested that in Eastern societies such as China, India, and the Republic of Korea, those in more powerful positions are expected to assist and support those in lower positions. At the same time, subordinates are expected to be loyal and obey their leader. In contrast, in Western societies, such as the United States, United Kingdom, and Germany, employees may prefer and expect greater independence from their leader. Extensive care and concern shown by an empowering leader could be seen as an intrusion.[43]

In general, the results of the study suggest that multinational managers should consider the cultural context of the management practices they implement. In particular, empowerment may backfire when used in a high power-distance culture. The study might also be interpreted as more evidence of the universal need for personal growth.

High-Performing Work Systems and National Culture

So far we have emphasized how differences in national culture might influence organizational behavior processes. Apparently, high-performance work systems (HPWSs) tend to be effective across different cultures. A group of researchers conducted a meta-analysis of the relationship between HPWSs and business performance for 156 high-performing work systems from 35,767 firms in 29 countries. For all the national cultures studied, HPWSs were positively related to business performance. National culture was measured on several of the dimensions of national culture, such as in-group collectivism and performance orientation, described earlier in the chapter. An important conclusion from this giant analysis is that a high-performing work system does not have to be adapted to a national culture.[44] One reason that this finding is not so surprising is that an HPWS is typically based on well-researched and fair human resource procedures that people from any culture would appreciate.

The accompanying Organizational Behavior in Action box illustrates the relevance of cultural diversity and cross-cultural organizational behavior in today's business world.

Initiatives to Enhance Cultural Diversity in Organizations

Organizations take many initiatives to help foster cultural diversity, including the type of program at MGM Resorts and the heavy reliance on minority group members at Capital One described previously. In this section, we first note the importance of programs for recruiting and hiring minority-group members. We then describe a diversity-training program, anti-bias training, along with cultural training for improving cross-cultural relationships including the development of cultural intelligence (CQ).

LEARNING OBJECTIVE 6 Appreciate the nature of diversity training and cultural training, including cultural intelligence and anti-bias training.

Recruitment of Minority-Group Members

A foundation step for creating a culturally diverse workplace is to recruit culturally diverse workers. The most successful programs for recruiting minorities and women into management and professional positions rely on the use of appropriate networks. For example, several traditionally black colleges specialize in producing information technology graduates. Furthermore, a number of employment placement agencies specialize in finding African Americans and Latinos for managerial and professional positions.

A minority recruiting program is likely to meet with high acceptance when it is not aimed against hiring majority-group members. Dennis Parker, director of the racial justice program of the American Civil Liberties Union, provides an insight into this delicate balance: "You can have a goal, even a numerical goal over a time period to increase the number of women or people of color. But this is different than saying, 'We're not going to hire many more white men.'"[45]

Diversity Training

Cultural training aims to help workers understand people from other cultures. Understanding can lead to dealing more effectively with them as work associates or customers. **Diversity training** has a slightly different purpose. It attempts to bring about workplace harmony by teaching people how to get along better with diverse work associates. Quite often the program is aimed at minimizing open expressions of racism and sexism. All forms of diversity training center on increasing people's awareness of and empathy for people who are different from themselves.

Diversity-training sessions focus on the ways that people of different races reflect different values, attitudes, and cultural backgrounds. Some diversity programs deal specifically with generational differences so people with different values based on age can work harmoniously. Diversity-training sessions can vary from several hours to several days. An

diversity training Training that attempts to bring about workplace harmony by teaching people how to get along better with diverse work associates.

Diversity training aims to improve relationships among diverse workers.

Western Union Works across Many Cultures

Western Union is a globally diverse company founded in 1851 in New York that originated with the now-extinct telegram that might be framed as the text messages of yesteryear. An example: "Congratulations. We will start you as department head for $5000 per year." Western Union (WU) is now a global money-transfer company. Across more than 200 countries and territories, the company has half a million agent locations. Services are offered over the telephone and at more than 150,000 automated teller machines (ATMs) and kiosks. CEO Hikmet Ersek says that the company has been connecting people and helping businesses to thrive, first in the United States, then in the world. He wants to bring the world closer, one person at a time.

Ersek is convinced that when money moves, better things can happen, such as a business expanding, a student attending college, an economy prospering, and jobs being created. He also explains that WU's purpose as a global company would not be possible without diversity and people. The company's culture celebrates diversity and inclusion. Company employees are expected to know what is going on in the world and how it affects WU customers.

WU has a distinctive type of customer who often interacts with a person in another country. Two types of people are served: the sender of the money and the person who receives it. The customer who is a sender can send money from a handheld phone, and the receiver can pick up the cash. Nongovernmental organizations (NGOs) can send money from their global headquarters in Paris, and their field workers can pick up the cash in a conflict zone.

According to Ersek, to build a unique physical and network like this, you cannot sit in an office in Denver or San Francisco. You have to be in and understand the diverse marketplaces in the world. Among the tasks that need doing are negotiating with reserve banks and finding the right agent for the right location. Every action you take must keep the voice of the customer in mind.

Globalization has helped WU not only with respect to goods and information but also in terms of the global workforce. The unique brand of WU has also been enabled by globalization. Not all people speak English, but they recognize Western Union. The company is a global language for moving money to support loved ones.

Multicultural skills are at a premium at WU. The customers have broadly diverse religious celebrations, school systems, languages, and beliefs. You need a multicultural understanding of these differences to stay close to WU customers—not only senders and receivers of money but also the bankers, regulators, and agents. You need multicultural competence to select the right agent for a given location or to create an app for a given country that reflects the WU brand in the right way.

In dealing with customers, you have to be willing to look beneath the surface of what the person is saying. Because the speaker may not be using his or her

essential part of relating more effectively to diverse groups is to empathize with their point of view. To help participants develop empathy, representatives of various groups explain their feelings related to workplace issues.

Evidence collected over the years suggests that diversity training is the most effective when it is integrated into other diversity-related activities, rather than being a stand-alone activity. A key diversity practice would be providing good career opportunities for women and minorities. A concern about diversity training is that it exaggerates stereotypes in order to promote understanding, such as propagating the belief that Latinos do not start meetings on time.[46]

More recently, diversity programs have been accused of focusing too much on underrepresented minorities and therefore not being inclusive enough. Diversity advisor Kara Helander says that leaders must recognize that some workers may resent or feel excluded from diversity programs focused on people from underrepresented ethnic backgrounds or the LGBTQ community.[47]

A suggestion for improving the effectiveness of diversity training is to pay more attention to the development of tolerance. The focus of tolerance is understanding different identities but not necessarily appreciating them totally.[48] The diversity trainer listens and accepts a point of view but does not have to agree. Take this example: Sven, a member of the diversity group from Sweden, talks for 10 minutes about the importance of company leadership sharing more of their compensation with lower-ranking workers. Tammy,

Western Union Works across Many Cultures *(Continued)*

primary language, the listener must actively participate in finding out what the person actually means by what is said.

Cultural diversity is important in making leadership assignments at WU. For example, about five years ago the company opened a new office in San Francisco with a team responsible for building WU Digital. The unit was assigned the responsibility of reinventing and expanding the money-transfer business for the mobile age. Instead of selecting a tech genius from Silicon Valley, Ersek chose the leader of its African business, Khalid Fellahi. Ersek wanted someone who had the multicultural competence referred to here—the understanding of WU's diverse customer base and their needs. Even a startup within the organization has to begin with the voice of the customer. Fellahi then hired 250 intelligent people from Silicon Valley, including the engineers the team needed.

Many people inside and outside the company were surprised by Ersek's decision to pull a leader out of Africa to set up and run a multimillion-dollar digital business in Silicon Valley. Even Fellahi was surprised. But Ersek believes that if you understand the voice of the customer, then all other good things will follow. The decision appeared to be the right one because the digital business has been the fastest-growing part of Western Union.

Ersek finds that people in the United States are more multicultural than they are given credit for. He says that business leaders in the United States adapt more easily to other cultures than do leaders within some other countries. Perhaps one reason is that immigrants have had such a strong influence in founding and building the country.

Ersek says that he is a migrant, having lived and worked in several countries. He is therefore committed to helping promote a world where multiculturalism and diversity become the norm and where the economic, intellectual capital, and cultural benefits of diverse populations are valued.

QUESTIONS

1. What do you think is a key message about cultural diversity and cross-cultural management contained in this story?

2. What might this story tell you about cross-cultural leadership?

Source: Original story created from facts and observations in the following sources: Hikmet Ersek, Lang Davidson, and Kausik Rajgopal, "Working across Many Cultures at Western Union," McKinsey & Company (www.mckinsey.com), January 2018, pp. 1–8; E. Hikmet, "Our Purpose Would Not Be Possible without Diversity," Western Union (www.westernunion.com/blog), p. 2. © 2018 Western Union Holdings Inc. "Our Behavior" Western Union (https://corporate.westernunion.com), p. 1. © 2015 Western Union Holdings Inc.; "Benefits: WU & You," Western Union (https://corporate.westernunion.com), p. 1.

---

another group member, responds, "I get what you are saying, Sven, but I still prefer capitalism."

The Skill-Development Exercise provides an opportunity to simulate a diversity-training program.

Anti-Bias Training

Closely related to diversity training is **anti-bias training** that helps employees discover their unconscious biases that may adversely affect certain demographic and cultural groups. Examples include being more likely to call back a Caucasian than a Latino or African American applicant for a second interview and not inviting a single parent to join a project that might require occasional weekend work.

Unconscious biases can shape diversity by rejecting people for certain assignments and not valuing their ideas. Anti-bias training has been used to identify and neutralize racial, age, gender, and political bias. An example of the latter is that Facebook Inc. was accused of suppressing news about conservative events and from conservative sources in its "trending topics" feature.[49]

Research conducted at Google indicates that almost everyone is a little bit sexist or racist.[50] Training can help us become aware of our unconscious biases and make appropriate adjustments. For example, a manager might believe that women Chinese American

anti-bias training A type of training that helps employees discover their unconscious biases that may adversely affect certain demographic groups.

workers want to occupy strictly technical roles and therefore do not adapt well to supervisor roles. After training, the manager would recognize that many Chinese American women are interested in and skilled at supervisory positions.

Unconscious bias training usually includes the administration of the Implicit Association Test, which is based on the logic of describing what comes to mind when a specific demographic or cultural group is mentioned. For example, "What association do you make to a 55-year-old man?" Or the person taking the test might be asked to attach a smiley face or a frowny face to a statement about an ethnic group to indicate whether they agree or disagree, such as "Indian Americans are great at coding."

Anti-bias training received extensive publicity in 2018 when it was administered at 8,000 Starbucks stores (cafés) during one afternoon. The trigger event for the anti–racial bias training was the arrest of two African American men at a Starbucks in Philadelphia. The two men were asked to leave after one was denied access to the restroom. Neither had yet ordered a beverage or food, but they were waiting for a business meeting. A Starbucks employee called the police, who arrested the men but released them almost immediately with no charges. The anti-bias training was combined with diversity training in such forms as presenting a video about the civil rights movement.[51]

A major concern about anti-bias training is that just because a person has an unconscious or hidden bias, it does not always follow that the bias will lead to discrimination. Take Conrad, for example, a construction site manager whose family has been in the construction business for generations. Conrad's hidden bias is that he believes that only Native Americans are highly skilled steeplejacks (good at dangerous climbing). Yet this bias does not stop Conrad from hiring other ethnic group members for these high-paying construction jobs.

Training in Cross-Cultural Relations

cultural training Training that attempts to help workers understand people from other cultures.

For many years, companies and government agencies have prepared their workers for assignments in other countries. The method most frequently chosen is **cultural training**, a set of learning experiences designed to help employees understand the customs, traditions, and beliefs of another culture. The globalization of business has created an impetus for cultural training. Even if a managerial worker interacts with another country remotely, knowledge of that culture is helpful in establishing good relationships.

culture shock A group of physical and psychological symptoms that can develop when a person is abruptly placed in a foreign culture.

A major goal of cultural training, especially for workers on overseas assignments, is to help them avoid **culture shock**. The condition refers to a group of physical and psychological symptoms that can develop when a person is abruptly placed in a foreign culture. Among the symptoms are excessive hand washing and concern for sanitation, fear of physical contact with others, fear of being mugged, and strong feelings of homesickness.[52] A partial explanation for culture shock is that, when placed in an unfamiliar environment and when people behave in ways we do not understand, we feel out of control.

Culture shock is a major contributor to the high failure rate of overseas assignments. Attention has also been paid to the culture shock problems of employees from other countries transferring to the United States. One problem is that they may find no fellow members of their country in the United States, whereas Americans can always find Americans in other countries. Another problem is that many people fear their children will be shot at on the way to or from school.[53] (Again, perceptions have a major influence on attitudes and actions, whether or not they are correct.)

Learning a foreign language is often part of cultural training, yet it can also be a separate activity. Knowledge of a second language is important because it builds better connections with people from other cultures than does having a reliance on a translator. Although English has become the universal language of business, many international business specialists believe that having employees who speak different languages has become a strategic business imperative. One finding is that 70 percent of employees feel more confident in their interaction with teams, partners, and vendors after successfully completing language training.[54]

Cultural Intelligence Training

An advanced form of learning how to deal effectively with people from other cultures is cultural intelligence training. **Cultural intelligence (CQ)** is an outsider's ability to interpret someone's unfamiliar and ambiguous behavior the same way that that person's compatriots would. (CQ refers to "cultural quotient," similar to IQ referring to "intelligence quotient.") Similar to emotional intelligence, cultural intelligence encompasses several different aspects of behavior. The four sources of cultural intelligence relate to the metacognitive, cognitive, emotional/motivational, and the physical, explained as follows:[55]

cultural intelligence (CQ) An outsider's ability to interpret someone's unfamiliar and ambiguous behavior in the same way that that person's compatriots would interpret the behavior.

1. *Metacognitive (higher-order intelligence).* The metacognitive aspect of cultural intelligence refers to high-level problem-solving ability used to organize and comprehend cultural knowledge. Metacognitive CQ facilitates individuals becoming more aware of others' cultural preferences and intentions before and during cultural interactions. Even thinking that there is much to be learned in a new cultural interaction requires considerable intelligence.
2. *Cognitive (the head).* The cognitive part of CQ refers to what a person knows and how he or she can acquire new knowledge. Here a person acquires facts about people from another culture, such as their passion for football (soccer in the United States), their business practices, and their promptness in paying bills. Another aspect of this source of cultural intelligence is figuring out how to learn more about the other culture.
3. *Emotional/motivational (the heart).* The emotional/motivational aspect of CQ refers to energizing one's actions and building personal confidence. Both confidence and motivation are needed to adapt to another culture. A man on a business trip to Italy might say to himself, "When I greet a work associate in a restaurant, can I really pull off kissing him on both cheeks? What if he thinks I'm weird?" With strong motivation, the same person might say, "I'll give it a try. I kind of greet my grandfather the same way back in the United States."
4. *The body (physical).* The body aspect of CQ is the action component. The body is the vehicle for translating intentions into actions and desires. Kissing the same-sex Italian work associate on both cheeks is the *physical* aspect just mentioned. We often have an idea of what we should do, but implementation is not so easy. We might know, for example, that when entering an Asian person's home we should take off our shoes, yet we might not actually remove them—thereby offending our Asian work (or personal life) associate.

A key part of the training is to learn the four contributors to CQ—higher-level intelligence, head, heart, and body. Instead of learning a few simple guidelines for working

Chapter 17 Cultural Diversity and Cross-Cultural Organizational Behavior effectively with people from another culture, the trainee is taught strategies for sizing up the environment to determine which course of action is best. The culturally intelligent overseas worker would learn how to figure out how much humor to interject into meetings, what kind of handshake is most appropriate, and so forth. The following excerpt will give a feel for what is involved in cultural intelligence training:

> An American manager is attempting to interpret a "Chinese smile." First, she needs to recognize that thinking about cultural differences is a worthwhile activity. Second, she needs to observe the various cues provided in addition to the smile gesture itself (e.g., other facial or bodily gestures) and to assemble them into a meaningful whole and make sense of what is really experienced by the Chinese employee. Third, she must have the requisite motivation (directed effort and self-confidence) to persist in the face of ambiguity of the situation. Fourth, she must choose, generate, and execute the right actions to respond appropriately, such as saying, "It pleases me that we are in agreement." If any of these elements is deficient, she will be less effective in dealing with the Chinese employee. A high CQ manager or professional has the capability with all three facets as they act in unison.

To practice high cultural intelligence, the mind, heart, and body would have to work together. You would have to figure out how you have to act with people from another culture, you would need motivation and confidence to change, and you would have to translate your knowledge and motivation into action. So when you are on a business trip to New Delhi, India, go ahead and hold your fork in your left hand! Recent research findings suggest that you are more likely to benefit from cultural intelligence training if you have a propensity to change cultural stereotypes.[56] In other words, you observe carefully to see if your stereotype about a given ethnic or racial group could profit from updating.

Cross-Cultural Differences in Diversity Programs

In this chapter we have described how cultural factors influence various aspects of organizational behavior. The effectiveness of diversity programs themselves is also affected by cultural factors. Attorneys Larry Turner and Allison Suflas caution that there are significant risks in attempting to implement a single diversity program across countries. In the United States, equal opportunity for individuals in many demographic groups is governed by federal legislation including Title VII of the Civil Rights Act (race, color, religion, gender, and national origin) and the Americans with Disabilities Act. States have their own legislation about discrimination that follows the federal law but can also be more stringent and more detailed. Disputes about diversity initiatives are often settled through the legal process. Many diversity programs developed by American employers had their origins in civil rights legislation.

A major difference between diversity programs in the United States and a few other countries is the use of quotas. Whereas in the United States, Title VII prohibits businesses from using quotas based on demographic factors such as race or sex, quotas have been embraced in many European and Asian countries. An exception to the U.S. restriction on quotas is that in 2014, a government compliance program established "goals" for individuals with disabilities. For example, government contractors are assigned a utilization goal that 7 percent of the workforce should be qualified people with disabilities.

Many European diversity initiatives focus on attaining gender diversity. The goal is to be attained by imposing quotas for upper-level executives and company board members. A specific goal the European Union requested is that all publicly listed companies in Europe sign a pledge to increase women's presence on corporate boards to 40 percent by 2020.[57]

In addition to the hundreds of diversity quotas established around the world, the effectiveness of diversity initiatives working well across borders is moderated by cultural readiness. For example, if a country has a long-standing tradition of limiting women's employment to low-paying service positions, a gender diversity program will have to move in small steps.

Implications for Managerial Practice

1. Perhaps the easiest way to get along with people from other cultures is to focus on similarities rather than differences. From a work standpoint, you might find that you and a teammate from another culture are both interested in attaining high-quality results in a short period of time. On a social level, you might find that the two of you carefully follow the World Cup (a truly international soccer/football event).

2. As a manager or cultural diversity specialist, it is important to keep selling the idea that diversity initiatives do not regard white males as the enemy. In contrast, diversity is meant to be inclusive. Many white males are concerned that diversity initiatives are a form of discrimination and that they will be accused of being "advantaged" because of their skin color.[58]

3. A managerial success factor is to become multicultural in terms of conducting business effectively with people from different cultures. The demand for multicultural workers continues to increase as the business world becomes increasingly global.

4. To perform well in many positions in the modern world, it may be necessary to develop a global mind-set, a feeling of comfort and confidence in dealing with workers from diverse countries. Developing a global mind-set requires perspective, a sincere interest in another country, and a sense of humor to recover from obvious slips.[59]

Summary of Key Points

1. *Understand the scope, competitive advantages, and potential problems associated with cultural diversity.* The true meaning of valuing diversity is respecting a wide range of cultural and individual differences and therefore being inclusive. Diversity is seen today as a mechanism for business success, including generating more ideas and serving customers better. To be diverse is to be different in some measurable, though not necessarily visible, way.

   Encouraging cultural diversity within an organization is socially responsible and also offers these potential advantages: increased sales and profits, cost reduction associated with turnover and lawsuits, better employee recruitment, better ideas for publicity and advertising, and creativity. A diverse staff can also help to avoid publicity and advertising that is offensive to a cultural or demographic group. The potential for conflict is high in culturally diverse groups, but mutual support within the group can decrease problems.

2. *Identify and explain key dimensions of cultural differences.* Ten values particularly helpful in understanding how national cultures differ are: individualism versus collectivism, power distance (respect for hierarchy), uncertainty avoidance, materialism versus concern for others, long-term versus short-term orientation, formality versus informality, urgent time orientation versus casual time orientation, high-context versus low-context cultures, work orientation/leisure orientation, and performance orientation.

3. *Explain what is required for managers and organizations to become multicultural.* Multicultural workers have the skills and attitudes to relate effectively to and motivate people across race, gender, social attitudes, and lifestyles. Multiculturalism is enhanced by cultural integration, cultural sensitivity, cultural agility, multicultural identities, and positive indifference to unimportant cultural differences. A multicultural organization values cultural diversity and is willing to encourage and even capitalize upon such diversity. To move toward being a multicultural organization, business firms take a variety of diversity initiatives.

4. *Be more aware of barriers to good cross-cultural relations.* Barriers to the good cross-cultural relations required of a multicultural organization include perceptual expectations that lead to discriminatory stereotypes and ethnocentrism, intergroup (based on group differences) versus interpersonal (based on individual differences) relations. Language differences, cultural assumptions, and biases also create barriers.

5. *Explain how motivation, ethics, appropriate negotiation skills, conflict resolution, and empowerment practices can vary across cultures.* Certain motivational approaches can apply cross-culturally. Some psychological needs, like attachment differences, cultural assumptions, and biases against another cultural group apply across cultures. A cultural belief in collective effort enhances the effectiveness of participative decision making. Coping with cross-cultural ethical codes challenges many international managers. A major issue is whether to abide by the home ethical codes or those of the foreign company and country.

   Managers need good negotiating skills to achieve their objectives in international business. Americans must adapt their traditional negotiating tactics to fit other cultures. For example, people from other cultures may want to work more slowly than Americans on reaching agreement. A starting point in cross-cultural negotiations is whether members of the culture tend to seek integrative or distributed outcomes. When working in other countries, managers must be sensitive to differences in the preferred model of resolving conflict. Empowerment is likely to work poorly in a high-power-distance culture such as India. However, continuous improvement works across cultures.

6. *Appreciate the nature of diversity training and cultural training, including cultural intelligence and anti-bias training.* Diversity training attempts to bring about workplace harmony by teaching people how to get along better with diverse work associates. Anti-bias training is currently popular. Cultural training is helpful in overcoming culture shock and contributing to better relations with various groups at home. Learning a foreign language is often part of cultural training, yet it can also be a separate activity. Cultural intelligence training is an advanced form of learning how to deal effectively with people from other cultures. The effectiveness of diversity programs can be affected by cultural factors such as the use of quotas and readiness to accept the changes proposed by diversity training.

Key Terms and Phrases

individualism, p. 390	formality, p. 391	multicultural organization, p. 395
collectivism, p. 390	informality, p. 391	ethnocentrism, p. 396
power distance, p. 390	urgent time orientation, p. 391	cultural assumption, p. 396
uncertainty avoidance, p. 390	casual time orientation, p. 391	diversity training, p. 401
materialism, p. 391	high-context culture, p. 391	anti-bias training, p. 403
concern for others, p. 391	low-context culture, p. 391	cultural training, p. 404
long-term orientation, p. 391	multicultural worker, p. 392	culture shock, p. 404
short-term orientation, p. 391	cultural sensitivity, p. 393	cultural intelligence (CQ), p. 405

Discussion Questions and Activities

1. What steps can you take to better prepare yourself to become a multicultural worker?
2. Commercial airlines go out of their way to be culturally homogeneous for certain positions. For example, the flight attendants on Singapore Airlines are from Singapore, Air India flight attendants are from India, and the Air France attendants and flight crew all speak French. Explain whether these airlines should be accused of practicing job discrimination and minimizing cultural diversity.
3. More business firms than most people recognize have appointed women, Latinos, and African Americans to senior executive posts, including CEO. Explain whether you think these companies should publicize these appointments to demonstrate to the world that they are culturally diverse?
4. Diversity specialists argue that a firm's employee mix (or base) should match its customer mix. Assume you are the general manager of a nursing home or a retirement village. Explain whether your employee base (or mix) should match your client base.
5. If you knew that group members all had "a strong leisure orientation," how would this information help you do a better job as a manager?
6. Working in a small group, think through the many group projects you might have had in school or on the job. Brainstorm a list of the advantages and disadvantages that have stemmed from having diverse groups.
7. Software is available to translate documents from one language into another, and devices are for sale that will give you a voice translation from one language to another. With this technology available, why should the multicultural worker bother learning another language?
8. Suppose one of your ethnic biases is valid, such as the one mentioned in the chapter about Native Americans being naturally good steeplejacks. Should you work to overcome this bias?
9. For many years, countless millions of young people in the United States completed all their schooling and participated in teams and school activities in a multicultural environment. Explain whether diversity training and cultural training are necessary for these people.
10. Visualize yourself as the sales manager of a company in a highly competitive field. Your highest-performing sales representative, Billy, appears to be culturally insensitive in such ways as referring to female workers as "girls," and doing imitations of the accents of workers who are not native-speakers of English. What are you going to do about Billy?

HR consultant Emma is conducting an on-premises workshop in anti-bias training for Star Growth Inc, a large telecommunications company. Although Star Growth was not plagued with complaints about discrimination against or limited growth opportunities for any particular group, company leadership wanted to foster a climate of cultural diversity and inclusion. The CEO said, "We are hiring Emma as much for prevention of problems as dealing with actual problems."

After delivering a 15-minute PowerPoint presentation on the meaning of implicit bias and how it might affect workplace relationships, Emma gives the 10 workshop participants this assignment: "I want each of you, one by one, to tell the group of any bias you think you might possibly have. Nothing you say will be placed on a hidden video and presented to management. So be as candid as you are willing to be. I want us all to learn what biases might really be like at Star Growth." Although visibly nervous, the workshop participants obliged Emma's request.

Derek: I'll go first at the risk of being hated by my colleagues. As a sales manager, when I am interviewing a candidate for a sales position and she is really a knock-out in appearance, I think she might not be so sharp intellectually. Sorry, folks, that's my bias.

Tanya: When I'm at a store purchasing something complicated, like a smart refrigerator or a giant-screen TV set, I'll approach an Asian sales associate first if possible—especially Indian Americans or Chinese Americans—because my bias is that they are smart and efficient.

Brice: If I see a young African American in our company wearing a lot of expensive "bling," I figure that he or she might be involved in crime on the outside. I know that's a horrible insult, but Emma asked us to be totally honest.

Connor: A few months ago I was tasked with the job of putting together a men's basketball team to compete in an industrial league. My first approach was to talk to or send texts to African American or African guys in the company. I figure they have more interest and natural ability in basketball. I hope I didn't hurt anybody's feelings.

Eva: When I need technical advice, I never ask anybody in the company over age 50. I figure that if you're not a digital native, you won't be very helpful with a tough tech problem.

Gianna: I never thought I was biased, but come to think of it, I do have one bias. If I need something done in a hurry, I avoid asking an obese person. I think he or she might be a little lazy.

Hudson: When the company recently announced that the new CFO had an MBA from Harvard, I was relieved. I figure that the best financial minds have attended elite schools.

Harley: Last year I had an opportunity to transfer to one of two departments. I avoided the department headed by a recently divorced middle-aged male because I thought there was a good chance that he would sexually harass me.

Ivan: Two weeks ago I had to visit our affiliated urgent-care clinic because I had cut a capillary in my finger. I requested being helped by a woman nurse because I believe that nursing is a job for a woman.

Crystal: I needed to add another member to my project. I purposely avoided inviting a millennial to join because I think that they have poor attendance records.

Lionel: We had to order new, complex telecommunication equipment. I suggested that we order the equipment from a German firm because I believe that Germans are the best manufacturing engineers.

Emma said, "Thanks for your candor. Let's reflect together on what we just learned about bias at Star Growth."

Case Questions

1. To what extent do you think that the employees' expression of their conscious biases in a workshop accomplishes anything worthwhile?
2. Which one or two of the biases expressed do you think might be harmful to a climate of cultural diversity at Star Growth?
3. If you were in this workshop, explain whether or not you would express any conscious bias you might have.

Endnotes

1. Original story created from facts and observations in the following sources: Michael C. Bush and Sarah Lewis-Kulin, "Hundred Best Companies to Work for 2018," *Fortune*, March 1, 2018, p. 58; Paolo Gaudiano and Ellen Hunt, "How Capital One Supports Diversity from Top to Bottom," *Forbes* (www.forbes.com), pp. 1–3; "Kane Hopkins—Capital One," *Diversity Journal* (www.diversityjournal.com), March 7, 2016, pp. 1–3.

2. U.S. Census data presented in Shelton Goode, "Are Employee Resource Groups Good for Business?" *HR Magazine*, September 2016, p. 24.

3. Cited in "The Key to More Workplace Diversity," *The Wall Street Journal*, March 14, 2018, p. B2.

4. Cited in Susan G. Hauser, "The Clone Danger," *Workforce Management*, April 2013, p. 39.

5. Rachel Feintzeig, "Study Finds Diversity Toll," *The Wall Street Journal*, July 24, 2014, p. D3.

6. Vivian Hunt, Larsina Yee, Sara Prince, and Sundiatu Dixon-Fyle, "Delivering through Diversity," McKinsey & Company (www.mckinsey.com), January 2018, p. 8.

7. Hunt, Yee, Prince, and Dixon-Fyle, "Delivering through Diversity," pp. 1–10.

8. Carolyn Magner, "Driver Deficit: Tapping into Drivers of Color," *The Driver Deficit* (www.ccjdigital.com), June 7, 2018, pp. 1–4.

9. David Rock and Heidi Grant Halverson, "Why Diverse Teams Are Smarter," *Harvard Business Review*, November 4, 2016, pp. 1–8.

10. Orlando C. Richard, Tim Barnett, Sean Dwyer, and Ken Chadwick, "Cultural Diversity in Management, Firm Performance, and the Moderating Role of Entrepreneurial Dimensions," *Academy of Management Journal*, April 2004, p. 263.

11. "Dunkin' Donuts Criticized for Blackface Ad Campaign" (www.detnews.com), August 30, 2013, pp. 1–2.

12. Wayne Ma, "Gap Apologizes for China T-Shirt," *The Wall Street Journal*, May 16, 2018, p. B3.

13. Samuel B. Bacharach, Peter A. Bamberger, and Dana B. Vashdi, "Diversity and Homophily at Work: Supportive Relations among White and African-American Peers," *Academy of Management Journal*, August 2005, pp. 619–644.

14. Ellen Emmerentze Jervell, "New Henkel CEO Makers Amends," *The Wall Street Journal*, July 28, 2016, p. B4.

15. Research reviewed in Michele J. Gelfand, Zeynep Aycan Miriam Erez, and Kwok Leung, "Cross-Cultural Industrial-Organizational Psychology and Organizational Behavior: A Hundred-Year Journey," *Journal of Applied Psychology*, March 2017, p. 522.

16. Geert Hofstede, *Culture's Consequences: International Differences in Work-Related Values* (Beverly Hills, CA: Sage, 1980); updated and expanded in "A Conversation with Geert Hofstede," *Organizational Dynamics*, Spring 1993, pp. 53–61; Jim Kennedy and Anna Everest, "Put Diversity in Context," *Personnel Journal*, September 1991, pp. 50–54.

17. Robert J. House et al., *Culture, Leadership, and Organizations: The GLOBE Study of 62 Societies* (Thousand Oaks, CA: Sage, 2004).

18. Huiwen Lian, Lance Ferris, and Douglas J. Brown, "Does Power-Distance Exacerbate or Mitigate the Effects of Abusive Supervision?" *Journal of Applied Psychology*, January 2012, pp. 107–123.

19. G. E. Miller, "The U.S. Is the Most Overworked Developed Nation in the World—When Do We Draw the Line?" 20 Something Finance (https://20somethingfinance.com), September 11, 2016, p. 3.

20. Susan Ricker, "Workplace Behavior around the World," *CareerBuilder*, November 10, 2013, p. 1.

21. John Schaubroeck and Simon S. K. Lam, "How Similarity to Peers and Supervisor Influences Organizational Advancement in Different Cultures," *Academy of Management Journal*, December 2002, pp. 1120–1136.

22. Anne Fisher, "Piercing the 'Bamboo Ceiling,'" *Fortune*, August 22, 2005, p. 122.

23. Jennifer Arnold, "Have You Gone Global?" *HR Magazine*, March 2018, pp. 22–23.

24. Research cited in Eric Krell, "Expats: Keeping Feet in Two Cultures," *HR Magazine*, December 2012, pp. 66–67.

25. Arvand V. Phatak, *International Dimensions of Management* (Boston: Kent, 1983), p. 167.

26. Juan Antonio Fernandez and Laurie Underwood, "Succeeding in China: The Voices of Experience," *Organizational Dynamics*, No. 4, 2005, pp. 404, 411–414.

27. Jack Scarborough, *The Origins of Cultural Differences and Their Impact on Management* (Westport, CT: Quorum, 2000).

28. Paula Caligiuri, *Cultural Agility: Building a Pipeline of Successful Global Professionals* (San Francisco, CA: Jossey-Bass, 2012), pp. 4–5.

29. Stacey R. Fitzsimmons, "Multicultural Employees: A Framework for Understanding How They Contribute to Organizations," *Academy of Management Review*, October 2013, pp. 525–549.

30. Tsedal Neeley, "How to Successfully Work across Countries, Languages, and Cultures," *Harvard Business Review*, August 28, 2017, pp. 1–7.

31. "MGM Resorts International Named among Nation's 2017 Top Companies for Diversity by DiversityInc," *Cision PR Newsletter* (www.prnewswire.com), May 10, 2017, p. 1.

32. "MGM International Named a 'Best Company for Diversity' by Leading Hispanic Business Publication," MGM Resorts International Investor Room (http://mgmresorts.investorroom.com), October 24, 2014, pp. 1–2; "MGM Resort's International Earns National Diversity Honor," MGM Resorts (www.mgmresortsdiversity.com), March 7, 2011, pp. 1–2.

33. Rita Pryllis, "SAP Feted for Gender Diversity," *Workforce*, April 2016, p. 17.

34. Harry C. Triandis, *Culture and Social Behavior* (New York: McGraw-Hill, 1994), pp. 249–259.

35. Joan C. Williams, "Hacking Tech's Diversity Problem," *Harvard Business Review*, October 2014, pp. 26–27.

36. Simon S. K. Lam, Xiao-Ping Chen, and John Schaubroeck, "Participative Decision Making and Employee Performance in Difficult Cultures: The Moderating Effects of Allocentrism/Idiocentrism and Efficacy," *Academy of Management Journal*, October 2002, pp. 905–914.

37. Erin Meyer, "Getting to Sí, Ja, Oui, Hai, and Da," *Harvard Business Review*, December 2015, pp. 74–80; John L. Graham

and Roy A. Herberger Jr., "Negotiators Abroad—Don't Shoot from the Hip," *Harvard Business Review*, July–August 1983, p. 167.

38. Marc Diener, "Culture Shock," *Entrepreneur*, July 2003, p. 77.

39. Jeanne M. Brett, Brian G. Gunia, and Brosh M. Teucher, "Culture and Negotiation Strategy: A Framework for Future Research," *Academy of Management Perspectives*, November 2017, pp. 291–292.

40. Brian Gunia, Jeanne Brett, and Amit Nandkeolyar, "In Global Negotiations, It's All about Trust," *Harvard Business Review*, December 2012, p. 26.

41. Catherine Tinsley, "Models of Conflict Resolution in Japanese, German, and American Cultures," *Journal of Applied Psychology*, April 1998, pp. 316–323.

42. Christopher Robert et al., "Empowerment and Continuous Improvement in the United States, Mexico, Poland, and India: Predicting Fit on the Dimensions of Power Distance and Individualism," *Journal of Applied Psychology*, October 2000, pp. 643–658.

43. Allan Lee, Sara Willis, and Amy Wee Tian, "Empowering Leadership: A Meta-Analytic Examination of Incremental Contribution, Mediation, and Moderation," *Journal of Organizational Behavior*, Vol. 38, 2017.

44. Tanja Rabal, Mevan Jayasinghe, Barry Gerhart, and Torsten M. Kühlmann, "A Meta-Analysis of Country Differences in the High-Performance Work System-Business Performance Relationship: The Roles of National Culture and Managerial Discretion," *Journal of Applied Psychology*, November 2014, pp. 1011–1041.

45. Lauren Weber, "Diversity Efforts Challenged," *The Wall Street Journal*, March 15, 2018, p. B5.

46. Gillian Flynn, "The Harsh Reality of Diversity Programs," *Workforce*, December 1998, p. 34.

47. John Simons, "Workplace Diversity Efforts Get a Reboot," *The Wall Street Journal*, February 15, 2017, p. B5.

48. Diether Gebert, Claudia Buengeler, and Kathrin Heinitz, "Tolerance: A Neglected Dimension in Diversity Training?" *Academy of Management Learning & Education*, September 2017, pp. 415–438.

49. Deepa Seetharaman and Natalie Andrews, "Facebook to Train against Bias," *The Wall Street Journal*, June 24, 2016, p. B3.

50. Farhad Manjoo, "Exposing Hidden Bias at Google," *New York Times* (www.nytimes.com), September 24, 2014, pp. 1–4.

51. Terry Tang, "Starbucks Training a First Step, Experts Say," *Associated Press*, May 29, 2018.

52. Triandis, *Culture and Social Behavior*, p. 263.

53. Sarah Fister Gale, "Now, You're Speaking My Language," *Workforce Management*, July 13, 2013, p. 10.

54. Ryan McMunn, "3 Ways Language Training Benefits Your Business," www.entrepreneur.com, August 7, 2017, p. 2.

55. Jacob Eisenberg et al., "Can Business Schools Make Students Culturally Competent? Effects of Cross-Cultural Management Courses on Cultural Intelligence," *Academy of Management Learning & Education*, December 2013, pp. 603–621; P. Christopher Earley and Elaine Mosakowski, "Toward Culture Intelligence Training: Turning Cultural Differences into a Workplace Advantage," *Academy of Management Executive*, August 2004, pp. 154–155.

56. Valerie Alexandra, "Predicting CQ Development in the Context of Experiential Cross-Cultural Training: The Role of Social Dominance Orientation and the Propensity to Change Stereotypes," *Academy of Management Learning & Education*, March 2018, pp. 62–78; Melody Manchi Chao, Riki Takeuchi, and Jiing-Lih Farh, "Enhancing Cultural Intelligence: The Roles of Implicit Culture Beliefs and Adjustment," *Personnel Psychology*, Number 1, 2017, pp. 257–292.

57. Larry Turner and Allison Suflas, "Global Diversity—One Program Won't Fit All," *HR Magazine*, May 2014, pp. 59–61.

58. Simons, "Workplace Diversity Efforts Get a Reboot," p. B5.

59. Mildred L. Culp, "New Mentality Compels Business Effectiveness . . . Global Mind-Set: Don't Leave Home without It," *WorkWise*®, December 6, 1998.

Glossary

A

Active Listening   Listening for full meaning without making premature judgments or interpretations.

Administrative Management   A school of management thought concerned primarily with how organizations should be structured and managed.

Anti-Bias Training   A type of training that helps employees discover their unconscious biases that may adversely affect certain demographic groups.

Artificial Intelligence   The ability of a computer program or machine to think and learn in a manner that emulates human intelligence.

Attitude   A predisposition to respond that exerts an influence on a person's response to a person, a thing, an idea, or a situation.

Attribution Theory   The process by which people ascribe causes to the behavior they perceive.

Avoidance Motivation   Rewarding by taking away an uncomfortable consequence.

B

Behavioral Approach to Leadership   An attempt to specify how the behavior of effective leaders differs from their less-effective counterparts.

Behavioral Approach to Management   The belief that specific attention to the workers' needs creates greater satisfaction and productivity.

Big Data   Enormous amounts of data that have the potential to be mined for information.

Blame   The tendency to place the responsibility for a negative outcome on a person, a thing, or the environment.

Bureaucracy   A rational, systematic, and precise form of organization in which rules, regulations, and techniques of control are precisely defined.

Burnout   A pattern of emotional, physical, and mental exhaustion in response to chronic job stressors.

Business Process Reengineering   The radical redesign of work to achieve substantial improvements in performance.

C

Casual Time Orientation   The perception of time as an unlimited and unending resource, leading to patience.

Centralization   The extent to which executives delegate authority to lower organizational units.

Charisma   The ability to lead others based on personal charm, magnetism, inspiration, and emotion.

Coaching (in relation to teams)   A direct interaction with the team with the intention of improving team processes to enhance performance.

Coercive Power   Controlling others through fear or threat of punishment.

Cognitive Dissonance   The situation in which the pieces of knowledge, information, attitudes, or beliefs held by an individual are contradictory.

Cognitive Intelligence   The capacity to acquire and apply knowledge, including solving problems.

Cognitive Learning Theory   A theory emphasizing that learning takes place in a complicated manner involving much more than acquiring habits and small skills.

Cognitive Skills   Mental ability and knowledge.

Collectivism   A value emphasizing that the group and society receive top priority.

Complexity   The number of different job titles and units within an organization.

Concern for Others   An emphasis on personal relations and a concern for the welfare of others. Usually measured along a continuum, with materialism at the opposite end.

Conflict   The opposition of persons or forces giving rise to some tension.

Confrontation and Problem Solving   A method of identifying the true source of conflict and resolving it systematically.

Consideration   The degree to which the leader creates an environment of emotional support, warmth, friendliness, and trust.

Contingency Approach to Management   The viewpoint that there is no one best way to manage people or work but that the best way depends on certain situational factors.

Contingency Theory of Leadership   The position that the best style of leadership depends on factors relating to group members and the work setting.

Corporate Social Responsibility   The idea that firms have an obligation to society beyond their economic obligations to owners or stockholders and also beyond those prescribed by law or contract.

Creative Self-Efficacy   The belief that one can be creative in a work role.

Creativity   The process of developing good ideas that can be put into action.

Crew   A group of specialists each of whom has specific roles, performs brief events that are closely synchronized with each other, and repeats these events under different environmental conditions.

Crisis Leadership The process of leading group members through a sudden and largely unanticipated, extremely negative, and emotionally upsetting circumstance.

Cross-Functional Team A work group composed of workers with different specialties but from about the same organizational level, who come together to accomplish a task.

Crowdsourcing The gathering of input or information relevant to a particular task by enlisting the services of many people either paid or unpaid, typically via the Internet.

Cultural Assumption A form of stereotype in which we attribute attitudes and behaviors to members of a group, without verifying our information.

Cultural Intelligence (CQ) An outsider's ability to interpret someone's unfamiliar and ambiguous behavior in the same way that that person's compatriots would interpret the behavior.

Cultural Sensitivity An awareness of and a willingness to investigate the reasons why people of another culture act as they do.

Cultural Training Training that attempts to help workers understand people from other cultures.

Culture Shock A group of physical and psychological symptoms that can develop when a person is abruptly placed in a foreign culture.

D

Decision The act of choosing among two or more alternatives in order to solve a problem.

Decision Criteria The standards of judgment used to evaluate alternatives.

Departmentalization The process of subdividing work into departments.

Difficult Person An individual who creates problems for others, yet has the skill and mental ability to do otherwise.

Diversity Training Training that attempts to bring about workplace harmony by teaching people how to get along better with diverse work associates.

Double-Loop Learning A change in behavior that occurs when people use feedback to confront the validity of the goal or the values implicit in the situation.

Downsizing The laying off of workers to reduce costs and increase efficiency.

E

E-Learning A web-based form of computer-based training.

Emotion A feeling such as anger, fear, joy, or surprise that underlies behavior.

Emotional Intelligence Qualities such as understanding one's own feelings, empathy for others, and the regulation of emotion to enhance living.

Emotional Labor The process of regulating both feelings and expressions to meet organizational goals.

Employee Engagement High levels of personal investment in the work tasks performed on the job.

Empowerment The process of sharing power with group members, thereby enhancing their feelings of self-efficacy.

Equity Theory The theory that employee satisfaction and motivation depend on how fairly the employees believe that they are treated in comparison to peers.

Ethics An individual's moral beliefs about what is right and wrong or good and bad.

Ethnocentrism The assumption that the ways of one's own culture are the best ways of doing things.

Evidence-Based Management Using research evidence to help make management decisions.

Expectancy A person's subjective estimate of the probability that a given level of performance will occur.

Expectancy Theory The theory that motivation results from deliberate choices to engage in activities in order to achieve worthwhile outcomes.

Experience of Flow Being "in the zone"; total absorption in one's work and intense concentration.

Expert Power The ability to influence others because of one's specialized knowledge, skills, or abilities.

Extinction Weakening or decreasing the frequency of undesirable behavior by removing the reward for such behavior.

F

Feedback Information about how well someone is doing in achieving goals. Also, messages sent back from the receiver to the sender of information.

Filtering The coloring and altering of information to make it more acceptable to the receiver.

Flat Organization Structure An organization structure with relatively few layers.

Formal Communication Channels The official pathways for sending information inside and outside an organization.

Formal Group A group deliberately formed by the organization to accomplish specific tasks and achieve goals.

Formal Organization Structure An official statement of reporting relationships, rules, and regulations.

Formality Attaching considerable importance to tradition, ceremony, social rules, and rank.

Formalization The degree to which expectations regarding the methods of work are specified, committed to writing, and enforced.

Frame of Reference A perspective and vantage point based on past experience.

Functional Departmentalization The grouping of people according to their expertise.

Fundamental Attribution Error The tendency to attribute behavior to internal causes when focusing on someone else's behavior.

G

g (general) Factor A major component of intelligence that contributes to problem-solving ability.

Goal What a person is trying to accomplish.

Grapevine The major informal communication channel in organizations.

Grit Perseverance and passion for long-term goals.

Group A collection of people who interact with one another, work toward some common purpose, and perceive themselves as a group.

Group Cohesiveness A situation that takes place when members work closely with each other, in a unified, cooperative manner.

Group Norms The guidelines for acceptable and unacceptable behaviors that are informally agreed on by group members.

Group Polarization A situation in which post-discussion attitudes tend to be more extreme than pre-discussion attitudes.

Groupthink A deterioration of mental efficiency, reality testing, and moral judgment in the interest of group cohesiveness.

H

Hawthorne Effect The tendency of people to behave differently when they receive attention because they respond to the demands of the situation.

Heuristics Simplified strategies that become rules of thumb in decision making.

High-Context Culture A culture that makes more extensive use of body language.

High-Performance Work System (HPWS) A system of HR practices designed to enhance employees' skills, engagement, and productivity in such a way that the workforce becomes a source of sustainable competitive advantage.

Horizontal Structure The arrangement of work by teams that are responsible for accomplishing a process.

Human Relations Movement An approach to dealing with workers based on the belief that there is an important link among managerial practices, morale, and productivity.

I

Implicit Leadership Theory An explanation of leadership contending that group members develop prototypes specifying the traits and abilities that characterize an ideal business leader.

Individual Differences Variations in how people respond to the same situation based on personal characteristics.

Individualism A mental set in which people see themselves first as individuals and believe that their own interests take priority.

Informal Communication Channels The unofficial network of channels that supplements the formal channels.

Informal Group A group that emerges over time through the interaction of workers, typically to satisfy a social or recreational purpose.

Informal Learning A planned learning that occurs in a setting without a formal classroom, lesson plan, instructor, or examination.

Informal Organization Structure A set of unofficial working relationships that emerges to take care of the events and transactions not covered by the formal structure.

Informality A casual attitude toward tradition, ceremony, social rules, and rank.

Information (or Communication) Overload A situation that occurs when people are so overloaded with information that they cannot respond effectively to messages, resulting in stress.

Initiating Structure The degree to which a leader establishes structure for group members.

Innovation The process of creating new ideas and their implementation or commercialization.

Instrumentality The individual's subjective estimate of the probability that performance will lead to certain outcomes.

Intellectual Capital Knowledge that transforms raw materials and makes them more valuable; it is also a capital asset consisting of intellectual material.

Intrinsic Motivation A person's beliefs about the extent to which an activity can satisfy his or her needs for competence and self-determination.

Intuition An experience-based way of knowing or reasoning in which weighing and balancing evidence are done automatically.

J

Job Characteristics Model A method of job design that focuses on the task and interpersonal demands of a job.

Job Crafting The physical and mental changes workers make in the task or relationship aspects of their job.

Job Demands–Job Control Model An explanation of job stress contending that workers experience the most stress when the demands of the job are high yet they have little control over the activity.

Job Enrichment The process of making a job more motivational and satisfying by adding variety, responsibility, and managerial decision making.

Job Satisfaction The amount of pleasure or contentment associated with a job.

K

Knowledge Management (KM) The systematic sharing of information to achieve advances in innovation, efficiency, and competitive advantage.

L

Large-Scale Organizational Change The method used to accomplish a major change in the firm's strategy and culture.

Leader–Member Exchange (LMX) Model The model that recognizes that leaders develop unique working relationships with each group member.

Leader Political Support Tactics of organizational politics and influence engaged in by leaders to provide followers with necessary resources to advance individual, group, or organizational objectives.

Leadership The ability to inspire confidence and support among the people on whose competence and commitment performance depends.

Leadership Style The relatively consistent pattern of behavior that characterizes a leader.

Learning A relatively permanent change in behavior based on practice or experience.

Learning Organization An organization that is skilled at creating, acquiring, and transferring knowledge and at modifying behavior to reflect new knowledge and insights.

Learning Style A person's particular way of learning, reflecting the fact that people learn best in different ways.

Legitimate Power Power based on one's formal position within the hierarchy of the organization.

Linguistic Style A person's characteristic speaking pattern, involving the amount of directness used, pacing and pausing, word choice, and the use of jokes, figures of speech, questions, and apologies.

Locus of Control The way in which people look at causation in their lives.

Long-Term Orientation In describing national culture, taking a long-range perspective.

Low-Context Culture A culture that makes less use of body language.

M

Machiavellianism A tendency to manipulate others for personal gain.

Management by Walking Around The process of managers intermingling freely with workers on the shop floor, in the office, and with customers.

Maslow's Hierarchy of Needs A classical theory of motivation that arranges human needs into a pyramid-shaped model, with basic physiological needs at the bottom and self-actualization needs at the top.

Materialism An emphasis on assertiveness and the acquisition of money and material objects; usually measured along a continuum, with concern for others at the opposite end.

Matrix Organization Structure An organization consisting of a project structure superimposed on a functional structure.

Message A purpose or an idea to be conveyed in a communication event.

Meta-Analysis A quantitative or statistical review of the literature on a particular subject; an examination of a range of studies for the purpose of reaching a combined result or best estimate.

Metacommunicate To communicate about your communication to help overcome barriers or resolve a problem.

Micromanagement Supervising group members too closely and second-guessing their decisions.

Mindfulness Concentrating on the present moment without making judgments about what is happening.

Mixed Signals Communication breakdown resulting from the sending of different messages about the same topic to different audiences.

Modeling Imitation; learning a skill by observing another person performing that skill.

Motivation In a work setting, the process by which behavior is mobilized and sustained in the interest of achieving organizational goals.

Multicultural Organization An organization that values cultural diversity and is willing to encourage and even capitalize on such diversity.

Multicultural Worker A worker with the skills and attitudes to relate effectively to and motivate people across race, gender, age, social attitudes, and lifestyles, and to conduct business in a diverse, international environment. Also, an employee who has more than one cultural identity, thereby belonging to multiple worlds.

N

Need for Achievement The desire to accomplish something difficult for its own sake.

Need for Affiliation The desire to establish and maintain friendly and warm relationships with others.

Need for Power The desire to control other people, to influence their behavior, and to be responsible for them.

Negative Lifestyle Factors Behavior patterns predisposing a person to job stress, including poor exercise and eating habits and heavy consumption of caffeine, alcohol, tobacco, and other drugs.

Negotiating and Bargaining Conferring with another person in order to resolve a problem.

Network Organization A spherical structure that can rotate self-managing teams and other resources around a common knowledge base.

Network Structure (or Virtual Organization) A temporary association of otherwise independent firms linked by technology to share expenses, employee talents, and access to one another's markets.

New Age Workplace Human-friendly spaces that accommodate both the digitalization of work and an emphasis on collaboration.

Noise Anything that disrupts communication, including the attitude and emotions of the receiver.

Nominal Group Technique (NGT) An approach to developing creative alternatives that requires group members to generate alternative solutions independently.

Nomophobia A form of anxiety stemming from having no access to a smartphone or the phone battery being dangerously low.

Nonverbal Communication The transmission of messages by means other than words.

O

Offshoring The practice of having work performed by a company in an overseas location.

Open-Door Policy An understanding in which any employee can bring a gripe to the attention of upper-level management without checking with his or her immediate manager.

Operant Conditioning Learning that takes place as a consequence of behavior.

Organization A collection of people working together to achieve a common purpose (or simply a big group).

Organization Development (OD) Any strategy, method, or technique for making organizations more effective by bringing about constructive, planned change.

Organization Structure The arrangement of people and tasks to accomplish organizational goals.

Organizational Behavior (OB) The study of human behavior in the workplace, of the interaction between people and the organization, and the organization itself.

Organizational Citizenship Behavior (OCB) Behaviors that express a willingness to work for the good of an organization even without the promise of a specific reward.

Organizational Culture A system of shared values and beliefs that influence worker behavior.

Organizational Design The process of creating a structure that best fits a purpose, strategy, and environment.

Organizational Effectiveness The extent to which an organization is productive and satisfies the demands of its interested parties.

Organizational Politics Informal approaches to gaining power through means other than merit or luck.

Outsource   The practice of having work performed by groups outside the organization.

P

Perception   The various ways in which people interpret things in the outside world and how they act on the basis of these interpretations.

Personality   The persistent and enduring behavior patterns of an individual that are expressed in a wide variety of situations.

Personality Clash   An antagonistic relationship between two people based on differences in personal attributes, preferences, interests, values, and styles.

Personalized Power   The use of power primarily for the sake of personal aggrandizement and gain.

Person–Role Conflict   A condition that occurs when the demands made by the organization or a manager clash with the basic values of the individual.

Political Skill   A combination of social astuteness with the capacity to adjust and adapt behavior to different situational demands.

Positive Organizational Behavior   The study and application of human resource strengths and psychological capacities that can be measured, developed, and managed for performance improvement.

Positive Reinforcement   The application of a pleasurable or valued consequence when a person exhibits the desired response.

Positive Reinforcement Program   The application of reinforcement theory for motivating people in work settings.

Power   The potential or ability to influence decisions and control resources.

Power Distance   The extent to which employees accept the idea that members of an organization have different levels of power.

Practical Intelligence   A type of intelligence required for adapting to an environment to suit an individual's needs.

Proactive Personality   A relatively stable tendency to effect environmental change.

Problem   A discrepancy between the ideal and the real.

Procrastinate   Delaying to take action without a valid reason.

Product/Service Departmentalization   The arrangement of departments according to the products or services they provide.

Project   A temporary group of specialists working together under one manager to accomplish a fixed objective.

Prosocial Motivation   The desire to expend effort to help others.

Psychological Safety   The belief that you will not be punished or humiliated for speaking up with ideas, questions, concerns, or mistakes.

Punishment   The presentation of an undesirable consequence for a specific behavior.

R

Referent Power   The ability to influence others that stems from one's desirable traits and characteristics; it is the basis for charisma.

Reinforcement Theory   The contention that behavior is determined by its consequences.

Relationship Conflict   Conflict that focuses on personalized, individually oriented issues.

Relaxation Response   A general-purpose method of learning to relax by oneself, which includes making oneself quiet and comfortable.

Reshoring   The bringing of jobs back to a country that outsourced these jobs previously.

Resource Dependence Perspective   The need of the organization for a continuing flow of human resources, money, customers, technological inputs, and material to continue to function.

Reward Power   Controlling others through rewards or the promise of rewards.

Role Ambiguity   A condition in which the job holder receives confused or poorly defined role expectations.

Role Conflict   Having to choose between competing demands or expectations.

S

s (special) Factors   Components of intelligence that contribute to problem-solving ability.

Scientific Management   The application of scientific methods to increase workers' productivity.

Self-Awareness   Understanding oneself and insightfully processing feedback about oneself to improve personal effectiveness.

Self-Determination Theory   The idea that people are active agents, rather than passive reactors to, environmental forces.

Self-Efficacy   The feeling of being an effective and competent person with respect to a task.

Self-Managed Work Team   A formally recognized group of employees responsible for an entire work process or segment that delivers a product or service to an internal or external customer.

Self-Serving Bias   An attribution error whereby people tend to attribute their achievements to good inner qualities, whereas they attribute their failures to adverse factors within the environment.

Semantics   The varying meanings people attach to words.

Servant Leader   A leader who serves constituents by working on their behalf to help them achieve their goals, not the leader's own goals.

Sexual Harassment   Unwanted sexually oriented behavior in the workplace that results in discomfort and/or interference with the job.

Shaping   Learning through the reinforcement or rewarding of small steps to build to the final or desired behavior.

Shared Team Leadership   A mutual influence process in which team members collaborate on decision making, share responsibility, and lead each other toward the attainment of goals.

Short-Term Orientation   In describing a national culture, a demand for immediate results.

Situational Control   The degree to which the leader can control and influence the outcomes of group effort.

Social Cognitive Theory   The explanation that observation, rather than trial and error and reward and punishment, is the key to learning.

Social Entrepreneurship An environmental approach to social problems such as homelessness, contaminated drinking water, and extreme poverty.

Social Learning The process of observing the behavior of others, recognizing its consequences, and altering behavior as a result.

Social Loafing Freeloading, or shirking individual responsibility when placed in a group setting and removed from individual accountability.

Social Responsibility The idea that firms have an obligation to society beyond their economic obligations to owners or stockholder and also beyond those prescribed by law or contract.

Socialization The process of coming to understand the values, norms, and customs essential for adapting to an organization.

Socialized Power The use of power to achieve constructive ends.

Span of Control The number of workers reporting directly to a manager.

Stock Option A financial incentive that gives employees the right to purchase a certain number of company shares at a specified price, generally the market price of the stock on the day the option is granted.

Stress The mental and physical condition that results from a perceived threat that cannot be dealt with readily.

Stressor Any force creating the stress reaction.

Subculture A pocket in which the organizational culture differs from the dominant culture, as well as other pockets of subculture.

Superordinate Goals Overarching goals that capture the imagination of people.

T

Task Conflict Conflict that focuses on substantive, issue-related differences related to the work itself.

Team A special type of group in which the members have complementary skills and are committed to a common purpose, a set of performance goals, and an approach to the task.

Team Efficacy A team's belief that it can successfully perform a specific task.

Teamwork A situation in which there is understanding and commitment to group goals on the part of all team members.

Telecommuting An arrangement in which employees use computers to perform their regular work responsibilities at home or in a satellite office; working at home and sending output electronically to the office.

Territorial Games Also known as "turf wars," behaviors that involve protecting and hoarding resources that give a person power, such as information, relationships, and decision-making authority.

Transformational Leader One who helps organizations and people make positive changes in the way they conduct their activities.

Triple Bottom Line The idea that organizations should prepare three different and separate bottom lines: the corporate bottom line; people, in terms of their well-being; and the planet, referring to environmental responsibility.

Two-Factor Theory of Work Motivation Herzberg's theory contending that there are two different sets of job factors. One set can satisfy and motivate people (motivators or satisfiers); the other set can only prevent dissatisfaction (dissatisfiers or hygiene factors).

U

Uncertainty Avoidance The extent to which people accept the unknown and tolerate risk and unconventional behavior.

Urgent Time Orientation The perception of time as a scarce resource, therefore leading to impatience.

V

Valence The value a person places on a particular outcome.

Value The importance a person attaches to something that serves as a guide to action.

Value Judgment An overall opinion of something based on a quick perception of its merit.

Virtual Team A group that conducts almost all of its collaborative work via electronic communication rather than face-to-face meetings.

W

Wellness Program A formal organization-sponsored activity to help employees stay well and avoid illness.

Whistle-Blower An employee who discloses organizational wrongdoing to parties who can take action.

Win–Win The belief that, after conflict has been resolved, both sides should gain something of value.

Work–Family Conflict Conflict that ensues when the individual has to perform multiple roles: worker; spouse; and, often, parent.

Organization Index

Name Index

Subject Index

organizational effectiveness, 345
organizational health, 347
person-organization fit, 346
productivity, quality, and engagement, 346
safety of workers, 346
socialization for learning, 345
stories for, 340
subculture, 343
values and, 340
well-known companies and, 344
Organizational and individual effectiveness, 6–7
Organizational health, 347
Organizational justice, 342
Organization development, 371–374
  high-performance work systems, 374
  large-scale change, 372–373
  process model for, 371–372
  transformational leadership for, 373
Outdoor (off-site) training, 227–228
Outsourcing, 328–331
  cloud computing and, 329
  offshoring, 330
  outsourcing to homes, 330–331
  scope of, 328–330
  reshoring, 329–330
  time-zone advantage, 330
Outsourcing to homes, 330–331
Overconfidence bias, 97

Participant observation, 4
Participative decision making, 364
Passion and creativity. 100
Pay-to-performance link, 152
People-oriented management practice, 7
Perception, 50–55
  attribution theory and blame, 53–55
  characteristics of stimulus, 51
  distortions and problems, 50–51
  locus of control, 54–55
  mental processes of people, 51–52
Perceptual expectations, 396
Performance orientation, 392
Personal growth and human behavior insight, 6
Personal mastery of job, 349
Personality, 27–34, 99–100, 238–243, 292
  clashes, 292
  creativity and, 99–100
  curvilinear relationship with performance, 34
  decision making and, 93
  Five Factor Model and, 27–28
  job behavior and, 31, 33–34

leadership traits and, 238–243
  nine major factors and traits, 28–31
  stress and, 305–306
Personality clashes, 292
Person-organization fit, 346
Person-role conflict, 58
Persuasive and power-oriented language, 183–184
Physiological needs, 116
Plausibility in negotiations, 299
Political blunders, 274, 275
Political skill, 274
Political support for change, 364
Politics (organizational), 270–277
  backstabbing, 274–275
  blunders, 274, 275
  control of dysfunctional type, 279–280
  decision making and, 95
  embrace or demolish, 275
  ethical considerations, 280
  ethical and positive tactics, 272–274
  factors contributing to, 271–272
  flattery for, 274
  leader political support, 270
  stealing credit, 275
  territorial games, 275
  unethical and negative tactics, 274–277
Position power, 265–266
Positive indifference for cultural relations, 375
Positive organizational behavior, 13
Positive reinforcement, 122, 145–147
Positive thinking and innovation, 377
Posture as nonverbal communication, 170
Power distance and culture, 390
Power in organizations, 265–270
  coercive type, 266
  empowerment, 269–270
  expectations of subordinates, 267–268
  expert type, 266
  hubris syndrome, 268
  implicit leadership theory, 267–268
  legitimate type, 265–266
  position type, 265–266
  referent type, 266
  resource dependence perspective, 267
  reward type, 267
  sources of, 265–269
  subordinate type, 267
Practical intelligence, 26–27
Praise as motivator, 149
Presentation technology, 166

Pride as motivator, 150–151
Proactivity and leadership, 240
Process model of organization development, 371
Processes within work group, 204
Procrastination and decision making, 97
Product and service departmentalization, 324
Productivity differences among people, 24
Projection, 52
Psychological safety in groups, 205
Punishment and motivation, 123, 145

Quality of work differences, 24
Quantitative vs. qualitative methods, 5

Rational persuasion, 277
Recognition as motivator, 148
Recruitment of minority group members, 401
Referent power, 266
Reinforcement theory, 121
Relationship management and emotional intelligence, 37
Relaxation response, 309
Remote working, 166–167
Research methods, 4
Reshoring of jobs, 329–330
Resistance to change, 364–365
Resource allocation and rewards, 341
Resource dependence perspective, 267
Reward power, 266
Rights of individuals, 74
Risk taking and thrill seeking, 30
Rites and rituals in organizations, 341
Role ambiguity, 306
Role conflict, 306
Role modeling for organizational change, 362
Role overload, 306
Roles within groups, 199–201
Rumors, 173

s (special) factors of intelligence, 26
Safety needs, 116
Scientific management, 10
Selective perception, 52
Self-actualization needs, 116–117
Self-assessment quizzes
  bureaucracy attitudes, 321
  concentration and focus, 101–102
  conscientiousness, 29
  cross-cultural attitudes and skills, 385
  flexibility, 375
  grit, 130